**W9-CTY-575**

## DATE DUE

| | | | |
|---|---|---|---|
| | | | |
| | | | |
| | | | |
| | | | |
| | | | |
| | | | |
| | | | |
| | | | |
| | | | |

# SOMETHING ABOUT THE AUTHOR®

Something about
the Author *was named
an "**Outstanding
Reference Source,**"
the highest honor given
by the American
Library Association
Reference and Adult
Services Division.*

ISSN 0276-816X

# SOMETHING ABOUT THE AUTHOR®

**Facts and Pictures about Authors
and Illustrators of Books for Young People**

EDITED BY
## KEVIN S. HILE

# VOLUME 78

**Gale Research Inc.** • *DETROIT* • *WASHINGTON, D.C.* • *LONDON*

## STAFF

*Editor:* Kevin S. Hile

*Associate Editor:* Marie Ellavich

*Managing Editor:* Joyce Nakamura

*Sketchwriters/Copyeditors:* Joseph O. Aimone, Joanna Brod, Craig Bryson, Robin Cook, Pamela S. Dear, Elizabeth A. Des Chenes, Stephen Desmond, Kathleen J. Edgar, David M. Galens, Ronie-Richele Garcia-Johnson, Scott Gillam, Mary Gillis, Jeff Hill, David Johnson, Denise E. Kasinec, Pat Matson Knapp, Sharyn Kolberg, Thomas F. McMahon, Mark F. Mikula, Mary L. Onorato, Tom Pendergast, Wendy Pfeffer, Jani Prescott, Anders J. Ramsay, Jordan Richmond, Vita Richmond, Terrie M. Rooney, Pamela L. Shelton, Geri J. Speace, Aarti D. Stephens, Diane Telgen, Linda Tidrick, Brandon Trenz, Arlene True, Polly A. Vedder, Thomas Wiloch, and Kathleen Wilson

*Research Manager:* Victoria B. Cariappa
*Research Supervisor:* Mary Rose Bonk
*Editorial Associates:* Reginald A. Carlton, Frank Vincent Castronova, Andrew Guy Malonis, and Norma Sawaya
*Editorial Assistants:* Laurel Sprague Bowden, Dawn Marie Conzett, Eva Marie Felts, Shirley Gates, Sharon McGilvray, Dana R. Schleiffers, and Amy B. Wieczorek

*Picture Permissions Supervisor:* Margaret A. Chamberlain
*Permissions Associates:* Pamela A. Hayes, Arlene Johnson, Keith Reed, and Barbara A. Wallace
*Permissions Assistant:* Susan Brohman

*Production Director:* Mary Beth Trimper
*Production Assistant:* Shanna Heilveil
*Art Director:* Cynthia Baldwin
*Macintosh Artist:* Sherrell Hobbs
*Camera Operator:* Willie Mathis

∞™ This book is printed on acid-free paper that meets the minimum requirements of American National Standard for Information Sciences—Permanence Paper for Printed Library Materials, ANSI Z39.48-1984.

Library of Congress Catalog Card Number 72-27107

ISBN 0-8103-2288-9  ISSN 0276-816X

Printed in the United States of America

Published simultaneously in the United Kingdom by Gale Research International Limited
(An affiliated company of Gale Research Inc.)

I(T)P™

The trademark **ITP** is used under license.

10 9 8 7 6 5 4 3 2 1

# Contents

Authors in Forthcoming Volumes  viii
Introduction  ix          Acknowledgments  xi

# Authors in Forthcoming Volumes

Below are some of the authors and illustrators that will be featured in upcoming volumes of *SATA*. These include new entries on the swiftly-rising stars of the field, as well as completely revised and updated entries (indicated with *) on some of the most notable and best-loved creators of books for children.

**\*Judy Blume:** A popular yet sometimes controversial author, Blume treats coming-of-age problems with frankness and a touch of humor in such books as *Otherwise Known as Sheila the Great* and *Just as Long as We're Together.*

**James Earl Carter:** With his *Talking Peace: A Vision for the Next Generation,* the former U.S. president uses his experience as a mediator for nations in conflict to help put the lives of young Americans into perspective.

**Cynthia DeFelice:** A former library media specialist, DeFelice has found a successful career as the author of *The Strange Night Writing of Jessamine Colter, Weasel,* and other acclaimed works. (Entry contains exclusive interview.)

**\*Virginia Hamilton:** Hamilton's *M. C. Higgins the Great* was the first book to win both the National Book Award and the Newbery Medal; her popular works offer a mix of realism, history, myth, and folklore.

**Annette Curtis Klause:** Klause's books about aliens and vampires have broken new ground in young adult literature. (Entry contains exclusive interview.)

**\*R. R. Knudson:** In works such as *Zanbanger, Fox Running,* and *Zan Hagan's Marathon,* Knudson uses her personal knowledge of sports to create quick-paced and often funny stories of athletic competition.

**John Peel:** Peel is the author of a number of *Dr. Who, Carmen Sandiego,* and *James Bond, Jr.* books, as well as the young adult science fiction book *Uptime, Downtime* and horror stories like *Shattered.*

**Anatoli Rybakov:** At one time best known in his native country for his children's books, Rybakov became internationally recognized in the 1980s as the author of novels critical of communist Russia.

**Brian Selznick:** With his debut picture book, *The Houdini Box,* Selznick won wide acclaim from reviewers for his sensitive story about the magic of the human heart, as well as for his evocative illustration style. (Entry contains exclusive interview.)

**Jerry Stanley:** Stanley, a historian by profession, has received enthusiastic reviews for his first two books, *Children of the Dust Bowl* and *I Am an American,* nonfiction works about people overcoming adversity during two difficult periods in American history. (Entry contains exclusive interview.)

**\*Brinton Turkle:** Turkle's popular illustrations have accompanied the texts of numerous authors, as well as his own charming stories, such as the ''Obadiah'' books, which have received both the Caldecott honor and Christopher Award.

**\*Cynthia Voigt:** A Newbery and Edgar Award winner, Voigt has been especially praised for her fine narrative technique and for creating memorable characters like the Tillerman children.

**Lee Wardlaw:** Young readers have been drawn to Wardlaw's novels, such as *Corey's Fire* and *Seventh-Grade Weirdo,* for their realistic characters who discover inner strength in the face of trying situations.

**\*Jane Breskin Zalben:** An illustrator of many children's works, Zalben has become best known for her series of picture books about Jewish holidays featuring a lovable bear family.

# Introduction

*Something about the Author* (SATA) is an ongoing reference series that deals with the lives and works of authors and illustrators of children's books. *SATA* includes not only well-known authors and illustrators whose books are widely read, but also those less prominent people whose works are just coming to be recognized. This series is often the only readily available information source on emerging writers or artists. You'll find *SATA* informative and entertaining whether you are a student, a librarian, an English teacher, a parent, or simply an adult who enjoys children's literature for its own sake.

## What's Inside SATA

*SATA* provides detailed information about authors and illustrators who span the full time range of children's literature, from early figures like John Newbery and L. Frank Baum to contemporary figures like Judy Blume and Richard Peck. Authors in the series represent primarily English-speaking countries, particularly the United States, Canada, and the United Kingdom. Also included, however, are authors from around the world whose works are available in English translation. The writings represented in *SATA* include those created intentionally for children and young adults as well as those written for a general audience and known to interest younger readers. These writings cover the entire spectrum of children's literature, including picture books, humor, folk and fairy tales, animal stories, mystery and adventure, science fiction and fantasy, historical fiction, poetry and nonsense verse, drama, biography, and nonfiction.

Obituaries are also included in *SATA* and are intended not only as death notices but as concise views of people's lives and work. Additionally, each edition features newly revised and updated entries for a selection of *SATA* listees who remain of interest to today's readers and who have been active enough to require extensive revision of their earlier biographies.

## Two Convenient Indexes

In response to suggestions from librarians, *SATA* indexes no longer appear in each volume, but are included in alternate (odd-numbered) volumes of the series, beginning with Volume 57.

*SATA* continues to include two indexes that cumulate with each alternate volume: the Illustrations Index, arranged by the name of the illustrator, gives the number of the volume and page where the illustrator's work appears in the current volume as well as all preceding volumes in the series; the Author Index gives the number of the volume in which a person's Biographical Sketch or Obituary appears in the current volume as well as all preceding volumes in the series.

These indexes also include references to authors and illustrators who appear in Gale's *Yesterday's Authors of Books for Children, Children's Literature Review,* and the *Something about the Author Autobiography Series.*

## Easy-to-Use Entry Format

Whether you're already familiar with the *SATA* series or just getting acquainted, you will want to be aware of the kind of information that an entry provides. In every *SATA* entry the editors attempt to give as complete a picture of the person's life and work as possible. A typical entry in *SATA* includes the following clearly labeled information sections:

- *PERSONAL:* date and place of birth and death, parents' names and occupations, name of spouse, date of marriage, and names of children, educational institutions attended, degrees received, religious and political affiliations, hobbies and other interests.

- *ADDRESSES:* complete home, office, and agent addresses.

- *CAREER:* name of employer, position, and dates for each career post; military service.

- *MEMBER:* memberships and offices held in professional and civic organizations.

- *AWARDS, HONORS:* literary and professional awards received.

- *WRITINGS:* title-by-title chronological bibliography of books written and/or illustrated, listed by genre when known; lists of other notable publications, such as plays, screenplays, and periodical contributions.

- *ADAPTATIONS:* a list of films, television programs, plays, and other media presentations that have been adapted from the author's work.

- *WORK IN PROGRESS:* description of projects in progress.

- *SIDELIGHTS:* a biographical portrait of the author's development, either directly from the person—and often written specifically for the *SATA* entry—or gathered from diaries, letters, interviews, or other published sources.

- *FOR MORE INFORMATION SEE:* references for further reading.

- *EXTENSIVE ILLUSTRATIONS:* photographs, movie stills, manuscript samples, book covers, and other interesting visual materials supplement the text.

## How a SATA Entry Is Compiled

A *SATA* entry progresses through a series of steps. If the biographee is living, the *SATA* editors try to secure information directly from him or her through a questionnaire. From the information that the biographee supplies, the editors prepare an entry, filling in any essential missing details with research and/or telephone interviews. When necessary, the author or illustrator is sent a copy of the entry to check for accuracy and completeness.

If the biographee is deceased or cannot be reached by questionnaire, the *SATA* editors examine a wide variety of published sources to gather information for an entry. Biographical and bibliographic sources are consulted, as are book reviews, feature articles, published interviews, and material sometimes obtained from the biographee's family, publishers, agent, or other associates. Entries compiled entirely from secondary sources are marked with an asterisk (*).

## We Welcome Your Suggestions

We invite you to examine the entire *SATA* series, starting with this volume. Please write and tell us if we can make *SATA* even more helpful to you. Send comments and suggestions to: The Editor, *Something about the Author,* Gale Research Inc., 835 Penobscot Bldg., Detroit, MI 48226-4094.

# *Acknowledgments*

Grateful acknowledgment is made to the following publishers, authors, and artists whose works appear in this volume.

**DIANE WORFOLK ALLISON.** Photograph courtesy of Diane Worfolk Allison.

**JUDIE ANGELL.** Cover of *In Summertime It's Tuffy,* by Judie Angell. Copyright © 1977 by Judie Angell Gaberman. Reprinted by permission of Dell Books, a division of Bantam Doubleday Dell Publishing Group, Inc./ Jacket of *Yours Truly,* by Judie Angell. Jacket painting copyright © 1993 by Richard Elmer. Reprinted by permission of Orchard Books, a division of Franklin Watts, Inc./ Jacket of *Leave the Cooking to Me,* by Judie Angell. Copyright © 1990 by Judie Angell. Cover art copyright © 1990 by Ken Joudrey. Reprinted by permission of Bantam Books, a division of Bantam Doubleday Dell Publishing Group, Inc./ Jacket of *Suds: A New Daytime Drama,* by Judie Angell. Jacket painting by Jenny Rutherford. Copyright © 1983 by Bradbury Press. Reprinted by permission of Bradbury Press, an affiliate of Macmillan, Inc./ Jacket of *One-Way to Ansonia,* by Judie Angell. Jacket painting by Robert Casilla. Copyright © 1985 by Bradbury Press. Reprinted by permission of Bradbury Press, an affiliate of Macmillan, Inc.

**ELEANOR H. AYER.** Photograph courtesy of Eleanor H. Ayer.

**NANCY BENTLEY.** Illustration from *I've Got Your Nose!,* by Nancy Bentley. Text copyright © 1991 by Nancy Bentley. Illustrations copyright © 1991 by Don Madden. Reprinted by permission of Doubleday, a division of Bantam Doubleday Dell Publishing Group, Inc./ Photograph courtesy of Nancy Bentley.

**CLARA WIDESS BERKUS.** Photograph by Margaret Dodd, courtesy of Clara Widess Berkus.

**KATHRYN HOOK BERLAN.** Photograph by Joseph W. Darwal, courtesy of Kathryn Hook Berlan.

**BRUCE BERNARD.** Cover of *Van Gogh,* by Bruce Bernard. Copyright © 1992 by Dorling Kindersley Limited, London. Van Gogh's sketch book, flower vase, plaster statuette and sketches of moth, cicada, street scene and sunflowers, reprinted by permission of Vincent van Gogh Foundation/Vincent van Gogh Museum, Amsterdam. Painting of "Fourteen Sunflowers," reprinted by permission of the Trustees, The National Gallery, London.

**JON BLAKE.** Jacket of *Wriggly Pig,* by Jon Blake. Jacket illustration copyright © 1992 by Susan Jenkin-Pearce. Reprinted in the United States and Canada by permission of Tambourine Books, a division of William Morrow & Company, Inc. Reprinted in the British Commonwealth by permission of Hutchinson Children's Books.

**MARIBETH BOELTS.** Photograph courtesy of Maribeth Boelts.

**HESBA FAY BRINSMEAD.** Jacket of *Pastures of the Blue Crane,* by H. F. Brinsmead. Oxford University Press, 1964. Copyright © 1964 by H. F. Brinsmead. Jacket illustration by Annette McArthur-Onslow. Reprinted in the United States by permission of The Putnam Publishing Group. Reprinted in the British Commonwealth by permission of Oxford University Press.

**JEANNETTE CAINES.** Cover of *I Need a Lunchbox,* by Jeannette Caines. Cover art copyright © 1993 by Pat Cummings. Reprinted by permission of HarperCollins Publishers Inc./ Jacket of *Just Us Women,* by Jeannette Caines. Jacket art copyright © 1982 by Pat Cummings. Reprinted by permission of HarperCollins./ Photograph by Al Cetta.

**JANELL CANNON.** Jacket by Janell Cannon from her *Stellaluna.* Jacket illustration copyright © 1993 by Janell Cannon. Reprinted in the United States by permission of Harcourt Brace & Company. Reprinted in the British Commonwealth by permission of Janell Cannon and the Sandra Dijkstra Literary Agency.

**ANN CARTWRIGHT.** Jacket of *The Winter Hedgehog,* by Ann and Reg Cartwright. Copyright © 1989 by Ann and Reg Cartwright. Reprinted in the United States by permission of Macmillan Publishing Company, a division of Macmillan, Inc. Reprinted in Canada and the British Commonwealth by permission of Hutchinson Children's Books.

**MICHAEL CASSUTT.** Jacket of *The Star Country,* by Michael Cassutt. Copyright © 1986 by Cathy Hull. Reprinted by permission of Doubleday, a division of Bantam Doubleday Dell Publishing Group, Inc./ Photograph by Cindy Cassutt, courtesy of Michael Cassutt.

**JU-HONG CHENG.** Photograph courtesy of Ju-Hong Cheng.

**NANCY L. CLOUSE.** Cover by Nancy L. Clouse from her *Puzzle Maps U.S.A.* Copyright © 1990 by Nancy L. Clouse. Reprinted by permission of Henry Holt and Company, Inc.

**JUDITH LOVE COHEN.** Photograph courtesy of Judith Love Cohen.

**KINUKO CRAFT.** Jacket cover by Kinuko Craft from *Bailey's Window,* by Anne Lindbergh. Copyright © 1984 by Anne Lindbergh. Jacket illustration copyright © 1984 by Kinuko Craft. Reprinted by permission of Harcourt Brace & Company.

**CHARA CURTIS.** Photograph courtesy of Chara Curtis.

**DANIEL SOLOMON CUTLER.** Cover of *One Hundred Monkeys,* by Daniel Solomon Cutler. Illustrations copyright © 1991 by Marsha Winborn. Reprinted by permission of the publisher, Simon & Schuster Books for Young Readers, New York.

**SIS BOULOS DEANS.** Photograph courtesy of Sis Boulos Deans.

**DEBORAH DENNARD.** Photograph courtesy of Deborah Dennard.

**MICHELE DIETERICH.** Photograph courtesy of Michele Dieterich.

**HARRIETT DILLER.** Photograph courtesy of Harriett Diller.

**BILL DODDS.** Photograph courtesy of Camera Craft, Inc.

**JOAN DONALDSON.** Photograph by Louis Schabel, courtesy of Joan Donaldson.

**ARTHUR DORROS.** Jacket by Arthur Dorros from his *Ant Cities.* Jacket art copyright © 1987 by Arthur Dorros. Reprinted by permission of HarperCollins Publishers Inc./ Cover by Arthur Dorros from his *Alligator Shoes.* Copyright © 1982 by Arthur Dorros. Reprinted in the United States and Canada by permission of Dutton Children's Books, a division of Penguin Books USA Inc. Reprinted in the British Commonwealth by permission of Arthur Dorros./ Photograph courtesy of Arthur Dorros.

**JOHN DAVID DOWD.** Photograph courtesy of John David Dowd.

**ARLENE ERLBACH.** Photograph courtesy of Arlene Erlbach.

**DORIS FABER.** Photograph from *Harry Truman,* by Doris Faber. Copyright © 1972 by Doris Faber. Photograph by Edmund Trissell. Reprinted by permission of Edmund Trissell./ Cover of *Captive Rivers,* by Doris Faber. Copyright © 1966 by Doris Faber./ Photograph from *Bella Abzug,* by Doris Faber. Text copyright © 1976 by Doris Faber. Photograph by Dev O'Neill./ Cover of *Margaret Thatcher: Britain's "Iron Lady,"* by Doris Faber. Text copyright © 1985 by Doris Faber. Illustrations copyright © 1985 by Robert Masheris. Reprinted by permission of Viking Penguin, a division of Penguin Books USA Inc./ Cover of *Eleanor Roosevelt: First Lady of the World,* by Doris Faber. Text copyright © 1985 by Doris Faber. Illustrations copyright © 1985 by Donna Ruff. Reprinted by permission of Viking Penguin, a division of Penguin Books USA Inc.

**JEROME FORD.** Photograph from *The Grand Slam Collection: Have Fun Collecting Baseball Cards,* by Jerome Ford. Copyright © 1992 by Lerner Publications Company. Photograph by Maria Kaiser. Reprinted by permission of Maria Kaiser.

**EVELYN GALLARDO.** Photograph by Mary V. Ammon, courtesy of Evelyn Gallardo.

**BARBARA GIRION.** Illustration from *Joshua, the Czar, and the Chicken Bone Wish,* by Barbara Girion. Copyright © 1978 by Barbara Girion. Reprinted by permission of Charles Scribner's Sons, an imprint of Macmillan Publishing Company./ Cover of *Indian Summer,* by Barbara Girion. Copyright © 1990 by Barbara Girion. Reprinted by permission of Scholastic Inc./ Jacket of *Misty and Me,* by Barbara Girion. Copyright © 1979 by Barbara Girion. Jacket illustration by Fran Stiles. Typography design by Diana Hrisinko. Reprinted by permission of Charles Scribner's Sons, an imprint of Macmillan Publishing Company./ Photograph © Sharon Faulkner.

**GRACE GOLDBERG.** Photograph courtesy of Grace Goldberg.

**KAREN GRAVELLE.** Cover of *Teenagers Face to Face with Bereavement,* by Karen Gravelle and Charles Haskins. Cover copyright © 1989 by Julian Messner, a division of Simon & Schuster, Inc. Cover design by Antler & Baldwin, Inc. Cover photo by Robert Llewllyn/FourByFive. Reprinted by permission of Simon & Schuster, Inc./ Photograph courtesy of Karen Gravelle.

**KAREN HABER.** Photograph courtesy of Karen Haber.

**GAIL E. HALEY.** Illustration by Gail E. Haley from her *Birdsong.* Copyright © 1984 by Gail E. Haley. Reprinted by permission of Crown Publishers, Inc./ Illustration by Gail E. Haley from her *Jack and the Bean Tree.* Copyright © 1986 by Gail E. Haley. Reprinted by permission of Crown Publishers, Inc./ Photograph by George Flowers.

**MELANIE W. HALL.** Photograph courtesy of Melanie W. Hall.

**DIANE JOHNSTON HAMM.** Cover of *Rock-a-Bye Farm,* by Diane Johnston Hamm. Illustrations copyright © 1992 by Richard Brown. Reprinted by permission of the publisher, Simon & Schuster Books for Young Readers, New York./ Jacket of *Bunkhouse Journal,* by Diane Johnston. Jacket illustration copyright © 1990 by Toby Gowing. Reprinted by permission of Toby Gowing./ Photograph courtesy of Diane Johnston Hamm.

**KEVIN HAWKES.** Cover by Kevin Hawkes from his *Then the Troll Heard the Squeak.* Jacket illustrations copyright © 1991 by Kevin Hawkes. Reprinted by permission of Lothrop, Lee & Shepard Books, a division of William Morrow & Company, Inc./ Photograph by Jennifer Perkes.

**PATRICIA HERMES.** Cover of *Kevin Corbett Eats Flies,* by Patricia Hermes. Cover copyright © 1986 by Minstrel and Pocket Books, divisions of Simon & Schuster, Inc. Reprinted by permission of Pocket Books, a division of Simon & Schuster, Inc./ Jacket of *Mama, Let's Dance,* by Patricia Hermes. Jacket illustration copyright © 1991 by Ellen Thompson. Reprinted by permission of Little, Brown and Company./ Jacket of *A Place for Jeremy,* by Patricia Hermes. Copyright © 1987 by Patricia Hermes. Jacket illustration by Leland Neff. Reprinted by permission of Leland Neff./ Photograph by David Bravo.

**DOUGLAS HILL.** Cover of *Coyote the Trickster,* by Douglas Hill. Illustrations copyright © 1975 by Graham McCallum./ Cover of *Blade of the Poisoner,* by Douglas Hill. Jacket illustration copyright © 1987 by Jon Weiman. Reprinted by permission of Jon Weiman./ Jacket of *ColSec Rebellion,* by Douglas Hill. Atheneum, 1985. Jacket painting copyright © 1985 by Stephen Marchesi. Reprinted by permission of Stephen Marchesi.

**DEBORAH HITZEROTH.** Cover of *The Importance of Galileo Galilei,* by Deborah Hitzerotl and Sharon Heerboth. Copyright © 1992 by Lucent Books, Inc., P.O. Box 289011, San Diego, California, 92198-9011.

**RUSSELL HOBAN.** Jacket of *The Marzipan Pig,* by Russell Hoban. Text copyright © 1986 by Russell Hoban. Illustrations copyright © 1986 by Quentin Blake. Reprinted in the United States by permission of Farrar, Straus & Giroux, Inc. Reprinted in Canada and the British Commonwealth by permission of Quentin Blake./ Jacket of *Monsters,* by Russell Hoban. Jacket art copyright © 1989 by Quentin Blake. Reprinted by permission of Scholastic Inc./ Jacket of *Riddley Walker,* by Russell Hoban. Cover copyright © 1980 by Simon & Schuster, Inc. Jacket design by Fred Marcellino. Reprinted by permission of Simon & Schuster, Inc./ Video cover of *The Mouse and His Child,* by Russell Hoban. Layout and design copyright © 1985 by RCA/Columbia Pictures Home Video. Special thanks to Blockbuster Video, Royal Oak, MI, for the use of this video jacket cover./ Photograph by Jerry Bauer.

**SHARON HOLM.** Photograph courtesy of Sharon Holm.

**JAMES D. HOUSTON.** Photograph by Barbara Hall, courtesy of James D. Houston.

**JEANNE WAKATSUKI HOUSTON.** Cover of *Farewell to Manzanar,* by Jeanne Wakatsuki Houston & James D. Houston. Copyright © 1973 by James D. Houston. Reprinted by permission of Bantam Books, a division of Bantam Doubleday Dell Publishing Group, Inc./ Photograph courtesy of Jeanne Wakatsuki Houston.

**SATOMI ICHIKAWA.** Illustration by Satomi Ichikawa from her *A Child's Book of Seasons.* Copyright © 1975 by Satomi Ichikawa. Reprinted by permission of Satomi Ichikawa./ Illustration by Satomi Ichikawa from her *Nora's Stars.* Illustrations copyright © 1989 by Satomi Ichikawa. Reprinted in the United States by permission of Philomel Books. Reprinted in the British Commonwealth by permission of Hodder & Stoughton Publishers./ Photograph by Marianne Veron.

**LEE KAISER JOHNSON.** Photograph courtesy of Lee Kaiser Johnson.

**SUE KAISER JOHNSON.** Photograph courtesy of Sue Kaiser Johnson.

**JULIE JOHNSTON.** Jacket of *Hero of Lesser Causes,* by Julie Johnston. Copyright © 1992 by Julie Johnston. Reprinted by permission of Little, Brown and Company./ Photograph courtesy of Julie Johnston.

**FRANCOISE & FREDERIC JOOS.** Photograph courtesy of Francoise & Frederic Joos.

**ANDREW KAPLAN.** Cover of *Careers for Artistic Types,* by Andrew Kaplan. Copyright © 1991 by Millbrook Press. Cover photograph of woman and child by Kathy Fairfield. Cover photographs by Eddie Keating. Reprinted by permission of The Milllbrook Press Inc.

**JULIE KELEMEN.** Cover of *Prayer Is for Children,* by Julie Kelemen. Copyright © 1992 by Julie Kelemen. Cover and interior art by Chris Sharp. Reprinted by permission of Liguori Publications, Liguori MO 63057-9999./ Photograph by Mark C. Patterson, Fast Foto, Inc.

**ELIZABETH KEOWN.** Photograph courtesy of Elizabeth Keown.

**DAVID KIRBY.** Jacket of *The Cows Are Going to Paris,* by David Kirby and Allen Woodman. Jacket illustration copyright © 1991 by Chris L. Demarest. Jacket designed by Joy Chu. Reprinted by permission of Boyds Mills Press, Inc.

**L. PATRICIA KITE.** Photograph courtesy of L. Patricia Kite.

**ANITA LARSEN.** Cover of *The Roanoke Missing Persons Case,* by Anita Larsen. Copyright © 1992 by Crestwood House, Macmillan Publishing Company. Illustrations by James Watling. Reprinted by permission of Crestwood House, an imprint of Macmillan Publishing Company./ Photograph courtesy of Anita Larsen.

**LOUISE LAWRENCE.** Jacket of *The Warriors of Taan,* by Louise Lawrence. Jacket art copyright © 1988 by Alix Berenzy. Jacket copyright © 1988 by Harper & Row, Publishers, Inc. Reprinted by permission of HarperCollins Publishers Inc./ Jacket of *Andra,* by Louise Lawrence. Jacket copyright © 1991 by Anton Kimball. Jacket art copyright © 1991 by HarperCollins Publishers. Reprinted by permission of HarperCollins Publishers Inc./ Photograph courtesy of Louise Lawrence.

**SHEILA MacGILL-CALAHAN.** Photograph by Maria Fernandez.

**DOUG MAGEE.** Illustration from *All Aboard ABC,* by Doug Magee and Robert Newman. Copyright © 1990 by Doug Magee and Robert Newman. Reprinted by permission of Cobblehill Books, an affiliate of Dutton Children's Books, a division of Penguin Books USA Inc.

**FRANCES CARFI MATRANGA.** Photograph courtesy of Frances Carfi Matranga.

**CHARLES MIKOLAYCAK.** Illustration by Charles Mikolaycak from *The Changing Maze,* by Zilpha Keatley Snyder. Illustrations copyright © 1985 by Charles Mikolaycak. Reprinted by permission of Macmillan Publishing Company, a division of Macmillan, Inc./ Illustration by Charles Mikolaycak from *Babushka,* retold by Charles Mikolaycak. Copyright © 1984 by Charles Mikolaycak. Reprinted by permission of Holiday House, Inc.

**BETTY MILES.** Illustration from *Save the Earth: An Ecology Handbook for Kids,* by Betty Miles. Copyright ©1974 by Betty Miles. Illustrations by Claire A. Nivola. Reprinted by permission of Alfred A. Knopf, Inc./ Jacket of *Maudie and Me and the Dirty Book,* by Betty Miles. Cover art copyright © 1989 by Hodges Solieau. Reprinted by permission of Alfred A. Knopf, Inc./ Cover of *The Trouble with Thirteen,* by Betty Miles. Cover art copyright © 1989 by Vince Natale. Reprinted by permission of Alfred A. Knopf, Inc.

**WENDELL G. MINOR.** Illustration by Wendell G. Minor from *The Moon of the Owls,* by Jean Craighead George. Copyright © 1993 by Wendell G. Minor. Reprinted in the United States and Canada by permission of Wendell G. Minor. Reprinted in the British Commonwealth by permission of HarperCollins Publishers Inc./ Photograph courtesy of Wendell G. Minor.

**LIZA KETCHUM MURROW.** Cover of *The Ghost of Lost Island,* by Liza Ketchum Murrow. Cover copyright © 1991 by Minstrel and Pocket Books, divisions of Simon & Schuster, Inc. Cover art by Neal McPheeters. Reprinted by permission of Pocket Books, a division of Simon & Schuster, Inc./ Cover of *Fire in the Heart,* by Liza Ketchum Murrow. Copyright © 1989 by Liza Ketchum Murrow. Reprinted by permission of Troll Associates./ Cover of *West against the Wind,* by Liza Ketchum Murrow. Copyright © 1987 by Liza Ketchum Murrow. Reprinted by permission of Troll Associates./ Photograph courtesy of Lisa Ketchum Murrow.

**JOAN LOWERY NIXON.** Jacket of *The Orphan Train Quartet: In the Face of Danger,* by Joan Lowery Nixon. Copyright © 1988 by Joan Lowery Nixon and Daniel Weiss Associates, Inc. Cover art copyright © 1988 by Daniel Weiss Associates, Inc. Cover photograph copyright © 1988 by Marc X. Witz. Reprinted by permission of Bantam Books, a division of Bantam Doubleday Dell Publishing Group, Inc./ Cover of *The Orphan Train Quartet: A Family Apart,* by Joan Lowery Nixon. Copyright © 1987 by Joan Lowery Nixon and Daniel Weiss Associates, Inc. Cover art copyright © 1988 by Nigel Chamberlain. Reprinted by permission of Bantam Books, a division of Bantam Doubleday Dell Publishing Group, Inc./ Cover of *The Other Side of Dark,* by Joan Lowery Nixon. Copyright © 1986 by Joan Lowery Nixon. Reprinted by permission of Dell Books, a division of Bantam Doubleday Dell Publishing Group, Inc./ Cover of *The Kidnapping of Christina Lattimore,* by Joan Lowery Nixon. Copyright © 1979 by Joan Lowery Nixon. Reprinted by permission of Dell Books, a division of Bantam Doubleday Dell Publishing Group, Inc./ Jacket of *The Orphan Train Quartet: Caught in the Act,* by Joan Lowery Nixon. Copyright © 1988 by Joan Lowery Nixon and Daniel Weiss Associates, Inc. Cover art copyright © 1988 by Daniel Weiss Associates, Inc. Cover photograph copyright © 1988 by Marc X. Witz. Reprinted by permission of Bantam Books, a division of Bantam Doubleday Dell Publishing Group, Inc./ Jacket of *Ellis Island: Land of Hope,* by Joan Lowery Nixon. Copyright © 1992 by Joan Lowery Nixon and Daniel Weiss Associates, Inc. Cover art copyright © 1992 by Colin Backhouse. Reprinted by permission of Bantam Books, a division of Bantam Doubleday Dell Publishing Group, Inc./ Photograph by Kaye Marvins.

**JOSEPHINE NOBISSO.** Photograph courtesy of Josephine Nobisso.

**ELLEN CASSELS O'SHAUGHNESSY.** Photograph courtesy of Ellen Cassels O'Shaughnessy.

**TOM PAISLEY.** Jacket from *New York City Too Far from Tampa Blues,* by Tom Paisley. Copyright © 1975 by Tom Paisley. Jacket design by Richard Cuffari. Reprinted by permission of Holiday House, Inc./ Jacket of *Doris Fein: Legacy of Terror,* by Tom Paisley. Copyright © 1984 by Tom Paisley. Jacket art by Brad Hamann. Reprinted by permission of Holiday House, Inc./ Jacket of *The Dog Days of Arthur Cane,* by Tom Paisley. Copyright © 1976 by Thomas Paisley. Jacket design by Bernard Colonna. Reprinted by permission of Holiday House, Inc./ Jacket of *The Me Inside of Me,* by Tom Paisley. Copyright © 1985 by Tom Paisley. Jacket illustration by Michael Deraney. Reprinted by permission of Lerner Publications Company./ Photograph by Bob Campbell.

**BARBARA PARK.** Jacket of *Buddies,* by Barbara Park. Jacket painting copyright © 1985 by Richard Williams. Reprinted by permission of Alfred A. Knopf, Inc./ Cover of *The Kid in the Red Jacket,* by Barbara Park. Cover art copyright © 1987 by Rob Sauber. Reprinted by permission of Random House, Inc.

**WILLIAM BARTLETT PEET.** Illustration from *Encyclopedia of Walt Disney's Animated Characters,* by John Grant. Copyright © 1993 by The Walt Disney Company. Illustration taken from movie *The Sword and the Stone,* story by Bill Peet. Reprinted by permission of Hyperion Books for Children./ Cover by Bill Peet from his *Cock-a-Doodle Dudley.* Copyright © 1990 by William Peet. Reprinted by permission of Houghton Mifflin Company./ Jacket by Bill Peet from his *The Kweeks of Kookatumdee.* Jacket copyright © 1985 by Bill Peet. Reprinted by permission of Houghton Mifflin Company./ Illustration by Bill Peet from his *The Whingdingdilly.* Copyright © 1970 by Bill Peet. Reprinted by permission of Houghton Mifflin Company./ Photograph courtesy of William Peet.

**MARY E. PENSON.** Photograph courtesy of Mary E. Penson.

**RUSSELL M. PETERS.** Photograph courtesy of Russell M. Peters.

**WENDY PFEFFER.** Jacket of *Popcorn Park Zoo: A Haven with a Heart,* by Wendy Pfeffer. Copyright © 1992 by Wendy Pfeffer. Photographs © 1992 by J. Gerard Smith. Reprinted by permission of Julian Messner, a division of Simon & Schuster, Inc./ Photograph courtesy of Wendy Pfeffer.

**PAMELA POWELL.** Jacket of *The Turtle Watchers,* by Pamela Powell. Jacket illustration copyright © 1992 by Donna Perrone. Reprinted by permission of Viking Penguin, a division of Penguin Books USA Inc./ Photograph by Jiri Hrubec.

**EUGENE F. PROVENZO.** Cover of *47 Easy-to-Do Classic Science Experiments,* by Eugene F. Provenzo, Jr. and Asterie Baker Provenzo. Copyright © 1989 by Eugene F. Provenzo, Jr., Asterie Baker Provenzo, and Peter A. Zorn, Jr. Illustrations prepared by Peter A. Zorn, Jr. Cover design by Paul E. Kennedy. Reprinted by permission of Dover Publications, Inc.

**ANN RINALDI.** Cover of *The Last Silk Dress,* by Ann Rinaldi. Copyright © 1988 by Ann Rinaldi. Cover art copyright © 1990 by Lisa Falkenstern. Reprinted by permission of Bantam Books, a division of Bantam Doubleday Dell Publishing Group, Inc./ Cover of *Wolf by the Ears,* by Ann Rinaldi. Text copyright © 1991 by Ann Rinaldi. Reprinted by permission of Scholastic Inc./ Photograph by Bart Ehrenberg.

**ROBERT ROENNFELDT.** Photograph courtesy of Robert Roennfeldt.

**ROBERT ROPER.** Photograph courtesy of Robert Roper.

**JOHN RUEMMLER.** Photograph courtesy of John Ruemmler.

**MARGARET RYAN.** Cover of *Figure Skating,* by Margaret Ryan. Copyright © 1987 by Margaret Ryan. Cover design reprinted by permission of Franklin Watts, Inc. Cover photograph reprinted by permission of AP/Wide World Photos./ Photograph by Dency Kane.

**ANNE LINDBERGH SAPIEYEVSKY.** Jacket of *The Hunky-Dory Dairy,* by Anne Lindbergh. Jacket illustration copyright © 1986 by Julie Brinckloe. Reprinted by permission of Harcourt Brace & Company./ Jacket of *The Shadow on the Dial,* by Anne Lindbergh. Jacket art copyright © 1987 by Richard Jesse Watson. Jacket copyright © 1987 by Harper & Row, Publishers, Inc. Reprinted by permission of HarperCollins Publishers Inc./ Photograph by Sally Stone Halvorson.

**PAMELA SARGENT.** Jacket of *Homesmind,* by Pamela Sargent. Jacket art copyright © 1984 by David Palladini. Jacket copyright © 1984 by Harper & Row, Publishers, Inc./ Cover of *Alien Child,* by Pamela Sargent. Cover art copyright © 1988 by Vincent Nasta. Cover copyright © 1989 by Harper & Row Publishers, Inc. Reprinted by permission of HarperCollins Publishers Inc./ Photograph by Jerry Bauer.

**WILL SHETTERLY.** Cover of *Elsewhere,* by Will Shetterly. Copyright © 1991 by Will Shetterly and Terri Windling. Cover art by Dennis Nolan. Reprinted by permission of Tom Doherty Associates, Inc.

**ERICA SILVERMAN.** Cover of *On Grandma's Roof,* by Erica Silverman. Illustrations copyright © 1990 by Deborah Kogan. Reprinted by permission of Macmillan Publishing Company, a division of Macmillan, Inc./ Photograph by Marilyn Sanders.

**MARYA SMITH.** Photograph by Tom Fezzey, courtesy of Marya Smith.

**MARGARET SPRINGER.** Cover of *A Royal Ball,* by Margaret Springer. Illustrations copyright © 1992 by Tom O'Sullivan. Reprinted by permission of Boyds Mills Press, Inc./ Photograph courtesy of Margaret Springer.

**TRICIA SPRINGSTUBB.** Jacket of *Eunice (The Egg Salad) Gottlieb,* by Tricia Springstubb. Copyright © 1988 by Tricia Springstubb. Jacket illustration copyright © 1988 by Don Dailey. Reprinted by permission of Bantam Doubleday Dell Books for Young Readers./ Photograph courtesy of Tricia Springstubb.

**BARBARA SPURLL.** Illustration by Barbara Spurll from *Mustard,* by Betty Waterton. Illustrations copyright © 1992 by Barbara Spurll. Reprinted by permission of Scholastic Canada Ltd./ Photograph courtesy of Barbara Spurll.

**ERIK D. STOOPS.** Photograph courtesy of Erik D. Stoops.

**CYNTHIA STOWE.** Photograph courtesy of Cynthia Stowe.

**ROSEMARY SUTCLIFF.** Cover of *The Eagle of the Ninth,* by Rosemary Sutcliff. Cover art copyright © 1993 by Charles Mikolaycak. Reprinted by permission of Farrar, Straus & Giroux, Inc./ Jacket of *The Shining Company,* by Rosemary Sutcliff. Jacket art copyright © 1990 by Charles Mikolaycak. Reprinted by permission of Farrar, Straus & Giroux, Inc./ Cover of *Flame-Colored Taffeta,* by Rosemary Sutcliff. Cover art copyright © 1986 by Rachel Birkett. Reprinted by permission of Farrar, Straus & Giroux, Inc./ Jacket of *The Minstrel and the Dragon Pup,* by Rosemary Sutcliff. Jacket illustration copyright © 1993 by Emma Chichester Clark. Reprinted by permission of Candlewick Press, Cambridge, MA./ Photograph courtesy of Murray Pollinger.

**DAVE TAYLOR.** Photograph by James D. Markou, courtesy of Dave Taylor.

**WILLIAM TAYLOR.** Jacket of *Agnes the Sheep,* by William Taylor. Jacket painting © 1991 by David Gaadt. Reprinted by permission of Scholastic Inc.

**JOYCE CAROL THOMAS.** Jacket of *Journey,* by Joyce Carol Thomas. Jacket painting copyright © 1988 by Paul Davis. Reprinted by permission of Scholastic Inc./ Cover of *Marked by Fire,* by Joyce Carol Thomas. Copyright © 1982 by Joyce Carol Thomas. Reprinted by permission of Avon Books, New York./ Cover of *Bright Shadow,* by Joyce Carol Thomas. Copyright © 1983 by Joyce Carol Thomas. Reprinted by permission of Avon Books, New York./ Photograph by Steve Anderson, courtesy of Joyce Carol Thomas.

**STEPHANIE TOLAN.** Jacket of *The Witch of Maple Park,* by Stephanie Tolan. Jacket illustration copyright © 1992 by Helen Cogancherry. Reprinted by permission of Morrow Junior Books, a division of William Morrow & Company, Inc./ Jacket of *Plague Year,* by Stephanie Tolan. Jacket illustration copyright © 1990 by Ellen Thompson. Reprinted by permission of Ellen Thompson.

**NELLY S. TOLL.** Photograph by Herb Nelson.

**VALERIE TRIPP.** Photograph courtesy of Valerie Tripp.

**JEAN URE.** Cover of *Hi There, Supermouse!,* by Jean Ure. Hutchinson Junior Books Ltd., 1983. Copyright © 1983 by Jean Ure. Illustrations by Martin White. Reprinted by permission of William Morrow & Company, Inc./ Cover of *See You Thursday,* by Jean Ure. Copyright © 1981 by Jean Ure. Reprinted by permission of Dell Books, a division of Bantam Doubleday Dell Publishing Group, Inc./ Photograph courtesy of Jean Ure.

**LAUREL van der LINDE.** Photograph courtesy of Laurel van der Linde.

**JOAN MARIE VERBA.** Photograph courtesy of Joan Marie Verba.

**MARTHA M. VERTREACE.** Cover of *Kelly in the Mirror,* by Martha M. Vertreace. Illustrations © 1993 by Sandra Speidel. Reprinted by permission of Albert Whitman & Company. All rights reserved./ Photograph courtesy of Martha M. Vertreace.

**BARBARA BROOKS WALLACE.** Jacket of *Miss Switch to the Rescue,* by Barbara Brooks Wallace. Copyright © 1981 by Abingdon. Jacket and book design by Thelma Whitworth. Reprinted by permission of Abingdon Press./ Jacket of *The Contest Kid Strikes Again,* by Barbara Brooks Wallace. Copyright © 1980 by Abingdon. Illustrations by Gloria Kamen. Reprinted by permission of Abingdon Press./ Jacket of *Julia and the Third Bad Thing,* by Barbara Brooks Wallace. Illustrations copyright © 1975 by Follett Publishing Company, a division of Follett Corporation. Illustrations by Mike Eagle. Reprinted by permission of Mike Eagle./ Cover of *Peppermints in the Parlor,* by Barbara Brooks Wallace. Cover illustration copyright © 1993 by Richard Williams. Cover design by Rebecca Tachna. Reprinted by permission of Richard Williams./ Photograph courtesy of Barbara Brooks Wallace.

**DONNA WALSH SHEPHERD.** Photograph courtesy of Donna Walsh Shepherd.

**APRIL HALPRIN WAYLAND.** Photograph by Steve DeVorkin, courtesy of April Halprin Wayland.

**WILLIAM WEGMAN.** Illustration by William Wegman from *Little Red Riding Hood,* retold by William Wegman with Carole Kismaric and Marvin Heiferman. Text and photographs copyright © 1993 by William Wegman. Reprinted by permission of Hyperion Books for Children./ Photograph by Madeleine de Sinety.

**SUSAN WELLS.** Cover of *The Illustrated World of Oceans,* by Susan Wells. Copyright © 1991 by Ilex Publishers Limited. Reprinted in Canada and the United States by permission of the publisher, Simon & Schuster Books for Young Readers, New York.

**SHERLEY ANNE WILLIAMS.** Illustration from *Working Cotton,* by Sherley Anne Williams. Illustrations copyright © 1992 by Carole Byard. Reprinted by permission of Harcourt Brace & Company.

**PATRICIA WINDSOR.** Jacket of *How a Weirdo and a Ghost Can Change Your Entire Life,* by Patricia Windsor. Text copyright © 1986 by Patricia Windsor. Jacket design by Donna Jaseckas. Jacket illustration copyright © 1986 by Jacqueline Rogers. Reprinted by permission of Bantam Doubleday Dell Books for Young Readers./ Cover of *The Sandman's Eyes,* by Patricia Windsor. Copyright © 1985 by Patricia Windsor. Reprinted by permission of Dell Books, a division of Bantam Doubleday Dell Publishing Group, Inc./ Cover of *The Christmas Killer,* by Patricia Windsor. Copyright © 1991 by Patricia Windsor. Reprinted by permission of Scholastic Inc./ Photograph by Steve Altman.

**SUSAN WOJCIECHOWSKI.** Jacket of *And the Other, Gold,* by Susan Wojciechowski. Jacket painting by Toby Gowing. Jacket design by Sylvia Frezzolini. Copyright © 1987 by Orchard Books. Reprinted by permission of Orchard Books, a division of Franklin Watts, Inc./ Photograph courtesy of Susan Wojciechowski.

**JANET WOLF.** Jacket by Janet Wolf from *Rosie & the Yellow Ribbon,* by Paula DePaola. Copyright © 1991 by Janet Wolf. Reprinted by permission of Little, Brown and Company./ Photograph courtesy of Janet Wolf.

**VIRGINIA EUWER WOLFF.** Photograph courtesy of Virginia Euwer Wolff.

**HERBERT WONG YEE.** Photograph by Judy Yee.

**DEBORAH TURNEY ZAGWYN.** Photograph courtesy of Deborah Turney Zagwyn.

**CHARLOTTE ZOLOTOW.** Cover of *I Know a Lady,* by Charlotte Zolotow. Illustrations copyright © 1984 by James Stevenson. Reprinted by permission of Greenwillow Books, a division of William Morrow & Company, Inc./ Cover of *Do You Know What I'll Do?,* by Charlotte Zolotow. Illustrations copyright © 1958 by Garth Williams. Illustrations copyright © renewed 1986 by Garth Williams./ Cover of *This Quiet Lady,* by Charlotte Zolotow. Illustrations copyright © 1992 by Anita Lobel. Reprinted by permission of Greenwillow Books, a division of William Morrow & Company, Inc.

# SOMETHING ABOUT THE AUTHOR®

ABBOTT, Sarah
  See Zolotow, Charlotte S(hapiro)

*   *   *

ADAMS, Tricia
  See KITE, (L.) Patricia

*   *   *

ALBERTSON, Susan
  See WOJCIECHOWSKI, Susan

*   *   *

ALLISON, Diane Worfolk

## ■ Personal

Born in Mt. Kisco, NY; daughter of Frederic (a food inspector) and Dorothy (a secretary; maiden name, Russo) Worfolk; married C. Monroe Allison II (a sales executive), May 16, 1970; children: Jessica Mary, Paul Roy. *Education:* Macalester College, B.A., 1970; Midwest Montessori Training Center, certificate. *Religion:* Christian Scientist.

## ■ Addresses

*Home*—207 Sterling Place, Brooklyn, NY 11238.

DIANE WORFOLK ALLISON

## ■ Career

Children's book writer and illustrator. Ezzard Charles School, Chicago, IL, Montessori directress, 1972-76; Ancona Montessori School, Chicago, art director, 1980-81, integrated arts director and storyteller, 1982-83; Cultural Education Collaborative of Massachusetts, visiting artist and storyteller, 1986-90; Spectrum Educational Services, storyteller, 1992-93; freelance storyteller, songwriter, and illustrator, 1994—.

1

## ■ Awards, Honors

*This Is the Key to the Kingdom* was a *Reading Rainbow* selection, 1993.

## ■ Writings

### PICTURE BOOKS

*In Window Eight, the Moon Is Late,* Little, Brown, 1988.
*This Is the Key to the Kingdom,* Little, Brown, 1992.

### ILLUSTRATOR

Patricia Edwards, *Chester and Uncle Willoughby* (picture book), Little, Brown, 1987.
Ann Cameron, *Julian, Secret Agent,* Random House, 1988.
Polly Berends, *The Case of the Elevator Duck,* Random House, 1989.
Susan Saunders, *Tent Show,* Dutton, 1990.
Nancy White Carlstrom, *Wishing at Dawn in Summer* (picture book), Little, Brown, 1993.

### OTHER

Also author of poems and a series on modern art for children for the *Christian Science Monitor;* author of television scripts for *Beyond the Magic Door,* for ABC Chicago, and three-minute marketing films and commercials for Sears, Roebuck and Co. Allison's illustrations have appeared in various periodicals.

## ■ Work in Progress

"*Tanta,* about a friend's Czechoslovakian great aunt; *Just Papa and Me,* my mother's memories of vaudeville; a new musical based on a modern-day Peter Pan theme; illustrating for *Ladybug* magazine."

## ■ Sidelights

"I was born and raised in Mt. Kisco, New York, in a house where the town was down the hill and the 'estate' was up," Diane Worfolk Allison told *SATA.* "The town had a school with stern and dedicated teachers who admired my dancing and drawing and despaired at my absentmindedness. The estate had orchards, gardens, and woods where our feet sank deep in a carpet of needles. Our house had grownups who adored us, yelled at us, and trained us to be loving to all people, well-mannered at the table, and obedient, and who, to our great bliss, let us alone for hours. The library and book store furnished me with books, the ballet school with dance steps, the church with hope.

"Although I loved to dance, I always felt the only self-respecting job was saving the world. I thought about it deeply and designed many schemes. I came to the conclusion that the only way to do this was through education—especially the education of teachers and Soviet premiers. So the job was to instill a love of ideas and write the books that would, well, do the trick. They'd have to be beautiful, of course. There was nothing so infuriating as awful pictures in a book. Beautiful drawings had power. The words told the story, the pictures showed the love. Lines were wondrous to me, and shadowed forms, and expressions.

"When I grew up, childhood had become a foreign country. I'd forgotten the language. I became a Montessori teacher. Gradually my heart burned again the way it did when I was little. Then I could work on my books. Those drawings led to the illustrations in *Chester and Uncle Willoughby,* which led to *In Window Eight, the Moon Is Late,* then *This Is the Key to the Kingdom.* That book germinated from my love for a student I'd had long ago in Chicago who, though trapped in a grim life in a grim corner of the city, came to school filled with wonder and so many questions.

"At first, the book was a way to take her into my own childhood, to the woods and gardens, but that was not right. The book took three years. There were few crises I wasn't stabbed with during that long struggle, but each held a lesson, and then friends handed me keys. I finally saw that she had the kingdom within her all along, and so did I. And the key is there, too. The book has been criticized for the pale palette. I honestly could not paint it differently today. It is a dream world, and that is the palette of my dreams. Spiritually it's right, even if it's professionally all wrong.

"I am story-telling now. My ancestors were performers. It is not writing books, but it is telling about them. It's not painting, except with myself. It's not saving the world—not the whole world. But it's getting there, one smile at a time."

\*       \*       \*

## ANGELL, Judie 1937-
## (Fran Arrick, Maggie Twohill)

## ■ Personal

Born July 10, 1937, in New York, NY; daughter of David Gordon (an attorney) and Mildred (a teacher; maiden name, Rogoff) Angell; married Philip Gaberman (a pop and jazz music teacher and arranger), December 20, 1964; children: Mark David, Alexander. *Education:* Syracuse University, B.S., 1959. *Religion:* "Yes." *Hobbies and other interests:* Singing, painting, cats, listening to music.

## ■ Addresses

*Home*—South Salem, NY.

## ■ Career

Elementary school teacher in Brooklyn, NY, 1959-62; *TV Guide,* Radnor, PA, associate editor of New York City metropolitan edition, 1962-63; WNDT-TV (now WNET-TV), New York City, continuity writer, 1963-68; full-time writer, 1968—. Has worked variously as a switchboard operator and a waitress.

JUDIE ANGELL

■ **Awards, Honors**

Ethical Culture School Book Award, 1977, for *In Summertime It's Tuffy,* and 1979, for *A Word from Our Sponsor; or, My Friend Alfred;* Best Books for Young Adults citations, American Library Association, 1978, for *Steffie Can't Come Out to Play,* 1980, for *Tunnel Vision,* 1983, for *God's Radar,* and 1985, for *One-Way to Ansonia.*

■ **Writings**

*YOUNG ADULT NOVELS*

*In Summertime It's Tuffy,* Bradbury Press, 1977.
*Ronnie and Rosey,* Bradbury Press, 1977.
*Tina Gogo,* Bradbury Press, 1978.
*Secret Selves,* Bradbury Press, 1979.
*A Word from Our Sponsor; or, My Friend Alfred,* Bradbury Press, 1979.
*Dear Lola; or, How to Build Your Own Family: A Tale,* Bradbury Press, 1980.
*What's Best for You,* Bradbury Press, 1981.
*The Buffalo Nickel Blues Band,* Bradbury Press, 1982.
*First, the Good News,* Bradbury Press, 1983.
*Suds: A New Daytime Drama,* Bradbury Press, 1983.
*A Home Is to Share—and Share—and Share—,* Bradbury Press, 1984.
*One-Way to Ansonia,* Bradbury Press, 1985.
*The Weird Disappearance of Jordan Hall,* Orchard Books, 1987.
*Don't Rent My Room!,* Bantam Books, 1990.
*Leave the Cooking to Me,* Bantam Books, 1990.
*Yours Truly,* Orchard House, 1993.

*YOUNG ADULTS NOVELS; UNDER PSEUDONYM FRAN ARRICK*

*Steffie Can't Come Out to Play,* Bradbury Press, 1978.
*Tunnel Vision,* Bradbury Press, 1980.
*Chernowitz!,* Bradbury Press, 1981.
*God's Radar,* Bradbury Press, 1983.
*Nice Girl from Good Home,* Bradbury Press, 1984.
*Where'd You Get the Gun, Billy?,* Bantam Books, 1991.
*What You Don't Know Can Kill You,* Bantam Books, 1992.

*CHILDREN'S NOVELS; UNDER PSEUDONYM MAGGIE TWOHILL*

*Who Has the Lucky Duck in Class 4-B?,* Bradbury Press, 1984.
*Jeeter, Mason and the Magic Headset,* Bradbury Press, 1985.
*Bigmouth,* Bradbury Press, 1986.
*Valentine Frankenstein,* Bradbury Press, 1991.
*Superbowl Upset,* Bradbury Press, 1991.

*OTHER*

Contributor of short stories to anthologies, including *Sixteen: Short Stories by Outstanding Writers for Young Adults,* edited by Donald R. Gallo.

■ **Adaptations**

*Dear Lola; or, How to Build Your Own Family: A Tale* was adapted as the videotape *The Beniker Gang* by Scholastic, Lorimar Distribution, 1984; *Ronnie and Rosey* was recorded on audiocassette as part of the "Young Adult Cliffhangers Series" by Listening Library, 1985.

■ **Sidelights**

"As far back as I can remember, there have been two constants in my life—music and writing," Judie Angell stated in a publicity release for Bradbury Press. "The music was always there as background for the stories in my head, a rhythm to fit the mood." Angell, the author of popular novels for young people of various age groups, recalled the sound of the Victrola playing in the mid-1940s while she, an eight- or nine-year-old, fashioned stories in crayon about a girl who rescues various animals from perilous situations. Angell's concern for animals was eventually displaced by a passion for baseball, but her interest in music continued to develop; the works of Norwegian composer Edvard Grieg and Russian composer Pyotr Tchaikovsky provided the atmosphere as she depicted the painful defeats of the Brooklyn Dodgers. And as an adolescent in the 1950s the author recorded personal thoughts and feelings in a diary while listening to jazz and pop artist Nat King Cole or the musicals of Rodgers and Hammerstein.

Angell attended Syracuse University, and shortly after graduating in 1959 she accepted a position as a second-grade teacher in Brooklyn, New York. The author's first professional writing experiences involved composing blurbs for *TV Guide* and writing for a public television station during the 1960s. In 1964 Angell married Philip

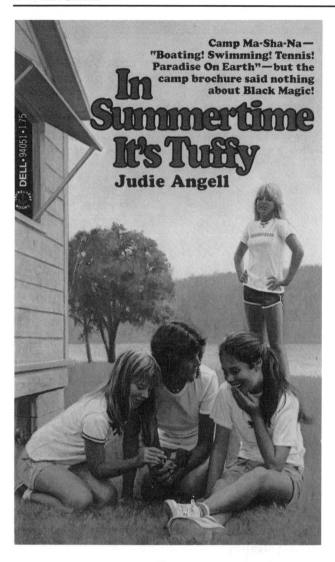

Camp Ma-Sha-Na—
"Boating! Swimming! Tennis!
Paradise On Earth"—but the
camp brochure said nothing
about Black Magic!

**In Summertime It's Tuffy**

Judie Angell

DELL · 94051 · 1.75

**Tuffy and her bunkmates at camp Ma-Sha-Na plot revenge against a hated camp counselor in Angell's humorous juvenile novel.**

Gaberman, a music teacher and arranger specializing in pop and jazz. They moved to an old house on a lake in South Salem, New York, where they raised their two sons, Mark and Alexander. Angell has been crafting works of fiction since 1968, and her musical inspirations have included jazz artists Cleo Laine and Mel Torme, stage musical writers Stephen Sondheim and Marvin Hamlisch, pop singer/songwriter Paul Simon, and classical composer Johann Sebastian Bach.

### Childhood Inspires Work

Angell considers each element of her youth and early adulthood helpful in her current work as a novelist for children and young adults. While her teaching and television writing served to strengthen her skills, her childhood stories and musical background inspired many of the characters and events in her books. The author has strong memories of the powerful emotions that pre-teens and teenagers experience and believes this to be her most important asset as a writer. "I take a lot of those feelings, hug them, wrap them carefully in some

words, and present them in a book with an invisible card that says, maybe this'll help a little—make you laugh—make you feel you're not alone," Angell related in a Bradbury Press publicity release. The author currently publishes three different categories of novels under separate pen names. She has been writing longest under the name Judie Angell, producing works for and about pre-teens and younger teenagers. Since the late 1970s, she has explored darker subjects for older teenagers under the pseudonym Fran Arrick. More recently, Angell has adopted the name Maggie Twohill to fashion books suited to a younger audience.

Blending serious emotions with humorous circumstances, Angell's novels explore both common and unique issues that young people face in their families, with their peers, and with authority figures. Most of her protagonists are experiencing important transitions in their lives, and they tend to be clever and creative in meeting the challenges involved in moving toward adulthood. Angell's first book, 1977's *In Summertime It's Tuffy,* is based on the author's fifteen summers away at camp as a camper, counselor-in-training, senior counselor, and dramatics counselor. The main character, eleven-year-old Betsy (whose summer nickname is Tuffy), and her friends were devised as "a composite of my friends and young charges during those years," the author explained. Amidst the typical camp activities— including swimming and arts and crafts—Tuffy gets to know her bunk mates, one of whom is overweight, another obsessively neat, and a third preoccupied with boys and clothes. Tuffy also befriends Iris, a new girl with creative talents and an interest in witchcraft. Iris, Tuffy eventually learns, has wealthy parents who send her to boarding school and summer camp while they travel the world. She is attempting to use black magic to force them to spend time with her. But the girls' more immediate problem is the heartless head counselor, Uncle Otto. Combining Tuffy's wit and Iris's voodoo, the two wage a war against him that lands them in hilarious straits.

Angell's knowledge of and love for music are evident in *The Buffalo Nickel Blues Band,* her 1982 work concerning a group of sixth- and seventh-grade musicians. Jewish pianist Eddie Levy, black drummer Ivy Sunday, and white Anglo-Saxon Protestant guitarist Georgie Higgins are close friends as well as members of a band. On the advice of Eddie's piano teacher, they concentrate on the blues and enlist two new instrumentalists: horn player Shelby Powell and a bassist who only admits to the name Reese. The two newcomers are somewhat odd and mysterious, but the band improves significantly and becomes better known. Eventually Reese and Shelby reveal their secrets, involving the band members and their parents in humorous antics. Holly Sanhuber asserted in *School Library Journal* that in spite of minor unrealistic elements, "the story is engaging, and readers are made to care for the players."

## Angell's Strong, Independent Characters

In 1980 Angell published *Dear Lola; or, How to Build Your Own Family: A Tale.* This work involves six residents of an orphanage—ranging in age from five to eighteen—each of whom has been either orphaned or deserted. Although they all depend on each other and are as close as any family, the orphanage continually threatens to separate them by placing the younger ones in foster homes. To avoid this fate, they decide to run away from the orphanage and live in a home of their own. Eighteen-year-old Arthur Beniker—whose nickname, Lola, is the pseudonym under which he writes a nationally-syndicated advice column—orchestrates the plan and provides emotional and financial support for the rest of the Benikers: ten-year-old Anne, who narrates the story, and her twin brother Al-William; eight-year-old Edmund, who is prone to temper tantrums; five-year-old Ben, who is constantly eating small objects; and thirteen-year-old James, whose need for privacy is so great that he rarely leaves his room or makes contact with anyone other than Lola. They travel in a van for three months, stopping at libraries where Lola reads to the group and researches child custody laws. When they are a safe distance from the orphanage, they rent and renovate a house in a small town. In this setting Lola works on his column and tutors James, the other

In this young adult novel by Angell, a girl from a broken family resolves to find someone to love after losing touch with her father. (Cover illustration by Richard Elmer.)

This soap opera spoof features a wealthy orphan who encounters—and survives—a number of unusual situations. (Cover illustration by Jenny Rutherford.)

children attend school, and they all help each other work out the difficulties that arise.

But the group attracts the attention of school authorities and suspicious neighbors. They attempt to persuade the community that they are siblings living with their ailing grandfather. But when the truth is discovered, Lola must prove in court that he is fit to be the children's guardian. He explains to the judge that for the first time in the Benikers' lives, they all have a stable, nurturing home environment. The judge is impressed by Lola's intentions, but when he insists that Lola identify his occupation, the resulting publicity costs Lola his job, and this in turn costs him legal custody of the children. The Benikers make another daring escape, however, and wind up picking fruit in California. Reviewers appreciated Angell's exploration of the rights of minors, and praised her ability to promote a willing suspension of disbelief. Marilyn R. Singer commented in *School Library Journal* that the book "will gladden the hearts of many young readers." In her review of the novel for *Publishers Weekly,* Jean F. Mercier described her reaction to *Dear Lola* in the words of poet William

Wordsworth: "'surprised by joy—impatient to get on with it.'"

In 1985, Angell published *One-Way to Ansonia,* a novel about a Jewish immigrant arriving in the United States in the late 1800s. The work was inspired in part by the experiences of the author's maternal grandmother. Ten-year-old Rose Olshansky and her four brothers and sisters travel by boat from their Russian village to New York City's Lower East Side, in order to attend their father's wedding. When they arrive they learn that their stepmother has only been informed about the youngest child, Celia. The apartment is too small to accommodate the others, so Rose and her three older siblings find separate homes with neighbors, working to pay for their room and board. Although Celia attends school, Rose must work at a factory, where she sews twelve hours a day for pennies. At the age of fourteen, she becomes determined to learn to read and write English and begins attending night school against her father's wishes. Walking to class one evening, she meets Hyman Rogoff, a young trade unionist who is attending a meeting in the same building. Unlike most men in their community, who view women only as child-bearers and house-

**Shirley has no problem running her own catering business, but has trouble keeping it a secret from her disapproving mother in *Leave the Cooking to Me.* (Cover illustration by Ken Joudrey.)**

keepers, Hyman appreciates Rose's intellect, and the two become friends. When her father selects a husband for Rose whom she does not like, she quickly proposes to Hyman and convinces her father to permit them to marry. But soon after their first baby is born, Hyman contracts pneumonia and Rose's best friend is killed at a union rally. Sixteen-year-old Rose decides she has had enough of the ghetto. Promising to send for Hyman when she is settled, she takes the baby and her savings to Grand Central Station. Choosing her destination on the basis of what she can afford, she buys a one-way ticket to Ansonia, Connecticut, a town with hills and trees where she hopes to start a new life. Although a *Bulletin of the Center for Children's Books* contributor felt that the "book is weakened" by Angell's focus on historical setting, Hanna B. Zeiger maintained in *Horn Book* that "Judie Angell has created a powerful, moving story rich in authentic images and characterization."

Angell's 1989 work, *Leave the Cooking to Me,* concerns a modern-day young woman who, like *One-Way to Ansonia*'s Rose, is determined to make her own way in the world. Fifteen-year-old Shirley Merton is seeking summer employment. Her mother, who runs her late husband's law firm, wants Shirley's work to be intellectually stimulating. However, the only jobs available involve bagging groceries or shelving library books. Then Shirley's friend Mary Kay's mother needs last-minute help preparing for a dinner party. Cooking has been Shirley's forte since she began fixing meals for her mother and younger sister several years earlier, so she agrees to lend her assistance and winds up doing most of the work. At the party, one of the guests is so impressed with the food that she assumes it was prepared by a professional. When she asks Shirley for the name of the caterer for whom she works, Shirley invents the name "Vanessa" and supplies her own phone number. Soon, the woman calls to ask Vanessa to cater a party, and Shirley makes the arrangements. She tells her mother she has found a job, but refuses to disclose any information about it.

Shirley hires Mary Kay and a few other friends as kitchen help and a charming boy to wait tables in exchange for tutoring. Although the fictional Vanessa does not appear at the function, the caterers are so competent that no one doubts the company's legitimacy. As other guests sample Shirley's fare, she is hired to cater more and more functions, and the business becomes extremely lucrative. But when Mrs. Merton finds her daughter's stash of money, she suspects Shirley is involved in drug dealing. But she gets a first-hand glimpse of Shirley's abilities when she is invited to a party catered by Vanessa.

## Writing as Fran Arrick

In the late 1970s, Angell adopted the pseudonym Fran Arrick and began producing novels about controversial topics for older teens. By depicting realistic family and community scenarios, the author brings prominent social issues such as suicide, prostitution, and acquired immunodeficiency syndrome (AIDS) into a personal

**A young Russian immigrant attempts to define her own life by attending school, joining a workers' union, and choosing her own husband in this story based on the life of Angell's grandmother. (Cover illustration by Robert Casilla.)**

context. *Tunnel Vision,* Arrick's 1980 work, begins with the death of Anthony, a bright, athletic, well-liked fifteen-year-old who hangs himself with his father's neckties and leaves no note. The novel explores the reactions of Anthony's friends and relations, revealing the events that led up to the suicide through flashbacks. Although he was depressed, Anthony was attuned to the needs of his parents, rebellious sister, and rape-victim girlfriend. While none of these characters is certain of the reason for Anthony's suicide, each one blames someone different, and as they share their grief, they all gain new strength. A neighborhood police officer who has investigated a number of teen suicides describes the common element among the victims: "It's like each of them was caught inside a tunnel and they couldn't see any end to it or anything at all outside." Although one *Kirkus Reviews* critic judged the book to be "inoffensive but uninspired," others praised it as authentically and humanly presented. Laura Geringer stated in *School Library Journal* that the characters' "struggle to come to terms with [Anthony's decision] rings true, and should prompt some heated discussions." *Publishers Weekly* contributor Jean F. Mercier declared that the "human-

ized cast grips the reader and can help, perhaps, to promote understanding of troubled teenagers."

In 1984 Angell examined the impact of sudden unemployment on a well-off family in *Nice Girl from Good Home.* Brady Hewitt is a successful advertising executive whose wife Deborah and teenage children Jeremy and Dory are accustomed to country clubs and designer clothing. When Brady loses his job and begins drinking, Deborah goes into denial and continues spending money as if nothing had happened. But then her husband puts their house up for sale, and she has a breakdown and is institutionalized. Echoing her mother's reaction, Dory buys an expensive dress, and Brady orders her to return it. She defies her father, making him furious, and then rebels by cutting school and spending time with trouble-makers who help her plan a bomb threat. Jeremy, meanwhile, determines to ease the family's financial straits. Forgoing college to start a house painting business, he suggests a job for his father that might help keep the family together. Audrey B. Eaglen remarked in *School Library Journal* that *Nice Girl from Good Home* "lacks the power of Arrick's *Tunnel Vision* ... because of a wildly unbelievable plot and flat characterization." However, a *Bulletin of the Center for Children's Books* contributor called the work "starkly realistic; the characters are convincing and their problems (and solutions) believable."

Angell uses a quiet town setting to present the problem of handgun violence in her 1991 novel, *Where'd You Get the Gun, Billy?* Billy, a high school student, shoots and kills his girlfriend, Lisa, and the entire community is deeply affected. One of Billy and Lisa's classmates, David, becomes intent on learning how Billy obtained the murder weapon. With Lisa's best friend Liz, David goes to the police station, where a lieutenant enumerates the ways in which guns are acquired, from permits to theft. The lieutenant then traces the revolver's hypothetical journey from legal owner to troubled teenager. His story implies that handguns are too readily available, but also points to the deeper societal ills that are the root causes of violence. While a *Publishers Weekly* reviewer decided that "the novel sacrifices verisimilitude for tabloid-style sensationalism," *School Library Journal's* Ellen Ramsay praised Arrick's approach to the issue: "With its straightforward style and episodic plot, [the novel] effectively examines the problem."

*What You Don't Know Can Kill You,* Arrick's 1992 novel, is narrated by thirteen-year-old Debra. Debra envies her attractive and intelligent eighteen-year-old sister, Ellen, who is dating Jack, a handsome college student. When a neighboring family is badly hurt in a car accident, Ellen volunteers to donate blood for a transfusion. When her blood is tested, however, Ellen learns that she has been infected with human immunodeficiency virus (HIV). HIV antibodies can be transmitted through unprotected sexual contact and eventually cause the deadly AIDS. Ellen did not practice safe sex because she thought her relationship with Jack was monogamous. But Jack confesses to having had an affair while at school. Ellen, Debra, and their parents are shocked and grief-stricken. Although Ellen remains healthy, the community soon learns about her condition and responds with hostility. Jack's guilt leads him to commit suicide, but Ellen's family is united by their struggle, and Debra vows never to engage in risky behavior. Reviewers responded favorably to the work, noting that the novel both reveals the ignorance and prejudice surrounding the AIDS virus and provides honest information. Susan R. Farber commented in *Voice of Youth Advocates,* "While the plot is not new, Debra's viewpoint and the family's deep grief make this an absorbing, emotional story." A *Publishers Weekly* critic found some of the dialogue unnatural, but added that *What You Don't Know Can Kill You* "should dispel notions of 'It can't happen to me' among careless, sexually active readers."

### Stories for Younger Children

In contrast to the novels she has written as Fran Arrick, which focus on harsh, serious topics for readers at the high school level, Angell's works under the pseudonym Maggie Twohill are lighter fare for middle school children. In the 1985 work, *Jeeter, Mason and the Magic Headset,* Jeeter Huff receives a radio headset and a Cabbage Patch doll, which she names Mason, for her tenth birthday. As Jeeter is skateboarding and listening to music, she is surprised to hear Mason speaking over the headset, warning her of an oncoming bike. After that, Mason makes a series of predictions—including one about Jeeter's father's job—all of which come true. Trouble arises when Jeeter's older sister Carol-Ann wants Mason to supply advice on attracting boys and passing exams. *School Library Journal* contributor Margaret Gross referred to the work as a "clever, lively tale for pre-adolescents. Characters are believable, the dialogue and action on-target."

*Valentine Frankenstein,* which Angell published under the Twohill pseudonym in 1991, is a more realistic story about friendship and popularity. Walter is a shy but sweet fifth-grader whose low opinion of himself causes his classmates to dislike him. As Valentine's Day draws near, Amanda—Walter's only friend—decides to boost his self-esteem by stuffing the class Valentine box with unsigned cards addressed to him. When he receives them at their holiday celebration, Walter is surprised and overjoyed. The other children suddenly take an interest in him, and he soon becomes the most popular boy in the class. But when Walter begins ignoring Amanda, she is both jealous and concerned and considers telling him the truth about the valentines. Nancy P. Reeder commented in *School Library Journal* that "Twohill has combined just the right amount of friendship and humor ... to create a readable, lighthearted story."

While the novels written under the names Judie Angell, Fran Arrick, and Maggie Twohill differ in terms of the characters' ages, subject matter, and level of difficulty, they are unified by the author's respect for young people. Angell reveals this through the strength and conviction of her protagonists as they come to terms

with the changes involved in growing up. Her frequent use of first-person narration allows her to tell stories through her young characters' insightful perceptions. Angell once reported that of all the rich childhood experience she brings to her writing, "Most important to me are the feelings I recall so well."

### ■ Works Cited

Angell, Judie, *Tunnel Vision,* Bradbury Press, 1980.

Eaglen, Audrey B., review of *Nice Girl from Good Home, School Library Journal,* December, 1984, p. 88.

Farber, Susan R., review of *What You Don't Know Can Kill You, Voice of Youth Advocates,* June, 1992, p. 91.

Geringer, Laura, review of *Tunnel Vision, School Library Journal,* April, 1980, pp. 119-20.

Gross, Margaret, review of *Jeeter, Mason and the Magic Headset, School Library Journal,* September, 1985, p. 140.

*Meet Judie Angell* (publicity release), Bradbury Press, c. 1978.

Mercier, Jean F., review of *Tunnel Vision, Publishers Weekly,* June 20, 1980, p. 87.

Mercier, Jean F., review of *Dear Lola, Publishers Weekly,* November 7, 1980, p. 61.

Review of *Nice Girl from Good Home, Bulletin of the Center for Children's Books,* December, 1984.

Review of *One-Way to Ansonia, Bulletin of the Center for Children's Books,* November, 1985.

Ramsay, Ellen, review of *Where'd You Get the Gun, Billy?, School Library Journal,* March, 1991, p. 211.

Reeder, Nancy P., review of *Valentine Frankenstein, School Library Journal,* January, 1992, p. 117.

Sanhuber, Holly, review of *The Buffalo Nickel Blues Band, School Library Journal,* August, 1982, p. 110.

Singer, Marilyn R., review of *Dear Lola, School Library Journal,* January, 1981, p. 56.

Review of *Tunnel Vision, Kirkus Reviews,* August 1, 1980, p. 983.

Review of *What You Don't Know Can Kill You, Publishers Weekly,* December 6, 1991, p. 74.

Review of *Where'd You Get the Gun, Billy?, Publishers Weekly,* December 21, 1990.

Zeiger, Hanna B., review of *One-Way to Ansonia, Horn Book,* March-April, 1986, pp. 205-206.

### ■ For More Information See

*BOOKS*

Gallo, Donald R., *Speaking for Ourselves: Autobiographical Sketches by Notable Authors of Books for Young Adults,* National Council of Teachers of English, 1990, pp. 8-9.

*PERIODICALS*

*Booklist,* November 1, 1979, p. 442.

*Bulletin of the Center for Children's Books,* January, 1980; November, 1985.

*Horn Book,* April, 1978; February, 1980; February, 1981.

*Kirkus Reviews,* January 1, 1980, p. 8; March 1, 1993, p. 296.

*New York Times Book Review,* October 9, 1977.

*Publishers Weekly,* February 28, 1977; April 23, 1982, p. 93; June 7, 1985, p. 81; December 22, 1989, p. 57; December 21, 1990, p. 57; November 15, 1991, p. 72; December 6, 1991, p. 74; March 22, 1993, p. 80.

*School Library Journal,* May, 1977, p. 58; November, 1979, p. 73; January, 1990, p. 120; April, 1993, p. 140.

*Washington Post Book World,* August 14, 1977.*

\*    \*    \*

## ARRICK, Fran
### See ANGELL, Judie

\*    \*    \*

## AYER, Eleanor H. 1947-

### ■ Personal

Born September 6, 1947, in Burlington, VT, daughter of William H. (a plumbing and heating contractor) and Shirley T. (an elementary school teacher; maiden name, Thomas) Hubbard; married John Ayer (a publisher); children: Madison, William. *Education:* Newhouse School of Journalism, Syracuse University, B.S., 1969, M.S., 1970.

### ■ Addresses

*Office*—P.O. Box 177, 541 Oak St., Frederick, CO 80530.

### ■ Career

Laubach Literacy Foundation, Syracuse, NY, associate editor for *News for You,* 1967-69; Laubach Literacy Foundation, Syracuse, associate editor for New Readers Press, 1969-70; *Jackson Hole Guide,* Jackson, WY, assistant editor, 1971; Jende-Hagan (book distribution and publishing company), Frederick, CO, co-founder, editor, and marketing manager, 1972—; Pruett Publishing Company, Boulder, CO, production/promotion coordinator, 1972; Shields Publishing Company, Fort Collins, CO, production/promotion coordinator, 1973-74; Renaissance House Publishing Company, Frederick, CO, editor and marketing manager, 1984—. Founder and writer for *The American Traveller* (travel guides), 1987—; free-lance writer. *Member:* Society of Children's Book Writers and Illustrators, Rocky Mountain Book Publishers Association, Mountains and Plains Booksellers Association, Colorado Authors' League.

### ■ Awards, Honors

Top Hand Award for young adult nonfiction, Colorado Authors' League, 1991, for *Teen Marriage;* Notable Children's Trade Book in the field of social studies, Children's Book Council and the National Council for Social Studies, 1992, for *Margaret Bourke-White;* Top

**ELEANOR H. AYER**

Hand Award for specialty writing, Colorado Authors' League, 1992, for *Southwest Traveler: The Anasazi: A Guide to Ancient Southwest Indians,* Top Hand Award for book-length nonfiction for young adults, Colorado Authors' League, 1992, for *The Value of Determination.*

### ■ Writings

*Green Light on the Tipple,* Platte 'N Press, 1978.

NONFICTION FOR YOUNG ADULTS

*Teen Marriage,* Rosen Publishing Group, 1990.
*Germany,* Rourke, 1990.
*The Value of Determination,* Rosen Publishing Group, 1991.
*Berlin,* New Discovery Books/Macmillan, 1992.
*Boris Yeltsin: Man of the People* (biography), Dillon Press/Macmillan, 1992.
*Margaret Bourke-White: Photographing the World* (biography), Dillon Press/Macmillan, 1992.
*Our Flag,* Millbrook Press, 1992.
*Our National Monuments,* Millbrook Press, 1992.
*The Anasazi,* Walker and Company, 1993.
*Everything You Need to Know about Teen Fatherhood,* Rosen Publishing Group, 1993.
*Teen Suicide: Is It Too Painful to Grow Up?* Twenty-first Century Books/Holt, 1993.
*Our Great Rivers and Waterways,* Millbrook Press, 1994.

Also author of revised editions of *Drug Abuse,* Rosen Publishing Group, 1991; *Sexual Abuse,* Rosen Publishing Group, 1992; *Family Violence,* Rosen Publishing Group, 1993.

*"COLORADO CHRONICLES" SERIES*

*Famous Colorado Men,* Platte 'N Press, 1980.
*Famous Colorado Women,* Platte 'N Press, 1981.
*Indians of Colorado,* illustrated by Jane Kline, Renaissance House, 1981.
*Hispanic Colorado,* illustrated by Kline, Renaissance House, 1982.
*Colorado Wildlife,* Platte 'N Press, 1983.
(Editor) *Colorado Businesses,* Renaissance House, 1984.
(Editor) Suzanne Thumhart, *Colorado Wonders,* illustrated by Kline, Renaissance House, 1986.
*Colorado Chronicles Index,* illustrated by Kline, Renaissance House, 1986.

*"TRAVEL GUIDES" SERIES*

*Colorado Traveler—Hall of Fame: A Gallery of the Rich and Famous,* Renaissance House, 1987.
*Colorado Traveler—Birds,* Renaissance House, 1987.
*Colorado Traveler—Parks and Monuments,* Renaissance House, 1987.
*Colorado Traveler—Wildflowers: A Guide to Colorado's Unique Varieties,* Renaissance House, 1987.
*Colorado Traveler—Skiing,* Renaissance House, 1987.
*Colorado Traveler—Discover Colorado,* Renaissance House, 1988.
*Arizona Traveler: Birds of Arizona—A Guide to Unique Varieties,* Renaissance House, 1988.
*Arizona Traveler: Discover Arizona—The Grand Canyon State,* Renaissance House, 1988.

*Arizona Traveler: Arizona Wildflowers,* Renaissance House, 1989.
*Arizona Traveler: Indians of Arizona,* Renaissance House, 1990.
*Southwest Traveler: A Guide to the Anasazi and Other Ancient Southwest Indians,* Renaissance House, 1991.
*California Traveler Earthquake Country: Traveling California's Fault Lines,* Renaissance House, 1992.
*California Traveler National Parks and Monuments: A Scenic Guide,* Renaissance House, 1992.

Also editor of volumes in the Colorado, Arizona, California, and Southwest Traveler series.

## ■ Work in Progress

*Ruth Bader Ginsburg,* and *The Holocaust Museum: America Keeps the Memory Alive* are under contract for Dillon Press (Macmillan), and *Depression* is under contract for Rosen Publishing Group. Ayer has completed manuscripts for *Parallel Journey* for Atheneum/Macmillan, and *Stress* for the Rosen Publishing Group. All are expected to be published in 1994.

## ■ For More Information See

*PERIODICALS*

*Booklist,* June 15, 1992, p. 1818; December 1, 1992.
*Kirkus Reviews,* January 1, 1993.
*School Library Journal,* October, 1992, p. 124; March, 1993, p. 205.
*Voice of Youth Advocate,* December, 1992, p. 298.

# B

## BARNHART, Clarence L(ewis) 1900-1993

*OBITUARY NOTICE*—See index for *SATA* sketch: Born December 30, 1900, near Plattsburg, MO; died of complications resulting from a fall, October 24, 1993, in Peekskill, NY. Lexicographer and editor. Keenly attuned to new words and changing usages in the English language, Barnhart oversaw the creation of a number of dictionaries and other reference works, including Random House's *American College Dictionary,* published in 1947. He also joined forces with the educational psychologist Edward L. Thorndike to produce a series of dictionaries designed for various levels of readers, from third-graders to college students. His *World Book Dictionary,* a family reference book, contained more than 250,000 entries. He began his own reference book company, Clarence L. Barnhart, Inc., in 1948, and from 1982 until his death Barnhart edited the *Barnhart Dictionary Companion* with his son Robert for Springer-Verlag.

*OBITUARIES AND OTHER SOURCES:*

*BOOKS*

*Who's Who in America,* 48th edition, Marquis, 1994, p. 186.

*PERIODICALS*

*Chicago Tribune,* October 31, 1993, section 2, p. 7.
*New York Times,* October 26, 1993, p. B10.
*Washington Post,* October 27, 1993, p. D5.

\*   \*   \*

## BENTLEY, Nancy 1946-

### ■ Personal

Born September 11, 1946, in East Orange, NJ; daughter of George E. (an instrument technician) and Antoinette Dorothy (a telephone company supervisor; maiden name, Grobosky) Bentley; married John Turner Atkinson (computer systems analyst) November 17, 1990. *Education:* Lake Erie College, B.A., 1968; University of

NANCY BENTLEY

Hawaii, M.Ed., 1974; University of Denver, M.A.L.S., 1981; attended Stanford University Publishing Course, 1983. *Politics:* Democrat. *Religion:* Catholic, Unitarian Universalist.

### ■ Addresses

*Home*—1220 West High Point Lane, Colorado Springs, CO 80904.

11

# ■ Career

Dancer-Fitzgerald-Sample, San Francisco, CA, production department assistant, 1968-70; San Mateo Educational Resources Center, San Mateo, CA, educational research assistant, 1972-74; Colorado Springs School District, Colorado Springs, CO, media specialist, 1974-78, teacher, 1979—. Creator and co-producer of videotape, *The Making of a Storybook: Mary Calhoun—Storyteller.* Member: Society of Children's Book Writers and Illustrators (former president, Rocky Mountain Region), Colorado Mountain Club, Common Cause.

# ■ Awards, Honors

*The Making of a Storybook: Mary Calhoun—Storyteller* was shown at Chicago International Children's Film Festival, 1991; Junior Literary Guild Selection, 1992, for *I've Got Your Nose;* Chautauqua Writer's Conference grant.

# ■ Writings

*I've Got Your Nose!,* Doubleday, 1991.
(With Donna Guthrie) *The Young Author's Do-it-Yourself Book: How to Write, Illustrate and Produce Your Own Book,* Millbrook Press, 1994.

*"BUSY BODY BOARD BOOK" SERIES; ILLUSTRATED BY KATY ARNSTEEN*

*Let's Go, Feet!,* Price, Stern, 1987.
*Do This, Hands!,* Price, Stern, 1987.
*Listen to This, Ears!,* Price, Stern, 1987.
*What's on Top, Head?,* Price, Stern, 1987.

*OTHER*

(Script writer) *I've Got Your Nose!* (videotape), Chip Taylor Communications, 1992.

Also author of script for videotape *The Making of a Storybook: Mary Calhoun—Storyteller,* 1991. Contributor to *Colorado Fever,* 1983-85.

# ■ Sidelights

Nancy Bentley told *SATA:* "Before I ever thought of becoming a writer I was a reader. I read so much in high school, locked away in my bedroom, perched on my favorite overstuffed chair, that my mother worried about me. I read partially to escape my loud and freewheeling family and partially to enter a lifelong journey into other worlds.

"Later I earned a master's degree in library science. It was a way of learning the organizational 'code' to a treasure trove of ideas. It was only much later, as an adult involved in education, that I began to try my hand at writing for children.

"Two of my continuing loves in life have been music and the outdoors. I sang in church choirs as a child and went on to participate in high school, college, and community choirs. In between I've studied opera and vocal music and continue to think that the most

Bentley's *I've Got Your Nose* features a witch who samples a number of noses in her search for the perfect fit. (Illustrated by Don Madden.)

wonderful job in the world would be to become an opera singer.

"My love of nature and the outdoors came together in many happy years spent as a Girl Scout. I was fortunate to participate in a Girl Scout Roundup in Vermont the year Maria Von Trapp talked to us. I still remember all ten thousand of us singing with her! Later as a Mariner Scout I was part of a crew that sailed from New York City to Mystic, Connecticut, on the *Yankee Schooner.* So it was a great honor for me to be selected as one of ten 'Women of Distinction' by the regional Pikes Peak Girl Scout Wagon Wheel Council in 1989.

"Although I grew up on the East Coast, I have spent most of my adult life living in the West—California, Hawaii, and now Colorado. I love to hike and ski (both downhill and cross-country) and am an amateur bird-watcher.

"I love books—I love reading them, sharing them with children, writing them! *I've Got Your Nose!* was written out of a childhood memory of one of my many uncles leaning down to 'steal my nose' with his fingers. The idea of losing or changing one's nose seemed utterly fascinating—then as well as now. *The Making of a Storybook: Mary Calhoun—Storyteller* was created for children, teachers, and librarians to see Mary up close and to explain how books and stories are created. *The Young Author's Do-it-Yourself Book: How to Write, Illustrate and Produce Your Own Book* was written in an effort to explain the publishing process to children and help them publish their own works."

**CLARA WIDESS BERKUS**

# BERKUS, Clara Widess 1909-

## ■ Personal

Born December 27, 1909, in Providence, RI; daughter of Calmon Max and Marion Beatrice (maiden name, Wolk) Widess; married Harry J. Berkus, 1932; children: Barry Alan, David William. *Education:* Attended University of California at Los Angeles, 1927-28, and University of California at Berkeley, 1929; University of Southern California, B.A., 1930. *Hobbies and other interests:* "Walking with friends and taking courses that open fresh areas of thought."

## ■ Career

Writer. *Member:* Society of Children's Book Writers and Illustrators, Monday Writers, Lena Passman Book Club, Pasadena Area Liberal Arts Center, Hadassah, Orton Dyslexia Society.

## ■ Writings

*Charlsie's Chuckle,* Woodbine Press, 1992.

## ■ Work in Progress

*A Boy and a Horse Named Dakota,* the story of the struggle of a boy with dyslexia to achieve his personal goal; *The Humpty, Dumpy, Grumpy, Day;* and *The Most Wonderful Things.*

## ■ Sidelights

"I began writing at an early age and received my first rejection slip at age nine," Clara Berkus told *SATA.* "At UCLA, I was a member of Tri-C and the local honorary journalism society, [and I was] society editor and a writer for the *Daily Bruin.* I studied playwriting at UCLA and at USC and later with George Abbot's play doctor, Martha Sheridan Stanton.... I published skits, short stories, articles, chiefly for children." During the 1960s, Berkus became active in grass roots politics and wrote publicity for candidates.

Berkus's first published book for children is *Charlsie's Chuckle,* a story about a boy with Down's syndrome who charms his town with his laugh. *School Library Journal* critic Constance A. Mellon wrote that Berkus's "conversational approach" in *Charlsie's Chuckle* "effectively introduces Down['s] syndrome without dwelling on potentially baffling points."

## ■ Works Cited

Mellon, Constance A., review of *Charlsie's Chuckle, School Library Journal,* March, 1993, p. 170.

\*       \*       \*

# BERLAN, Kathryn Hook 1946-

## ■ Personal

Born November 30, 1946, in Franklin County, OH; daughter of Robert Earl (owner of a hamburger and ice-cream shop) and Norma Jean (a porcelain artist; maiden name, Speaks) Hook; married Ronald George Berlan (an insurance underwriter) May 12, 1972; children: Michael David, Andrew Brian. *Education:* Ohio State University, B.S., 1969, additional studies, 1970-71; John Carroll University, M.Ed., 1993. *Religion:* Catholic. *Hobbies and other interests:* Children, nature, trees, hiking, reading, collecting, drawing, painting, building, gardening, horses.

## ■ Addresses

*Home*—5034 Hartley Dr., Lyndhurst, OH 44124.

## ■ Career

Hamilton Local Schools, Columbus, OH, third-grade teacher, 1969-70; Newark City Schools, Newark, OH, sixth-grade and elementary art teacher, 1971-77; Licking Valley Local Schools, Newark, second- and third-grade teacher, 1978-85. Freelance creator of workshops and teacher in-service projects, Cleveland, OH; Cleveland City Schools, creator and facilitator of classroom publishing project, 1991—. Owner and founder, Imagi-Books. Has given presentations for libraries and P.T.A. groups on writing with children. *Member:* International Reading Association, Society of Children's Book Writers and Illustrators.

## ■ Writings

*Andrew's Amazing Monsters,* Macmillan, 1993.

KATHRYN HOOK BERLAN

## ■ Work in Progress

*Tent Wars; Morning Glorious.*

## ■ Sidelights

Kathryn Hook Berlan told *SATA* that she "loved to daydream and create stories" in her mind as she was growing up in Ohio, but she "did not consider" herself to be a writer. Instead, she "loved drawing and painting," and was "especially adept at three-dimensional art, and loved to experiment with new materials." Berlan also explained to *SATA* that she was "an avid reader . . . . Through reading I could step into other worlds, make new friends of the characters that readers would love and miss at the book's end, but I still considered myself an artist, not a writer."

It was not until Berlan had been teaching school for some time that she began to seriously think about children's books. With her sons, Michael and Drew, and the young children she taught, she read children's books and "explored making books and imitating styles of famous illustrators such as Leo Leonni." Later, Berlan began to teach bookmaking. "Whole language teaching and young authors' conferences were the big buzz words in the Cleveland educational community," she told *SATA*. Berlan began to teach "freelance workshops to teachers and students in the suburban schools" of

Cleveland. "In my first workshop I saw that rare light a teacher sometimes sees in a child's eyes when something is happening in the classroom that really excites him; only I saw it in most of the students' eyes. I knew that this is what I wanted to do."

Berlan has since "taught thousands of children and many teachers how to create their own original books." She teaches classroom publishing at several elementary schools in Cleveland, and works with children—grades four through six—as they write newspapers and newsletters as well as create books. "There is magic in creating a three-dimensional book. It's like a sculpture. It clears away the assembly line fog of writing assignments and brings back the age of craftsmanship where the craftsman creates the product from start to finish. There is a feeling of ownership and pride that can't be beat."

\*    \*    \*

## BERNA, Paul 1910-1994

*OBITUARY NOTICE*—See index for *SATA* sketch: Born Jean Sabran on February 21, 1910, in Hyeres, France; died January 21, 1994, in Paris, France. Author. A prolific author of books for juvenile readers, Berna is best remembered for his mystery and adventure stories. After a stint as a journalist, he turned to writing children's books in the 1950s, publishing regularly until the early 1970s. Some of his novels for older children that have been translated into English include *Threshold of the Stars, The Clue of the Black Cat, The Secret of the Missing Boat,* and *The Mule on the Expressway.*

*OBITUARIES AND OTHER SOURCES:*

*BOOKS*

*Authors of Books for Young People,* 3rd edition, Scarecrow, 1990.

*PERIODICALS*

*New York Times,* January 28, 1994, p. B7.

\*    \*    \*

## BERNARD, Bruce

## ■ Personal

*Education:* Studied painting at St. Martin's School of Art.

## ■ Career

*Sunday Times Magazine* (London), picture editor, 1972-80; *Independent Magazine,* visual arts editor.

## ■ Writings

(Collector) *Photodiscovery: Masterworks of Photography, 1840-1940,* notes by Valerie Lloyd, Abrams, 1980.
*The Bible and Its Painters,* introduction by Lawrence Gowing, Macmillan, 1984.

**BRUCE BERNARD**

(Editor) *Vincent by Himself: A Selection of Van Gogh's Paintings and Drawings Together with Extracts from His Letters,* Little, Brown, 1985.

(Editor) *The Impressionist Revolution,* Orbis, 1986.

(Editor) *The Queen of Heaven: A Selection of Paintings of the Virgin Mary from the Twelfth to the Eighteenth Centuries,* introduction by Peter Levi, notes by Christopher Lloyd, Macdonald Orbis, 1987.

*Van Gogh,* Dorling Kindersley/Houghton, 1992.

## ■ Sidelights

Bruce Bernard came to prominence as the editor of *Photodiscovery: Masterworks of Photography 1840-1940,* a volume that, critics noted, treats the history of photography with the kind of respect usually reserved for painting. Bernard has also been praised for writing *The Bible and Its Painters* and his work as editor of *The Impressionist Revolution.* While most of his books have been geared toward an adult audience, however, more recently Bernard published *Van Gogh,* an art history book aimed at students in price, accessibility, and inclusiveness.

Part of a series on modern painters published by Dorling Kindersley, *Van Gogh* offers biographical material on the artist and images of his best known paintings as well as of objects that were included in the paintings, of his tools and preliminary sketches. In addition, extreme closeups of several paintings are featured in each of the volumes of the series so that students of art may examine brush strokes and application of pigments. Of *Van Gogh* Barbara Peklo Abrahams remarked in *School Library Journal* that the "visuals in these books are brilliant." And Joan Levin of *Library Journal* concluded: "The rich illustrations, informative text, and reasonable price recommend the series for public libraries."

## ■ Works Cited

Abrahams, Barbara Peklo, review of *Van Gogh, School Library Journal,* February, 1993, pp. 109-10.

Levin, Joan, review of *Van Gogh, Library Journal,* December, 1992, p. 130.

## ■ For More Information See

*PERIODICALS*

*Booklist,* June 15, 1981, pp. 1366-1367; October 15, 1984, p. 274.

*Christian Science Monitor,* December 12, 1984, p. 32.

*Los Angeles Times Book Review,* March 17, 1985, p. 10.

*New Statesman,* December 16, 1983, p. 29; January 9, 1987, p. 29.

*New York Times Book Review,* December 2, 1984, p. 11.

*Observer,* December 14, 1980, p. 29; December 18, 1983, p. 29; December 7, 1986, p. 29.

*Publishers Weekly,* October 10, 1980, p. 66; February 27, 1987, p. 156.

*Spectator,* December 6, 1980, pp. 17-18; December 17, 1983, p. 45; December 13, 1986, p. 37; November 28, 1987, p. 35; December 19, 1987, pp. 75, 77.

*Time,* December 10, 1984, p. 97.

*Times Educational Supplement,* January 6, 1984, p. 16.

*Times Literary Supplement,* November 14, 1980, p. 1299.

*Village Voice,* December 10, 1980, p. 55.*

**Bernard applied his experience in art history to this text specifically written for the student.**

## BETHANCOURT, T. Ernesto
See PAISLEY, Tom

\*   \*   \*

## BISHOP, Courtney
See RUEMMLER, John D(avid)

\*   \*   \*

## BLAKE, Jon 1954-

### ■ Personal

Born November 20, 1954, in Reading, England; son of Kenneth Thomas (an electrical contractor) and Ellen Jean (a sales assistant; maiden name, Bosley) Blake. *Education:* Attended York University, 1975-78.

### ■ Addresses

*Home*—12 Comet St., Adamsdown, Cardiff, Wales CF2 1JA, England. *Agent*—Gina Pollinger, 222 Old Brompton Rd., London SW5 0B2, England.

### ■ Career

Teacher of English and drama in Peterborough, England, 1979-80, and Nottingham, England, 1980-84; International Community Centre, Nottingham, assistant warden, 1984-85; part-time community education worker in Cardiff, Wales, 1988—.

### ■ Writings

*Yatesy's Rap* (young adult novel), Kestrel, 1986.
*Direct Action* (television play), broadcast on *Dramarama,* TVS, 1986.
*Net* (play), produced in Nottingham, England, at New Era Theatre, 1986.
*Showdown* (short stories), Kestrel, 1988.
*Geoffrey's First* (young adult novel), Walker Books, 1988.
*Trick or Treat?* (juvenile novel), illustrated by C. Ewen, Blackie and Son, 1988.
*Holiday in Happy Street* (young adult novel), Blackie and Son, 1989.
*Oddly* (juvenile novel), illustrated by John Farman, Kestrel, 1989.
*Roboskool* (juvenile novel), Blackie and Son, 1990.
*Roboskool: The Revenge* (juvenile novel), Blackie and Son, 1991.
*The King of Rock and Roll* (juvenile novel), Walker Books, 1991.
*The Likely Stories* (juvenile novel), Kestrel, 1991.
*Wriggly Pig* (juvenile), illustrated by Susie Jenkin-Pearce, Hutchinson, 1991.
*Binka and the Banana Boat* (juvenile), Collins, 1991.
*Impo* (juvenile), illustrated by Arthur Robins, Walker Books, 1991.

Mr. and Mrs. Pig think that things would be much better if little Wriggly Pig would just sit still in this picture book written by Jon Blake. (Illustrated by Susie Jenkin-Pearce.)

*Daley B.* (juvenile), illustrated by Axel Scheffler, Walker Books, 1991.
*Pilot Bird and Gums* (juvenile), Collins, 1991.
*The Birdwoman of Normal Street* (play), produced in Wrexham, England, at Wrexham Arts Centre, 1991.
*The Melody of Oddly* (juvenile novel), Kestrel, in press.

### ■ Sidelights

Jon Blake is a playwright and author of books for young people that are often noted for their humorous portrayal of common problems. In *Showdown,* a collection of three stories aimed at adolescent boys, Blake mixes realistic language and settings with comic elements and fast-paced action. In one story, "Be Honest," the main character gets into continual trouble by keeping his vow to be completely honest, including being falsely charged with assault. Teresa Scragg, reviewing *Showdown* for *School Librarian,* praised the stories for their "realistic language and authentic, often very funny, dialogue."

In *Geoffrey's First,* the main character deals with his feelings of inadequacy by being rude and eccentric until the presence of a girl allows him to face the world more honestly. David Bennett of *Books for Keeps* praised the humor in *Geoffrey's First* but cautioned that it might make some parents angry. *Oddly,* another humorous novel aimed at boys, concerns a servant-robot that two boys get from their aunt, allowing them to quickly adapt to a life of leisure. In a *Books for Keeps* review, Pam Harwood noted the "frenetic pace" of "this zanily funny story" after one of the boys alters Oddly the robot's programming. This change causes Oddly to have feelings, changing the boys' view of their comfortable new lifestyle. *School Librarian* contributor Joyce Banks remarked: "The style is matter-of-fact, the content ridiculous, and the two combine to make a very enjoyable story."

Blake has also contributed to the series "First Thrillers," from Blackie Publishers. *Trick or Treat?* concerns two young children sent to stay with their mother's aunt while their mother takes her final tests for her university degree. Upon their arrival at the great aunt's home, the children become convinced that her handyman is a murderer and begin sneaking around at night, snooping through the man's possessions and rescuing their aunt from being poisoned. A reviewer for *Junior Bookshelf* felt that children really did not need to be introduced to the genre of the thriller, but added that "the story is easily read and exciting."

*Holiday on Happy Street* is another mystery for intermediate readers. In this novel, Ben Lewis writes a poem about the clown that symbolizes a fast food chain and wins a trip to Happy Street Burger Paradise. At first he enjoys himself, though he wonders why he is not allowed to visit the nearby beach. The mystery is solved when he meets a girl named Becky. She shows him that the bricks used to build Happy Street Burger Paradise were made from beach sand. The loss of sand threatens the stability of the cliff on which the restaurant rests, and the area is likely to collapse. Although *Junior Bookshelf* found the resolution of *Holiday on Happy Street* "a disappointment," the reviewer also noted the fine writing style with which Blake presented his tale.

Michael Lockwood, who reviewed Blake's *The King of Rock and Roll* for *School Librarian,* noted a mythic and symbolic level to this humorous novel that comments on class stereotypes and issues of identity. Three bored young people are invited to help out a local theater group by scavenging for props. In the process they meet the king of the title, who sits royally in a stuffed armchair in the local junkyard. The kids soon decide to stage a revival for the aging rock star. Lockwood summarized: "The plot is skillfully worked out ... and reads on one level as a jokey suspense story ... but more experienced readers will realise other meanings."

### Wacky Animals Trying to Belong

Blake's books from 1991 often feature animals as their principal characters. *Wriggly Pig,* a story for young readers, garnered praise for its humorous depiction of a young pig who cannot keep still, ruining a series of family outings for his perfectly-behaved siblings and parents. At the end of an exhausting day, they decide to take their wriggly relative to the doctor to see what can be done about him, but Wriggly slips away, runs into a mail box and is knocked unconscious. When Wriggly finally awakens, he finds that his family is at last able to accept him the way he is, and they all wriggle happily home. A *Publishers Weekly* reviewer found the story "thin," but also felt it contained "a gentle sweetness." Writing in *School Library Journal,* Jane Marino complained that the book's meaning was unclear. "Is wriggling wrong or is correcting it wrong—or maybe neither?," Marino wondered, concluding that other authors have dealt with the subject of problem behavior more effectively. *Wilson Library Bulletin* reviewers Donnarae MacCann and Olga Richard, on the other hand, complimented the author's "consistent whimsicality" in *Wriggly Pig,* adding that "Blake writes a spare, rhythmic text with poetic precision."

For even younger children, Blake wrote *Daley B.,* which is about a rabbit who does not realize he is a rabbit until he tries on several identities that do not suit him, including one that almost makes him a meal for a weasel. *School Library Journal* contributor Lori A. Janick found little to praise in this "unexceptional" tale accompanied by "simple cartoon illustrations." But a reviewer for *Publishers Weekly* remarked, "With its three distinguishing voices—a narrator's, Daley B.'s, and the sinister weasel's—Blake's lighthearted tale begs to be read aloud."

### ■ Works Cited

Banks, Joyce, review of *Oddly, School Librarian,* May, 1990, p. 67.

Bennett, David, review of *Geoffrey's First, Books for Keeps,* January, 1990.

Review of *Daley B., Publishers Weekly,* June 29, 1992, pp. 61-62.

Harwood, Pam, review of *Oddly, Books for Keeps,* September, 1991.

Janick, Lori A., review of *Daley B., School Library Journal,* September, 1992, p. 198.

Lockwood, Michael, review of *The King of Rock and Roll, School Librarian,* August, 1991, p. 104.

MacCann, Donnarae, and Olga Richard, review of *Wriggly Pig, Wilson Library Bulletin,* October, 1992, pp. 82-83.

Marino, Jane, review of *Wriggly Pig, School Library Journal,* August, 1992, p. 132.

Scragg, Teresa, review of *Showdown, School Librarian,* February, 1989, p. 27.

Review of *Trick or Treat?, Junior Bookshelf,* April, 1989, p. 67.

Review of *Wriggly Pig, Publishers Weekly,* May 18, 1992, p. 68.

### ■ For More Information See

*PERIODICALS*

*Booklist,* June 1, 1992, p. 1764.

*Children's Book Review Service,* August, 1992, p. 157.

*Junior Bookshelf,* June, 1990, pp. 146-147.

*School Librarian,* November, 1991, p. 138.

*Times Educational Supplement,* February 14, 1992, p. 31.

**MARIBETH BOELTS**

# BOELTS, Maribeth 1964-

## ■ Personal

Born January 19, 1964, in Waterloo, IA; daughter of Gerald Clifford (a machinist) and Dorothy Angela (a registered nurse; maiden name, Shimek) Condon; married Darwin Dale Boelts (a firefighter), August 1, 1983; children: Adam, Hannah. *Education:* University of Northern Iowa, B.A., 1987; Hawkeye Institute of Technology, emergency medical technician certification, 1988. *Politics:* Democrat. *Religion:* Christian Reformed. *Hobbies and other interests:* Reading, exercise, spending time with husband and children.

## ■ Addresses

*Home*—3710 Veralta Dr., Cedar Falls, IA 50613.

## ■ Career

St. John/St. Nicholas School, Evansdale, IA, preschool teacher, 1988-91; substitute teacher, 1991—; *Waterloo Courier,* Waterloo, IA, freelance feature writer, 1992—. Has held many church-related positions. *Member:* Society of Children's Book Writers and Illustrators, National Writer's Union, National League of American PEN Women.

## ■ Writings

*With My Mom, with My Dad,* Pacific Press, 1992.
*Kids to the Rescue!: First Aid Techniques for Kids,* Parenting Press, 1992.
*Tornado,* Paulist Press, 1993.
*Dry Days, Wet Nights,* A. Whitman, 1994.
*Grace and Joe,* A. Whitman, 1994.
*The Lulla-Book,* A. Whitman, 1994.
*Summer's End,* Houghton, in press.

## ■ Work in Progress

"I usually try to have two or three stories on file to work on at any given time—with a backlog of ideas."

## ■ Sidelights

Maribeth Boelts explained her decision to write children's books to *SATA:* "I grew up in a family of readers, spending long hours at the Waterloo Public Library, filling my backpack every Saturday with Beverly Cleary, Laura Ingalls Wilder, and *Boy's Life* magazine (much more exciting, I thought, than anything out for girls at the time.) The writing joined the reading when I was in first grade, and from that [first] poem on, I was hooked on words. I continued to write through high school and into college, but as a twenty-year-old married college student with a newborn baby, pursuing an actual writing career seemed like a frivolous dream. I needed a job, and because I liked kids and had always liked school, teaching seemed a reasonable choice. After three years of teaching, however, I realized that the writing, like an impatient child, wouldn't wait. I quit my job, taking with me a file folder of ideas from the children I taught and the two young children I had at home. I wrote a few really bad children's stories, received a lot of rejections, did some more research, spent hours reading children's books, and then wrote some more. Eventually, I got some good news from a publisher, and that was all I needed for fuel.

"Currently, I try to write daily, mostly for children, but I also do freelance feature writing for our local newspaper. Substitute teaching helps me with ideas and is something I also enjoy. I feel that as long as there are children around me, our own, or the others I am privileged to meet, there will be stories to write."

\*      \*      \*

# BOOKMAN, Charlotte
## See Zolotow, Charlotte S(hapiro)

\*      \*      \*

# BOULLE, Pierre (Francois Marie-Louis) 1912-1994

*OBITUARY NOTICE*—See index for *SATA* sketch: Born February 20, 1912, in Avignon, France; died January 30, 1994, in France. Novelist and screenwriter.

Boulle's writings vary from espionage and adventure novels to futuristic fantasies, many of which were praised by reviewers for their suspenseful plots and revealing psychological portraits. After taking an engineering degree in France, Boulle worked in Indochina on a rubber plantation, later becoming part of the French resistance in Asia during World War II. His wartime experiences, including a stint as a prisoner of war of the Vichy French forces, provided a backdrop for his war novels. The best known of these is *Le Pont de la riviere Kwai,* published in English as *The Bridge on the River Kwai,* which Boulle later adapted into an award-winning film. Another noted screen adaption was made of his futuristic 1963 story *Planet of the Apes,* which envisions a world in which apes have evolved as the dominant intelligent species and reign over the primal humans. Boulle reminisces about his own World War II imprisonment in his 1967 autobiography *My Own River Kwai.* His other books include *William Conrad, Le Sacrilege malais, Jardin de Kanashima,* and his last work, *A Nous Deux, Satan,* which was published in 1992.

*OBITUARIES AND OTHER SOURCES:*

BOOKS

*Twentieth-Century Science Fiction Writers,* 3rd edition, St. James, 1991.

*PERIODICALS*

*Chicago Tribune,* February 1, 1994, Section 3, p. 13.

\*   \*   \*

# BRIDE, Nadja
## See NOBISSO, Josephine

\*   \*   \*

# BRINSMEAD, H(esba) F(ay) 1922-
## (Pixie Hungerford)

## ■ Personal

Born March 15, 1922, in Blue Mountains, New South Wales, Australia; daughter of Edward K. G. (a missionary to Indonesia and sawmill operator) and May (Lambert) Hungerford; married Reginald Brinsmead (owner of a spray contracting company), February 11, 1943; children: Bernard Hungerford, Ken Hungerford. *Education:* Attended Avondale College for one year. *Politics:* Australian Democrat. *Religion:* Christian.

## ■ Addresses

*Home*—Weathertop, Shamara Rd., Terranora, New South Wales, Australia 2485.

## ■ Career

Governess for two years in Tasmania; teacher of speech therapy in western Victoria, Australia, 1945-48; kindergarten supervisor in Melbourne, Australia, for two

**H. F. BRINSMEAD**

years; amateur actress with Box Hill City Drama Group, Melbourne, 1950-60; began writing after a trip to Indonesia, 1957; full-time writer, 1960—.

## ■ Awards, Honors

Mary Gilmore Award, 1963, and Australian Children's Book Council book of the year award, 1965, both for *Pastures of the Blue Crane;* Australian Children's Book Council book of the year award, 1972, for *Longtime Passing;* Elizabethan Medal for *Isle of the Sea Horse.*

## ■ Writings

*FOR YOUNG ADULTS*

*Pastures of the Blue Crane,* illustrated by Annette Macarthur-Onslow, Oxford University Press, 1964, Coward, 1966.
*Season of the Briar,* illustrated by William Papas, Oxford University Press, 1965, Coward, 1967.
*Beat of the City,* illustrated by Papas, Oxford University Press, 1966, Coward, 1968.
*A Sapphire for September,* illustrated by Victor Ambrus, Oxford University Press, 1967.
*Isle of the Sea Horse,* illustrated by Peter Farmer, Oxford University Press, 1969.
*Listen to the Wind,* illustrated by Robert Mickelwright, Oxford University Press, 1970.
*Who Calls from Afar?,* illustrated by Ian Ribbons, Oxford University Press, 1971.
*Longtime Passing,* Angus & Robertson, 1971.
*Echo in the Wilderness,* illustrated by Graham Humphreys, Oxford University Press, 1972.

*Under the Silkwood,* illustrated by Michael Payne, Cassell, 1975.

*The Wind Harp,* Cassell, 1977.

*The Ballad of Benny Perhaps,* Cassell, 1978.

*The Honey Forest* (based on her children's serial of the same title), illustrated by Louise Hogan, Hodder & Stoughton, 1978.

*Once There Was a Swagman,* illustrated by Noela Young, Oxford University Press, 1979.

*High Dive, and Free Is Lonely,* illustrated by Craig Smith, Hodder & Stoughton, 1979.

*Longtime Dreaming,* Angus & Robertson, 1982.

*Time for Tarquinia,* illustrated by Bruce Riddell, Hodder & Stoughton, 1982.

*Christmas at Longtime,* illustrated by John Caldwell, Angus & Robertson, 1984.

*The Sand Forest,* Angus & Robertson, 1986.

*When You Come to the Ferry,* Hodder & Stoughton, 1988.

*Bianca and Roja,* Independent Publishers Group, 1992.

*The Silver Train to Midnight,* Margaret Hamilton Publishing, 1993.

*FOR ADULTS*

*I Will Not Say the Day Is Done,* Alternative Publishing, 1983.

*OTHER*

Also author of two children's serials, "The Honey Forest," 1960, and "The Apple Ship," 1962, and of short stories for Australian Broadcasting Commission. Contributor to anthologies, including *Beneath the Sun,* Collins, 1972; *The Cool Man,* Angus & Robertson, 1973; *A Handful of Ghosts,* Hodder & Stoughton, 1976; and *A Swag of Australian,* edited by Leon Garfield and Ward Lock. Contributor of articles and stories, sometimes under name Pixie Hungerford, to *Country, Women's Weekly, Australian Letters,* and other periodicals.

## ■ Adaptations

*Pastures of the Blue Crane* and *Beat of the City* were made into television series by the Australian Broadcasting Commission.

## ■ Sidelights

H. F. Brinsmead is an Australian writer who is best known for her novels about teenagers. Tackling the issues that arise from racial or class prejudice, Brinsmead's characters are enriched by a vitality that reflects the author's own personality; her heroines are particularly memorable. Brinsmead has been especially praised for her "Longtime" series of books, which glean autobiographical scenes from her unusual early years in the frontier of the Australian Blue Mountains rain forest.

Brinsmead had a unique childhood. Her parents, sometime missionaries in Indonesia, moved to the rural Blue Mountains with the hope that healthier surroundings would cure their oldest daughter, who was very ill. Whereas modern medicine could offer them no cure, the move did the trick. Later, Brinsmead was born in a bark hut; she was the youngest of five children. Brinsmead enjoyed a free life, learning through correspondence courses and earning money by picking her mother's cultivated violets. Although she loved to read and listen to stories, she did not do particularly well at spelling or arithmetic—problems she still has to this day. As a child, she wanted to be a writer and would tell this to any adult who asked. She usually received the same reaction—polite indulgence—from all of them.

At the age of thirteen, Brinsmead was taken away from her tasks of working in her father's sawmill and milking the family cow to attend a boarding school in a suburb of Sydney. Although some of her school work was mediocre, she showed talent in composition writing. As she admitted in her *Something about the Author Autobiography Series* entry, "My maths were appalling, as was my spelling.... But when the teacher corrected the composition homework, he refused to believe that I had written it myself. Naturally, I was quickly reduced to tears." Impressed by the young Brinsmead's talent, her teacher pointed out her strengths to the headmaster. Later, the headmaster encouraged her to apply for a cadetship with the Sydney *Morning Herald.* But somehow she never got around to it. After high school, Brinsmead spent a summer picking raspberries in Tasmania, where she met her future husband, Reg Brinsmead. She attended college for a while, but soon lost interest in becoming a teacher.

The couple moved several times around Australia, and Brinsmead took odd jobs. At the time, she was also active in the theater and was offered a job acting on television. Her husband worried about the late hours inherent in this kind of work, so he sent her on a vacation to Singapore as a distraction. While on the boat, Brinsmead made her first attempt at writing a book. Upon her return home, she took a correspondence course in journalism and began to sell her stories. When one of her clients stopped taking freelance work, she decided to use her time to write *Pastures of the Blue Crane.*

The book was well received and heralded a new era for teenage fiction in Australia. The main character, Amaryllis Mereweather, is a vibrant, good-looking girl who is the heiress to her father's fortune. During the course of the book, she finds out that she is part Pacific Islander. The conflicts and resolutions that come with learning about her racial history are explored in the rest of the book.

Brinsmead also launched a series that is loosely based on her colorful childhood in the Blue Mountains. *Longtime Passing,* 1971, *Longtime Dreaming,* 1982, *Christmas at Longtime,* 1983, and *Once There Was a Swagman,* 1979, look nostalgically at the Australia of the 1920s. They focus on the pioneer Truelance family and are narrated from the point of view of Teddy, the youngest child.

Noted for her vital characters and skillful touch with both people and places, Brinsmead has built a solid

**Ryl learns about her family's past and about her own abilities when she joins her long-lost grandfather on a farm in northern Australia in this novel by Brinsmead.**

body of fiction. Her writing was prompted by what she thought was a need in the world of young adult fiction. She commented in *Bookbird* that "I pictured myself turning out books that would *not* be so unsophisticated as to insult the young (and often deep) intelligence—yet not so filled with adult experience far beyond their own." She now feels that there are enough topics to keep her busy. "No need to put the cover on the typewriter!" she declared.

### ■ Works Cited

Brinsmead, H. F., "How and Why I Write for Young People," *Bookbird*, December 15, 1969, pp. 24-26.
Brinsmead, Hesba, entry in *Something about the Author Autobiography Series*, Volume 5, Gale, 1988, pp. 53-67.

### ■ For More Information See

*BOOKS*

Chevalier, Tracy, editor, *Twentieth-Century Children's Writers*, 3rd edition, St. James, 1989.
*Contemporary Literary Criticism*, Volume 21, Gale, 1982.

Crouch, Marcus, *The Nesbit Tradition: The Children's Novel in England 1956-70*, Ernest Benn, 1972.
Eyre, Frank, *British Children's Books in the Twentieth Century*, Longman Books, 1971.
Townsend, John Rowe, *A Sense of Story: Essays on Contemporary Writers for Children*, Lippincott, 1971.

\* \* \*

## BROWN, Margery (Wheeler)

### ■ Personal

Born in Durham, NC; daughter of John Leonidas and Margaret (Hervey) Wheeler; married Richard E. Brown, December 22, 1936 (deceased); children: Janice (Mrs. Jan E. Carden). *Education:* Spelman College, B.A.; Ohio State University, art studies, 1932-34. *Religion:* Presbyterian.

### ■ Addresses

*Home*—245 Reynolds Terrace, Orange, NJ 07050.

**MARGERY BROWN**

## ■ Career

Writer and illustrator. Art teacher in Newark, NJ, 1948-74.

## ■ Writings

*JUVENILE*

(And illustrator) *That Ruby,* Reilly & Lee, 1969.
(And illustrator) *Animals Made by Me,* Putnam, 1970.
(And illustrator) *The Second Stone,* Putnam, 1974.
(And illustrator) *Yesterday I Climbed a Mountain,* Putnam, 1976.
(And illustrator) *No Jon, No Jon, No!,* Houghton, 1981.
*Afro-Bets: Book of Shapes,* illustrated by Culverson Blair, Just Us Books, 1991.

*Afro-Bets: Book of Colors: Meet the Color Family,* illustrated by Blair, Just Us Books, 1991.

*ILLUSTRATOR*

Gordon Allred, *Old Crackfoot,* Obolensky, 1965.
Allred, *Dori the Mallard,* Astor-Honor, 1968.
*I'm Glad I'm Me,* Putnam, 1971.

*OTHER*

Contributor to *Life* and *School Arts.*

## ■ Work in Progress

Stories for and about inner city children.

# C

**JEANNETTE CAINES**

# CAINES, Jeannette (Franklin) 1938-

## ■ Personal

Born in 1938, in New York, NY; married; children: two.

## ■ Addresses

*Home*—Freeport, Long Island, NY.

## ■ Career

Writer of children's books. Affiliated with Harper & Row (a publishing company), New York City. Member of Coalition of 100 Black Women, Council on Adoptable Children, and Negro Business and Professional Women of Nassau County. Councilwoman of Christ Lutheran Church, Nassau County. *Member:* Salvation Army (former member of board of directors).

## ■ Awards, Honors

Certificate of merit and appreciation, National Black Child Development Institute.

## ■ Writings

*Abby,* illustrated by Steven Kellogg, Harper, 1973.
*Daddy,* illustrated by Ronald Himler, Harper, 1977.
*Window Wishing,* illustrated by Kevin Brooks, Harper, 1981.
*Just Us Women,* illustrated by Pat Cummings, Harper, 1982.
*Chilly Stomach,* illustrated by Cummings, Harper, 1986.
*I Need a Lunch Box,* Harper, 1988.

## ■ Sidelights

Jeannette Caines creates children's books populated with black characters who love life and their families. Lauded by critics for presenting positive stories about black culture, Caines is especially praised for the understanding she brings to her child protagonists. Her work is also acknowledged for its depiction of positive black males. "Jeannette's books ... don't finish neat," wrote Allen Raymond in *Early Years.* "There are few words, big pictures. Each story is simply a tiny vignette, a minuscule peek into the lives of others."

Her first effort, 1973's *Abby,* discusses the relationship between a young, adopted girl and Kevin, her older brother. Kevin used to read to Abby from her baby book, which told the story of when she became part of the family. But one day he announces he cannot be bothered any longer. A *Kirkus Reviews* contributor remarked that the resolution of this story "provides assurance for adopted children," when Kevin relents and even asks their mother if he can take his little sister to show-and-tell the next week. A reviewer for *Publishers Weekly,* found the story "endearing."

Caines's second book, *Daddy,* depicts the Saturday visitation of a divorced father with his daughter Windy. In a *New York Times Book Review* article, Judith Viorst called *Daddy* "a warm-hearted effort," and noted that a more realistic work might have also depicted times when the father does not show up, or is in a bad mood. Similarly, a *Kirkus Reviews* critic wrote that Caines implies every visit with the divorced father is an "idyll of fun, games, and affection." Michele Reed Taborn noticed in a *School Library Journal* review that in *Daddy* the only negative aspect of having divorced parents is the "wrinkles in [her] stomach" that Windy gets when she worries about her father. Taborn concluded that *Daddy* is a "gentle, evocative book."

"Window wishing" is Grandma's name for window shopping in Caines's next book, which tells of two children who spend vacations with their unusual grandmother every year. A *Bulletin of the Center for Children's Books* critic called *Window Wishing* "mild, pleasant, a nice family story," featuring a grandmother who wears tennis shoes, flies kites, and does not like to cook. A contributor for *Kirkus Reviews,* while calling the plot in *Window Washing* weak, concluded, "Each of the situations reflects child likings and feelings."

*Just Us Women,* Caines's fourth volume, is another evocation of a close relationship between two generations of females in a black family. Hazel Rochman, reviewing the book for *School Library Journal,* praised the "unhurried rhythm" of the text, which she believed reinforces the easy relationship between a little girl and her Aunt Martha, who joyfully leave behind the men and boys to drive to North Carolina to visit relatives. A *Publishers Weekly* reviewer described the two protagonists as "kindred souls ... going along their own, sweet way." And Barbara Karlin in the *Los Angeles Times Book Review* called *Just Us Women* "a beautifully simple story."

The title of Caines's next book, *Chilly Stomach,* describes the way the story's protagonist, Sandy, feels whenever her Uncle Jim tickles her or kisses her on the lips. The little girl is afraid to tell her parents for fear they will be angry, and so she shares her secret with her friend Jill instead. Sandy hopes that Jill will tell her own parents and they will inform Sandy's parents. While praising the accuracy of Caines's depiction of the feelings of children in this situation, some critics felt that the author did not provide a clear resolution to Sandy's dilemma. A reviewer for *Bulletin of the Center for Children's Books* found the ending "too subtle for young children," who should be reassured that no matter how frightened they are, they should always tell someone if they are being molested. A *Publishers*

*Weekly* critic remarked that *Chilly Stomach* treats the subject "in a way that may frighten children without educating them." And Karen K. Radtke concluded in her review in *School Library Journal* that the book's ending requires discussion between the child reader and an adult. Radtke added that the volume "should not be dumped in the picture book section; it belongs in parents' or teachers' collections."

In Caines's next book, *I Need a Lunch Box,* the author returns to the subject of relations between siblings, particularly when one goes off to school, leaving the other behind. In what a *Kirkus Reviews* writer called "a straightforward story about a rite of passage," a little boy becomes envious of his older sister as she collects the items she needs to start first grade, including a lunch box. The boy's mother says he cannot have a lunch box of his own until he, too, is ready to start school. This inspires him to dream of differently sized and shaped lunch boxes for each day of the week. While some reviewers noted the happy family atmosphere and the realistic story of *I Need a Lunch Box,* others wondered whether parents would be bothered when the little boy's father contradicts the mother by giving him a lunch box of his own on his sister's first day of school. Leda Schubert wrote in a *School Library Journal* review, however, that this latter development is "buried in the happy ending."

## ■ Works Cited

Review of *Abby, Kirkus Reviews,* October 1, 1973, p. 1090.
Review of *Abby, Publishers Weekly,* December 17, 1973, p. 38.

A girl and her aunt leave the men behind when they take a trip to North Carolina in this picture book written by Caines and illustrated by Pat Cummings.

Caines's stories have been praised for their positive portraits of black children and families, as in this book in which a little boy is told he must wait until he starts school to get a lunch box. (Cover illustration by Pat Cummings.)

Review of *Chilly Stomach, Bulletin of the Center for Children's Books,* July, 1986, p. 203.
Review of *Chilly Stomach, Publishers Weekly,* April 25, 1986, p. 74.
Review of *Daddy, Kirkus Reviews,* March 15, 1977, pp. 279-280.
Review of *I Need a Lunch Box, Kirkus Reviews,* July 15, 1988, p. 1057.
Review of *Just Us Women, Publishers Weekly,* November 19, 1982, pp. 76-77.
Karlin, Barbara, review of *Just Us Women, Los Angeles Times Book Review,* October 1, 1984, p. 4.
Radtke, Karen K., review of *Chilly Stomach, School Library Journal,* August, 1986, p. 79.
Raymond, Allen, "Jeannette Caines: A Proud Author, with Good Reason," *Early Years,* March, 1983, pp. 24-25.
Rochman, Hazel, review of *Just Us Women, School Library Journal,* September, 1982, p. 105.
Schubert, Leda, review of *I Need a Lunch Box, School Library Journal,* December, 1988, p. 83.
Taborn, Michele Reed, review of *Daddy, School Library Journal,* November, 1978, p. 41.
Viorst, Judith, review of *Daddy, New York Times Book Review,* April 17, 1977, p. 50.
Review of *Window Wishing, Bulletin of the Center for Children's Books,* October, 1980, p. 27.
Review of *Window Wishing, Kirkus Reviews,* October 1, 1980, pp. 1291-1292.

### ■ For More Information See

*BOOKS*

*Children's Literature Review,* Volume 24, Gale, 1992.

Rollock, Barbara, *Black Authors and Illustrators of Children's Books,* Garland, 1988.

*PERIODICALS*

*School Library Journal,* March, 1981, p. 129.*

\*  \*  \*

## CANNON, Janell 1957-

### ■ Personal

Born November 3, 1957, in St. Paul, MN; daughter of Burton H. and Nancy A. Cannon. *Hobbies and other interests:* Travel, bicycling, reading.

### ■ Addresses

*Office*—P.O. Box 1362, Carlsbad, CA 92018. *Agent*—Sandra Dijkstra, 1155 Camino Del Mar, Del Mar, CA 92014.

### ■ Career

Carlsbad Library, Carlsbad, CA, graphic artist, 1981-93; freelance author and illustrator, 1993—. *Member:* Bat Conservation International.

### ■ Awards, Honors

American Library Association John Cotton Dana, 1985; Children's Summer Reading Program "Supervet."

### ■ Writings

(And illustrator) *Stellaluna,* Harcourt, 1993.

In Janell Cannon's debut picture book, a lost fruit bat is befriended by a family of birds but has trouble adapting to their unfamiliar habits. (Cover illustration by the author.)

## ■ Work in Progress

A picture book featuring the journey of a mythical creature, due in spring, 1995, for Harcourt.

## ■ Sidelights

"As a kid, I always was drawing," Janell Cannon told *SATA.* "In the classroom, doodling was my way of getting through slow lectures without falling asleep. I liked the idea that I appeared to be taking notes. In high school, the habit escalated into carrying an 18' x 24' sketchbook from class to class. It fit perfectly over the desk, and I could wildly draw without marring the desk surface. I loved black Bic pens and did most of my drawings with them. Being a left-hander, the side of my hand tended to drag over the ink while drawing, and so I walked about for most of my school years with an ink-blackened hand. My academic career was not exemplary, but I sure got a lot of practice at my art."

Janell Cannon's first book, *Stellaluna,* tells the story of a baby fruit bat who is separated from her mother during an attack by an owl. Stellaluna falls into a nest of baby birds and is quickly accepted into the family. The birds teach the little bat to eat worms instead of fruit, to stay awake all day, and to sleep in the nest instead of hanging upside down from a branch. But despite Stellaluna's willingness to attempt this strange behavior, she is neither comfortable nor very good at being a bird. Stellaluna is soon discovered by a group of fruit bats who recognize her as one of their own and help her find her real mother.

Her mother teaches Stellaluna to improve the skills—such as finding fruit to eat—that come more naturally to her as a bat. The book concludes with two pages of facts about bats, an addition that critics note reinforces the usefulness of this picture book as an introduction to the subject for younger children. A review of *Stellaluna* in *Publishers Weekly* praised the humor and ease with which Cannon tells this story of tolerance in friendship and the value of self-knowledge. Reviewing the book for *School Library Journal,* Marianne Saccardi called *Stellaluna* "a promising debut" and dubbed the author's illustrations "lovely." *Publishers Weekly* also praised the author's illustrations, calling Cannon's images "striking" and set off by a "luminous precision."

## ■ Works Cited

Saccardi, Marianne, review of *Stellaluna, School Library Journal,* June, 1993, p. 70.
Review of *Stellaluna, Publishers Weekly,* April 26, 1993.

\*　　\*　　\*

# CARTWRIGHT, Ann 1940-

## ■ Personal

Born October 28, 1940, in England; daughter of John William and Mary (Glover) Harrison; married Reg

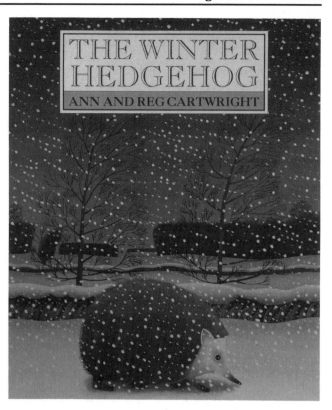

A young hedgehog decides to experience the mysteries of winter rather than hibernate in this tale by Ann Cartwright. (Cover illustration by Reg Cartwright.)

Cartwright (an illustrator), March 31, 1962; children: Simon, James. *Education:* Leicester Polytechnic, B.A. (with honors), 1984.

## ■ Addresses

*Home and office*—29 Church Rd., Kibworth Beauchamp, Leicestershire LE8 0NB, England. *Agent*—Eunice McMullen, 38 Clewer Hill Rd., Windsor, Berkshire SL4 4BW, England.

## ■ Career

Publisher of prints and greeting cards in Leicestershire, England, 1990—; writer.

## ■ Writings

*ILLUSTRATED BY HUSBAND, REG CARTWRIGHT*

*Norah's Ark,* Hutchinson, 1984.
*The Proud and Fearless Lion,* Hutchinson, 1986.
*The Last Dodo,* Hutchinson, 1989.
*The Winter Hedgehog,* Hutchinson, 1989.
*Polly and the Privet Bird,* Hutchinson, 1990.
*Jackdaw,* Random House, 1993.

Also author of *The Lighthouse,* 1993.

## ■ Sidelights

Ann Cartwright and her husband Reg have made a very successful partnership in the production of children's picture books. Ann handles the writing and Reg produces his distinctive brand of illustration to complement the text. "It's often local everyday sights which evoke ideas for stories," Cartwright told *SATA*. "Reg and I had the inspiration for the character in *Norah's Ark* when we saw a local farmer's wife herding cattle along a country lane near our village."

*Norah's Ark* plays on the flood theme apparent in the title, when, in anticipation of a great downpour, a villager named Norah persuades her livestock to help her build an ark. They manage to do this by turning the barn upside down and making it shipshape through the addition of walls, floors, and decking. Eventually the flood waters subside and Norah and her animals disembark, no worse for wear. Critics consistently praised the illustrations in *Norah's Ark* for their vivid, dramatic quality, although a reviewer for the *Bulletin of the Center for Children's Books* criticized the "persistent note of cuteness" in the writing.

*The Proud and Fearless Lion*, the Cartwrights' next work, was well received. As a reviewer for *Growing Point* noted, the story is an "intriguing offshoot" of Aesop's lion and mouse fable. In Cartwright's version, a loud lion is cured of a sore throat by a mouse and neighboring animals who bring him honey and eucalyptus. The lion later comes to their rescue.

### Exploring Environmentalist Themes

Cartwright told Felicity Newson of the *Leicester Mercury*, "We hope that at some level our stories will help to make five year olds aware of the environment as well as entertain them." *The Last Dodo*, "a lovely book," according to one *Junior Bookshelf* reviewer, provides an environmental lesson with its tale of a king who desires to eat the only Dodo egg in the world. *The Winter Hedgehog* also touches on some environmental themes; in this book, a hedgehog leaves his nest while the other hedgehogs hibernate, in order to experience the wonder and beauty of the winter. In the words of another reviewer for *Junior Bookshelf*, *The Winter Hedgehog* is "developed with much verbal eloquence."

Created after Cartwright and her husband saw a topiary bird in a gamekeeper's garden, *Polly and the Privet Bird* is the story of an eccentric woman who shears her overgrown privet bush into a topiary bird and flies away on it. Hearing the cries of children, she rescues a child and then brings groceries to her neighbors. While children are excited at the sight of Polly and her bird, grown-ups cannot or will not see her. "Well, if they won't look they won't see," explain the children. When their parents finally decide to explore the claims of the children, it's too late—the bird has turned back into a bush. A reviewer for *Kirkus Reviews* concluded, "All in all, [the book is] an appealing fantasy."

Today, Cartwright and her husband continue to create children's books together. "Reg and I walk in the Leicestershire and Northamptonshire countryside to discuss our story ideas," she explained to *SATA*. "Back at our house, where Reg has a second floor studio and I have a third floor study, the ideas are further developed." She continued, "After the story is finished and approved by an editor, the illustrations follow, and it's always a great joy to see the words materialise in Reg's visuals."

### ■ Works Cited

Cartwright, Ann, *Polly and the Privet Bird*, Hutchinson, 1990.
Review of *The Last Dodo*, *Junior Bookshelf*, October, 1989, p. 213.
Newson, Felicity, "As Live as a Dodo," *Leicester Mercury*, May 31, 1989, p. 5.
Review of *Norah's Ark*, *Bulletin of the Center for Children's Books*, September, 1985.
Review of *Polly and the Privet Bird*, *Kirkus Reviews*, December 15, 1992, p. 1588.
Review of *The Proud and Fearless Lion*, *Growing Point*, March, 1987, p. 4765.
Review of *The Winter Hedgehog*, *Junior Bookshelf*, February, 1990, p. 13.

### ■ For More Information See

*PERIODICALS*

*Publishers Weekly*, November 29, 1991, p. 51.
*School Library Journal*, April, 1985, p. 75.

\* \* \*

# CASSUTT, Michael (Joseph) 1954-

## ■ Personal

Born April 13, 1954, in Owatonna, MN; son of Florian Francis (a baseball player, coach, and teacher) and Joyce (a teacher; maiden name, Williams) Cassutt; married Cynthia Stratton (a magazine editor), August 19, 1978; children: Ryan Spencer, Alexandra Lee. *Education:* University of Arizona, B.A., 1975. *Politics:* Democrat. *Religion:* Roman Catholic.

## ■ Addresses

*Home*—12241 Hillslope St., Studio City, CA 91604-3604. *Agent*—(literary) Richard Curtis Assoc., 171 East 74th St., New York, NY 10021; (television/film) Creative Artists Agency, 9830 Wilshire Blvd., Beverly Hills, CA 90212-1825.

## ■ Career

KHYT Radio, Tucson, AZ, disc jockey and operations manager, 1975-78; CBS Television, Los Angeles, CA, held various positions including children's programming executive, 1979-85; freelance writer and television producer, 1985—. *Member:* Science Fiction and Fantasy Writers of America (vice-president, 1988-89), Writers Guild of America—West, Academy of Television Arts and Sciences.

MICHAEL CASSUTT

# ■ Awards, Honors

Nancy B. Reynolds Award, Center for Population Options, 1989, for "First Love Trilogy" episode of television series *TV 101*.

# ■ Writings

*The Star Country* (science fiction), Doubleday, 1986.
*Who's Who in Space: The First Twenty-five Years* (reference), G. K. Hall, 1987, 2nd edition published as *Who's Who in Space: The International Space Year*, 1993.
*Dragon Season* (fantasy), Tor Books, 1991.

*TELEVISION AND FILM*

Author of teleplays for *Love, Sidney*, National Broadcasting Co. (NBC-TV), 1982; *Gloria*, Columbia Broadcasting Systems (CBS-TV), 1982; *It's Not Easy*, American Broadcasting Co. (ABC-TV), 1983; *Alice*, CBS-TV, 1983-84; *Dungeons and Dragons*, CBS-TV, 1985; *Rocky Road*, (syndicated), 1985; *Misfits of Science*, NBC-TV, 1985; *The Twilight Zone*, CBS-TV, 1985-87; *Centurions*, (syndicated), 1986; *Simon and Simon*, CBS-TV,

1986; *The Wizard*, CBS-TV, 1987; *Max Headroom*, ABC-TV, 1987-88; *Beauty and the Beast*, CBS-TV, 1988; *TV 101*, CBS-TV, 1988-89; *CBS Storybreak*, CBS-TV, 1989; *WIOU*, CBS-TV, 1990; *Eerie, Indiana*, NBC-TV, 1992; *Sirens*, ABC-TV, 1993, and *Sea Quest*, NBC-TV, 1993. Author of screenplay *Dungeonmaster II: Mestema's Challenge*, Empire Films.

*OTHER*

(Author of introduction) Valentin Lebedev, *Diary of a Cosmonaut: Two Hundred Eleven Days in Space*, PhytoResource Research, 1988.
(Editor with Andrew Greeley and Martin H. Greenberg) *Sacred Visions* (science fiction anthology), Tor Books, 1991.
(With Donald K. "Deke" Slayton) *Deke! U.S. Manned Space: Mercury to the Shuttle*, Forge, 1994.

Contributor of short stories to periodicals, including *Magazine of Fantasy and Science Fiction, Isaac Asimov's SF Magazine, Mike Shayne Mystery Magazine*, and *Amazing Science Fiction;* contributor of short stories to anthologies; contributor of nonfiction articles to periodicals, including *Science Fiction Review, McGill's Guide to Space Science, Spaceflight, Orbiter, Omni, L-5 News, Future Life, Starlog*, and *Space World*.

# ■ Work in Progress

*Mount Thunder*, a novel.

# ■ Sidelights

"For years I've been pursuing three parallel writing careers," Michael Cassutt told *SATA*, "prose fiction, especially science fiction and fantasy; non-fiction, most of it on the subject of space flight; and TV scriptwriting.

"A number of well-meaning friends have suggested I'd be further along in any one of these fields if I dropped the other two, but I'm reluctant to do that, even though it makes for awkward moments at social occasions. How do I introduce myself? Am I a science fiction writer or an aerospace historian or a television scriptwriter? In weak moments I tailor the answer to suit the situation.

"Anyway, there's a hidden benefit to this apparent lack of commitment: whenever I get tired of one type of project, I can turn to something completely different. This means I rarely appear to be blocked, though under oath I would have to admit I'm stuck as often as any other writer.

"More seriously, I'd also point out that I became interested in space flight in the mid-1960s, just as it was changing from science fiction into reality. For me the truest sort of SF, even though I've rarely written it, is about exploring other worlds. And I owe my television career in part to SF, since my first two staff positions were on *The Twilight Zone* and *Max Headroom*. So there's really no inconsistency, is there?"

Michael Cassutt's first novel, *The Star Country,* is set in the year 2038, in a world where the United States has broken up into smaller nation-states and the Soviet Union and China have destroyed each other. When representatives of an alien nation arrive on earth to deliver the Genesis File, a package of advanced knowledge and technology, they have difficulty finding any person or nation worthy of receiving it. Then a young Iowa farmer rescues one of the aliens after he crashes near the commune on which the man lives. A *Kirkus Reviews* critic claimed *The Star Country* possessed a "brisk, reasonably gripping narrative." Bill Collins in *Fantasy Review,* however, noted several flaws in the book's plotting, but concluded: "If one doesn't read too critically, the time passes pleasantly." Gerald Jonas of the *New York Times Book Review,* on the other hand, commended the "generosity of vision" that inspired the author to spend as much time with his humble characters as he does with his elite ones and called *The Star Country* "a pleasantly small-scale book about world-shaking events."

Cassutt's next project, *Who's Who in Space: The First Twenty-five Years,* is a comprehensive reference book on astronauts and others involved in space travel in the United States and other countries. The book features short biographies, photographs, and appendices detailing all spaceflights, with information on crew members, launch and landing dates, and accomplishments. *Booklist* praised Cassutt's biographies as "objective and very readable," and recommended the book as "the first source to include information on all astronauts from all nations."

Cassutt returned to novel writing with the publication of *Dragon Season,* a fantasy tale about Rick Walsh, an Air Force lieutenant who returns from overseas duty to discover he is the father of a baby boy whose mother is missing. Rick's search for her leads him to a parallel world ruled by a god named Griffon and populated with dragon-like creatures and buildings that grow. Patricia S. Franz of *Kliatt* liked the fast-paced adventure story, and concluded: "Cassutt tells a story that most fantasy/SF readers will enjoy."

### ■ Works Cited

Collins, Bill, review of *The Star Country, Fantasy Review,* October, 1986, p. 22.

Franz, Patricia S., review of *Dragon Season, Kliatt,* April, 1992, p. 12.

Jonas, Gerald, review of *The Star Country, New York Times Book Review,* September 21, 1986.

Review of *The Star Country, Kirkus Reviews,* July 1, 1986, p. 976.

Review of *Who's Who in Space: The First Twenty-five Years, Booklist,* June 15, 1987, p. 1584.

### ■ For More Information See

*PERIODICALS*

*Publishers Weekly,* June 20, 1986, p. 94.
*School Library Journal,* May, 1988.

**In this science fiction thriller by Cassutt, alien visitors hesitate to hand over the knowledge that could help rejuvenate a post-apocalyptic Earth.** (Cover illustration by Cathy Hull.)

*Voice of Youth Advocates,* June, 1992, p. 108.

\* \* \*

## CHEN, Ju-Hong 1941-

### ■ Personal

Born October 12, 1941, in Shanghai, China; married Zheng-Fei Lin (a physician), 1976; children: Mi-Le Chen.

### ■ Addresses

*Office*—7920 Southeast Washington St., Portland, OR 97215.

### ■ Career

Freelance artist and illustrator.

### ■ Awards, Honors

Honor book for illustration, Parent's Choice, 1987, for *The Magic Leaf.*

**JU-HONG CHEN**

### ■ Illustrator

*The Magic Leaf,* Atheneum, 1987.
*The Tigers Bought Pink Lemonade,* Atheneum, 1988.
Susan Nunes, *Tiddalick the Frog,* Atheneum, 1989.
*A Song of Stars,* Holiday House, 1990.
*The Fourth Question,* Holiday House, 1991.
Caryn Yacowitz, *The Jade Stone,* Holiday House, 1992.
*The Tale of Aladdin and the Wonderful Lamp,* edited by
    Eric A. Kimmel, Holiday House, 1992.

### ■ Sidelights

"When I was a young boy," Ju-Hong Chen told *SATA,*
"I remember a common scene on the streets of Shanghai: children clustering around the *Little Man Picture Book* rental booths. Old men would sit inside these stalls under a cool winter sun, and 'rent-out' miniature illustrated books to those youngsters who might afford a penny or two for a literary treat. These books were not great works of art, mainly tales of good guys fighting the baddies, but the children of Shanghai lapped them up, furiously thumbing through them to reach the end, as they could not take them home. So frequently handled, the books were gray and spotted with thumbprints, not a few of my own! My love of illustrating was born there. I was about twelve years old when I dared myself to create

art to accompany these stories. Ever since, art has been a part of my career.

"When I illustrate a story written by someone else, I read it many times until I feel the desire in me to tell the tale myself—only I use paint and brush, rather than words, to relate it. I don't believe that a single standard art style can work for every story. Each tale has its unique focus, tone, and mood; I always try to be sensitive to the particular story I am illustrating, to be true to its theme and tenor. Always, it is a challenge to create a fresh medley of characters, a vividly enticing landscape. And always, it proves to be a rich, creative reward."

\* \* \*

## CHURCH, Kristine
### See JENSEN, Kristine Mary

\* \* \*

## CLOUSE, Nancy L. 1938-

### ■ Personal

Born December 31, 1938, in Jackson, MI; daughter of Beryl (a farmer) and Margaret (a homemaker) Luttenton; married Roger W. Clouse (a teacher), April 6, 1963; children: Susan. *Education:* Michigan State University, B.A., 1960, M.A., 1963. *Hobbies and other interests:* Reading, theater, art.

### ■ Addresses

*Home*—4157 Cummings Ct. NW, Grand Rapids, MI 49504. *Office*—Rm. 445 Main Bldg., Grand Rapids Community College, 143 Bostwick NE, Grand Rapids, MI 49503.

### ■ Career

Art educator, 1960—; Grand Rapids Community College, Grand Rapids, MI, art instructor, 1968-94. *Member:* Michigan Watercolor Society, Grand Rapids Art Museum, Muskegon Art Museum.

### ■ Writings

(And illustrator) *Puzzle Maps U.S.A.,* Holt, 1990.
(Illustrator) Verna Aardema, reteller, *Sebgugugu the Glutton: A Bantu Tale from Rwanda,* Eerdmans, 1993.
(Illustrator) Virginia Kroll, *Pink Paper Swans,* Eerdmans, 1994.

*Puzzle Maps U.S.A.* has been translated into Spanish.

### ■ Sidelights

"I have been an art educator since 1960, working with elementary, secondary, and adult art students," Nancy L. Clouse told *SATA.*

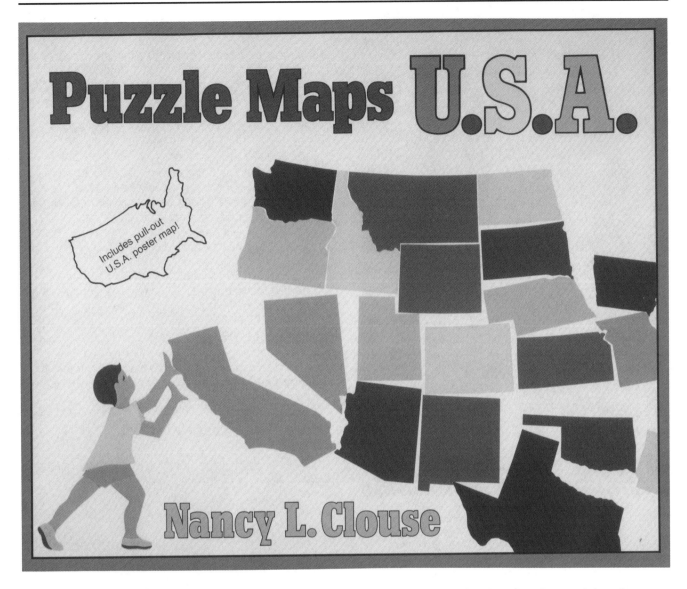

**Nancy L. Clouse uses the shapes of the fifty states as the basis for her book of educational and entertaining pictures.** (Cover illustration by the author.)

"I presently teach art history, drawing, and art education methods at Grand Rapids Community College. I recently pursued an interest in children's literature relying on my art background. In 1990, Henry Holt released my book *Puzzle Maps U.S.A.,* which I wrote and illustrated with cut paper. This led to a cut paper rendition of Verna Aardema's African folktale from Rwanda called *Sebgugugu the Glutton.* I continue teaching art at Grand Rapids Community College while at the same time working with young children discussing the making of books and images for books."

■ **For More Information See**

*PERIODICALS*

*Publishers Weekly,* April 13, 1990, p. 64.
*School Library Journal,* May, 1990, pp. 95-96.

## COHEN, Judith Love 1933-

■ **Personal**

Born August 16, 1933, in Brooklyn, NY; daughter of Maurice Bernard (a soft drink manufacturer) and Sarah (a homemaker; maiden name, Roisman) Cohen; married Bernard Siegel (divorced, 1965); married Thomas W. Black, January 20, 1965 (divorced, 1980); married David Katz (a teacher), February 20, 1981; children: (first marriage) Neil G., Howard K., Constance Rachel; (second marriage) T. Jack. *Education:* Attended Brooklyn College, 1950-52; University of Southern California, B.S., 1957, M.S., 1962; University of California, Los Angeles, M.E., 1982. *Politics:* Conservative. *Religion:* Jewish.

JUDITH LOVE COHEN

## ■ Addresses

*Office*—c/o Cascade Pass, 10734 Jefferson Blvd., Number 235, Culver City, CA 90230.

## ■ Career

Author of children's books, journalist, playwright, and engineer. TRW-Aerospace, Redondo Beach, CA, project manager, 1959-90; Command Systems Group-Aerospace, Torrance, CA, project manager, 1990-92; freelance consulting engineer, 1993—. *Member:* Society of Women Engineers (chair of Los Angeles section), Los Angeles Technical Societies Council (secretary), Tau Beta Pi, Eta Kappa Nu.

## ■ Awards, Honors

Outstanding Engineer award, Institute for the Advancement of Engineering, 1977; certificate of recognition, National Aeronautics and Space Administration (NASA), 1991, for contributions made to the Hubble Space Telescope Program.

## ■ Writings

*A Passover to Remember* (play), first produced at Act One Stage, Los Angeles, CA, 1985.
*You Can Be a Woman Engineer,* Cascade Pass, 1991.
(With Margot Siegel) *You Can Be a Woman Architect,* Cascade Pass, 1992.
(With Flo McAlary) *You Can Be a Woman Marine Biologist,* illustrated by David A. Katz, Cascade Pass, 1992.
(With Betsy Bryan) *You Can Be a Woman Egyptologist,* illustrated by Katz, Cascade Pass, 1993.
(With Diane Gabriel) *You Can Be a Woman Paleontologist,* illustrated by Katz, Cascade Pass, 1993.
(With Valerie Thompson) *You Can Be a Woman Zoologist,* illustrated by Katz, Cascade Pass, 1993.

Also contributor of a monthly column to *Engineer of California* magazine, 1977—. Many of Cohen's books are available in Spanish.

## ■ Work in Progress

*Life after Aerospace; Starting Your Own Business; What Makes a Good Marriage;* (with Sharon Franks) *You Can Be an Oceanographer.*

## ■ For More Information See

*PERIODICALS*

*Science Books and Films,* May, 1992.

\*     \*     \*

## COLIN, Ann
   See URE, Jean

\*     \*     \*

## CURTIS, Chara M(ahar) 1950-

## ■ Personal

Born May 14, 1950, in Fairmont, MN; daughter of Harold Richard (a radio news and sports reporter) and Gloria Estelle (a writer; maiden name, LaValleur) Mahar Shemorry. *Education:* Attended Morningside College, Sioux City, IA.

## ■ Addresses

*Home*—6021 Saxon Rd., Acme, WA 98220.

## ■ Career

Songwriter, 1971—; Screen Gems—EMI Music, professional staff, 1976-81; assistant to film director John Cherry, 1983-86. Writer, 1986—. Conducts "Writing Wild" workshops. *Member:* Society of Children's Book Writers and Illustrators.

**CHARA M. CURTIS**

### ■ Writings

*All I See Is Part of Me,* illustrated by Cynthia Aldrich, Illumination Arts, 1989.
*Fun Is a Feeling,* illustrated by Aldrich, Illumination Arts, 1992.
*How Far to Heaven,* illustrated by Alfred Currier, Illumination Arts, 1993.

### ■ Work in Progress

Children's books *Kitty on the Counter (and Other Household Horrors)* and *Lullaby with the Bogeyman* (tentative title); *Family of Love,* a book of poetry (love themes); songs.

### ■ Sidelights

"I write metaphorically of the human experience, believing that proper art carries a dual message level—psychological and metaphysical," Chara M. Curtis told *SATA.* "Sometimes employing a plot—and sometimes not—I strive to create that moment of awe known as aesthetic arrest. Knowing that imagination is often stimulated by crisis, I also recognize that, even as children, we are capable of being held in the wonder of a sunset." Curtis adds, "I see words as palette paints and paper as canvas. I write, striving for the Mona Lisa's smile."

Before she began writing children's books, Curtis worked in Nashville's music industry for over ten years. She collaborated with other songwriters such as Wayne Carson and Mark James, who are famous for tunes such as "Suspicious Minds" and "Always on My Mind." Curtis told *SATA,* "My most beneficial education has been derived through apprenticeships—collaborations with other successful writers. I began early, under the tutelage of my word-wise mother." Curtis also created scenes and dialogue with writer/director John Cherry for Disney Productions' "Ernest" film series. Although she continues to write songs, she is also producing more books for children, as well as writing poetry.

"I write every day," Curtis explains. "The form this writing takes is never predetermined.... I enter into a thought or object completely, thrilled by the newness of each experience. I hear its story, its history and yearnings, its wisdom and confusion, its passion. I hear its voice, but it has no hands, so I offer mine so that its life can be recorded. Sound crazy? It is. And fun!"

\*    \*    \*

## CUTLER, Daniel S(olomon) 1951-

### ■ Personal

Born June 27, 1951, in Detroit, MI; son of Aaron Zelig (a chemist) and Simi (a homemaker; maiden name, Bernstein) Cutler; divorced; children: Naomi Tamar. *Education:* Wayne State University, B.F.A., 1974; University of Michigan, M.S., 1979.

### ■ Addresses

*Office*—Veterans Administration Medical Center, 2215, Fuller Rd., Ann Arbor, MI 48105.

### ■ Career

Veterans Administration Medical Center, Ann Arbor, MI, medical illustrator, 1978—. Lectures on the subject of illustration.

### ■ Writings

*The Bible Cookbook,* Morrow, 1985.
*One Hundred Monkeys,* illustrations by Marsha Winborn, Simon & Schuster, 1991.

Contributing editor, *Step-By-Step Graphics.*

### ■ Sidelights

Daniel S. Cutler told *SATA:* "I am a medical artist. My drawings and paintings are used to illustrate medical books and lectures by medical scientists. People often ask me if I also do any artwork that is 'creative.' Well, thinking up a way to portray a complicated medical

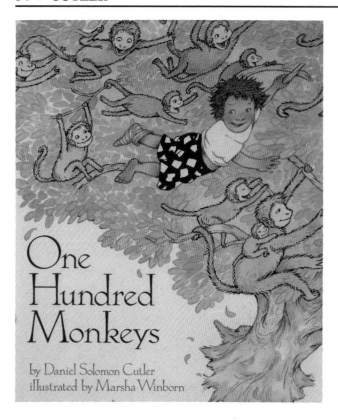

One
Hundred
Monkeys

by Daniel Solomon Cutler
illustrated by Marsha Winborn

**A young boy has a wild time hanging out at the monkey school, until the teacher there discovers he is tail-less in this enthusiastic story by Daniel S. Cutler.** (Cover illustration by Marsha Winborn.)

subject is actually very creative work. It satisfies the artist in me. Still, I understand these people are asking whether I create to express myself. For that I usually write—stories like *One Hundred Monkeys.*

"Marsha Winborn, an artist with a lot of experience illustrating children's books, created the pictures. I didn't know Marsha; we've never met. Many people with ideas for stories think they need to find a friend to illustrate their words before approaching a publisher. The opposite is true: publishers would rather find their own illustrator for a story they like. There are many technical considerations in preparing good children's book illustrations that inexperienced artists don't know about. These matters are very interesting to me. I often interview other artists and write about how they work in a magazine called *Step-By-Step Graphics* (which is translated into Spanish, Japanese and Italian). I also give lectures on the subject.

"There is a scene in *One Hundred Monkeys* in which the monkeys address their teacher as '*Madame*'—in French. That is because the incident actually occurred when I was in seventh grade French class. Like the boy in the story I was being a smart mouth and got into trouble!"*

# D

## DANIEL, Colin
### See WINDSOR, Patricia

\*   \*   \*

## DEANS, Sis Boulos 1955-

### ■ Personal

Born November 4, 1955, in Portland, ME; daughter of James (an electrician) and Velma (a nurse; maiden name, Pellitier) Boulos; married John Deans (a farrier [shoes horses]), October 7, 1978; children: Jessica Emily, Rachel Marie, Emma Lee. *Education:* University of Maine, Orono, A.S. (animal medical technology), 1976; Maine Medical Center School of Surgical Technology, 1985. *Politics:* Democrat. *Religion:* Roman Catholic. *Hobbies and other interests:* Camping, photography, sports.

### ■ Addresses

*Home*—260 Gray Rd., Gorham, ME 04038.

### ■ Career

Mercy Hospital, Portland, ME, surgical technician, 1985—. Has worked variously as a lifeguard, a waitress, a writing instructor, and nine years as an animal medical technician for veterinarians. *Member:* Association of Surgical Technologists, Maine Writers and Publishers Alliance.

### ■ Awards, Honors

*The Legend of Blazing Bear* was a Maine Writers and Publishers Alliance best-selling children's book for 1992.

### ■ Writings

*Chick-a-dee-dee-dee: A Very Special Bird,* illustrated by Nantz Comyns, Gannett Books, 1987.

**SIS BOULOS DEANS**

*Emily Bee and the Kingdom of Flowers,* illustrated by Nantz Comyns, Gannett Books, 1988.
*The Legend of Blazing Bear,* illustrated by Nantz Comyns, Windswept House Publishers, 1992.

Also author of adult short fiction, poetry, and plays, published in periodicals, including *Tableau, New England Sampler,* and *Portland Review of the Arts.*

### ■ Work in Progress

*Brick Walls,* a young adult novel; *Summer of the Gang,* a book for middle readers; *Jessica's Christmas Pageant* and *Olivia's Operation,* two children's books.

### ■ Sidelights

Sis Boulos Deans is a very, very busy woman. "I'm hyper, work well under pressure, and require little

35

sleep," she told *SATA*. Her home is always a center of activity. She shares a farm in Maine with her husband, their three daughters, two horses, two dogs, a cat, a rabbit, and three chickens. "My husband and children share my love for camping, and vacations for us usually involve sleeping in a tent," Deans says. "My girls swim competitively, and are also active in other sports, church, and school activities, so I'm usually en route to a pool or a ball field.

"Besides being a wife, mother, and writer, I work three days and a night of call in the operating room as a surgical technician. My specialty is orthopedics; my favorite cases are total knee and hip replacements. People usually ask how I manage to balance such a hectic life and still write. My answer: 'I write when normal people are sleeping.' Which is true—it's the only time our house is quiet.

"For me, writing is like breathing—something that comes naturally and is a necessity of life. Since childhood, I've been motivated by a creative desire to capture with words the world around me. Dialogue is one of my favorite vehicles, and humor is usually in the driver's seat." In addition to children's books, Deans has written plays and stories for adults. "I didn't start writing children's books until my eldest daughter was four," she told *SATA*. "After seeing one of my short stories published in a magazine that she was too young to read, she said, 'Momma, you write for everyone but me.' My guilt kicked in, and I immediately called Nantz Comyns, a good friend and an artist I'd known since college. 'Nantz,' I said, 'I'm going to write a kid's book and you're going to illustrate it.'"

Since then, Deans and Comyns have worked on three books together. Their latest book, *The Legend of Blazing Bear*, was the Maine Writers and Publishers Alliance best-selling children's book for 1992. In the book, an Abenaki father gently teaches his son through storytelling, emphasizing his nation's culture and customs. However, Jeanette K. Cakouros in the *Maine Sunday Telegram* declares that *Blazing Bear* is "more than a storybook," citing the book's added glossary of American Indian words and terms, a chart of Maine's Kennebec and Abenaki Indians, a map showing the locations and place names of the tribes, a bibliography for further reading, and, of course, colorful artwork. "Nantz and I have an excellent working relationship," Deans explains, "and our successful collaborations have been, and continue to be, rewarding and fun."

### ■ Works Cited

Cakouros, Jeanette K., review of *The Legend of Blazing Bear, Maine Sunday Telegram,* September 20, 1992.

### ■ For More Information See

*PERIODICALS*

*School Library Journal,* February, 1993, p. 92.

# DENNARD, Deborah 1953-

### ■ Personal

Born October 8, 1953, in Houston, TX; daughter of Margaret (Kelly) Ward; married Robert Marion Dennard (an engineer), December 22, 1973. *Education:* Texas A & M University, B.A., 1976. *Religion:* Methodist. *Hobbies and other interests:* Community theater, dogs, music, bird watching, tap dancing, travel.

### ■ Career

Fort Worth Zoo, Fort Worth, TX, zoo educator, 1976-92. *Member:* Society of Children's Book Writers and Illustrators.

### ■ Writings

*How Wise Is an Owl?,* illustrated by Michelle Neavill, Carolrhoda, 1993.
*Do Cats Have Nine Lives?,* illustrated by Jackie Ubanovic, Carolrhoda, 1993.
*Can Elephants Drink through Their Noses?,* illustrated by Terry Boles, Carolrhoda, 1993.
*Travis and the Better Mousetrap,* Cobblehill Books, in press.

### ■ Work in Progress

"I am always doing research for at least ten projects at once. All (or most) of my projects are animal or nature

**DEBORAH DENNARD**

oriented. Some are serious, some are frivolous, all are fun."

## ■ Sidelights

Deborah Dennard told *SATA:* "As a newly published author, still in a state of shock over my first three books, I feel that the greatest motivation behind my writing is a desire to excite children, and hopefully to inspire in them a lifelong interest in reading, animals, and nature. I am available as a visiting author, an activity which I greatly enjoy, and hope to continue publishing both my nonfiction and fiction works in the future. What could be more exciting than to see your name on the cover of a book?"

\*   \*   \*

# DIETERICH, Michele M. 1962-

## ■ Personal

Born June 8, 1962, in Ohio; daughter of Don (an engineer) and Barbara (an artist; maiden name, Sigler) Dieterich. *Education:* Boston University, B.S. (magna cum laude), 1984.

## ■ Addresses

*Home and office*—P.O. Box 7273, Bozeman, MT 58715.

**MICHELE M. DIETERICH**

## ■ Career

Artist and writer. Freelance commercial artist in Newport Beach, CA; *Mountain Biker International,* London, England, itinerant correspondent; *Happenings Magazine,* Bozeman, MT, staff writer and art critic. Contributing photographer to *Mountain Biker International.* Member of Gallatin County Search and Rescue.

## ■ Writings

*Skiing,* photographs by Bob Allen, Wayland Publishers, 1991.

Also contributor to *Mountain City Biking, Bicycle Guide,* and *Happenings Magazine.* Contributor of photographs to *Mountain Biking,* by Allen, Wayland Publishing, 1991.

## ■ Work in Progress

A children's book about experiencing art; traveling in Guatemala and Peru to research a novel about shamanism.

## ■ Sidelights

Michele M. Dieterich told *SATA:* "I recently finished a short book about skiing for children between the ages of ten and thirteen. I had wondered if the idea was a bit redundant until I wandered through a variety of libraries in England and the United States in search of something—anything—about snow sports written for children. The few books I discovered were concise, well written, and informative, but they were written for adults in reference to children or written in a manner that forgets children are aware, intelligent individuals with a unique understanding of the world, especially those in the age group that my book targets.

"It was a pleasure to write directly to children and to encourage children to read by touching upon a subject most enjoyable to them. I believe that just writing for children on an intelligent level can and will encourage them to read. And why not broach subjects of all kinds to children, who are most receptive to new ideas and who are like sponges for knowledge? It is my theory that children are listless about reading because vibrant, provocative subjects are often unavailable to them. When I was young, I was a voracious reader bored by what I found in the children's section of the library. I often ventured into the adult areas, picking up everything I could find that looked intriguing, getting a bit lost by technical language, but being fascinated by the topics.

"Since my interests in writing follow from my life choices, I have mostly written about skiing, mountain biking, art, and travel. I would love to write about both art and travel for children in an experiential format. For example, art as a subject would not be a list of famous artists and paintings and museums, but how to experience and relate to art. What it means to enjoy a painting or sculpture on all levels, I believe, would be reiterating something children already feel when they see art. While children can and should be the most receptive to art, they are unsure of the significance of their reactions. It is tough to rarely be taken seriously.

"Different cultures and places on this planet could be related to children so well in an adventure format. I believe that the best way to reach children about something they are completely removed from is to tell it in the form of a mystical, but reality-filled story of travel. I would really like to introduce alien cultures and religions to children through the people and places [I've] experienced.

"Meanwhile I am skiing, rock climbing, ice climbing, telemarking, biking, running, and hiking in Bozeman, Montana. On the scribe side of things, I am currently writing a series on local artists for a regional arts magazine, and, of course, writing proposals."

*      *      *

## DILLER, Harriett 1953-

### ■ Personal

Born August 9, 1953, in Lancaster, SC; daughter of Neal (an office services manager) and Betty (a college professor; maiden name, Hovis) Hodges; married Jeffrey Diller (a member of the clergy), August 21, 1976; children: Adam, Michael. *Education:* Davidson College, B.A., 1975. *Politics:* Democrat. *Religion:* United Church of Christ. *Hobbies and other interests:* Bicycling, reading, watching baseball and football.

### ■ Addresses

*Home and office*—590 East King St., Chambersburg, PA 17201.

### ■ Career

Freelance writer, 1979—.

### ■ Writings

*Celebrations That Matter,* Augsburg, 1990.
*Grandaddy's Highway,* illustrated by Henri Sorensen, Boyds Mills, 1993.
*The Waiting Day,* Green Tiger Press, 1994.

### ■ Sidelights

Harriett Diller told *SATA:* "I'm often asked how I chose to write for children, and I give a different answer each time. The truth is, I really don't know. Or maybe the truth is, there are so many reasons that I could give a different one to everybody who ever asks and never run out of sincere answers.

"I'm always intimidated by the kind of writer who is called a natural storyteller, because I'm not a natural

**HARRIETT DILLER**

storyteller at all. I would rather hide in a closet than tell a story. Or listen to other people tell stories. I consider myself to be more of a collage artist than a storyteller. I take what I hear, see, feel, read, and think, and try to form them into a story."

In Diller's 1993 book, *Grandaddy's Highway,* young Maggie and her grandfather imagine their way across the country in a pretend truck, traveling west through Pittsburgh, Chicago, the West, and finally to the Pacific Ocean. A *Publishers Weekly* critic praises Diller's tale as a "warm intergenerational story [that] offers a subtle geography lesson in the form of a loosely structured fantasy." And *School Library Journal* contributor Sharron McElmeel notes that Henri Sorensen's accompanying illustrations "have a dreamy element that highlights the fantasy."

### ■ Works Cited

Review of *Grandaddy's Highway, Publishers Weekly,* February 1, 1993, p. 95.
McElmeel, Sharron, review of *Grandaddy's Highway, School Library Journal,* May, 1993, p. 83.

# ■ For More Information See

*PERIODICALS*

*Children's Book Review Service,* April, 1993, p. 103.
*Kirkus Reviews,* March 15, 1993, p. 369.

\* \* \*

# DODDS, Bill 1952-

## ■ Personal

Born July 24, 1952, in Des Moines, IA; son of John J. (a lawyer) and Margaret (a homemaker; maiden name, Farrell) Dodds; married Monica Faudree (a social worker), March 23, 1974; children: Tom, Carrie, Andy. *Education:* Attended St. Thomas Seminary, 1970-72; University of Washington, B.A., 1974. *Religion:* Roman Catholic.

## ■ Addresses

c/o Boyds Mills Press, 910 Church St., Honesdale, PA 18431.

## ■ Career

Catholic Youth Organization, Seattle, WA, retreat leader, 1974-76; King County Advocates for Retarded Citizens, Seattle, WA, recreation center assistant director, 1976-78; *The Progress,* Seattle, WA, reporter and editor, 1978-88. Freelance writer of fiction and nonfiction for adults and children, 1988—. Volunteer for Special Olympics, Catholic Worker Family Kitchen, Knights of Columbus. *Member:* Catholic Press Association.

## ■ Awards, Honors

International Three-Day Writing Contest award, 1990; twenty-five regional, state, and national writing and editing awards from the Catholic Press Association, the Society of Professional Journalists, and the Washington Press Association.

## ■ Writings

*JUVENILE*

*The Hidden Fortune,* Liguori Publications, 1991.
*My Sister Annie,* Boyds Mills Press, 1993.
*Bedtime Parables,* Our Sunday Visitor, 1993.

*OTHER*

(Coauthor) *Speaking Out, Fighting Back: Personal Experiences of Women Who Survived Childhood Sexual Abuse in the Home,* Madrona Publications, 1985.
*How to Be a Catholic Mother* (humor), Meadowbrook, 1990.
*Dads, Catholic Style* (humor/inspirational/spirituality), Servant Publications, 1990.
*How to Survive Your 40th Birthday* (humor), Meadowbrook, 1990.
*O Father: A Murder Mystery,* Pulp, 1991.

*How I Flunked Penmanship and Other Tales of Growing Up Catholic,* Servant Publications, 1991.
*The Parents' Guide to Dirty Tricks* (humor), Meadowbrook, 1989, reprinted as *How to Outsmart Your Kids: The Parents' Guide to Dirty Tricks,* 1993.

Also contributor to *Keeping Your Kids Catholic,* Servant Publications, 1989, and *Kids Pick the Funniest Poems,* Meadowbrook, 1991. Author of weekly family humor column, "Dad Knows Best," 1983-88, syndicated nationally in Catholic papers, 1983-85; co-author (with wife, Monica) of Catholic News Service monthly advice column and family advice column for *Columbia Magazine;* also columnist for and contributor to periodicals including *Columbia Magazine, Our Sunday Visitor, New Covenant, Catholic Digest, Liguorian, National Catholic Reporter, St. Anthony Messenger, Salt, U.S. Catholic,* and *Woman's World.*

## ■ Sidelights

Bill Dodds told *SATA:* "I love writing (and reading) because I had five very special teachers: two in grade school, one in high school and two in college. They not only taught me the basics, they encouraged me to develop the talent they saw in me.

"I didn't like to read when I was young. I have one brother and three sisters and I was the only one in my family who never received a certificate for reading ten

**BILL DODDS**

books during summer vacation. I'm not sure I read even one. It wasn't until I was in high school (a boarding school) that I began to read for fun.

"Almost all my books have a lot of humor in them, the kind that doesn't make fun of anyone in a mean way. I really like making people laugh, especially kids."

### ■ For More Information See

*PERIODICALS*

*Booklist,* February 15, 1993, p. 1059; March 1, 1993, p. 1229.
*Children's Book Review Service,* March, 1993, p. 92.
*Quill and Quire,* July, 1991, p. 50.
*School Library Journal,* February, 1993, p. 92.

\*    \*    \*

## DONALDSON, Joan 1953-

### ■ Personal

Born May 24, 1953, in Mount Clemens, MI; daughter of James (an engineer) and Ruth (a homemaker and artist; maiden name, Schnoor) Donaldson; married John Van Voorhees (a farmer), October 18, 1975; children: (adopted) Mateo, Carlos. *Education:* Hope College, B.A., 1975. *Religion:* Anabaptist (Mennonite). *Hobbies and other interests:* Traditional music and dance, Spencerian script, knitting lace, gardening.

### ■ Addresses

*Home*—Pleasant Hill Farm, Route 4, Fennville, MI 49408. *Agent*—Colleen Mohyde, Doe Coover Agency, 58 Sagamore Ave., Medford, MA 02155.

### ■ Career

Organic fruit farmer, 1975—. Hope College, Hope, MI, teaching associate of dance, 1981-84. Michigan Literacy Tutor, folk dance instructor with Community Education, musician for church services, 1982-87. Quiltmaker, creating commissioned pieces of folk art. *Member:* Comhaltas Ceoltoirr Eireann (traditional music and dance association of Ireland), Bread for the World, Michigan Organic Growers, Lacy Knitters.

### ■ Awards, Honors

Allegan County Homemaker of the Year, 1986; Michigan State Fair Homemaker of the Year, 1987.

### ■ Writings

*The Real Pretend,* illustrated by Tasha Tudor, Checkerboard Press, 1992.
*Great American Quilts 1994,* Oxmoor House, 1994.

Contributor of articles to *Practical Homeschooling.*

### ■ Work in Progress

A biography of Platt Rogers Spencer, master penman; a book about international adoption called *Forever Family.*

### ■ Sidelights

Joan Donaldson told *SATA:* "The values of simplicity, self-reliance and community, as seen from a Christian viewpoint, have shaped and governed the goals of my life. Together with my husband, John, we have established an organic fruit farm and worked to be good stewards of our land by planting trees and building up the soil. We built our own passive solar post-and-beam home from salvaged materials, plus numerous small outbuildings.

"Recently, with the help of our friends, we raised an enormous old-fashioned barn and experienced the satisfaction of large scale cooperation. This barn now holds our Summer Solstice celebrations, centered in different folk traditions. Our friends help create these affairs as they blend their talents in music, dance and drama. During last year's party we took a trip Through the Looking Glass. After playing pink flamingo croquet, [Lewis] Carroll's characters gave out the clues for the treasure hunt. The clues were written in verse and printed backwards on the back of a playing card.

**JOAN DONALDSON**

Finally, a play based on 'Jabberwocky' finished the revelry.

"Behind the barn, up on Pleasant Hill, resides a wind generator to produce our electricity. In spite of this limited electrical current, our farm seems to be slipping back in time as we work our oxen, milk goats, heat and cook with a wood cookstove, and try to hold to plainer values that result in a quiet, pastoral lifestyle.

"I approach my writing from the perspective of an organic farmer, homemaker, and folk artist. As a writer, I draw on the experiences and lessons learned from those roles. Writing and telling stories has been a part of my life since I was six years old. I still have a book of collected stories and poems I wrote, illustrated, and bound when I was ten. Now when I am dismayed over my children's spelling (whom I homeschool), I turn to my youthful writings to recall my own spelling mistakes.

"Pencil and paper are where stories begin for me. Having many jobs to fill each day, I snatch time for writing whenever time arises. But a blessing of manual labor is that ideas can flourish in your mind even if your hands are busy packing fruit or quilting. Recently I discovered a dear writer friend, and together we critique and encourage each other as writers and homemakers. I feel this sharing is important, and when speaking to 'young authors' groups I advise them to seek out someone who is willing to read their works a dozen times.

"As a child I read constantly and in my early dreams about being an author, I knew I wanted to give back a little of what I had claimed as a young reader. Now I hope to present a glimpse into my own 'far from the madding crowd' lifestyle. I would like to give children a sense of simpler values, the delights of nurturing, and the joys to be found in community. With these thoughts in mind I pray about my stories and begin to write."

\*      \*      \*

## DORROS, Arthur (M.) 1950-

### ■ Personal

Surname is pronounced "doh-rohs"; born May 19, 1950, in Washington, D.C.; son of Sidney Dorros (an educator) and Dorothy Louise Dorros (a nurse); married Sandra Marulanda (a teacher, translator, and editor), May, 1986; children: Alex. *Education:* University of Wisconsin, B.A., 1972; Pacific Oaks College, postgraduate studies and teaching certification, 1979. *Hobbies and other interests:* Filmmaking, building, carpentry, horticulture, hiking in Central and South America, Asia, and Spanish language and literature.

### ■ Addresses

*Agent*—Ruth Cohen, Inc., P.O. Box 7626, Menlo Park, CA 94025.

### ■ Career

Writer and illustrator, 1979—. Worked variously as a builder, carpenter, draftsman, photographer, horticultural worker, and longshoreman; teacher in elementary and junior high schools and adult education in Seattle, WA, and New York City for six years; artist in residence for more than a dozen New York City public schools, running programs in creative writing, bookmaking, and video; University of Washington, former teacher of courses on writing in the classroom; consultant in libraries and schools; director of Children's Writing Workshop, presenting seminars and workshops on writing to students, teachers and administrators in schools, libraries, and at conferences internationally. *Member:* Authors Guild, Authors League of America.

### ■ Awards, Honors

Reading Rainbow Book selection, 1986, for *Alligator Shoes,* 1989, for *Ant Cities,* and 1993, for *Abuela; Ant Cities, Feel the Wind,* and *Rain Forest Secrets* were selected as Outstanding Science Books by the National Science Teachers Association Children's Book Council, 1987, 1989, and 1990 respectively; *Tonight Is Carnaval* was named to Booklink's Best of Year list, 1991; *Abuela* was named an American Library Association notable book, 1991, *Horn Book* 20 Best citation, 1991, for *Abuela;* Parent's Choice, 1991, for *Abuela;* Notable

**ARTHUR DORROS**

**After spending a night frolicking in a shoe store, Alvin alligator realizes he likes his natural footwear the best in Dorros's self-illustrated picture book.** (Cover illustration by the author.)

Book in Field of Social Studies, 1991, for *Tonight Is Carnaval;* 25 Best of the Year, *Boston Globe,* 1991, for *Abuela;* Book of Distinction, *Hungry Mind Review,* 1991, for *Abuela;* American Book Association Pick of Lists citation, 1992, for *This Is My House;* Books for Children List, Children's Literature Center in the Library of Congress, 1992, for *Abuela* and *Tonight Is Carnaval.*

# ■ Writings

*JUVENILE*

*Tonight Is Carnaval,* Dutton, 1991, translated into Spanish by wife, Sandra Marulanda Dorros, as *Por Fin Es Carnaval,* illustrated by Club de Madres Virgenes del Carmen, Dutton, 1991.
*Abuela,* illustrated by Elisa Kleven, Dutton, 1991.

*SELF-ILLUSTRATED; JUVENILE*

*Pretzels,* Greenwillow, 1981.
*Alligator Shoes,* Dutton, 1982.
*Yum Yum* (board book for toddlers), Harper, 1987.
*Splash Splash* (board book for toddlers), Harper, 1987.
*Ant Cities* (nonfiction), Harper, 1987.
*Feel the Wind* (nonfiction), Harper, 1989.
*Rain Forest Secrets* (nonfiction), Scholastic, 1990.
*Me and My Shadow* (nonfiction), Scholastic, 1990.
*Follow the Water from Brook to Ocean* (nonfiction), HarperCollins, 1991.
*This Is My House* (nonfiction) Scholastic, 1992.

*Animal Tracks* (nonfiction), Scholastic, 1992.
*Radio Man/Don Radio,* Spanish translation by S. M. Dorros, HarperCollins, 1993.
*Elephant Families* (nonfiction), HarperCollins, 1994.

Also illustrator of children's books *Charlie's House, What Makes Day and Night,* and *Magic Secrets.*

*OTHER*

Scriptwriter and photographer for filmstrips, including "Teaching Reading, a Search for the Right Combination," released by the National School Public Relations Association, and "Sharing a Lifetime of Learning," released by the National Education Association. Author and director of *Portrait of A Neighborhood* and other videos. Contributor of articles and illustrations published in periodicals and purchased by Dodd-Mead Publishers and *USA Today.*

# ■ Work in Progress

*A Tree Is Growing,* for Scholastic, 1995; *Isla,* for Dutton, 1995.

# ■ Sidelights

As Arthur Dorros wrote in a profile for Scholastic Books, he "never imagined that" he "would be making books someday" when he was a child growing up in Washington, D.C. Nevertheless, the award-winning children's author loved to read and draw and was enthralled with animals. His family and friends fostered his latent talent. "First there was my grandfather, who would occasionally send me letters, all with the same drawing of a bird on them," he wrote in his profile. "Then there was the ninety-year-old neighbor who made sculptures out of tree roots he found, and my mother who kept a set of oil pastels in a drawer and would provide ... art supplies or a bottle of tempera paint at the drop of a hat. And my father was a great storyteller."

Despite this environment, Dorros did not pursue drawing through elementary and junior high school. Dorros remembers that he grew frustrated with his attempts to draw, and, as so he "quit drawing in the fifth grade." He did not begin to draw again until he reached high school and had to draw amoebas and animals in biology class. He has been drawing ever since. Dorros makes a point of encouraging children to persist in their endeavors despite frustration. When he gives bookmaking seminars and workshops in schools internationally, he tells children that they should continue to create even if they make mistakes. Jeff Green of the *Oakland Press* reported that Dorros told a group of children: "I wasn't born an author. I had to learn, just like you guys. You have to keep on trying and don't let anyone make you stop."

## Of Pretzels and Alligator Shoes

Dorros himself began to create picture books at the age of twenty-nine, after exchanging stories with children who wandered close to watch him remodel houses. "I found I really enjoyed swapping stories, and my interest in making pictures had continued," he explained in his

Scholastic Books profile. His first book, *Pretzels,* provides a whimsical account of the invention of the pretzel. The silly crew members of the *Bungle* let the anchor chain rust away, and the ship's cook, I Fryem Fine, replaces it with biscuit dough. When the salt encrusted, dough anchor chain is no longer needed, the cook shapes it into a twisted biscuit. First Mate Pretzel loves the cook's invention so much that it is named after him. Two other tales, "The Jungle" and "A New Land," are also included in this account of the *Bungle* crew's adventures. With Dorros' "knack for writing straight-faced nonsense" and the book's "droll" pictures, concluded a commentator for *Kirkus Reviews, Pretzels* is "mighty companionable." A reviewer for the *Bulletin of the Center for Children's Books* wrote that the "ineptitude of the characters" and "humor in the writing style" may be enjoyed by children. A reviewer for *School Library Journal* decided that the stories have a "refreshing, slightly off-the-wall feel.... Kids will enjoy the absurdities."

Dorros' next published work, *Alligator Shoes,* was inspired by his earliest childhood memory: sitting on an alligator's tail. In *Alligator Shoes,* an alligator fascinated with footwear visits a shoe store. Locked in after closing time, he tries on pair after pair, and finally falls asleep. When he wakes up in the morning, he hears a woman say that she would like a pair of alligator shoes. Realizing that not having shoes is better than becoming shoes, the alligator flees. *Alligator Shoes* was eventually selected as a Reading Rainbow book.

The publication of *Ant Cities* in 1987 marked Dorros' debut as a writer of children's nonfiction. In *Ant Cities,* Dorros uses text and cartoon-like illustrations to explain ants and their various activities, from processing food to caring for eggs. Instructions for building an ant farm are also provided. A reviewer for the *Bulletin of the Center for Children's Books* characterized the illustrations as "inviting" and "informative." Ellen Loughran, writing for *School Library Journal,* noted that the book would be a "useful addition to the science section." *Ant Cities* was selected as an Outstanding Science Book of 1987 by the National Science Teachers Association Children's Book Council. *Feel the Wind,* published in 1989, and *Rain Forest Secrets,* released in 1990, also earned this distinction, and his other picture books about science—*Me and My Shadow, Follow the Water from Brook to Ocean,* and *Animal Tracks*—have also been well received.

## Bilingual Texts

Dorros, who spent a year living in South America and speaks Spanish, made a much-needed contribution to children's literature in the United States with the publication of *Abuela* and *Tonight Is Carnaval,* which was translated by his wife, Sandra Marulanda Dorros, and released in Spanish as *Por Fin Es Carnaval.* Both volumes were published by Dutton in 1991. In *Abuela,* Rosalba imagines that she and her Abuela (grandmother) fly together over New York City. While the text is primarily English, Spanish words are interspersed

throughout the story. Readers may infer meaning from the text or look up these words in the glossary provided. Elisa Kleven's vivid illustrations complement the text and the resulting book is, according to Molly Ivins, "just joyful." In a review for *New York Times Book Review* Ivins asserted that *Abuela* "is a book to set any young child dreaming." Kate McClelland, writing in *School Library Journal,* concluded that the "innovative fantasy" will enrich "intellectually curious children who are intrigued by the exploration of another language."

In *Tonight Is Carnaval,* a young boy tells of his community's preparation for *carnaval.* The tapestries, or *arpilleras,* sewn by Club de Madres Virgen del Carmen of Lima, Peru, illustrate the beauty and excitement of the cultural event Dorros describes. A reviewer for *Horn Book* described the book as "brilliant, beautiful ... affirmative and valuable." Both *Abuela* and *Tonight Is Carnaval* have won several awards, including selection to the Books for Children List recommended by the Children's Literature Center in the Library of Congress.

Arthur Dorros also wrote *Radio Man/Don Radio,* and his wife provided the Spanish translation. The story centers on friends Diego and David, children who are members of migrant farm worker families. Diego, who constantly listens to the radio, has earned the nickname of "Radio Man" from David. The boys lose touch with one another when Diego's family begins a journey to Washington state, where they intend to work in the apple orchards. Diego, however, finds a way to contact David through the radio. Reviewer Janice Del Negro noted in *Booklist* that the illustrations provided by Dorros provide "a solid sense of place and reflect the

**Dorros applies his writing and artistic skills to nonfiction in this book about how ants live and work together.** (Cover illustration by the author.)

strong family ties and efforts at community Dorros conveys in his story."

The nonfiction book *This Is My House* conveys the respect and admiration for other cultures communicated by *Abuela, Tonight Is Carnaval, Radio Man/Don Radio*. In this book, Dorros describes twenty-two houses around the world and discusses the climate in which they are built, the people whom they shelter, and their construction. These dwellings range from stone houses in Bolivia, to the car in which an otherwise homeless family in the United States lives. The phrase, "This is my house" is included on every page in the language of the people who occupy each house. Mary Lou Budd, writing for the *School Library Journal,* praises this "engaging" book by noting that there is "unlimited value in the succinct, interesting text and pictures" and that the watercolors are "bright" and "pleasing."

Arthur Dorros lives with his Colombian-born wife and his bilingual son, Alex, in Seattle, Washington. He continues to write children's books and to teach children how to create books for themselves in his workshops. He told *SATA,* "I very much enjoy visiting schools and working with children on their own writing and illustration. Everyone has stories to tell."

## ■ Works Cited

Review of *Ant Cities, Bulletin of the Center for Children's Books,* March, 1987.
Budd, Mary Lou, review of *This Is My House, School Library Journal,* September, 1992, p. 215-216.
Del Negro, Janice, review of *Radio Man/Don Radio, Booklist,* January 15, 1994.
Dorros, Arthur, *Arthur Dorros* (publicity profile), Scholastic Books, c. 1992.
Green, Jeff, "Children's Authors Visit Area Schools," *Oakland Press,* April 18, 1991.
Ivins, Molly, review of *Abuela, New York Times Book Review,* December 8, 1991, p. 26.
Loughran, Ellen, review of *Ant Cities, School Library Journal,* August, 1987, pp. 66-67.
McClelland, Kate, review of *Abuela, School Library Journal,* October, 1991, pp. 90-94.
Review of *Pretzels, Kirkus Reviews,* November 1, 1981.
Review of *Pretzels, School Library Journal,* December, 1981, p. 74.
Review of *Pretzels, Bulletin of the Center for Children's Books,* January, 1982.
Review of *Tonight Is Carnaval, Horn Book,* May, 1991, p. 360.

## ■ For More Information See

*PERIODICALS*

*Junior Bookshelf,* February, 1990, p. 25.
*Kirkus Reviews,* August 15, 1990, p. 1167.
*Publishers Weekly,* August 14, 1987, p. 100; November 15, 1991, p. 71; August 3, 1992, p. 70.
*School Library Journal,* May, 1990, p. 96; September, 1991, p. 245.

# DOWD, John David 1945-

## ■ Personal

Born March 12, 1945, in Dargaville, New Zealand; son of Daniel H. H. (a dentist) and Audrey Belle Judd (a dental technician); married Beatrice Thiboutot (an editor and translator), June 19, 1976; children: Dylan Xavier, Olympia Hardy. *Education:* Attended Auckland University. *Hobbies and other interests:* Gardening, scuba diving, sea kayaking.

## ■ Addresses

*Home*—Box 91323, West Vancouver, British Columbia, Canada V7V 3N9.

## ■ Career

Freelance photographer and writer, 1970-80; commercial scuba diver in the North Sea, United Kingdom, and Scotland, 1976-77; Ecomarine Ocean Kayak Center, British Columbia, Canada, owner and manager, 1980-90; *Sea Kayaker Magazine,* Seattle, WA, owner and editor, 1984-89. Writer for children, 1990—. Adventure tour operator, South America, 1971-72; led kayak expedition in Caribbean, 1977-78. Outward Bound Instructor in United Kingdom, New Zealand, and Canada. Former president and founding member of Trade Association of Sea Kayaking (TASK), Seattle, WA. *Member:* Society of Children's Book Writers and Illustrators.

## ■ Writings

*JUVENILE*

*Ring of Tall Trees,* Alaska Northwest, 1992.
*Abalone Summer,* Alaska Northwest, 1993.

*OTHER*

*Sea Kayaking: A Manual for Long-Distance Touring,* University of Washington Press, 1981.

## ■ Work in Progress

*Hogsty Reef, Elk in the Fields, The Butterfly* (all complete manuscripts); *Flight from the Generals;* and *Rare and Endangered.*

## ■ Sidelights

John David Dowd told *SATA:* "In 1990 I reassessed my priorities and discovered that when I matched them with a time allotment, the lists matched almost perfectly—if one was inverted. At the time I was president of three companies and a trade association. My wife averaged twelve hours a day editing a magazine and we hired people to help care for our children. As a result of our reassessment, we sold all business interests and I have spent the past three years writing children's books and 'doing things' with my family. In particular, we traveled more together, visiting Japan, Bali, New Zea-

**JOHN DAVID DOWD**

land, Fiji, the U.K., France. This year, we drove across the U.S.A. and Canada.

"I left university in Auckland in 1965, then spent the next fifteen years travelling the world, systematically seeking adventure. I hitchhiked South America, Europe, North Africa, and the Mid-East to India. I kayaked South Chile (Punta Arenas to Puerto Montt), Indonesia and the Caribbean. I dived on the North Sea oil rigs and worked as a freelance photographer in London, as well as an Outward Bound school instructor around the world.

"I had decided to write at an early age, so I kept logbooks throughout my travels and considered myself to be 'loading' up with writable adventures and experiences. It had not occurred to me to write children's books until, living in Vancouver, B.C., I became a father and discovered that I enjoyed telling my kids stories. All my books to date are based upon adventures from my past. Because I write from personal experience, research is limited to checking details. My kids' stuff tends to involve the resolution of problems through action, with a minimum amount of introspection. This has been my experience with children. For me, writing is fun—another adventure—and when it stops being that way, I'll do something else."

## ■ For More Information See

*PERIODICALS*

*Booklist,* April 1, 1989, p. 1340.
*Kliatt,* winter, 1982, p. 71.
*Library Journal,* January, 1981, p. 1942.
*Quill and Quire,* September, 1992, p. 76.
*School Library Journal,* January, 1993, pp. 97-98.

# E–F

ELLEN, Jaye
See NIXON, Joan Lowery

\*    \*    \*

## ERLBACH, Arlene 1948-

### ■ Personal

Born October 8, 1948, in Cleveland, OH; daughter of Morris (in sales) and Lillian (maiden name, Fried) Faverman; married Herb Erlbach (a computer trainer and consultant), November 27, 1977; children: Matthew. *Education:* Kent State University, B.S. (communications), 1971; Northeastern Illinois University, Chicago, M.S. (special education), 1989. *Politics:* Liberal. *Religion:* "Jewish (non-practicing)." *Hobbies and other interests:* Animals.

### ■ Addresses

*Home and office*—5829 Capulina Ave., Morton Grove, IL 60053. *Agent*—Lettie Lee, The Ann Elmo Agency, Inc., 60 East 42nd St., New York, NY 10165.

### ■ Career

Writer. Schoolteacher in Illinois. *Member:* Society of Children's Book Writers and Illustrators, Romance Writers of America, The Young Adult Network, Children's Reading Round Table.

### ■ Awards, Honors

Golden Medallion for best young adult novel, Romance Writers of America, 1987, for *Does Your Nose Get in the Way, Too?*

### ■ Writings

*Does Your Nose Get in the Way, Too?,* Crosswinds, 1987.
*Guys, Dating, and Other Disasters,* Crosswinds, 1987.
*Drop out Blues,* Crosswinds, 1988.

**ARLENE ERLBACH**

*Hurricanes* (nonfiction), Children's Press, 1993.
*Peanut Butter* (nonfiction), Lerner Publications, 1994.

### ■ Work in Progress

*The Best Friend Book;* research on the welfare system, children's rights, and background for a biography of Florence Kelley.

46

## ■ Sidelights

"I've always loved to write and make up stories," Arlene Erlbach told *SATA*. "When I was in grade school I'd make up stories about children while I lay in bed." It was not until much later, however, that Erlbach paid attention to the praise her writing had earned from teachers and professors and submitted a novel for publication.

The book, *Does Your Nose Get in the Way Too?*, follows a teenage girl, Henny Zimmerman, through the trials of Highland High School, where her lack of inclusion in fashionable cliques has created a personal crisis for her. Henny thinks cosmetic surgery to reduce the size of her nose will solve her problems, but her father refuses to permit her to have the operation. Despite her nose, which she finally realizes isn't bad at all, Henny establishes a romantic relationship which relieves her anxiety.

In a *Voice of Youth Advocates* review of *Does Your Nose Get in the Way, Too?*, Joan Wilson complemented Erlbach's "genuine sympathy for the heroine." But Joyce Adams Burner took a contrary point of view in a *School Library Journal* review, calling the "characters stereotyped and run of the mill." Burner went on to express serious concern about the message of the book, speculating that it might convince certain teens to succumb to peer pressure.

Henny also appears in Erlbach's second book, *Guys, Dating, and Other Disasters,* in which a school assignment dealing with marriage runs a parallel course with the impending marriage of Henny's widowed father. Erlbach's third book, *Drop Out Blues*, is about two cousins who drop out of school and move in together. Commenting on her inspirations for writing, Erlbach related to *SATA:* "I get ideas from my childhood, my son's experiences, the news and kids at the school where I teach. In addition to being an author, I teach elementary school. I am in charge of my school's Young Authors' Program. It gives me great joy to encourage children in reading and writing."

## ■ Works Cited

Burner, Joyce Adams, review of *Does Your Nose Get in the Way, Too?*, *School Library Journal*, September, 1987, p. 195.

Wilson, Joan, review of *Does Your Nose Get in the Way, Too?*, *Voice of Youth Advocates,* October, 1987, pp. 200-201.

## ■ For More Information See

*PERIODICALS*

*School Library Journal*, October, 1987, pp. 149-150.
*Voice of Youth Advocates,* June, 1988, p. 85; December, 1987, p. 234.*

## FABER, Doris (Greenberg) 1924-

## ■ Personal

Born January 29, 1924, in New York, NY; daughter of Harry (a clothing manufacturer) and Florence (Greenwald) Greenberg; married Harold Faber (a writer and editor for the *New York Times*), June 21, 1951; children: Alice, Marjorie. *Education:* Attended Goucher College, 1940-42; New York University, B.A., 1943.

## ■ Addresses

*Home*—R.D. 1, Ancram, NY 12502.

## ■ Career

*New York Times,* New York City, reporter, 1943-51; nonfiction writer.

## ■ Awards, Honors

*Robert Frost: America's Poet* and *Printer's Devil to Publisher: Adolph S. Ochs of the New York Times* were both named Junior Literary Guild selections; *Oh, Lizzie!: The Life of Elizabeth Cady Stanton* was named a *Book World* Honor Book; *The Life of Lorena Hickok: E. R.'s Friend* was named a Book-of-the-Month Club alternate selection.

## ■ Writings

*JUVENILE*

*Elaine Stinson: Campus Reporter,* Knopf, 1955.
*The Wonderful Tumble of Timothy Smith,* Knopf, 1958.
*Behind the Headlines: The Story of Newspapers,* Pantheon, 1963.
*The Life of Pocahontas,* Prentice-Hall, 1963.
*Luther Burbank: Partner of Nature,* Garrard, 1963.
*Printer's Devil to Publisher: Adolph S. Ochs of the New York Times,* Messner, 1963.
*Horace Greeley: The People's Editor,* Prentice-Hall, 1964.
*The Miracle of Vitamins,* Putnam, 1964.
*Robert Frost: America's Poet,* Prentice-Hall, 1964.
*Clarence Darrow: Defender of the People,* illustrated by Paul Frame, Prentice-Hall, 1965.
*Captive Rivers: The Story of Big Dams,* Putnam, 1966.
*Enrico Fermi: Atomic Pioneer,* Prentice-Hall, 1966.
*John Jay,* Putnam, 1966.
*Rose Greenhow: Spy for the Confederacy,* Putnam, 1967.
*Petticoat Politics: How American Women Won the Right to Vote,* Lothrop, 1967.
(With husband, Harold Faber) *American Heroes of the 20th Century,* Random House, 1967.
*The Mothers of American Presidents,* New American Library, 1968.
*Anne Hutchinson,* Garrard, 1970.
*I Will Be Heard: The Life of William Lloyd Garrison,* Lothrop, 1970.
*Lucretia Mott: Foe of Slavery,* illustrated by Russell Hoover, Garrard, 1971.

One of Faber's books on U.S. leaders, *Harry Truman* introduces young readers to the story of the thirty-third president.

*Oh, Lizzie!: The Life of Elizabeth Cady Stanton,* Lothrop, 1972.
*Enough!: The Revolt of the American Consumer,* Farrar, Straus, 1972.
*Harry Truman,* Abelard-Schuman, 1972.
*The Perfect Life: The Shakers in America,* Farrar, Straus, 1974.
*Franklin Delano Roosevelt,* Abelard-Schuman, 1975.
*Bella Abzug,* Lothrop, 1976.
*Dwight Eisenhower,* Abelard-Schuman, 1977.
(With H. Faber) *The Assassination of Martin Luther King, Jr.,* F. Watts, 1978.
*Wall Street: A Story of Fortunes and Finance,* Harper, 1979.
*Love and Rivalry: Three Exceptional Pairs of Sisters,* Viking, 1983.
*Eleanor Roosevelt: First Lady of the World,* illustrated by Doris Ruff, Viking, 1985.
*Margaret Thatcher: Britain's "Iron Lady,"* illustrated by Robert Masheris, Viking, 1985.
(With H. Faber) *Martin Luther King, Jr.,* Messner, 1986.
(With H. Faber) *Mahatma Gandhi,* Messner, 1986.
(With H. Faber) *We the People: The Story of the United States Constitution since 1787,* Scribner, 1987.
(With H. Faber) *American Government: Great Lives,* Scribner, 1988.
*The Amish,* illustrated by Michael E. Erkel, Doubleday, 1991.
(With H. Faber) *Nature and the Environment: Great Lives,* Scribner, 1991.
*Calamity Jane: Her Life and Her Legend,* Houghton, 1992.

*FOR ADULTS*

*The Presidents' Mothers,* St. Martin's Press, 1978.

*The Life of Lorena Hickok: E. R.'s Friend,* Morrow, 1980.
(With H. Faber) *The Birth of a Nation: The Early Years of the United States,* Scribner, 1989.
*Smithsonian Book of the First Ladies,* Holt, 1993.

*OTHER*

Also contributor of occasional feature stories to newspapers.

## ■ Sidelights

"Before starting to write books, I worked for eight years as a reporter for the *New York Times*," Doris Faber told *SATA*, "and since retiring to raise a family I've continued to do freelance pieces for various special sections of the *Times*. After living in Westchester nearly twenty years, we moved in 1971 to a farm we had bought in 1968, thinking it would be merely a weekend retreat. My husband and I are now doing our writing and editing (and organic vegetable growing) away from the noise and tensions of the New York metropolitan area. Our new home is a rundown dairy farm, with a quirky old Victorian farmhouse, both of which we're trying to rehabilitate in between sessions at the typewriter."

Whether written on her own or with her husband Harold, Doris Faber's books have garnered praise for

Doris Faber was praised for her clear explanations of scientific and social concepts in this book on the workings and effects of dams.

the clarity and vivacity with which they introduce middle readers and young adults to important figures and issues in history, science, and politics. Her first biographical subjects included Horace Greeley, the nineteenth-century American politician and journalist, Robert Frost, the twentieth-century American poet, and Clarence Darrow, the controversial lawyer whose victories in the courtroom altered American life. In regard to *Clarence Darrow,* a reviewer for *Kirkus Reviews* noted the author's "lively" presentation of her subject's strategies. William Jay Jacobs of the *New York Times Book Review* was less pleased with Faber's prose, but concluded: "Although stylistically commonplace, [*Clarence Darrow*] conveys much of Darrow's intriguing personality."

Faber's *Enrico Fermi: Atomic Pioneer,* which describes the life and work of an early atomic scientist, was praised for its deft explanations of complex issues and events. Faber continued in a scientific vein in her next work, *Captive Rivers: The Story of the Big Dams,* which garnered praise for its clear delineation of both the science and the social issues surrounding the building of large dams worldwide. Della Thomas remarked in the *Library Journal,* "Respect for young readers is shown by

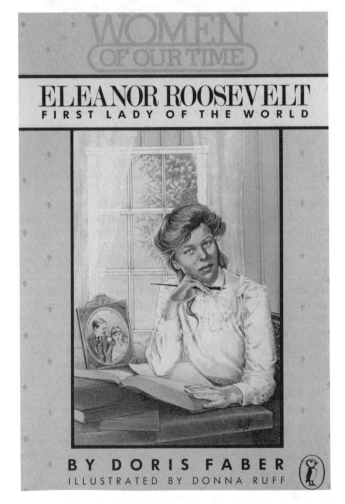

The personal and political life of first lady Eleanor Roosevelt is featured in this volume, one of Faber's many books on notable twentieth-century women. (Cover illustration by Donna Ruff.)

the straightforward style and exact vocabulary" of the author's descriptions. And a *Booklist* critic called *Captive Rivers* "absorbing and thorough."

## Presidential Biographies Earn Praise

Faber's numerous biographies of prominent men, several of which are about former U.S. presidents, have made successful additions to the ranks of nonfiction titles available to young adults. Her *Harry Truman,* which is about the thirty-third president of the United States, was praised by a reviewer for the *Bulletin of the Center for Children's Books* for its "direct and simple style." And while *Publishers Weekly* contributor Jean Mercier felt that *Harry Truman* is unnecessarily adulatory of the late president, she called the biography "perfectly adequate and easy reading for the younger reader." *Harry Truman* was followed by *Franklin Delano Roosevelt,* which garnered praise for its effective inclusion of personal details about the longest-serving president in United States history. One *Publishers Weekly* reviewer called it "a fair and well-balanced exploration" of Roosevelt. Of *Dwight Eisenhower,* Faber's next biography of a president, critic Sandra A. Collins praised the clarity of the writing in an *School Library Journal* article, finding the book to be an "accurate and objective" overall.

Throughout her career, Faber has periodically focussed on important or influential women as the subjects for her books. An early example of this is *Petticoat Politics: How American Women Won the Right to Vote,* a history of the women's suffragist movement in the United States. A contributor to *Kirkus Reviews* felt this work relies more heavily on personal facts about the movement's leaders than about their political strategies, dubbing it "a girl's book" that would tempt only those "more feminine than feminist." However, Marion Marx of *Horn Book* wrote that the "book shows clearly and with sympathy how the struggle began, developed, and was resolved."

Faber followed *Petticoat Politics* with *The Mothers of American Presidents,* a book that discusses what is known about women whom a *Kirkus Reviews* contributor described as "the unwitting very first ladies" in the lives of the presidents. With extended treatment given to twelve women and shorter biographies for the remaining mothers, Faber highlights traits such as the level of education and religious beliefs shared by the presidents' mothers. Because some of what is learned about the presidents' mothers is less than flattering, the *Kirkus Reviews* writer called *The Mothers of American Presidents* "a shrewd, conversational assessment." Lavinia Russ in *Publishers Weekly* similarly described Faber's anecdotes as "not sentimental but flavorsome and witty." *The Presidents' Mothers* covers similar ground for adult readers.

## Women Featured in Further Biographies

Faber continued writing about women in her next biography, *Lucretia Mott: Foe of Slavery,* which a commentator for the *Bulletin of the Center for Chil-

*dren's Books* judged to be "more bland than is typical of Faber, [but] this is a useful biography." *The Life of Lorena Hickok: E. R.'s Friend,* provides another example of Faber's interest in influential women. This work, written for adults, outlines the life of the first female journalist to have a byline on the front page of the *New York Times,* with a special focus on the years when she was a close friend of first lady Eleanor Roosevelt. Reviewers were titillated by the details Faber uncovered concerning the intimate friendship between these two powerful women. Faber's biography of Eleanor Roosevelt for young adults, subtitled *First Lady of the World,* garnered praise for its depiction of the first lady's life.

*Oh, Lizzie!: The Story of Elizabeth Cady Stanton* is a full-length biography for young adults of an early hero of the women's suffragist movement that Faber first outlined in *Petticoat Politics.* Reviewers noted the author's usual focus on the personal life of her subject, which a commentator for *Kirkus Reviews* found "irresistibly inspiring." A critic for the *Bulletin of the Center for Children's Books,* on the other hand, said Faber's "solid research" was marred by her "recurrent fictionalization" of the small details of Stanton's life.

*Bella Abzug,* Faber's biography of the contemporary feminist lawyer, mother, and congresswoman, also earned the author praise. A reviewer for the *Bulletin of the Center for Children's Books* called the biography, which is based on Faber's interviews with Abzug, her family, colleagues and employees, "objective, factual, written with vitality, and it makes the subject's personality come alive." Other critics praised the ease with which Faber presents a balanced yet insightful picture of a woman renowned for her controversial outspokenness. A *Kirkus Reviews* critic characterized Faber's stance as "admiring but never slavish"; and in her review of *Bella Abzug* in *School Library Journal,* Whitney Rogge concluded: "This is an enthusiastic and candid biography in a conversational style that makes lively, informative reading."

*Love and Rivalry: Three Exceptional Pairs of Sisters* is another collective biography with female subjects that critics found unique and interesting. In this work, Faber examines the relationships that author Harriet Beecher Stowe, poet Emily Dickinson, and actress Charlotte Cushman each shared with their less famous siblings. In the *School Library Journal,* Gayle Berge called *Love and Rivalry* "well documented and researched," and a commentator for *Bulletin of the Center for Children's Books* praised the author's "perceptive ... analysis of the relationships" of these people. Ann A. Flowers concluded in *Horn Book* that *Love and Rivalry* is "an intelligent, thoughtful book which deals with important themes and subject matter."

Faber is the author of two more biographies for young adults on famous women. The first, *Margaret Thatcher: Britain's "Iron Lady,"* while praised for its inclusion of interesting information on the British leader's life and the workings of her country's political system, was panned for its "tone of being condescending," in the

For the biography *Bella Abzug,* Faber interviewed the feminist lawyer and congresswoman as part of her research on the life and career of this outspoken public figure.

words of a reviewer for *Bulletin of the Center for Children's Books.* In addition, Ann W. Moore wrote in the *School Library Journal* that she discovered errors of fact in the book's statements on dates, figures, and sequence of events. Faber's other biography concerns a legendary figure of the American West, Calamity Jane, and is also, according to a reviewer for *Bulletin of the Center for Children's Books,* "an intriguing commentary on how legends are made." In this work, Faber attempts to sort out what actually happened to the woman born Martha Jane Cannary from the stories she herself and others invented about her life on the Western frontier. Though in a *School Library Journal* review Mary Mueller refuted Faber's contention that Calamity Jane was an early example of an emancipated woman, she did admit that the book is "well researched."

Faber is also the author of *Enough!: The Revolt of the American Consumer,* which outlines the history of consumer protection agencies from the 1880s to the present. A critic for *Kirkus Reviews* called this "a routine, uncontroversial review" of the issues and personalities involved. Faber's *Wall Street: A Story of Fortunes and Finance,* another historical overview of an American institution, was more positively received by its critics. Margaret L. Chatham of *School Library Journal* found the book "entertaining" after a slow start,

WOMEN OF OUR TIME

MARGARET THATCHER
BRITAIN'S "IRON LADY"

BY DORIS FABER
ILLUSTRATED BY ROBERT MASHERIS

**This biographical work details Margaret Thatcher's journey from her youth as a grocer's daughter to her powerful position as prime minister of Great Britain.** (Cover illustration by Robert Masheris.)

and a commentator for *Kirkus Reviews* noted that *Wall Street* "will ... leave young readers with a better understanding of how things work than will the usual definition-ridden visit to the floor."

In *The Perfect Life: The Shakers in America,* Faber paints a "thoughtful" portrait of this religious movement, according to a commentator for *Kirkus Reviews.* *Horn Book* contributor Paul Heins noted that Faber not only introduces young people to the history and doctrine of this religion, but also to the effect of their communities on the surrounding neighborhood. Faber covers similar ground in *The Amish,* which relates the history of another religious minority that sought refuge in America. In reviewing *The Amish,* Jeanne Marie Clancy commented in the *School Library Journal* on the "remarkable simplicity and clarity" of Faber's prose.

### Collaborates with Husband

Doris Faber has also written several books with her husband, Harold Faber. Their first collaboration for young adults was *Martin Luther King, Jr.,* which was praised for its "simple, eloquent style" by *School*

*Library Journal* critic Gale P. Jackson. This was followed by *Mahatma Gandhi,* a biography of the twentieth-century religious leader whose influence has been felt worldwide. In the *School Library Journal,* Todd Morning commented on the book's "clear, concise, and straightforward account" of Gandhi's life that nevertheless leaves out much of the historical context for his struggles. Similarly, *Kirkus Reviews* found this biography overly "cautious" yet "a reliable" source of information about the man's life.

The Fabers have also authored several patriotic books for young people. The first, *We the People: The Story of the United States Constitution since 1787,* was written in honor of the two-hundredth anniversary of the document that embodies the spirit of the American Revolution. "A combination of solid research and interest-holding prose makes this book a well-written, briskly moving introduction to Constitutional history," according to David A. Lindsey in a *School Library Journal* review. *Great Lives: American Government,* another book on which the couple worked together, offers short biographies of some influential figures in the history of American politics. A *Horn Book* reviewer judged the biographies to be "finely crafted, reflective accounts." Elizabeth S. Watson, in another *Horn Book* article, called the Fabers' next history, *The Birth of a Nation: The Early Years of the United States,* "a marvelous blend of research, interpretation, and explanation." Lindsey added in the *School Library Journal,* "Once again the Fabers have put to excellent use their well-honed skills as researcher/writers to create a solidly researched, interest-holding" book.

The Fabers have also joined forces to produce *Great Lives: Nature and the Environment,* a "crisply written" collective biography of twenty-five environmentalists, according to Renee Blumenkrantz in the *School Library Journal.* In the *Voice of Youth Advocates,* Luvada Kuhn praised the "enthusiasm" and "sense of discovery" the Fabers bring to their accounts of both famous and little-known figures in the areas of naturalism, conservation, and environmentalism.

### ■ Works Cited

Review of *Bella Abzug, Bulletin of the Center for Children's Books,* December, 1976, p. 56.

Review of *Bella Abzug, Kirkus Reviews,* September 1, 1976, p. 984.

Berge, Gayle, review of *Love and Rivalry: Three Exceptional Pairs of Sisters, School Library Journal,* January, 1984, p. 85.

Blumenkrantz, Renee, review of *Great Lives: Nature and the Environment, School Library Journal,* October, 1991, pp. 134, 138.

Review of *Calamity Jane: Her Life and Her Legend, Bulletin of the Center for Children's Books,* November, 1992, pp. 71-72.

Review of *Captive Rivers: The Story of Big Dams, Booklist,* April 15, 1966, p. 830.

Chatham, Margaret L., review of *Wall Street: A Story of Fortunes and Finance, School Library Journal,* May, 1979, p. 71.

Clancy, Jeanne Marie, review of *The Amish, School Library Journal,* May, 1991, pp. 88-89.

Review of *Clarence Darrow: Defender of the People, Kirkus Reviews,* January 15, 1965, p. 61.

Collins, Sandra A., review of *Dwight Eisenhower, School Library Journal,* April, 1977, p. 66.

Review of *Enough!: The Revolt of the American Consumer, Kirkus Reviews,* November 15, 1972, pp. 1315-1316.

Flowers, Ann A., review of *Love and Rivalry: Three Pairs of Exceptional Sisters, Horn Book,* February, 1984, p. 72.

Review of *Franklin Delano Roosevelt, Publishers Weekly,* October 7, 1974, p. 63.

Review of *Great Lives: American Government, Horn Book,* March-April, 1989, p. 225.

Review of *Harry Truman, Bulletin of the Center for Children's Books,* May, 1973, p. 136.

Heins, Paul, review of *The Perfect Life: The Shakers in America, Horn Book,* August, 1974, pp. 388-389.

Jackson, Gale P., review of *Martin Luther King, Jr., School Library Journal,* August, 1986, p. 100.

Jacobs, William Jay, review of *Clarence Darrow: Defender of the People, New York Times Book Review,* July 25, 1965, p. 20.

Kuhn, Luvada, review of *Great Lives: Nature and the Environment, Voice of Youth Advocates,* February, 1992, p. 392.

Lindsey, David A., review of *We the People: The Story of the United States Constitution, School Library Journal,* May, 1987, p. 110.

Lindsey, David A., review of *The Birth of a Nation: The Early Years of the United States, School Library Journal,* July, 1989, p. 94.

Review of *Love and Rivalry: Three Exceptional Pairs of Sisters, Bulletin of the Center for Children's Books,* February, 1984, p. 106.

Review of *Lucretia Mott: Foe of Slavery, Bulletin of the Center for Children's Books,* January, 1972, p. 73.

Review of *Mahatma Gandhi, Kirkus Reviews,* December 1, 1986, p. 1799.

Review of *Margaret Thatcher: Britain's "Iron Lady," Bulletin of the Center for Children's Books,* October, 1985, p. 25.

Marx, Marion, review of *Petticoat Politics: How American Women Won the Right to Vote, Horn Book,* April, 1968, p. 192.

Mercier, Jean, review of *Harry Truman, Publishers Weekly,* April 2, 1973, p. 65.

Moore, Ann W., review of *Margaret Thatcher: Britain's "Iron Lady," School Library Journal,* December 1985, pp. 87-88.

Morning, Todd, review of *Mahatma Gandhi, School Library Journal,* December, 1986, p. 101.

Review of *The Mothers of American Presidents, Kirkus Reviews,* May 15, 1968, p. 518.

Mueller, Mary, review of *Calamity Jane: Her Life and Her Legend, School Library Journal,* October, 1992, p. 148-149.

Review of *Oh, Lizzie!: The Story of Elizabeth Cady Stanton, Bulletin of the Center for Children's Books,* May, 1972, p. 138.

Review of *Oh, Lizzie!: The Story of Elizabeth Cady Stanton, Kirkus Reviews,* December 15, 1972, p. 1423.

Review of *The Perfect Life: The Shakers in America, Kirkus Reviews,* January 1, 1975, p. 12.

Review of *Petticoat Politics: How American Women Won the Right to Vote, Kirkus Reviews,* October 15, 1967, pp. 1286-1287.

Rogge, Whitney, review of *Bella Abzug, School Library Journal,* November, 1976, p. 57.

Russ, Lavinia, review of *The Mothers of American Presidents, Publishers Weekly,* April 22, 1968, p. 49.

Thomas, Della, review of *Captive Rivers: The Story of Big Dams, Library Journal,* March 15, 1966, pp. 1717-1718.

Review of *Wall Street: A Story of Fortunes and Finance, Kirkus Reviews,* May 15, 1979, p. 581.

Watson, Elizabeth A., review of *The Birth of a Nation: The Early Years of the United States, Horn Book,* November, 1989, pp. 794-795.

## ■ For More Information See

*PERIODICALS*

*Bulletin of the Center for Children's Books,* June, 1965, p.146.

*Horn Book,* January-February, 1993, p. 97.

*Kirkus Reviews,* January 1, 1966, pp. 12-13; January 15, 1966, pp. 62-63.

*Library Journal,* July, 1968, p. 2649; December 15, 1971, p. 4197; May, 1972, p. 138.

*New York Times Book Review,* August 18, 1974, p. 8; July 9, 1978, pp. 18, 20; February 17, 1980, pp. 3, 25.

*Publishers Weekly,* June 1, 1970, p. 67.

*School Library Journal,* March, 1975, p. 95; August, 1985, p. 64.

*Times Literary Supplement,* July 11, 1980, pp. 787-788.

\*    \*    \*

## FEYDY, Anne Lindbergh
## See SAPIEYEVSKI, Anne Lindbergh

\*    \*    \*

## FORD, Jerome W. 1949-
## (Jerry Ford)

## ■ Personal

Born November 30, 1949, in Pipestone, MN; son of L. Eldon Ford (a farmer) and Opal Marie Yackley Ford Barron (a homemaker and painter); married Martha Patricia Bates (an administrative assistant), April 26, 1975; children: Maggie, Louis. *Education:* Northern Arizona University, B.S., 1979. *Politics:* Independent. *Religion:* Presbyterian.

## ■ Addresses

*Agent*—c/o Publicity Director, Lerner Publications Co., 241 First Ave. N., Minneapolis, MN 55401.

## ■ Career

*Scottsdale Progress,* Scottsdale, AZ, sports reporter, 1971-77; *Arizona Daily Sun,* Flagstaff, AZ, sports reporter, 1977-79; *Logan Herald & Journal,* Logan, Utah, entertainment/news reporter, 1979-84; *Decatur Herald Review,* Decatur, IL, news editor, 1984-88; *Holland Sentinel,* Holland, MI, managing editor, 1988-90.

## ■ Writings

(Under name Jerry Ford) *The Grand Slam Collection: Have Fun Collecting Baseball Cards,* Lerner Publications, 1993.

## ■ Sidelights

Jerome W. Ford told *SATA:* "When I was sixteen, I decided I wanted to be a writer. I learned writing in the newspaper business. Now I am working on a variety of projects which are competing for my attention, time, and energy. Writing is probably the toughest thing to do, and do well. But when you get a key segment right, so that it fits into a story, it is very satisfactory. What is really a kick, however, is to get a book published and have it start selling."

**Readers are instructed in the history and value of baseball cards in Ford's *The Grand Slam Collection.***

## ■ For More Information See

*PERIODICALS*

*Horn Book Guide,* fall, 1992, p. 319.
*School Library Journal,* December, 1992, p. 118.*

\*        \*        \*

## FORD, Jerry
## See FORD, Jerome W.

\*        \*        \*

## FRANKEL, Ellen 1951-

## ■ Personal

Born May 22, 1951, in New York, NY; daughter of David (a certified public accountant) and Ann (Gordon) Frankel; married Herb Levine (a professor), August 3, 1975; children: Sarah Pearl, Les. *Education:* University of Michigan, B.A., 1972; Princeton University, Ph.D., 1978. *Religion:* Jewish.

## ■ Addresses

*Office*—Jewish Publication Society of America, 1930 Chestnut St., Philadelphia, PA 19103.

## ■ Career

Teacher at Franklin and Marshall College, Lancaster, PA, Drexel University, Philadelphia, PA, and Millersville University, Millersville, PA, 1977-85; freelance writer, 1981-89; B'nai B'rith Book Club, Washington, D.C., editor, 1990; Jewish Publication Society of America, Philadelphia, editor in chief, 1991—. Storyteller, 1988—; business consultant.

## ■ Writings

*Choosing to Be Chosen* (stories for children), illustrated by Janna Paiss, Ktav, 1985.
*George Washington and the Constitution,* Bantam, 1987.
*The Classic Tales: Four Thousand Years of Jewish Lore,* J. Aronson, 1989.
(With Betsy Teutsch) *The Encyclopedia of Jewish Symbols,* J. Aronson, 1992.

Contributor of articles, poems, stories, and reviews to periodicals, including *Moment, Jewish Monthly, Judaism,* and *Jewish Spectator;* contributor of children's stories to *Shofar.*

## ■ For More Information See

*PERIODICALS*

*Booklist,* November 1, 1989, p. 502.
*Library Journal,* June 15, 1989, p. 61.

# G

**EVELYN GALLARDO**

## GALLARDO, Evelyn 1948-

### ■ Personal

Surname is pronounced "guy-*are*-doe"; born October 10, 1948, in Los Angeles, CA; daughter of Carlos (a construction supervisor) and Molly (a homemaker; maiden name, Subia) Gallardo; married David Leon Root (a consultant), January 2, 1992; children: Dawn Andrea. *Education:* Attended University of California, Los Angeles. *Politics:* Democrat.

### ■ Addresses

*Home and office*—2208 The Strand, B, Manhattan Beach, CA 90266. *Agent*—Susan Cohen, Writers House, Inc., 21 West 26th St., New York, NY 10010.

### ■ Career

Writer and photographer, 1988—. Educational Travel Services, instructor, 1989—. *Member:* Young International People Protecting the Environments of the Earth (advisory board member), International Primate Protection League (West Coast/USA representative), Orangutan Foundation International, National Wildlife Federation, Society of Children's Book Writers and Illustrators, South Bay Area Reading Council.

### ■ Awards, Honors

Outstanding Support for Anti-poaching Patrol, Digit Fund, 1989; Magazine Merit Honor Certificate, Society of Children's Book Writers and Illustrators, 1990.

### ■ Writings

*Among the Orangutans: The Birute Galdikas Story,* Chronicle Books, 1993.

Also contributing author to *Endangered Wildlife,* GINN Publishing, 1993. Contributor to numerous magazines, including *International Primate Protection League News, Ranger Rick Magazine, EarthWhile, Mini-World Magazine,* and *The Easy Reader.* Gallardo's photographs have appeared on the cover of *Jane Goodall's Animal World: Gorillas,* in books, including *The Dark Romance of Dian Fossey* and numerous McGraw Hill college textbooks, and in magazines and newspapers, including *Science Magazine, Animal Magazine, Zoolife, Earthwatch, Owl Magazine, Terre Sauvage, GEO,* and the *Los Angeles Times.*

## ■ Work in Progress

*Farewell Orphan Ape,* a story about a former pet orangutan, and *The Fossey Files,* the story of Gallardo's involvement with Dr. Dian Fossey, publication expected in 1995.

## ■ Sidelights

Evelyn Gallardo told *SATA:* "I'm a Los Angeles born Mexican-American writer whose fascination for great apes stems from childhood. I fell in love with King Kong at the age of three, which launched my lifelong devotion to primates.

"Nature photography and travel are my passions. I've photographed gorillas in Africa and orangutans in Borneo. In 1975, I spent nine months in South America and hitched cargo boats up the Amazon river. I've also been to Nepal, India, Costa Rica, Japan, Thailand, China, Singapore, and Mexico.

"After working with orangutans for Birute Galdikas in Borneo in 1984 and 1987, I discovered her desire to involve children in her efforts to save the apes from extinction. I wrote *Among the Orangutans* to give kids a candid look at the life of a field scientist and the mysterious apes she studies and to spur children's imaginations to seek creative ways to help orangutans survive."

## ■ For More Information See

*PERIODICALS*

*Los Angeles Times,* July 16, 1987; May 27, 1988, pp. 8, 15; July 29, 1988, p. 2.
*News-Pilot,* December 19, 1988.
*Publishers Weekly,* March 22, 1993.
*South Pasadena Review* (Pasadena, CA), February 25, 1987.

\*   \*   \*

## GARNER, David 1958-

## ■ Personal

Born February 11, 1958, in Mt. Kisco, NY. *Education:* Attended Rhode Island School of Design, 1976-78; Cooper Union, B.F.A., 1980.

## ■ Addresses

*Home*—301 West 110th St., New York, NY 10026.

## ■ Career

Art director, Jordan, Case & McGrath Advertising, 1980-83; designer, Eisenman & Enock, Inc., 1983-84; senior art director, Russek Advertising, 1985-86; owner, David Garner Design & Illustration, 1987—.

## ■ Awards, Honors

American Institute of Graphic Arts awards, 1981 and 1989; Communication Arts Annual award, 1981; Art Director's Club award, 1982; Print Regional Design Annual award, 1986 and 1987.

## ■ Illustrator

*FOR CHILDREN*

H. I. Peeples, *Ice Cream,* Contemporary Books, 1988.
*The Mommy Book,* Lyle, 1990.
Ellen O'Shaughnessy, *Somebody Called Me a Retard Today—And My Heart Felt Sad,* Walker, 1992.

*OTHER*

Alice Lee, *Field Guide to Retirement: Fourteen Lifestyle Opportunities and Options for a Successful Retirement,* Doubleday, 1991.

## ■ Sidelights

David Garner told *SATA:* "Although I started my career as an art director at an advertising agency, I always enjoyed drawing. As a matter of fact, I was always drawing. Even as a young child I used to 'paint by the numbers.' When I was in high school I was chosen as 'best artist' by my classmates. So I always combined my sense of design with my illustration talents. And even now I do both graphic design and illustration and enjoy them equally."

\*   \*   \*

## GIRION, Barbara 1937-

## ■ Personal

Born November 20, 1937, in New York, NY; daughter of Samuel and Blanche Belle (Taub) Warren; married Heywood Jay Girion (a direct-mail advertising executive), November 27, 1957; children: Jeffrey, Eric, Laurie Sue. *Education:* Montclair State College, B.A., 1958; graduate study at Kean College and New School for Social Research. *Politics:* "I vote in every election." *Religion:* Jewish. *Hobbies and other interests:* Travel.

## ■ Addresses

*Home and office*—25 Wildwood Dr., Short Hills, NJ 07078. *Agent*—Donald Farbee, 98 Park Ave., New York, NY 10016.

## ■ Career

Junior high school teacher of history in Hillside, NJ, 1958-62; substitute special education teacher, 1962-68; writer, 1968—. Hofstra University, guest lecturer, 1976, 1978-79, currently instructor in creative writing and writing for young people; University of Rhode Island, guest lecturer, 1980-81; also instructor in writing at University of Hawaii and University of Rhode Island. Engaged in community theater and public relations

**BARBARA GIRION**

work, 1962-70; member of Hillside Democratic Committee, 1962-67; president of Hillside Community Players, 1965-68; speaker for women's groups; workshop director. Member of board of governors of Jewish Community Federation of Metropolitan New Jersey, 1973-78; member of board of directors of West Orange Young Men's-Young Women's Hebrew Association, 1973—; member of board of trustees of Jewish Education Association, 1973-78, and *Jewish News,* 1976—. Member of Council of Jewish Federations and Welfare Funds, 1973-78. *Member:* Authors League of America, Authors Guild, Society of Children's Book Writers and Illustrators (New York regional adviser).

## ■ Awards, Honors

National Young Leadership Award from Council of Jewish Federations and Welfare Funds, 1973, for multimedia script *Like a Bridge; A Tangle of Roots* was named one of the Best Books for Young Adults by the American Library Association, 1979, and won the Kenneth B. Smilen/*Present Tense* Magazine Award for Best Book for Children with a Jewish content, 1980; *Like Everybody Else* was named an International Reading Association/Children's Book Council Children's Choice, 1981; *A Handful of Stars* was named Best Book for Young Adults by the American Library Association, 1982; New Jersey Institute of Technology award, 1983, for *In the Middle of a Rainbow.*

## ■ Writings

### CHILDREN'S FICTION

*The Boy with the Special Face,* Abingdon, 1978.
*Joshua, the Czar, and the Chicken Bone Wish,* illustrated by Richard Cuffari, Scribner, 1978, published as *The Chicken Bone Wish,* Scholastic, 1982.
*Misty and Me,* Scribner, 1979.

### YOUNG ADULT FICTION

*A Tangle of Roots,* Scribner's, 1979.
*Like Everybody Else,* Scribner's, 1980.
*A Handful of Stars,* Scribner's, 1981.
*In the Middle of a Rainbow,* Scribner's, 1983.
*A Very Brief Season* (short stories), Scribner's, 1984.
*Front Page Exclusive,* Dell, 1987.
*Portfolio to Fame,* Dell, 1987.
*Prescription for Success,* Dell, 1987.
*Prime Time Attraction,* Dell, 1987.
*Indian Summer,* Scholastic, 1990.

### OTHER

Also author of scripts for children and adults, including *A Time to Love,* 1973, and *Like a Bridge,* 1975. Contributor to magazines, including *Co-Ed, Seventeen, Young Miss,* and *Young World,* and to newspapers. Editor of Hillside *Democratic* (newspaper), 1961-66.

## ■ Sidelights

Barbara Girion, whose fiction for children and young adults explores the trials and triumphs of growing up, has won praise for the warmth and humor of her stories and for her perceptive, believable portrayals of her characters and their lives. A longtime resident of the

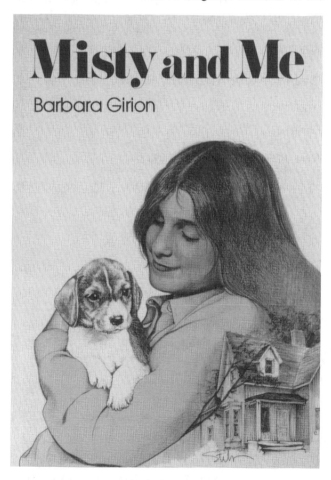

**Owning a puppy is only one of the new responsibilities sixth-grade Kim takes on in *Misty and Me* (Cover illustration by Fran Stiles.)**

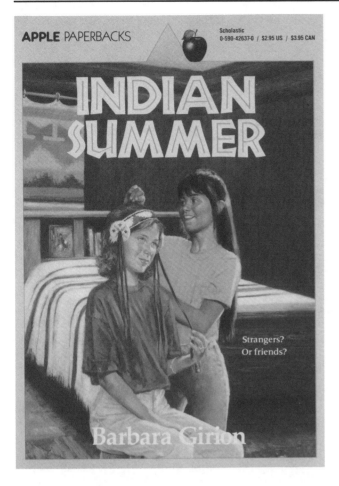

APPLE PAPERBACKS

Scholastic
0-590-42637-0 / $2.95 US / $3.95 CAN

INDIAN SUMMER

Strangers?
Or friends?

Barbara Girion

**A white girl from the city and a Native American girl living on a reservation try to overcome their differences when they room together for the summer in Girion's juvenile novel.**

New Jersey suburbs near New York City, Girion once wanted to be a singer, dancer, and actress. She studied dance and dramatics, and appeared in summer stock and community theater productions. But, she once told *SATA,* she was always a voracious reader. "No matter how many times my mother would tell me, 'Lights out,' I'd put my head under the covers with a flashlight or sneak into the bathroom and read and read and read. It's lucky I ate a lot of carrots or my eyesight would be fading from all the dark corners I've read in." Girion also taught junior high school for several years. But "even though I liked teaching," she added, "I kept writing. I combined my two loves, writing and theater, to write scripts and education programs for adults and children."

### Candid Portrayals of Teens

Many of Girion's books deal with the everyday problems of young adulthood. In *Misty and Me,* for example, sixth grader Kim wants a dog. Instead, she finds herself with new responsibilities when her mother takes a full-time job. First love is the theme of *In the Middle of the Rainbow,* whose sixteen-year-old protagonist also struggles with the demands of a part-time job and pressure for good grades so she can win a college scholarship.

Other Girion novels deal with weightier topics, such as intercultural tensions in *Indian Summer,* epilepsy in *A Handful of Stars,* and the death of a parent in *A Tangle of Roots.*

Reviewers have particularly high praise for *A Handful of Stars,* in which graduating high school senior Julie Meyers recalls the dramatic changes wrought by her diagnosis with epilepsy during her sophomore year. Writing in the *Bulletin of the Center for Children's Books,* a reviewer praises the book's "candid" treatment of the "resentment, despair, and anger that Julie must overcome." A *Publishers Weekly* reviewer finds the novel "astringently unsentimental, spiced by wit and the more moving for these qualities." *School Library Journal* contributor Marilyn Kaye concludes that *A Handful of Stars* "rises above the usual problem novel format to become a provocative and sensitive portrayal of one young girl's ordeal."

Beth, the sixteen-year-old protagonist of *A Tangle of Roots,* must also deal with a shattering upheaval when her mother dies suddenly. Commending Girion's insightful treatment of Beth's reactions to her loss and the many changes that subsequently occur in her life, a reviewer for the *Bulletin of the Center for Children's Books* praises the book's "honesty and sensitivity" as well as its "perceptive characterization."

Reviewers have also been enthusiastic about the short stories in Girion's collection *A Very Brief Season,* which center on the conflicts teenage girls experience during the "very brief season" that precedes adulthood. Jean F. Mercier describes Girion's stories in *Publishers Weekly* as "finely wrought"; and *School Library Journal* writer Charlene J. Lenzen praises Girion's character development and suggests that her stories "will strike a responsive chord in many teens."

Girion once commented that she draws on childhood memories as well as adult experiences when writing her books. "I try to remember what it was like when I was growing up, and most of the time I can. I remember the days I felt so happy when the boy I liked smiled at me, or the days I wanted to crawl under a rock because a favorite teacher yelled at me for a missed assignment. I remember the fun times with my family and also the times when I thought no one in the world understood or cared about me."

"I write about the people and things I know," she once told *SATA.* "My husband Heywood is a direct-mail advertising executive. We have three children. They give me lots of inspiration, although they don't always like everything I write . . . . Most of my magazine stories come from real life. 'Rip-off!,' the story of a teen-age shoplifter that I wrote for *Co-Ed,* was based on an item in our local paper about two teens caught in a department store. I also eavesdrop a lot. My children try to hide in the closet when they talk on the telephone so I won't overhear them."

"*In Joshua, the Czar, and the Chicken-Bone Wish,*" Girion continued, "I used our old family custom of breaking chicken bones and wishing. The story takes place at Deerfield School, which Jeff, Eric, and Laurie [Girion's children] attended. I won't say who Joshua (the klutz) is, but the fabulous Czar he meets is somewhat like my Russian grandfather, who told fantastic stories of Siberia. When Laurie and her classmates signed up for disco dancing lessons in the sixth grade," she added, "their adventures gave me a couple of funny chapters for *Misty and Me.*"

## Sitting Down to Write

Yet despite her love of writing, Girion told *SATA* she often finds it hard work. "It's hard to sit down and write every day, though I try to keep to a schedule. Sometimes I do anything to waste time, just as I did when I was in school and had an assignment due. I water the plants, clean out drawers, make a peanut butter sandwich on toasted rye, wash the dishes, and run around the block with Misty, our mostly-beagle puppy.... Sometimes I can be found talking to myself," she disclosed, "and I have to admit that I'm writing dialog for a book out loud. If I'm not near my typewriter I scribble ideas on anything handy: a laundry ticket, a brown paper bag— even a grocery list. Once my husband opened his briefcase at an important meeting and started reading from his notes: 'Chapter 13; Beth meets a tennis pro in Miami and they have a fabulous time....' (That was from *A Tangle of Roots.*) It wouldn't have been so bad except that the executives at the meeting wanted to know what happened after Chapter 13!"

"I have my own writing room," she later commented, "and no one is allowed in while I'm working. Sometimes I won't even answer the telephone. I write on pink paper first and then I switch to yellow and then to blue. I don't use white paper until I'm sure that I have the story as perfect as I can make it. When I'm working hard, the floor looks like a pastel blizzard hit it because I rip the pages out of my typewriter and throw them around the room. I don't clean up until I'm finished with a chapter, and sometimes I have to crawl around on my hands and knees looking through all the papers to try and find a sentence that I wrote two days before!"

More recently, Girion added in a letter to *SATA,* "I finally entered the twentieth century in time for the twenty-first century. I learned to work on a word processor. It took me a long time to get used to it as I am terrified of anything more involved than a toaster. But now I not only have a computer at home but I've also acquired a lightweight portable to carry around with me. Actually, it is not as much fun as having papers of all colors strewn around the room, but I am still a messy writer and have books, mail, and other papers toppling off the couch and desk. Of course, all these technical advancements are just tools, and I still have to force myself to sit down and write, putting down word after word, hoping that the words will turn into sentences and the sentences into paragraphs and—hopefully—the paragraphs will turn into a story."

Girion drew on memories of her own family to create the characters in *Joshua, the Czar, and the Chicken Bone Wish.* (Illustrated by Richard Cuffari.)

Girion believes that identifying fully with her characters enables her to write about experiences and situations with which she has not dealt personally. "I try to put myself in my characters' places," she commented to *SATA.* "What would I do if that happened to me? What would I say? How would I act? The second chapter of *A Tangle of Roots* tells how sixteen-year-old Beth Frankle reacts to the sudden death of her mother. When that chapter appeared in *Seventeen,* I received letters from many young readers telling me of the tragedies that had occurred in their own families. The book continues the story of Beth after her mother's death. People sometimes ask if the book is autobiographical. It isn't; you can write about feelings and events even if you haven't been involved with them personally."

"Writing is one of the most exciting professions in the world," Girion remarked. "After the hard work of writing and rewriting comes the fun of seeing a story in print, getting letters from young readers and parents who have enjoyed it, and meeting lots of new and interesting people, some of whom become close friends. I enjoy traveling around the country speaking at schools and universities about my books. That's the reward for all the times I have to sit alone in a room and write. After all, you can't call up a friend and say, 'Do you want to hear a nice sentence?' After the writing comes the rewriting, checking the galleys, and then the day you actually hold a book in your hand. That's when I clean up my writing room, take my family out to dinner to celebrate, and start thinking about the next story!"

"I guess the most exciting thing about being a writer," she added, "is walking into a library and seeing a book you've written on the shelf. I'm still not used to it."

### ■ Works Cited

Review of *A Handful of Stars, Publishers Weekly,* October 23, 1981, pp. 62-63.

Review of *A Handful of Stars, Bulletin of the Center for Children's Books,* March, 1982, p. 128.

Kaye, Marilyn, review of *A Handful of Stars, School Library Journal,* January, 1982, p. 77.

Lenzen, Charlene J., review of *A Very Brief Season, School Library Journal,* September, 1984, p. 128.

Mercier, Jean F., review of *A Very Brief Season, Publishers Weekly,* May 25, 1984.

Review of *A Tangle of Roots, Bulletin of the Center for Children's Books,* November, 1979, pp. 47-48.

### ■ For More Information See

*BOOKS*

*Something about the Author Autobiography Series,* Volume 14, Gale, 1992, pp. 105-124.

*PERIODICALS*

*Bulletin of the Center for Children's Books,* October, 1978, p. 29; April, 1979, p. 136; April, 1980, p. 152; March, 1981, p. 133; July, 1984, p. 204; June, 1990, p. 239.

*Horn Book,* April, 1980, p. 172; February, 1982, p. 52.

*Kirkus Reviews,* January 1, 1979, p. 5; April 1, 1979, p. 392.

*Kliatt,* September, 1987, p. 14.

*Los Angeles Times Book Review,* July 25, 1982, p. 9.

*Publishers Weekly,* May 29, 1987, p. 81; June 26, 1987, p. 73.

*School Library Journal,* November, 1978, p. 44; March, 1979, p. 139; May, 1979, p. 71; January, 1980, p. 69; February, 1981, p. 65; October, 1983, p. 167; October, 1987, p. 151; June, 1990, p. 120.

*Voice of Youth Advocates,* April, 1982, p. 34; December, 1983, p. 279; December, 1987, p. 240; April, 1988, p. 32; June, 1990, pp. 102-103.

\* \* \*

## GOLDBERG, Grace 1956-

### ■ Personal

Born October 24, 1956, in Chattanooga, TN; daughter of William B. Thompson (an investor) and Kathryn Finley (a writer and artist); children: Adam Charles, William Blair. *Education:* Received degree from Schuler School of Fine Arts, Baltimore, MD, 1978.

**GRACE GOLDBERG**

### ■ Addresses

*Home and office*—65 Port Rd., Kennebunk, ME 04043.

### ■ Career

Children's book illustrator. Instructor in illustration techniques and airbrush, Maine College of Art. *Exhibitions:* Exhibited art at First Annual Young Professional Artists Show, Baltimore, MD, c. 1976.

### ■ Illustrator

Tim Dietz, *Whales and Man,* Yankee Publishers, 1987.

Eve Knowles, *The Amazing Marsh: Alex Discovers a Hidden World,* Down East Books, 1988.

D. Kovacs, *The Whale's Tale,* Marvel Entertainment Group, 1988.

Linda Cunningham, *The Copper Angel of Piper's Mill, and How She Saved Her Town,* Down East Books, 1989.

Tina Anton, *Sharks, Sharks, Sharks,* Raintree Publishers, 1989.

J. Nelson, *Animals Change Their Clothes,* Modern Curriculum Press, 1990.

Judy Nayer, *The Happy Little Dinosaur,* McClanahan, 1990.

Nelson, *Hatched from an Egg,* Modern Curriculum Press, 1990.

Jo Albee, *The Lost Kitten* (picture book), McClanahan, 1991.

Linda P. Butler, *Maxine and the Ghost Dog* (picture book), McClanahan, 1992.

*"FACTS AT YOUR FINGERTIPS" SERIES; WRITTEN BY JUDY NAYER*

*Sea Creatures,* McClanahan, 1992.

*Jungle Life,* McClanahan, 1992.

*Reptiles,* McClanahan, 1992.

*Animals at Night,* McClanahan, 1992.

*OTHER*

Also illustrator of "Facts at Your Fingertips: Second Series," featuring *Dinosaurs, Mammals, Insects,* and *Space,* McClanahan, 1993. Illustrator of textbooks for publishers including Harcourt, Houghton, Macmillan, and Modern Curriculum Press. Contributor to *Highlights for Children* and *Clue* magazine.

■ **Work in Progress**

A new series of four board books for McClanahan.

■ **Sidelights**

"From an early age," Grace Goldberg told *SATA,* "I have had a passion for drawing and an intense interest in wildlife. Throughout my life I have strived to integrate my love of these subjects through the study of both. In illustrating books, I found an avenue that is most conducive to both interests, allowing not only a perfect opportunity to expand my scientific knowledge and research but also a chance to develop and diversify my artistic abilities through the varied mediums required for different publications. This broad spectrum is essential as I continue to try to challenge myself in my work.

"In 1973 I started, in earnest, an education in art that had begun in my childhood. I attended the Schuler School of Fine Arts in Baltimore, Maryland, where I graduated in 1978. While in my third year there, I was one of ten students chosen throughout the state to be featured in the First Annual Young Professional Artists Show, sponsored by the exclusive Charcoal Club of Baltimore. In 1977 I was again selected, this time in a show featuring five artists. I received numerous awards and commissions both during and after my early training, including works for the Stieff Silver Company and the National Aquarium.

"After moving to Maine in 1981, I shifted my efforts from showing in fine arts galleries to publishing. My first nationally distributed hardcover book, *Whales and Man,* by Tim Dietz (Yankee Publishers), was released in 1987 and has been followed by eighteen children's books, including publications by Modern Curriculum Press, Raintree Publishers, and McClanahan and Company."

\*    \*    \*

## GRAVELLE, Karen 1942-

■ **Personal**

Born July 22, 1942, in Alexandria, VA; daughter of Gordon Karl (an urban traffic commissioner) and Aileen (a housewife; maiden name, Clark) Gravelle. *Education:* University of Oregon, B.A., 1965; Catholic University of America, M.S.W., 1969; City University of New York, Ph.D., 1981.

**KAREN GRAVELLE**

■ **Addresses**

*Home*—New York, NY. *Office*—55 West 70th St., New York, NY 10023.

■ **Career**

Hospital for Special Surgery, New York City, medical social worker, 1969-70; Greenwich House Counseling Center, New York City, therapist, 1970-75; Hunter College of the City University of New York, New York City, adjunct lecturer, 1978-81, visiting assistant professor of psychology, 1982; Hamilton College, Clinton, NY, visiting assistant professor of psychology, 1981; Cancer Research Institute, New York City, director of public information, 1983-84; Fox Chase Cancer Center, Philadelphia, PA, senior science editor, 1985-86; Renaissance Medical Group, New York City, supervisor of behavioral modification support program for obese patients, 1986-87. Free-lance writer, editor, and photographer, 1982—. *Member:* Authors Guild, Authors League of America.

■ **Awards, Honors**

Best Book Award, Young Adult Library Services Association/American Library Association, 1993, for *Teenage Fathers: An Inside View.*

■ **Writings**

*FOR CHILDREN*

*Feather* (fiction), Weekly Reader, 1985.
*Fun Facts about Creatures,* Weekly Reader, 1986.

(With Ann Squire) *Animal Talk,* Messner, 1988.
*Lizards,* F. Watts, 1991.
*Animal Societies,* F. Watts, 1993.

*FOR YOUNG ADULTS*

(With Bertram A. John) *Teenagers Face to Face with Cancer,* Messner, 1989.
(With Charles Haskins) *Teenagers Face to Face with Bereavement,* Messner, 1989.
*Understanding Birth Defects,* F. Watts, 1990.
(With Leslie Peterson) *Teenage Fathers: An Inside View,* Messner, 1992.
(With Susan H. Fischer) *Where Are My Birth Parents?: A Guide for Teenage Adoptees,* Walker & Co., 1993.

*OTHER*

(With Robert Rivlin) *Deciphering the Senses: The Expanding World of Human Perception* (adult nonfiction), Simon & Schuster, 1984.

Contributor of articles to scholarly journals, including *Animal Behavior* and *Sociobiology.*

## ■ Work in Progress

*Listening to Native American Teens,* to be published by F. Watts.

## ■ Sidelights

Karen Gravelle once commented that her fascination with how people and animals experience the world is the motivating factor behind her work. She has explored these ideas through her work as a psychotherapist, college professor, free-lance writer, editor, and photographer. In particular, her books for children and young adults are attempts to understand the turbulent and confusing experiences of adolescence.

Gravelle's first book for young adults, *Teenagers Face to Face with Cancer,* is based on interviews with sixteen adolescents who were battling cancer. Gravelle and her coauthor, John A. Bertram, grouped the adolescents' stories by theme to provide answers to questions that teens with cancer often ask, including the difficult question: "What if I die?" Types of cancer, treatments, doctors, family matters, and coping techniques are also discussed by the interviewees and authors. A *Kirkus Reviews* writer concluded that this "honest treatment" of cancer would "help and reassure other teenage cancer patients, as well as their friends and relatives."

*Teenagers Face to Face with Bereavement,* written by Gravelle and Charles Haskins, utilizes an interview structure similar to *Teenagers Face to Face with Cancer* to provide information about death and the loss of loved ones. In the book seventeen teenagers comment on their relationships with parents, siblings, and friends, their feelings at the time of death and at the funeral, and the emotions they experience at later stages of grief. The authors provide guidance and advice while highlighting positive actions teenagers can take to help them rebuild their lives after the death of a loved one. As Libby K.

This book by Gravelle and Charles Haskins uses interviews with teenagers to examine the emotions young people may experience when coping with the death of a loved one.

White pointed out in the *School Library Journal,* "Both interviewees and compilers offer hope and comfort. The compilers endorse survivor counseling and point to successful outcomes of peer group therapy."

After publishing *Understanding Birth Defects,* another book for young adults, Gravelle went on to write *Teenage Fathers: An Inside View* with Leslie Peterson. The third book in the Simon & Schuster interview series presents in-depth discussions with thirteen teenage fathers and was designated a 1993 Young Adult Library Services Association/American Library Association best book. This "well laid out and informative" book, as a writer for *Kirkus Reviews* described it, allows readers to examine the diverse situations, backgrounds, and characteristics of these fathers as well as to understand the challenges presented by fatherhood. *Booklist* contributor Stephanie Zvirin described the interviews as "filled with disillusionment, fear, anger, and occasionally real joy," and described their words as a "dramatic, eye-opening portrayal of what teen fathers face when their desires and expectations collide with reality." In *Voice of Youth Advocates,* Sister Mary Veronica concluded that the book is "an important addition to young adult collections, both school and public libraries" and advised that young men should listen to the advice of teenage fathers: "Wait, don't rush into a relationship which could change your life and all of your dreams."

Gravelle provided another important resource for young people with the book, *Where Are My Birth Parents?: A Guide for Teenage Adoptees.* Co-written with Susan Fischer, this book describes the process of and problems of searching for birth parents. The authors provide advice on what to expect from birth mothers as well as adoptive parents throughout the search. A list of search and support groups is included.

Gravelle has contributed books to the world of children's literature as well. *Feather,* Gravelle's first work of fiction, is the story of a convalescent girl and a trapped pigeon. *Fun Facts about Creatures* provides interesting information about reptiles and insects. *Animal Talk,* written with Ann Squire, discusses animal communication with other animals and humans and was described by Beth Ames Herbert of *Booklist* as a "fascinating" book. And *Lizards* describes the differences and similarities between the lives of humans and lizards.

Gravelle has worked as a free-lance writer, editor, and photographer since 1982. She once explained that her interest in photography is directly related to her desire to understand the world from the point of view of the picture's subject.

■ **Works Cited**

Herbert, Beth Ames, review of *Animal Talk, Booklist,* October 15, 1988, p. 408.
Review of *Teenage Fathers, Kirkus Reviews,* August 15, 1992, p. 1061.
Review of *Teenagers Face to Face with Cancer, Kirkus Reviews,* December 1, 1986, p. 1800.
Veronica, Sister Mary, review of *Teenage Fathers, Voice of Youth Advocates,* December, 1992, p. 307.
White, Libby K., review of *Teenagers Face to Face with Bereavement, School Library Journal,* July, 1989, p. 95.
Zvirin, Stephanie, review of *Teenage Fathers, Booklist,* October 15, 1992, p. 413.

■ **For More Information See**

*PERIODICALS*

*Kirkus Reviews,* June 1, 1989, p. 836; June 15, 1993, p. 785.
*School Library Journal,* February, 1987, p. 90.

\*　　\*　　\*

**GREGORY, Jean**
**See URE, Jean**

\*　　\*　　\*

**GUSTAFSON, Anita**
**See LARSEN, Anita**

# H

**KAREN HABER**

## HABER, Karen 1955-

### ◼ Personal

Born January 7, 1955, in Bronxville, NY; daughter of David Haber and Edythe Cohen Marinoff; married Robert Silverberg (a writer), February 14, 1987. *Education:* Cedar Crest College, B.A., 1976. *Hobbies and other interests:* Antiques, music, theater, gardening, and crafts.

### ◼ Addresses

*Home*—P.O. Box 13160, Station E, Oakland, CA 94661. *Agent*—Chris Lott, Ralph Vicinanza Ltd., 111 Eighth Ave., Suite 1501, New York, NY 10011.

### ◼ Career

Writer, editor, and journalist. *Member:* Science Fiction and Fantasy Writers of America, Friends of Ethnic Art (board member, 1992—).

### ◼ Writings

(With husband, Robert Silverberg) *The Mutant Season,* Bantam/Spectra, 1990.
*Thieves' Carnival* (novella), Tor Books, 1990.
*The Mutant Prime,* Bantam/Spectra, 1991.
*Mutant Star,* Bantam/Spectra, 1992.
*Mutant Legacy,* Bantam/Spectra, 1993.

Also author of numerous short stories and articles which have appeared in *Isaac Asimov's Science Fiction Magazine, Magazine of Fantasy and Science Fiction, Full Spectrum, Fires of the Past, Women of Darkness,* and *Journeys to the Twilight Zone,* as well as other journals and anthologies. Coeditor with Silverberg of *Universe,* an anthology of original science fiction stories published by Bantam Doubleday Dell.

### ◼ Sidelights

"I think that love of reading inevitably leads to writing," Karen Haber told *SATA.* "That was certainly the case for me: I was an early reader, drawn to books, magazines, and even the backs of cereal boxes. A trip to the library with my parents was a marvelous treat: I could roam the stacks, pulling out any books I fancied, and actually bring them home with me. By the time I was in grade school, I was writing my own little stories and had composed two books by the age of sixteen—now safely buried.

"After college, I pursued journalism because I enjoyed the people, the diversity, and the stimulation. What I didn't enjoy were the hours and low pay. Eventually, I was lured by fiction, and I found the field rewarding both artistically and in terms of compensation. (I like to have things both ways, however, and I still dally with a couple of articles a year, primarily on art-related topics.) I find writing to be an intriguing, slow-motion form of communication, peculiar for the quasi-intimate relationship it creates between reader and writer.

"Science fiction and fantasy keep the imagination fresh and vital. Dealing with what might be is so often more interesting than writing about what is: a broadening exercise for both reader and writer—one hopes."

\* \* \*

## HAINS, Harriet
### See WATSON, Carol

\* \* \*

## HALEY, Gail E(inhart) 1939-

### ■ Personal

Born November 4, 1939, in Charlotte, NC; daughter of George C. (an advertising manager and artist) and P. Louise Bell (an artist) Einhart; married Joseph A. Haley (a mathematician), August 15, 1959 (marriage ended); married David Considine (a professor of mass media), September 3, 1983; children: Marguerite Madeline, Geoffrey David. *Education:* Attended Richmond Professional Institute, 1957-59, and University of Virginia, 1960-64.

### ■ Addresses

*Office*—Department of Language, Reading and Exceptionalities, Appalachian State University, Boone, NC 28608. *Agent*—Sheldon Fogelman, 10 East 40th St., New York, NY 10016.

### ■ Career

Artist, author, and illustrator of children's books and educational material. Appalachian State University, Boone, NC, currently writer in residence. Toured Great Britain in one-woman multimedia show "Get into a Book." Actively involved in the design and utilization of puppetry in education. *Exhibitions:* Graphics and illustrations exhibited at libraries and museums in the southern United States and New York; work included in permanent collections at the University of Minnesota, Jacksonville (FL) Children's Museum, and the University of Southern Mississippi. *Member:* Union Internationale de la Marionnette, Puppeteers of America.

### ■ Awards, Honors

*Boston Globe-Horn Book* honor award for illustration, 1970, and Caldecott Medal, American Library Association, 1971, both for *A Story, a Story;* Czechoslovak Children's Film Festival Award for best animated children's film of the year, 1974; Kate Greenaway Medal for illustration, British Library Association, 1977, and Kadai Tosho award (Japan), both for *The*

**GAIL E. HALEY**

*Post Office Cat;* Parents' Choice Award for illustration, 1980, for *The Green Man;* Children's Book Council children's choice selection for *Birdsong,* 1984; National Council for the Social Studies Notable Children's Book award, 1986, for *Jack and the Beantree;* Kerlan Award, University of Minnesota Kerlan Collection, 1989, for lifetime achievement and contribution to children's literature.

### ■ Writings

*FOR CHILDREN; SELF-ILLUSTRATED*

*My Kingdom for a Dragon,* Cozet Print Shop, 1962.
*The Wonderful Magical World of Marguerite: With the Entire Cast of Characters Including Rocks, Roses, Mushrooms, Daisies, Violets, Snails, Butterflies, Breezes, and Above All—the Sun,* McGraw, 1964.
*Round Stories about Our World,* Follett, 1966.
*Round Stories about Things That Grow,* Follett, 1966.
*Round Stories about Things That Live in Water,* Follett, 1966.
*Round Stories about Things that Live on Land,* Follett, 1966.
(Reteller) *A Story, a Story: An African Tale,* Atheneum, 1970.
*Noah's Ark,* Atheneum, 1971.
*Jack Joett's Ride,* Viking, 1973.
*The Abominable Swampman,* Viking, 1975.
*The Post Office Cat,* Scribner's, 1976.
*Go Away, Stay Away!,* Scribner's, 1977.

*Costumes for Plays and Playing,* Methuen, 1978.
*The Green Man,* Scribner's, 1979.
*A Story, a Day,* Methuen, 1979.
*Gail Haley's Costume Book,* Magnet Books, Volume 1: *Dress Up and Have Fun,* 1979, Volume 2: *Dress Up and Play,* 1980.
*Birdsong,* Crown, 1984.
*Jack and the Bean Tree,* Crown, 1986.
*Jack and the Fire Dragon,* Crown, 1988.
*Sea Tale,* Dutton, 1990.
(Reteller) *Puss in Boots,* Dutton, 1991.
*Mountain Jack Tales,* Dutton, 1992.
*Dream Peddler,* Dutton, 1993.

*ILLUSTRATOR*

Francelia Butler, editor, *The Skip Rope Book,* Dial, 1962.
Jane Yolen, editor, *One, Two, Buckle My Shoe: A Book of Counting Rhymes,* Doubleday, 1964.
James Holding, *The Three Wishes of Hu,* Putnam, 1964.
Bernice Kohn, *Koalas,* Prentice-Hall, 1965.
Lois Wyse, *P.S., Happy Anniversary,* World Publishing, 1966.
Hannah Rush, *The Peek-A-Boo Book of Puppies and Kittens,* T Nelson, 1966.
Solveig Russell, *Which Is Which?,* Prentice-Hall, 1966.
(With others) E. L. Konigsburg, *All Together, One at a Time,* Atheneum, 1971, 2nd edition, Macmillan, 1989.

Also illustrator of syndicated column, "Parents and Children," written by Arnold F. Arnold.

*FOR ADULTS; NONFICTION*

*Play People: Puppetry in Education,* Appalachian State University, 1988.

(With husband, David Considine) *Visual Messages: Integrating Imagery into Instruction, K-12 Resource,* Libraries Unlimited, 1992.
(With Considine and Lyn Lacy) *Imagine That: Developing Critical Viewing and Thinking Skills through Children's Books,* Libraries Unlimited, in press.

Contributor of articles to periodicals, including *The New Advocate, Children's Literature Association Quarterly,* and *Puppetry Journal.* Author and narrator of *Wood and Linoleum Illustration,* Weston Woods, 1978.

## ■ Adaptations

*A Story, a Story* (filmstrip), Weston Woods, 1972.
*A Story, a Story* (animated film), Weston Woods, 1973.
*Jack Jouett's Ride* (filmstrip), Weston Woods, 1975.
*Jack Jouett's Ride* (animated film), Weston Woods, 1975.
*Taleb and His Lamb* (film; based on *A Story, a Story*), Arthur Barr Productions, 1975.
*Go Away, Stay Away* (filmstrip), Weston Woods, 1978.
*Jack and the Bean Tree* (filmstrip), Weston Woods, 1987.
*Tradition and Technique: Creating Jack and the Bean Tree* (filmstrip), Weston Woods, 1987.

## ■ Sidelights

Since the early 1960s, author and illustrator Gail E. Haley has produced books with strong, socially relevant themes that entertain and educate children about the world in which they live. Her works include messages about the environment, ecology, racism, and illiteracy. Haley is also a noted reteller of stories based on myth and folklore. She was the first illustrator to receive the two most prestigious awards for illustration in children's literature: the Caldecott Medal for *A Story, a Story* in

**Haley's colorful illustrations complement her magical tale of a girl who receives the gift to understand the language of birds in *Birdsong*.**

1971, and its British equivalent, the Kate Greenaway Medal, for *The Post Office Cat* in 1976. Haley is widely acclaimed as an artist who skillfully utilizes a variety of media and styles to convey visually the essence of her ideas.

Haley was born in Charlotte, North Carolina, and raised in nearby Shuffletown, a rural community complete with sprawling farms and open woods, which she avidly explored. She received much attention as the first child of George and Louise Einhart, and her precociousness was encouraged from a very young age. When she was four years old, her father was drafted into the infantry; the entire family made an unplanned, week-long trip aboard a military train to his California base. This was the beginning of Haley's lifelong love of travel and adventure.

### Family Encourages Reading and Writing

Following her father's departure to Japan, Haley and her mother returned to Charlotte to live with Haley's grandparents. "My grandmother, who had grown up in Kings Mountain, North Carolina, was my mentor and earliest fan," Haley wrote in her essay for the *Something about the Author Autobiography Series* (*SAAS*). "She worked in an engraving house, and she brought me endless supplies of paper, pencils, empty books, silk cords, and anything else I might need to be creative.... My grandparents and aunt spoiled me rotten. Whatever I drew was beautiful. My stories were brilliant."

When World War II ended, Haley's family was reunited, and they returned to their home in Shuffletown. By this time Haley was in the second grade but had not yet learned to read. Her father taught her in a matter of days, beginning an enduring love of books. Haley devoured as much literature as she could during the long bus rides (ten miles each way) to and from school, including some material that was not allowed at home. She acquired her first typewriter at age ten and immediately began writing her first "book," which was about a crusader from a Middle-Eastern country. Her stories became more advanced as she grew older.

Haley became a big sister when she was eight years old and again when she was twelve. Rather than feeling deprived of the spotlight, she was delighted by her younger sisters and enjoyed telling them stories, making dolls and tiny accessories and even wooden puppets like the one her father had made for her. Haley reveled in the Saturday mornings she spent in town with her father in his office at the *Charlotte Observer* and was significantly influenced by her experiences there. "The art department was like an alchemist's laboratory," Haley said in *SAAS*. "There were jars of rubber cement, airbrushes, kneaded erasers, french curves, T squares, and machines to create almost any kind of line imaginable to mankind. I would hang around the artists for hours, watching the magic they did. Then I'd wander around the building talking to the writers.... The act of communicating through the printed word was something I knew I wanted to be a part of."

After graduating from high school, Haley attended art school for two years in Richmond, Virginia, a compromise she and her parents reached following their refusal to allow her to attend the school of her choice in New York City. Haley undertook a double major and studied graphics and painting as well as fashion illustration. She met her first husband while in school and, following graduation, was married at the age of nineteen. A job as a technical illustrator left her unfulfilled, and when she had accumulated enough money she returned to school. It was there that she received encouragement from a professor, Charles Smith, to pursue her interest in writing and illustrating children's books seriously. Later, when she had written a half dozen books, Haley traveled to New York to call on publishers but was unable to sell her work. She waited for several months before taking matters into her own hands.

"I borrowed five hundred dollars from the bank, bought a stack of woodblocks, some ink and paper," said Haley in *SAAS*. "I wrote an allegory about my need to write and illustrate books. It was called *My Kingdom for a Dragon* and told the story of a knight who made friends with a dragon, even though he realized it would cost him his knighthood and the princess whom he loved." Haley produced the book with the help of a local printer, traveled to Washington to secure the copyright, and then made her first sale of 250 copies to Brentano's bookstore. She besieged the publishing industry with the remaining copies and sent copies to writers and illustrators she admired, asking their advice about how to get started.

### Breakthrough Book Wins Caldecott

Several years after her first marriage ended, Haley spent a year in the Caribbean. Her experiences there led her to research Caribbean folklore and eventually write and illustrate *A Story, a Story,* the Caldecott Award-winning retelling of the Ashanti myth of the Sky God, Ananse. Haley is credited as the first children's author to introduce the concept of a black God. Several years later the film version of *A Story, a Story* won the Czechoslovak Children's Film Festival Award. Following this success, Haley's retelling of *Noah's Ark* was published. The book, inspired in part by her two children, focused on the conservation of natural resources and the importance of educating children about ecology.

Haley has always drawn story ideas from her surroundings, as was the case when the family moved from New York to Virginia, where she wrote *Jack Joett's Ride*. She examined library archives and traveled to England in order to research the history of the local Revolutionary War hero before writing her book. It met with great success and was made into an animated film.

Within a year the family moved to England and Haley's work went in a new direction. Inspired by the British custom of "employing" cats in post offices to catch mice, she wrote and illustrated the award-winning *The Post Office Cat*. This book went on to win an important Japanese book award. Also while in London, Haley

**Haley adds a folksy flavor to a traditional fairy tale in her self-illustrated *Jack and the Bean Tree*.**

researched the origins of the country's mythical "Green Man" and produced another popular book based on this figure; in 1990 she served as advisor for the BBC television production of *Return of the Green Man.*

By 1983 Haley had returned to the United States and remarried. She and her husband David Considine joined the faculty at Appalachian State University in North Carolina, where Haley taught courses in writing and illustrating for children as well as a course in puppetry. The rich, Blue Ridge mountain folklore became a new source of story ideas for Haley, and her subsequent books with mountain themes include *Jack and the Bean Tree* and *Jack and the Fire Dragon.*

In 1984 Haley's love of puppetry and children's theater culminated in a presentation of her work at the Smithsonian Institute; from 1983 to 1993, she also kept a marionette collection at Appalachian State to which she regularly added puppets she had acquired during her world travels to Bali, Thailand, and Australia. "Puppets are an extension of my work with picture books," she

said in *SAAS.* "They allow me to use the skills I've gained over the years, plus the added dimensions of form, music, and movement." Haley is also the author of a 1988 nonfiction work about puppets for adults, *Play People: Puppetry in Education.*

Today, Haley continues to write and illustrate original works for children and considers herself fortunate to be permitted to live in the "special world of childhood even as an adult," she said in the *Third Book of Junior Authors.* "I address my books to all adults who recall and cherish their childhood." As she fretted in the *36th Yearbook* of the Claremont Reading Conference, however, the childhood world that today's adults experienced is very different from the one in which modern children live. "The very concept of active play, curiosity, experimentation, manipulative doing and reading are being extinguished," she wrote as early as 1972. Haley later added, "Mass culture and passive consumption are antithetical to the idea that childhood is a special stage of human development requiring shelter, care, and nurturance." "In today's world," she remarked almost twenty years later in her *SAAS* entry, "children's literature is marketed, packaged, and sold like any other product in any other industry.... The industry wants a 'safe, marketable' product." It is important to Haley, therefore, to tell stories that exceed the industry's norms, because it "is through stories that we hear and are willing to share; that we communicate our culture, and, through communication, that we grow."

### ■ Works Cited

De Montreville, Doris, and Donna Hill, editors, *Third Book of Junior Authors,* H. W. Wilson, 1972, pp. 117-118.

Haley, Gale E., "Children—the Vanishing Species," *36th Yearbook* (Claremont Reading Conference), 1972, pp. 72-76.

Haley, Gail E., essay in *Something about the Author Autobiography Series,* Volume 13, Gale, 1991, pp. 89-103.

### ■ For More Information See

*BOOKS*

*Children's Literature Review,* Volume 21, Gale, 1990.

Kingman, Lee, and others, compilers, *Illustrators of Children's Books: 1967-1976,* Horn Book, 1978.

Kingman, Lee, editor, *Newbery and Caldecott Medal Books: 1966-1975,* Horn Book, 1975.

Kirkpatrick, D. L., *Twentieth-Century Children's Writers,* St. Martin's, 1978.

*PERIODICALS*

*School Library Journal,* April, 1986.

\* \* \*

## HALL, Melanie 1949-

### ■ Personal

Born November 20, 1949, in Gloucester, MA; daughter of Edward A. (a doctor) and Doris (a housewife; maiden name, Goldfield) Winsten; married Ronald Hall (an artist and musician), 1982. *Education:* Attended Rhode Island School of Design, 1967-70; Pratt Institute, B.F.A., 1978; Marywood College, M.A., 1993. *Hobbies and other interests:* Archery, reading, meditation.

### ■ Addresses

*Home and office*—Cat's Paw Studio, 22 Krom Rd., Olivebridge, NY 12461.

### ■ Career

Worked variously as a painter, museum curator, printer's assistant, editorial illustrator, graphic designer, and fashion illustrator. Children's book illustrator, 1991—. *Member:* Society of Children's Book Writers and Illustrators.

**MELANIE HALL**

### ■ Awards, Honors

Received an award for work exhibited at the Original Art Show, Society of Illustrators, 1992; Don Freeman Grant, Society of Children's Book Writers, 1993.

### ■ Illustrator

Charles Temple, *On the Riverbank,* Houghton, 1992.

Washington Irving, *The Legend of Sleepy Hollow,* adapted by Freya Littledale, Scholastic, 1992.

(Contributor) *The Very Best of Children's Book Illustration,* compiled by the Society of Illustrators, Northlight Books, 1993.

*Weather,* edited by Lee Bennett Hopkins, HarperCollins, 1994.

Patrick Lewis, *July Is a Mad Mosquito,* Atheneum, 1994.

Temple, *Shanty Boat,* Houghton, 1994.

### ■ Work in Progress

*A Very Berry Red Dress,* by Nancy Carlstrom White, for Philomel, 1994.

### ■ Sidelights

"Illustrating children's books is a dream come true for me," Melanie Hall told *SATA.* "When I was a little girl I made a series of books called 'The Fun Book,' which came out seasonally and were filled with illustrations, rebuses, puzzles, and stories. I laugh to myself remembering how I sat on the beach with colored pencils and paper finishing up the latest fun book so I wouldn't be late for the deadline. I didn't know that was a taste of what was to come.

"I've had a checkered career as a painter, museum curator, printer's assistant, editorial illustrator, graphic designer, and fashion illustrator. I wasn't very happy. One day, while sitting at my drawing table doing my umpteenth fashion illustration, I wondered, 'Will I be doing this boring stuff when I'm sixty?' I complained to my girlfriend, 'I want to do children's books!' She replied, 'Well, why don't you?' At that moment, lights flashed and bells rang. I said to myself, 'Yeah, why don't I? What's stopping me?' Everything fell into place. I went back to school and learned how to do children's books.

"The day I got my first book contract changed my life forever. After my editor, Matilda Welter of Houghton Mifflin, offered me *On the Riverbank,* I jumped up and down and whooped for joy. I tried to sound calm, cool, and collected but failed miserably. Matilda chuckled appreciatively at my delight. I told her, 'This is the day all my dreams come true,' quoting Bob Dylan's song 'New Morning.' Afterwards, I called up every member of my family and every friend to crow about the news. I am completely happy now and love what I do!"

■ **For More Information See**

*PERIODICALS*

*Artist's Magazine,* May, 1992; January, 1994.

        \*     \*     \*

## HAMM, Diane Johnston 1949-

■ **Personal**

Born November 10, 1949, in Portland, OR; daughter of Harold David (a rancher, logger, and real estate agent) and Claire (a nurse; maiden name, Trueworthy) Johnston; married Jeffrey Hamm (a transportation director), December 29, 1971; children: Nathan, Jesse, Valarie. *Education:* Attended Beloit College, 1968-70; Montana State University, B.A., 1971; University of Washington, M.Ed., 1979. *Hobbies and other interests:* Carpentry, drawing, reading, travel.

■ **Addresses**

*Office*—525 Benton St., Port Townsend, WA 98368.

■ **Career**

Freelance writer, 1971—. Barranquilla, Colombia, teacher and community extension worker, 1973-75; Community School, Seattle, WA, workshop counselor, 1981-83; has also taught in Mexico and Spain. Health

clinic, volunteer counselor, 1990—. *Member:* Society of Children's Book Writers and Illustrators.

■ **Awards, Honors**

Outstanding Juvenile Fiction—Western Heritage Wrangler Award, National Cowboy Hall of Fame, 1990, and Reluctant Reader Choice, American Library Association, 1991, both for *Bunkhouse Journal;* Alternate Book of the Month Selection, 1992, for *Rockabye Farm.*

■ **Writings**

*FOR CHILDREN*

*Grandma Drives A Motor Bed,* illustrated by Charles Robinson, A. Whitman, 1987.
*How Many Feet in the Bed,* illustrated by Kate Salley Palmer, Simon & Schuster, 1991.
*Laney's Lost Momma,* illustrated by Sally G. Ward, A. Whitman, 1991.
*Rockabye Farm,* illustrated by Rick Brown, Simon & Schuster, 1992.

*FOR YOUNG ADULTS*

*Bunkhouse Journal,* Scribner's, 1990.
*Second Family,* Scribner's, 1992.

■ **Work in Progress**

Two self-illustrated children's books, *Sleep Tight, Blue Ram* and *Let's Have a Picnic,* and a novel for young adults, *Borderline.*

**DIANE JOHNSTON HAMM**

This young adult novel by Hamm follows the life and thoughts of a teenage ranch hand who has run away from his alcoholic father. (Cover illustration by Toby Gowing.)

## ■ Sidelights

"I grew up in rural Western Montana with three brothers and a sister in a television-free home," Diane Johnston Hamm told *SATA* in discussing the development of her writing skills. "As a young person I was a prolific letter and journal writer, and I discovered as I grew older that it was easier for me to express myself in writing than it was in person.... Writing allows me to explore what is important to me. When a manuscript is accepted, my observations go public."

Hamm's first book, *Grandma Drives a Motor Bed,* describes the observations of a curious little boy who visits his bedridden grandmother and joins friends, family, and professionals in caring for her. Reviewing the book for *School Library Journal,* Virginia Opocensky describes it as a "realistic story of age and infirmity" filled with "gentle understanding and steadfast love," while a reviewer for the *Bulletin of the Center for Children's Books* suggests that it should be useful to children attempting to understand "their own experience of gerontological problems." *How Many Feet in the Bed,* is a counting book for young children. In this

"warm and cozy" book, as a reviewer for the *Children's Book Review Service* describes it, a mother, father, baby, and two children lounge in the bed on Sunday morning, and the little girl counts ten feet until, one by one, the family members leave the bed to begin the day.

*Laney's Lost Momma* is for somewhat older children. When Laney's mother disappears in the department store, both Laney and her mother remember Momma's warnings that Laney should never leave a store without her. After a frantic search, Laney asks a salesman for help, and Laney and her mother are reunited. Deborah Abbott, writing for *Booklist,* assures readers that "Hamm handles the traumatic experience adroitly, including the emotional jitters of both mother and child." *Rockabye Farm,* another book for young children, will, according to a *Publishers Weekly* critic, "surely soothe youngsters." The farmer in this bedtime story rocks his baby to sleep and then his dog, chicken, cow, and horse as well. After all this work, the farmer sits in a chair and rocks himself to sleep. "With its low-key humor and lullaby cadence, the book is as warm and reassuring as a hug," Marge Loch-Wouters writes in the *School Library Journal.*

Hamm was inspired to write her first book for young adults after reading the published letters of a pioneer woman. In *Bunkhouse Journal,* a novel set in 1910-11, sixteen-year-old Sandy Mannix has run away from his alcoholic father in Denver. His journal entries record his life on a ranch and his attempts to deal with the anger and guilt he feels towards his father. Through the relationships he develops on the ranch, including a blossoming romance, he begins to forge a new life for himself and makes the decision to depart for college. Gladys Hardcastle writes in *Voice of Youth Advocates* that readers should find Sandy to be an engaging and realistic character: "The writing style and vocabulary of a 16 year old are exceptionally well represented and highly believable, as well as beautifully expressed." Martha V. Parravano praises Hamm's "sense of people, time and place" in *Horn Book,* and a reviewer for *Publishers Weekly* concludes that "Hamm's novel offers many rewards."

In *Second Family,* a "realistic and touching novel," according to Kay Weisman in *Booklist,* "Hamm portrays the themes of loneliness and adjusting to new life situations." When Catherine Donovue, a divorcee, and her twelve-year-old son, Rodney, move in to live with lonely Mr. Torkleson, a widower, all three have difficulties adjusting to each other and to their new life situations. Eventually, despite Catherine's attempts to busy herself with graduate school and Rodney's shoplifting scheme, the three learn to respect each other and communicate more effectively. Maria B. Salvadore, writing in *School Library Journal,* comments that "this contemporary, realistic novel moves swiftly to a credible, satisfying conclusion."

Hamm's books for children and young adults encompass a wide variety of characters and situations. Explaining her ability to create realistic and engaging works, Hamm commented to *SATA:* "I am more a 'muser' than a storyteller. I always start by wondering— wondering about a situation or a character trait. Story line develops from there." Hamm, who has lived in Mexico, Colombia, and Spain, and now lives in Washington state with her husband and children, has been writing since the 1970s and is developing her talent for drawing. "It suits my style to be at one time wayfarer, researcher, philosopher, and guide," she told *SATA.* "I trust that I will never write a story that does not leave both me and the reader feeling strengthened and hopeful."

## ■ Works Cited

Abbott, Deborah, review of *Laney's Lost Momma, Booklist,* January 1, 1992, p. 834.
Review of *Bunkhouse Journal, Publishers Weekly,* August 31, 1990, p. 69.
Review of *Grandma Drives a Motor Bed, Bulletin of the Center for Children's Books,* December, 1987.
Hardcastle, Gladys, review of *Bunkhouse Journal, Voice of Youth Advocates,* December, 1990, p. 282.
Review of *How Many Feet in the Bed, Children's Book Review Service,* September, 1991, p. 2.
Loch-Wouters, Marge, review of *Rockabye Farm, School Library Journal,* July 1992, p. 59.
Opocensky, Virginia, review of *Grandma Drives a Motor Bed, School Library Journal,* January, 1988, pp. 65-66.
Parravano, Martha V., review of *Bunkhouse Journal, Horn Book,* November, 1990, p. 748.
Review of *Rockabye Farm, Publishers Weekly,* June 22, 1992, p. 60.
Salvadore, Maria B., review of *Second Family, School Library Journal,* January 1993, p. 106.

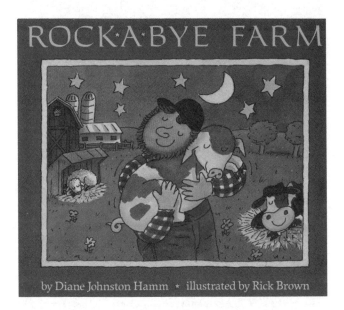

After rocking his baby to sleep, a farmer puts the rest of his farm to bed as well in Hamm's affectionate bedtime book. (Illustrated by Rick Brown.)

Weisman, Kay, review of *Second Family, Booklist,* November 1, 1992, p. 513.

## ■ For More Information See

*PERIODICALS*

*Booklist,* December 15, 1987, p. 707; March 15, 1991, p. 1481; July, 1991, p. 2050.
*Bulletin of the Center for Children's Books,* December, 1987, p. 65.
*School Library Journal,* December, 1990, p. 102; October, 1991, p. 95; December, 1991, p. 92.

\*　　\*　　\*

## HAWKES, Kevin 1959-

## ■ Personal

Born August 28, 1959, in Sherman, TX; son of Joseph (a military officer) and Carma (a homemaker; maiden name, Wiser) Hawkes; married Karen Perkes (a medical technologist), December, 1982; children: Spencer, Jessie, Ian. *Education:* Utah State University, B.A., 1985. *Religion:* Church of Jesus Christ of Latter-Day Saints (Mormon). *Hobbies and other interests:* Gardening, bicycling, beach-combing, soccer, painting.

## ■ Addresses

*Home*—Peaks Island, ME.

## ■ Career

Book store clerk, Boston, MA 1986-87; freelance illustrator in Boston, 1987-90, and Portland, ME, 1990—; children's book author and illustrator, 1990—. Scoutmaster, Varsity Scout Coach, 1986-88. *Member:* Society of Children's Book Writers and Illustrators.

## ■ Writings

*SELF-ILLUSTRATED*

*Then the Troll Heard the Squeak,* Lothrop, 1991.
*His Royal Buckliness,* Lothrop, 1992.

*ILLUSTRATOR*

Joyce Maxner, *Lady Bugatti,* Lothrop Books, 1991.
Marvin Terban, *Hey, Hay! A Wagonful of Funny Homonym Riddles,* Clairon, 1991.
Walter de la Mare, *The Turnip,* D. R. Godine, 1992.
Caroline Stutson, *By the Light of the Halloween Moon,* Lothrop, 1993.
Kathryn Lasky, *The Librarian Who Measured the Earth,* Little, Brown, 1994.

## ■ Work in Progress

Illustrating *The Nose* by Nicolai Golgol, as retold for children by Catherine Cowan, and *My Friend the Piano* by Cowan, both for Lothrop.

**KEVIN HAWKES**

## ■ Sidelights

After earning a degree in illustration at Utah State University in 1985 and working in a Boston bookstore, Kevin Hawkes began his career as an illustrator. His talent for creating rich images and writing whimsical tales led to the publication of his first book, *Then the Troll Heard the Squeak,* which was described by *Kirkus Reviews* as "witty, innovative, and lots of fun: a fine debut." In this book, limerick-style verse communicates the tale of a little girl who delights in jumping on her bed in the middle of the night. One night, this habit causes an especially disruptive ruckus in her tall, old Victorian house—it topples her brother's block tower, sends her grandmother's dentures flying, causes the maid to slip, and forces the gardener to snip his moustache instead of the plant he had intended to trim. Finally, a troll living in the basement is awakened. The annoyed troll springs up the stairs to Miss Terry's room, frightens Miss Terry and, instead of punishing her, eats the bed.

*Then the Troll Heard the Squeak* was well received by critics. According to Ann A. Flowers of *Horn Book,* the "wonderfully ghoulish illustrations ... will both chill and amuse young readers." A *Publishers Weekly* critic also praised the book: "Unusual, imaginative perspectives and open-sided views of the old Victorian house are a real delight." Hawkes once explained the "ghoulish" aspect of his work this way: "Much of my writing stems from the issues of my early childhood. My artwork often has a darker, European look to it, perhaps the result of my stay as a child in Europe."

"My work certainly reflects my own personal sense of humor," Hawkes also noted. This humor is exemplified in Hawkes' second self-illustrated book, *His Royal Buckliness.* In this story, a little boy (Lord Buckley) is kidnapped by giants who crown him king and force him to live in their cold country. The homesick Lord Buckley sends a message in a bottle, and his own countrymen soon arrive to rescue him. Their gift of spring wins the friendship of the giants, and "in the end, they parted friends"—Lord Buckley is free to return home. Judith Gloyer, a reviewer for *School Library Journal,* writes that the rhyming story is "charmingly rendered," and a *Kirkus Reviews* contributor notes that Hawkes' illustrations "glow with vitality and humor."

An understanding of Hawkes' work would be incomplete without an appreciation of the illustrations he has created for children's books written by other authors, including Joyce Maxner's *Lady Bugatti* and Marvin Terban's *Hey! Hay!*

## ■ Works Cited

Flowers, Ann A., review of *Then the Troll Heard the Squeak, Horn Book,* May, 1991, p. 314.

Gloyer, Judith, review of *His Royal Buckliness, School Library Journal,* December, 1992.

Review of *His Royal Buckliness, Kirkus Reviews,* November 1, 1992, p. 1377.

**In Hawkes's debut picture book, Little Miss Terry's habit of jumping on the bed causes chaos in her house and wakes up a very annoyed troll who lives in the basement. (Cover illustration by the author.)**

Review of *Then the Troll Heard the Squeak, Kirkus Reviews,* February 15, 1991, p. 248.
Review of *Then the Troll Heard the Squeak, Publishers Weekly,* December 21, 1990, pp. 55-56.

## ■ For More Information See

*PERIODICALS*

*Publishers Weekly,* October 26, 1992, pp. 70-71.
*School Library Journal,* June, 1991, p. 78.

\*     \*     \*

## HERMES, Patricia 1936-

### ■ Personal

Born February 21, 1936, in Brooklyn, NY; daughter of Fred Joseph (a bank vice president) and Jessie Gould Martin; married Matthew E. Hermes (a research and development director for a chemical company), August 24, 1957 (divorced, 1984); children: Paul, Mark, Timothy, Matthew, Jr., Jennifer. *Education:* St. John's University, B.A., 1957.

### ■ Addresses

*Home and office*—1414 Melville Ave., Fairfield, CT 06430. *Agent*—Dorothy Markinko, McIntosh & Otis, Inc., 310 Madison Ave., New York, NY 10017.

### ■ Career

Rollingcrest Junior High School, Takoma Park, MD, teacher of English and social studies, 1957-58; Delcastle Technical High School, Delcastle, DE, teacher of homebound children, 1972-73; writer, 1977—. Teacher of gifted middle-grade children, Norfolk, VA, 1981-82;

PATRICIA HERMES

adult education instructor. *Member:* Authors Guild, Authors League of America, Society of Children's Book Writers and Illustrators.

### ■ Awards, Honors

Best Book for Young Adults citation, American Library Association, 1985, and Notable Children's Trade Book in the Field of Social Studies citation, National Council for Social Studies/Children's Book Council Joint Committee, both for *A Solitary Secret;* Children's Choice Award, 1987, for *Kevin Corbett Eats Flies;* Crabbery Award and Children's Choice Award, International Reading Association/Children's Book Council, both for *What If They Knew?;* Children's Choice Award for *Friends Are Like That;* Pine Tree Book Award, Iowa Young Reader Medal, Hawaii Nene Award, California Young Reader Medal, Notable Children's Trade Book in the Field of Social Studies citation, National Council for Social Studies/Children's Book Council Joint Committee, all for *You Shouldn't Have to Say Goodbye;* Notable Children's Trade Book in the Field of Social Studies citation, National Council for Social Studies/Children's Book Council Joint Committee, for *Who Will Take Care of Me?;* Children's Choice Award for *Heads, I Win;* Best Book of the Year citation, *School Library Journal,* and Children's Choice Award, both for *Mama, Let's Dance.*

### ■ Writings

*FOR MIDDLE-GRADE READERS*

*What If They Knew?,* Harcourt, 1980.
*Nobody's Fault?,* Harcourt, 1981.
*Who Will Take Care of Me?,* Harcourt, 1984.
*Kevin Corbett Eats Flies,* illustrations by Carol Newsom, Harcourt, 1986.
*A Place for Jeremy* (sequel to *What If They Knew?*), Harcourt, 1987.
*Heads, I Win* (sequel to *Kevin Corbett Eats Flies*), illustrations by Newsom, Harcourt, 1989.
*I Hate Being Gifted!,* Putnam, 1990.
(Adaptor) *My Girl,* Simon & Schuster, 1991.
*Take Care of My Girl,* Little, Brown, 1992.
*Someone to Count On,* Little, Brown, 1993.
*Nothing But Trouble, Trouble, Trouble,* Scholastic, 1993.
*On Winter's Wind,* Little, Brown, in press.

*FOR YOUNG ADULTS*

*You Shouldn't Have to Say Goodbye,* Harcourt, 1982.
*Friends Are Like That,* Harcourt, 1984.
*A Solitary Secret,* Harcourt, 1985.
*A Time to Listen: Preventing Youth Suicide* (nonfiction), Harcourt, 1987.
*Be Still My Heart,* Putnam, 1990.
*Mama, Let's Dance,* Little, Brown, 1991.
(Adaptor) *My Girl II,* Simon & Schuster, 1994.

*OTHER*

Contributor to textbooks, including *On Reading and Writing for Kids.* Contributor to magazines, including *Woman's Day, Life and Health, Connecticut, American Baby,* and *Mother's Day,* and newspapers, including the

*New York Times. What If They Knew?* has been translated into French, Portuguese, and Japanese; *Friends Are Like That,* Japanese; *A Solitary Secret,* Danish; and *Mama, Let's Dance,* Italian.

## ■ Work in Progress

A series, including *The Cousins' Club,* and *I'll Pulverize You William!*

## ■ Sidelights

"As adults, we often try to deceive ourselves that childhood is a safe, pleasant place to be. It isn't—at least, some of the time. For me, it is important to say this to young people so children know they are not alone," Patricia Hermes once commented. While many of Hermes's characters experience difficult and trying times—life in foster care, uncaring parents, unaccepting classmates—most of the author's young protagonists use these unsettling periods to gain strength and wisdom. And in spite of these difficulties, they manage to have fun, mischief, and a great deal of joy.

Hermes was always interested in books and writing. "I loved to write when I was a kid," she remarked in an interview with *Something about the Author* (*SATA*). "I was an avid reader as a kid, just buried in books." Hermes noted that since there were very few books specifically for children and young adults in those days, she spent a lot of time reading classic literature: "I lived with *The Secret Garden.*" Hermes also loved the "Green Gables" books by L. M. Montgomery, *Tom Sawyer* and *Huckleberry Finn,* the Grimm brothers' fairy tales, *A Child's Garden of Verses, The Yearling,* and *Heidi.*

Hermes got a lot of practice reading and writing because once she came down with rheumatic fever, "Which in those days was a big deal. You recuperated by spending months in bed." When not stuck in bed or in the hospital, Hermes—like many of her female characters— was an active tomboy. When she went to college, Hermes majored in speech and English. After graduating, she married and taught school for a short time; she also raised a large family. Hermes returned to teaching for several years after her children were older, eventually deciding that it was not what she wanted to do. It was about this time that the author became interested in writing professionally.

"I've always written for myself. I never thought of writing for anybody else," Hermes explained to *SATA.* She eventually took a class at the New School for Social Research in writing nonfiction for adults, a course taught by Russell Freedman, who later won the Newbery Award for his biography of Abraham Lincoln. After finishing a few articles, Hermes "took some things I wrote in the course and sent them out to publishers and to my utter amazement, people started buying them. You get hooked pretty quickly that way." Hermes continued to write nonfiction articles for several years, including many pieces on SIDS (sudden infant death syndrome), which had caused the death of one of her children. One of Hermes's first articles was sold to the *New York Times.*

## Young Readers, Tough Issues

After that article appeared in the *Times,* Hermes turned to fiction writing for children, completing her first novel, *What If They Knew?.* In her first young adult book, *You Shouldn't Have to Say Goodbye,* Hermes presents twelve-year-old Sarah, who is losing her mother to cancer. While confronting this crisis, Sarah moves between fear for her mother and her own daily concerns. In the end, Sarah is left with a journal her mother has written, a book that offers guidance in dealing with life's various trials. "This is moving, but it's not maudlin, although Mom's fortitude and equanimity may be more exemplary than typical," commented a *Bulletin of the Center for Children's Books* contributor.

A book for younger children dealing with death and abandonment is Hermes's *Who Will Take Care of Me?* In this story, Mark and his retarded younger brother Pete live with their grandmother. When she dies, the boys run away to the woods to keep Pete from being sent

**In this sequel to Hermes's *What if They Knew?,* Jeremy returns to her grandparent's Brooklyn home while she waits for the arrival of her parents and their new adopted baby. (Cover illustration by Leland Neff.)**

Kevin teams up with Bailey, an antagonistic classmate, to find a new love interest for his father, who wants to move out of town in Hermes's humorous juvenile novel. (Cover illustration by Joanne L. Scribner.)

Three children try to live on their own after being abandoned by their mother, but eventually must ask outsiders for help in this novel by Hermes. (Cover illustration by Ellen Thompson.)

away to a special school. *School Library Journal* critic Nancy Berkowitz found Mark "sympathetic" and Pete's characterization "honest and unsentimental."

Hermes' first book for young adults, the award-winning *A Solitary Secret,* "is a spellbinding book that drops the reader deep into the soul" of a girl who has endured incest, noted *Voice of Youth Advocates* contributor Marijo Duncan. The unnamed teen, who ages from fourteen to eighteen during the story, tells her story via a journal. Eventually, she shares her secret with a friend's parent.

Two books featuring elementary school friends Kevin Corbett and foster child Bailey Wharton are *Kevin Corbett Eats Flies* and *Heads, I Win.* The title for *Kevin Corbett Eats Flies* "came about because my daughter came home and told me there was a kid in her class eating dead flies off the windowsill," Hermes related in her interview. "As soon as she said that, I said, 'There's the title for my next book.'" In *Kevin Corbett,* the hero regularly gains his classmates' attention by tackling bizarre stunts, like eating flies or the class goldfish. Kevin meets his match, however, in tough but likeable

Bailey, who eventually becomes his friend. *Heads, I Win* focuses on Bailey's life both in school and with Ms. Henderson and her four-year-old son. Bailey is afraid that her social worker wants to move her to yet another foster home; to help combat this fear, she decides to run for the class presidency to show everyone how well she is doing in school. Kevin volunteers to be Bailey's campaign manager, "and their analysis of how best to 'buy' individual students makes up much of the humor of the book," wrote Candy Colborn in *School Library Journal,* adding that the "characters are well drawn, and the fifth-grade in-fighting is very realistic."

Another book for middle-grade children is *A Place for Jeremy,* the sequel to *What If They Knew?* Jeremy spends part of her fifth-grade year with her grandparents in Brooklyn while her parents are abroad and in the process of adopting a baby. Jeremy calls the unknown child "Stupid Baby," fearing that the infant will steals her parents' affections. A *Publishers Weekly* contributor remarked that "scenes between Jeremy and her grandfather are heartwarming."

## Love, Alienation, and Abandonment

According to the author, *Be Still My Heart* "came about because I saw a girl and a boy in a school hallway, just looking at each other with this adoration in their eyes, and I thought, 'I've got to write about that.'" In the novel, Allison loves David, who loves Leslie, Allison's best friend. David and Allison are brought together when a teacher's husband develops AIDS and becomes a victim of discrimination. The book features an unusual character in the Countess—Allison's grandmother—who advocates the use of condoms. While some reviewers found the story stereotypical and lacking depth, "this book shows through its female characters that looks aren't everything to all boys, and that intelligence, enthusiasm, and conviction are just as appealing," declared *School Library Journal* contributor Kathryn Havris.

Hermes tackles the plight of the gifted children in *I Hate Being Gifted!* The story's main character, KT, is proud to be in a class for gifted children, but hates being separated from her two best friends. When another girl threatens to usurp her place in the trio, KT has to learn that intellectual pursuits and a social life are compatible. "KT's narrative voice is authentic and fresh; many readers will recognize themselves and their classmates in this slice of sixth grade life," observed a reviewer for *Publishers Weekly*.

Writing for *Horn Book*, Mary M. Burns maintained that *Mama, Let's Dance* "tugs at the heart without manipulating its audience." The story involves three children—ages sixteen, eleven, and seven—who are left to fend for themselves when their mother abandons them. The children pretend nothing has changed until the youngest becomes seriously ill and the siblings realize that they must reach out to their neighbors for help. Carolyn Noah of *School Library Journal* found *Mama* a "tightly woven tale," in which "rhythmic, homey text and genuine characters resonate with authenticity."

An unusual living situation and a missing parent are also the subjects of *Take Care of My Girl*. Eleven-year-old Brady lives in an old house with her grandfather Jake. Years before, Brady's father left to "save the whales" and hasn't been heard from since. Over the course of the story, a school project and Jake's failing health make finding Brady's missing parent a priority. "Hermes writes movingly of a young girl's search for the meaning of family," declared Cindy Darling Codell in *School Library Journal*. And *Booklist* contributor Janice Del Negro found "the story's weak beginning is overcome by a slowly accelerating plot, and loose ends ... are tidily if summarily accounted for in a rosy conclusion."

*A Time to Listen* is Hermes's nonfiction guide intended to help young adults understand issues related to suicide. The book consists of interviews with teens who have tried suicide, parents and friends of victims, and a therapist specializing in the problems confronting young people. "The interviews are probing, but sensitive to the privacy of subjects," commented Libby K. White in *School Library Journal*. "The great myths of teen suicide ... are refuted." *A Time to Listen* includes suggestions for helping depressed friends and overall, it is "a sensible, approachable book for those who need it," concluded Rosemary Moran in *Voice of Youth Advocates*.

Part of becoming a children's writer, Hermes told *SATA*, is that there is a childlike part of us "we never lose, if we're lucky. Every good teacher has that. I think that child is a part of me, and she needs to speak—and does—through my books. I don't write for some child out there, I write for the child in me." When asked if she had any advice for young writers, Hermes said, "If I could preach for a minute, I'd say 'If you're going to be a writer, you must be a reader.' It doesn't matter what you read. Forget what those teachers tell you. You don't have to read 'good' literature. Read anything, because eventually, if you become a reader you will someday find good literature. No, there's nothing wrong with trivial reading. Also don't throw away anything you've ever written. I tell kids that if their mothers get in cleaning fits, tell them they can throw away their school books, or their baby brother, but do not throw away anything they've written."

## ■ Works Cited

Berkowitz, Nancy, review of *Who Will Take Care of Me?, School Library Journal*, October, 1983, p. 158.

Burns, Mary M., review of *Mama, Let's Dance, Horn Book,* January/February, 1992, p. 70.

Codell, Cindy Darling, review of *Take Care of My Girl, School Library Journal*, December, 1992, p. 112.

Colborn, Candy, review of *Heads, I Win, School Library Journal,* August, 1988, p. 95.

Del Negro, Janice, review of *Take Care of My Girl, Booklist,* November 15, 1992.

Duncan, Marijo, review of *A Solitary Secret, Voice of Youth Advocates,* December, 1985, p. 320.

Havris, Kathryn, review of *Be Still My Heart, School Library Journal,* December, 1989, p. 118.

Hermes, Patricia, telephone interview conducted by Jani Prescott for *Something about the Author,* August 13, 1993.

Review of *I Hate Being Gifted!, Publishers Weekly,* November 23, 1990, p. 66.

Moran, Rosemary, review of *A Time to Listen, Voice of Youth Advocates,* June, 1988, p. 101.

Noah, Carol, review of *Mama, Let's Dance, School Library Journal,* September, 1991, p. 253.

Review of *A Place for Jeremy, Publishers Weekly,* April 24, 1987, p. 70.

White, Libby K., review of *A Time to Listen, School Library Journal,* March, 1988, p. 220.

Review of *You Shouldn't Have to Say Goodbye, Bulletin of the Center for Children's Books,* March, 1983, p. 127.

# ■ For More Information See

*PERIODICALS*

*Booklist,* October 15, 1989, p. 826.
*Bulletin of the Center for Children's Books,* February, 1983, p. 76; July/August, 1983, p. 211; June, 1985, p. 185; February, 1990, p. 138; December, 1991, p. 91.
*Publishers Weekly,* November 24, 1989, p. 72; October 4, 1991, p. 89; November 2, 1992, p. 72.
*Science Books and Films,* September/October, 1988, p. 4.
*School Library Journal,* August, 1985, p. 76; May, 1993, p. 23; April, 1994, p. 128.
*Wilson Library Bulletin,* February, 1986, p. 47; October, 1989, p. 106.

*—Sketch by Jani Prescott*

\*        \*        \*

# HILL, Douglas (Arthur) 1935-
## (Martin Hillman)

## ■ Personal

Born April 6, 1935, in Brandon, Manitoba, Canada; married Gail Robinson, 1958 (divorced, 1978); children: Michael Julian. *Education:* University of Saskatchewan, B.A. (with honors), 1957; attended University of Toronto, 1957-59.

## ■ Addresses

*Home*—3 Hillfield Ave., London N8 7DU, England.
*Agent*—Sheila Watson, Watson Little Ltd., 12 Egbert St., London NW1 8LJ, England.

## ■ Career

Aldus Books, London, England, series editor, 1962-64; freelance writer, 1964—; literary editor, London *Tribune,* 1971-84. Science fiction advisor, Rupert Hart-Davis, 1966-68, Mayflower Books, 1969-71, J. M. Dent & Sons, 1972-74, and Pan Books, 1974-80. *Member:* Society of Authors (England), Children's Book Circle.

## ■ Awards, Honors

Received grants from the Canada Council of Arts, 1966, 1968, 1969, and 1970; Parents' Choice Award, 1987, for *Blade of the Poisoner.*

## ■ Writings

*YOUNG ADULT FICTION*

*Galactic Warlord,* Gollancz, 1979, Atheneum, 1980.
*Deathwing over Veynaa,* Gollancz, 1980, Atheneum, 1981.
*Day of the Starwind,* Gollancz, 1980, Atheneum, 1981.
*Planet of the Warlord,* Gollancz, 1981, Atheneum, 1982.
*Young Legionary: The Earlier Adventures of Keill Randor,* Gollancz, 1982, Atheneum, 1983.

*The Huntsman,* Atheneum, 1982.
*Have Your Own Extraterrestrial Adventure,* Sparrow, 1983.
*Warriors of the Wasteland,* Atheneum, 1983.
*Alien Citadel,* Atheneum, 1984.
*Exiles of ColSec,* Atheneum, 1984.
*The Moon Monsters,* illustrated by Jeremy Ford, Heinemann, 1984.
*The Caves of Klydor,* Gollancz, 1984, Atheneum, 1985.
*ColSec Rebellion,* Atheneum, 1985.
*How Jennifer (and Speckle) Saved the Earth,* illustrated by Andre Amstutz, Heinemann, 1986.
*Blade of the Poisoner,* McElderry, 1987.
*Master of Fiends,* Gollancz, 1987, McElderry, 1988.
*Goblin Party,* illustrated by Paul Demayer, Gollancz, 1988.
*Penelope's Pendant,* illustrated by Annabel Spenceley, Pan-Macmillan, 1990, illustrated by Steve Johnson, Doubleday, 1990.
*The Unicorn Dream,* Heinemann, 1992.
*The Voyage of Mudjack,* Methuen, 1993.
*The World of the Stiks,* Transworld, 1994.
*Penelope's Protest,* Pan, 1994.

*FOR CHILDREN*

(With Gail Robinson) *Coyote the Trickster: Legends of the North American Indians,* illustrated by Graham McCallum, Chatto & Windus, 1975, Crane Russak, 1976.
*The Exploits of Hercules,* illustrated by Tom Barling, Pan, 1978.
(With John Elkington, Joel Merkower, and Julia Hailes) *The Young Green Consumer Guide,* Gollancz, 1990, published as *Going Green: A Kid's Handbook to Saving the Planet,* Viking, 1990.

*ADULT FICTION*

*The Fraxilly Fracas,* Gollancz, 1989.
*The Colloghi Conspiracy,* Gollancz, 1990.
*The Lightless Dome,* Pan, 1993.
*The Leafless Forest,* Pan, 1994.

*EDITOR*

*The Peasants' Revolt: A Collection of Contemporary Documents,* Jackdaw, 1966.
*The Way of the Werewolf,* Panther, 1966.
*Window on the Future,* Hart Davis, 1966.
*The Devil His Due,* Hart Davis, 1967, Avon, 1969.
*Warlocks and Warriors,* Mayflower, 1971.
*Tribune 40,* Quartet, 1977.
*The Shape of Sex to Come,* Pan, 1978.
*Alien Worlds,* Heinemann, 1981.
*Planetfall,* Oxford University Press, 1986.

*OTHER*

(With Pat Williams) *The Supernatural,* Aldus, 1965, Hawthorn, 1966.
*The Opening of the Canadian West,* Day, 1967.
*Magic and Superstition,* Hamlyn, 1968.
*John Keats,* Morgan Grampian, 1968.
*Regency London,* Macdonald, 1969.
*Fortune Telling,* Hamlyn, 1970.

*A Hundred Years of Georgian London,* Macdonald, 1970, Hastings House, 1971.

*Return from the Dead,* Macdonald, 1970, published as *The History of Ghosts, Vampires, and Werewolves,* Harrow, 1973.

(Under pseudonym Martin Hillman) *Bridging a Continent,* Aldus, 1971, revised edition, Reader's Digest, 1978.

*The Scots to Canada,* Gentry, 1972.

*The Comet,* Wildwood, 1973.

*Northern Ireland,* Cambridge University Press, 1974.

(With others) *Witchcraft, Magic, and the Supernatural,* Octopus, 1974.

*The English to New England,* Potter, 1975.

*Fortune Telling: A Guide to Reading the Future,* Hamlyn, 1978.

(Reteller) *The Illustrated "Faerie Queene,"* Newsweek, 1980.

Contributor to anthologies, including *Poetmeat Anthology of British Poetry,* 1965; *Young British Poets,* 1967; and *Poems from Poetry and Jazz in Concert,* 1969. Contributor to periodicals, including *Ambit, Poetry Review, Tribune, Poetry One, Solstice, Arts in Society, Poesie Vivante,* and *Canadian Forum.*

## ■ Sidelights

"Diversity seems to be the keynote," commented Douglas Hill about his broad range of writing, which includes poetry, history, folklore, occultism, science, and science fiction for adults and young people, as well as work as both an editor and publisher's consultant. "[It] often seems [I work] an eight-day week and a twenty-five-hour day, but it's still the best way to live and to earn a living I know."

Hill was born in Brandon, Manitoba, in 1935, the son of a locomotive engineer and a nurse. He spent his childhood in Canada and attended the University of Saskatchewan in Saskatoon where he earned a bachelor of arts degree with honors in 1957. He spent the next two years in graduate study at the University of Toronto, and then worked for newspapers in Canada before moving to England in 1959. In 1962, Hill was hired as an editor at London's Aldus Books Ltd., and worked there until 1964, when he began his freelance writing career in earnest.

### Beginning a Freelance Career

In 1965, Hill's first book *The Supernatural,* written with coauthor Pat Williams, was published. Thus began what would be a long string of nonfiction books on history, the supernatural, popular folklore, literary biography, and other topics. In 1966, Hill's second book, *The Peasant's Revolt,* was published, quickly followed by an anthology called *Window on the Future* and 1967's *The Opening of the Canadian West,* a popular narrative history.

For a brief period between 1967 and 1968, Hill served as associate editor of *New Worlds,* Britain's only science fiction magazine and an avant garde leader in science fiction periodicals of the time. As a freelance writer, he continued writing nonfiction books as well as contributing articles and book reviews to magazines. In 1971, Hill began working for the *Tribune,* a London weekly. There, he reviewed science fiction and soon began writing it on his own, first in short story form and later in full length books.

During the 1970s, Hill spent more time writing science fiction. He also wrote two books for children: *Coyote the Trickster: Legends of the North American Indians,* which was coauthored by Gail Robinson, and *The Exploits of Hercules.* By 1979, Hill had published his first full-length science-fiction book for children, *Galactic Warlord.*

Like many science fiction writers, Hill's fascination with the genre began in childhood when he was a self-proclaimed addict of Buck Rogers, Flash Gordon, and other science-fiction heroes of the time. "When I began writing SF for young readers—after some ten years and nearly 20 books of adult nonfiction—I felt it had to be a simple enough process," Hill noted in *The Writer.* "I

**With Gail Robinson, Douglas Hill retells various "Trickster" legends of Native North Americans in this entertaining collection for children.** (Cover illustration by Graham McCallum.)

could clearly remember what I liked reading when I was 12 or 13, so I set out to write along those lines." He began writing space adventures because "as a kid I had liked reading about adventures on other worlds; I'd had an idea for an interplanetary hero with a particular problem and purpose; and I was encouraged by the fact that television and films were creating a huge audience for space adventure, even in 1977 B.S.W. (Before Star Wars)."

Hill's character, Keill Randor (the "Last Legionary") was featured in a quartet of "Last Legionary" books: *Galactic Warlord, Deathwing Over Veynaa, Day of the Starwind,* and *Planet of the Warlord.* The series begins after the Legions of Moros, mercenaries who fight tyranny in the universe, are destroyed along with their planet. Only Randor remains and the series describes his adventures as he embarks on a search for a mysterious enemy.

## Two Trilogies

Following the "Last Legionary" quartet, Hill published his "Huntsman" trilogy over the next three years, beginning with 1982's *The Huntsman.* In this trilogy, Hill's hero Finn leads the fight against an alien dictatorship, the Slavers, who rule the world after a holocaust and are determined to destroy the remains of humanity left on Earth. Hill's "ColSec" trilogy, which includes *Exiles of ColSec, The Caves of Klydor,* and *ColSec Rebellion,* tells the story of a group of five young people from a chaotic oppressed future Earth who try to establish a colony on the planet Klydor. In the conclusion of the trilogy, the governors of Earth who sent the young people to Klydor (in hopes they would not survive) arrive for an inspection and find, to their disbelief, the group very much alive. Allied with Lathan, an explorer supposedly lost in space, the young people strand the governors on the planet and return to Earth to rally a force of rebels and evacuate them to Klydor, a base from which to fight the tyrannous ColSec organization.

In the 1987 book *Blade of the Poisoner,* Hill shifts from planetary worlds to a quasi-medieval fantasy world of magic inhabited by a submissive population. Mysterious "Talents" who emerge occasionally are ruthlessly pursued by the evil Prince Mephtik. The hero, Jarral, follows his three elders—Archer the kinetic, Scythe, who has multiple sight, and Mandra, who can invade the minds of others—and his talent emerges slowly, is nurtured, and is finally tested in a battle against the prince. Hill's medieval-like tale of sword and sorcery enforces one of his common themes—the triumph of good over evil.

The battle of good versus evil, as well as fast action and strong central characters, are trademarks of Hill's science fiction work. In *The Writer,* he described the importance of those three elements: "The adventure element [of science fiction] seemed paramount at first, mainly because I [had] never written anything like it. I had stumbled, probably by instinct, onto the first main

prerequisite, a clearly defined and fairly fundamental 'good vs. evil' plot—otherwise defined as a good guy against a number of bad guys.... The characters must be clearly defined and distinguishable ... and of course, science fiction requires you to place emphasis on drama and suspense and action."

Hill's 1990 book, *Penelope's Pendant,* is also set in a fantasy realm. The book's central character is a girl who finds a damaged pendant while beachcombing and discovers it is magical. As she experiments with it, she finds that the magic is somewhat tarnished, like the pendant itself. At night, she dreams of a small creature earnestly searching her room and soon discovers the creature is very real. The creature, a cobold (related to gnomes and elves) reluctantly agrees to let Penelope keep the pendant, but urges caution and restraint. The story tells of her adventures with the pendant, concluding with her use of it when she is chased by members of a gang. "Hill's fantasy is both believable and refreshing," noted a reviewer for *Booklist.* "Fast action, deftly-drawn characters, and the triumph of good over evil add up to a thoroughly satisfying read."

**One of Hill's many science fiction novels for young adults, this book features a band of youths who plot to overthrow the dictatorial Earth government that controls their new home planet and other space colonies.** (Cover illustration by Stephen Marchesi.)

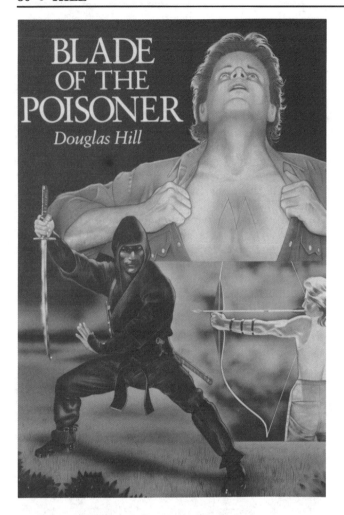

**Jarral's newfound powers allow good to triumph over evil in this tale of magic and fantasy by Hill.** (Cover illustration by Jon Weiman.)

### Versatility Displayed in Poetry

Hill has also published poetry. In fact, his first professional sale as a writer was a poem. His verse has been included in several poetry anthologies as well as numerous periodicals. Hill described himself in *Contemporary Poets* as "a poet who makes his living writing nonfiction prose, journalism, etc.," adding that "I am still in the process of developing my own 'voice.'" He considers his dominant themes to be "loneliness, fear, the minor and less minor horrors of 20th-century human relationships—with a scattering of love poems, comic poems and exercises in various degrees of human rhetoric." Hill added: "Much of my *materia poetica* comes from my fairly ordinary experience, but I rarely get personal and am not averse to elements of fantasy."

Hill believes that science fiction—even on television and in films—can be an important motivator for young people to read books. "That might seem a contradiction, but consider—SF is imaginative fiction, and the imagination flourishes best when it has room to operate," Hill wrote in *The Writer*. While television and film provide so much detail that there is little room left for imagination, a science fiction book, with its brief descriptive passages, leaves room for young readers to use their own imaginations. "Children may well see not only that the SF they enjoy at the movies or on TV has its counterparts in book form," Hill wrote, "but that the written word can offer more exciting, positive lasting pleasures."

### ■ Works Cited

*Contemporary Poets,* St. James Press, 1973, pp. 503-504.

Hill, Douglas Arthur, "Science Fiction for Young Readers," *The Writer,* January, 1984, pp. 15-18.

Review of *Penelope's Pendant, Booklist,* March 15, 1991, p. 1493.

### ■ For More Information See

BOOKS

Wingrove, David, editor, *The Science Fiction Sourcebook,* Van Nostrand, 1984.

PERIODICALS

*Junior Bookshelf,* December, 1985, p. 278.

\* \* \*

## HILLMAN, Martin
   See HILL, Douglas (Arthur)

\* \* \*

## HITZEROTH, Deborah L. 1961-

### ■ Personal

Born June 13, 1961, in Missouri; daughter of Gary (an engineer) and Kathy (a nurse; maiden name, Boll) Hughes; married Ryan Hitzeroth (an engineer), June 11, 1988. *Education:* University of Missouri—Columbia, B.A., 1983; graduate study at San Diego State University.

### ■ Addresses

*Home*—5800 Quantrell #304, Alexandria, VA 22312.

### ■ Career

*Waco Tribune Herald,* Waco, TX, reporter, 1983-86; American Association of Colleges of Podiatric Medicine, director of public affairs, 1988-89; American Airlines, customer service representative, 1992—.

### ■ Awards, Honors

Recipient of awards for featuring writing.

### ■ Writings

*Radar: The Silent Detector,* Lucent Books, 1990.
(With sister, Sharon Heerboth) *Movies: The World on Film,* Lucent Books, 1991.

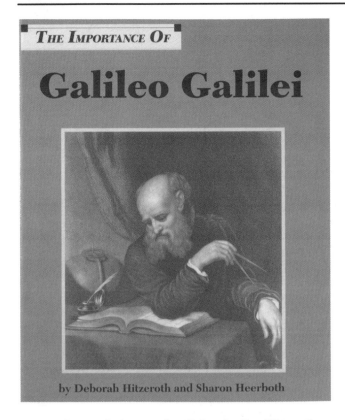

THE IMPORTANCE OF

# Galileo Galilei

by Deborah Hitzeroth and Sharon Heerboth

**In this nonfiction work, Deborah L. Hitzeroth examines the accomplishments of the Galileo Galilei and current thought regarding his work.**

*Telescopes: Searching the Heavens,* Lucent Books, 1991.
(With Heerboth) *The Importance of Galileo Galilei,* Lucent Books, 1992.
(With sister, Sharon [Heerboth] Leon) *The Importance of Isaac Newton,* Lucent Books, 1992.
*Guns: Tools of Destructive Force,* Lucent Books, 1994.

Also contributor of articles to *Journal of Podiatric Medicine, Fort Worth Magazine,* and *Landscape News.*

## ■ Sidelights

Deborah L. Hitzeroth told *SATA:* "I grew up in a university town where the best known division was the department of journalism and the major industry was the media. With this type of background, I was convinced by third grade that I wanted to be 'a writer.' I spent the next twenty years trying to make my dream a reality. I'm currently working with educational books for junior high and high school students, but my next goal is to move into the field of fiction."

\*        \*        \*

## HOBAN, Russell (Conwell) 1925-

## ■ Personal

Born February 4, 1925, in Lansdale, PA; son of Abram T. (an advertising manager for the *Jewish Daily Forward*) and Jeanette (Dimmerman) Hoban; married Lillian Aberman (an illustrator), January 31, 1944 (divorced, 1975); married Gundula Ahl (a bookseller), 1975; children: (first marriage) Phoebe, Abrom, Esme, Julia; (second marriage) Jachin Boaz, Wieland, Benjamin. *Education:* Attended Philadelphia Museum School of Industrial Art, 1941-43. *Hobbies and other interests:* Stones, short wave radio listening.

## ■ Addresses

*Home and office*—Fulham, London, England. *Agent*—David Higham Associates Ltd., 5-8 Lower John St., Golden Sq., London W1R 4HA, England.

## ■ Career

Novelist and author of children's books, 1967—. Artist and illustrator for magazine and advertising studios, New York City, 1945-51; Fletcher Smith Film Studio, New York City, story board artist and character designer, 1951; Batten, Barton, Durstine & Osborn, Inc., New York City, television art director, 1952-57; J. Walter Thompson Co., New York City, television art director, 1956; free-lance illustrator for advertising agencies and magazines, including *Time, Life, Fortune, Saturday Evening Post,* and *True,* 1957-65; Doyle, Dane, Bembach, New York City, copywriter, 1965-67. Art instructor at the Famous Artists Schools, Westport, CT, and School of Visual Arts, New York City. *Military service:* U.S. Army, Infantry, 1943-45; served in Italian cam-

**RUSSELL HOBAN**

paign; received Bronze Star. *Member:* Authors Guild, Authors League of America, Society of Authors, PEN.

## ■ Awards, Honors

*Bread and Jam for Frances* was selected as a Library of Congress Children's book, 1964; Boys' Club Junior Book Award, 1968, for *Charlie the Tramp; Emmet Otter's Jug-Band Christmas* was selected as one of *School Library Journal's* Best Books, 1971, and received the Lewis Carroll Shelf Award and the Christopher Award, both 1972; Whitbread Literary Award, 1974, and International Board on Books for Young People Honor List, 1976, both for *How Tom Beat Captain Najork and His Hired Sportsmen; A Near Thing for Captain Najork* was selected as one of the best illustrated children's books of the year by the *New York Times,* 1976; *Riddley Walker* received the John W. Campbell Memorial Award for the best science fiction novel of the year from Science Fiction Research Association, 1981, and was nominated as the most distinguished book of fiction by National Book Critics Circle and for the Nebula Award by Science Fiction Writers of America, both 1982, and the Australian Science Fiction Achievement Award, 1983; Recognition of Merit, George G. Stone Center for Children's Books, 1982, for his contributions to books for younger children; *The Sorely Trying Day, The Mouse and His Child, How Tom Beat Captain Najork and His Hired Sportsmen,* and *Dinner at Alberta's* have all been named notable books by the American Library Association; *Letitia Rabbit's String Song* was a Junior Literary Guild selection.

## ■ Writings

*CHILDREN'S FICTION*

*Bedtime for Frances,* illustrations by Garth Williams, Harper, 1960.

*Herman the Loser,* illustrations by Lillian Hoban, Harper, 1961.

*The Song in My Drum,* illustrations by L. Hoban, Harper, 1961.

*London Men and English Men,* illustrations by L. Hoban, Harper, 1962.

(With L. Hoban) *Some Snow Said Hello,* Harper, 1963.

*The Sorely Trying Day,* illustrations by L. Hoban, Harper, 1964.

*A Baby Sister for Frances,* illustrations by L. Hoban, Harper, 1964.

*Nothing to Do,* illustrations by L. Hoban, Harper, 1964.

*Bread and Jam for Frances,* illustrations by L. Hoban, Harper, 1964.

*Tom and the Two Handles,* illustrations by L. Hoban, Harper, 1965.

*The Story of Hester Mouse Who Became a Writer and Saved Most of Her Sisters and Brothers and Some of Her Aunts and Uncles from the Owl,* illustrations by L. Hoban, Norton, 1965.

*What Happened When Jack and Daisy Tried to Fool the Tooth Fairies,* illustrations by L. Hoban, Scholastic Book Services, 1965.

*Henry and the Monstrous Din,* illustrations by L. Hoban, Harper, 1966.

*The Little Brute Family,* illustrations by L. Hoban, Macmillan, 1966.

(With L. Hoban) *Save My Place,* Norton, 1967.

*Charlie the Tramp,* illustrations by L. Hoban, Four Winds, 1967, published with record, Scholastic Book Services, 1970.

*The Mouse and His Child* (novel), illustrations by L. Hoban, Harper, 1967.

*A Birthday for Frances,* illustrations by L. Hoban, Harper, 1968.

*The Stone Doll of Sister Brute,* illustrations by L. Hoban, Macmillan, 1968.

*Harvey's Hideout,* illustrations by L. Hoban, Parents' Magazine Press, 1969.

*Best Friends for Frances,* illustrations by L. Hoban, Harper, 1969.

*Ugly Bird,* illustrations by L. Hoban, Macmillan, 1969.

*The Mole Family's Christmas,* illustrations by L. Hoban, Parents' Magazine Press, 1969.

*A Bargain for Frances,* illustrations by L. Hoban, Harper, 1970.

*Emmet Otter's Jug-Band Christmas,* illustrations by L. Hoban, Parents' Magazine Press, 1971.

*The Sea-Thing Child,* illustrations by son, Abrom Hoban, Harper, 1972.

*Letitia Rabbit's String Song,* illustrations by Mary Chalmers, Coward, 1973.

*How Tom Beat Captain Najork and His Hired Sportsmen,* illustrations by Quentin Blake, Atheneum, 1974.

*Ten What?: A Mystery Counting Book,* illustrations by Sylvie Selig, J. Cape, 1974, Scribner's, 1975.

*Crocodile and Pierrot: A See the Story Book,* illustrations by Selig, J. Cape, 1975, Scribner's, 1977.

*Dinner at Alberta's,* pictures by James Marshall, Crowell, 1975.

*A Near Thing for Captain Najork,* illustrations by Blake, J. Cape, 1975, Atheneum, 1976.

*Arthur's New Power,* illustrations by Byron Barton, Crowell, 1978.

*The Twenty-Elephant Restaurant,* illustrations by Emily Arnold McCully, Atheneum, 1978, published in England with illustrations by Blake, J. Cape, 1980.

*La Corona and the Tin Frog* (originally published in *Puffin Annual,* 1974), illustrations by Nicola Bayley, J. Cape, 1978, Merrimack Book Service, 1981.

*The Dancing Tigers,* illustrations by David Gentlemen, J. Cape, 1979, Merrimack Book Service, 1981.

*Flat Cat,* illustrations by Clive Scruton, Philomel, 1980.

*Ace Dragon Ltd.,* illustrations by Blake, J. Cape, 1980, Merrimack Book Service, 1981.

*They Came from Aargh!,* illustrations by Colin McNaughton, Philomel, 1981.

*The Serpent Tower,* illustrations by David Scott, Methuen/Walker, 1981.

*The Great Fruit Gum Robbery,* illustrations by McNaughton, Methuen, 1981, published as *The Great Gum Drop Robbery,* Philomel, 1982.

*The Battle of Zormla,* illustrations by McNaughton, Philomel, 1982.

*The Flight of Bembel Rudzuk,* illustrations by McNaughton, Philomel, 1982.

*Big John Turkle,* illustrations by Martin Baynton, Walker Books, 1983, Holt, 1984.

*Jim Frog,* illustrations by Baynton, Walker Books, 1983, Holt, 1984.

*Lavinia Bat,* illustrations by Baynton, Holt, 1984.

*Charlie Meadows,* illustrations by Baynton, Holt, 1984.

*The Rain Door,* illustrations by Blake, J. Cape, 1986, HarperCollins, 1987.

*The Marzipan Pig,* illustrations by Blake, J. Cape, 1986.

*Ponders,* illustrations by Baynton, Walker Books, 1988.

*Monsters,* illustrations by Blake, Scholastic, Inc., 1989.

*Jim Hedgehog and the Lonesome Tower,* illustrations by Betsy Lewin, Clarion Books, 1990.

*Jim Hedgehog's Supernatural Christmas,* illustrations by Lewin, Houghton, 1992.

*M.O.L.E.,* illustrated by J. Pienkowski, Cape, 1994.

*CHILDREN'S VERSE*

*Goodnight,* illustrations by L. Hoban, Norton, 1966.

*The Pedaling Man, and Other Poems,* illustrations by L. Hoban, Norton, 1968.

*Egg Thoughts, and Other Frances Songs,* illustrations by L. Hoban, Harper, 1972.

*SELF-ILLUSTRATED CHILDREN'S NONFICTION*

*What Does It Do and How Does It Work?: Power Shovel, Dump Truck, and Other Heavy Machines,* Harper, 1959.

*The Atomic Submarine: A Practice Combat Patrol under the Sea,* Harper, 1960.

*NOVELS*

*The Lion of Boaz-Jachin and Jachin-Boaz,* Stein & Day, 1973.

*Kleinzeit: A Novel,* Viking, 1974.

*Turtle Diary,* J. Cape, 1975, Random House, 1976.

*Riddley Walker,* J. Cape, 1980, Summit Books, 1981.

*Pilgermann,* Summit Books, 1983.

*The Medusa Frequency,* edited by Gary Fisketjohn, Atlantic Monthly, 1987.

*OTHER*

(Illustrator) W. R. Burnett, *The Roar of the Crowd: Conversations with an Ex-Big-Leaguer,* C. N. Potter, 1964.

*The Carrier Frequency* (play), first produced in London, England, 1984.

*Riddley Walker* (stage adaptation of his novel), first produced in Manchester, England, 1986.

(Author of introduction) Wilhelm K. Grimm, *Household Tales,* illustrations by Mervyn Peake, Schocken, 1987.

Also author of television play, *Come and Find Me,* 1980. Contributor to *The Thorny Paradise: Writers on Writing for Children,* edited by Edward Blishen, Kestrel, 1975. Also contributor of articles to *Granta, Fiction Magazine,* and *Holiday.* Hoban's papers are included in the Kerlan Collection at the University of Minnesota.

## ■ Adaptations

*The Mouse and His Child* was made into a feature-length animated film by Fario-Lockhart-Sanrio Productions in 1977 and featured the voices of Cloris Leachman, Andy Devine, and Peter Ustinov (who also read an abridged version of the novel for a Caedmon recording in 1977); Glynnis Johns recorded selections from *Bedtime for Frances, A Baby Sister for Frances, Bread and Jam for Frances,* and *A Birthday for Frances* in a sound recording entitled "Frances," as well as selections from *A Bargain for Frances, Best Friends for Frances,* and *Egg Thoughts, and Other Frances Songs* in a sound recording entitled "A Bargain for Frances and Other Stories," both by Caedmon in 1977; *Turtle Diary* was adapted for the screen by United British Artists/Brittanic in 1986, featuring a screenplay by Harold Pinter and starring Glenda Jackson and Ben Kingsley; *The Marzipan Pig* was adapted as a 1990 animated film produced by Michael Sporn and Italtoons Corp.

RCA/Columbia Pictures
Home Video

**Considered a modern classic by many critics, Hoban's story of two toy mice searching for happiness was later adapted as a 1977 animated feature.**

# ■ Sidelights

"Russell Hoban is a writer whose genius is expressed with equal brilliance in books both for children and for adults," writes Alida Allison in the *Dictionary of Literary Biography*. Largely self-educated, Hoban has moved masterfully from artist and illustrator to the author of children's fables and adult allegorical fiction. Praising his "unerring ear for dialogue," his "memorable depiction of scenes," and his "wise and warm stories notable for delightful plots and originality of language," Allison considers Hoban to be "much more than just a clever and observant writer. His works are permeated with an honest, often painful, and always uncompromising urge toward self-identity." Noting that "this theme of identity becomes more apparent, more complex as Hoban's works have become longer and more penetrating," Allison states that " . . . Hoban's writing has leaped and bounded—paralleling upheavals in his own life."

In an interview with Rhonda M. Bunbury in *Children's Literature in Education,* Hoban indicates that as a child he was "good with words and good with drawing. It just happened my parents more or less seized on the drawing and thought that I'd probably end up being a great painter. I did become an illustrator, but I think that the drawing formula was always a little bit poisoned by the expectations that were laid on me, while the writing was allowed to be my own thing." He wrote poetry and short stories in school, and won several prizes. Having attended the Philadelphia Museum School of Industrial Art, Hoban worked as a freelance illustrator before he began writing children's stories. He would drive throughout Connecticut, occasionally stopping at construction sites and sketching the machinery being used. A friend saw his work and suggested that it might make a good children's book; Hoban's first published work was about construction equipment: *What Does It Do and How Does It Work?: Power Shovel, Dump Truck, and Other Heavy Machines.*

## Hoban's Famous Characters

Although Hoban has since originated several well-known characters in children's literature, including Charlie the Tramp, Emmet Otter, the Mouse and his Child, and Manny Rat, he is especially recognized for a series of bedtime books about an anthropomorphic badger named Frances. Reviewers generally concur that these stories depict ordinary family life with much humor, wit, and style. Benjamin DeMott suggests in the *Atlantic Monthly* that "these books are unique, first, because the adults in their pages are usually humorous, precise of speech, and understandingly conversant with general life, and second, because the author confronts—not unfancifully but without kinky secret garden stuff—problems with which ordinary parents and children have to cope." *Bedtime for Frances,* for instance, concerns nighttime fears and is regarded by many as a classic in children's literature; and according to a *Saturday Review* contributor, "The exasperated humor of this book could only derive from actual parental experience, and no doubt parents will enjoy it."

As with *The Mouse and His Child,* there are philosophical overtones to this simple tale of how a candy pig passes along its feelings of longing to a mouse and an owl. (Cover illustration by Quentin Blake.)

"Hoban has established himself as a writer with a rare understanding of childhood (and parental) psychology, sensitively and humorously portrayed in familiar family situations," writes Allison. He and his first wife, Lillian, also an illustrator and author of books for children, collaborated on many successful works, including several in the Frances series. Allison notes that although their work together was usually well received, "there were pans as well as paeans." While some books have been faulted for "excessive coziness, for sentimentality, and for stereotyped male-female roles," Allison adds that a more general criticism of their work together is that "it tends toward repetition." However, in their *Children and Books* May Hill Arbuthnot and Zena Sutherland find that all of Hoban's stories about Frances show "affection for and understanding of children" as well as "contribute to a small child's understanding of himself, his relationships with other people, and the fulfillment of his emotional needs." Further, they say, "These characters are indeed ourselves in fur." Yet as a *Times Literary Supplement* contributor observes, "Excellent as [the Frances books] are, they give no hint that the author had in him such a blockbuster of a book as *The Mouse and His Child.*"

Revered in England as a modern children's classic, *The Mouse and His Child* is described in the *New York Times Book Review* by Barbara Wersba as a story about two wind-up toy mice who are discarded from a toyshop and are then "buffeted from place to place as they seek the lost paradise of their first home—a doll house—and their first 'family,' a toy elephant and seal." Ill equipped for the baffling, threatening world into which they are tossed, the mouse and his child innocently confront the unknown and its inherent treachery and violence, as well as their own fears. The book explores not only the transience and inconstancy of life but the struggle to persevere also. "Helpless when they are not wound up, unable to stop when they *are*, [the mice] are fated like all mechanical things to breakage, rust and disintegration as humans are to death," writes Margaret Blount in her *Animal Land: The Creatures of Children's Fiction.* "As an adult," says Blount, "it is impossible to read [the book] unmoved." Distressed, however, by the "continuing images of cruelty and decay," Penelope Farmer remarks in *Children's Literature in Education* that *The Mouse and His Child* is "like Beckett for children." But assessing whatever cruelty and decay there is in the novel as the "artful rendering of the facts of life," Allison affirms, "If there is betrayal, there is also self-sacrifice. If there is loss, there is also love. If there is homelessness, there is also destination. The mouse child gets his family in the end; children's literature gets a masterpiece."

"Like the best of books, [*The Mouse and His Child*] is a book from which one can peel layer after layer of meaning," says the *Times Literary Supplement* contributor. Some critics, however, wonder whether it is a children's book at all. Wersba, for instance, feels that "it is the mouse, his child and their search we care about not—metaphysics—and the intellectual trappings of this story are unnecessary." Hoban responds to such assessments in an essay for *Books for Your Children:* "When I wrote [*The Mouse and His Child*] I didn't think it was [a children's book]. I was writing as much book as I was capable of at the time. No concessions were made in style or content. It was my first novel and ... it was the fullest response I could make to being alive and in the world." Hoban indicates to Bunbury that the book has become his favorite book for children, the one that has given him the most satisfaction: "Though it may not be the best of my novels, it is the closest to my heart because of that." Believing the book reveals "an absolute respect for its subject—which means its readers as well," Isabel Quigley adds in the *Spectator* that she's "still not sure just who is going to read it but that hardly seems to matter.... It will last." Hoban feels that within its limitations, the book is suitable for children. "Its heroes and heroines found out what they were and it wasn't enough, so they found out how to be more," he says in his essay. "That's not a bad thought to be going with."

## Ventures into Science Fiction

Nominated as the most distinguished book of fiction by the National Book Critics Circle, and for the Nebula Award by the Science Fiction Writers of America, *Riddley Walker* received the John W. Campbell Memorial Award from the Science Fiction Research Association as the year's best science fiction novel and the

Australian Science Fiction Achievement Award. *Riddley Walker* imagines a world and civilization decades after a nuclear holocaust; the story of what remains is narrated in a fragmented, phonetical English by a twelve-year-old boy struggling to comprehend the past so that its magnificence might be recaptured. "Set in a remote future and composed in an English nobody ever spoke or wrote," writes DeMott in the *New York Times,* "this short, swiftly paced tale juxtaposes preliterate fable and Beckettian wit, Boschian monstrosities and a hero with Huck Finn's heart and charm, lighting by El Greco and jokes by Punch and Judy. It is a wrenchingly vivid report on the texture of life after Doomsday."

Detecting similarities in *Riddley Walker* to other contemporary works such as Anthony Burgess's *A Clockwork Orange,* John Gardner's *Grendel,* and the works of William Golding, DeMott believes that "in vision and execution, this is an exceptionally original work, and Russell Hoban is actually his own best source." *Riddley Walker* "is not 'like' anything," concurs Victoria Glendinning in the *Listener.* As A. Alvarez expresses in the *New York Review of Books,* Hoban has "transformed what might have been just another fantasy of the future into a novel of exceptional depth and originality."

Critically lauded and especially popular in England, *Riddley Walker* has been particularly commended for its inventive language, which Alvarez thinks "reflects with extraordinary precision both the narrator's understanding and the desolate landscape he moves through." Reviewing the book in the *Washington Post Book World,* Michael Dirda believes that "what is marvelous in all this is the way Hoban makes us experience the uncanny familiarity of this world, while also making it a strange and animistic place, where words almost have a life of their own." "What Hoban has done," Barbara A. Bannon further suggests in a *Publishers Weekly* interview with Hoban, "is to invent a world and a language to go with it, and in doing both he remains a storyteller, which is the most significant achievement of 'Riddley Walker.'"

Alvarez calls *Riddley Walker* an "artistic tour de force in every possible way," but Natalie Maynor and Richard F. Patteson suggest in *Critique* that even more than that, it is "perhaps the most sophisticated work of fiction ever to speculate about man's future on earth and the implications for a potentially destructive technology." Eliot Fremont-Smith maintains in the *Village Voice* that "the reality of the human situation now is so horrendous and bizarre that to get a hold on it requires all our faculties, including the imaginative. We can't do it through plain fact and arms controllers' reasoning alone.... Read *Riddley,* too." Although Kelly Cherry refers to the novel in the *Chicago Tribune Book World* as a "philosophical essay in fictional drag," DeMott thinks that Hoban's focus on what has been lost in civilization "summons the reader to dwell anew on that within civilization which is separate from, opposite to, power and its appurtenances, ravages, triumphs." *Riddley Walker,* says DeMott, is "haunting and fiercely

**Hoban's switch to science fiction proved successful with the publication of this post-apocalyptic adventure, which has been praised for its originality and insight.**

imagined and—this matters most—intensely ponderable."

Hoban is the author of nearly sixty books; although most are for children, for whom he continues to write, adults have found much in his books to appreciate as well. The world that Hoban often explores may be a child's world, but it is a world seen in its complexity. "In my books there aren't characters who are simply bad or simply good," Hoban tells Fred Hauptfuhrer in *People.* "Nothing in life is that simple." Writing for adults has added both breadth and depth to Hoban's work; and as his work has grown in complexity, he has commented upon the process by which an idea evolves into a book. As he explains to Bannon, "There always seems to be something in my mind waiting to put something together with some primary thought I will encounter. It's like looking out of the window and listening to the radio at the same time. I am committed to what comes to me, however it links up."

In an essay appearing in *The Thorny Paradise: Writers on Writing for Children,* Hoban addresses an intrinsic characteristic of his writing for both children and adults: "If in my meandering I have seemed to offer tangled

thinking more than worked-out thoughts, it has not been through self-indulgence; I have wanted to join the action of my being with that of my readers in a collective being. Collectively we must possess and be repossessed by the past that we alter with our present, must surrender the vanity of personal identity to something more valuable." Underlying the most powerful of Hoban's works, according to Allison, is the idea that "we must struggle for meaning and identity and place against the random element of loss in the attempt to gain 'self-winding.'" She considers Hoban a "great writer because he makes unsentimental reality into art."

## ■ Works Cited

Allison, Alida, "Russell Hoban," *Dictionary of Literary Biography,* Volume 52: *American Writers for Children since 1960: Fiction,* Gale, 1986, pp. 192-202.

Alvarez, A., "Past, Present & Future," *New York Review of Books,* November 19, 1981, pp. 16-18.

Arbuthnot, May Hill, and Zena Sutherland, *Children and Books,* 4th edition, Scott, Foresman, 1972.

Bannon, Barbara A., *Publishers Weekly,* May 15, 1981.

Review of *Bedtime for Frances, Saturday Review,* May 7, 1960.

Blount, Margaret, *Animal Land: The Creatures of Children's Fiction,* Morrow, 1974.

Cherry, Kelly, *Chicago Tribune Book World,* July 12, 1981.

**In one of Hoban's more recent children's books, John spends much of his time drawing gruesome monsters that become surprisingly real. (Cover illustration by Quentin Blake.)**

DeMott, Benjamin, "The Way You Slide," *Atlantic Monthly,* August, 1976, pp. 83-84.

DeMott, Benjamin, "2,000 Years after the Berstyn Fyr," *New York Times,* June 28, 1981, pp. 1, 25.

Dirda, Michael, "Riddling Out a Canterbury Tale," *Washington Post Book World,* June 7, 1981, pp. 1, 14.

Farmer, Penelope, *Children's Literature in Education,* March, 1972.

Fremont-Smith, Eliot, *Village Voice,* June 15, 1982.

Glendinning, Victoria, "The 1 Big 1," *Listener,* October 30, 1980, p. 589.

Hoban, Russell, *The Thorny Paradise: Writers on Writing for Children,* edited by Edward Blishen, Kestrel, 1975.

Hoban, Russell, "'The Mouse and His Child': Yes, It's a Children's Book," *Books for Your Children,* winter, 1976, p. 3.

Hoban, Russell, interview with Fred Hauptfuhrer, *People,* August 10, 1981.

Hoban, Russell, interview with Rhonda M. Bunbury, *Children's Literature in Education,* fall, 1986, pp. 139-149.

Maynor, Natalie, and Richard F. Patterson, *Critique,* fall, 1984.

Review of *The Mouse and His Child, Times Literary Supplement,* April 3, 1969, p. 357.

Quigley, Isabel, "Nice Mice," *Spectator,* May 16, 1969, pp. 654-655.

Wersba, Barbara, review of *The Mouse and His Child, New York Times Book Review,* February 4, 1968.

## ■ For More Information See

*BOOKS*

*Children's Literature Review,* Volume 3, Gale, 1978.

*Contemporary Literary Criticism,* Gale, Volume 7, 1977; Volume 25, 1983.

*Twentieth-Century Children's Writers,* 3rd edition, St. James Press, 1989.

*PERIODICALS*

*American Artist,* October, 1961.

*Antioch Review,* summer, 1982.

*Atlantic Monthly,* December, 1983.

*Bulletin of the Center for Children's Books,* September, 1990, p. 9.

*Children's Literature in Education,* spring, 1976.

*Educational Foundation for Nuclear Science,* June, 1982.

*Encounter,* June, 1981.

*Globe and Mail* (Toronto), March 29, 1986.

*Harper's,* April, 1983.

*Horn Book,* January, 1991, p. 64.

*Junior Bookshelf,* July, 1963; February, 1994, p. 15.

*Los Angeles Times,* February 14, 1986.

*New Statesman,* May 25, 1973; April 11, 1975.

*Newsweek,* March 1, 1976; June 29, 1981; December 7, 1981; May 30, 1983; February 17, 1986.

*New Yorker,* March 22, 1976; July 20, 1981; August 8, 1983.

*New York Times,* November 1, 1981; June 20, 1983; February 14, 1986.

*New York Times Book Review,* March 21, 1976; June 6, 1982; May 29, 1983; November 27, 1983.

*Observer* (London), March 13, 1983.

*Publishers Weekly,* March 23, 1992, p. 72.

*Saturday Review,* May 1, 1976; December, 1981.

*School Library Journal,* June, 1992, p. 95; October, 1992, p. 41.

*Spectator,* April 5, 1975; March 12, 1983.

*Time,* February 16, 1976; June 22, 1981; May 16, 1983.

*Times* (London), January 7, 1982; March 24, 1983.

*Times Literary Supplement,* March 16, 1973; March 29, 1974; October 31, 1980; March 7, 1986; April 3, 1987; September 4, 1987.

*Washington Post,* February 28, 1986.

*Washington Post Book World,* June 27, 1982; May 29, 1983; July 12, 1987; October 14, 1990.

*Wilton Bulletin* (Wilton, CT), September 26, 1962.*

\* \* \*

# HOLM, Sharon Lane 1955-

## ■ Personal

Born December 31, 1955, in Newark, NJ; daughter of James (employed by Bell Systems) and Bridget (a mother; maiden name, Favero) Lane; married Gregory W. Holm (employed by Pepsi Co. International), November 21, 1981; children: Michael James. *Education:* Fort Lauderdale Art Institute, 1979. *Politics:* "Undecided." *Religion:* Catholic.

## ■ Addresses

*Home and office*—1 Sweetcake Mt. Rd., New Fairfield, CT 06812. *Agent*—Cornell and McCarthy, 2-D Cross Highway, Westport, CT.

**SHARON LANE HOLM**

# Career

Illustrator. Has worked as an art director at a number of agencies and studios in Boca Raton and Fort Lauderdale, FL, and in Danbury, CT. Freelance designer, illustrator, and consultant. *Member:* M.E.O.W./Help for Pets and other animal welfare organizations, Society of Children's Book Writers and Illustrators.

# Awards, Honors

Twelve Addys (regional advertising award); Outstanding Achievement Award, Fort Lauderdale Art Institute, 1979; five public service awards for advertising/design; three Scholastic Art Awards.

# Illustrator

Robert Gardner, *Celebrating Earth Day: A Sourcebook of Activities and Experiments,* Millbrook Press, 1992.
Martin J. Gutnik, *Experiments That Explore Acid Rain,* Millbrook Press, 1992.
*Experiments That Explore Oil Spills,* Millbrook Press, 1992.
Gutnik, *Experiments That Explore Recycling,* Millbrook Press, 1992.
*Experiments That Explore the Greenhouse Effect,* Millbrook Press, 1992.
Gutnik, *Experiments That Explore Energy,* Millbrook Press, 1993.
*The Mind at Work,* Millbrook Press, 1993.
*The United States Navy,* Millbrook Press, 1993.
*The United States Airforce,* Millbrook Press, 1993.
*The Marines,* Millbrook Press, 1993.
*The Coast Guard,* Millbrook Press, 1993.
*The United States Army,* Millbrook Press, 1993.
*Crafts for Halloween,* Millbrook Press, 1993.
*Crafts for Kwanzaa,* Millbrook Press, 1993.
*Crafts for Valentine's Day,* Millbrook Press, 1994.
Kathy Ross, *Crafts for Earth Day,* Millbrook Press, 1994.
*Simple Nature Projects,* Millbrook Press, 1994.

Holm's illustrations have appeared in various educational workbooks for Houghton Mifflin, Macmillan/McGraw Hill, and Harcourt Brace Jovanovich.

# Sidelights

"With over thirteen years' experience as an award-winning art director, I decided that I had always wanted to be an illustrator, specifically a children's book illustrator," Sharon Lane Holm told *SATA.* "Three years ago the opportunity arose to go out on my own and see if I could seriously 'make it' as a children's book illustrator. I had already freelanced some illustrations, but never as a full-time job. With a lot of hard work, I am now a full-fledged children's book illustrator! I love my job. Each project is new and exciting and I feel my art must reflect that enthusiasm. The children of today are so much more visually attuned because of video games and television.

"Due to my experience as an art director, I am better able to offer my work in a variety of styles, from a more serious scientific approach to a cutesy, whimsical approach. I do a lot of educational illustration at the moment, but would love to expand my art horizons and do a more mass-market, juvenile type of book illustrating. I'd love to educate, but with a touch of humor and whimsy. I think that best describes my style of illustrating."

\* \* \*

# HOUSTON, James D. 1933-

# Personal

Born November 10, 1933, in San Francisco, CA; son of Albert Dudley and Alice Loretta (Wilson) Houston; married Jeanne Toyo Wakatsuki, 1957; children: Corinne, Joshua, Gabrielle. *Education:* San Jose State College (now University), B.A., 1956; Stanford University, M.A., 1962.

# Addresses

*Home*—2-1130 East Cliff Dr., Santa Cruz, CA 95062.

**JAMES D. HOUSTON**

## ■ Career

Cabrillo College, Aptos, CA, instructor in English, 1962-64; guitar instructor in Santa Cruz, CA, 1964-66; Stanford University, lecturer in English, 1967-68; University of California, Santa Cruz, lecturer in writing, 1969—. Writer in residence, Villa Montalvo, Saratoga, CA, spring, 1980 and 1992, and Centrum Foundation, Port Townsend, WA, winter, 1992; distinguished visiting writer, University of Hawaii at Manoa, spring, 1983, University of Oregon, Eugene, 1994; visiting writer, University of Michigan, fall, 1985; Allen T. Gilliland Chair in Telecommunications, San Jose State University, 1985. Member of California Council for the Humanities, 1983-87. *Military service:* U.S. Air Force, 1957-60; became lieutenant. *Member:* PEN, Writers Guild of America—West.

## ■ Awards, Honors

Winner, U.S. Air Force Short Story Contest, 1959; Wallace Stegner creative writing fellow, Stanford University, 1966-67; Joseph Henry Jackson Award, San Francisco Foundation, 1967, for *Gig;* faculty research grant, University of California, 1972; Humanitas Prize, 1976, and Christopher Award, both for screenplay, *Farewell to Manzanar;* creative writing grant, National Endowment for the Arts, 1976-77; small press grant, National Endowment for the Arts, 1977; travel grant to Asia, Arts America Program, fall, 1981, and 1984; Before Columbus Foundation American Book Award, 1983, for *Californians: Searching for the Golden State;* Library of Congress, Award Story, PEN Syndicated Fiction Project, 1990.

## ■ Writings

*FICTION*

*Between Battles* (novel), Dial, 1968.
*Gig* (novel), Dial, 1969.
*A Native Son of the Golden West* (novel), Dial, 1971.
*The Adventures of Charlie Bates* (short stories), Capra, 1973, enlarged edition published as *Gasoline: The Automotive Adventures of Charlie Bates,* 1980.
*Continental Drift* (novel), Knopf, 1978.
*Love Life* (novel), Knopf, 1985.

*NONFICTION*

(With wife, Jeanne Wakatsuki Houston) *Farewell to Manzanar: A True Story of Japanese American Experience during and after the World War II Internment,* Houghton, 1973.
*Three Songs for My Father,* Capra, 1974.
(With J. W. Houston and John Korty) *Farewell to Manzanar* (screenplay), Universal and MCA-TV, 1976.
*Californians: Searching for the Golden State,* Knopf, 1982.
*One Can Think about Life after the Fish Is in the Canoe and Other Coastal Sketches* (bound with *Beyond Manzanar and Other Views of Asian-American Womanhood* by J. W. Houston), Capra, 1985.

*The Men in My Life, and Other More or Less True Recollections of Kinship,* Creative Arts, 1987.

*OTHER*

*Writing from the Inside* (textbook), Addison-Wesley, 1973.
(With John R. Brodie) *Open Field* (biography), Houghton, 1973.
(Editor with Gerald Haslam) *California Heartland: Writings from the Great Central Valley,* Capra, 1978.
(Editor and contributor) *West Coast Fiction: Modern Writing from California, Oregon and Washington,* Bantam, 1979.
(With Robert Moesle) *San Jose Collects Robert Moesle,* San Jose Museum of Art, 1988.

Contributor to anthologies, including *Writers and Their Craft,* Wayne State University Press, 1989; *Dreamers and Desperadoes,* Dell, 1993; *Remembering Ray,* Capra Press, 1993; and *A Thousand Leagues of Blue,* Sierra Club, 1994. Contributor of short stories and articles to *Playboy, Rolling Stone, New York Times, Los Angeles Times,* and *Mother Jones.*

Author of documentary teleplays *Li'a,* 1988, *Listen to the Forest,* 1991, *The Hawaiian Way,* 1993, all for the *Hawaiian Legacy Series,* produced by the Asian/Pacific Foundation. Also author of teleplay, *Barrio,* with J. W. Houston, developed by National Broadcasting Co. (NBC).

## ■ Sidelights

See entry for Jeanne Wakatsuki Houston.

\*     \*     \*

# HOUSTON, Jeanne (Toyo) Wakatsuki 1934-

## ■ Personal

Born September 26, 1934, in California; daughter of Ko (a fisherman) and Riku (Sugai) Wakatsuki; married James D. Houston (a writer), 1957; children: Corinne, Joshua, Gabrielle. *Education:* University of San Jose, B.A., 1956; also attended Sorbonne, University of Paris.

## ■ Addresses

*Home*—2-1130 East Cliff Dr., Santa Cruz, CA 95062. *Agent*—George Diskant, Diskant and Associates, 1033 Gayley Ave., Suite 202, Los Angeles, CA 90024.

## ■ Career

Writer. Group worker and juvenile probation officer in San Mateo, CA, 1955-57. *Member:* Writers Guild, Screen Writers Guild.

**JEANNE WAKATSUKI HOUSTON**

## ■ Awards, Honors

Humanitas Prize, 1976, and Christopher Award, both for screenplay *Farewell to Manzanar;* award from National Women's Political Caucus; Wonder Woman Award, 1984.

## ■ Writings

(With husband, James D. Houston) *Farewell to Manzanar: A True Story of Japanese American Experience during and after the World War II Internment* (nonfiction), Houghton, 1973.

(With J. D. Houston and John Korty) *Farewell to Manzanar* (screenplay), Universal and MCA-TV, 1976.

(With Paul G. Hensler) *Don't Cry, It's Only Thunder* (nonfiction), Doubleday, 1984.

*Beyond Manzanar: Views of Asian-American Womanhood* (bound with *One Can Think about Life after the Fish Is in the Canoe and Other Coastal Sketches* by J. D. Houston), Capra, 1985.

Also author of teleplay *Barrio,* with J. D. Houston, developed by National Broadcasting Co. (NBC). Contributor to magazines.

## ■ Work in Progress

*Fire Horse Woman,* a novel about a picture bride at the turn of the century.

## ■ Sidelights

With the publication of Jeanne Wakatsuki Houston's book, *Farewell to Manzanar* (coauthored with her husband, James D. Houston), she "became, quite unintentionally, a voice for a heretofore silent segment of society," according to a *Los Angeles Times* reporter. After the Japanese attack at Pearl Harbor in 1941, President Roosevelt signed an order that gave the War Department the authority to evacuate all Japanese-Americans on the West Coast for the sake of national security. The daughter of first and second generation Japanese-American parents, Houston describes herself in the *Los Angeles Times* as "almost third-generation American." Yet she and her family, along with thousands of other Japanese-Americans, were interned at a

Houston gives a frank, unsentimental portrayal of life in a Japanese-American internment camp during World War II in this personal account of her family's experiences.

work camp during World War II. *Farewell to Manzanar* tells the experience of wrongful internment and its lasting effects upon the author and the members of her family.

The Wakatsukis were one of the first families interned at the Manzanar camp, and one of the last to be released. *Farewell to Manzanar* describes the indignities of life in the camp and the harmful effects it had on Houston's family, particularly her father. As a *New Yorker* critic observes, "Her father was too old to bend with the humiliations of the camp.... His story is at the heart of this book, and his daughter tells it with great dignity." In the *Saturday Review,* Dorothy Rabinowitz calls *Farewell to Manzanar* "a tale remarkably lacking in either self-pity or solemnity." Though a *New York Times Book Review* critic faulted the book for not examining the broader political implications of the U.S. government imprisoning a segment of its population based solely upon its ethnic heritage, he also praised the narrative as "vivid," and "dramatic." A *Publishers Weekly* reviewer emphasized the government's mistreatment of children along with their parents in its review of this "sober and moving personal account."

Houston further explored the tribulations of post-World War II Asian-Americans in her 1985 book, *Beyond Manzanar: Views of Asian-American Womanhood.* Using a combination of essays and short fiction, she describes the difficulty she and other women found in trying to assimilate with American culture while maintaining the traditions of her Japanese heritage. "Her descriptions of how she handles this challenge ... constitute the book's most substantial assets," commented James W. Byrkit in *Western American Litera-* ture. *Los Angeles Times Book Review* contributor Jonathan Kirsch, too, found the book a worthwhile endeavor. "Jeanne Houston writes poignantly of the chasms of myth and expectation that must be spanned when a Japanese-American woman marries 'a blond Samurai,'" wrote Kirsch.

## ■ Works Cited

Byrkit, James W., review of *Beyond Manzanar, Western American Literature,* summer, 1986, p. 184.

Review of *Farewell to Manzanar, New York Times Book Review,* January 13, 1974, p. 31.

Review of *Farewell to Manzanar, Publishers Weekly,* August 20, 1973, p. 78.

Review of *Farewell to Manzanar, New Yorker,* November 5, 1973.

Review of *Farewell to Manzanar, Los Angeles Times,* November 15, 1984.

Kirsch, Jonathan, review of *Beyond Manzanar, Los Angeles Times Book Review,* August 11, 1985.

Rabinowitz, Dorothy, review of *Farewell to Manzanar, Saturday Review,* November 6, 1973, p. 34.

## ■ For More Information See

*PERIODICALS*

*Washington Post,* February 27, 1984.

\*    \*    \*

## HUNGERFORD, Pixie
## See BRINSMEAD, H(esba) F(ay)

# I

**SATOMI ICHIKAWA**

## ICHIKAWA, Satomi 1949-

### ■ Personal

Born January 15, 1949, in Gifu, Japan; moved to Paris, France, 1971; daughter of Harumi (a teacher) and Nobuko Ichikawa. *Hobbies and other interests:* Collecting dolls (used), piano, dance.

### ■ Career

Author and illustrator of books for children, 1974—.
*Exhibitions:* Gallery Printemps Ginza, Japan, 1984.

### ■ Awards, Honors

Special mention for Prix "Critici in Erba," Bologna Children's Book Fair, 1978, for *Suzette et Nicolas au marche* (*Suzanne and Nicholas at the Market*); Kodansha Prize (Japan), 1978, for illustrations in *Sun through Small Leaves: Poems of Spring;* Sankei Prize (Japan), 1981, for illustrations in *Keep Running, Allen!; Dance, Tanya* was named an American Library Association notable book.

### ■ Writings

*SELF-ILLUSTRATED*

*A Child's Book of Seasons* (poetry), Heinemann, 1975, Parents' Magazine Press, 1976.
*Friends,* Heinemann, 1976, Parents' Magazine Press, 1977.
*Suzanne and Nicholas in the Garden,* translation by Denise Sheldon, F. Watts, 1977, St. Martin's Press, 1986 (originally published as *Suzette et Nicolas dans leur jardin,* Gautier-Languereau, 1976).
*Suzanne and Nicholas at the Market,* translation by Sheldon, F. Watts, 1977, (originally published as *Suzette et Nicolas au marché,* Gautier-Languereau, 1977), adaptation by Robina Beckles Wilson published as *Sophie and Nicky Go to Market,* Heinemann, 1984.
*Let's Play,* Philomel, 1981.
*Children through Four Seasons,* Kaisei-sha (Japan), 1981.
*Angels Descending from the Sky,* Kaisei-sha, 1983.
*Children in Paris* (two volumes), Kaisei-sha, 1984.
*Nora's Castle,* Philomel, 1986 (originally published as *Furui oshiro no otomodachi,* Kaisei-sha, 1984).
*Beloved Dolls,* Kaisei-sha, 1985.
*Nora's Stars,* translated from the Japanese, Philomel, 1989.
*Nora's Duck,* translated from the Japanese, Philomel, 1991.
*Nora's Roses,* translated from the Japanese, Philomel, 1993.
*Fickle Barbara,* Philomel, 1993.

*Nora's Surprise,* translated from the Japanese, Philomel, 1994.

*ILLUSTRATOR*

Elaine Moss, compiler, *From Morn to Midnight* (poetry), Crowell, 1977.

Clyde R. Bulla, *Keep Running, Allen!,* Crowell, 1978.

Marie-France Mangin, *Suzanne and Nicholas and the Four Seasons,* F. Watts, 1978 (originally published as *Suzette et Nicolas et l'horloge des 4 saisons,* Gautier-Languereau, 1978), translation by Joan Chevalier published in the United States as *Suzette and Nicholas and the Seasons Clock,* Philomel, 1982, adaptation by Robina Beckles Wilson published as *Sophie and Nicky and the Four Seasons,* Heinemann, c. 1985.

Cynthia Mitchell, *Playtime* (poetry), Heinemann, 1978, Collins, 1979.

Mitchell, compiler, *Under the Cherry Tree* (poetry), Collins, 1979.

Michelle Lochak and Mangin, *Suzette and Nicholas and the Sunijudi Circus,* translation by Chevalier, Philomel, 1980 (originally published as *Suzette et Nicolas et le cirque des enfants,* Gautier-Languereau, 1979).

Marcelle Verite, *Suzette et Nicolas au Zoo,* Gautier-Languereau, 1980.

Wilson, *Sun through Small Leaves: Poems of Spring,* Collins, 1980.

Martine Jaureguiberry, *The Wonderful Rainy Week: A Book of Indoor Games,* translation by Chevalier, Philomel, 1983 (originally published as *La joyeuse semaine de Suzette et Nicolas,* Gautier-Languereau, 1981).

Resie Pouyanne, *Suzette et Nicolas: L'Annee en fetes,* Gautier-Languereau, 1982.

Wilson, *Merry Christmas! Children at Christmastime around the World,* Philomel, 1983.

Resie Pouyanne, *Suzette et Nicolas font le tour du monde,* Gautier-Languereau, 1984.

Mitchell, editor, *Here a Little Child I Stand: Poems of Prayer and Praise for Children,* Putnam, 1985.

Elizabeth Laird, *Happy Birthday!: A Book of Birthday Celebrations,* Philomel, 1988.

Sylvia Clouzeau, *Butterfingers,* translated from the French by Didi Charney, Aladdin Books, 1988.

Mangin, *Sophie and Simon,* Macmillan, 1988.

Patricia Lee Gauch, *Dance, Tanya,* Philomel, 1989.

Laird, *Rosy's Garden: A Child's Keepsake of Flowers,* Philomel, 1990.

Gauch, *Bravo, Tanya,* Philomel, 1992.

Gauch, *Tanya and Emily in a Pas de Deux,* Philomel, 1994.

### ■ Work in Progress

*Nora and Benji* and *A Girl Who Loves Ribbons,* for Philomel.

### ■ Sidelights

Unlike many prominent illustrators, Japanese-born Satomi Ichikawa had not been drawing for years before submitting her work to publishers, and she had not thought, as a child, that she would be interested in illustrating children's books. "I had no idea what I wanted to become," she once told *SATA.* "I took a general course of study for women in college. Girls in Japan were usually expected to work for a few years after college and then get married."

To reunite with Italian friends she had met in Japan, Ichikawa traveled to Italy, and from there took a trip to France. When she explored Paris, as she recalled, "I felt at home right away.... Japan is beautiful, all of my family is there, but I grew up in the countryside where people are more conservative and where traditions tend to be restrictive." In Paris, Ichikawa "discovered true freedom of spirit." She decided to live permanently in Paris, and while working as an *au pair* (a live-in governess) to support herself, she began to study French.

It was at that time that Ichikawa encountered the work of illustrator Maurice Boutet de Monvel, who died in 1913, and began to search for his books in second-hand book shops. "I didn't know whether Boutet de Monvel was alive or dead," she told Herbert R. Lottman in *Publishers Weekly.* "But I fell in love with his work and wanted to try something of my own. In Paris you are nothing if you don't work."

Inspired by Boutet de Monvel's example, Ichikawa began to draw. "Since I had never drawn before, I started by observing real life in the gardens and in the playgrounds of Paris," she once related to *SATA.* While she viewed the reality she was drawing with the images of Boutet de Monvel in mind, Ichikawa gradually began to develop her own style. "Although I am Japanese," she explained, "my drawings are more European, because my awakening happened here. While I lived in Japan I never paid much attention to its special beauty, so that

**Ichikawa first showcased her talents as an illustrator and writer in *A Child's Book of Seasons.***

In *Nora's Stars,* one of several "Nora" books by Ichikawa, a little girl's toy animals come to life and gather up the stars from the sky. (Illustration by the author.)

it is difficult for me to draw Japanese children and scenes."

As Lottman noted in *Publishers Weekly,* "Ichikawa's initial attempts to have her work published were filled with as much verve and undaunted sense of adventure as the rest of her life." During a vacation in England, Ichikawa walked into a London bookstore and copied the names and addresses of children's book editors from the books on the shelf. She then visited the editor with the closest address, Heinemann. After perusing the thirty drawings Ichikawa had brought with her, the editor decided to publish her illustrations and the ideas behind them as *A Child's Book of Seasons.* In a review for *Horn Book,* Ethel L. Heins described the illustrations as "charming, beautifully composed." Ichikawa's career as an illustrator had begun.

## Suzanne, Nicholas, and Nora, Too

Since the publication of that first work, Ichikawa has seen her own books and books that she has illustrated

published in various languages in England, France, the United States, and Japan. Especially notable among these books is the "Suzanne and Nicholas" series. In the first, *Suzanne and Nicholas in the Garden,* the children enjoy a summer day in the garden. When Nicolas informs Suzette that another world exists outside the garden, Suzette decides that the garden is big enough, "for the moment." As Gayle Celizic wrote in the *School Library Journal,* the book may convey a "sense of peace and contentment."

Also prominent in Ichikawa's work is the series of "Nora" books. The inspiration for the creation of the first of these came from Ichikawa's summer stay in a friend's castle. As she once remembered in *SATA,* "There was no electricity, and every night I went to my room with a candle—going up and down stairs and walking along endless hallways. I stayed there for a month and a half and had no intention of working. But I was so inspired that I wrote the story of a little girl visiting this castle and in every room she discovers a presence—a king, an old piano—reminders of another life." Ichikawa especially enjoyed the creation of *Nora's Castle,* the first book which she developed "from beginning to end—a very satisfying experience," she said, adding, "I have come to see that this is the best way to work."

The books have been well received. *Nora's Stars,* in which Nora's toys come alive at night and help her gather the stars from the sky, was described as "charming" and "cozy" by Jane Yolen in the *Los Angeles Times Book Review.* Sally R. Dow, writing for *School Library Journal,* noted the "whimsical mood of this quiet bedtime fantasy." In *Nora's Duck,* Nora finds a wounded duckling and takes it to Doctor John, who provides care and a home for other stricken animals on his farm. Doctor John lovingly tends to the duckling and Nora takes it back to its pond to be reunited with its mother. Ann A. Flowers wrote in *Horn Book* that the "quiet delicacy" of Ichikawa's illustrations "mirrors the compassion and trust of the story." A reviewer for *Kirkus Reviews* commented that Ichikawa's "sweet, precise style is perfect for this idyll"; and Jody McCoy related in *School Library Journal* that the book is an "excellent choice to encourage discussion of the humane treatment of animals." In *Nora's Roses,* Nora preserves the only rose left from the bush she has enjoyed by drawing it. Carolyn Phelan of *Booklist* observed that Ichikawa's technique "captures ... the beauty of a rose in bloom, and the determination of a young child." A critic for *Quill & Quire* also praised Ichikawa, proclaiming that her "illustrative technique is a delight."

Ichikawa told *SATA* that the books *Dance, Tanya; Bravo, Tanya;* and *Tanya and Emily in a Pas de Deux* are very important in her life. "This is the first time that my love for dance and my drawing have joined," she said. "Thanks to P. L. Gauch, who wrote these stories of Tanya especially for me!" Denise Wilms said of *Dance, Tanya* in *Booklist,* "Gauch's sweet story gains strength from Ichikawa's soft watercolor paintings." *Bravo, Tanya* also was commended by a *Kirkus Reviews* contributor, who wrote that "Ichikawa captures the joy and energy of the dance in her sensitive paintings."

Boutet de Monvel's work "is kept alive" through Ichikawa's art, according to Michael Patrick Hearn in a *Horn Book* article, noting that her illustrations continue to delight children around the world. Ichikawa works every day, in ink and aquarelle, to complete two commissioned books a year "and one uncommissioned one if I have the time," she once told *SATA.* Ichikawa continues to live in Paris at Rue Campagne Premiere, in the same studio complex that Pablo Picasso inhabited as a young artist. Because, according to her, an "artist must feel complete freedom in order to create," her work is enriched by her life in the city. Ichikawa once asserted, "Coming to Paris was a rebirth for me."

## ■ Works Cited

Review of *Bravo, Tanya, Kirkus Reviews,* April 1, 1992, p. 464.

Celizic, Gayle, review of *Suzette and Nicholas in the Garden, School Library Journal,* March, 1987, p. 146.

Dow, Sally R., review of *Nora's Stars, School Library Journal,* July, 1989, pp. 66-67.

Flowers, Ann A., review of *Nora's Duck, Horn Book,* March, 1992, p. 191.

Hearn, Michael Patrick, *Horn Book,* April, 1979, p. 180.

Heins, Ethel L., review of *A Child's Book of Seasons, Horn Book,* June, 1976, pp. 280-281.

Lottman, Herbert R., "In the Studio with Satomi Ichikawa," *Publishers Weekly,* June 7, 1993, p. 19.

McCoy, Jody, review of *Nora's Duck, School Library Journal,* November, 1991, pp. 97-98.

Review of *Nora's Duck, Kirkus Reviews,* November 1, 1991, p. 1404.

Review of *Nora's Roses, Quill and Quire,* April, 1993, p. 36.

Phelan, Carolyn, review of *Nora's Roses, Booklist,* March 15, 1993, p. 1360.

Wilms, Denise, review of *Dance, Tanya, Booklist,* September 1, 1989, pp. 70-71.

Yolen, Jane, review of *Nora's Stars, Los Angeles Times Book Review,* June 4, 1989, p. 11.

## ■ For More Information See

*PERIODICALS*

*Booklist,* May 1, 1992, p. 1610.
*Children's Book Review Service,* May, 1988, p. 109.
*Horn Book,* April, 1978, p. 181.
*Junior Bookshelf,* February, 1992, p. 10.
*Kirkus Reviews,* August 1, 1989, p. 1156.
*Publishers Weekly,* March 16, 1990, p. 68.
*Quill and Quire,* May, 1992, p. 36.
*School Library Journal,* August, 1988, p. 90; March, 1992, p. 214; May, 1994, p. 96.

# J

## JENSEN, Kristine Mary 1961- (Kristine Church)

### ■ Personal

Born July 2, 1961, in Mount Isa, Australia; daughter of William George and May Church; married Hans Peter Jensen, March 16, 1983; children: Jamie-May, Isaac. *Education:* A.A., 1980; B.A., 1985.

### ■ Addresses

*Home*—52 Delta St., Toowoomba, 4350, Australia.

### ■ Career

"At the moment—motherhood."

### ■ Writings

UNDER NAME KRISTINE CHURCH

*For the Person Who Has Everything: A Book about Nothing,* Nu-Wave (Australia), 1984.
*Grandad Barnett's Beard,* Collins/Ingram (Australia), 1989.
*My Brother John,* illustrated by Kilmeny Niland, Collins/Ingram, 1990, Tambourine, 1991.

### ■ Work in Progress

Two children's books: *Sue's New Blue Shoes* and *Where's Max?*

### ■ Adaptations

*My Brother John* has been issued on ABC cassette with other stories.

### ■ Sidelights

"I began writing children's books because I love the way children see the world," Kristine Mary Jensen told *SATA.* "Stories have to be short and clear, and fire their imaginations to keep their interest.

"All and no writers have influenced my work, because I find that if I read too many children's stories by others I feel inadequate! I constantly remind myself that I have my own unique style, and that is important for all writers to remember—especially with such a competitive market.

"Being a feminist makes me aware of stereotyping in my work, so I often detest older stories for children. I'm sick of wicked witches and mothers baking in the kitchen—but I won't waffle about that.

"Why do I write?," Jensen concluded, "Because the ideas and words seem always to be there, and I love them dearly."

*My Brother John* is a picture book in which a small girl tells how her elder brother, John, knows exactly how to chase off the "monsters" that lurk under the bed, in the bathroom, and in the treehouse. But when a real live frog turns up, John needs some help from his sister to handle the situation.

### ■ For More Information See

PERIODICALS

*Children's Book Review Service,* January, 1992, p. 50.
*Kirkus Reviews,* August 15, 1991, pp. 1095-1096.
*School Library Journal,* October, 1991, p. 86.

\* \* \*

## JOHNSON, Lee Kaiser 1962-

### ■ Personal

Born Lee Dunnagan Johnson, May 21, 1962, in Fort Defiance, AZ; son of Charles R. (an editor and college professor) and Ava Dale (a writer and teacher; maiden name, Plummer) Johnson; married Sue Kaiser (a writer, home school teacher, and full-time mother), July 9, 1982; children: Andrea, Eric, Elicia, Josiah. *Education:* Macalester College, B.A. (physics and computer science), 1984. *Politics:* "Peace, justice, children, environ-

**LEE KAISER JOHNSON**

ment, consistent life ethic, make a difference." *Religion:* "Christian, everyday natural spirituality." *Hobbies and other interests:* "Fishing with my kids, inventing, weight lifting."

## ■ Addresses

*Home*—5921 Concord Ave., Edina, MN 55424.

## ■ Career

Writer, teacher, professional speaker. Control Data Corp., Minneapolis, MN, software engineer, 1984-88; Perkin Elmer Corp., Eden Prairie, MN, software engineer, 1988-90; Kaiser Johnson Consulting, Edina, MN, parenting speaker, 1989—; Advance/Possis Technical Services, St. Louis Park, MN, consulting engineer, 1991—. Involved in various parenting and child care groups. *Member:* Early Childhood Family Education (member of advisory council, 1987-88), Phi Beta Kappa.

## ■ Writings

(With wife, Sue Kaiser Johnson) *If I Ran the Family,* Free Spirit Publishing, 1992.

Also coauthor of a series of articles about personal and family growth in the regional monthly newspaper, *Stepping Up Towards Wholeness.*

## ■ Work in Progress

*I Can't Get to Sleep, My Sister's a Creep,* a children's picture book, with Sue Kaiser Johnson; "other stories for picture books that are based in children's life experiences, stories from grandparents, concept books."

## ■ Sidelights

Lee Kaiser Johnson told *SATA:* "After a childhood filled with vivid memories of my solo large projects of many types (restoring a classic car, building a salt-water aquarium, designing and building a rocket-plane model, and drawing political cartoons), I found myself the (overwhelmed) father of four young children and the lucky husband of their mother. Her example was an inspiration to me of awareness, sensitivity to the rewards of parenting, and of deep intuition and valuing of childhood.

"Together and individually, we attended four years of Early Childhood Family Education (ECFE) classes, and I took on Mr. Rogers as a surprise role model. Now I enjoy sharing some of the appreciation and enjoyment of youthful love of life that my kids have re-awakened in me. I hope the little kid in me can connect with his peers in kids and grownups everywhere!"

\*      \*      \*

## JOHNSON, Sue Kaiser 1963--

## ■ Personal

Born February 7, 1963, in Minneapolis, MN; daughter of Patrick (a dispatcher) and Alvera (a homemaker; maiden name, Wolters); married Lee Dunnagan Johnson (an engineer and writer), July 9, 1982; children: Andrea, Eric, Elicia, Josiah. *Education:* Normandale Community College, A.A., 1983. *Politics:* "Pro life, children's issues, environmental issues, consistent life ethic." *Religion:* Catholic. *Hobbies and other interests:* "I love to read self-help and parenting books, play tennis, swim, play board games with my children, and travel."

## ■ Addresses

*Home*—5921 Concord Ave., Edina, MN 55424.

## ■ Career

Writer, home school teacher, and mother. Kaiser Johnson Consulting, Edina, MN, parenting speaker, 1989—, consultant, early childhood family education, 1991—. *Member:* Greenpeace, Nature Conservancy, Feminists for Life, Minnesota Homeschooling Alliance.

## ■ Writings

(With husband, Lee Kaiser Johnson) *If I Ran the Family,* Free Spirit Publishing, 1992.

**SUE KAISER JOHNSON**

Also coauthor of a series of articles about personal and family growth in the regional monthly newspaper, *Stepping Up Towards Wholeness.*

### ■ Work in Progress

*I Can't Get to Sleep, My Sister's a Creep,* a children's picture book, with Lee Kaiser Johnson; compiling stories from grandparents.

### ■ Sidelights

"I have always dreamt of being a parent and staying home with my kids," Sue Kaiser Johnson told *SATA.* "My dream came true with the birth of our first daughter, and I have been lucky enough to be at home with all of my children. In our state, we have an Early Childhood Education Program, which really helped me realize how wonderful parenting is. I learned what a gift children are. These insights made me want to write a children's book based on the rights of all children, so that parents and children could not only enjoy sitting down and reading it together, but would gain insight into a healthier way of parenting. I want all children to know how special they are and writing books for them seems the best way to reach them. I have always dreamt of being a writer too. I feel very fortunate to have been able to accomplish my dreams."

# JOHNSTON, Julie 1941-

### ■ Personal

Born January 21, 1941, in Smith Falls, Ontario, Canada; daughter of J. A. B. (a lawyer) and Sarah Mae (a homemaker; maiden name, Patterson) Dulmage; married Basil W. Johnston (an orthopedic surgeon), 1963; children: Leslie, Lauren, Andrea, Melissa. *Education:* University of Toronto, received degree, 1963; Trent University, B.A., 1984. *Hobbies and other interests:* Old wooden boats, vegetable gardening, bicycling, hiking, travelling, reading, and stone masonry.

### ■ Addresses

*Home and office*—463 Hunter St. W., Peterborough, Ontario, Canada K9H 2M7.

### ■ Career

Occupational therapist at a school for mentally handicapped children, Smith's Falls, Ontario, 1963-65; Rehabilitation Centre, Kingston, Ontario, occupational therapist, 1965-69. Peterborough Board of Education, Continuing Education Department, creative writing instructor, 1988-89. *Member:* Canadian Society of Children's Authors, Illustrators, and Performers (CANSCAIP), Canadian Children's Book Centre, The Writer's Union of Canada, Ottawa Independent Writers.

**JULIE JOHNSTON**

## ■ Awards, Honors

Runner-up, *Chatelaine* Fiction Contest, 1979, for the short story "Canadian Content"; first prize, Solange Karsh Award, Birks Gold Medal, and cash prize, Canadian Playwriting Competition, Ottawa Little Theatre, 1979, for *There's Going to Be a Frost;* Kawartha Region Best Play award, 1980, for *There's Going to Be a Frost* and co-winner for best play, 1984, for *Lucid Intervals;* Canadian Library Association Young Adult Honour Book, 1993, shortlisting for Mister Christie's Book Award, 1993, National Chapter of Canada Independent Order Daughters of the Empire (IODE) Violet Downey Book Award, 1993, Governor General's Literary Award for children's literature, 1993, *School Library Journal* Best Book, 1994, New York Public Library's 1994 Books for the Teen Age list selection, Ontario Library Association 1994 Silver Birch Award nomination, and American Library Association notable book selection, all for *Hero of Lesser Causes.*

## ■ Writings

*There's Going to Be a Frost* (one-act play), first produced at the Sears Drama Festival, 1980.
*Lucid Intervals* (one-act play), first produced at the Sears Drama Festival, 1984.
*Hero of Lesser Causes* (young adult novel), Lester Publishing, 1992, Joy Street Books, 1993.
*Adam and Eve and Pinch-Me* (young adult novel), Little, Brown, 1994.

Contributor of the novella *The Window Seat* to *Women's Weekly Omnibus,* 1984, and the story "Mirrors" to the anthology *The Blue Jean Collection,* Thistledown Press, 1992. Contributor of fiction to periodicals, including *Women's Weekly Buzz, Chatelaine, Woman and Home,* and *Matrix;* contributor of nonfiction to periodicals, including *Wine Tidings, Homemakers, Doctor's Review,* and *Canadian Author and Bookman.* Johnston's work has been translated into French.

## ■ Work in Progress

A screenplay based on *Hero of Lesser Causes* for Canadian producer Roy Krost, proposed production date 1994-95.

## ■ Sidelights

Julie Johnston won praise for her first novel for young adults, *Hero of Lesser Causes,* which reviewer Deborah Stevenson described in a *Bulletin of the Center for Children's Books* review as a "touching and funny story of sibling maturation." Set in Canada in 1946, the book begins as twelve-year-old Keely sees her brother Patrick paralyzed by polio after swimming in a public pool. Keely and her brother, just a year apart in age, are close friends, and Keely cannot imagine her life without him. Yet Patrick seems a different person as he becomes more and more bitter about his disease. Patrick's frustration and depression moves Keely to concoct wild plans to cheer and heal him. One of these plans is to find

Keely Connor is an optimistic girl with a rich imagination, but her efforts to cheer up her polio-stricken brother might not be enough to save him from a deep depression.

the fiance of Patrick's nurse, who is missing and presumed dead in World War II. Despite her efforts, Patrick's emotional condition grows increasingly serious. Finally, after an attempted suicide, Patrick begins to understand that his life is worth living, and he responds to Keely's optimism.

*Hero of Lesser Causes* was well received. A *Kirkus Reviews* writer noted that the book was "a fine first novel," while a *Publishers Weekly* review found that the book "accelerates into a spectacular novel, balancing coming-of-age-angst with the grief from a sudden, devastating affliction." Cindy Darling Codell praised the book in *School Library Journal* as being "wonderfully simple, yet layered with meaning." Nancy Vasilakis, a reviewer for *Horn Book,* appreciated the "unique period details" which "create a strong sense of the place and the time without slowing down the action." *Hero of Lesser Causes* earned Johnston Canada's prestigious Governor General's Literary Award in 1993.

Explaining her approach to writing, Johnston told *SATA:* "Fiction is about developing characters who never existed but might have, and allowing them to do things that never happened but could have. It's making up the truth. What I enjoy most about writing fiction is burrowing so deeply into these characters that I am in tune with how they think, how they sound, and how they see the world. The only way I can do this is to explore every facet of myself and use bits for every character—good, bad, or ridiculous. Creating a character is like going on an archeological dig of the soul. Truth is what I'm digging for; the trick is in recognizing it. When I agonize over my own flaws and failures, or rejoice in chunks of good fortune, I find myself storing it all away in some closet in my mind to use as a hand-me-down for a future character. While I'm grubbing around under the surface of things I sometimes find the one true passion that rules a character's life."

## ■ Works Cited

Codell, Cindy Darling, review of *Hero of Lesser Causes, School Library Journal,* June, 1993, p. 107.
Review of *Hero of Lesser Causes, Kirkus Reviews,* May 15, 1993, p. 663.
Review of *Hero of Lesser Causes, Publishers Weekly,* May 24, 1993, p. 89.
Stevenson, Deborah, review of *Hero of Lesser Causes, Bulletin of the Center for Children's Books,* April, 1993, p. 254.
Vasilakis, Nancy, review of *Hero of Lesser Causes, Horn Book,* August, 1993, p. 457.

## ■ For More Information See

*PERIODICALS*

*Booklist,* July, 1993, p. 1966.
*Children's Book News,* spring, 1992, p. 17.
*Emergency Librarian,* March, 1993, p. 14.
*Publishers Weekly,* July 12, 1993, p. 24.
*Quill and Quire,* April, 1992, p. 31.
*Toronto Star,* December 22, 1992.

\* \* \*

## JOOS, Francoise 1956-

## ■ Personal

Born February 5, 1956, in Alsace, France; daughter of Marius (an insurance company manager) and Denise (maiden name, Jehaumasse) Dalpra; married Frederic Joos (an illustrator), July 3, 1984.

## ■ Addresses

*Home*—27, Avenue Guillaume le Conpeuraut 14150, Ouistreham, Riva Bella, France.

## ■ Career

Author.

## ■ Writings

*Puss in Palace,* illustrations by husband, Frederic Joos, Andersen Press, 1988.
*Sarah and the Stone Man,* illustrations by Frederic Joos, Andersen Press, 1988.
*The Golden Snowflake,* illustrations by Frederic Joos, Little, Brown, 1991.

## ■ Sidelights

"I have always been fond of books," Francoise Joos told *SATA.* "I met Frederic Joos, my husband, in the bookshop where I worked. At the time, I was thinking of doing translations—which I have done since—but I never dreamt of writing anything by myself.

"Frederic talked to me about children's books and all the illustrators he loved. Soon afterwards, he began to draw for children's magazines and to illustrate books, but I still did not think of writing even though he urged me to try. Then one day, Klaus Flugge from the Andersen Press, for whom Frederic had illustrated *Sorry Miss Folio,* advised Frederic to write his own stories and, very naturally, we collaborated. There came our first story, *Sarah and the Stone Man,* then another book and *The Golden Snowflake.* We find it so interesting to have, as we live together, the opportunity to marry the pictures and the text, and the text with the pictures at the same time—and not one after the other. We would like so much to be able to share with children more and more an atmosphere of tenderness and hope, an aspiration for inner and outward freedom, dream, mind and heart opening, which we think are basic clues for a harmonious growth in all of us: little ones as well as so-called grown-ups."

\* \* \*

## JOOS, Frederic 1953-

## ■ Personal

Born April 23, 1953, in Alger, Algeria; son of Olivier Joos (a commercial manager) and Angelica Joos-Taller; married Francoise Dalpra (a writer), July 3, 1984.

## ■ Addresses

*Home and office*—27, Avenue Guillaume le Conpeuraut 14150, Ouistreham, Riva Bella, France.

## ■ Career

Building designer, musician, and illustrator.

## ■ Illustrator

J. Held and C. Held, *Le Drole de Dictionnaire,* Editions Milan, 1986.
Beatrice Rouer, *La Patate du Marche,* Editions Milan, 1987.

**FRANCOISE AND FREDERIC JOOS**

Jo Furtado, *Sorry Miss Folio!*, Andersen Press, 1988, Kane/Miller, 1988.

Francoise Joos, *Puss in Palace*, Andersen Press, 1988.

Francoise Joos, *Sarah and the Stone Man*, Andersen Press, 1988.

Furtado, *Special Visitors*, Andersen Press, 1988.

Francoise Joos, *The Golden Snowflake*, Little, Brown, 1991.

## ■ Sidelights

Frederic Joos told *SATA:* "I should have liked to enter an Art School, but my parents thought this was not good, so I became a building designer, which sounded much more serious. However, I disliked it: while in the army, I prepared an illustration-press-book and as soon as I left the army a big regional advertising agency took me on as a designer. Meanwhile, I was singing and playing acoustic guitar in a 'progressive rock group.' We were giving concerts and even recorded an L.P. Three years later, I had had enough of this very busy life and went wandering on the roads of France (with a friend and a ... donkey). But a year later, I also had had enough of it.

"I settled down as a free-lance roughman and designer in Nancy (the East of France), and little by little I developed the various aspects of the profession. Children's magazines began to call me also and I enjoyed more and more drawing for children. In fact, I had always had the desire to do so. One day, my wife and I decided to visit Bologne's bookfair—a jolly opportunity to visit Italy! There we stopped in front of the Andersen Press stand and, without knowing who he was, began to talk with David McKee, a famous illustrator for Andersen Press we both admired a lot. Back in Nancy, I received a first order to illustrate a story for Andersen Press, Jo Furtado's *Sorry Miss Folio!* Then there came *Sarah and the Stone Man* and *Puss in Palace,* both by my wife, *Special Visitors* by Jo Furtado, and now *The Golden Snowflake,* with my wife again.

"During these years, I never stopped doing posters and all sorts of work for the advertising and cultural fields. I also draw a lot for magazines, and I am fond of exploring all the possible techniques I can. Now we live at the seaside, in Normandy, and we hope that the fresh wind from the sea and our long talks with the seagulls will inspire us with many stories for children, for I swear I have not had enough of it at all!"

# K

## KAPLAN, Andrew 1960-

### ■ Personal

Born April 26, 1960, in New York, NY; son of Jerome Kaplan (an editor and writer) and Thelma Kaplan (a career counselor; maiden name, Cornon). *Education:* Cornell University, B.A., 1982.

### ■ Addresses

*Home and office*—25 Tudor City Pl., Apt. 1205, New York, NY 10017.

### ■ Career

*Curriculum Concepts,* New York City, editor and writer, 1982-85; freelance writer and editor, 1985—.

### ■ Writings

*Careers for Sports Fans,* Millbrook Press, 1991.
*Careers for Computer Buffs,* Millbrook Press, 1991.
*Careers for Artistic Types,* Millbrook Press, 1991.
*Careers for Outdoor Types,* Millbrook Press, 1991.
*Careers for Number Lovers,* Millbrook Press, 1991.
*Careers for Wordsmiths,* Millbrook Press, 1991.
*War of the Raven,* Avon, 1991.

### ■ Work in Progress

Research on "career changers" and "oral histories of neighborhood residents."

### ■ Sidelights

Andrew Kaplan told *SATA:* "Glancing at the 'personal' section of this entry, you would see that my father is an editor and writer and my mother is a career counselor. At that point, you might look at my 'writings' section, which includes six books in which I profiled eighty-four people in different careers, and decide 'Kaplan's books represent the combined effects of his parents' influence. Case closed.' However, although the match seems

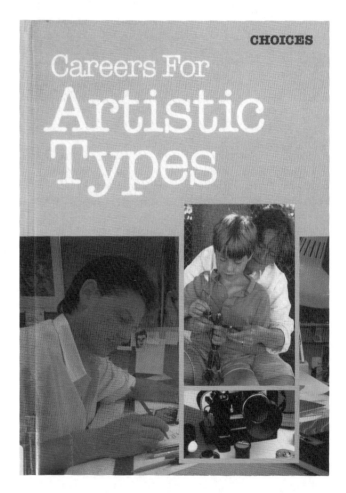

In one of Andrew Kaplan's many books about career possibilities, the author shows young readers how they might use their artistic talents to earn a living in fourteen different professions.

almost perfect, I deny it. There's no connection whatsoever. In fact, the very drawing of that conclusion would only prove, one more time, that pop-psychology has overrun our culture and is leading us to misunderstand the events and people which we're analyzing. What's the real answer? No one knows for sure, least of all me. All I can tell you is that I've always liked stories, books, and movies, and talking to people and listening to their stories. Even if those stories are made up. Or, perhaps, especially if they're made up."

\*     \*     \*

## KELEMEN, Julie 1959-

### ■ Personal

Born September 17, 1959, in St. Louis, MO; daughter of Joseph (a professor of electrical engineering) and Marcella (a family counseling office administrator; maiden name, Voss) Kelemen; married Toby W. Paone (a union organizer), September 30, 1989. *Education:* Western Michigan University, B.A. (magna cum laude), 1981, Washington University, M.F.A. (writing), 1986. *Hobbies and other interests:* Foreign languages, ethnic cooking, gardening, early television trivia and memorabilia, Africana, "hanging out with kids," computers, dogs.

### ■ Addresses

*Home and office*—6408 South Kingshighway, St. Louis, MO 63109-3741.

**JULIE KELEMEN**

### ■ Career

Central Institute for the Deaf, St. Louis, MO, technical writer/editor, 1986-87; Liguori Publications, Liguori, MO, associate editor, book and pamphlet department, 1987-90, associate editor, Parish Education Products, 1990-93. Adjunct English instructor at St. Louis Community College, St. Louis, and St. Charles County Community College, St. Peters, MO, 1993—. *Member:* Society of Children's Book Writers and Illustrators, St. Louis Writers' Guild (secretary, 1990-92; president, 1992-93).

### ■ Awards, Honors

First prize, James Nash Memorial Writing Contest, St. Louis Writer's Guild, 1987, for the short story "Zero O'Clock."

### ■ Writings

*Lent Is for Children,* Liguori, 1987.
*Advent Is for Children,* Liguori, 1988.
*Prayer Is for Children,* Liguori, 1992.

### ■ Work in Progress

"A book of stories that take place in Nigeria, where I lived as a child; I'm also trying to expand into trade children's publishing from the children's religious field where I've been for the past seven years."

### ■ Sidelights

"During the late sixties, I was in the second and third grades in Nigeria where my father taught college," Julie Kelemen remembered for *SATA.* "I went to school with mostly African children—Yorubas, Ibos, Hausas, Fulanis. These were fascinating, fun years of learning about West African culture.

"My family returned to the United States in 1968. On the news and in magazines I remember looking, aghast, at images of Martin Luther King after he'd been shot. Bobby Kennedy had just been shot. Race riots were erupting. Riot police came out in full force at the Democratic National Convention. The horror of these images sharply contrasted with the racial harmony I'd experienced in Nigeria. Returning to America was more of a culture shock than going to Nigeria. My sadness about this contrast remains with me today.

"I was both blessed, and cursed, with a harmonious, pleasant exposure to African culture at a young age. I say 'cursed' because I fear intercultural tolerance won't happen in the United States in my lifetime. Thus, I tend to involve myself in ventures (including writing) that promote intercultural understanding and harmony.

"I seriously began considering a writing career in Mrs. Groening's sixth grade class at St. Joseph's school in Kalamazoo, Michigan. One day, Mrs. Groening had us read aloud stories we'd written. When my turn came, I

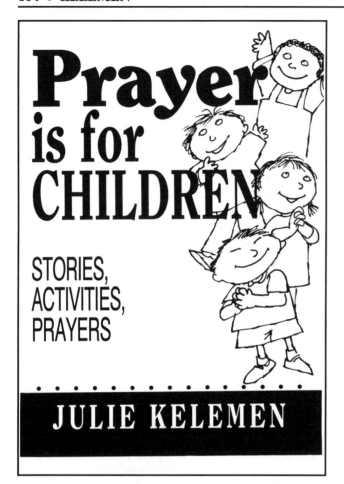

**Keleman teaches children how to talk with God in this guide, which combines fun illustrations, activities, and interesting tidbits of information to effectively deliver her message.**

gulped and read my science fiction tale about earthlings visiting another planet and finding nice creatures, for a change. When I finished, there were a few seconds of insufferable silence. Then ... the whole class burst into applause (they hadn't clapped for anyone else's story).

"Wish I'd saved the story. All I remember is a character named Barney and the last line: '... and they feasted on goodiak soup.'

"Three children's authors have influenced me more than any others—Shel Silverstein, Dr. Seuss, and Bernadette McCarver Snyder. They've perfected the art of exploring controversial or complicated elements of life without boring or offending their readers. They're true masters of silliness, and silliness is serious business in kids' writing! Viva la silly!

"To be a successful children's author, four things are necessary (in addition to the ability to write coherently). First, talk *with* (not at) children whenever you can. Take them seriously. Listen more than you talk. Second, be confident and take your desire to write for children seriously. Lots of folks won't want you to do it. They think it's frivolous. Stand firm. Repeat 'I am a writer' to yourself every day, then DO it. Third, have a vivid

memory of, and respect for, your own childhood—knowing what it is to be a child. Fourth, maintain a childlike attitude and outlook, even if you're eighty. That means cultivating hope, wonder, and silliness when cynicism and worry try to crawl under the door. I have to work on that every day!"

\*   \*   \*

## KEOWN, Elizabeth 1913-

### ■ Personal

Born December 23, 1913, in Frankfort, IN; daughter of John (a merchant) and Mary (Horlacher) Dorner; married Arthur D. Keown (a social worker), August 19, 1939; children: Mary M. Todd, Martha E. Swank, Arthur J. *Education:* Attended Indiana University, 1932-34; University of Michigan, B.A. (with honors), 1939; Wayne State University, teacher certification, 1967.

### ■ Addresses

*Agent*—c/o Publicity Director, Atheneum Publishers, 866 3rd Ave., New York, NY 10022.

### ■ Career

County Department of Welfare, Frankfort, IN, social worker, 1936; Detroit Children's Aid Society, Detroit, MI, social worker, 1937; Michigan Children's Aid Society, Detroit, field representative, 1937-41; Detroit Public Preschool, Detroit, teacher, 1968-73. Volunteer for kindergarten classes, Detroit, 1973-84; volunteer in bilingual kindergarten, Dearborn, MI, 1986—. *Member:* American Association of University Women.

### ■ Writings

*Emily's Snowball, The World's Biggest,* illustrated by Irene Trivas, Atheneum, 1992.

### ■ Work in Progress

*Less Is Sometimes Best,* a children's picture book.

### ■ Sidelights

"I was the youngest of six children, and when I was very little, my parents were always busy," Elizabeth Keown told *SATA.* "My youngest brother and I lived in a fantasy world of our own, dominated by Mrs. Sabee, who was crazy and stole babies. Then there were the outrageous monster stories my oldest brother would tell. My mother was concerned! Nevertheless, a few years later I was telling the same kind of stories to the younger children in the family."

Keown called it "a happy day" when she received her first library card. "I became an avid reader, and the stories I would tell became slightly more civilized. When our three children were young, my husband and I read

**ELIZABETH KEOWN**

to them constantly, and I became acquainted with children's literature."

Her experiences as a volunteer in Detroit's Head Start program spurred Keown into going back to school. She obtained her teaching certification and taught in the same project where she had formerly been a volunteer. As a teacher, she used picture books as the basis of many of her lessons. When she retired from teaching, Keown returned again to become a kindergarten volunteer in the inner city neighborhood where she had taught.

"Only a very few of these children had participated in the Head Start program," she commented, "and they had so much to learn! One winter there was a tremendous amount of snow. The kindergarten children never grew tired of making snowballs. So, to help them develop the concept of size in a meaningful context and gain some understanding of seasonal changes, I wrote and illustrated *Emily's Snowball, The World's Biggest.* The story tells how, step by step, Emily's little snowball becomes bigger and bigger, and is found truly to be the WORLD'S BIGGEST. People come to see it! Children climb it! Then the sun gets warmer and slowly the snowball starts melting and turning to water and gets littler and littler. Finally the last puddle is gone, but happy memories remain."

Keown has continued her volunteer work with kindergarten students, and she reads her stories in elementary classrooms: "I do my best," she said, "to encourage young children to write."

## KILE, Joan 1940-

### ■ Personal

Born in 1940 in Milford Center, OH; married; husband's name, Burke; children: Grant Cole. *Education:* Middle Tennessee State University, M.Ed.

### ■ Addresses

*Home*—104 Stable Ct., Franklin, TN 37064.

### ■ Career

School teacher in public and private schools; writer, narrator, director, and producer for the Mustard Seed Gospel Radio Program, Nashville, TN; writer.

### ■ Writings

*"MUSTY THE MUSTARD SEED" SERIES*

*God's Mustard Seed,* illustrated by Teresa Ragland, Musty the Mustard Seed Books, 1993.
*God's Rugged Cross,* Musty the Mustard Seed Books, 1994.
*God's Fruit Tree,* Musty the Mustard Seed Books, 1994.
*God's Fig Tree,* Musty the Mustard Seed Books, 1994.

### ■ Sidelights

Joan Kile's idea for the "Musty the Mustard Seed" books was conceived during the three years that she wrote, narrated, directed, and produced the Mustard Seed Gospel Radio Program in Nashville, Tennessee. The books are written from the scripts of the radio programs, and many children who participated in the programs came up with picture ideas for the illustrations of the "Musty the Mustard Seed" series. Kile told *SATA* that she "hopes the books will be used to teach the gospel message to children throughout the world."

\*    \*    \*

## KIRBY, David K(irk) 1944-

### ■ Personal

Born November 29, 1944, in Baton Rouge, LA; son of Thomas Austin (a professor) and Josie (a teacher; maiden name, Dyson) Kirby; married Judy Kates (a teacher), March 21, 1969 (marriage ended); married Barbara Hamby (a writer), June 11, 1981; children: William, Ian. *Education:* Louisiana State University, B.A., 1966; Johns Hopkins University, Ph.D., 1969.

### ■ Addresses

*Home*—1168 Seminole Dr., Tallahassee, FL 32301-4656. *Office*—English Department, Florida State University, Tallahassee, FL 32306-1036.

**THE COWS ARE GOING TO PARIS**
by DAVID KIRBY & ALLEN WOODMAN          Illustrated by CHRIS L. DEMAREST

**A herd of cattle decide it's time to trade places with a trainload of humans and take a trip to Paris, where they live high on the hog in David K. Kirby's whimsical romp.** (Cover illustration by Chris L. Demarest.)

## ■ Career

Florida State University, Tallahassee, assistant professor, 1969-74, associate professor, 1974-89, McKenzie Professor of English, 1989—, visiting member of faculty at Florida State University Study Center in Florence, Italy, 1973—. Has conducted workshops and seminars for groups including elementary school children and prison inmates. *Member:* Associated Writing Programs, Melville Society, National Book Critics Circle.

## ■ Awards, Honors

Pushcart Prize Outstanding Writer Citations, 1978 and 1984, for poetry, and 1987, for nonfiction; Florida Arts Council grants, 1983, 1989; first-place poetry prizes from *Kansas Quarterly,* 1983, *Southern Poetry Review,* 1985, and *Fine Madness,* 1989; fellowship, National Endowment for the Arts, 1985; Brittingham Prize in Poetry, University of Wisconsin, 1987, for *Saving the Young Men of Vienna;* College of Arts and Sciences

Teaching Award, 1990; University Teaching Award, 1992.

## ■ Writings

*FOR CHILDREN*

(With Allen Woodman) *The Cows Are Going to Paris,* illustrated by Chris L. Demarest, Boyds Mills, 1991.
(With Woodman) *The Bear Who Came to Stay,* Bradbury, in press.

*OTHER*

(Editor with Kenneth H. Baldwin) *Individual and Community: Variations on a Theme in American Fiction,* Duke University Press, 1975.
*American Fiction to 1900: Guide to Information Sources,* Gale, 1975.
*The Opera Lover,* Anhinga, 1977.
*Grace King,* Twayne, 1980.
*America's Hive of Honey: Foreign Influences on American Fiction through Henry James,* Scarecrow, 1980.

*The Sun Rises in the Evening: Monism and Quietism in Western Culture,* Scarecrow, 1982.
*Sarah Bernhardt's Leg* (poetry), Cleveland State University Poetry Center, 1983.
*The Plural World,* Garland, 1984.
(Editor) *Dictionary of Contemporary Thought,* Macmillan, 1984.
*Diving for Poems,* Word Beat, 1985.
*Saving the Young Men of Vienna* (poetry), University of Wisconsin Press, 1987.
*Writing Poetry: Where Poems Come from and How to Write Them,* Writer, 1989.
*Mark Strand and the Poet's Place in Contemporary Culture,* Missouri University Press, 1990.
*The Portrait of a Lady,* Macmillan, 1991.
*Boyishness in American Culture: The Charms and Dangers of Social Immaturity,* Mellen, 1991.
*Herman Melville,* Continuum, 1993.

Contributor of poems, reviews, and essays to *New York Times Book Review, Times Literary Supplement, Village Voice, The Writer, Quarterly, Southern Review, Sewanee Review, Ploughshares, College English, Virginia Quarterly Review, Christian Science Monitor, Gettysburg Review,* and others.

### ■ Sidelights

David Kirby told *SATA:* "I like to alternate between two kinds of writing. In articles, reviews, and books of literary criticism, I try to be as clear as possible about the world we live in now. That's my sole goal in that type of writing: clarity. But in my poems and children's books, I try to re-enter a time when trees talked, when wizards roamed the earth, and animals dressed up like human beings. I count it a bad day when I don't spend a few hours in each of these worlds, the real one and the magic one."

### ■ For More Information See

*PERIODICALS*

*Antioch Review,* winter, 1991, p. 153.
*Booklist,* December 15, 1991, pp. 769-770.
*Chattahoochee Review,* spring, 1989, pp. 1-13.
*Choice,* December, 1990, p. 629.
*Washington Post,* July 13, 1993, p. E7.

\* \* \*

## KITE, (L.) Patricia 1940-
### (Tricia Adams)

### ■ Personal

Born February 2, 1940, in New York; daughter of Oscar (in business) and Sarah (a lawyer and homemaker; maiden name, Evenchick) Padams; married Ronald G. Kite (a physician), 1962 (divorced, 1975); children: Rachel, Karen, Laura Kite-Raney, Sally. *Education:* Attended University of California, Los Angeles, 1957-60; University of California Medical Center, San Francisco, B.S., 1961; graduate study at University of

**PATRICIA KITE**

California, Berkeley, 1962-70; California State University, Hayward, biology teaching credential, 1971; San Jose University, M.S., 1982. *Politics:* Democrat. *Hobbies and other interests:* Gardening, walking, people.

### ■ Addresses

*Home*—5318 Stirling Ct., Newark, CA 94560-1352.

### ■ Career

Science Communications, owner, 1975—; producer of the television program *The Writing Life,* 1984-90; Institute of Children's Literature, instructor, 1990—; member of Union Sanitary District Board of Directors, 1992—. *Member:* Society of Children's Book Writers and Illustrators, Pacific Coast Entomology Society, California Writer's Club, Northern California Science Writers.

### ■ Awards, Honors

Short fiction award from California Writer's Club, 1977; award from National Society of Newspaper Columnists, 1984, for syndicated column "On My Own"; awards from Garden Writers of America, 1988, 1989, and 1990.

# ■ Writings

*FOR CHILDREN*

*Noah's Ark,* Greenhaven Press, 1989.
*Down in the Sea: The Octopus,* Albert Whitman, 1993.
*Down in the Sea: The Jellyfish,* Albert Whitman, 1993.
*Down in the Sea: The Sea Slug,* Albert Whitman, 1994.
*Down in the Sea: The Crab,* Albert Whitman, 1994.

Contributor of stories and articles to periodicals, including *Highlights for Children, Ranger Rick,* and *Odyssey.*

*FOR ADULTS*

*How to Be Successfully Interviewed by the Press,* privately printed, 1982.
*Freelance Interview Tips and Tricks,* privately printed, 1983.
(Under pseudonym Tricia Adams) *Between the Sheets* (humorous romance novel), Berkley-Jove, 1984.
(With R. F. Nelson) *How to Self-Promote Your Book,* privately printed, 1984.
*Controlling Lawn and Garden Insects,* Ortho Books, 1987.
*A Cutting Garden for California,* B. B. Mackey Books, 1990.
*Suddenly Single Mother's Survival Guide,* Mills & Sanderson, 1991.
*Home Gardener's Problem Solver,* Ortho Books, 1993.

Author of syndicated newspaper column "On My Own," 1984-92; contributor of articles and stories to periodicals.

# ■ Work in Progress

*Indoor Gardening for Children* (tentative title), for Barron's Educational Series.

# ■ Sidelights

Patricia Kite told *SATA:* "I began my writing career quite by accident, volunteering to write public service announcements for the Sierra Club. At the time, I was a newly singled parent of children ages eleven, eight, six, and four months. Although my original intention was to write science for children, this is not the easiest field to break into. In the interim, I wrote Occupational Safety and Health Administration (OSHA) compliance, hazardous waste material transport, and security management documents, garden entomology for the layperson, materials on home decorating and Victoriana, and general interest newspaper features. From 1984 to 1992, I syndicated a national newspaper column on single parenting. From 1984 to 1990, I produced a cable television program, *The Writing Life,* which aired on fourteen channels. All in all, I've done about two thousand interviews and pride myself on capturing the true flavor of the individual, through print or visual media.

"Along the way, I sold quite a few children's stories and articles. These went to *Highlights for Children, Ranger Rick, Junior Trails, The Friend, Odyssey,* etc. Several

pieces have been reprinted in school texts. I'm delighted to finally be writing K-3 science, my goal of eighteen years. Of particular joy is working with the California Academy of Science staff. And I do love to research. Old books, new books are a joy, and a library is like a second home."

# ■ For More Information See

*PERIODICALS*

*Argus,* June, 1984.
*Booklist,* March 1, 1990, p. 1337; March 15, 1993, p. 1353.
*Children's Book Watch,* December, 1992, p. 6.
*Children's Book Review Service,* May, 1993, p. 114.
*Grit,* November, 1984.
*Kirkus Reviews,* January 1, 1993, p. 63.
*Library Journal,* July, 1991, p. 177.
*School Library Journal,* March, 1993, p. 191; May, 1994, p. 124.

\*    \*    \*

# KORMAN, Bernice 1937-

# ■ Personal

Born July 23, 1937, in Montreal, Quebec, Canada; daughter of George (a manufacturer) and Claire (Schwartz) Silverman; married Charles Isaac Korman (an accountant), June 26, 1960; children: Gordon. *Education:* Concordia University, Montreal, B.A., 1958. *Hobbies and other interests:* Swimming, music, baseball.

# ■ Addresses

*Home*—20 Dersingham Crescent, Thornhill, Ontario L3T 4E7, Canada. *Agent*—Curtis Brown Ltd., Ten Astor Place, New York, NY 10003.

# ■ Career

Columnist for the *Suburban* (English-language weekly newspaper), 1964-81; Teleterm, Inc., Markham, Ontario, executive assistant, 1980—. *Member:* Canadian Society of Children's Authors, Illustrators, and Performers.

# ■ Writings

(With son, Gordon Korman) *The D-Poems of Jeremy Bloom,* Scholastic Inc., 1992.

Also author of a weekly column, "Bernice's Banter," published in the *Suburban,* 1964-81.

# ■ Work in Progress

A sequel to *The D-Poems of Jeremy Bloom;* several Regency romances.

# ■ Sidelights

Although *The D-Poems of Jeremy Bloom* has done well, Bernice Korman considers her personal claim to fame to be the fact that she is the mother of young-adult novelist Gordon Korman. "To collaborate with him on a book was a delight," she told *SATA,* "but it was merely an extension of the years I spent typing and editing his grammar—he started writing at age twelve!"

Korman is currently at work on more poems, and a sequel to *The D-Poems of Jeremy Bloom* is in the works. "And I'm hard at work writing Regency romances, a genre I enjoy," she commented. She continues to find the writing process as rewarding as seeing her finished work in print: "For those who believe that the act of creating a book is at least half of the art, you ought to see Gordon and Bernice Korman collaborating! If laughter and sheer enjoyment count for anything, we've found the system!"

# L

## LACOE, Addie
### [A pseudonym]

### ■ Personal

Surname pronounced "Lah-*coh*"; born October 18, in Scranton, PA; daughter of Milt and Norah; married; husband's name, George; children: Dolly, Ellie, Rick, Andrea, Deborah, Amy. *Religion:* Church of Jesus Christ of Latter-Day Saints.

### ■ Addresses

*Office*—The Village Bookstore, 47 Southwick Rd., Westfield, MA 01085.

### ■ Career

Writer.

### ■ Writings

*Just Not the Same,* illustrated by Pau Estrada, Houghton, 1992.

### ■ Work in Progress

*Mama, Lindsey, and Chaos* for Millbrook Press.

### ■ Sidelights

Addie Lacoe told *SATA:* "The real-life Addie Lacoe was the youngest child in a large farming family. Born in the nineteenth century, she died when she was about ten years old, before she had much of a chance to make a name for herself. Most of my stories are fantasy, science fiction, or horror, so I thought it appropriate to use a ghostly pen name.

"I also enjoy making up stories for and about young people. I've been about every kind of mother there can be: a birth mother, an adoptive mother, a step-mother, a foster mother, a grandmother, and a mother-in-law. I try to keep in mind what it was like to be a child."

### ■ For More Information See

*PERIODICALS*

*Booklist,* September 15, 1992, pp. 155-156.
*Publishers Weekly,* September 28, 1992, pp. 78-79.
*School Library Journal,* November, 1992, p. 72.

\* \* \*

## LARSEN, Anita 1942-
### (Anita Gustafson; Dana White, a pseudonym)

### ■ Personal

Born December 29, 1942, in Hastings, NE; daughter of Donald and Zelda Larsen; married Brian Gustafson, 1963 (divorced, 1985). *Education:* Buena Vista College, B.A. (cum laude), 1967; Drake University, M.A., 1973.

### ■ Addresses

*Home*—310 Burch, Box 6402, Taos, NM 87571.

### ■ Career

Drake University, Des Moines, IA, lecturer in theater history, manager of publicity for theater arts department, and teaching assistant in English department; Alta High School, Alta, IA, English and speech teacher, 1969-73; Charlie's Showplace (dinner theater), Des Moines, resident company, 1974; CMF & Z (advertising agency), Des Moines, copywriter, 1983; Institute of Children's Literature, instructor, 1984-92. Freelance writer, communications consultant, critic, actress, and speaker at workshops and seminars, 1975—. *Member:* Society of Children's Book Writers and Illustrators, National Writer's Union, American Federation of Television and Radio Artists (AFTRA), Southwest Writers Workshop, Taos Archeological Society, Alpha Psi Omega, Sigma Tau Delta.

ANITA LARSEN

### ■ Awards, Honors

*Guilty or Innocent?* was named an American Library Association (ALA) Notable Book, 1986; *Some Feet Have Noses* was named an ALA Notable Book and an outstanding science trade book for children by the Children's Book Council, both 1983; first place award in Children's Division, Southwest Writers Workshop, 1993, for *Amanda's Angel.*

### ■ Writings

*Monster Rolling Skull and Other Native American Stories,* Crowell, 1980.
(Under name Anita Gustafson) *Burrowing Birds,* Lothrop, 1981.
(Under name Anita Gustafson) *Some Feet Have Noses,* Lothrop, 1983.
(Under name Anita Gustafson) *Guilty or Innocent?,* Holt, 1985.
*Lost ... and Never Found,* Scholastic, 1984.
(Under pseudonym Dana White) *Jason Saves the Kitten,* Weekly Reader Books, 1984.
(Under name Anita Gustafson) *The Case of the Purloined Park,* National Park Producers Council, 1985.
*Lost ... and Never Found II,* Scholastic, 1991.
*True Crimes and How They Were Solved,* Scholastic, 1993.
*Psychic Sleuths,* New Directions, 1994.

*"HISTORY'S MYSTERIES" SERIES*

*The Roanoke Missing Persons Case,* illustrated by James Watling, Crestwood House, 1992.

*The Rosenbergs,* illustrated by Marcy Ramsey, Crestwood House, 1992.
*Amelia Earhart: Missing, Declared Dead,* Crestwood House, 1992.
*Raoul Wallenberg: Missing Diplomat,* illustrated by Watling, Crestwood House, 1992.
*Montezuma's Missing Treasure,* illustrated by Pamela Johnson, Crestwood House, 1992.

*PLAYS; UNDER NAME ANITA GUSTAFSON*

*Felix Culpa* (full-length), first produced at American Shakespeare Theater, Stratford, CT, 1974.
*The Hungerbear and the Fried Egg Spatters* (one-act) [and] *Fish of April* (one-act), first produced at Fargo ETC, 1975.
*Tale of the Mouse* (juvenile; first produced at Dallas Theater Center, Dallas, TX), Pioneer Drama, 1977.
(Contributor) *Asbestos Curtain* (includes "The Transcendental Mediator"), International Thespian Society, 1978.
*Fox Boy's Night Vision* (juvenile; first produced by Five Flags Theater Company, Dubuque, IA, 1982), portions reprinted in *Writing for Children and Teenagers* by Lee Wyndham, Writers Digest Books, 1988.

*"AT RISK" SERIES; EDITOR, EXCEPT WHERE NOTED*

Jean Dick, *Bomb Squads and SWAT Teams,* Crestwood House, 1988.
Gail Stewart, *Stuntpeople,* Crestwood House, 1988.
Stewart, *Offshore Oil Rig Workers,* Crestwood House, 1988.
Shirley Keran, *Underwater Specialists,* Crestwood House, 1988.
Nancy J. Nielsen, *Helicopter Pilots,* Crestwood House, 1988.
Stewart, *Smokejumpers and Forest Firefighters,* Crestwood House, 1988.
Stewart, *Coal Miners,* Crestwood House, 1988.
(Under pseudonym Dana White) *High-Rise Workers,* Crestwood House, 1988.

*"THE FACTS ABOUT" SERIES; EDITOR*

Renardo Barden, *Fears and Phobias,* Crestwood House, 1989.
JoAnn Bren Guernsey, *Teenage Pregnancy,* Crestwood House, 1989.
Caroline Evensen Lazo, *Divorce,* Crestwood House, 1989.
Gail Stewart, *Peer Pressure,* Crestwood House, 1989.
Stewart, *Death,* Crestwood House, 1989.
Laurie Beckelman, *The Homeless,* Crestwood House, 1989.
Marilyn Bailey, *Single-Parent Families,* Crestwood House, 1989.
Barden, *Gangs,* Crestwood House, 1989.
Stewart, *Child Abuse,* Crestwood House, 1989.
Judy Monroe, *Latchkey Children,* Crestwood House, 1989.
Stewart, *Discrimination,* Crestwood House, 1989.
Stewart, *Adoption,* Crestwood House, 1989.

*OTHER*

Under the names Anita Larsen and Anita Gustafson, and under the pseudonym Dana White, contributor of fiction and articles to periodicals, including *Ranger Rick, Minnesota Monthly, Publishers Weekly, Bookfinders,* and *Country Homes.* Author of book review columns in periodicals, including *Des Moines Register and St. Paul Pioneer Press Dispatch.* Author of commercial and technical copy, including scripts for Pillsbury, Massey-Ferguson, 3M, and Fuller Company. Speechwriter for numerous companies. Editor of books for Iowa State University Press, Wallace-Homestead Book Company, Greenhaven Books, and Carolhoda Books. Packager of books series.

## ■ Work in Progress

All under the name Anita Larsen: *Amanda's Angel,* an upper elementary fiction book; *Janssen House, Deadline,* and *Scraps,* adult suspense books; a screenplay titled *The So-What Summer.*

## ■ Sidelights

Anita Larsen told *SATA:* "One way or another, I've always hung out with words. I've taught English and drama to high school and university students, as well as writing to correspondence students. I've done commercial and editorial writing. I've edited books and packaged series of them. I've acted on stage and camera and written all kinds of scripts. I suppose, however, that if I had to pick just one pursuit that I've loved above all others, it would be theater—from publicity to box office to the 'glamour stuff.' Unfortunately, I listened to advice that said theater wasn't a real career. My best advice to aspiring artists of any kind is to not listen to what other people think is real. Instead, I would hope that those who want to act (or write or paint or dance or be a musician) would already know deep down what's real for them—and then have the courage to run their own races.

"All my dogs get books. My dog Moppet, for example, was rescued from beneath an Iowa farmer's machine shed. She was the smallest puppy, and that must have made an impression on her. All her life, she begged piteously and 'buried' bones in carpeted corners so she could find them later if she needed them. She looked and behaved like the trickster Coyote; this inspired my first book. When Moppet died, I framed her photographs and buried her in my midwestern garden so she could hear the cicadas and, every other year, the acorn-rain from the surrounding oaks. She liked that.

"Magnetic Lady Tibor, alias Meg, was a Vizsla who lived with me for many years. A true aristocrat, Meg had a puppy habit of bolting like bad news from nowhere and attacking my feet. 'Why me?' I asked her. No answer. Big grin. 'Why my feet?' No answer. Big kiss. Meg's inordinate interest in my feet inspired my third book. She now sleeps beside the Camino Real where there is a mountain view she especially liked. And wildflowers. She liked flowers, too.

Larsen has written several "History's Mysteries" books, including this one about the baffling disappearance of a sixteenth-century English colony. (Cover illustration by James Watling.)

"Ami, my dog, is still in the juvenile-delinquent phase I am told Chesapeake Bay retrievers go through until they are older than two years. She is a Taos dog, which means that although she is American Kennel Club bred and born, no one has gotten around to getting the paperwork done. And so far, neither have I. That is, I haven't gotten around to writing a book about or for her.

"If I had to pick favorite children's book writers, I would probably settle on Robert Cormier, Gary Paulsen, and Margaret Mahy. The latter, especially, seems wonderfully able to find the magic for so many age levels, which I think is the mark of a 'real' writer. But there are so many other truly wonderful writers working for young people today—and I read so many of them for my book review columns—that it's hard to whittle down to specific names of writers."

## ■ For More Information See

*PERIODICALS*

*Booklist,* August, 1992, p. 2003.
*Horn Book Guide,* fall, 1992, p. 337.

School Library Journal, February, 1989, p. 92; September, 1992, p. 268; October 1992, p. 130.

\*   \*   \*

## LAWRENCE, Louise 1943-

### ■ Personal

Born Elizabeth Rhoda Holden, June 5, 1943, in Leatherhead, Surrey, England; daughter of Fred (a bricklayer) and Rhoda Edith (a cook; maiden name, Cowles) Holden; married second husband, Graham Mace, August 28, 1987; children: Rachel Louise, Ralph Lawrence, Rebecca Jane. *Education:* Educated at Poplar Road Primary School, Leatherhead, 1948-54; Lydney Grammar School, Gloucestershire, 1955-60. *Politics:* "Bewildered by." *Religion:* "Searching for."

### ■ Addresses

*Home*—22 Church Rd., Cinderford, Gloucestershire GL14 2EA, England. *Agent*—A. M. Heath, 79 St. Martin's Lane, London WC2N 4AA, England.

**LOUISE LAWRENCE**

### ■ Career

Assistant librarian, Gloucestershire Country Library, 1961-63, and at Forest of Dean branches, 1969-71; writer, 1971—.

### ■ Writings

*YOUNG ADULT FICTION*

*Andra,* Collins, 1971.
*The Power of Stars: A Story of Suspense,* Harper, 1972.
*The Wyndcliffe: A Story of Suspense,* Collins, 1974, Harper, 1975.
*Sing and Scatter Daisies* (sequel to *The Wyndcliffe*), Harper, 1977.
*Star Lord,* Harper, 1978, Bodley Head, 1987.
*Cat Call,* Harper, 1980.
*The Earth Witch,* Harper, 1981, Collins, 1982.
*Calling B for Butterfly,* Harper, 1982, revised edition, Bodley Head, 1988.
*The Dram Road,* Harper, 1983.
*Children of the Dust,* Harper, 1985.
*Moonwind,* Harper, 1986.
*The Warriors of Taan,* Bodley Head, 1986, Harper, 1988.
*Extinction Is Forever and Other Stories,* HarperCollins, 1990.
*Keeper of the Universe* Clarion Books, 1992, published in England as *Ben-Harran's Castle,* Bodley Head, 1992.

### ■ Sidelights

Louise Lawrence has built a large and loyal following on the strength of her fantasy and science fiction novels. Though often set in the dim past or far-flung future, her stories usually address the same issues and concerns that face people today. In a review of *Star Lord,* a *Junior Bookshelf* critic remarks, "Louise Lawrence does not deal in worn-out cliches. What is more her space fiction is firmly based in the real world." "Her stories are essentially humane," offers another *Junior Bookshelf* contributor in a review of *Extinction Is Forever.* "She shirks none of the technical problems of the genre, but most of all she writes about individuals and their personal dilemmas, whether they are in this world or off-world." Paul Heins, writing in *Horn Book,* concludes that Lawrence so skillfully balances the mundane and the fantastic that "she has made the unbelievable believable."

As a child, the author told the *Sixth Book of Junior Authors & Illustrators,* Lawrence was drawn to storytelling by her grandfather. "He had the power to frighten me witless. He peopled the hills with giants and fairies and mythical beasts, monsters of his own ghoulish imagination. And he fostered mine—taught me of trees and flowers, how to dabble in ponds, where the birds nested, and how to distinguish their songs."

Even so, Lawrence's transformation into a professional author was not an easy one. "What motivated me into writing my first (unpublished) book at the age of twenty-two was fear of mental stagnation," she once commented. "What gave rise to that fear was being married with small children, totally isolated socially and environmentally in a remote farmhouse, with a husband who had no time for me. I didn't choose to become a writer. An idea came to me and I felt compelled to set it down, and in six weeks I had written a very bad book."

Despite the poor quality of her initial work, Lawrence persevered. "I wrote to occupy my mind, as a hobby, as a way of escaping from unhappy reality into worlds of fantasy. I wrote because I was compelled to write ... and it got a hold on me like a drug," she said. Lawrence wrote a total of four "very bad" books before selling *Andra,* her first published work. "I decided to become a professional writer," she continued in *Sixth Book of Junior Authors & Illustrators,* "left my husband, and set out to survive alone."

Set two thousand years in the future, *Andra* tells of a young girl who receives a "brain graft," a donation of frozen tissue taken from a boy who died in the 1980s. Soon after the procedure, young Andra is filled with strange, rebellious thoughts: she sees her society not as a technological Utopia but as a restrictive machine designed to limit individual freedom. Fired by memories of a free society, Andra becomes the leader of a youth movement bent on overturning the rule of the city director. Though several critics found the scientific concepts in *Andra* somewhat implausible, *School Library Journal* contributor Lucinda Snyder Whitehurst described the book as "both hopeful and sorrowful. *Andra* is a fascinating story about the power of one individual following a dream."

Since the 1971 publication of *Andra,* Lawrence has continued to deliver exciting stories often featuring young female protagonists. In 1988's *The Warriors of Taan,* she depicts a planet in which the two genders have been rigidly segregated: the warlike men control their sphere through force and intimidation, while the more cerebral women, known as the Sisterhood, prefer reason and cunning. Both groups, however, must contend with the Earth colonists who have come to claim their planet; the only way to regain Taan is for the two groups to merge, to produce a hero whose might is tempered by feminine wiles. *School Library Journal* critic Pam Spencer calls *The Warriors of Taan* a "'can't-put-down' book" that is "filled with adventure, symbolism, and wonderful writing, from opening sentence to last line."

In 1992's *Keeper of the Universe,* Lawrence pits her young characters against and intimidating opponent: the devil. In the novel, Lucifer is actually Ben-Harran, a member of the intergalactic High Council of Atui that rules the planets. Earth, along with several other planets, falls under the rule of Ben-Harran, who, despite his rather demonic reputation, steadfastly refuses to intervene in the affairs of his planets. Unfortunately, Ben-Harran's hands-off policy leads to the destruction of one planet, Zeeda, and he is brought to trial by the High Council on charges of genocide. Representatives from

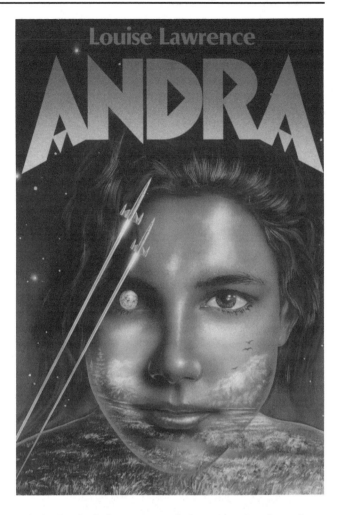

A brain graft from a twentieth-century boy into the brain of a young girl who lives in a strict society of the distant future plants the seeds of rebellion in Lawrence's first novel. (Cover illustration by Anton Kimball.)

his other planets, including Earth, are called in to testify either for or against Ben-Harran. Though a *Kirkus Reviews* writer calls *Keeper of the Universe* "talky, didactic [and] more polemic than science fiction [should be]," many other critics praised the book. It is, according to a *Junior Bookshelf* contributor, "an absorbing and exciting story concerned with problems which have their contemporary counterparts in real life," and a *Publishers Weekly* reviewer finds that the story "succeeds because of its trenchant humor, capped by a deliciously ironic final twist."

"The thing about Louise Lawrence is that, carefully as she works at the science, one suspects that it is the fiction (i.e. the people) which really concerns her," declares one *Junior Bookshelf* critic. "We are riveted to the ground ... watching the protagonists as they work out their destinies.... It demands, and deserves, the reader's total surrender."

As to writing, the author admits in the *Sixth Book of Junior Authors & Illustrators,* "it remains a strange and magical process, and it was never I who chose to write

**When the Outworlders from Earth begin to destroy the delicate balance of life on Taan, can the native warriors defeat the technologically advanced invaders armed only with crossbows and the help of the mysterious Stonewraiths? (Cover illustration by Alix Berenzy.)**

the books but the books that chose me to write them. Each one came to me unasked for, like watching a film being projected onto a screen inside my head ... the whole story from beginning to end compelling me to write it."

## ■ Works Cited

Review of *Ben-Harran's Castle, Junior Bookshelf,* December, 1992, p. 267.

Review of *Extinction Is Forever, Junior Bookshelf,* October, 1990, p. 253.

Heins, Paul, review of *The Earth Witch, Horn Book,* June, 1981, p. 310.

Review of *Keeper of the Universe, Publishers Weekly,* April 26, 1993, p. 80.

Review of *Keeper of the Universe, Kirkus Reviews,* March 15, 1993, p. 373.

Lawrence, Louise, autobiographical essay in *Sixth Book of Junior Authors & Illustrators,* edited by Sally Homes Holtze, H. W. Wilson, 1989.

Spencer, Pam, review of *The Warriors of Taan, School Library Journal,* February, 1988, p. 84.

Review of *Star Lord, Junior Bookshelf,* February, 1988, p. 48.

Whitehurst, Lucinda Snyder, review of *Andra, School Library Journal,* May, 1991, p. 112.

## ■ For More Information See

*BOOKS*

*Twentieth Century Children's Writers,* St. Martin's, 1989.

*PERIODICALS*

*Bulletin of the Center for Children's Books,* December, 1978, p. 65; July, 1980, p. 218.

*Horn Book,* August, 1977, p. 450; December, 1982, p. 659; January, 1986, p. 92.

*Kirkus Reviews,* March 15, 1980, p. 371; March 15, 1991, p. 395.

*Publishers Weekly,* May 30, 1977, p. 45; December 25, 1987, p. 75.

*School Library Journal,* April, 1977, p. 77; August, 1980, p. 77.

*Times Literary Supplement,* April 2, 1971, p. 383; April 28, 1972, p. 484; November 28, 1986, p. 1347.

*Voice of Youth Advocate,* October, 1993, p. 232.

*—Sketch by Brandon Trenz*

\*    \*    \*

**LINDBERGH, Anne**
**See SAPIEYEVSKI, Anne Lindbergh**

# M

**SHEILA MacGILL-CALLAHAN**

## MacGILL-CALLAHAN, Sheila 1926-

### ■ Personal

Born July 20, 1926, in London, England; daughter of Patrick (a writer) and Margaret (a writer; maiden name, Gibbons) MacGill; married Leo P. Callahan (a teacher), 1956; children: Patrick, Mary Messite, Deborah Knowlton, Justin. *Politics:* Socialist-Democrat. *Religion:* Roman Catholic. *Hobbies and other interests:* Neighborhood activist, politics, interior decorating, collecting old toys.

### ■ Addresses

*Home*—401 Beach 47 St., Far Rockaway, NY 11691. *Agent*—Susan Cohen, Writers House Inc., 21 West 26th St., New York, NY 10010.

### ■ Career

CWA-CIO (labor union), New York City, organizer, steward, and educational council chair, 1947-57; Radio Free Europe, New York City, 1958-60; Writer's House Inc., New York City, reader, factotum, 1987-1993. Full-time writer, 1993—. *Member:* Society of Children's Book Writers and Illustrators, Jewish Arts Center, Authors Guild, Authors League of America, Mystery Writers of America, Smithsonian.

### ■ Awards, Honors

Notable book citation, National Council of Social Studies, and Outstanding Science Trade Book designation, National Science Teachers Association, both 1991, both for *And Still the Turtle Watched.*

### ■ Writings

*Death in a Far Country* (fiction), St. Martin's, 1993.

*JUVENILE*

*And Still the Turtle Watched,* illustrated by Barry Moser, Dial, 1991.
*The Children of Lir,* illustrated by Genady Spirin, Dial, 1993.

### ■ Work in Progress

Sequel to *Death in a Far Country;* a children's version of Gilgamesh; and *Children of the Dead End,* an adaptation of a children's book published by Patrick MacGill.

### ■ Sidelights

"I come from a writing family," Sheila MacGill-Callahan told *SATA*. "My father, Patrick MacGill, who died in 1963, was known as 'the Navy Poet.' His two most famous books, *Children of the Dead End* and *The Rat Pit,* are still in print from Caliban Books in London. My mother, Margaret Gibbons MacGill, wrote romance novels of the type that are published today by Harlequin and Silhouette. Unfortunately, they are no longer available.

"My two sisters are both editors, one retired and one active. They each have a hardcover book to their credit. One niece is well known as a regular contributor to Catholic magazines; my daughter Deborah is an aspiring writer as is my son, Justin. One might say that it is in the genes.

"My first love was the ballet. I grew too tall (5'10") so I switched to acting, but I found that my ambition was bigger than my talent. When I stayed at home with the children I tried to write but was not successful. I kept trying off and on without success for the next twenty-five years.

"Finally, when I retired from one of my brainless jobs, I decided to give it one more try. I saw a job advertised in the *New York Times* for a receptionist at a literary agency, Writers House Inc. I applied, was hired, and (after a decent interval) sneaked one of my manuscripts into a pile going to an agent. The rest is my personal history. Dial Books bought *And Still the Turtle Watched.* Then, in quick succession, they contracted for five more books and St. Martin's Press bought my adult mystery, *Death in a Far Country* and gave me a two-book contract because they wanted a sequel. The moral of this story is: IF YOU CAN'T LICK THEM, JOIN THEM!"

\*    \*    \*

## MAGEE, Doug 1947-

### ■ Personal

Born January 24, 1947, in Rome, NY; son of Robert (in sales) and Ruth (a teacher; maiden name, Coe); married Mary Hedahl (an actor), March 17, 1991; children: Timothy Maxwell, Joseph Neilon. *Education:* Amherst College, B.A., 1969; Union Theological Seminary, M.Div., 1973. *Politics:* "Very far to the left." *Religion:* "Hmmm."

### ■ Addresses

*Home*—309 East 108th St., No. 5A, New York, NY 10029. *Office*—1659 Lexington Ave., New York, NY 10029.

### ■ Career

Writer.

**Doug Magee and Robert Newman use photographs of everyday items anyone can see on a train trip to illustrate *All Aboard ABC.***

### ■ Writings

*FOR CHILDREN*

(And photographer) *Trucks You Can Count On,* Dodd, Mead, 1985.
(Author and photographer with Robert Newman) *All Aboard ABC,* Dutton, 1991.
(Author and photographer with Newman) *Let's Fly From A to Z,* Dutton, 1992.

*NONFICTION*

*Slow Coming Dark: Interviews from Death Row,* Pilgrim Press, 1980.
*What Murder Leaves Behind: The Victim's Family,* Dodd, Mead, 1983.

*FOR TELEVISION*

*Somebody Has to Shoot the Picture,* HBO, 1990.
*Conviction: The Kitty Dodds Story,* CBS, 1993.

### ■ For More Information See

*PERIODICALS*

*Booklist,* October 15, 1980, p. 289; April 1, 1985, p. 1121; October 1, 1990, p. 336; October 15, 1992, p. 435.

*Bulletin of the Center for Children's Books,* July-August, 1985; September, 1990, p. 12.
*Choice,* April, 1981, p. 1167.
*Christian Science Monitor,* March 30, 1981, p. 19.
*Library Journal,* October, 1980, p. 2100; June 1, 1983, p. 1152.
*New York Review of Books,* March 5, 1981, p. 6.
*Publishers Weekly,* May 13, 1983, p. 46; September 28, 1990, p. 100.
*School Library Journal,* May, 1985, p. 79; November, 1990, p. 96; November, 1992, p. 85.
*Village Voice,* March 1, 1981, p. 37; August 30, 1983, p. 40.

\*   \*   \*

# MATRANGA, Frances Carfi 1922-

## ■ Personal

Born May 18, 1922, in North Tarrytown, NY; daughter of Joseph (a contractor) and Nellie (maiden name, Corallo) Carfi; married Philip Matranga, Sr. (a driver for Anchor Motors), November 2, 1941; children: Philip, Jr., Paul, Peter, Francine. *Education:* Voice lessons for light opera with Maestro Leon Ardin at Carnegie Hall, New York City, 1941-42. *Politics:* Republican. *Religion:* Christian. *Hobbies and other interests:* "Reading! (And not just fiction. I LOVE to read.)"

**FRANCES CARFI MATRANGA**

## ■ Addresses

*Home and office*—1600 Harmony Dr., Port Charlotte, FL 33952-2703.

## ■ Career

Freelance writer. Co-founder, writers' workshops, Port Charlotte, FL, 1975-83. *Member:* Society of Children's Book Writers and Illustrators.

## ■ Awards, Honors

Runner-up, CBS-TV Scriptwriting Competition, 1959; first prize, New York Writers Guild Fiction Contest, 1960, for "Death Trap"; honorable mention, National Writers Club fiction contest, 1975, for "Fourthborn"; honorable mention, National Writers Club fiction contest, 1976, for "That's My Mama!"; second place for fiction, Evangelical Press Association Convention, 1980, for "The Dare"; also recipient of two prizes and four honor certificates from the annual *Writer's Digest* international competitions.

## ■ Writings

*JUVENILE*

*Follow the Leader,* Concordia, 1982.
*The Perfect Friend,* Concordia, 1985.
*The Contest,* Concordia, 1986.
*One Step at a Time,* Concordia, 1987.

*"NINA CRISTINA MYSTERY" SERIES*

*The Secret behind the Blue Door,* Baker Books, 1981.
*The Mysterious Prowler,* Victor Books, 1984.
*The Forgotten Treasure,* Victor Books, 1986
*The Mystery of the Missing Will,* Victor Books, 1986.
*The Big Top Mystery,* Victor Books, 1987.

*PICTURE BOOKS*

*My Book of Prayers,* illustrated by Vic Mitchell, Standard Publishing, 1985.
*I'm Glad I'm Me,* illustrated by Joanne (Jodi) McCallum, Standard Publishing, 1991.

*ADULT FICTION*

*Land of Shadows,* Manor Books, 1977.
*Summer Magic,* Dell, 1979.
*Destiny in Rome,* Dell, 1979.
*Angel Face,* Barbour Books, 1994.

*Land of Shadows, Summer Magic,* and *Destiny in Rome* have been translated into six different languages.

*OTHER*

Also author/illustrator of two activity books, Standard Publishing, 1983. contributor of stories and poems to anthologies for children. Also contributor to more than three hundred periodicals, including *Mystery Digest, Cricket, Junior Scholastic, Christian Life, Popular Psychology,* and *Woman's World.*

# ■ Work in Progress

"Sammy's Visit to Heaven," an article about a sixteen-year-old's extraordinary spiritual experience; two children's books: *Pixie Dinkerdoo and the Lollipop Kitten* and *Marjorie's Revenge.*

# ■ Sidelights

"Ever since I was little," Frances Carfi Matranga told *SATA,* "I loved hearing stories, and books fascinated me. My mother was a terrific storyteller, and I pestered her constantly. By the time I was eight, I was devouring book after book. I would take out ten books at a time from my hometown Warner Library, using my mother's card as well as my own. How I loved that beautiful library! It became my second home. I would read my borrowed books one after another, and even sat by my bedroom window reading in the moonlight when I was supposed to be sleeping. I wore eyeglasses at the time and ever since, and one day my mom told me I was born with the marks of glasses on my nose. Hmm ... interesting.

"At age fourteen, I spent the summer creating short stories. At fifteen and sixteen, I was writing poetry. Two were published in an anthology. I did some writing for my high school paper, and one of my teachers said I should become a writer. At the time, however, I was more interested in music. I had a lyric soprano voice and solo parts in school musicals, in my church, and for many a bride from different churches who wanted me to sing at her wedding ceremony. I later won a county talent show—three times in a row—and was asked to tour Westchester County. Due to circumstances, I couldn't accept the offer, nor could I tour the United States after appearing on *Ted Mack's Talent Show.* Married at nineteen, I then studied voice at Carnegie Hall in New York City for two years under Maestro Leon Ardin. I sang semi-classical and some opera. My teacher was preparing me to sing in a theater with which he was associated. But after the births of my first two sons, I ended my lessons and stayed home to take care of them. That's when I began freelance writing in earnest, learning as I went along. It took ten years to make my first sale, but I never gave up.

"That first literary acceptance came in 1952, fifteen dollars from *True Story Magazine* for a humorous but embarrassing incident that happened when I was a teenager. I got conked on the nose while singing on stage before an audience. The other performer—a girl dressed as a boy—had a small basket of fruit hanging by its handle on the curved end of the cane held over her shoulder. She misjudged the distance between us as she turned away from me, and *bingo*—my poor nose! With scarlet face, I managed to finish my song.

"I have worked hard as a freelance writer and it has been uphill all the way. You really have to love your work to stick to it, for the money as a freelancer is nothing to brag about and you're alone so much of the time. The good Lord gave me several talents, and although writing and designing greeting cards was more profitable for me, writing fiction suits me best. You don't wear eyeglasses singing on stage, but writers and spectacles go together. Born with the marks of eyeglasses on my nose? Hmm....

"My way of writing is to sit in a comfortable armchair with a clipboard on my lap. I use the backs of rejection letters (I save the personal ones) to do my first draft of a story or book chapter in pencil. I then correct each page as I finish it before continuing on. I'm one of those writers who can't seem to go on to the next page unless I first improve the one I'm working on. When the changes please me, I'm encouraged to start the next page. Some authors will finish the story or chapter or the whole novel before making corrections and that's fine. I just can't seem to work that way. The next day I will again read what I've written and make several more corrections. Then, inevitably, when I keyboard the manuscript onto my computer, a few more changes take place.

"My advice to aspiring writers is to read read read, especially the kind of literature you would like to write, whether fiction or nonfiction. If reading isn't important to you, I doubt you have what it takes to be a writer. But if you enjoy reading and are set on writing, study the monthly *Writer's Digest* and/or *The Writer.* Join a writer's critique group, if possible. Don't get discouraged. Remember, it took me ten years to make my first sale and only because I persevered. Why did I persevere? My whole heart was in it, that's why, and I believed in myself. Don't give up your dream too easily."

\*     \*     \*

# McCULLOCH, Sarah
## See URE, Jean

\*     \*     \*

# McKELVEY, Carole A. 1942-

## ■ Personal

Born October 1, 1942, in Alton, IL; daughter of Francis A. (a printer) and Geraldine (a homemaker) Conner; married George McKelvey (a comedian), May, 1965; children: Ian, Heather, Fawn. *Education:* Foothills College, A.A., 1962; attended San Francisco State College (now University), 1962-64.

## ■ Addresses

*Home and office*—2181 South Cook, Denver, CO 80210. *Agent*—Natasha Kein Literary Agency, Portland, OR 97208-2908.

## ■ Career

Freelance journalist in and around Los Angeles, CA, 1966-73, and in Evergreen, CO, 1976-77; Burbank Daily

Review, Burbank, CA, editor, 1973-74; Canyon Courier, Evergreen, editor, 1977-80, managing editor, 1980; Sentinel Newspapers, Denver, CO, editor, 1980; Rocky Mountain News, Denver, editor, 1980-88, staff writer, 1988-90; freelance writer, 1990—. General manager, *Granby Sky Hi News* and *Kremmling Middle Park Times,* 1980. Wits End Comedy Club, Westminster, CO, owner. Rocky Mountain Women's Institute, University of Denver, associate, 1990—; Attachment Center at Evergreen, member of board of directors. Guest on television and radio programs; lecturer. *Member:* National Federation of Press Women, Women in Communications, Journalism and Women's Symposium (member of board of directors), Colorado Press Association, Colorado Press Women (member of board of directors), Colorado Authors League, Denver Women's Press Club.

## ■ Awards, Honors

Best News Story Award, Valley Press Club, 1974; Sweepstakes Award, Colorado Press Association, 1975, for newswriting; certificate of outstanding leadership, National School Safety Center, 1988; Colorado Press Women Award, 1989, for *High Risk;* five annual awards, National Federation of Press Women.

## ■ Writings

(With Ken Magid) *High Risk: Children without a Conscience,* Bantam, 1988.

Also author, with sister Jo Ellen Stevens, of *Suffer the Little Children: An Examination of the Adoption Process,* Bantam. Contributor of articles to national magazines and newspapers. Newspaper columnist.

## ■ Work in Progress

Research on families, women, and children.

## ■ For More Information See

PERIODICALS

*Los Angeles Times Book Review,* February 21, 1988, p. 13.

\*   \*   \*

## MIKOLAYCAK, Charles 1937-1993

## ■ Personal

Surname is pronounced "*Mike*-o-lay-chak"; born January 26, 1937, in Scranton, PA; died of cancer, June 23, 1993, in Manhattan, NY; son of John Anthony and Helen (Gruscelak) Mikolaycak; married Carole Kismaric (an editor and writer), October 1, 1970. *Education:* Pratt Institute, B.F.A., 1958; attended New York University, 1958-59. *Hobbies and other interests:* Reading, theater, films, travel.

CHARLES MIKOLAYCAK

## ■ Addresses

*Home*—64 East 91st St., New York, NY 10128.

## ■ Career

Free-lance illustrator and designer. DuCrot Studios, Hamburg, Germany, illustrator and designer, 1959; Time-Life Books, New York City, designer, 1963-76; Syracuse University, Syracuse, NY, guest instructor, 1976-88. Work represented in "The Fine Art of Children's Book Illustrations" exhibit at the Port Washington, Long Island, Public Library, 1986, in the Kerlan Collection at the University of Minnesota, the Festival Art Collection at Keene State College, the Mazza Collection at Findlay College, and in a permanent collection at the International Youth Library, Munich, Germany. *Military service:* U.S. Army, 1960-62; became sergeant. *Member:* Society of Children's Book Writers and Illustrators.

## ■ Awards, Honors

American Institute of Graphic Arts Children's Book Show selections, 1967, 1968, 1970, 1973, for *The Feast Day,* 1974, for *Shipwreck,* 1977, 1980, and 1986; Chicago Book Clinic Best of the Year Show selections, 1967, 1971, and 1972; Printing Industries of America Graphic Design Awards, 1967, for *Great Wolf and the Good Woodsman,* 1970, for *Mourka, the Mighty Cat,* 1971, 1972, and 1973; Charles W. Follett Award, 1969, for *Banner over Me;* Society of Illustrators Gold Medal for book art direction, 1970; New Jersey Institute of Technology Award, 1970, for *Russian Tales of Fabulous Beasts and Marvels;* American Institute of Graphic Arts selections for entry in Biennial of Illustrations, Bratislava, 1973, for *How the Hare Told the Truth,* and 1984, for *Peter and the Wolf;* Children's Book Council Children's Book Showcase selection, 1975, for *Shipwreck;*

Many of the stories Mikolaycak has illustrated are legends, folktales, or fairy tales, like this work by Zilpha Keatley Snyder, *The Changing Maze.*

American Library Association (ALA) notable book citations, 1975, for *How Wilka Went to Sea and Other Tales from West of the Urals,* and 1981, for *I Am Joseph;* Brooklyn Museum Art Books for Children citations, 1977, 1978, and 1979, for *Great Wolf and the Good Woodsmen;* New York Graphics award, 1980, for *The Surprising Things Maui Did;* Parents' Choice Award for illustration, 1982, for *Peter and the Wolf,* and 1988, for *The Rumor of Pavel and Paali; New York Times* best illustrated books of 1984 citation, for *Babushka: An Old Russian Folktale; Horn Book* Fanfare list citation, 1984, for *The Highwayman;* Golden Kite Honor Book Award for illustration, 1986, for *Juma and the Magic Jinn;* University of Minnesota Kerlan Award, 1987, in recognition of singular attainments in the creation of children's literature; National Jewish Book Award for illustration, 1988, for *Exodus.*

## ■ Writings

(Reteller with wife, Carole Kismaric, and illustrator) *The Boy Who Tried to Cheat Death* (Norwegian folktale), Doubleday, 1971.

(Reteller and illustrator) *Babushka: An Old Russian Folktale,* Holiday House, 1984.

(Reteller and illustrator) *Orpheus,* Harcourt, 1992.

*ILLUSTRATOR AND/OR DESIGNER OF CHILDREN'S BOOKS*

Helen Hoover, *Great Wolf and the Good Woodsman,* Parents Magazine Press, 1967.

Margery Greenleaf, *Banner over Me,* Follett, 1968.

Jacob and Wilhelm Grimm, *Little Red Riding Hood,* C. R. Gibson, 1968.

J. and W. Grimm, *Grimm's Golden Goose,* Random House, 1969.

Jane Lee Hyndman (under pseudonym Lee Wyndham), *Mourka, the Mighty Cat,* Parents Magazine Press, 1969.

Hyndman (under pseudonym Lee Wyndham), *Russian Tales of Fabulous Beasts and Marvels,* Parents Magazine Press, 1969.

Cynthia King, *In the Morning of Time: The Story of the Norse God Balder,* Four Winds, 1970.

Barbara Rinkoff, *The Pretzel Hero: A Story of Old Vienna,* Parents Magazine Press, 1970.

Eric Sundell, *The Feral Child,* Abelard-Schuman, 1971.

Margaret Hodges, reteller, *The Gorgon's Head: A Myth from the Isles of Greece,* Little, Brown, 1972.

Barbara K. Walker, *How the Hare Told the Truth about His Horse,* Parents Magazine Press, 1972.

Edwin Fadiman, Jr., *The Feast Day,* Little, Brown, 1973.

Vera G. Cumberlege, *Shipwreck,* Follett, 1974.

Mirra Ginsburg, translator and editor, *How Wilka Went to Sea and Other Tales from West of the Urals,* Crown, 1975.

Marion L. Starkey, *The Tall Man from Boston,* Crown, 1975.

Jerzy Ficowsky, *Sister of the Birds and Other Gypsy Tales,* translated from the Polish by Lucia Borski, Abingdon, 1976.

Doris Gates, *A Fair Wind for Troy,* Viking, 1976.

Norma Farber, *Six Impossible Things before Breakfast,* Addison-Wesley, 1977.

Avi, *Captain Grey,* Pantheon, 1977.

Farber, *Three Wanderers from Wapping,* Addison-Wesley, 1978.

Barbara Cohen, *The Binding of Isaac,* Lothrop, 1978.

Ewa Reid and Barbara Reid, *The Cobbler's Reward,* Macmillan, 1978.

Richard Kennedy, *Delta Baby and Two Sea Songs,* Addison-Wesley, 1979.

Jay Williams, *The Surprising Things Maui Did,* Four Winds, 1979.

Elizabeth Winthrop, *Journey to the Bright Kingdom,* Holiday House, 1979.

William H. Armstrong, *The Tale of Tawny and Dingo,* Harper, 1979.

Ginsburg, *The Twelve Clever Brothers and Other Fools,* Lippincott, 1979.

Earlene Long, *Johnny's Egg,* Addison-Wesley, 1980.

Cohen, *I Am Joseph,* Lothrop, 1980.

Anne Pellowski, *The Nine Crying Dolls: A Story from Poland,* Philomel Books/U.S. Committee for UNICEF, 1980.

Loretta Holz, *The Christmas Spider: A Puppet Play from Poland and Other Traditional Games, Crafts, and Activities,* Philomel Books/U.S. Committee for UNICEF, 1980.

Anne Laurin, *Perfect Crane,* Harper, 1981.

Bernard Evslin, *Signs and Wonders: Tales from the Old Testament,* Four Winds, 1981.

Sergei Prokofiev, *Peter and the Wolf,* translated from the Russian by Maria Carlson, Viking, 1982, published with cassette, Live Oak Media, 1987.

Jan Wahl, *Tiger Hunt,* Harcourt, 1982.

Winthrop, *A Child Is Born: The Christmas Story,* Holiday House, 1983.

Alfred Noyes, *The Highwayman,* Lothrop, 1983.

Eve Bunting, *The Man Who Could Call Down Owls,* Macmillan, 1984.

Zilpha K. Snyder, *The Changing Maze,* Macmillan, 1985.

Winthrop, editor, *He Is Risen: The Easter Story,* Holiday House, 1985.

Joy Anderson, *Juma and the Magic Jinn,* Lothrop, 1986.

Jane Yolen, editor, *The Lullaby Songbook,* Harcourt, 1986.

Miriam Chaikin, *Exodus,* Holiday House, 1987.

Carole Kismaric, reteller, *The Rumor of Pavel and Paali: A Ukrainian Folktale,* Harper, 1988.

Kismaric, reteller, *A Gift from Saint Nicholas,* Holiday House, 1988.

Walt Whitman, *Voyages: Poems,* compiled by Lee Bennett Hopkins, Harcourt, 1988.

Yolen, reteller, *Tam Lin: An Old Ballad,* Harcourt, 1990.

Ellin Greene, reteller, *The Legend of the Christmas Rose,* Holiday House, 1990.

Eric A. Kimmel, *Bearhead: A Russian Folktale,* Holiday House, 1991.

Hodges, reteller, *The Hero of Bremen,* Holiday House, 1993.

*PICTURE EDITOR AND/OR DESIGNER*

Ken Dallison, *When Zeppelins Flew,* Time-Life, 1969.

Fred Freeman, *Duel of the Ironclads,* Time-Life, 1969.

Paul Williams, *The Warrior Knights,* Time-Life, 1969.

Carole Kismaric, *On Leadership,* I.B.M., 1974.

Robert Elson, *Prelude to War,* Time-Life, 1976.

Robert Wernick, *Blitzkrieg,* Time-Life, 1976.

Leonard Mosley, *The Battle of Britain,* Time-Life, 1976.

Robert Adams, *Beauty in Photography: Essays in Defense of Traditional Values,* Aperture, 1981.

Adams, *Summer Nights,* Aperture, 1985.

*OTHER*

(Illustrator) Donald Hall, *Old Home Day* (history), Harcourt, 1994.

Also creator of the Constitution Poster Triptych, a three-poster set celebrating the bicentennial of the U.S. Constitution, 1986.

### ■ Sidelights

Award-winning children's illustrator and book designer Charles Mikolaycak recreated his own boyhood and the historical worlds of others in his works. His drawings deal with everything from biblical stories to the recreations of old folktales and vary in composition from brilliant, lushly colored pictures to more somber black-and-white depictions. "I have found the perfect vehicle for myself—the picture book," Mikolaycak once said in the *Fifth Book of Junior Authors and Illustrators.* "I cast

In his retelling of an old Russian folktale, Mikolaycak illustrates Babushka's travels through time and around the world as she searches for the Christ Child.

the roles, dress the performers, design the sets, choose the moment to be illustrated and tell a story in visual terms. What an opportunity!"

Born in Scranton, Pennsylvania, Mikolaycak became and remained an only child after his twin brother died a few months following their birth. He remembered making his first drawing in the fourth grade, after which his interest in illustration increased steadily. By the time he was ten years old, Mikolaycak was drawing more seriously and most, if not all, of his drawings were of movie posters. "Throughout grade school, I drew in my spare time—on the kitchen table with its smooth, cool porcelain surface, on the linoleum floor, on a tablet on the rug in front of the radio," he recalled in an essay for the *Something about the Author Autobiography Series* (*SAAS*). "In the seventh grade I first became aware of drawing as illustration."

Mikolaycak's world opened up even further in high school when he realized that he actually wanted to do something with his drawing ability. Along with taking an art class at school, Mikolaycak's parents also enrolled him in an outside painting class. During these same years, Mikolaycak began accompanying his parents to a nearby summer playhouse, explaining in his *SAAS* essay: "This was a beginning of my love for, and fascination with, the theater." Beginning to think about his future, Mikolaycak noticed a small advertisement for Pratt Institute in the back of the *New York Times Magazine.* He applied and was accepted.

"It was during the years at Pratt I started discovering who I really was and who I was capable of becoming," Mikolaycak remarked in his autobiographical essay. "For the first time in my life I was surrounded by people, friends who had the same interests—not a football player in the crowd." Graduating with a B.F.A. degree, Mikolaycak knew he wanted to illustrate but didn't know for whom or where. This decision was made when he was contacted by Mr. and Mrs. Dudley DuCrot. The couple had a small advertising agency in New Jersey, but wanted to return to Germany, where they had met, and establish a designer's studio. They got Mikolaycak's name from Pratt, and in April of 1960 he sailed for Hamburg. Although the advertising accounts were not very exciting, Mikolaycak planned to stay in Germany for a year before returning to New York to do magazine illustrating. His stay was cut short, though, when he was drafted into the U.S. Army toward the end of the summer.

Returning home, Mikolaycak discovered that the regional quotas were filled, and not wanting to volunteer, he moved into an apartment in Brooklyn and began illustrating for such teen magazines as *Seventeen, Calling All Girls,* and *Datebook.* The army then decided that they did need Mikolaycak, and following basic training he was assigned to the graphics department in the Pentagon. After being discharged in 1962, he spent a summer at home in Pennsylvania before moving back to Brooklyn and beginning his career as an illustrator. Mikolaycak spent many hours dropping off portfolios before receiving calls from Elizabeth Armstrong, who wanted to be his agent, and from Edward Hamilton, who offered him a job as an assistant to the designer at Time-Life Books. So Mikolaycak began spending his days at Time-Life, using his nights and weekends to do the illustration jobs that Armstrong got for him. After doing his first children's book, *Great Wolf and the Good Woodsman,* Mikolaycak was hooked, and when Time-Life decided to relocate, he chose to become a full-time illustrator.

"I am an illustrator because I must illustrate, and I am a book designer because I love books," Mikolaycak once told *SATA.* "Obviously the field in which the two meet is the one which makes me most happy—children's books. I can usually find something in most stories which makes me excited; be it a locale or period of time requiring great research, or a sense of fantasy which permits me to exercise my own fantasies pictorially, or great writing which forces me to try to match it in visual images." Although most of Mikolaycak's work consists of illustrations for other authors' works, he has written a few of his own books. His 1984 retelling of *Babushka: An Old Russian Folktale* details the story of a peasant woman who was too busy cleaning her house to accompany the three kings as they followed the star. She later repented and spent the rest of her life searching for baby Jesus, leaving gifts for children as she went along. Mikolaycak "has captured the haunting, ethereal qualities of *Babushka,*" asserted Lisa Lane in a *Christian Science Monitor* review. And Jean F. Mercier, writing in *Publishers Weekly,* concluded that "Mikolaycak's adaptation stands out as an astonishingly original feat."

"I am particularly fond of epics and folk tales," Mikolaycak once remarked. "I don't care how many times they have been illustrated before; the challenge is to find the truth for myself and depict it. When I illustrate I am aware of many things; storytelling, graphic design, sequence of images and my own interests in which I can indulge. I never 'draw-down' to a projected audience. I feel children are most surprisingly capable of meeting a challenge and instinctively understand a drawing. Perhaps it will lead them to ask a question or wonder in silence—either will help them to learn or to extend themselves. I have experienced that if I am satisfied with one of my books, both children and adults will often get from it more than I ever realized I was putting into it."

## ■ Works Cited

Lane, Lisa, "Christmas Roundup of Books for Young Children," *Christian Science Monitor,* December 7, 1984, p. B6.

Mercier, Jean F., review of *Babushka, Publishers Weekly,* December 14, 1984, p. 54.

Mikolaycak, Charles, essay in *Fifth Book of Junior Authors and Illustrators,* edited by Sally Holmes Holtze, H. W. Wilson, 1983, pp. 216-217.

Mikolaycak, Charles, essay in *Something about the Author Autobiography Series,* Volume 4, Gale, 1987.

## ■ For More Information See

*BOOKS*

Freedman, Russell, *Holiday House, The First 50 Years,* Holiday House, 1985, pp. 96-97.

Roginski, Jim, *Behind the Covers,* Libraries Unlimited, 1985, pp. 138-53.

*PERIODICALS*

*Horn Book,* November, 1983; March-April, 1986, pp. 167-73.

*Language Arts,* October, 1981, pp. 850-57.

*Library Journal,* November 15, 1971, p. 3902.

*New Advocate,* spring, 1990, pp. 111-15.

*New York Times Book Review,* February 19, 1984; November 4, 1984, p. 22; September 25, 1988, p. 51; March 26, 1989; December 9, 1990, p. 30.

*Publishers Weekly,* September 27, 1971, p. 66.

*School Library Journal,* April, 1988, pp. 73-74.

*Washington Post Book World,* November 7, 1971, p. 4.

*Wilson Library Bulletin,* February, 1989, pp. 82-83.

*OBITUARIES:*

*PERIODICALS*

*Chicago Tribune,* June 27, 1993, Section 2, p. 6.

*New York Times,* June 25, 1993, p. B7.*

\* \* \*

## MILES, Betty 1928-

## ■ Personal

Born May 16, 1928, in Chicago, IL; daughter of David D. (an editor) and Helen (an editor; maiden name, Otte)

**BETTY MILES**

Baker; married Matthew B. Miles (a social psychologist), September 27, 1949; children: Sara, David Baker, Ellen. *Education:* Antioch College, B.A., 1950.

## ■ Addresses

*Home*—94 Sparkill Ave., Tappan, NY 10983.

## ■ Career

New Lincoln School, Manhattan, New York, began as secretary, became assistant kindergarten teacher, 1950-51; Bank Street College of Education, New York City, publications associate, 1958-1965; instructor in children's language and literature 1971—. Freelance writer, 1965—. Consultant to Random House Beginner Books, National Coordinating Council on Drug Education, and the Children's Television Workshop (*Sesame Street*). *Member:* Authors Guild, Authors League of America, PEN.

## ■ Awards, Honors

Distinguished Achievement Award, Educational Press Association, 1973; Child Association Book of the Year and Outstanding Science Books for Children Award, both 1974, both for *Save the Earth: An Ecology Handbook for Kids;* Child Association Book of the Year, 1974, for *The Real Me;* Mark Twain Award, 1984, and Georgia Children's Book Award, 1986, both for *The Secret Life of the Underwear Champ.*

## ■ Writings

### PICTURE BOOKS

*A House for Everyone,* illustrated by Jo Lowrey, Knopf, 1958.

*What is the World?,* illustrated by Remy Charlip, Knopf, 1958.
*The Cooking Book,* illustrated by Lowrey, Knopf, 1959.
*Having a Friend,* illustrated by Eric Blegvad, Knopf, 1959.
*A Day of Summer,* illustrated by Charlip, Knopf, 1960.
*A Day of Winter,* illustrated by Charlip, Knopf, 1961.
*Mr. Turtle's Mystery,* illustrated by Margot Tomes, Knopf, 1961.
*The Feast on Sullivan Street,* illustrated by Kurt Werth, Knopf, 1963.
(With Joan Blos) *Joe Finds a Way,* illustrated by Lee Ames, Singer, 1967.
*A Day of Autumn,* illustrated by Marjorie Auerbach, Knopf, 1967.
*A Day of Spring,* illustrated by Auerbach, Knopf, 1970.
(With Blos) *Just Think,* illustrated by Pat Grant Porter, Knopf, 1971.
*Around and Around—Love,* Knopf, 1975.
*How to Read,* illustrated by Sylvie Wickstrom, Knopf, 1994.

### FICTION FOR YOUNG PEOPLE

*The Real Me,* Knopf, 1974.
*All It Takes Is Practice,* Knopf, 1976.
*Just the Beginning,* Knopf, 1976.
*Looking On,* Knopf, 1978.
*The Trouble with Thirteen,* Knopf, 1979.
*Maudie and Me and the Dirty Book,* Knopf, 1980.
*The Secret Life of the Underwear Champ,* Knopf, 1981.
*I Would If I Could,* Knopf, 1982.
*Sink or Swim,* Knopf, 1986.

### OTHER

*Save the Earth: An Ecology Handbook for Kids,* Knopf, 1974, new revised edition published as *Save the Earth: An Action Handbook for Kids,* 1991.

Also editor and author of film and television scripts and pamphlets, such as *Super Me,* written for the National Coordinating Council on Drug Education in 1975, and *Little Miss Muppet Fights Back,* Feminists on Children's Media. Contributor of articles to numerous magazines; contributor of story to *Free to Be You and Me,* McGraw-Hill, 1974. Associate editor of *The Bank Street Readers,* Macmillan, 1965-69.

## ■ Sidelights

"I always hope, when my ideas have become a book, that my readers will enjoy sharing experiences and feelings with my characters—and with me," Betty Miles once commented. Miles has provided her readers with a wide range of experiences through her books, which include fiction and nonfiction for various ages. Miles's work touches on topics of current interest, such as ecology, censorship, and discrimination, as well as subjects of perennial interest for young people: growing pains, social adjustment, personal responsibility, and self-worth. "I always hope that what I write will be useful to children," the author wrote in her *Something about the Author Autobiography Series* (*SAAS*) entry. "I

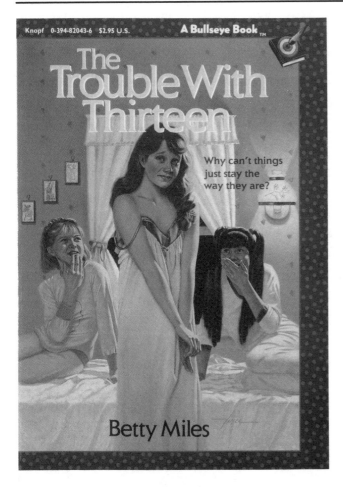

Knopf  0-394-82043-6  $2.95 U.S.  **A Bullseye Book**™

**The Trouble With Thirteen**

Why can't things just stay the way they are?

Betty Miles

**In one of her more didactic books, Miles tells how
Annie must learn to deal with the problems of growing
up before her friends all leave her behind.** (Cover
illustration by Vince Natale.)

hope that reading will help them, as it has helped me, to
find what all of us are searching for, which is ourselves."

Stories played an important role in the author's childhood. Even before she learned to read, Miles enjoyed
listening to the tales and poems her parents recited and
read to her: "Just the sound of the words pleased me,"
she remarked. Her missionary parents' home was filled
with books—Bible stories, A. A. Milne's "Pooh" books,
and Beatrix Potter's tales of Peter Rabbit. Her mother
read to her and often took her to the library to choose
her own books. "But learning to read for myself, at five,
was most exciting of all," Miles related in *SAAS*. "*What
I read has long since vanished from my memory, but I
can still remember the feel of my first soft, thin primer
and see, in my mind's eye, its bright blue cover and the
orange and blue pictures inside.*" Later, Miles spent
summers reading through the generations of children's
books in her grandmother's bookcase.

### From Baghdad to First Book

Nevertheless, Miles's childhood had some lonely moments. She was raised in Baghdad, Iraq, where her
parents served as missionaries, and the family returned
to the United States when Miles was six. The move,

while exciting, was a big adjustment, she recalled: "The
sudden, hearty American strangeness of small-town
Ohio to a shy, only child with an English accent, golden
curls, and a total innocence of American ways remains
sharp in my memory." She was switched from a first
grade to a second grade class when she started school,
and being left-handed also marked her as different. "In
a humiliating reversal, I was demoted back to the first
class ... when it was discovered that I could not really
write at all," Miles noted in her *SAAS* entry. For an hour
each day she was retrained with the first graders to write
with her right hand.

Miles soon adjusted, however, and excelled as a student.
She wrote her first poems in elementary school, and she
was amazed when something she had written impressed
her teacher. She also loved to read poetry. A favorite
book was Louis Untermeyer's anthology *The Singing
World,* in which she especially liked the humorous
verses of Lewis Carroll and Edward Lear. Later, she
enjoyed James Thurber, P. G. Wodehouse, and other
writers whose funny tales provided relief from the
tensions of adolescence. In high school, she pursued
writing by working on the school newspaper. As she
related in *SAAS,* "This was the closest I ever came, in
school, to real vocational education. I loved the craft
and the pressure and the collegiality of work on the
*Echo.*" A year as coeditor of the paper led to an interest
in journalism, and later at Antioch College she edited
the school paper and worked on a small town newspaper.

Married during her last year of college, Miles supported
her husband as he studied for a graduate degree in
education. Her first job was at Manhattan's New
Lincoln School, a progressive private school where she
moved from office secretary to teacher's assistant in the
kindergarten. The teacher she worked for read aloud to
the children daily, and she encouraged Miles to share
the task. Searching out suitable books for her students
led her to begin writing her own, so Miles enrolled at
Bank Street College of Education, where years later she
would teach a similar course herself. At Bank Street, she
joined the Writers' Laboratory, a group of children's
book authors who critiqued each others' manuscripts
and provided support and encouragement.

During this period, Miles took time off from work to
raise a family, which gave her another perspective on
children's books. "Matt and I read to them for endless
hours—the rhythms of Farmer Small and Little Bear
and so many others still resonate in my memory—and I
learned about picture books from the real experts in
children's literature," the author recalled in *SAAS.* She
continued working on her own manuscripts and collected three years' worth of rejection slips before her first
book, *A House for Everyone,* was accepted by Knopf,
which has been her publisher ever since.

That book, which explains how different kinds of
families live together, shows what Miles calls her
"didactic streak." "I think young readers deserve to
have their questions taken seriously in books," she

commented in her autobiographical essay. Thus, a much later novel, *The Trouble with Thirteen,* deals with the growing pains of twelve-year-old Annie, whose parents are separating. As Annie must deal with her upcoming move and separation from her best friend Rachel, as well as the death of her pet dog, she learns to accept the troubles life brings. Calling the book "fresh, funny, [and] tightly crafted," *Christian Science Monitor* reviewer Christine McDonnell notes that Miles "has written a convincing, satisfying story of friendship and puberty." M. B. Nickerson similarly comments that Annie and Rachel "are distinct, fully drawn characters" who make the plot "balanced and believable .... The book is a winner."

## Addressing Real-Life Issues in Fiction

Dealing with ordinary problems such as Annie and Rachel experience is a central concern of Miles's work, along with young peoples' concern with fairness and social justice. As an editor of the Bank Street Readers, she helped to create one of the first multicultural primer series in the United States. Later, with the group Feminists on Children's Media, she pressed for fairer representation of girls and women in children's literature at a time when most standard texts showed boys in active, positive roles and girls in silent, supportive positions.

But while Miles was working to change portrayals of girls in reading material for children, stereotypes of women persisted in real life. She recalled in *SAAS,* "Women who wanted to change things were damned as strident and unnatural and ridiculed in flippant jokes." Tired of having requests for fairness characterized as "radical," Miles was inspired to write her first novel for young readers, *The Real Me.* In the book, Barbara Fisher is an ordinary middle-schooler who becomes involved in women's liberation issues when she questions why girls are denied paper routes and aren't allowed to take tennis for their physical education class.

Barbara's story, and her eventual triumph, is told in "a breezy, pert, first-person chronicle" that is "fast-paced and funny," according to a *Horn Book* contributor. A *Publishers Weekly* reviewer similarly comments that *The Real Me* is a "low-keyed, attractively paced ... uncontrived picture" of a "believable" heroine. Readers also find Barbara's achievements inspiring; as Miles related in *SAAS,* "from the letters I got and still get about that book, it is clear that it does provide support and reassurance to many young readers. I feel good about that."

Miles has touched on other real-life issues in her books. *All It Takes Is Practice* deals with racial discrimination in its story of an interracial family that moves into a white, middle-class neighborhood. Kate Harris of *Maudie and Me and the Dirty Book* faces censorship when she reads a book about a puppy's birth to a first grade class. Miles's 1974 nonfiction work *Save the Earth: An Ecology Handbook for Kids* was one of the first books for kids on helping the environment. "I wanted to show ...

how knowledge, forward planning and hard work can lead to useful solutions," she once wrote. In 1991, she published a more comprehensive update, *Save the Earth, an Action Handbook for Kids,* which includes a report on significant environmental projects carried out by young people.

Miles writes out of her own experience and passion, but she finds that writing changes the very things she writes about. *I Would If I Could,* the story of a girl who doesn't know how to ride a bike, began as a reminiscence from Miles's own childhood. "I remember—I could never forget—how awful I felt to be ten years old and unable to ride a bike," the author recalled in *SAAS.* But when she began to set down her memories of that time in her life, she discovered "that memory doesn't make good fiction: it is selective, unreliable, fragmentary and, often, unbelievable. Right away, I found I had to jog mine" by conducting research. The experience taught her, as she told *SATA,* that "fiction is always a mix of reality and imagination."

"In the end," Miles concluded in *SAAS,* "I write about things I care about—like friendship, and the complicated love of people living together in families. Like the pressures children feel to grow up fast, and the losses they face as they grow .... Like the ordinary goodness of people, so common and so often unremarked, which

*Save the Earth: An Ecology Handbook for Kids,* was one of the first ecology books written for a young audience. (Illustrations by Claire A. Nivola.)

Censorship is the issue first-grade student Kate Harris must face when the picture book she reads in class is condemned by some adults as being "smut." (Cover illustration by Patricia Henderson Lincoln.)

is the theme of *Sink or Swim*. And like the lifelong process of changing and growing."

## ■ Works Cited

McDonnell, Christine, review of *The Trouble with Thirteen*, *Christian Science Monitor*, October 15, 1979, p. B2.

Miles, Betty, essay published in *Something about the Author Autobiography Series*, Volume 9, Gale, 1990.

Nickerson, M. B., review of *The Trouble with Thirteen*, *School Library Journal*, October, 1979, p. 153.

Review of *The Real Me*, *Horn Book*, April, 1975, p. 150.

Review of *The Real Me*, *Publishers Weekly*, October 28, 1974, p. 49.

## ■ For More Information See

*PERIODICALS*

*Bulletin of the Center for Children's Books*, January, 1975, p. 83; February, 1977, p. 95; February, 1980, p. 113; June, 1980, p. 197; April, 1986, p. 154.

*Horn Book*, June, 1980, p. 300; June, 1982, p. 290.

*New York Times Book Review*, April 21, 1974, p. 8; July 27, 1980, p. 22.

*School Library Journal*, April, 1976, p. 76; December, 1976, p. 70; May, 1980, p. 69; April, 1982, p. 73; March, 1986, p. 168.

\*    \*    \*

## MINOR, Wendell G. 1944-

## ■ Personal

Born March 17, 1944, in Aurora, IL; son of Gordon and Marjorie (a nursery school director; maiden name, Sebby) Minor; married Florence Friedmann (a studio coordinator for Wendell Minor design), October 14, 1978. *Education:* Graduated from Ringling School of Art and Design, 1966; attended Kansas City Art Institute, 1967, and Art Students League, New York City, 1975-76. *Hobbies and other interests:* Wildlife photography, bird watching.

## ■ Addresses

*Home and office*—15 Old North Rd., P.O. Box 1135, Washington, CT 06793.

**WENDELL G. MINOR**

# ■ Career

Hallmark Cards, Kansas City, MO, 1966-67; illustrator with Paul Bacon, New York City, 1968-70; freelance illustrator, 1970—. Lecturer on the environment and other topics at colleges and universities. *Exhibitions:* Exhibitor in one man shows, "Wendell Minor!!15 Years of Cover Art" at the Society of Illustrators' Museum of American Illustration; "The Book and Editorial Art of Wendell Minor" at the University of North Florida, Jacksonville; "Twenty-five Works by Wendell Minor" at the Ringling School of Art and Design; "An American Perspective" at the Society of Illustrators' Museum of American Illustration; and at the Elizabeth Stone Gallery, Birmingham, MI. Works are held in permanent collections at the Muskegon Museum of Art, at Illinois State Museum, in Findlay University's Mazza Collection, at the Museum of American Illustration, by NASA, the U.S. Air Force, the Library of Congress, the U.S. Coast Guard, and the USO, and in the private collections of authors David McCullough, Toni Morrison, Carl Bernstein, Mary Higgins Clark, Anton Myrer, Steve Tesich, Pat Conroy, Donald Harington, Michael Korda, Paul Theroux, and Marc Norman, among others. *Member:* Society of Illustrators (member of board of directors, 1982-91; president, 1989-91), National Wildlife Federation, Audubon Society, Humane Society of the United States, American Society for the Prevention of Cruelty to Animals.

# ■ Awards, Honors

Award from the California Library Association, 1992, for *Sierra;* John and Patricia Beatty Award; silver medals from the Society of Illustrators and the New York Art Directors Club.

# ■ Illustrator

*CHILDREN'S BOOKS, EXCEPT WHERE INDICATED*

Diane Siebert, *Mojave,* HarperCollins, 1988.
Siebert, *Heartland,* HarperCollins 1989.
Siebert, *Sierra,* HarperCollins, 1991.
Charlotte Zolotow, *The Seashore Book,* HarperCollins, 1992.
Jean Craighead George, *The Moon of the Owls,* HarperCollins, 1993.
Eve Bunting, *Red Fox Running,* Clarion Books, 1993.
George, *Everglades,* HarperCollins, 1994.

Also illustrator of *Julie's Choice* by Jean Craighead George, in press; illustrator of covers of adult books, including *Sula,* Knopf; *The Prince of Tides,* Houghton; *Mexico,* Random House; *The Last Convertible,* Putnam; and *House,* Houghton.

# ■ Sidelights

According to Margaret Miner in *Voices,* Wendell G. Minor is "an artist publishers turn to when they need a jacket for an important book, such as David McCullough's biography of [President Harry S] Truman and Fannie Flagg's *Fried Green Tomatoes.*" Minor has designed stamps for the U.S. Postal Service (including North Dakota's Centennial stamp) and was chosen as one of a six-member team commissioned by NASA to record, in pictures, the space shuttle *Discovery*'s return to flight. His one-man exhibits have been shown at museums, and he has earned more than two-hundred awards for his work.

Minor was born in Aurora, Illinois, in 1944. By the time he was nine years old, he was taking art classes and began to realize his talent. As he told Ann W. Davis in the *Kane County Chronicle,* "In the fifth grade, I remember Mrs. (Elroya) Brown would get after me for scribbling and sketching on the edges of my test papers." Minor cultivated his talent throughout his secondary school years, working as the art director of the school newspaper, and serving as editor in chief of his high school yearbook. After graduation, Minor attended the Ringling School of Art and Design in Sarasota, Florida.

While at college, Minor was recruited by Hallmark Cards and trained in a special program. During the year-and-a-half he spent with Hallmark, he attended classes at the Kansas City Art Institute. After a short time spent back in Aurora working for a design firm, Minor decided to move to New York City to begin his career in 1968. After just two weeks, he found a job with artist Paul Bacon. Working for Bacon allowed him to make the transition to working on his own in 1970. Since that time, Minor estimates that he has designed more than one thousand book jackets.

Minor is committed to helping children learn about the environment by illustrating many books on environmental subjects. He said in *Voices,* "I think we have to talk about bonding children to nature. When we lived in an agrarian society, we did it naturally. Now we have to teach it." His commitment to environmentalism is especially apparent in the three books he has illustrated for author Diane Siebert: *Mojave, Sierra,* and *Heartland.* Minor makes a point of constructing some scenes based on the perspectives of animals. Such detail necessitates thorough research; Minor made special trips to understand these places, or worked from memory and his own photographs. Minor explained to Davis: "My love of nature, history, etc. is funneled through these visuals. I want to synthesize this information into something for the next generation." He conducted careful yet enjoyable research for *Everglades,* another nature book for children written by Jean Craighead George. The illustrations for this book are especially important to Minor because, as he told Davis, the book is "a perfect way to teach the food chain to children."

Minor fulfills his commitment to environmentalism in many other ways. He is a member of several environmental organizations and frequently lectures at colleges and universities about environmental themes. And as president of the Society of Illustrators, Minor organized an exhibition entitled, "Art for Survival: The Illustrator and the Environment."

Many of Minor's illustrations for children's books reflect his love of nature, as in *The Moon of the Owls,* written by Jean Craighead George.

## ■ Works Cited

Davis, Ann W., "Artist Draws on His Life Experience," *Kane County Chronicle,* August 12, 1992.

Miner, Margaret, "Introducing Nature, Art," *Voices,* August 26, 1992, p. 42.

## ■ For More Information See

*BOOKS*

*The Very Best of Children's Book Illustration,* North Light Books, 1993.

*PERIODICALS*

*Boston Phoenix,* November 15, 1983, Section 3, pp. 2, 10.

\*　　\*　　\*

## MURROW, Liza Ketchum 1946-

## ■ Personal

Born June 17, 1946, in Albany, NY; daughter of Richard M. (a writer and historian) and Barbara (a sheep farmer and conservationist; maiden name, Bray) Ketchum; children: Derek, Ethan. *Education:* Sarah Lawrence College, B.A., 1968; Antioch Graduate School

of Education, M.Ed., 1971. *Hobbies and other interests:* Hiking, skiing, wilderness activities, studying Italian and other foreign languages.

## ■ Addresses

*Home and office*—74 South Main St., No. 2, Brattleboro, VT *Agent*—Gail Hochman, Brandt & Brandt, 1501 Broadway, New York, NY 10036.

## ■ Career

Teacher and writer. Meetinghouse School, Marlboro, VT, founder and director, 1973-78; participant in the Vermont Council of the Arts Artist in Education Program, 1988-91; adjunct faculty member at Antioch Graduate School and University of Vermont; leader of writing workshops; consultant. Brattleboro AIDS Project, volunteer and buddy. *Member:* Authors Guild, Authors League of America, Society for Children's Book Writers and Illustrators, Teachers and Writers Collaborative, Vermont Nature Conservancy.

## ■ Awards, Honors

Virginia Jefferson Cup Honor Book, Virginia Library Association, 1988, for *West against the Wind;* best young adult novel for 1990, American Library Association, and Mark Twain Award list for 1991-92, both for *Fire in the Heart;* Mark Twain Award list and Sequoyah Award list, both 1993-94, both for *The Ghost of Lost Island;* Junior Literary Guild selection and Children's Choice Book, both for *Good-Bye, Sammy.*

LIZA KETCHUM MURROW

# ■ Writings

*YOUNG ADULT NOVELS*

*West against the Wind,* Holiday House, 1987.
*Fire in the Heart* (companion book to *West against the Wind*), Holiday House, 1989.
*Twelve Days in August* (sequel to *Fire in the Heart*), Holiday House, 1993.

*"WOMEN SCIENTISTS" SERIES*

*Lolly Cochran, Veterinarian,* The Teachers' Laboratory (Brattleboro, VT), 1989.
*Susan Humphris, Geologist,* The Teachers' Laboratory, 1989.

*OTHER*

(With Casey Murrow) *Children Come First: The Inspired Work of English Primary Schools,* American Heritage Press, 1971.
*Good-Bye, Sammy* (picture book), illustrated by Gail Owens, Holiday House, 1989.
*Dancing on the Table,* illustrated by Ron Himler, Holiday House, 1990.
*The Ghost of Lost Island,* Holiday House, 1991.
*Allergic to My Family,* Holiday House, 1992.

Contributor of articles to periodicals, including *Society of Children's Book Writers and Illustrators Bulletin, Country Journal, New England Gardener,* and *Teachers and Writers.* Poetry published in *Poems in a Time of War,* an anthology published in Brattleboro, VT, in 1991.

# ■ Work in Progress

An adult novel about the relationship between art and science; *The Power of Dreams* (working title), a children's book about Vaudeville set in 1913.

# ■ Sidelights

"I started writing in second grade," Liza Ketchum Murrow told *SATA,* "creating tiny, palm-sized books about a girl who escaped all her troubles by riding off on the back of a fleet-footed white stallion. I wrote these books under the covers at night, with a flashlight, when my parents thought I had gone to sleep. I was lucky to have parents who encouraged my creative endeavors; my mother was a dancer and very involved in the arts, my father a writer and historian. Books and stories and music were always a part of our household, and my parents entered into the imaginary world my brother and I created with our stuffed animals, pretending, with us, that these were real characters, each with a different voice and distinctive personality.

"I spent every summer in Vermont with my grandmother. When I wasn't exploring the woods, swimming in the stream, or reading in my tree house, I put on plays with my dramatic older cousins, or played all kinds of games with my friend Sally; we dressed in my grandmother's old party gowns and created a string of imaginary, outlandish characters who lived under a weeping elm

tree near the brook. For years I thought I might be an actress; I used to hang out at the local summer theater, got involved with dramatic productions in high school, and spent a summer at the Neighborhood Playhouse in New York. This early involvement with drama, though short-lived, was excellent training for developing characters in fiction.

"After college I began teaching, studied and wrote about education in England, and founded a school in Vermont. During those years, the inner creative lives of children became very important to me. I listened with amazement to the poems, songs, and stories that poured from children's hearts. My own children were born and delighted me with their ability to paint, draw, and build. While I was teaching full time, I tried to write on the side, but was unable to produce more than a few magazine articles. A friend, knowing of my secret desire to create novels, asked, 'If you like kids so much, why haven't you written a book for them?' This was the spark that began my first young adult novel, *West against the Wind.*

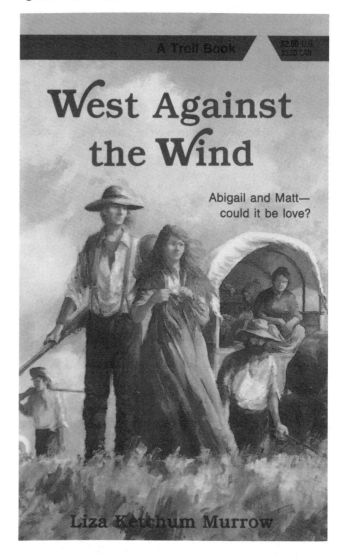

In Murrow's debut novel, a girl traveling to California in the 1800s becomes interested in a mysterious young man who joins her family on their difficult trip.

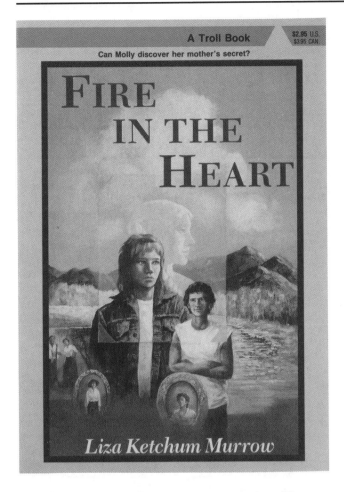

A Troll Book
$2.95 U.S.
$3.95 CAN.

Can Molly discover her mother's secret?

FIRE IN THE HEART

Liza Ketchum Murrow

**In this young adult novel by Murrow, an unusual letter starts Molly on a search for the reasons behind her mother's death, leading her to discover some interesting facts about her ancestors.**

"Many of the interests and issues that were important to me as a child have found their way into my books. My love for my grandparents led to the creation of many older characters, who appear as guides, mentors, or companions for my younger characters. My love for music creeps into many of my books, as does my passion for equality and fairness, my strong feelings about prejudice, my belief that every child deserves a chance to follow her own dream, to pursue the talents she brings to the world.

## Local Soccer Team Inspires Book

"When I start a story, the ideas may come from my own experiences, from those of my sons, or from students I know. My most recent book, *Twelve Days in August,* is about homophobia. The novel began when I watched a local group of kids on a soccer team tease and bait a fellow teammate because they thought he was gay. Their coach ignored the teasing, and when the boy—a talented player—left the team, I thought: What if things had worked out differently? Those two words—'What If?'—stimulate many of my stories. Although the germ of a book may lie in an experience that's familiar to me, once the characters begin to develop, they take the story into

their own hands and the outcome of the book is often a surprise.

"I also enjoy traveling, and feel at home exploring cities and small towns as well as wilderness areas. Whenever I visit a new place, I take photographs, read the local newspaper, and talk to local people, jotting down details in my journal, because sometimes a story evolves from one of these trips. Thus a spooky island off the Maine coast became the setting for *The Ghost of Lost Island.* Watching a fire devour houses and chaparral in southern California caused me to place a fictional heroine, Rosie Maxwell, on the roof of her family's home during a brush fire in *Allergic to My Family.* Recently, driving through Leadville, Colorado, I discovered an opera house perfectly preserved since the turn of the century. I spent a long afternoon there, imagining the empty seats filled with an expectant audience and poking around in the musty dressing rooms. My most recent novel, *The Power of Dreams,* ends with Teresa LeClair, the young heroine, belting out a song from that elegant Colorado stage."

Murrow's first novel for young adults, *West against the Wind,* tells the story of Abigail and her family's trek across the country to California in 1850. Murrow describes the dangers and monotony of the trip through Abigail's eyes. As she approaches womanhood, she hopes for another kind of life in California, where she can "be herself, for the very first time." Reviewers praised the depth of characterization, the swiftly-moving plot, and the insights gained by viewing the difficult journey through the eyes of a young girl.

At the center of Murrow's next novel for young adults, *Fire in the Heart,* is a mystery that leads fourteen-year-old Molly O'Connor to discover the connection between her mother's death ten years ago and her ancestors, including Abby from *West against the Wind.* Molly sifts through family photos, listens to family stories, and reads old letters, discovering unknown aspects of the woman who was her mother, and clues which may lead her to the nugget of gold buried by Abigail Parker in California, which her mother was seeking when she was killed in an accident. Reviewing *Fire in the Heart* for *Children's Book Review Service,* Ann Kalkhoff praised Murrow's "sensitivity to the fears and doubts of youth."

Murrow has also written several books for younger children, beginning with *Good-Bye, Sammy,* a picture book based on an event in the life of the author's son, Ethan. In a story that, according to a *Kirkus Reviews* critic, "provides a good model for dealing with trouble, large or small," *Good-Bye, Sammy* tells of a boy who accidentally leaves his treasured stuffed rabbit on an airplane, but, with the help of his sympathetic parents, becomes resigned to the loss. Writing in *Booklist,* Ilene Cooper remarked: "Murrow does a fine job of tracing the stages of grief" that the little boy goes through. Other reviews noted that the ending, in which the little boy accepts a new toy to replace Sammy, will be reassuring to the book's audience.

### Exploring Family Relationships

For slightly older children, Murrow has written *Dancing on the Table,* which highlights the friendship between Jenny, who is eight, and her grandmother Nana. Jenny and Nana spend special times together at Nana's house in Maine until the older woman announces that she is moving to New York to get married. Jenny tries to use a magic rabbit's foot to prevent her grandmother's wedding, but even Hurricane Wanda won't stop Nana from going on her honeymoon, and Jenny must save the day she had hoped to ruin.

For the same age group, Murrow published *Allergic to My Family,* which tells of another disgruntled young girl whose high spirits get her both into and out of trouble. Nine-year-old Rosie is unhappy because no one in her large family pays any attention to her, and when her parents announce that another child is on the way, Rosie is about to give up hope of ever having her talents recognized. In a review in *Booklist,* Chris Sherman remarked: "Rosie is a spirited and funny heroine, and her antics are completely believable." *School Library Journal* contributor Alexandra Marris noted: "Despite all of the chaos, Rosie's love for her family runs deeply and shines brightly." *Allergic to My Family* also garnered praise for its humorous depiction of realistic family relationships, and for its satisfying conclusion, in which Rosie finally gets a chance to prove herself to her family. A *Publishers Weekly* critic concluded, "Murrow adroitly conveys the joys and frustrations of being a member of a large household."

With *The Ghost of Lost Island* Murrow returns to the mystery genre in a story about twelve-year-old Gabe, who is invited—without his bossy older sister—to help shear sheep on Lost Island with his grandfather. Gabe becomes convinced that there is someone else on the island—perhaps the milk maid whose tragic story Grandfather told. When Gabe's sister Ginny arrives, they work together for the first time to solve the mystery and rescue the woman who haunts the island.

Murrow's *Twelve Days in August,* a novel for older teens, tells the story of prejudice against homosexuals on a high school soccer team in Vermont. Alex Beekman is the new kid in town, and when he shows up at soccer practice one day, he upsets the long-standing rivalry between the team's two former best players, Todd and Randy. When Randy's badgering remarks about Alex's supposed homosexuality go unchecked by the coach, encouraging the rest of the team to join in, Alex eventually quits, putting Todd, who is interested in Alex's twin sister, in an uncomfortable position. But when Todd's uncle shares his own painful stories of being teased about his homosexuality, Todd finds the courage to stand up to Randy and the rest of the team. Gerry Larson, reviewing *Twelve Days in August* for *School Library Journal,* remarked, "The game of soccer ... is a dynamic metaphor for Todd's emotional and intellectual growth." Susan DeRonne of *Booklist* also appreciated the book's sports element, "especially when

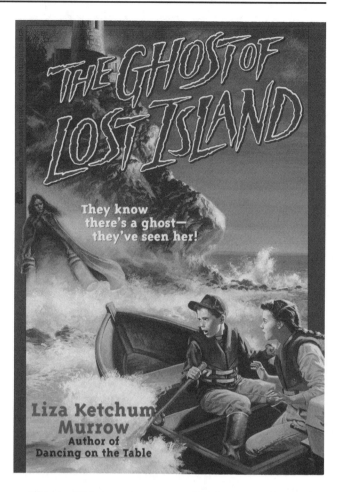

Gabe is glad to have his older sister around when they set out to find a ghost that appears on an island off the coast of Maine. (Cover illustration by Neal McPheeters.)

the dynamics of interpersonal relationships cause the team to falter."

### ■ Works Cited

Review of *Allergic to My Family, Publishers Weekly,* March 16, 1992.

Cooper, Ilene, review of *Good-Bye, Sammy, Booklist,* April, 1989.

DeRonne, Susan, review of *Twelve Days in August, Booklist,* March 1, 1993.

Review of *Good-Bye, Sammy, Kirkus Reviews,* April, 1989.

Kalkhoff, Ann, review of *Fire in the Heart, Children's Book Review Service,* June, 1989.

Larson, Gerry, review of *Twelve Days in August, School Library Journal,* March, 1993.

Marris, Alexandra, review of *Allergic to My Family, School Library Journal,* July, 1992.

Murrow, Liza Ketchum, *West against the Wind,* Holiday House, 1987.

Sherman, Chris, review of *Allergic to My Family, Booklist,* April 15, 1992.

## ■ For More Information See

*PERIODICALS*

*Booktalker,* September, 1989, p. 6.

*Bulletin of the Center for Children's Books,* December, 1987; May 9, 1991.
*Kirkus Reviews,* May 1, 1992.
*School Library Journal,* December, 1987.

# N–O

## NEUBERGER, Julia 1950-

### ■ Personal

Born February 27, 1950, in London, England; daughter of Walter Manfred (a civil servant) and Alice (an art critic; maiden name, Rosenthal) Schwab; married Anthony John Neuberger (an academic), September 17, 1973; children: Harriet Elinor Clare, Matthew Benedick Robert. *Education:* Newnham College, Cambridge, B.A. (with honors), 1973, M.A. (with honors), 1975; attended Leo Baeck College, London. *Politics:* Liberal Democrat.

### ■ Addresses

*Home*—36 Orlando Rd., London SW4 0LF, England. *Agent*—Carol Smith, 25 Hornton Ct., Kensington High St., London W8, England.

### ■ Career

Became rabbi, 1977. Rabbi of a Jewish congregation in London, England, 1977-89; King's Fund Institute, London, visiting fellow, 1989-91; Harvard Medical School, Boston, MA, visiting fellow, 1991-92. Leo Baeck College, lecturer. Royal College of Nursing, vice-president; member of board of trustees, Runnymede Trust and Citizenship Foundation; member of council, St. George's House, Windsor, Ontario, and St. George's Hospital Medical School. *Member:* Royal Society of Arts (fellow), Patients Association (chair, 1988-91), Groucho Club.

### ■ Awards, Honors

Harkness fellow, Commonwealth Fund of New York, 1991-92.

### ■ Writings

#### JUVENILE

*Judaism,* Dinosaur, 1986, published as *The Story of the Jews,* illustrated by Chris and Hilary Evans, Cambridge University Press, 1986.

#### FOR ADULTS

*Caring for Dying People of Different Faiths,* Lisa Sainsbury Foundation, 1986.
(Editor) *Days of Decision,* four volumes, Macmillan, 1987.
*Whatever's Happening to Women?: Promises, Practices, and Payoffs,* Kyle Cathie, 1991.
(Editor with John A. White) *A Necessary End: Attitudes to Death,* Macmillan, 1991.
(Editor) *Anthology of Women's Spiritual Poetry,* Kyle Cathie, 1992.

Also author of *The Things That Matter* and *Research Ethics Committees in the United Kingdom.* Contributor of articles and reviews to professional journals and newspapers.

### ■ Work in Progress

Research on professional values and attitudes and on the nature of professional ethics and codes.

### ■ Sidelights

Julia Neuberger once commented: "The rabbinic life made me concerned about those of other faiths in 'client' positions. It also made me interested in the hospice movement. Later research has made me curious about what shapes professional attitudes and made me question whether professions have values at all."

### ■ For More Information See

#### PERIODICALS

*School Librarian,* February, 1987, p. 76.*

* * *

## NEWMAN, Daisy 1904-1994

*OBITUARY NOTICE*—See index for *SATA* sketch: Born May 9, 1904, in Southport, Lancashire, England; died of heart failure, January 25, 1994, in Lexington,

MA. Author. An active member of the Quaker community in Cambridge, Massachusetts, Newman often wrote about Quaker life and history, including her history of American Quakers, *A Procession of Friends.* Her list of novels contains a number of titles for young adults, such as 1945's *Now That April's There,* 1968's *Mount Joy,* and 1975's *I Take Thee Serenity.* Other works by Newman include the novel *Indian Summer of the Heart,* published in 1982, and her 1987 autobiography, *A Golden String.*

*OBITUARIES AND OTHER SOURCES:*

BOOKS

*The Writers Directory: 1992-1994,* St. James Press, 1991.

PERIODICALS

*New York Times,* January 30, 1994, p. 38.

\*　　\*　　\*

# NIXON, Joan Lowery 1927-
## (Jaye Ellen)

## ■ Personal

Born February 3, 1927, in Los Angeles, CA; daughter of Joseph Michael (an accountant) and Margaret (Meyer) Lowery; married Hershell H. Nixon (a petroleum geologist), August 6, 1949; children: Kathleen Nixon Brush, Maureen Nixon Quinlan, Joseph Michael, Eileen Nixon McGowan. *Education:* University of Southern California, B.A., 1947; California State College, certificate in elementary education, 1949. *Religion:* Roman Catholic.

## ■ Addresses

*Home*—10215 Cedar Creek Dr., Houston, TX 77042. *Agent*—Amy Berkower, Writers House Inc., 21 West 26th St., New York, NY 10010.

## ■ Career

Writer. Elementary school teacher in Los Angeles, CA, 1947-50; Midland College, Midland, TX, instructor in creative writing, 1971-73; University of Houston, Houston, TX, instructor in creative writing, 1974-78; has taught creative writing in numerous publics schools in Texas. *Member:* Authors Guild, Authors League of America, Society of Children's Book Writers and Illustrators (charter member and former member of board of directors), Mystery Writers of America (former regional vice-president of Southwest chapter and member of national board of directors), Western Writers of America, Kappa Delta Alumnae Association.

## ■ Awards, Honors

Steck-Vaughn Award, Texas Institute of Letters, 1975, for *The Alligator under the Bed;* Edgar Allan Poe Award nomination, Mystery Writers of America, 1975, for *The Mysterious Red Tape Gang,* 1985, for *The Ghosts of*

*Now,* and 1992, for *The Weekend Was Murder!;* Outstanding Science Trade Book for children, National Science Teachers Association and Children's Book Council Joint Committee, 1979, for *Volcanoes: Nature's Fireworks,* 1980, for *Glaciers: Nature's Frozen Rivers,* and 1981, for *Earthquakes: Nature in Motion;* Edgar Allan Poe Award for best juvenile mystery, Mystery Writers of America, 1980, for *The Kidnapping of Christina Lattimore,* 1981, for *The Seance,* and 1987, for *The Other Side of Dark;* Crabbery Award, Oxon Hill branch of Prince George's County (MD) Library, 1984, for *Magnolia's Mixed-Up Magic;* Golden Spur, Western Writers of America, 1988, for *A Family Apart,* and 1989, for *In the Face of Danger;* Young Hoosier Award, 1988, for *A Deadly Game of Magic,* and 1989, for *The Dark and Deadly Pool;* Colorado Blue Spruce Young Adult Award, 1988, Virginia Young Adult Silver Cup, 1989, Oklahoma Sequoyah Young Adult Book Award, 1989, Iowa Teen Award, 1989, California Young Readers Medal, 1990, and Utah Young Adult Award, 1991, all for *The Other Side of Dark;* California Young Readers Medal, 1990, for *The Stalker;* Nevada Young Adult Award, 1992, Nebraska Golden Sower Young Adult Award, 1993, and Detroit Public Library Children's Choice Award, 1994, all for *Whispers from the Dead;* Virginia Young Adult Silver Cup, 1993, for *A Family Apart.*

**JOAN LOWERY NIXON**

# ■ Writings

*FICTION; FOR YOUNG PEOPLE*

*The Mystery of Hurricane Castle,* illustrated by Velma Ilsley, Criterion, 1964.

*The Mystery of the Grinning Idol,* illustrated by Alvin Smith, Criterion, 1965.

*The Mystery of the Hidden Cockatoo,* illustrated by Richard Lewis, Criterion, 1966.

*The Mystery of the Haunted Woods* (sequel to *The Mystery of Hurricane Castle*), illustrated by Theresa Brudi, Criterion, 1967.

*The Mystery of the Secret Stowaway,* illustrated by Joan Drescher, Criterion, 1968.

*Delbert, the Plainclothes Detective,* illustrated by Philip Smith, Criterion, 1971.

*The Alligator under the Bed,* illustrated by Jan Hughes, Putnam, 1974.

*The Mysterious Red Tape Gang,* illustrated by Joan Sandin, Putnam, 1974, published in paperback as *The Adventures of the Red Tape Gang,* illustrations by Steven H. Stroud, Scholastic, 1983.

*The Secret Box Mystery,* illustrated by Leigh Grant, Putnam, 1974.

*The Mysterious Prowler,* illustrated by Berthe Amoss, Harcourt, 1976.

*The Boy Who Could Find Anything,* illustrated by Syd Hoff, Harcourt, 1978.

*Danger in Dinosaur Valley,* illustrated by Marc Simont, Putnam, 1978.

*Muffie Mouse and the Busy Birthday,* illustrated by Geoffrey Hayes, Seabury, 1978, published as *Muffy and the Birthday Party,* Scholastic, 1979.

*Bigfoot Makes a Movie,* illustrated by Hoff, Putnam, 1979.

*The Kidnapping of Christina Lattimore,* Harcourt, 1979.

*Gloria Chipmunk, Star!,* illustrated by Diane Dawson, Houghton, 1980, published in paperback with illustrations by Hayes, Scholastic, 1980.

*Casey and the Great Idea,* illustrated by Amy Rowen, Dutton, 1980.

*The Seance,* Harcourt, 1980.

*The Spotlight Gang and the Backstage Ghost,* Harlequin, 1981.

*The Specter,* Delacorte, 1982, published in England as *The Spectre,* Granada, 1983.

(Under pseudonym Jaye Ellen) *The Trouble with Charlie,* Bantam, 1982.

*Days of Fear,* photographs by Joan Menschenfreund, Dutton, 1983.

*The Gift,* illustrated by Andrew Glass, Macmillan, 1983.

*A Deadly Game of Magic,* Harcourt, 1983.

*Magnolia's Mixed-Up Magic,* illustrated by Linda Bucholtz-Ross, Putnam, 1983.

*The Ghosts of Now,* Delacorte, 1984.

*The House on Hackman's Hill,* Scholastic, 1985.

*The Stalker,* Delacorte, 1985.

*The Other Side of Dark,* Delacorte, 1986.

*Haunted Island,* Scholastic, 1987.

*Secret, Silent Screams,* Delacorte, 1988.

*If You Were a Writer* (picture book), illustrated by Bruce Degen, Four Winds Press, 1988.

*The Island of Dangerous Dreams,* Dell, 1989.

*Whispers from the Dead,* Delacorte, 1989.

*A Candidate for Murder,* Delacorte, 1991.

*High Trail to Danger,* Bantam, 1991.

*Honeycutt Street Celebrities,* Dell, 1991.

*The Mystery Box,* Dell, 1991.

*Watch out for Dinosaurs,* Dell, 1991.

*The Haunted House on Honeycutt Street,* Dell, 1991.

*A Deadly Promise* (sequel to *High Trail to Danger*), Bantam, 1992.

*The Name of the Game Was Murder,* Delacorte, 1993.

*Will You Give Me a Dream?* (picture book), illustrated by Degen, Four Winds Press, 1994.

*When I Am Eight* (picture book), illustrated by Dick Gackenbach, Dial, 1994.

*Shadowmaker* (mystery), Delacorte, 1994.

*The Statue That Walks at Night,* Disney Press, 1995.

*The Legend of the Lost Mine,* Disney Press, 1995.

*The Haunted Theater,* Disney Press, 1995.

*The Thief at Piney Point Manor,* Disney Press, 1995.

*House of Fear* (young adult mystery), Delacorte, 1995.

Also contributor to anthologies, including *Stories for Free Children,* edited by Letty Cottin Pogrebin, McGraw-Hill, 1982; *Short Circuits: Thirteen Shocking Stories by Outstanding Writers for Young Adults,* edited by Donald Gallo, Delacorte, 1992; and *Don't Give Up the Ghost,* edited by David Gale, Delacorte, 1993.

*"FIRST READ-ALONE MYSTERIES" SERIES; ILLUSTRATED BY JIM CUMMINS*

*The New Year's Mystery,* Albert Whitman, 1979.

*The Halloween Mystery,* Albert Whitman, 1979.

*The Valentine Mystery,* Albert Whitman, 1979.

*The Happy Birthday Mystery,* Albert Whitman, 1979.

*The Thanksgiving Mystery,* Albert Whitman, 1980.

*The April Fool Mystery,* Albert Whitman, 1980.

*The Easter Mystery,* Albert Whitman, 1981.

*The Christmas Eve Mystery,* Albert Whitman, 1981.

*"CLAUDE AND SHIRLEY" SERIES*

*If You Say So, Claude,* illustrated by Lorinda Bryan Cauley, Warne, 1980.

*Beats Me, Claude,* illustrated by Tracey Campbell Pearson, Viking, 1986.

*Fat Chance, Claude,* illustrated by Pearson, Viking Kestrel, 1987.

*You Bet Your Britches, Claude,* illustrated by Pearson, Viking, 1989.

*That's the Spirit, Claude,* Viking, 1992.

*"KLEEP: SPACE DETECTIVE" SERIES; ILLUSTRATED BY PAUL FRAME*

*Kidnapped on Astarr,* Garrard, 1981.

*Mysterious Queen of Magic,* Garrard, 1981.

*Mystery Dolls from Planet Urd,* Garrard, 1981.

*"MAGGIE" SERIES; YOUNG ADULT NOVELS*

*Maggie, Too,* illustrations by Darrel Millsap, Harcourt, 1985.

*And Maggie Makes Three,* Harcourt, 1986.

*Maggie Forevermore,* Harcourt, 1987.

*"ORPHAN TRAIN ADVENTURES"; YOUNG ADULT NOVELS*

*A Family Apart,* Bantam, 1987.
*Caught in the Act,* Bantam, 1988.
*In the Face of Danger,* Bantam, 1988.
*A Place to Belong,* Bantam, 1989.
*A Dangerous Promise,* Delacorte, 1994.

*"HOLLYWOOD DAUGHTERS" TRILOGY; YOUNG ADULT NOVELS*

*Star Baby,* Bantam, 1989.
*Overnight Sensation,* Bantam, 1990.
*Encore,* Bantam, 1990.

*"MARY ELIZABETH" SERIES; YOUNG ADULT NOVELS*

*The Dark and Deadly Pool,* Delacorte, 1987.
*The Weekend Was Murder!,* Delacorte, 1992.

*"ELLIS ISLAND" SERIES*

*Land of Hope,* Bantam, 1992.
*Land of Promise,* Bantam, 1993.
*Land of Dreams,* Bantam, 1994.

*OTHER*

(With others) *This I Can Be* (textbook for eighth graders), Benefic, 1975.
(With others) *People and Me* (textbook for seventh graders), Benefic, 1975.
*Five Loaves and Two Fishes: Feeding of Five Thousand for Beginning Readers; John 6:1-15 for Children,* illustrated by Aline Cunningham, Concordia, 1976.
*Who Is My Neighbor?: The Good Samaritan for Beginning Readers; Luke 10:29-37 for Children,* illustrated by Cunningham, Concordia, 1976.
*The Son Who Came Home Again: The Prodigal Son for Beginning Readers; Luke 15:11-32 for Children,* illustrated by Cunningham, Concordia, 1977.
*Writing Mysteries for Young People* (for adults), The Writer, 1977.
(With husband, Hershell H. Nixon) *Oil and Gas: From Fossils to Fuels* (nonfiction), illustrated by Jean Day Zallinger, Harcourt, 1977.
(With H. Nixon) *Volcanoes: Nature's Fireworks* (nonfiction), Dodd, 1978.
*When God Listens,* illustrated by James McIlrath, Our Sunday Visitor, 1978.
*When God Speaks,* illustrated by McIlrath, Our Sunday Visitor, 1978.
*The Grandmother's Book* (for adults), Abingdon Press, 1979.
*The Butterfly Tree,* illustrated by McIlrath, Our Sunday Visitor, 1979.
*Before You Were Born,* illustrated by McIlrath, Our Sunday Visitor, 1980.
(With H. Nixon) *Glaciers: Nature's Frozen Rivers* (nonfiction), Dodd, 1980.
(With H. Nixon) *Earthquakes: Nature in Motion* (nonfiction), Dodd, 1981.
(With H. Nixon) *Land under the Sea* (nonfiction), Dodd, 1985.
(Author of introduction) Cynthia Manson, editor, *Tales from Ellery Queen's Mystery Magazine: Short Stories for Young Adults,* Harcourt, 1986.

*My Baby* (nonfiction), Mental Health Association (Houston, TX), 1994.

Author of introduction to *The Railway Children* by E. Nesbit, Bantam. Also author of nonfiction sections of *The Writer's Handbook,* The Writer, 1978, 1988, and 1992; *Writing Mysteries: A Handbook by the Mystery Writers of America,* edited by Sue Grafton, Writers Digest Books, 1992; and *The Fine Art of Murder, the Mystery Reader's Indispensable Companion,* compiled by the editors of *Mystery Scene* magazine, Carroll & Graf, 1993. Also contributor to magazines, including *West Coast Review of Books, The Writer, American Home, Parents, Woman's Day,* and *Ms.* Humor columnist for the *Houston Post.*

## ■ Sidelights

"Writing is hard," wrote Joan Lowery Nixon in her entry for the *Something about the Author Autobiography Series* (*SAAS*). "It's not easy. But it's such a fulfilling, enjoyable occupation that it's worth all the effort. There are days in which ideas flow and I can hardly type fast enough as I try to get every word down on paper, but there are other days during which I feel as though I'm painfully removing every word from my brain with a pair of pliers." Whether flowing freely or pried with pliers, Nixon's words have already won her the Mystery Writers of America's coveted Edgar Award for best juvenile mystery three times—the first writer to do so—and three of her other works have been nominated for that honor, including her 1992 novel *The Weekend Was Murder!* "In the field of young adult mystery writers, a field crowded with authors," stated Melissa Fletcher Stoeltje in the *Houston Chronicle Magazine,* "she is by all accounts the grande dame."

Nixon was born in Los Angeles, California. She lived with her parents, grandparents, and two younger sisters in a large double house. Nixon recalls that at a very young age she wanted to be a writer. When she was three, she began teaching herself to read by memorizing the words in her favorite books. She also followed her mother around, saying, "Write this down. I have a poem." She created verses for every holiday or family celebration, writing in *SAAS* that "from the time I discovered mysteries I was in love with them." Her first published work, a poem, appeared in *Children's Playmate* magazine when she was ten years old.

In her childhood home, one of the items in the playroom that stimulated her imagination was a puppet theater for which the young Nixon composed and performed plays with her younger sisters and neighborhood children. "Under my mother's direction," she once said in *SATA,* "we wrote our scripts, based on some of the classic fairy tales, such as 'Peter Rabbit' and the traditional 'Punch and Judy,' and took our shows—on a volunteer basis—to children's hospitals and orphanages and schools for many years. One moment I shall always remember: when we put on our puppet show for a group of very young Japanese children, none of whom spoke English. I realized that day the power of 'story telling' and laughter

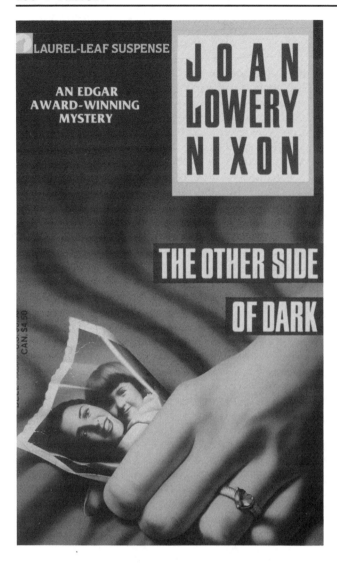

**A girl tries to identify her mother's murderer after being in a coma for four years in this thriller by Nixon.**

and friendship, as these little ones, unable to understand the dialogue, still responded to the puppets with as much enthusiasm as any audience we had ever met."

Nixon first attended Seventy-fourth Street elementary school in Los Angeles only two blocks from her home, and then Horace Mann Junior High. When Nixon was twelve, her grandfather died and the family moved to a large stucco house in East Hollywood. From her bedroom, which she shared with her grandmother, Nixon could see the lights from the Hollywood theaters. "We had some famous neighbors," she recalled in *SAAS:* "the producer-director, Cecil B. DeMille; the comedian, W. C. Fields; and the champion prizefighter, Jack Dempsey."

### Teacher Inspires Career

After entering ninth grade at Le Conte Junior High in Hollywood, Nixon became interested in journalism and almost at once became editor of the school newspaper. This was in 1941, the year of the attack on Pearl Harbor. Nixon tried to volunteer as a writer of propaganda for

the Red Cross, but her offer was ignored. Instead, the next year when she entered Hollywood High School, she wrote letters to lonely servicemen and helped serve breakfast to them in the school cafeteria. It was also at Hollywood High that Nixon met her favorite teacher, Miss Bertha Standfast. During the next three years, she enrolled in every English class taught by this lady, seeking her support in her writing. "I treasured the direction and encouragement Miss Standfast gave to me," she declared. "'You have talent,' she'd tell me. 'You're going to be a writer.' It was she who insisted that I major in journalism when I went to college." At the age of seventeen, Nixon wrote her first article for a magazine, selling it to *Ford Times.*

One week after her high school graduation, Nixon entered the University of Southern California as a journalism student. "My training in journalism taught me discipline," she remembered in *SATA.* "For one thing, I learned to create at the typewriter. We took our exams on the typewriter. Journalism taught me to focus because I had to sit down and *write,* whether I felt like it or not—no waiting for inspiration. I learned the skill of finding the important facts in a story, and how to isolate them from all of the unnecessary details."

Nixon's degree in journalism did not lead to a job in that field, partly because of competition from returning war correspondents. But the Los Angeles School District was in need of teachers, so she found work as a substitute for kindergarten through third grade classes. Soon she received an assignment to teach kindergarten at Ramona Elementary School, at the same time taking night school education courses at the nearby Los Angeles City College campus.

While at USC, Nixon also met her future husband, Hershell "Nick" Nixon, who was a student majoring in naval science. Two weeks after their first date they became engaged, but, as she stated in *SAAS,* "Nick still had over a year left to serve on his six-year hitch, so off he went to China for ten months. He was back for a few weeks, then off again to Hawaii for a few months." Their marriage was postponed until after he finished his stint in the Navy, but the couple was finally united on August 6, 1949. During the three years Nixon taught at Ramona, their first daughter, Kathleen Mary, was born.

In 1952 Nick graduated from USC, having changed his major to geology. His first job, which was with the Shell Oil Company, sent the young family to Billings, Montana. They later returned to California, but continued to move among different cities, eventually going to Corpus Christi, Texas. By the time they moved to Corpus Christi, Kathy had been joined by Maureen, Joe, and the youngest, Eileen. "I shed many tears over that move to Texas," Nixon recalled. "All I knew about the state was that it was full of cattle and cactus, and I didn't want to leave my family, my friends, and my beautiful state of California."

The move to Texas, however, marked an important event in Nixon's life. When she read an announcement of the upcoming Southwest Writers Conference only a little while after her arrival, she became enthusiastic about writing for children. "I had children, I had taught children, and I have the vivid kind of memory which enables me to remember all the details I saw and the emotions I felt when I was a child," she reminisced. "I made a mental note to myself. Maybe I'd try writing something for children." Kathy and Maureen discussed this development and, states the author, announced to their mother, "We've decided. If you're going to write for children, you have to write a book, and it has to be a mystery, and you have to put us in it." Nixon worked every Wednesday from nine a.m to three p.m. "All week I wrote in my mind, dialogue and scenes coming together, demanding to be written as I shoved them back. 'Not yet!' I'd say with a groan. 'Wait until I can get to my typewriter.'" Each day after school, Nixon read the material she had completed that day to her children. Often she used their suggestions (such as Kathy's "Put something funny in it.") Nixon even joined the Byliners, a local group of writers who read and criticized each

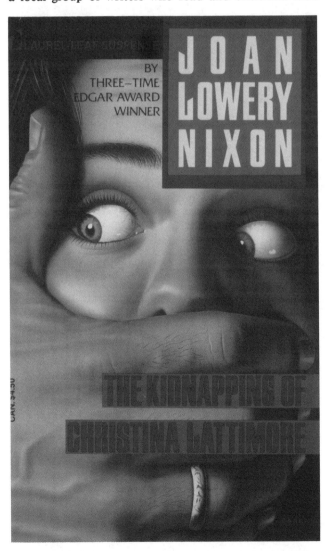

**In one of Nixon's many mystery novels, a young woman is accused of conspiring with the people who have kidnapped her.**

other's manuscripts. Despite all this input, *The Mystery of Hurricane Castle* was rejected twelve times by different publishers before Criterion finally accepted it.

*The Mystery of Hurricane Castle* tells the story of two girls—the Nickson sisters, Kathy and Maureen—and their younger brother, Danny, who are left behind during an evacuation of the Gulf of Texas area just before a hurricane. The book follows them as they seek shelter in a house that, according to local legend, is haunted. Nixon declares in *The Writer* that the plot of the book came from a family experience: "When we moved to Corpus Christi, Texas, we found ourselves in the middle of a hurricane. The eye of the storm missed our city, but the force of the rain, wind, and waves caused tremendous damage." "The area had been evacuated," Nixon continues, "but I wondered what someone would have done who couldn't leave—who, for some reason, had been left behind in the confusion. The beach houses could not withstand the force of the storm, or stay intact, but what if high on the hill there stood a stone 'castle,' strong enough to survive the storm and to shelter its occupants? And what if this castle were known to have as its only occupant a ghost?" As it turns out, Kathy's interest in painting helps the children to unmask the "ghost."

That first book persuaded Nixon to continue writing. After *Hurricane Castle,* she wrote *The Mystery of the Grinning Idol,* a story about smuggling Mexican artifacts (which starred her youngest child, Eileen), and *The Mystery of the Hidden Cockatoo,* about a jewelled pin lost in a house in the French Quarter of New Orleans, before bringing the Nicksons back in *The Mystery of the Haunted Woods.* Son Joe finally got a starring role in *The Mystery of the Secret Stowaway.* Nixon soon found herself busy writing children's books, teaching creative writing classes at local children's schools, libraries, and colleges, and writing a humor column for the *Houston Post.* Nixon said in *SAAS* that it "soon became apparent that I would have to make a decision about the direction of my career," for " . . . the careful time I spent on the work from the students in my writing classes subtracted from the time I had for my own writing. It was a difficult decision, but I gave up teaching." This decision allowed her to devote every morning to writing, a hard task, she says in her autobiographical sketch, "but it's such a fulfilling, enjoyable occupation that it's worth all the effort."

### Edgar Award-Winning Mysteries

Nixon's earliest work was for young readers—it was not until later in her career that she began writing for young adults. In 1975, Nixon and her daughter Kathy attended the first International Crime Writers Congress in London, England, where a speaker's comment encouraged her to try writing a mystery for young adults. This book became *The Kidnapping of Christina Lattimore,* which was awarded the Edgar for best juvenile mystery by the Mystery Writers of America in 1980. *The Kidnapping of Christina Lattimore* tells in the title character's own words her ordeal of being kidnapped, held for ransom, and then suspected of having engineered the whole project to get money from her grandmother for a school trip. When she is rescued, she dedicates herself to bringing the criminals to justice and proving that she did not try to defraud her grandmother. *New York Times Book Review* contributor Paxton Davis found this part of the novel particularly intriguing, writing that "Christina's inability to persuade the authorities or her family that she was not an accomplice in the crime makes for good narrative."

One year after *The Kidnapping of Christina Lattimore* won the Edgar, Nixon repeated the accomplishment with *The Seance,* and in 1987 *The Other Side of Dark* made her a three-time recipient of the prize. The latter book presents quite a different type of problem to the reader. Seventeen-year-old Stacy wakes up to find that she has lost four years of her life in a coma after an intruder has shot her and killed her mother. Not only does she have to adapt to a new lifestyle and catch up on the missing years, but she also has to identify the killer before she becomes his next victim. "Stacy is a vivid character," David Gale wrote in *School Library Journal,* "whose need to be brought up to date provides some comic moments."

Besides her acclaimed mysteries, Nixon has won awards for her historical fiction. Two volumes of her "Orphan Train" quintet, *A Family Apart* and *In the Face of Danger,* won the Golden Spur Award—the Western Writers of America's equivalent of the Edgar. The idea, she said in *Artists and Authors for Young Adults (AAYA),* came from a publisher who asked her if she had ever heard of the "Orphan Train Children." The historical Children's Aid Society, an organization of social activists, operated between 1854 and 1929 to place more than 100,000 children with foster families in the West. The children—not necessarily orphans—were usually from immigrant families living in slums in New York City.

Such is the case with Nixon's fictional Kelly family, first generation immigrants living in New York shortly before the Civil War. In *A Family Apart,* Nixon tells how, after the oldest boy is arrested for petty robbery, the widowed Mrs. Kelly realizes that she can no longer provide for her six children. She accepts the offer of Mr. Charles Loring Brace, a social activist, to have them placed with other families in the West. When the Kellys reach St. Louis, Missouri, however, they find to their dismay that they will be adopted by different people and must split up. *A Family Apart* goes on to show how Frances Mary, the oldest girl, and Petey, the youngest boy, are adopted by the Cummings, an abolitionist couple living in Kansas who help escaping slaves flee north. Megan, the second-oldest girl, is chosen by prairie farmers Ben and Emma Browder, and in *In the Face of Danger* she learns to overcome her grief about her family's disintegration and her lack of self-esteem. Ten-year-old Danny and his little sister Peg end up with a family named Swenson in *A Place to Belong,* while Mike—the would-be thief whose activities precipitated

the family's exodus—finds a home with a German family named Friedrich in *Caught in the Act.*

Nixon's popular "Claude and Shirley" series for younger readers is set in the American West. In a series of adventures ranging from *If You Say So, Claude,* in which the pioneer couple leave their noisy mining town for the peace of the Texas frontier, to *You Bet Your Britches, Claude,* in which the couple adopts a little boy and girl, Nixon displays a sense of humor that echoes the West's traditional "tall tales." A reviewer for *Publishers Weekly* appreciated the humor in the book, calling it a "rib-tickling yarn," while Betsy Hearne, writing in the *Bulletin of the Center for Children's Books,* further added that it contains "endearing characters, adroit writing, and an action-packed feminist pioneer."

Published in 1991, *High Trail to Danger* originates in nineteenth-century Chicago, where teenage sisters Sarah and Samantha are coping with the death of their mother. When greedy relatives assume control of the

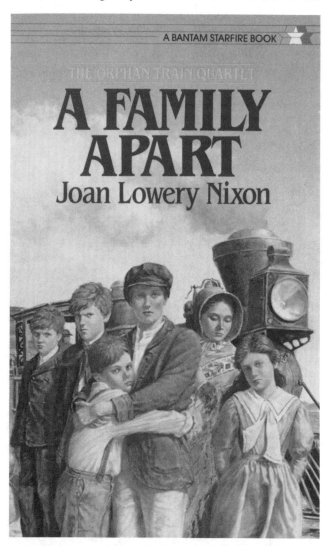

**Sent West with her five siblings to be adopted, Frances dons a disguise to keep from being split up from her youngest brother, Petey. (Cover illustration by Nigel Chamberlain.)**

**Megan Kelly tries to overcome the curse of a gypsy and the hardships of life on the prairie in this "Orphan Train" novel.**

**The second book in the "Orphan Train" stories, this novel follows Mike Kelly, who suspects that his adoptive father may be a murderer.**

family boardinghouse, seventeen-year-old Sarah is encouraged by her younger sister to try to find their father, who left over a decade earlier to try to strike it rich in the silver mines of Colorado. During the journey Sarah confronts a number of seedy characters as well as a pair of Western suitors. *A Deadly Promise,* published in 1992, continues the story with Sarah summoning her sister to Colorado to help in a quest to restore their father's good name by proving that he was not involved in a murder plot.

### That Western State of Mind

"The West to me is a state of mind," Nixon declared in *The Writer.* "While immersed in stories set west of the Mississippi in the last half of the eighteen-hundreds, modern readers are discovering concepts like *sacrifice* and *self-denial* and *unwavering commitment to an ideal*—concepts that are not too common in today's very different world." "Writing western historical novels for young adults is immensely satisfying," she concluded. "It gives me the opportunity to show that

history isn't simply a collection of dates and wars and kings and presidents, but that *children* have always helped make history, that *children* are not only important to the past but are helping to shape history being made today."

In 1992, Nixon returned to the setting of New York in *Land of Hope,* the first book in her "Ellis Island" series. The story focuses on Rebekah Levinsky, a Jewish immigrant from Russia who comes to Ellis Island with her family to avoid persecution in her native country. Set in the early 1900s, *Land of Hope* features promises of opportunity for the family when they arrive in the United States. When they arrive in America, however, they find life to be much more difficult than they imagined it would be. Nixon also draws on her own past for inspiration. Her "Hollywood Daughters" series, she related in *AAYA,* was based on "some of the kids I knew at Hollywood High during the 1940s—kids who had been stars as children but who were 'has-beens' by the time they were teenagers." Nixon's "Maggie" stories deal with the problems of growing up in an unstable

**Nixon portrays the difficult life of a family of immigrants arriving in the United States, and one girl's determination to succeed in her new country, in this volume of the "Ellis Island" series.** (Cover illustration by Colin Backhouse.)

environment. Young Maggie lost her mother in an accident several years before the opening chapters of *Maggie, Too,* and she has little contact with her film-maker father. Maggie becomes openly resentful when her father announces his plans to remarry (a twenty-one-year-old starlet) and packs her off to spend the summer with her librarian grandmother (also named Maggie) in Texas. Over the course of the book and its two sequels, *And Maggie Makes Three* and *Maggie Forevermore,* Maggie learns to love her grandmother, to lose her resentment toward her father and his new wife, and to appreciate her own life. "Generation to generation, emotions don't change," Nixon stated in *The Writer.* "Loneliness, fear, joy, sorrow, embarrassment.... External situations may differ greatly, but the emotions they cause are always the same. Our basic needs—such as the need to be loved, to be comforted, and to be secure—remain constant."

Commenting on her own writing processes, Nixon noted in *SAAS* that "even imaginary characters can have wills of their own," and related that she sees her characters in her dreams and hears them talking about the story. She always has two levels in her mystery novels, "a problem to solve, and a mystery to solve," she stated. "Later the characters can weave them together." In *The Writer* Nixon shared her secret of writing successfully for teenagers: "Appreciating them, really liking them—this, too, I think, is an essential part of the answer." Her message to young people, she declares in *SAAS,* is: "For those of you who have hopes of becoming writers, it's important to know that you'll need that determination and persistence and the courage to continue, no matter what might happen."

Nixon's popularity shows no signs of flagging. Why is her work so popular with young people? "It's because her writing gives them a feeling of hope," Nick Nixon told Stoeltje. "Through her heroines, she tells children that anything is possible for them. 'Be strong, be confident. You can do things.'" And she remains constantly inventive. Even a trip in a hot-air balloon doesn't stop her imagination: while admiring the desert scenery around Sedona, Arizona, "I glanced down and a man just happened to be in his driveway, putting something in the trunk of his car," she told Stoeltje. "I said to Nick, 'Suppose he had just committed a crime and was stuffing the body bags in the trunk?' And Nick sort of gave this exasperated sigh and said, 'Can't you just enjoy this lovely scenery and forget about mysteries for a while?'"

## ■ Works Cited

Davis, Paxton, review of *The Kidnapping of Christina Lattimore, New York Times Book Review,* May 13, 1979, p. 27.

Review of *Fat Chance, Claude, Publishers Weekly,* September 25, 1987, p. 107.

Gale, David, review of *The Other Side of Dark, School Library Journal,* September, 1986, pp. 145-146.

Hearne, Betsy, review of *Fat Chance, Claude, Bulletin of the Center for Children's Books,* September, 1987, p. 15.

Nixon, Joan Lowery, "Clues to the Juvenile Mystery," *The Writer,* February, 1977, pp. 23-26.

Nixon, Joan Lowery, autobiographical sketch in *Something about the Author Autobiography Series,* Volume 9, Gale, 1990, pp. 267-284.

Nixon, Joan Lowery, "Writing Mysteries Young Adults Want to Read," *The Writer,* July, 1991, pp. 18-20.

Nixon, Joan Lowery, "Writing the Western Novel for Young Adults," *The Writer,* June, 1992, pp. 21-23.

Nixon, Joan Lowery, "Joan Lowery Nixon," *Authors and Artists for Young Adults,* Volume 12, Gale, 1994.

Stoeltje, Melissa Fletcher, "Murder for Gentle Readers," *Houston Chronicle Magazine,* June 20, 1993, pp. 8-11.

## ■ For More Information See

*BOOKS*

*Children's Literature Review,* Volume 24, Gale, 1991.

*Twentieth-Century Children's Writers,* 3rd edition, St. James, 1989, pp. 723-724.

Ward, Martha E., *Authors of Books for Young People,*
    3rd edition, Scarecrow Press, 1990.

*PERIODICALS*

*Bulletin of the Center for Children's Books,* March, 1992,
    p. 189.
*Horn Book,* November, 1986, p. 748.
*Los Angeles Times Book Review,* November 23, 1986, p.
    12.
*New York Times Book Review,* February 27, 1983, p. 37;
    October 9, 1988.
*Publishers Weekly,* February 22, 1980, p. 108; Decem-
    ber 5, 1980, p. 52; April 1, 1983, p. 103; April 22,
    1983, p. 104; October 5, 1984, p. 91; May 30, 1986,
    p. 67; November 28, 1986, p. 77; October 9, 1987,
    p. 89; October 23, 1987, p. 73; December 11, 1987,
    p. 66; August 12, 1988, p. 462; September 9, 1988,
    pp. 133-134; September 8, 1989, p. 67; October 13,
    1989, p. 55; November 10, 1989, p. 62; March 15,
    1991, p. 59; June 14, 1991, p. 58; April 27, 1992.
*School Library Journal,* April, 1976, p. 58; January,
    1979, p. 45; September, 1979, p. 160; December,
    1979, p. 97; May, 1980, p. 85; September, 1980, p.
    62; November, 1980, p. 66; October, 1981, p. 157;
    December, 1981, p. 82; December, 1982, p. 81;
    May, 1983, p. 74; October, 1983, p. 152; December,
    1984, p. 102; May, 1985, p. 111; September, 1985,
    pp. 137-138; September, 1986, p. 138; January,
    1987; March, 1987, p. 164; May, 1987, p. 102;
    December, 1987, p. 75; February, 1988, p. 85-86;
    August, 1988, p. 97; November, 1988, p. 94;
    September, 1989, pp. 275-276; November, 1989, p.
    128; January, 1990, p. 87; May, 1990, p. 126;
    March, 1991, pp. 194, 216; July, 1991, p. 88;
    March, 1992, pp. 240, 259; March, 1993, p. 222;
    February, 1994, p. 104; May, 1994, p. 117.
*School Library Media Quarterly,* fall, 1982.
*Voice of Youth Advocates,* December, 1986, p. 221;
    October, 1987, p. 204; December, 1987, p. 236;
    August, 1988, p. 134; December, 1988, pp. 240-241;
    February, 1989, p. 288; August, 1989, p. 160;
    October, 1989, p. 215; June, 1990, p. 108; Decem-
    ber, 1990, p. 287; February, 1991, p. 355; August,
    1991, p. 174; April, 1992, pp. 18, 34; October, 1992,
    p. 228; June, 1993, p. 93; February, 1994, p. 371.
*The Writer,* September, 1972.

\*       \*       \*

# NOBISSO, Josephine 1953-
## (Nuria Wood, Nadja Bride)

## ■ Personal

Born February 9, 1953, in Bronx, NY; daughter of
Ralph (a mason contractor) and Maria (a homemaker;
maiden name, Zamboli) Nobisso; married Victor Jude
(an antiques restorer), July 26, 1981; children: one
daughter. *Education:* State University of New York—
New Paltz, B.S. (cum laude), 1974; attended Universita
di Urbino, Italy, 1971-74. *Religion:* Roman Catholic.
*Hobbies and other interests:* Hiking, reading, collecting

**JOSEPHINE NOBISSO**

children's books, yoga, family days, vegetarianism,
contemplative walks.

## ■ Addresses

*Home and office*—P.O. Box 1396, Quoque, NY 11959.

## ■ Career

Self-employed writer and lecturer, 1971—. New York
State certified teacher with a specialization in early
childhood. Writing instructor and creator of copyright-
ed writing program: "The Nobisso Recommendations—
Guiding Students to Write in Their Authentic Voices."
*Member:* Society of Children's Book Writers and Illus-
trators, Writers Guild, Authors League of America,
Westhampton Writers Festival.

## ■ Awards, Honors

"Best Kids' Book of the Year," *Parents* magazine, 1989,
for *Grandpa Loved;* "Friend of Education Award,"
Delta Kappa Gamma Beta Pi, 1991.

## ■ Writings

*FOR YOUNG READERS*

*Grandpa Loved,* illustrated by Maureen Hyde, Green
    Tiger Press, 1989.
*Grandma's Scrapbook,* illustrated by Hyde, Simon &
    Schuster, 1991.
*Shh! The Whale Is Smiling,* illustrated by Hyde, Simon
    & Schuster, 1992.
*For the Sake of a Cake,* illustrated by Anton Krajnc,
    Rizzoli International, 1993.
*Hot Cha Cha,* Candlewick Press, in press.

*NOVELS*

(As Nuria Wood) *With No Regrets,* Berkley, 1983.
(As Nuria Wood) *The Family Plan,* Berkley, 1984.
(As Nadja Bride) *Hide and Seek,* Quest, 1985.

## ■ Work in Progress

*Time Travels Well* (a novel for young adults); screenplay and novelization titled, *The Psychic Life of Esther Cane* (for adults); numerous picture books.

## ■ Sidelights

Josephine Nobisso told *SATA:* "The incidents in my family are the stuff of legend. There was the grandfather who appeared to his ten children even though he was hundreds of miles away, the grandmother who unearthed an ancient urn that toppled every dish in the farmhouse in its fury to be re-buried, and the perfectly healthy grandfather whose prediction to die upon seeing the birth of a certain grandchild (me, I'm afraid to say), came true.

"My books find their source in the densely atmospheric and passionately happy world that was my childhood. If an author's voice is a function of her personality, then I can hope that mine is 'sharply original' for that's what my work is often called.

"It has taken some of my stories up to twenty years to see the light of day as published books. But I persevere, believing, as a playwright once said, that 'hope is an orientation of the heart. It is not the conviction that something will turn out well, but the certainty that something makes sense, regardless of how it turns out.'

"I was born in the Bronx, and raised on both sides of the Atlantic (and sometimes *on* the Atlantic as my fortuitous adventures included many things from luxury ocean liners to twelve-passenger freighter crossings). I attended Catholic schools until my last two years of high school. I married my childhood sweetheart, and we renewed our vows after many years.

"Although English was not the primary language spoken in my home, some far-sighted and kind teachers inscribed my name in my high school lobby for 'Excellence in English.' My B.S. in foreign languages came cum laude from SUNY—New Paltz, but I spent most of my semesters abroad in Europe, finishing in three years. I'm a certified teacher with a specialization in early childhood.

"My years of bungling through writing helped me eventually to develop a most innovative writing method, full of surprising strategies. What's next? My writing life constitutes a full-time commitment, and my life is all of a piece. I'm writing all the time (even in my dreams!), planning workshops, running my office and home, and waking up very early to accomplish it all."

# O'CONOR, Jane 1958-

## ■ Personal

Born August 13, 1958; daughter of Andrew J. (an attorney) and Carol (a housewife; maiden name, Hedman) O'Conor. *Education:* Attended summer graphic design course at Kansas City Art Institute, 1978; University of Iowa, B.F.A., teaching certificate in art (kindergarten to grade twelve), 1980; studied continuing education in illustration, Rhode Island School of Design, 1987-90.

## ■ Addresses

*Home and office*—65 Best St., Portland, ME 04103.

## ■ Career

Freelance illustrator, 1988—. Marshall Fields and Co., Chicago, IL, window display senior designer, 1982-86; freelance window display designer, Providence, RI; Court Appointed Child Advocate, Providence, RI.

## ■ Illustrator

Carla Heymsfeld, *Coaching Ms. Parker,* Bradbury Press, 1992.
*The LADO Dictionary,* Prentice Hall, 1992.

Also illustrator of high school french and spanish language text books for Heinle and Heinle Publishing and an English as a second language dictionary for Prentice Hall; illustrations have also appeared in the *Chicago Reader* and *Casco Bay Weekly.*

## ■ Sidelights

Jane O'Conor told *SATA:* "Being an illustrator requires a lot of decision making. I may ultimately go with my original inspiration for an illustration assignment, but not until I have thought long and hard about as many other concepts possible.

"It is my favorite part of the creative process, because one idea leads to another, and very soon the excitement takes over and the possibilities seem endless. Of course, this is when I have to start making choices as to which ideas really work and which do not. The best way to find this out is by starting to sketch.

"I give this phase a lot of time and thought, drawing and redrawing—it's kind of like thinking out loud only on paper! I also look at a lot of reference material, so that I am accurately drawing certain objects or figures. This means going to the library a lot or actually obtaining the needed object in order to draw it from life or having friends pose for you. I have found that people really enjoy helping me with research, because they feel like they are part of the creating, too.

"I think that if I have done all the preliminary steps as much to my satisfaction as possible, the work on the final illustration not only captures the essence of the piece, but it is simply much more enjoyable to do. Making an illustration is not just a technical process for me—it requires a lot of different thought processes, and I enjoy every one of them. There is so much satisfaction in looking at a finished piece that looks *and* feels right—you have to have both elements."

\* \* \*

# O'SHAUGHNESSY, Ellen Cassels 1937-

## ■ Personal

Born October 1, 1937, in Columbia, SC; daughter of Melvin O. (a professional golfer) and Grace Ellen (a writer; maiden name, Cassels) Hemphill; married John F. O'Shaughnessy (a teacher), December, 1979 (divorced, March, 1990); children: John H., Anne H. Sloan. *Education:* Attended University of South Carolina, 1955-57, and Golden Gate University, 1974; International University, B.A., 1977; Fielding Institute, M.A., 1979. *Politics:* Republican. *Religion:* Protestant. *Hobbies and other interests:* Painting acrylics for children (carousel horses).

ELLEN CASSELS O'SHAUGHNESSY

## ■ Addresses

*Home*—P.O. Box 51063, Pacific Grove, CA 93950.

## ■ Career

Monterey Peninsula Unified School District, Monterey, CA, teacher's aide and art instructor, 1968-74; Pacific Grove Unified School District, Pacific Grove, credentialed adult school teacher and teacher's aide, 1974-82, special education consultant, 1984-85; Psychological Services, Fort Ord, CA, intern, 1976; substitute teacher for special education classes, 1983-84; Synthesis (publishing company), Pacific Grove, CA, owner, writer, and publisher, 1984—.

## ■ Writings

*Teaching Art to Children,* privately printed, 1974.
*Synthesis* (symbolic-language series for developmentally disabled and non-reading adults), Synthesis, 1981.
*You Love to Cook Book* (symbolic-language cookbook), Synthesis, 1983.
*I Could Ride on the Carousel Longer,* Synthesis, 1989.
*Somebody Called Me a Retard Today ... And My Heart Felt Sad,* Walker, 1992.

## ■ Work in Progress

"A very easy-to-understand method for learning to play piano ... ideal for developmentally disabled adults."

## ■ Sidelights

Ellen O'Shaughnessy's career as a writer and publisher grew out of her years of experience as a teacher of developmentally disabled adults. She developed a symbolic language called Synthesis and created a series of books and a cookbook for her students, incorporating her work into a project for her M.A. degree in psychology. "This project took three years of research, and it works!" O'Shaughnessy explained to *SATA.*

"I feel the most comfortable with my students and friends who are disabled because of their strengths and love. We laugh a lot and genuinely care about one another. I wrote *Somebody Called Me a Retard Today ... And My Heart Felt Sad* for them because we get teased a lot. It seems that many people are critical or pull back when the handicap is on the outside and are far *less* critical when the handicap is on the inside.

"When I get an idea for a book, I become compulsive and preoccupied," O'Shaughnessy noted. "When the project is finished, I come back to reality and find that colors are much brighter than I remembered. I sometimes wonder just where this 'place' is that I go to and how I know when to come back."

O'Shaughnessy, who was described as "one very special woman" by Susan Cantrell in the *The Californian,* explained her motivation for writing: "What I hope to achieve through the books I write is not always clear to me. I want to do more than entertain. I think that I want children (or adults) to be moved or changed in attitude or understanding after reading one of my books. When I developed a language and books for developmentally disabled adults and they could 'read' for the first time in [their lives], we all wept with excitement. That's what I'm trying to say … I hope that my books have impact."

O'Shaughnessy has this advice for aspiring writers: "Since I wrote a very simple little book with what I consider to be a message for children—to *be kind*—I suggest that any young authors forget about the competi-

tion and send your manuscript to a publisher! Your message may be just what is needed at the time. Just mail it in and be patient. If it is rejected, just mail it out again. Keep your spirits up. Remember how many great writers have been rejected over and over and then found success!"

## ■ Works Cited

Cantrell, Susan, "Woman Brings Touch of Art to Blind Children," *The Californian,* June 11, 1990.
Review of *Somebody Called Me a Retard Today … And My Heart Felt Sad, Kirkus Reviews,* October 15, 1992.

# P

TOM PAISLEY

## PAISLEY, Tom 1932-
### (T. Ernesto Bethancourt)

### ■ Personal

Name originally Thomas E. Passailaigue; name changed to Tom Paisley; born October 2, 1932, in Brooklyn, NY; son of Aubrey Ernesto (a truck driver) and Dorothy (Charest) Passailaigue; married Nancy Yasue Soyeshima, May 9, 1970; children: Kimi, Dorothea. *Education:* Attended City College of the City University of New York. *Politics:* Registered Democrat. *Hobbies and other interests:* Old cars, old movies.

### ■ Addresses

*Home and office*—P.O. Box 787, Alta Loma, CA 91701.

### ■ Career

Writer, singer, musician, composer, lyricist, actor, and critic. Biographer of recording artists, RCA Records and CBS Records, 1969-76; staff lyricist, Notable Music, 1970-71. Has held various other odd jobs, including a stint during the 1950s as an undercover claims investigator for the New York office of Lloyd's of London. *Military service:* U.S. Navy, 1950-53. *Member:* PEN International, American Society of Composers, Authors and Publishers, Mystery Writers of America, Writers Guild of America—West, Authors Guild, Authors League of America, American Federation of Musicians, Southern California Council on Literature for Children and Young People, The Bank Dicks (W. C. Fields fan club).

### ■ Awards, Honors

American Society of Composers, Authors and Publishers Popular Division Award, 1970-71, for "Cities"; named "Kentucky Colonel" by governor of Kentucky, 1976; *Tune in Yesterday* was named a notable children's book in the field of the social studies, National Council on Social Studies—Children's Book Council, 1978; "Author of the Year Award," University of California at Irvine, 1978; American Library Association "Best of the Best Books, 1970-83" citation, for *Tune in Yesterday;* Excellence in a Series award, Southern California Council on Literature for Children and Young People, 1983, for "Doris Fein" series; Central Missouri State University Distinguished Body of Work award, 1984; Children's Choice Award for *Nightmare Town.*

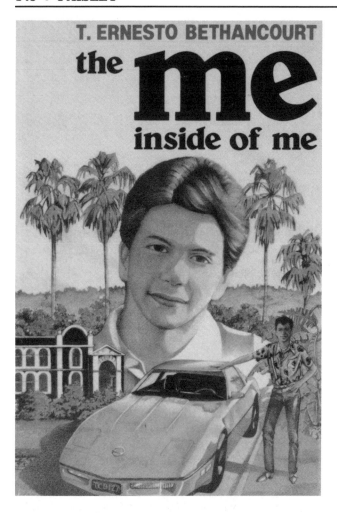

**T. ERNESTO BETHANCOURT**
**the me inside of me**

One of the works written under Paisley's pseudonym, T. Ernesto Bethancourt, this book features a Latino teen who has some trouble adjusting to his new life when he suddenly receives one million dollars. (Cover illustration by Michael Deraney.)

## ■ Writings

*JUVENILE NOVELS; UNDER PSEUDONYM T. ERNESTO BETHANCOURT*

*New York City Too Far from Tampa Blues,* Holiday House, 1975.
*The Dog Days of Arthur Cane,* Holiday House, 1976.
*The Mortal Instruments,* Holiday House, 1977.
*Tune in Yesterday,* Holiday House, 1978.
*Dr. Doom: Superstar,* Holiday House, 1978.
*Instruments of Darkness,* Holiday House, 1979.
*Nightmare Town,* Holiday House, 1979.
*Where the Deer and Cantaloupe Play,* Oak Tree, 1981.
*T.H.U.M.B.B.: The Hippest Underground Marching Band in Brooklyn,* Holiday House, 1983.
*The Tomorrow Connection,* Holiday House, 1984.
*The Great Computer Dating Caper,* Crown, 1984.
*The Me Inside of Me,* Lerner Publications, 1985.

*"DORIS FEIN" SERIES; UNDER PSEUDONYM T. ERNESTO BETHANCOURT*

*Doris Fein: Superspy,* Holiday House, 1980.
*Quartz Boyar,* Holiday House, 1980.

*Phantom of the Casino,* Holiday House, 1981.
*The Mad Samurai,* Holiday House, 1981.
*Deadly Aphrodite,* Holiday House, 1982.
*Murder Is No Joke,* Holiday House, 1982.
*Dead Heat at Long Beach,* Holiday House, 1983.
*Legacy of Terror,* Holiday House, 1984.

*OTHER*

*That's Together* (television script), WTTW-TV (Chicago), 1974.
*The New Americans* (television script), KCET-TV (Los Angeles), 1981.

Also author of several collections of short stories for the General Learning Corporation; author of lesson in television series *Skills Essential to Learning,* Agency for Instructional Television, 1979; author of "Easy to Read" adaptations of classics, all published by Pittman Fearon Publishing, including *Dr. Jekyll and Mr. Hyde, The Time Machine, Frankenstein, The Three Musketeers,* and *The Last of the Mohicans.* Lyricist for *Music,* Silver Burdett, three volumes, 1973-75; also lyricist/librettist for Off-Broadway play *Cities,* 1971, and contributor to *Weigh-in, Way Out,* 1970. Contributor of unattributed pieces to text books. Former contributing editor to *Stereo Review* and *High Fidelity.*

## ■ Adaptations

*New York City Too Far from Tampa Blues* was adapted for television by NBC in 1979; *The Dog Days of Arthur Cane* was adapted for television by ABC in 1984.

## ■ Sidelights

Throughout his life, Tom Paisley has devoted his creative energies to a wide array of literary and musical genres. He is, however, best known and most successful in the field of young adult literature, having penned over twenty novels under the name T. Ernesto Bethancourt between 1975 and 1984. However, to pigeon-hole Paisley merely as an author of novels for young adults is to overlook the numerous other facets of a diverse "Renaissance man" of our time.

Born Thomas E. Passailaigue (pronounced Pas-a-laig) on October 2, 1932, in Brooklyn, New York, he took on the name Paisley in the early 1960s. He explains that as his career as a folk musician—both singing and playing guitar—began to blossom, and with the psychedelic movement taking hold, changing his name to "Paisley" seemed appropriate. Besides, he once told *SATA,* "if you put *Passailaigue* up in lights, you'd die of the heat." Later, he chose "Bethancourt," a family name on his father's side, for publication.

The son of Aubrey Ernesto and Dorothy (Charest) Passailaigue, Paisley spent most of his youth in Brooklyn. His father, a native of the Dominican Republic who was raised in Santurice, Puerto Rico (near old San Juan), came to New York with his parents and brothers just before World War I. Paisley's mother was born in Pelham, New York, and was of French-Canadian descent. Until Paisley was ten, his father worked as a truck driver in New York. In 1942, his parents "took a shot" and moved to the Tampa, Florida, area where they had friends. "It didn't work out too well," Paisley recalled in an interview for *SATA,* "and we came back to New York in 1944 and my father took his old job." This experience was later to provide some of the background for Paisley's first novel, *New York City Too Far from Tampa Blues.*

Though while in high school he had dreamt of becoming a writer, Paisley enlisted in the navy shortly after graduating in 1950 and was surprised to find himself in the midst of the Korean War one month later. Serving in the military during a war "wasn't my idea at all. I enlisted in May and the war broke out in June," he explained. During his three years in the navy, he served as an electronics and radar technician. As a result of his service in the navy, however, Paisley was eligible for the "GI Bill," which paid for the many classes he took as a part-time student at City College of the City University of New York, where he enrolled in the pre-law program upon his return to the city.

### Musical Career

Although not a professional musician until after he got out of the navy, Paisley performed publicly as a musician, primarily as a singer, from the age of ten. "I think I was ten years old when I first sang at somebody's bar mitzvah on Bedford Avenue in Brooklyn. I always was a singer," he noted. However, Paisley did not perform commercially until he was of age because, he recalled, "the only places that hired live music served booze and New York City regulations required that you had to be over eighteen to perform." During high school, he was in the school chorus and performed for two years with New York City's All City Chorus, but he did not return to music immediately after his discharge from the navy. Rather, Paisley took a full-time job during the day in the insurance business, investigating casualty claims for Lloyd's of London, while going to college at night. It was while working for the New York agents of Lloyd's that Paisley accidently stumbled onto the folk music scene.

Lloyd's of London "took on all these absurd risks,... and I was a claims investigator—I was a general snoop to see if somebody's claim was legit," Paisley explained. "On one occasion, I was following this fellow who was supposedly totally disabled in a gym [accident] and I tracked him up to a place that had live music—a piano player—and he did a lot of strenuous mambo dancing. But after a while, there I was standing there nursing a beer ... and I went out to my car and got my guitar out of the trunk and started playing and singing with the piano player. At the end of the evening, the owner of the place gave me a $20 bill and said 'come back on a weekend and we can do okay.' I came back on a weekend and discovered I was making more on a weekend than the insurance company was paying me in a week. And that was my downfall," he noted, adding

that afterward he gave up claims investigations for the more lucrative world of folk music.

This was a heady time to be involved in folk music, Paisley observed, pointing out that at the same time he was getting his start in the business, others, whose fame in the musical world would later eclipse his own, were doing the same and in the same clubs. "I remember when Bobby Dylan first came to town," he said in his interview. "I remember when Peter, Paul and Mary were working separately. They weren't big news then—they were just starting," he related. During this time he also met and befriended blues guitarist Josh White, whom he refers to as "the man who taught me how to play blues guitar." And after learning the blues guitar from White, the legendary blues man approached Paisley and asked him to accompany his daughter, a singer in her own right, on a tour, serving as her guitar player. At one point, Paisley even recorded a solo album during this period, though the record was never released.

**With the help of a new friend, Tom leaves shoe-shining behind and begins a successful music career in this humorous first novel by Paisley. (Cover illustration by Richard Cuffari.)**

**The Dog Days of Arthur Cane**

T. Ernesto Bethancourt

**A pampered suburban youth sees a different side of life when he is mysteriously transformed into a dog.** (Cover illustration by Bernard Colonna.)

### First Taste of Writing

It was also during this time that Paisley got his real beginning in writing, penning songs he performed himself as well as reviewing records and performances for several publications, including *Stereo Review* and *High Fidelity*. Additionally, during this time Paisley began to take work writing liner notes for several record companies, including RCA and Columbia Records. Apparently pleased with his work on the liner notes, the record companies then began to solicit Paisley to write artist press biographies.

It was "by accident," however, that a few years later Paisley wrote his first novel. "When my first daughter was born, I thought 'My God, she could get to be a teenager and, if for some reason we couldn't talk or I was dead or something equally fascinating, she might wonder what I was all about,' and I started an autobiography," he recalled. Coincidentally, it was indirectly through his work as a musician that Paisley's first novel was published. "I was writing in long hand at a table in a night club I was working at. I was writing between shows and a customer saw me writing and asked to read it. She was very interested in it and put me in touch with some

people." Unlike many aspiring novelists, Paisley did not have to endure the repeated rejection which often precedes the publication of a first novel. In fact, he explained that this "friend of a friend" took the work to Holiday House which resulted in a contract to publish the book. Paisley's "autobiography" had become fiction, and it was published as the novel *New York City Too Far from Tampa Blues*. "Holiday House just kind of automatically bought the next fifteen novels as I wrote them," he added.

Just as Paisley did not set out to be a novelist, neither did he set out to write literature for young adults. However, because he was writing his first work for his daughter to read when she became a teenager—though she had just been born at the time—Paisley naturally wrote it in a style that a teenager would find easy to read and enjoyable. The result is a streetwise story of a half-Hispanic singer-guitarist (also named Tom) who works to get out of the city by becoming part of a successful musical duo. "The whole book is a loose, funny, nonstop rap ... that makes you feel you're listening to [Tom's] spontaneous recollections," a *Kirkus Reviews* contributor notes. *Publishers Weekly* contributor Jean F. Mercier similarly calls the book "real" and "joyously satisfying." And while he finds some of the characters stereotyped, John F. Caviston states in *School Library Journal* that the novel is a "skillfully written, consistently irreverent commentary about life in the tenements and on the streets of the city."

The success of Paisley's first novel led him to write others in the same genre. His follow-up book, *The Dog Days of Arthur Cane,* shows the trials of a privileged Long Island teenager who is transformed into a dog by a classmate's curse. How the experience changes Arthur "is not only wise, it is very funny, and I loved it for its warmth and honesty," Rosalyn Drexler comments in the *New York Times Book Review. The Mortal Instruments* is a science fiction thriller about a street kid from Spanish Harlem who eerily becomes a type of superman; *Publishers Weekly* critic Sybil Steinberg calls it a "sophisticated, superbly crafted SF thriller." And *Tune in Yesterday* makes similar use of science fiction elements in presenting two boys who find a gateway to the past and use it to travel to the jazz age of 1942.

"The first novel was very, very successful, as was the second, the third and the fourth," the author noted in his interview. It was not until Paisley moved to California in 1977, however, that he devoted his full time and energy to being a writer—and then only out of necessity. "Until I came out here, my primary living was as a performer/entertainer. But I came out to California and found that what people pay outrageous money to hear in New York City, they wouldn't go around the corner to hear in California," he chuckled. At that point, Paisley said he decided that "if I was going to survive, I had better write more books."

It was also through his writing that Paisley found he was able to present his political beliefs and values without doing so in a condescending manner. He found that he could weave into the fabric of his novels his abhorrence of the bigotry and hatred that has historically been, and continues today, to be directed at minorities. The author does not deny that political themes recur in his works. In fact, he defines the essential themes which form the structure for his work as "basic values"—among these are honesty, belief in truth, and belief in working through the system. "And if the system doesn't work, demanding to know why instead of attempting to destroy it—that's tied to belief in the system. You don't throw bombs, you go to the voting place," he explained. In some of his works, these sentiments are expressed very subtly in the form of minorities holding non-traditional positions. In others they are much more overtly apparent in the form of direct elements of the plot.

### Doris Fein Mysteries

In several of his "Doris Fein" mystery novels, for instance, Paisley explores the topic of the internment of Japanese Americans in the United States during World War II. During this time, the United States government rounded up many Japanese Americans and detained them in "camps"—a violation of liberties that was allowed to occur largely because of the widespread anti-Japanese sentiments which gripped the country following the Japanese bombing of Pearl Harbor. This issue is of particular interest and importance to Paisley because his wife's parents were among those Japanese Americans interned.

Among the most popular of his novels, the Doris Fein series chronicles the adventures of a teenage girl sleuth. The series includes eight novels published in rapid succession between 1980 and 1984, beginning with *Doris Fein: Superspy*. At this time, the author explained, "there had been books written from the point of view of an internee. I told the story from the outside by introducing a New York City Police detective sergeant named Suzuki. Through him I told the story of the internment." Doris becomes involved with Detective Suzuki in the first novel, in which a trip to New York to visit her aunt and uncle turns into a missing persons case. While the story follows the traditional mystery format, *Doris Fein: Superspy* is distinguished by the "candor" with which Doris, a Jew, and the detective "discuss minority groups and bias," as well as Doris's "cheerful honesty about her feelings," as a *Bulletin for the Center for Children's Books* critic writes.

Paisley pointed out that one reviewer referred to Doris Fein as "Nancy Drew of the 1980s, except that she possesses a sense of humor." He grudgingly concedes the similarity between his girl detective and the earlier version. "I had always cordially loathed Nancy Drew. But this girl detective I invented is a nice, middle-class Jewish girl from Southern California, she's five-foot-four, she's got mousy blond hair and great teeth because her uncle Saul is a dentist. She's constantly fighting a battle with her weight. She's even left-handed," he quipped. Many reviewers find Doris an enjoyable character; in *Horn Book* Mary M. Burns calls her "an

The adolescent sleuth featured in Paisley's "Doris Fein" mysteries often finds herself dealing with issues of race and prejudice. (Cover illustration by Brad Hamann.)

intelligent, self-confident teenager with remarkable intuition and a well-developed sense of humor," while Micki S. Nevett notes in *Voice of Youth Advocates* that Doris "is as spunky and feisty as ever" in the sixth installment of the series.

Paisley has made a point of including a number of other minority characters in his works. "I've consistently depicted minorities in non-stereotypical roles," he pointed out in his interview. "Minorities are primarily misunderstood because people are looking at them from the outside in. I thought maybe through my work people would see that minorities are like anybody else—they have the same goals: a decent job, to live like a person, the hope that your kids grow up to live better than you did." In *Where the Deer and Cantaloupe Play*, for example, a Hispanic boy is intrigued by cowboys and the Wild West, particularly when his great-grandfather, a former cavalry soldier and cowboy, comes to visit. *The Me Inside of Me* depicts an orphaned Latino whose sudden millions place him in a prestigious if prejudiced private school. Paisley has also penned sequels to *Tune in Yesterday* and his first novel.

The political and social sentiments expressed in Paisley's works are really just an extension of the positions Paisley, like many others of his generation, struggled to express during the 1960s and 1970s. "I demonstrated extensively for civil rights in the 1960s, got knocked about in protests.... I did all of that," he said in his interview. In fact, it was the opportunity in 1960 to campaign for John F. Kennedy, who for Paisley represented the ideals of the younger generation, which brought the then-musician home from Paris where he had been living briefly. And though his political activity is much more limited these days, he pointed out that there are still issues from time to time that cause him to join the political fray. "Every now and then something outrageous happens and the bell rings and, like an old fighter, I come out of the corner with my hands up, though not as quickly as I once did," he stated. Among the issues that have caused him to become politically active in recent years are women's rights ("I have two daughters—I want them to know they have a future besides working at the phone company or marrying some putz with a surf board") and gay rights. And, of course, these issues continue to appear in Paisley's works, though he is adamant that his writing never carries a "message."

Paisley is currently working on a novel which focuses on three homosexual characters who he describes as being "sympathetically portrayed." Much of the subject matter for the work, which deals with homosexuals in different areas of the performing arts, is drawn from Paisley's own years in that field. "In a field where what you are able to do is the only criterion, minorities will flourish because what they 'are' is secondary to what they do. This is true of any minority and it is especially true of gays, blacks and Latinos because, outside of sports, that's the only way you can cross the line," he declared.

### Just Getting Kids to Read

And though Paisley believes the political themes that are woven into his work are important, he does not set about to convert anyone to his political doctrine through his writing. In fact, he insists that the most important thing he hopes his readers will get out of his novels is "a good time." "You must ask what is the function of young adult literature? What is the function of juvenile literature? It is simply to get kids into the idea of reading, to convey that reading is a good thing. You want to establish the reading habit through stimulating the imagination. Everybody is under the impression that you have to write something elevating with a moral or a message and all that crap. In juvenile literature you don't have to do that," he asserted. The function of a writer for young adults, Paisley added, "is to interest the kid in reading and trust that the kid has the intelligence, once they go on to other forms, to make up his or her own mind." Paisley feels strongly that authors of works for young adults should not moralize or preach, because "preaching implies condescension and condescension is the kiss of death for any adoles-cent—talk down to a kid and you've lost the kid as an audience."

And what does he do when he is not writing or playing music (he still occasionally pens a song)? Among his hobbies, Paisley counts old cars and old movies. He notes that his love for old movies developed when he was a boy and his family did not have a television. It was regular trips to the Saturday matinee at the local movie house that got him hooked, he added. As for old cars, Paisley calls himself a "car nut." "I've been a car nut for years. That's one of the few redeeming things about living in Southern California—you can drive down any major thoroughfare and see some of the greatest cars in the world," he observed. And, of course, he has owned one of the old classics himself—a 1969 Cadillac Deville convertible which he has refurbished and sold. Most of all, however, Paisley says his main concern remains avoiding a nine-to-five job, which he boasts he has successfully done since the night in 1957 when he left the insurance claims investigation business for a spot in the foot lights of the folk music scene. "Anything to keep from holding a nine-to-five job. And I've done that wonderfully well since I discovered that guy phonying up a back injury in Yonkers. Since then, I've held one day job—for thirteen months I was assistant copy chief at an advertising agency in New York. Oh God, did I hate it. But actually that's a pretty good track record. It hasn't always been swell but at least I've managed to keep alive in the arts all these years."

### ■ Works Cited

Burns, Mary M., review of *Doris Fein: Superspy, Horn Book,* August, 1980, p. 413.

Caviston, John F., review of *New York City Too Far from Tampa Blues, School Library Journal,* September, 1975, p. 117.

Review of *Doris Fein, Superspy, Bulletin of the Center for Children's Books,* May, 1980, p. 167.

Drexler, Rosalyn, review of *The Dog Days of Arthur Cane, New York Times Book Review,* October 17, 1976, p. 41.

Mercier, Jean F., review of *New York City Too Far from Tampa Blues, Publishers Weekly,* April 28, 1975, p. 45.

Nevett, Micki S., review of *Doris Fein: Murder Is No Joke, Voice of Youth Advocates,* June, 1983, p. 96.

Review of *New York City Too Far from Tampa Blues, Kirkus Review,* April 15, 1975, pp. 464-465.

Paisley, Tom, interview conducted by Craig Bryson for *Something about the Author,* August 7, 1993.

Steinberg, Sybil, review of *The Mortal Instruments, Publishers Weekly,* February 14, 1977, p. 83.

### ■ For More Information See

*BOOKS*

*Children's Literature Review,* Volume 3, Gale, 1978.

*PERIODICALS*

*Bulletin of the Center for Children's Books,* December, 1982, p. 62; January, 1984, p. 83.

*Horn Book,* August, 1977, pp. 448-449; August, 1978, p. 400; August, 1979, p. 419; August, 1981, p. 429; March/April, 1985, p. 184.
*Kirkus Reviews,* March 15, 1977, p. 289.
*New York Times Book Review,* April 30, 1978, p. 44; July 8, 1979, p. 31; October 5, 1980, p. 30.
*School Library Journal,* January, 1977, p. 99; May, 1978, p. 73; September, 1979, p. 152; May, 1981, p. 62; April, 1984, p. 121; December, 1984, p. 88.
*Voice of Youth Advocates,* October, 1980, p. 25; August/October, 1986, p. 139.
*West Coast Review of Books,* Volume 2, number 6, 1976, p. 47.

—*Sketch by Craig Bryson*

\* \* \*

# PARK, Barbara 1947-

## ■ Personal

Born April 21, 1947, in Mount Holly, NJ; daughter of Brooke (a banker and merchant) and Doris (a secretary; maiden name, Mickle) Tidswell; married Richard A. Park (in real estate), June 28, 1969; children: Steven Allen, David Matthew. *Education:* Attended Rider College, 1965-67; University of Alabama, B.S., 1969.

**BARBARA PARK**

## ■ Addresses

Paradise Valley, AZ.

## ■ Career

Author of books for young people. *Member:* PEN International, Authors Guild, Authors League of America.

## ■ Awards, Honors

IRA Children's Choice Award, 1983 for *Beanpole,* 1987, for *The Kid in the Red Jacket;* Young Hoosier Award, 1985, for *Operation: Dump the Chump;* Georgia Children's Book Award, Maud Hart Lovelace Book Award, and Texas Bluebonnet Award, all 1985, and Utah Children's Book Award, 1987, all for *Skinnybones;* Parents' Choice Award, 1985, for *Buddies,* 1987, for *The Kid in the Red Jacket,* 1990, for *Maxie, Rosie, and Earl—Partners in Grime,* and 1991, for *Rosie Swanson—Fourth Grade Geek for President;* Milner Award, 1986; Tennessee Children's Choice Book Award, 1986, for *Operation: Dump the Chump,* and 1987, for *Skinnybones;* Library of Congress Book of the Year, 1987, for *The Kid in the Red Jacket;* West Virginia Honor Book, 1990, for *The Kid in the Red Jacket,* and 1991, for *My Mother Got Married (And Other Disasters).*

## ■ Writings

*YOUNG ADULT FICTION*

*Don't Make Me Smile,* Knopf, 1981.
*Operation: Dump the Chump,* Knopf, 1982.
*Skinnybones,* Knopf, 1982.
*Beanpole,* Knopf, 1983.
*Buddies,* Knopf, 1985.
*The Kid in the Red Jacket,* Knopf, 1987.
*Almost Starring Skinnybones,* Knopf, 1988.
*My Mother Got Married (And Other Disasters),* Knopf, 1989.
*Maxie, Rosie, and Earl—Partners in Grime,* Knopf, 1990.
*Rosie Swanson—Fourth Grade Geek for President,* Knopf, 1991.
*Dear God, Help!!! Love, Earl,* Knopf, 1993.
*Mick Harte Was Here,* Knopf, 1995.

*"JUNIE B. JONES" SERIES; FOR BEGINNING READERS*

*Junie B. Jones and the Stupid Smelly Bus,* Random House, 1992.
*Junie B. Jones and a Little Monkey Business,* Random House, 1993.
*Junie B. Jones and Her Big Fat Mouth,* Random House, 1993.
*Junie B. Jones and Some Sneaky Spying,* Random House, 1994.

## ■ Work in Progress

More titles in the *Junie B. Jones* series; a middle grade novel.

## ■ Sidelights

Barbara Park has succeeded in winning wide recognition as "one of the funniest writers around," says Ilene Cooper in *Booklist*. As a writer of comic children's literature, she is able to make people laugh at the foibles and language of such characters as Skinnybones, Junie B. Jones, Molly Vera Thompson, and a host of other lively characters that exist within the pages of her books for young adults.

How does a writer get children as well as adults to laugh at some of the serious problems of growing up? During an interview with *SATA*, Park recalled her editor asking the same question at a conference for writers of children's literature. The editor observed that there were two types of juvenile fiction writers—those who are still children themselves and those who observe children. Then, pointing to Park who was seated at the back of the audience, the editor proclaimed Park an example of the first group of writers.

Park does not quarrel with this characterization. In *From the Inside Out—The Author Speaks,* Park wrote, "Being a child isn't an illness—it's not something you ever really 'get over.' In fact, if you're lucky, there are lots of things about being a kid that can stick with you forever. And I for one wouldn't have it any other way."

Park was "lucky." "I was the class clown," she told *SATA*. As a child she was able to make people laugh. Discovering how to channel the "funny" part of her personality took a while for Park. "I did not have a burning desire to become a writer," she revealed, "nor did I have any burning desire to become a writer." Early in her marriage, while her husband Richard was serving in the Air Force, she decided that writing might be a good outlet for her sense of humor. And the idea of working at home, while raising her family, became very appealing.

Park's first efforts at adult fiction were disappointing. There was a badly edited story for a newspaper magazine that lost the humor of her first printed piece, along with many rejections of stories that she realizes now were not very good. For a short time Park backed away from writing adult literature, feeling that she was unable to master it. Then in 1978 her son brought home a book by Judy Blume called *Tales of a Fourth Grade Nothing*. Park read the book and felt that Blume had captured the type of humor with which she felt at home. Her job now was to see herself as a writer of children's fiction.

Park told *SATA* that she made a solemn promise to dedicate two years to her writing, with hopes of getting a children's novel published. Since her boys were in school and her husband was making a good living, she had the luxury of being able to write full time. "There are writers who would have given anything to have had as much time available to write as I did," she said. "And I decided I would be a fool not to take advantage of it." Writing humor for children came easily to Park, and using her boys as inspiration she set out to write books that would not only deal with juvenile problems and frustrations but, most importantly, make the reader laugh in the process.

Brainstorming for *Operation: Dump the Chump* followed her resolution to have a book published within the deadline period she had set for herself. In this book an eleven-year-old named Oscar Winkle plans to have his seven-and-a half-year-old brother Robert "dumped" on an elderly couple living next door, the Hensons, through a series of intrigues that ultimately misfire. Oscar ends up having to do time at the Hensons instead, leaving his irritating younger brother time to do such things as spoil Oscar's favorite Christmas cards, spy on him while he tries on new underwear, and spill a box of "black widow" spiders on his bedroom floor. *Operation: Dump the Chump* was rejected three times before it was accepted by Knopf. After the publisher accepted the book, Park was asked if she had any other manuscripts. She did, and *Skinnybones* and *Don't Make Me Smile* were also published by Knopf.

### Writing Better Books

Park explained to *SATA* that while she was happy about meeting her deadline for publication, she was not

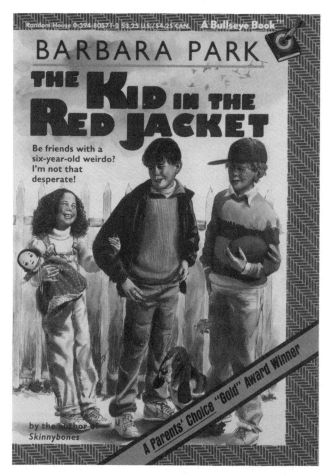

Howard doesn't want to admit he hangs around with a first-grader, but his friendship with a younger neighbor helps him overcome the loneliness of being in a new town. (Cover illustration by Rob Sauber.)

altogether satisfied with the results of these three early works. "The kids liked them—especially *Skinnybones*—and I was glad about that," she said. When asked which were the first books she was happy with, she replied, "I felt that *My Mother Got Married (And Other Disasters)* and *The Kid in the Red Jacket* accomplished what I set out to do better than the earlier ones."

*The Kid in the Red Jacket* is about ten-year-old Howard Jetter, who has to move from Arizona to Massachusetts when his father is transferred by his company to that state. Howard's adjustment to his new environment is complicated by a lonely little girl, Molly Vera Thompson, who adopts him as her buddy. Howard is embarrassed by Molly's attentions and finds their age differences—he is in the fifth grade and she is in the first—insurmountable. When Howard points out this large age difference to her, she responds by saying, "My Uncle Russell likes to hang around with me and he's thirty-seven or fifty."

In *From the Inside Out,* Park said that "Molly Vera Thompson was probably the character I had the most fun creating. Like most six-year-olds, she said almost anything that came to her mind, and I was constantly surprised by the wild and funny things she would do." In her earlier stories Park felt more comfortable writing about boys since she had the experience of raising her two sons, but with *Beanpole, Buddies,* and *The Kid in the Red Jacket,* she discovered "that girl characters can be just as much fun."

The girl's summer camp setting of *Buddies* gave Park the opportunity to explore a number of sharply contrasting girl characters. The fourteen-year-old Dinah Feeney decides to spend two weeks at Camp Miniwawa. On the way to camp, she meets Fern Wadley, a social misfit who bonds to Dinah much to her dismay. Dinah's attempt to be nice to Fern is stymied by her desire to make friends with two top personalities in the camp: Marilyn Powers, whose grandfather owns the camp, and Cassandra Leigh Barnhill, who has all the looks and social refinements Dinah finds attractive. In her desire to be a part of the triangle of the "in" group, Dinah turns against her "nerd" dependent with a cruel and dangerous act. She shoves Fern out of their canoe into the water with the other two girls looking on to prove that she can get rid of the nerd.

After the camp show, which features a cannibal act that the girls had performed with Fern as the one being eaten, Fern thinks she is now one of the group. But when she is later shoved into the water by Dinah she realizes that she has been rejected. She spends the rest of her time at camp wounded, sitting by herself away from everyone else in a secluded part of the campground. Dinah feels guilty whenever she sees her, but does not approach Fern to apologize.

The story of *Buddies* was suggested by a situation Park's son experienced. He knew a boy who had no friends and Park suggested that he should be nice to him as an act of kindness. He made a false attempt at kindness to follow

Turning against a nerdy camper to please her popular friends, Dinah soon finds herself rejected instead. (Cover illustration by Richard Williams.)

his mother's advice, but the friendless boy soon began to call her son at all times and to follow him wherever he went. By trying to do the right thing, the larger problem of how to cut off the friendless person without hurting his feelings was raised.

Park recalled for *SATA* a comment a teacher made about *Buddies:* "She didn't like *Buddies* because the problems were not resolved in the story. It would be nice if everything could be tied up neatly so that Fern becomes the ugly duckling who turns into the swan or the friends are forgiven. But most times in life things are not tied up so easily. I show how the characters handle a situation with the implication that next time they might be able to handle it better—or they might not be able to. We don't know."

Pursuing the subject of "messages" in fiction, Park told *SATA:* "I don't write books to try to impart heavy morals or messages. I don't particularly like it when teachers ask students to list what 'lessons' they have learned from one of my stories. It's not my style to wave a self-righteous finger in a reader's face and warn 'Now see what will happen to you if you do that?' I don't believe that in order to be worthwhile a book must try to teach some weighty lesson for life."

Park counts J. D. Salinger's *Catcher in the Rye* among the many books that have influenced her. After reading it for the first time in the tenth grade, *Catcher in the Rye* became "my favorite book. It was the first book I saw as a person and not as a book, and that is the way I want my books to be to readers. I want all my books to be people! There is an incredible honesty expressed in the character of Holden Caufield and each person can take much out of the truth it expresses."

### The Junie B. Jones Series

*SATA* asked Park why she had turned from middle grade readers to write the Junie B. Jones stories about a young girl starting kindergarten. She replied that Junie B. Jones came about mainly because Random House wanted her to help kick off their "First Stepping Stone" series of titles for independent readers. There was some question if she could handle the grade level because her writing style relies on the use of flashbacks and innuendos that might be beyond the grasp of beginning readers.

Park had already created the character of the first grader Molly Vera Thompson, and she was ready to accept the challenge of the kindergartner Junie B. Jones. In the first of the series, *Junie B. Jones and the Stupid Smelly Bus*, Junie is afraid to ride home on the bus because she has been told that some mean kids will pour chocolate milk in her hair. Instead of going on the bus she hides out in a supply closet and is finally found when she calls 911.

The reviewers of *Junie B. Jones and the Stupid Smelly Bus* gave it high praise. Ilene Cooper in *Booklist* called Junie B. "a cross between Lily Tomlin's Edith Ann and Eloise." Gale W. Sherman wrote in the *School Library Journal* that "younger kids will enjoy listening to it when read aloud. It's a real hoot!"

Asked whether growing up in Mt. Holly, New Jersey, or living in Phoenix, Arizona, or anywhere else, had influenced her writing, Park told *SATA*, "not particularly. I've found that one place is pretty much like another and that people are (pretty much) people. Sometimes I use an Arizona or California setting at the urging of my editor to put some geographical location for a character. I prefer not to do that and I shy away from such specifics. In *The Kid in the Red Jacket* I had Howard move from Arizona to Massachusetts just as opposites to make it harder for him to adjust."

Park has found that the most asked question she receives from students when she visits with them is how one becomes a writer. Most of the time she has to remind them that writers are not celebrities, that they have a regular life and that it is a job like any other. "That means if you have something to say you have to work hard, expect rejections just like you may have to go on a number of interviews before you land the right job," she tells them.

As far as attending writing classes, she herself did not go to them because she felt that in a classroom setting she would write for a grade instead of develop her own ideas. "There are some things a teacher could help you with, like how to develop a plot or the teacher could be your editor, but I don't think you can teach someone how to write something funny. You don't have to be funny to write a mystery—that takes a different mind. The important thing is to find out where your strengths lie."

### ■ Works Cited

Cooper, Ilene, review of *Junie B. Jones and the Stupid Smelly Bus, Booklist,* December 1, 1992.

Park, Barbara, *The Kid in the Red Jacket,* Knopf, 1987.

Park, Barbara, *From the Inside Out—the Author Speaks* (pamphlet), Knopf, 1992.

Park, Barbara, in an interview conducted by Jordan Richman for *Something about the Author,* July 28, 1993.

Sherman, Gale, review of *Junie B. Jones and the Stupid Smelly Bus, School Library Journal,* November, 1992.

### ■ For More Information See

*BOOKS*

*Children's Literature Review,* Volume 34, Gale, 1994.

*PERIODICALS*

*Booklist,* August, 1991.

*Bulletin of the Center for Children's Books,* September, 1990; October, 1991.

*Horn Book Guide,* spring, 1992.

*Kirkus Reviews,* September 1, 1991; August 1, 1992; January 1, 1993.

*Publishers Weekly,* August 30, 1991; July 20, 1992.

*—Sketch by Jordan Richman*

\*     \*     \*

## PEALE, Norman Vincent 1898-1993

*OBITUARY NOTICE*—See index for *SATA* sketch: Born May 31, 1898, in Bowersville, OH; died after a stroke, December 24, 1993, in Pawling, NY. Minister, lecturer, and author. Beginning in the 1930s, Peale cultivated an enormous following with his pioneering blend of religion and popular psychology that stressed simple prayer and positive thinking to overcome the troubles of life, achieve a spiritual happiness, and reap material wealth. He preached his message to thousands of appreciative followers, including such notables as Presidents Eisenhower and Nixon and numerous prominent business leaders. His advice and teachings were captured in a number of successful books which feature short, memorable maxims and steps to success. Most notable is his *The Power of Positive Thinking,* which appeared on bestseller lists for three years during the mid-1950s. Anticipating the glut of self-help books that would become widely popular in the 1970s and 1980s,

Peale was initially criticized by some theologians, who considered his message to be overly simplistic and misleading. The continued high sales of the title, however, made it one of the most widely purchased religious books in history. The success of *The Power of Positive Thinking* propelled Peale and his wife, Ruth, into other ventures designed to promote his ideas, including a television program and the periodical *Guideposts.* Peale retired from his ministry at the Marble Collegiate Church in 1984 after having served for fifty-two years at the institution, which is part of the Reformed Church in America denomination. He continued to write in his retirement, crowning his list of over forty books with titles such as *The Power of Positive Living, This Incredible Century,* and *Bible Power for Daily Living.* He also penned a number of works about the life of Jesus for children, such as *The Coming of the King, He Was a Child,* and *The Story of Jesus.* Peale was the recipient of numerous awards and honorary degrees during his lifetime, including the Presidential Medal of Freedom, awarded by President Ronald Reagan in 1984.

*OBITUARIES AND OTHER SOURCES:*

BOOKS

*Who's Who in America,* 48th edition, Marquis, 1994.

*PERIODICALS*

*Los Angeles Times,* December 26, 1993, p. A1.
*New York Times,* December 26, 1993, p. 40; December 30, 1993, p. B6.
*Times* (London), December 27, 1993, p. 15.
*Washington Post,* December 26, 1993, p. B5.

\*     \*     \*

# PEET, Bill
## See PEET, William Bartlett

\*     \*     \*

# PEET, William Bartlett 1915-
## (Bill Peet)

### ■ Personal

Surname altered to Peet about 1947, though not legally changed; born January 29, 1915, in Grandview, IN; son of Orion Hopkins (a salesman) and Emma (a teacher; maiden name, Thorpe) Peet; married Margaret Brunst, November 30, 1937; children: Bill, Jr., Stephen. *Education:* Attended John Herron Art Institute, 1933-36.

### ■ Career

Author and illustrator of children's books. Worked briefly as an artist for a greeting card company in the Midwest, 1936-37; Walt Disney Studios, Hollywood, CA, began as sketch artist and continuity illustrator for motion picture industry, became screenwriter, 1937-64.

**WILLIAM BARTLETT PEET**

### ■ Awards, Honors

Prizes for paintings at exhibits in Indianapolis and Chicago, 1934-37; John Herron Art Institute citation, 1958, for being one of the outstanding students in the history of the school; *Box Office* Blue Ribbon award, 1961, 1964, for best screenplay; Indiana Author's Day Award for most distinguished Hoosier book of the year for children, 1967, for *Capyboppy;* Southern California Council on Literature for Children and Young People Award for illustration, 1967, for *Farewell to Shady Glade;* named outstanding Hoosier author of children's literature, 1967; Colorado Children's Book Award and California Reading Association Young Reader Medal, both 1976, both for *How Droofus the Dragon Lost His Head;* Little Archer Award from the University of Wisconsin—Oshkosh, 1977, for *Cyrus, the Unsinkable Sea Serpent;* Georgia Picture Book Award, 1979, and California Reading Association Young Reader Medal, 1980, both for *Big Bad Bruce;* International Reading Association "Children's Choice" award, 1982, for *Encore for Eleanor;* California Reading Association's Significant Author Award, 1983; George G. Stone Center Recognition of Merit Award for body of work, 1985; Caldecott honor book, 1989, for *Bill Peet: An Autobiography,* which also won the Southern California Children's Book Writer's Medal; Annie Award for distinguished contribution to the art of animation.

Fanciful rhymes and colorful illustrations fill this tale of a society of bird-like creatures and their island home. (Cover illustration by the author.)

# ■ Writings

*FOR CHILDREN; SELF-ILLUSTRATED; UNDER NAME BILL PEET*

*Goliath II*, Golden Press, 1959.
*Chester the Worldly Pig*, Houghton, 1965.
*Farewell to Shady Glade*, Houghton, 1966.
*Capyboppy*, Houghton, 1966.
*Buford, the Little Bighorn*, Houghton, 1967.
*Jennifer and Josephine*, Houghton, 1967.
*Fly, Homer, Fly*, Houghton, 1969.
*The Whingdingdilly*, Houghton, 1970.
*The Wump World*, Houghton, 1970.
*How Droofus the Dragon Lost His Head*, Houghton, 1971.
*The Ant and the Elephant*, Houghton, 1972.
*The Spooky Tail of Prewitt Peacock*, Houghton, 1972.
*Merle the High Flying Squirrel*, Houghton, 1974.
*Cyrus the Unsinkable Sea Serpent*, Houghton, 1975.
*The Gnats of Knotty Pine*, Houghton, 1975.
*Big Bad Bruce*, Houghton, 1977.
*Eli*, Houghton, 1978.
*Cowardly Clyde*, Houghton, 1979.
*Encore for Eleanor*, Houghton, 1981.
*Pamela Camel*, Houghton, 1984.
*Jethro and Joel Were a Troll*, Houghton, 1987.
*Cock-a-Doodle Dudley*, Houghton, 1990.

*CHILDREN'S VERSE; SELF-ILLUSTRATED; UNDER NAME BILL PEET*

*Hubert's Hair-Raising Adventure*, Houghton, 1959.
*Huge Harold*, Houghton, 1961.

*Smokey*, Houghton, 1962.
*The Pinkish, Purplish, Bluish Egg*, Houghton, 1963.
*Randy's Dandy Lions*, Houghton, 1964.
*Ella*, Houghton, 1964.
*Kermit the Hermit*, Houghton, 1965.
*The Caboose Who Got Loose*, Houghton, 1971.
*Countdown to Christmas*, Golden Gate, 1972.
*The Luckiest One of All*, Houghton, 1982.
*No Such Things*, Houghton, 1983.
*The Kweeks of Kookatumdee*, Houghton, 1985.
*Zella, Zack, and Zodiac*, Houghton, 1986.

*OTHER; UNDER NAME BILL PEET*

*Bill Peet: An Autobiography*, Houghton, 1989.

Author and illustrator of Walt Disney films *One Hundred and One Dalmatians*, 1961, and *The Sword in the Stone*, 1963, and, with others, of *Pinocchio*, 1940, *Dumbo*, 1941, *Fantasia*, 1941, *Song of the South*, 1946, *Cinderella*, 1950, *Alice in Wonderland*, 1951, *Peter Pan*, 1953, *Sleeping Beauty*, 1959, and short subjects.

Peet's books have been translated into many languages, including French, German, Japanese, and Swedish, and many have been issued in Braille.

# ■ Sidelights

William Bartlett Peet's lively drawings were familiar to moviegoers long before he began publishing books for children. As an illustrator for Walt Disney Studios, Peet contributed drawings to such animated classics as *Pinocchio, Fantasia, Cinderella,* and *Peter Pan,* and was the screenwriter for *One Hundred and One Dalmatians* and *The Sword in the Stone.* He left Disney in 1964 and since that time has been populating his books with warm animal characters such as Pamela Camel, Buford the Little Bighorn, and Merle the High Flying Squirrel. His children's books, which are all still in print, have won numerous awards and, according to Jim Trelease in the *New York Times Book Review,* "Children in four states have chosen him as their 'favorite author' in annual state polls."

Peet was born in 1915 near Indianapolis, Indiana. Before he was three years old, his father was drafted into the army to serve during World War I. His father had just finished training camp when the war ended, but he never rejoined his family, preferring the life of an itinerant salesman. Peet recalls in *Bill Peet: An Autobiography* that since he had never known his father, he didn't miss him, and he remembers fondly the years he spent living with his grandmother, mother, and brothers. In the attic of his grandmother's home, Peet discovered his love for drawing, a love that would remain with him his entire life.

### Bad Student Finds Success

But drawing sometimes caused Peet trouble. He was not very interested in traditional schoolwork, and constantly drew in the margins of his textbooks, on his desk, and on his ever-present pad of paper. Although the habit irritated many of his teachers, Peet says that "when it came time for the used book sales my illustrated books were best sellers." Peet told *Christian Science Monitor* interviewer Marshall Ingwerson about a teacher who once pleasantly surprised him: "This particular teacher snatched my tablet away just as the others had done and marched to the front of the room with it. Then turning to the class she said, 'I want you to see what William has been doing!' Then with an amused smile the teacher turned the pages for all to see. After returning the tablet she encouraged me with, 'I hope you will do something with your drawing someday.'"

The summer before Peet started high school, his father returned home. It was an unhappy reunion and his beloved grandmother died soon afterward as Peet looked on, helpless. His newly poor family was forced to move frequently, and Peet had to attend one of the country's largest high schools. By the end of his first year he had failed every class except physical education, and his parents' constant quarrelling drove him and his brothers apart. At the suggestion of a childhood friend that he take more art classes, Peet dropped some of his academic courses and excelled in each of the art classes he took. His success gave him the momentum to pass his other classes, and in his senior year he received a scholarship to the John Herron Art Institute in Indianapolis. Peet was in his element at the art institute, commenting in his autobiography: "It was all peaches and cream, with no devilish academic problems to boggle my mind."

**Peet presents another of his entertaining animal characters in this self-illustrated book.**

After leaving school in 1937, "a poor year to start a career as a painter, or a career of any kind for that matter," he remembers, he sold some of his paintings and filled in the colors on greeting cards for a company in Dayton, Ohio. But he still could not make enough money to support a family. However, when Walt Disney Studios responded to a letter he had written and invited him to report to their California offices for a tryout, Peet shared the roads going west during the Great Depression with many other poor Americans hoping to find jobs in California. He arrived just two days before he was to try out for his new job. All the potential illustrators were placed in a large room where they practiced drawing versions of Mickey Mouse, Donald Duck, and Goofy over and over again, trying to master Disney's roundish drawing style. Peet made the cut and worked for months as an "in-betweener," the person responsible for filling in all the motion sequences of the characters. His steady job allowed him to marry Margaret, his art school sweetheart. But the repetitious work soon wore on him. "After drawing [Donald Duck] a few thousand times I had begun to despise [him] ...," recalls Peet in his autobiography. "It was too much! I went berserk and shouted at the top of my voice, 'NO MORE DUCKS!!!' much to the horror of my fellow in-betweeners." He stormed off the job, swearing not to return.

When Peet returned the next day to retrieve his jacket, he found an envelope on his desk, which he expected to be his dismissal notice. But when he opened it, he found that he was being assigned instead to work on the new Disney movie, *Pinocchio*. This move signalled the beginning of Peet's gradual climb in the Disney organization, for he progressed from creating small background characters to designing progressively larger and more important scenes, eventually writing the entire screenplay and drawing the story boards for *One Hundred and One Dalmatians* and *The Sword in the Stone.* Although Peet certainly had a great deal of success in his twenty-seven year career with Disney, all was not idyllic. Peet, who says in his autobiography that he designed the character of Captain Hook in *Peter Pan* to resemble Walt Disney in looks and in temperament, began to realize in the late 1950s that he needed to escape the stifling demands of adapting someone else's ideas, of continually having his own work changed, and of getting little credit for the work he did. He told *Los Angeles Times* writer Myrna Oliver that "Walt was very sensitive about credit. He would say 'Dammit, we are all in this together. But what he meant was 'the credit is all *mine.*' I knew that *we* stood for Walter Elias. Everything came out 'Walt Disney presents' and the rest of our names might as well have been in the phone book."

## Goodbye to Disney

As Peet's dissatisfaction with Disney grew, he began to devote his free time to developing drawings, characters, and stories of his own. He had no problem with the illustrations, but writing the stories proved difficult. "It finally occurred to me that as long as it was Walt Disney's [story], I could write it," Peet recalls in his

The rather predictable life of a dog takes a fantastic turn when a witch turns him into a strange new creature in Peet's self-illustrated tale *The Whingdingdilly*.

Before his success as a children's book author and illustrator, Peet worked as an animator and screenwriter for Walt Disney films such as *The Sword and the Stone.*

autobiography. "But when it came to doing a book for myself, I could never complete one." Peet managed to publish a few books by the time he began designing the animals for the new Disney film, *The Jungle Book;* but he and Disney were soon at odds over the voice for a character, and after the short-tempered Disney belittled him, he decided to quit. On his birthday in 1964, Peet became a full-time author of children's books.

Out from under the Disney shadow, Peet was able to develop more inventive stories; his first upon leaving was *Randy's Dandy Lions,* a tale of five timid circus lions too nervous to perform. Although Peet has said that the trainer represents Walt Disney, and he the lions, he is glad that he never worked up the gumption to roar back at the trainer as his lions finally do. Peet's favorite book is *Chester the Worldly Pig,* a book that he says in his autobiography "is the one book of mine that reflects my past more than any others." The story traces the adventures of Chester as he leaves the farm to join a circus, only to leave the circus to become a big star on his own.

The author enjoys visiting elementary schools to talk with and draw for children, and once received an idea for a book from them. Peet would often ask the excited students to guess what he was drawing on their blackboard, and they usually knew the answer before he was halfway through. One day, however, Peet outsmarted them by changing the animal as he drew, and soon he

had come up with a combination of giraffe, elephant, camel, zebra, reindeer, rhino, and dog that became the basis for *Whingdingdilly,* his story of a dog who wishes to be different, and finds a witch to help him make his dream come true. Children return Peet's attention by writing him thousands of letters. The author told Oliver, "My favorite compliment from the kids is 'We think your books are funny and make us laugh.' If you are trying to get kids to read, a book should be entertaining. If it isn't fun, it becomes a chore."

Peet's books have attracted much critical attention and have earned him numerous awards. His long experience as an animator shows in his cartoonish drawings; an illustrated page by Peet is always filled with detail and action, and characters come to life before the reader's eyes. Rachel Fordyce notes in *Twentieth-Century Children's Writers* that Peet's books "have an exotic patina of fantasy and realistic detail," and that "the pictures are strong enough to stand on their own." While his characters make the reader laugh, they also draw sympathy. In *American Picture Books from Noah's Ark to The Beast Within,* Barbara Bader calls Peet "the most humane of cartoonists," and Trelease comments that "his characters are less eccentric and have a dollop more warmth than Dr. Seuss' and like Dr. Seuss, Mr. Peet often writes with a message in mind, using animal characters in a fable-like but not didactic fashion." Peet's animal characters are often misfits, but through their resourcefulness and compassion they are able to succeed. Not every critic likes Peet's work, however. For example, *Listener* contributor Derwent May insists that the grotesque drawings in *The Whingdingdilly* make it a "coarse and upsetting fantasy." But a *Bulletin of the Center for Children's Books* reviewer contends that children will not be bothered by these elements of Peet's work, for they are having too much fun laughing at Peet's ridiculous drawings.

Peet enjoys the turn that his career has taken, telling Ingwerson: "So my early ambition to illustrate animal stories was finally realized, and a little bit more, since I had never considered writing one. This way I can write about things I like to draw, which makes it more fun than work. And I still carry a tablet around with me and sneak a drawing into it now and then. Sometimes I feel like I'm basically doing the same thing as when I was six years old: drawing lions and tigers in books."

## ■ Works Cited

Bader, Barbara, "The Storytellers," in *American Picture Books from Noah's Ark to The Beast Within,* Macmillan, 1976, pp. 199-210.

*Bulletin of the Center for Children's Books,* June, 1986, p. 194.

Fordyce, Rachel, essay in *Twentieth-Century Children's Writers,* 3rd edition, edited by Tracy Chevalier, St. James, 1989, pp. 771-772.

Ingwerson, Marshall, "It's Just as If I Was Still Six—Drawing Lions in Books," *Christian Science Monitor,* November 9, 1981.

May, Derwent, "Nun's Tale," *Listener,* November 11, 1971, p. 665.

Oliver, Myrna, "For Bill Peet, Work Is a Flight of Fancy," *Los Angeles Times,* December 23, 1990, pp. E1, E14.

Peet, Bill, *Bill Peet: An Autobiography,* Houghton, 1989.

Trelease, Jim, "Disney Animator to Durable Author," *New York Times Book Review,* March 11, 1984, p. 23.

### ■ For More Information See

*BOOKS*

*Books for Children, 1960-1965,* American Library Association, 1966.

Kingman, Lee, and others, compilers, *Illustrators of Children's Books: 1957-1966,* Horn Book, 1968.

Kingman, Lee, and others, compilers, *Illustrators of Children's Books: 1967-1976,* Horn Book, 1978.

Larrick, Nancy, *A Parent's Guide to Children's Reading,* 3rd edition, Doubleday, 1969.

*PERIODICALS*

*Horn Book,* June, 1971.

*Library Journal,* September, 1970.

*New York Times Book Review,* May 21, 1989, pp. 31, 46.

*       *       *

# PENSON, Mary E. 1917-

### ■ Personal

Born September 14, 1917, in Riverside, IL; daughter of William F. and Estelle (maiden name, Auslander) Schramm; married John B. Penson (a commercial artist), April, 1940 (deceased); children: John B., Bonnie

**MARY E. PENSON**

Blanton, Marge Anderson, James W. *Education:* Northern Illinois University, B.S., 1960, M.S., 1963. *Politics:* "I vote my conscience." *Religion:* Unitarian. *Hobbies and other interests:* Traveling.

### ■ Addresses

*Home*—2608 Fallcreek St., Arlington, TX 76014.

### ■ Career

DeKalb High School, DeKalb, IL, English teacher, 1963-80. Served in various offices of the Arlington, TX, branch of the American Association of University Women (AAUW), and as a docent at Fielder Museum, Arlington. *Member:* Society of Children's Book Writers and Illustrators.

### ■ Writings

*You're an Orphan, Mollie Brown!,* Texas Christian University Press, 1993.

### ■ Work in Progress

Two more "Mollie" books and several novels for young adults.

### ■ Sidelights

"Ever since I can remember I have been writing," Mary E. Penson told *SATA.* "One of my prized possessions is a beautiful copy of *Heidi* given to me as a writing award by the Elmhurst Public Library and the local PTA when I was in the fifth grade. In high school I wrote for the newspaper. In college I wrote for *Towers,* the literary magazine, and as a high school English teacher I sponsored *New Pennies,* the literary magazine, and taught creative writing."

Penson taught creative writing at the secondary level for seventeen years; her students consistently won prizes for their works in competitions held by *Atlantic Monthly* and *Scholastic Magazine.* She has been a guest speaker on creative writing at the University of Illinois Articulation Conference, the Illinois Teachers of English Association Conference, and the National Scholastic Press Association Convention. Penson noted that she has demonstrated the teaching of creative writing to the gifted under a grant from the State of Illinois, served as a judge of literary magazines for the National Scholastic Press, and judged the Annual Excellence in Writing program sponsored by the National Council of Teachers of English.

Penson told *SATA,* "In retirement I finally had time to practice what I preached and started writing children's stories and novels. Six years later, with a drawer full of rejected material, I sold my first short story. Now I write regularly for the Christian press and have just had my first novel, *You're an Orphan, Mollie Brown!,* published by Texas Christian University Press. A second Mollie

Brown book is in the works as are several contemporary novels for the junior high crowd."

* * *

## PETERS, Russell M. 1929-

### ■ Personal

Born January 5, 1929, in Mashpee, MA; son of Steven Amos (a selectman) and Clara (an activist; maiden name, Miles) Peters; married Ann M. Gilmore (a lawyer), 1950; children: Amanda. *Education:* Morgan State University, B.S., 1956; Harvard Graduate School of Education, Ed.M., 1980. *Politics:* Democrat. *Religion:* Indian Spiritualist. *Hobbies and other interests:* Research on Indian history, golf.

### ■ Addresses

*Home*—128 Williams St., Jamaica Plain, MA 02130.

### ■ Career

Honeywell Information Systems, Wellesley Hills, MA, marketing representative, 1961-74; Federal Energy Management Agency, Boston, MA, technical hazards specialist, 1987—. Mashpee Wampanoag Tribal Council, president, 1974-80, 1992—. Northeast American Indian Center, board of directors, 1993. Member of

**RUSSELL M. PETERS**

Repatriation Committee of Peabody Museum, Harvard; board member of Massachusetts Foundation for the Humanities. *Military service:* U.S. Army, 1946-53; served in infantry; became captain. *Member:* Indian Spiritual and Cultural Council, Inc.

### ■ Awards, Honors

Massachusetts Institute of Technology fellowship, 1978-79.

### ■ Writings

*Wampanoags of Mashpee,* Russell M. Peters, 1987.
*Clambake,* Lerner Publications Co., 1991.
*Regalia,* Sundance, 1993.

### ■ Work in Progress

Research on significant Indian leaders.

### ■ Sidelights

"My primary topic is 'The Wampanoags of Mashpee,'" Russell M. Peters told *SATA.* "This tribe met the English when they landed in Plymouth in 1620, yet little is known about this tribe of Indians who have maintained a distinct Indian community. I am dedicated to write about, create visual material [about], and promote the native people who survived the settlement of America. I want to make Wampanoag a word that Americans will associate with the Pilgrims, Thanksgiving, and Indian pride.

"I am president of the Mashpee Wampanoag Indian Tribal Council and work to achieve federal recognition for our tribe. Our biggest struggle is to maintain our identity as Indian people in a society that constantly attempts to extinguish native customs and traditions. Writing and research is a way to make our presence felt, and to continue the spirit of the Wampanoag."

* * *

## PFEFFER, Wendy 1929-

### ■ Personal

Surname is pronounced *Pef*-er; born August 27, 1929, in Upper Darby, PA; daughter of Wendell (a high school principal and college professor) and Margaret (a homemaker; maiden name, Nelson) Sooy; married Thomas Pfeffer (an engineer), March 17, 1951; children: Steven T., Diane Kianka. *Education:* Glassboro State College, B.S., 1950. *Hobbies and other interests:* Sailing, playing bridge, traveling, reading, collecting antiques, cross country skiing, walking.

### ■ Addresses

*Home*—3 Timberlane Dr., Pennington, NJ 08534. *Agent*—Renee Cho, McIntosh and Otis, 310 Madison Ave., New York, NY 10017.

**WENDY PFEFFER**

## ■ Career

First grade teacher in Pitman, NJ, 1950-53; Pennington Presbyterian Nursery School, co-founder, director, and early childhood specialist, 1961-91; free-lance writer, 1981—. Jointure for Community Adult Education, writer's workshop teacher, 1986; member of focus group for Mercer County libraries, 1993; speaker and instructor for creative writing workshops. *Member:* Society of Children's Book Writers and Illustrators, Association for Supervision and Curriculum Development, Popcorn Park Wildlife Club, Patti Lee Gauch Writer's Workshop.

## ■ Writings

*Writing Children's Books: Getting Started: A Home Study Course,* Fruition Publications, 1985.
*Starting a Day Care Business, a Rewarding Career: A Home Study Course,* Fruition Publications, 1989.
*The Gooney War,* illustrated by Mari Goering, Betterway Publications, 1990.
*All About Me: Developing Self Image and Self-Esteem with Hands-On Learning Activities,* edited by Mary B. Minucci and Mary L. Johansen, First Teacher, 1990.
*The World of Nature,* edited by Margery Kranyik and Mary L. Johansen, First Teacher, 1990.
(Coauthor) *The Sandbox,* Child's Play, 1991.
*Popcorn Park Zoo: A Haven with a Heart,* photographs by J. Gerard Smith, Messner, 1992.
*From Tadpole to Frog,* HarperCollins, 1994.
*Goldfish,* HarperCollins, in press.

Contributor to *Past and Promise: Lives of New Jersey Women,* 1990. Also author of numerous stories and articles for publications, including *The Grade Teacher, The Friend, Children's Digest, The Instructor, National Association of Young Writers News,* and *First Teacher.*

## ■ Work in Progress

Several projects, including *Baby Wolves Live in Loving Families, Spiderlings,* and *Sea Turtles,* as well as writing for Silver Burdette Ginn's new elementary science program.

## ■ Sidelights

Wendy Pfeffer told *SATA:* "I grew up in a household of mathematics and language. My father, a professor of mathematics, was in demand as a speaker on 'Magical Mathematics' as well as 'The Origin of Words and Phrases.' Two brief examples of his thousands are: 'COP' being short for 'Constabulary of Police,' and 'TIP' which stood for 'To Insure Promptness.' I was also introduced to the Latin derivatives of words at a very early age.

"Despite all this introduction into the world of words, my love of language probably came from my grandfather who was a medical doctor but would rather have been writing. He did find time to pen one novel and

**Pfeffer presents an introduction to a special zoo that takes in the animals no one else wants.**

spent many pleasant hours dramatizing stories for his spellbound grandchildren.

"I have always loved to read and dramatize stories for young children. Even though not all of my publications are specifically for children, they all deal with children directly or indirectly. Working with children has helped me to write for children, but just working with children doesn't provide all the insight necessary to know what makes a good children's book. A fine writing teacher once told me, 'To write for children, you must find the child in you.'

"From the time I was very young I wanted to write. When I learned to print, the first thing I did was to compose a story like *Hansel and Gretel*. In fact, it *was Hansel and Gretel*. When I was a little older, I kept a diary, then was editor of both the high school newspaper and yearbook. Years later, as I read and dramatized books while teaching young children, I felt that gnawing urge to write again. In fact, I knew I had to write.

"The majority of my work is nonfiction, which, in order to be successful, must be as compelling as fiction. Research is basic to nonfiction and interests me because I learn so much from it. Besides, as I research one topic I always have a file going to add ideas for other topics.

"I enjoy working with children of all ages, leading creative writing workshops, and speaking to school groups on writing. My presentations vary depending on the ages and interests of the children. Even though I stopped teaching to have more time to write, now I feel I have the best of both worlds, working with children and writing. As I said before, I must write—so I do. For me, writing is a challenge and a joy."

## ■ For More Information See

*PERIODICALS*

*Asbury Park Press,* July 1, 1992.
*Booklist,* September 1, 1990, p. 62; June 1, 1992, p. 1760.
*NJEA Review,* October 1992, p. 50.
*Kirkus Reviews,* June 15, 1992, p. 783.
*Library Talk,* September/October, 1992.
*Retirement Life,* May, 1992, p. 38.
*School Library Journal,* November, 1990, p. 98; July, 1992, p. 87.
*Science Books and Films,* October, 1992.

\*     \*     \*

## POWELL, Pamela 1960-

## ■ Personal

Born March 5, 1960, in Boston, MA; daughter of George L. and Doris (a secretary at the Museum of Fine Arts; maiden name, Cox) Powell. *Education:* Attended Wesleyan University, 1979-80; Goddard College, B.A., 1983. *Politics:* Democrat (liberal). *Religion:* Non-deno-

**PAMELA POWELL**

minational Christian. *Hobbies and other interests:* Ice skating, swimming, cross-country skiing, sailing/boats.

## ■ Addresses

*Home*—1320 8th St., Anacortes, WA 98221.

## ■ Career

Writer, 1984—. Operation Crossroads Africa, West Indies, group leader (summers), 1984-85; Outward Bound School, Boston, MA, Rockland, ME, Maryland, and Florida, instructor, 1988-92; World Horizons, Minto, AK, group leader (summer), 1992; Pacific Crest Outward Bound School, Anacortes, WA, instructor, 1993—. English as a Second Language teacher, Prague, Czechoslovakia, 1990-91; author in residence, Cambridge, MA, 1993. Worked on boats as a deckhand, mate, first mate, and captain, in waters off North and South America, 1978—. Instructor in writing; teaches writing workshops for children and adults. *Member:* Society of Children's Book Writers and Illustrators.

## ■ Awards, Honors

Edna St. Vincent Millay Fellowship, Austerlitz, NY, 1990; Arlington Arts Council Grant, Arlington, MA, 1992; third prize for "Write Now" short story contest in the *Ottawa Citizen,* 1992; Walden Fellowship (residency), Gold Hill, OR, 1993.

## ■ Writings

*The Turtle Watchers,* Viking/Penguin, 1992.

Contributor to books, including *Filtered Images: Women Remembering Their Grandmothers* (anthology), edited by Susan Aglietti, Vintage '45 Press, 1991. Contributor to *Kennebec: A Portfolio of Maine Writing* (literary journal); and to magazines and newspapers, including *Sail, Cruising World,* Annapolis *Capital,* and *Ottawa Citizen.*

## ■ Work in Progress

Research on Czech village life and diseases caused by environmental pollution for a second novel for children (set in Czechoslovakia), tentatively titled *The Village Cure; Cellar Boats,* a picture book; and a screenplay.

## ■ Sidelights

"I've always loved to read. I guess around sixth grade was when I first loved writing stories," Pamela Powell told *SATA.* "My favorite teacher, Mr. Seldin, encouraged us to fill our notebooks with stories, poems, or whatever we wanted to write. He used to read to us out

**When three sisters witness a mother turtle laying her eggs, they decide to help protect the nest from the many forces that threaten it in this ecological tale by Powell.** (Cover illustration by Donna Perrone.)

loud too, as did my mother and my English godmother, Pamela, whom I was named after.

"The times I've spent on the water, outdoors and traveling has fed my writing. I have many experiences to draw on. Writing fiction is wonderful because you never know which characters will emerge from where.

"I began working on boats when I was eighteen; after graduating from high school I became a deckhand on a ferry boat in Boston. I loved learning to throw the lines (we would have contests to see who could get a 'ringer' on the first try), and steering. Eventually I acquired enough 'sea time' to sit for my coast guard exam and got my captain's license. These days I mostly use the license as a captain/instructor in the Outward Bound Schools that have sea programs in Maine, Boston, Maryland, Florida, and Washington State, where I now live.

"I am a firm believer in following your heart. Often I don't know what I will be doing for the coming months, but something always seems to work out. It's that way with writing too. I don't usually follow a plan for my writing, but rather see what emerges. I have traveled a great deal, in the Caribbean where I lived for three years and found the inspiration for my first novel, *The Turtle Watchers,* and in Europe, the setting for my next book.

"I like to spend enough time in a place to get a good sense of what the people and place are really like; living and working in a place is a great way to immerse myself. Then once the place is truly embedded in my heart I like to write about it. Often I'm no longer in the place when I'm writing about it, but I remind myself of the atmosphere by listening to music, and hanging postcards and maps above my desk.

"I am fortunate to have found support for my writing early on. A recent gift—a writer's residency in southern Oregon—six weeks to write without any other responsibilities! It came as a real blessing, as I hadn't had a steady home of my own in about ten years! Now I am settling down in the watery area of Puget Sound, and am very glad to be here.

"Among my very favorite writers and books are those for children: Madeline L'Engle, E. B. White, C. S. Lewis, Louisa May Alcott. Their books are among the ones that made me who I am. I am very grateful to them for that. Reading books for kids is still one of my greatest pleasures! And if I can give a child joy and maybe tears through my writing, and in that way change their lives a little, then I feel I have succeeded."

\*     \*     \*

# PROVENZO, Eugene (F., Jr.) 1949-

## ■ Personal

Born December 2, 1949, in Buffalo, NY; son of Eugene F. (a social studies teacher and high school principal) and Therese (an elementary school principal; maiden name, King) Provenzo; married Asterie Baker (a writer), December 24, 1973. *Education:* University of Rochester, B.A. (with honors), 1972; Washington University, M.A., 1974; Graduate Institute of Education, Ph.D., 1976. *Hobbies and other interests:* Designing toys, cooking.

### ■ Addresses

*Home*—4939 Riviera Dr., Coral Gables, FL 33146. *Office*—School of Education, P.O. Box 248065, University of Miami, Coral Gables, FL 33124.

### ■ Career

University of Miami, Coral Gables, FL, faculty member, 1976-85, professor of education, 1985—, research coordinator and associate dean for research of School of Education, 1986-88; writer.

### ■ Awards, Honors

Newbery Library fellow, 1978; National Endowment for the Humanities fellow, 1984 and 1991.

### ■ Writings

*JUVENILE; WITH WIFE, ASTERIE BAKER PROVENZO*

*The Historian's Toybox: Children's Toys from the Past You Make Yourself,* illustrated by Peter A. Zorn, Jr., Prentice-Hall, 1979, published as *Easy-to-Make Old-Fashioned Toys,* Dover, 1989.
*Rediscovering Photography,* illustrated by Zorn, Oak Tree, 1979.
*Rediscovering Astronomy,* illustrated by Zorn, Oak Tree, 1980.
*Play It Again: Board Games from the Past You Can Make and Play Yourself,* illustrated by Zorn, Prentice-Hall, 1981, published as *Favorite Board Games You Can Make and Play,* Dover, 1990.
*Forty-seven Easy-to-Do Science Experiments,* illustrated by Zorn, Dover, 1989.

*JUVENILE; WITH PETER A. ZORN, JR., AND ASTERIE BAKER PROVENZO*

*Spad XIII and Spad VII,* Crown, 1982.
*Fokker Dr. 1 Triplanes,* Crown, 1982.
*The Ford Trimotor 5-AT,* Crown, 1982.
*The Spirit of Louis Ryan NYP,* Crown, 1982.

*OTHER*

(With Andrew D. Young) *The History of the St. Louis Car Company,* Howell-North Books, 1978.
(With Betty Hall and others) *The Historian as Detective,* CEMREL, Inc., 1979.
(With Arlene Brett) *The Complete Block Book,* photographs by Michael Carlebach, Syracuse University Press, 1983.
(With H. Warren Button) *History of Education and Culture in America,* Prentice-Hall, 1983, revised edition, 1989.

**With his wife, Asterie, Eugene Provenzo compiled a number of experiments that allow young people to learn about important scientific discoveries.**

(With Asterie Baker Provenzo) *Pursuing the Past: Oral History, Photography, Family History, and Cemeteries,* Volume 1, Addison-Wesley, 1983.
(Editor and author of introduction, with mother, Therese M. Provenzo) *Mary H. Lewis, an Adventure with Children,* University Press of America, 1985.
*An Introduction to Education in American Society,* C. E. Merrill, 1986.
*Beyond the Gutenberg Galaxy: Microcomputers and the Emergence of Post-Typographic Culture,* Teachers College Press, 1986.
(With Marilyn Cohn and Robert Kottkamp) *To Be a Teacher: Cases, Concepts, Observation Guides,* Random House, 1987.
*Religious Fundamentalism and American Education: The Battle for the Public Schools,* State University of New York Press, 1990.
*Video Kids: Making Sense of Nintendo,* Harvard University Press, 1991.
(With Brett and Robin Moore) *The Complete Playground Book,* photographs by Carlebach and Moore, Syracuse University Press, 1991.
(With Brett) *Adaptive Technology and the Microcomputer Revolution,* State University of New York Press, 1991.

(With Michael Carlebach) *Farm Security Administration Photographs of Florida,* University Press of Florida, 1993.

(Editor with Paul Farber and Gunilla Holm) *Schooling in the Light of Popular Culture,* State University of New York Press, 1994.

Also author of *Education and the International Expositions, 1876-1904,* University Press of Florida Editor, with Paul Farber and Gunilla Holm, of *Education and Popular Culture in the United States,* State University of New York Press. Work represented in anthologies, including *Educational Equity: Integrating Equity into Perspective Teacher Education,* Eric Clearinghouse on Teacher Education, 1981; *Allied in Educational Reform,* edited by Jerome M. Rosow and Robert Zager, Jossey-Bass, 1989; and *Literacy Online: The Promise (and Peril) of Reading and Writing with Computers,* edited by Myron Tuman, University of Pittsburgh Press, 1991. Coeditor, "Education and Culture Series," State University of New York Press, 1990—. Contributor of articles and reviews to periodicals.

## ■ Work in Progress

Research on education and culture and on computers and society.

## ■ Sidelights

Eugene Provenzo once commented: "While I was in graduate school, I focused primarily on historical and philosophical training, but I also received extensive background in ethnography and field-based research, as well as archival preservation and exhibit work. My career as a researcher has been interdisciplinary in nature.

"Throughout my work, the primary focus has been on education as a social and cultural phenomenon. A particularly important concern has been the role of the teacher in American society. Cross-disciplinary methods, as well as philosophical questions related to the process of inquiry and the sociology of knowledge, are also of primary interest to me. In addition, I have followed personal interests related to the impact of computers on contemporary culture and education, local and regional history, and the history of toys, toy design, and evaluation.

"Collaboration is an integral part of my work. I see myself as someone who learns through the process of research and writing. Undertaking various research projects with people in related fields of inquiry has played a critical role in my postgraduate education.

"As a professor and educational researcher, I am committed to relating theory to practice. I have worked closely with schools and teachers, and I consider myself a 'scholar-teacher' working to advance the profession."

## ■ For More Information See

*PERIODICALS*

*Booklist,* May 15, 1980, p. 1337.
*Library Journal,* November 1, 1979, p. 2337.
*New Statesman and Society,* December 20, 1991, p. 49.
*New York Times Book Review,* December 22, 1991, p. 2.
*School Library Journal,* October, 1981, p. 153.
*Times Educational Supplement,* November 29, 1991.

# R

## RINALDI, Ann 1934-

### ■ Personal

Born August 27, 1934, in New York, NY; daughter of Michael (a newspaper manager) and Marcella (Dumarest) Feis; married Ronald P. Rinaldi (a chief lineman for Public Service Gas & Electric), July, 1960; children: Ronald P., Jr., Marcella. *Education:* Attended high school in New Brunswick, NJ.

### ■ Addresses

*Home and office*—302 Miller Ave., Somerville, NJ 08876.

### ■ Career

Writer. *Somerset Messenger Gazette,* Somerset, NJ, columnist, 1969-70; *Trentonian,* Trenton, NJ, columnist, feature writer, and editorial writer, 1970-91. Lecturer, making visits to schools and educational conferences around the United States. Former member, Brigade of the American Revolution.

### ■ Awards, Honors

First place awards for newspaper columns, New Jersey Press Association, 1978, 1989; National History Award for contributions in "bringing history to life," Daughters of the American Revolution, 1991, for her historical novels; several second place awards for newspaper columns; *Time Enough for Drums, The Last Silk Dress, A Break with Charity* and *Wolf by the Ears* were named American Library Association Best Books for Young Adults.

### ■ Writings

*YOUNG ADULT NOVELS*

*Term Paper,* Walker, 1980.
*Promises Are for Keeping,* Walker, 1982.
*But in the Fall I'm Leaving,* Holiday House, 1985.
*Time Enough for Drums,* Holiday House, 1986.

**ANN RINALDI**

*The Good Side of My Heart,* Holiday House, 1987.
*The Last Silk Dress,* Holiday House, 1988.
*Wolf by the Ears,* Scholastic, 1991.
*A Ride into Morning: The Story of Tempe Wick,* Harcourt, 1991.
*A Break with Charity: A Story about the Salem Witch Trials,* Harcourt, 1992.
*In My Father's House,* Scholastic, 1993.
*The Fifth of March: The Story of the Boston Massacre,* Harcourt, 1993.

*A Stitch in Time* (first book in the "Quilt Trilogy"), Scholastic, 1994.

OTHER

Contributor of columns, editorials, and stories to the *Trentonian;* author of self-syndicated column to eighteen daily papers in New York, New Jersey, and Pennsylvania, 1969-70.

## ■ Work in Progress

A picture book about colors, in verse form, completed; continuing work—which began with *A Stitch in Time*—on "an historical trilogy for Scholastic, involving a Salem, Massachusetts, family from 1787 to 1850"; four Revolutionary War novels for Harcourt.

## ■ Sidelights

Although she worked for twenty-one years as an award-winning newspaper columnist, Ann Rinaldi is better known as an author of historically based, young adult fiction. Three of her novels focus on the period of the American Revolutionary War and combine historically accurate details with her own imaginative contributions. Other works, though, are not historically based or are based in other historical periods, including her well-received 1992 novel, *A Break with Charity: A Story of the Salem Witch Trials,* which focuses on the hysteria surrounding the famous trials in colonial Massachusetts.

"I was my mother's fifth child, and she died right after I was born," Rinaldi once told *SATA.* "For two years I lived in Brooklyn with an aunt and uncle who wanted to adopt me. In the household were a lot of older teenage cousins who pampered and spoiled me, but my father came one day and took me home abruptly. The only happy part of my childhood ended."

Although Rinaldi's father worked for a newspaper as a manager, the author continued, "he did everything he could to prevent me from becoming a writer. At school they attempted to take out of me what spirit had eluded my stepmother. My father did not believe in college for his daughters, so I was sent into the business world to become a secretary." Rinaldi worked in typing pools for several years until her marriage; after having two children, she began to write fiction again. She wished to become a novelist, but her work was "terrible," she recalled.

Rinaldi's introduction to professional writing came through the newspaper business, which she has been in since 1969. Though she was not formally educated to be a journalist, Rinaldi moved gradually into the business, starting out by writing a weekly column for the Somerset *Messenger Gazette* in her New Jersey hometown. Two years later, she approached the editor of the *Trentonian,* a larger daily newspaper in nearby Trenton, and was hired to write two columns a week. Several years later she had increased her responsibilities with the newspaper to writing feature stories and soft news as well as her regular columns. Finally, in 1979, she successfully crossed over from the world of newspaper writing to that of young adult novelist by reworking and extending a short story she had been working on for years, turning it into her first novel, *Term Paper.*

Though she had not set out to write a novel for young adults, that is exactly what Rinaldi realized she had in her first serious work. "My good friend was writing for young adults and succeeding very well and I realized that what I had was a young adult novel," she once noted, since "it was a story with a fourteen-year-old protagonist." The term paper of the title is written by Nicki as an attempt to articulate her feelings about her father's death; the assignment was given to her by a substitute English teacher who just happens to be Nicki's much-older brother. Through her efforts to finish the paper, Nicki matures and learns to understand how events have affected other members of the family. The result, according to *School Library Journal* contributor A. B. Hart, is a work that "declares strongly for family obligations of love and forgiveness." Nicki also appears in a sequel, *Promises Are for Keeps,* which details the hospital volunteer service she performs as a way to make up for some childish pranks. The book stands well on its own, M. K. Chelton writes in *Voice of Youth Advocates,* and "Nicki sounds like a real kid, not an imitation."

### Interest in the Revolutionary War

Around the time her second novel was published, Rinaldi's son Ron, then a high school student, became interested in Revolutionary War history, joining a war reenactment group after his mother wrote some stories about the organization and its activities for the *Trentonian.* After Rinaldi's daughter began to participate as well, the entire family became involved in the battle reenactments. Rinaldi credits this activity with sparking her interest in writing young adult novels about the Revolutionary War.

In the "Acknowledgement" to *Wolf by the Ears,* Rinaldi explains that as her son was growing up, his heroes were the founding fathers of the United States: George Washington, Thomas Jefferson, John Adams, and Benjamin Franklin, among others. "These people helped form [my son's] foundation for life which, when tested, held strong," Rinaldi notes. "It is for this reason that I write historical fiction for young people. If I can 'turn them on' to our country's past, and seize their imaginations as Ron's was seized, then I may succeed in doing something really worthwhile."

Although she had trouble at first convincing publishers that young adults would be interested in reading a historical novel, she eventually published her first work based on the Revolutionary War, *Time Enough for Drums,* in 1986. This novel tells the story of Jemima Emerson, a fifteen-year-old resident of Trenton, New Jersey, who watches in fascination as the American struggle for independence from Great Britain divides her town and her family. The novel is based roughly on the historical background of Washington's retreat before the battle of Trenton, though Rinaldi makes the story accessible by adding intrigue, romance, and a variety of interesting characters to the historical facts. As the plot develops, the war comes closer and closer to Trenton and finally into the town itself, with the British even invading Jemima's family's home. During all this, the reader witnesses Jemima growing from child to woman and learning many painful lessons in the process.

While she was trying to convince publishers that young readers would appreciate historical fiction, Rinaldi wrote her fifth young adult novel, *The Good Side of My Heart,* in which she returns to a contemporary setting. The work is consistent with Rinaldi's earlier efforts, however, in that the protagonist is a teenage girl, this time named Brie, who previously appeared in *But in the Fall I'm Leaving.* The story follows Brie's ups and downs as she dates and falls in love with Josh, a handsome but somewhat troubled youth. As in Rinaldi's other novels, in *The Good Side of My Heart* the protagonist is able to overcome a grave dilemma. In this case, she must deal with a shocking secret that Josh carries with him. Though learning Josh's secret at first devastates Brie, she is finally able to find the strength to deal with and ultimately overcome the trauma that results from learning Josh's secret.

### The Civil War and Slavery

In 1988, Rinaldi's *The Last Silk Dress,* another "coming of age" novel, was published. She returns to a historical setting, although this time it is that of the Civil War and based on an actual incident involving the capture of a Confederate balloon. The teenage female protagonist must again overcome the tumultuous and chaotic conditions caused both by the war and the corrupt society in which her family lives. As the novel progresses, Susan Chilmark gradually comes to understand the world around her and even to challenge it. Zena Sutherland, writing in the *New York Times Book Review,* praises Rinaldi for her "convincing" portrayal of Susan's awakening to the realities of racial inequality. *The Last Silk Dress,* Sutherland concludes, is "interesting not only for its theme and story, but also for the evidence it gives of Ms. Rinaldi's respect for her adolescent audience."

In *Wolf by the Ears,* one of the two Rinaldi novels published in 1991, the author returns to the Colonial era to follow the partially fictionalized tale of Harriet Hemings, whom some historians believe to be the illegitimate daughter (by a slave mother) of Thomas Jefferson. In her "Author's Note" section of the work, Rinaldi explains that it was, in part, the alienation which Jefferson's assumed illegitimate children must have felt which appealed to her. "The theme of alienation has always appealed to me," she notes. "My own mother had died when I was born. I never knew her family or even saw a picture of her until I was married. So there was always a part of me I could not acknowledge, a part of me I yearned to understand." As a result, she continues, "when looking for a real figure in American history to write about in connection with

alienation, I recalled Harriet Hemings and her brothers."

While Rinaldi did a great deal of research about Hemings and Thomas Jefferson, she ultimately had to fill in the historical gaps by creating many of the details of her character's life. "Using every fact I could find about Monticello, Thomas Jefferson and the Hemings family, I put my story together," she writes. "My research, however, only told me bits and pieces about Harriet Hemings. And, so, within a framework of fact, I invented my own Harriet." A slave who looks almost white, Harriet is perplexed by her role on Jefferson's plantation and struggles to find a place for herself in society. "Harriet's plight is poignant, and she is a finely drawn, believable character," Bruce Anne Shook observes in *School Library Journal.* Sister Mary Veronica also praises the novel, writing in *Voice of Youth Advocates* that "it is history brought to life by a skillful and imaginative author."

**Growing up in the South during the Civil War is not easy for Susan Chilmark, as she slowly realizes that her support for the Confederates and her dashing, older brother may be misguided.** (Cover illustration by Lisa Falkenstern.)

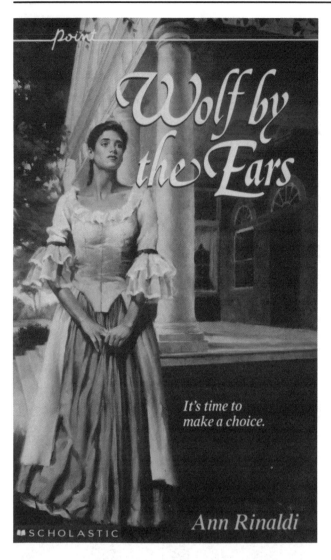

When slavery means living in a happy home with friends and family, is it still undesirable? Rinaldi puts a twist on the issue by exploring the life of Thomas Jefferson's daughter, Harriet Hemings.

Rinaldi's second work published in 1991 was *A Ride into Morning.* Also focusing on the Revolutionary War, this novel follows the tale of Tempe Wick who, along with her cousin, Mary Cooper, must run her farm despite the ravages of the war going on all around them. In her 1992 release, *A Break with Charity: A Story of the Salem Witch Trials,* Rinaldi remains in the historical vein, trading the Revolutionary War for the witch trials of 1692. As usual, Rinaldi uses historical fact for the basis of her story and fills in the gaps with her own imagination. The author again uses a teenage girl as the protagonist: Susanna English. An acquaintance of the girls accused of instigating the witch trials, Susanna narrates the story from the perspective of fourteen years after the event. Early on, she is told by one of the girls that they are only making their accusations as a means of seeking freedom from the harsh Puritan code of conduct. However, she watches as the girls become so wrapped up in the situation that they actually begin to believe their own lies and, ultimately, even threaten

Susanna with accusations of involvement in the occult if she betrays them.

As with her earlier works, Rinaldi has received generally positive reviews for *A Break with Charity,* many critics pointing out that she obviously did extensive research before writing the book. Carolyn Noah, writing in *School Library Journal,* praises Rinaldi's historical accurateness as well as her well-constructed plot. "The plot is rich with details and names that will be familiar to those who have read about the trials," Noah writes. While she faults the characters as "rigid," she concludes that *A Break with Charity* "portrays an excruciating era in American history from a unique perspective." Similar praise for the work was echoed by other critics. *Voice of Youth Advocates* contributor Sally Kotarsky declares that Rinaldi has "once again chosen a historical character who quickly draws the reader into the story." And a critic for *Kirkus Reviews* asserts that Rinaldi has created "an enthralling, authentic story that makes the results of compounding malicious lies with false confessions of terrified victims tragically believable."

"I write young adult novels because I like it," Rinaldi once commented. "But, as with my first book, I don't write for young people. I just write, I have an aim to write good stuff for them, to treat them as people, not write down to them with stories about romance and acne and the spring dance. Real life, as I know it, as I've learned it to be from my newspaper experience and own past, goes into my books.... I draw all my characters fully, give my adults as many problems and as much dimension as the young protagonist. I give them good, literary writing."

## ■ Works Cited

Review of *A Break with Charity, Kirkus Reviews,* July 15, 1992, p. 924.

Chelton, M. K., review of *Promises Are for Keeping, Voice of Youth Advocates,* August, 1982, p. 36.

Hart, A. B., review of *Term Paper, School Library Journal,* January, 1981, p. 72.

Kotarsky, Sally, review of *A Break with Charity, Voice of Youth Advocates,* December, 1992, p. 285.

Noah, Carolyn, review of *A Break with Charity, School Library Journal,* September, 1992, p. 279.

Rinaldi, Ann, *Wolf by the Ears,* Scholastic, 1991, pp. vii-viii, ix-xi.

Shook, Bruce Anne, review of *Wolf by the Ears, School Library Journal,* April, 1991, pp. 142-143.

Sister Mary Veronica, review of *Wolf by the Ears, Voice of Youth Advocates,* June, 1991, p. 101.

Sutherland, Zena, review of *The Last Silk Dress, New York Times Book Review,* April 10, 1988, p. 38.

## ■ For More Information See

*PERIODICALS*

*Book Report,* January, 1993, p. 48.

*Bulletin of the Center for Children's Books,* October, 1980, p. 39; September, 1992, p. 22; December, 1993, p. 132; April, 1994, p. 269.

*Children's Book Review Service,* October, 1992, p. 23.
*Library Journal,* October 1, 1980, p. 2122.
*Publishers Weekly,* August 3, 1992, p. 72; November 8, 1993, p. 78; January 24, 1994, p. 56.
*School Library Journal,* April, 1982, p. 84; May, 1986, pp. 108-109; August, 1987, p. 98; May, 1988, p. 112-113; May, 1991, p. 113; January, 1994, pp. 132-134; May, 1994, p. 132.
*Voice of Youth Advocates,* February, 1981, p. 32; December, 1988, p. 241; February, 1994, p. 390; April, 1994, p. 30.

*—Sketch by Craig Bryson*

\* \* \*

# ROENNFELDT, Robert 1953-

## ■ Personal

Born October 10, 1953, in Chicago, IL; son of Victor George (a minister) and Ivy Edna (a music teacher; maiden name, Jarick) Roennfeldt; married Lyn Amanda Reimers, November 10, 1985; children: Michael Lyndon, Nathan Mark. *Education:* Gordon Institute of Technology, diploma, 1975. *Religion:* Lutheran.

## ■ Addresses

*Home*—9 Childs Rd., Mount Barker S.A. 5251, Australia; and c/o Publicity Director, Orchard Books, 387 Park Ave. S., New York, NY 10016.

## ■ Career

Pressure Point Art Studio, Melbourne, Victoria, Australia, began as graphic artist, became art director, 1975-82; freelance author and illustrator, 1982—.

## ■ Awards, Honors

Australian Children's Book Council Award shortlist, picture book category, 1988, for *What's That Noise?* by Mary Roennfeldt.

## ■ Writings

*SELF-ILLUSTRATED*

*Tiddalick, the Frog Who Caused a Flood,* Puffin, 1980.
*A Day on the Avenue,* Kestrel, 1983.
*The Marmalade Cat,* Omnibus Books, 1991.

Also contributor of children's stories to periodicals, including *Reading Time.*

*ILLUSTRATOR*

Mary Roennfeldt, *What's That Noise?,* Omnibus Books, 1987, Orchard Books, 1992.
Lilith Norman, *The Paddock: A Story in Praise of the Earth,* Random House (Australia), 1992.
Judy Fitzpatrick, *Ella Bella Brown and the Christmas Play,* Ashton Scholastic, 1993.

**ROBERT ROENNFELDT**

Jenny Wagner, *The Werewolf Knight,* Random House (Australia), 1994.

Also illustrator of numerous books for educational publishers, including *I Spy.*

## ■ Sidelights

Robert Roennfeldt told *SATA:* "I was born in Chicago, while my parents were on a study visit. They returned to Australia in 1955. I was two years old." He first thought of becoming an artist at the age of ten, when a teacher asked to keep the best painting he had done during the school year, "a picture of a dark and wet night." He was working as a graphic artist in a small art studio when he published his first book, *Tiddalick, the Frog Who Caused a Flood,* which recounts an Aboriginal legend. After the success of this first venture, Roennfeldt turned freelance to work on his subsequent books.

"When I'm illustrating a book," Roennfeldt told *SATA,* "I envisage what the final artwork would look like hanging on a wall in a frame. That's just my way of wanting to show off my work in more ways than one. Because I do look at a printed picture book as an art form also. I'm not so much influenced by what other artists do, as pursuing my own course of discovery. I still have my favorite artists, though.

"No two books I've done, so far, look the same. Some books tend toward cartoon illustrations, others more toward realism. The mediums I've used are as various as scraper board and watercolor to oil pastel and crayon.

My work is now generally mixed media: colored pencil, acrylic paint and oil pastel."

He later added that regardless of the style or medium he chooses, the one element common to all his work is "texture."

## ■ For More Information See

*BOOKS*

*The Picture People, Illustrators of Contemporary Picture Books,* Margaret Hamilton Books, 1993, pp. 76-77.
*The 2nd Authors and Illustrators Scrapbook,* Omnibus Books, 1992, pp. 84-87.

*PERIODICALS*

*Book World,* November 11, 1984, p. 18.
*Emergency Library,* November, 1987, p. 53.
*Growing Point,* March, 1984, p. 4221.
*Junior Bookshelf,* April, 1984, p. 62; June, 1984, p. 120.
*Magpies,* July, 1992, p. 26.
*School Library Journal,* October, 1984, p. 150; November, 1992, p. 106.

\*      \*      \*

## ROPER, Robert 1946-

## ■ Personal

Born June 10, 1946, in New York, NY; son of Burt (an attorney) and Miriam (a teacher; maiden name, Wickner) Roper; married Summer Brenner (a writer); children: Michael Doise, Caitlin. *Education:* Swarthmore College, B.A., 1968; University of California, Berkeley, M.A., 1969.

## ■ Addresses

*Home*—1321 Milvia St., Berkeley, CA 94709.
*Agent*—Robbins Office, 866 2nd Ave., 5th Floor, New York, NY, 10017.

## ■ Career

Writer, 1972—.

## ■ Awards, Honors

National Endowment for the Arts grant; Ingram Merril Award; Stegner Fellowship.

## ■ Writings

*FOR YOUNG ADULTS*

*In Caverns of Blue Ice,* Sierra Club Books, 1991.

*FOR ADULTS*

*Royo County Tales,* Morrow, 1973.
*On Spider Creek,* Simon & Schuster, 1978.
*Mexico Days,* Weidenfeld & Nicholson, 1989.
*The Trespassers,* Ticknor & Fields, 1992.
*Cuervo Tales,* Ticknor & Fields, 1993.

## ■ Work in Progress

*The Abode of Snows,* a sequel to *In Caverns of Blue Ice.*

## ■ Sidelights

Best known as the author of the critically acclaimed adult novels *Royo County Tales* and *Mexico Days,* Robert Roper has also written *In Caverns of Blue Ice,* a work for young adults which presents a fictionalized account of the life of Louise DeMaistre, the first woman certified as an Alpine mountain guide. *In Caverns of Blue Ice* "was a story I wanted kids to read," Roper told *SATA.* "It originated in little bits of stories I would fold up and drop in my daughter's lunch bag each day. Finally she demanded that I tell her the *whole* story of Louise DeMaistre, the famous French girl mountainclimber, and so I began my book."

The daughter of a famous mountaineer, DeMaistre began climbing the French Alps in the 1950s, while she was still a girl. Roper's book chronicles her progress as a climber and details some of the more exciting experiences of her career, including the rescue of a group of Canadian climbers. The book reaches its climax with DeMaistre's near tragic ascent of Changamal, a peak in the Himalayas. Exhausted after climbing to the summit of Changamal, Louise and a Canadian climber, Lawrence Darnley, find themselves in serious trouble. Seeking refuge from the cold, the climbers huddle together in a crevasse. Louise and Darnley, readers are informed in the epilogue, later marry and their daughter, Martine, inherits their love of climbing.

"Louise's struggle to maintain her identity as a woman while competing with men in a high risk, physical environment will inform many readers about the possibilities and challenges they too may face in the pursuit of their dreams," noted Joel Shoemaker in a *School*

**ROBERT ROPER**

*Library Journal* review. Another critic expressed similar feelings in the *Los Angeles Times Book Review* by writing that Louise's story might inspire some young women to get out of shopping malls and into nature. Several critics also offered praise for the accurate and engaging description of the often dangerous climbs. Jane Van Wiemokly, for one example, commented in *Voice of Youth Advocates,* "I am not a mountain climber nor have I ever had any interest in it, but I found myself turning page after page engrossed by the climbing situations." Van Wiemokly also noted that the glossary of mountaineering terms provided at the beginning of the book is helpful.

Young adult readers who enjoy *In Caverns of Blue Ice* will be pleased to hear that Roper is considering continuing the story of Louise's family where *In Caverns* left off. "I hope someday to write a sequel to *In Caverns,*" Roper told *SATA,* "the story of Louise's daughter, Martine, to be called *The Abode of Snows.*"

### ■ Works Cited

Review of *In Caverns of Blue Ice, Los Angeles Times Book Review,* June 30, 1991, p. 13.
Shoemaker, Joel, review of *In Caverns of Blue Ice, School Library Journal,* June, 1991, p. 112.
Van Wiemokly, Jane, review of *In Caverns of Blue Ice, Voice of Youth Advocates,* June, 1991, p. 101.

### ■ For More Information See

*PERIODICALS*

*Bulletin of the Center for Children's Books,* April, 1991, p. 203.
*Kirkus Reviews,* May 1, 1993, p. 555.
*New York Times Book Review,* September 16, 1973, p. 4; November 8, 1992, p. 67.
*Publishers Weekly,* January 9, 1978, p. 72; June 16, 1989, p. 57.

\*    \*    \*

## RUEMMLER, John D(avid) 1948-
### (Courtney Bishop)

### ■ Personal

Surname is pronounced Rum-ler; Born June 8, 1948, in Granite City, IL; son of Adam L. (a press operator) and Rose C. (Kowalinski) Ruemmler; married Patricia Anne Spencer (an educator), July 2, 1982; children: Jessica Caitlin, Adam Dylan. *Education:* University of Illinois, B.A., 1970. *Politics:* Liberal Democrat. *Religion:* Lean Buddhist. *Hobbies and other interests:* Hiking, travel, reading.

### ■ Addresses

*Home*—1611 Jamestown Dr., Charlottesville, VA 22901. *Office*—c/o Studio 500, 815 West Main St., Charlottesville, VA 22903.

**JOHN D. RUEMMLER**

### ■ Career

Writer, 1980—; Iron Crown Enterprises, Charlottesville, VA, writer and editor, 1983-90; Writer's Digest School and Institute of Children's Literature, Charlottesville, writing instructor, 1990—. Volunteers in Service to America (VISTA), Corning, NY, teen crisis counselor, 1972, supervisor, Teen Center, Corning, 1972-73; has also worked as a public school teacher, a billing clerk, and a steel worker. *Member:* Society of Children's Book Writers and Illustrators, National Writer's Club, National Writer's Union, Phi Beta Kappa.

### ■ Awards, Honors

Eaton Literary Award, 1988, for *Hitler Does Hollywood.*

### ■ Writings

*Mirkwood,* Iron Crown Enterprises, 1981.
*Rangers of the North,* Iron Crown Enterprises, 1982.
*Night of the Nazgul,* Iron Crown Enterprises, 1984.
(Under pseudonym Courtney Bishop) *Brothers in Arms,* Lynx Publications, 1988.
*Smoke on the Water,* Shoe Tree Press, 1992.

Also author of the comic novel *Hitler Does Hollywood.*

# ■ Work in Progress

*Waterfall,* a middle-grade novel; *Prisoner in the White House,* a biography of Louisa Adams; research for a biographical novel about Edgar Allan Poe.

# ■ Sidelights

John Ruemmler's first six published works of fiction have sold over four hundred thousand copies around the world. He credits this success in part to his "travels here and abroad—like my anti-poverty work and my job with big business in Manhattan—[which] have broadened my understanding of people from all walks of life," he told *SATA.* In addition, Ruemmler has worked as a steel mill laborer, a billing clerk, an instructor of adult basic education, a teen crisis counselor, an editor, and an instructor for a writing school. "Writing is an attitude, a way of looking at life," Ruemmler further remarked. "The key is to develop that attitude into something productive, and to do that most new writers need instruction as well as imagination."

Ruemmler's novel for young adults, *Smoke on the Water,* tells of the relationship between an English colonist, Thomas Spencer, and a Powhatan Native American, Eagle Owl, who are at first enemies but eventually come to understand each other. Although these two boys inhabit different cultures, their lives and interests are similar, and the troubles they face, such as racism and parent-child relationships, are similar to the concerns of contemporary young adults. A critic for the *Bulletin of the Center for Children's Books* pointed out that "the boys live almost parallel lives ... complete with enemy rivals for the attention of the girl each boy loves." As a *Publishers Weekly* reviewer noted, "despite a profound language barrier—they communicate a wish to be friends and serve as a 'bridge of understanding between their peoples.'"

This bridge, however, crumbles with the massacre of 1622 in which the Powhatans killed three hundred Jamestown settlers. Although he had earlier defied the wishes of the elders and helped Thomas escape from the Powhatans, Eagle Owl finally joins the warriors of his tribe, and Thomas similarly must unite with the colonists. The boys' very similarity necessitates the destruction of their fragile friendship; such alliances cannot survive social conflict. Gerry Larson concluded in the *School Library Journal* that *Smoke on the Water* is "a beautifully written, well researched, and valuable source of information on early America."

# ■ Works Cited

Larson, Gerry, review of *Smoke on the Water, School Library Journal,* November, 1992, p. 124.
Review of *Smoke on the Water, Bulletin of the Center for Children's Books,* January, 1993, p. 156.
Review of *Smoke on the Water, Publishers Weekly,* June 22, 1992, p. 64.

# RYAN, Margaret 1950-

# ■ Personal

Born June 23, 1950, in Trenton, NJ; daughter of Thomas Michael (an accountant) and Anne (a secretary; maiden name, Jansen) Ryan; married Steven Lerner (a computer salesman), August 29, 1974; children: Emily Ryan. *Education:* University of Pennsylvania, B.A., 1972; Syracuse University, M.A., 1974; attended Columbia University, 1976.

# ■ Addresses

*Home*—250 West 104th St., No. 63, New York, NY 10025.

# ■ Career

Ryan Business Writing, speechwriter and owner, 1976—. New York State Poets in Public Service, teacher, 1987-1991. *Member:* Poetry Society of America, National Association of Female Executives.

# ■ Awards, Honors

College poetry prize, *Mademoiselle* magazine, 1972; Davidson Prize for Sonnets, Poetry Society of America, 1986; New York Foundation for the Arts fellowship, 1987.

**MARGARET RYAN**

# ■ Writings

*So, You Have to Give a Speech!,* F. Watts, 1987.
*Figure Skating,* F. Watts, 1987.
*How to Read and Write Poems,* F. Watts, 1992.

*POETRY*

*Filling Out a Life,* Front Street Press, 1981.
*Black Raspberries,* Parsonage Press, 1988.

# ■ Work in Progress

Revised edition of *So, You Have to Give a Speech!;* poetry manuscript.

# ■ Sidelights

Margaret Ryan told *SATA:* "I knew I wanted to be a writer from the time I was seven years old. We were asked to write a composition about spring during class; it was second grade. All my classmates struggled and chewed their pencils and thought and wrote and scratched out. I closed my eyes, and could see spring: a deep green lawn dotted with dandelions; lilacs in bloom at the edge of the lawn; a robin foraging for worms. I wrote down what I saw. My teacher read it out loud to the class ... I liked the recognition of my talent; I was a shy child who rarely spoke in class, so it was nice to have a voice, finally, even if it was the teacher's voice reading my words. I knew then that I would be a writer.

"I began to write poems when I was in high school. I liked reading poems: Shakespeare's sonnets, e. e. cummings, Edna St. Vincent Millay, Ernest Downson, Edgar Allan Poe. So I began trying to write poems of my own when I was about fifteen. At that time, folk music was very popular, and there was an emphasis on the lyrics of popular songs. So writing poems seemed like a very natural thing to do. Again, I learned that I was good at it: I submitted works to my high school literary magazine, and they were published. It was a great pleasure to see my poems in print.

"In college, I was lucky to have a wonderful Latin teacher who taught Catullus and Ovid and Horace as poems, real living poems, not as artifacts of a dead language. Through him I learned much about the form of poetry, its structure and subtlety. For a time I thought I, too, would like to be a Latin teacher. But then when I was a senior in college, I won the *Mademoiselle* magazine poetry contest and I knew I only wanted to be a poet. So I went to graduate school in creative writing, in Syracuse.

"I met my husband there. We were married in 1974 and moved to New York City. Guess what? There were no jobs for poets! In fact, it was the middle of a recession, and there were very few jobs at all. I got work in an advertising agency that did ads and catalogs for art galleries in New York. I was chosen because I knew how to spell the word 'Renaissance,' and no one else applying for the job could spell it!

**Ryan's love of figure skating led her to write this book, which teaches the sport using easy-to-understand explanations.**

"Eventually, I found work as a speechwriter. It is in many ways like writing poetry: you are writing for the voice; it must be rhythmical and interesting to the ear; it has to tell a story and be convincing. You also have to learn a lot of interesting facts, which can then be used in poems.

"Here's how I came to write a book about writing poetry: from a poetry workshop I was in, I knew an editor at Franklin Watts. He knew I was also a speechwriter, and asked me to do a book about it for high school students. So I wrote *So, You Have to Give a Speech!*

"Later, they asked me if I would like to write a book about something else, and I suggested *Figure Skating.* I have loved skating since I was a child, and it's always nice to write about something you love. Then a new editor came to Franklin Watts, and wanted to do a book about poetry. He called me because on the jacket of the speech book it said I was also a poet.

"I had then been teaching children how to read and write poems for several years, through a program called Poets in Public Service. I taught in schools all around New York City: kindergartens and high schools, middle schools and grade schools, in the city and in the suburbs, and everywhere I saw how much children liked poetry if they could just read it without too much emphasis on 'what it meant.' I had my own daughter by then, too, and I knew that making things—poems, pictures, puppets, cookies, anything creative—made kids feel better about themselves. So I agreed to write the book.

"It was hard to do, because I love poetry so much and know so much about it. I had trouble deciding what was most important to say in five thousand words—which is hardly anything. I wanted to make sure I communicated some of the conventions of poetry, and the excitement of poetry, and answered the kinds of questions I had about poems when I was a child. Finding the pictures was fun. It was great to think up visual ways of representing ideas like repetition or metaphor.

"I still write poems and meet with a group of poets once a month or so to discuss what we've written. And I still write speeches for business executives. And I'm working on revising the first book I did for Franklin Watts, on giving speeches, to include some information on recent speeches, such as those given by Bill Clinton and George Bush during the election [in 1992].

"But poetry is my first love, and I am assembling a third collection of poems. They are mostly about love, but some are about growing up with my brother, others are about my daughter, and some are even about my work. But even in those poems, they are about how I love the things of this world, and love to name them, too."

■ **For More Information See**

*PERIODICALS*

*Booklist,* April 15, 1987, p. 1270; February 1, 1988, p. 936.

*Book Report,* May, 1987, p. 56; March, 1988, p. 49.

*Library Talk,* May, 1993, p. 11.

*School Library Journal,* August, 1987, p. 98; March, 1988, p. 209; January, 1992, p. 132.

*Voice of Youth Advocates,* August, 1987, p. 139.

*Wilson Library Journal,* June, 1987, p. 65.

# S

ANNE LINDBERGH SAPIEYEVSKI

## SAPIEYEVSKI, Anne Lindbergh 1940-1993
## (Anne Lindbergh Feydy, Anne Lindbergh)

### ■ Personal

Born October 2, 1940, in New York, NY; died of cancer, December 10, 1993, in Thetford Center, VT; daughter of Charles Augustus (an aviator) and Anne (a writer; maiden name, Morrow) Lindbergh; married Julien Feydy (divorced); married Jerzy Sapieyevski (a composer and conductor), January, 1978 (divorced); married Noel Perrin (a writer and college professor), 1988; children: (first marriage) Charles, Constance; (second marriage) Marek (son). *Education:* Attended Radcliffe College and Sorbonne, University of Paris. *Hobbies and other interests:* Reading, walking ("preferably alone"), swimming, listening to music.

### ■ Addresses

*Home*—Washington, D.C. *Agent*—Harriet Wasserman, 230 East 48th St., New York, NY 10017.

### ■ Career

Writer.

### ■ Writings

*FOR CHILDREN; UNDER NAME ANNE LINDBERGH*

*North to the Orient,* Harcourt, 1966.
*The Unicorn & Other Poems,* Random, 1972.
*Osprey Island,* illustrated by Maggie Kaufman Smith, Houghton, 1974.
*War Within & Without: Diaries & Letters, Nineteen Thirty-Nine to Nineteen Forty-Four,* Harcourt, 1980.
*The People in Pineapple Place,* Harcourt, 1982.
*Nobody's Orphan,* Harcourt, 1983.
*Bailey's Window,* illustrated by Kinuko Craft, Harcourt, 1984.
*The Worry Week,* illustrated by Kathryn Hewitt, Harcourt, 1985.
*Hour of Lead,* Redpath, 1986.
*The Hunky-Dory Dairy,* illustrated by Julie Brinkloe, Harcourt, 1986.
*The Shadow on the Dial,* HarperCollins, 1987.
*Next Time, Take Care,* illustrated by Susan Hoguet, Harcourt, 1987.
*The Prisoner of Pineapple Place,* Avon, 1988.
*Tidy Lady,* illustrated by Hoguet, Harcourt, 1989.
*Dearly Beloved,* Buccaneer Books, 1991.
*Gift from the Sea,* Random, 1991.
*Three Lives to Live,* Little, Brown, 1992.
*Travel Far, Pay No Fare,* HarperCollins, 1992.
*Nick of Time,* Little, Brown, 1994.

*OTHER*

Contributor of short stories, some under name Anne Lindbergh Feydy, to periodicals, including *Vogue* and *Redbook.*

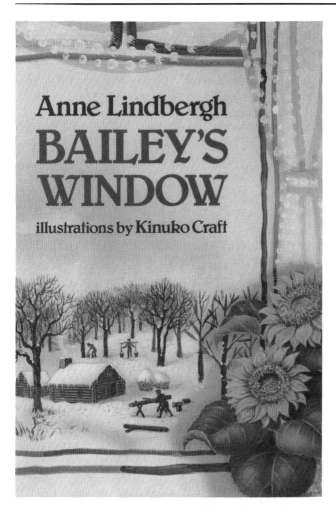

Anne Lindbergh
BAILEY'S
WINDOW
illustrations by Kinuko Craft

Fantasy and adventure are in store for Anna and Carl when their cousin Bailey discovers he can enter the pictures he draws on the wall next to his bed. (Cover illustration by Kinuko Craft.)

## ■ Sidelights

Anne Lindbergh Sapieyevski, daughter of aviator Charles Lindbergh and writer Anne Morrow Lindbergh, once told Jean F. Mercier in a *Publishers Weekly* interview how her parents had influenced her writing: "I would willingly hand anything over to my mother, and she would willingly read it," Sapieyevski recalled. "But, you know, she's too much of a mother. She would offer support rather than suggestions: 'it's very nice, dear,' no direct literary criticism.... My father was much more helpful." According to Sapieyevski, Charles Lindbergh "never stopped trying to perfect his own work," and he was similarly scrupulous about editing his daughter's manuscripts. "He visited me in Paris, the year before he died, and spent days going over my manuscript and saying things like, 'this is repetitive; this is too long.' I was just dizzy from the comments! But *he* was right too. He was absolutely able to take a book apart and find all the weak spots."

One of Sapieyevski's first books to gain significant note was her 1982 story *The People in Pineapple Place.* In this tale, August Brown is a young boy who has just moved to Washington D.C. with his mother, following his parents' divorce. He is lonely and unhappy until he discovers Pineapple Place, a magical street where time stands still. There August makes friends with seven children who help him see that his new home can be a happy and fun place. Due to Pineapple Place's nature, however, the street periodically moves from place to place, and when it prepares to leave the Washington D.C. area, August must learn to live in his new home without his friends. A *Publishers Weekly* reviewer called the book "witty" and "touching," with "continuing surprises." And Kathleen Leverich, writing in the *New York Times Book Review,* stated that Sapieyevski "brings vitality and charm to her descriptions."

For her 1983 book *Nobody's Orphan,* Sapieyevski created a story about a young girl named Martha, who, unhappy with her home life, becomes convinced that she is adopted. Her feelings are solidified when she meets an elderly couple who she is sure are her real grandparents. With the help of some understanding people, she finds happiness by the tale's end. One of the characters, an elderly, talkative man named Amory, is based partly on Sapieyevski's father. "Amory quotes nonstop from Calvin Coolidge and Robert Service," she explained to Mercier, "the way my father used to, at home." When Sapieyevski's editor advised her to check the accuracy of Amory's quotations, however, she discovered that Coolidge and Service "had never said any such things. My father had made up all of those 'quotes' himself." Katharine Bruner wrote in *School Library Journal* that the author's "characterizations ... ring true."

## Fantasies and Realism

While a number of Sapieyevski's books—like *Nobody's Orphan*—deal with events in the everyday world, a good portion of her writing deals with fantastic elements woven into reality. She commented that children are often the best audiences for this type of fiction because "a child is quite likely to challenge the logical and accept the fantastic." For her next book, *Bailey's Window,* Sapieyevski tested her readers' willingness to accept the whimsical. The title character is a pesky boy who must spend the summer with his aunt, uncle, and cousins while his parents attend to urgent business. Unhappy with being dumped off by his parents, Bailey proceeds to disrupt the summer activities of his cousins. Feeling unwanted and shunned, Bailey retreats to the attic of the house, where, hot and bored, he discovers that by drawing a picture with crayons, he can then enter that picture and explore a whole new world. He decides to share his newfound power with his cousins, and the children soon become friends as they embark on a series of adventures. A *Publishers Weekly* reviewer called *Bailey's Window* a "grand, spellbinding adventure," and *School Library Journal* contributor Nancy Berkowitz characterized the dialogue as "natural," while also praising the story's humor.

In her next book, 1985's *The Worry Week,* Sapieyevski returned to realism with her story of three sisters who trick their parents and arrange a week alone at their favorite vacation spot: a summer house in Maine. Comparing the book favorably to its predecessors, a *Publishers Weekly* reviewer called the book "enchanting." Sapieyevski followed the book with two more in 1986, *Hour of Lead* and *The Hunky-Dory Dairy,* which tells the magical story of a young girl and her single mother taking a time-traveling trip through an old dairy.

*The Shadow on the Dial,* published in 1987, is another of Sapieyevski's novels that centers on reality-based fantasy. Siblings Dawn and Marcus are taken to stay with their cranky, bachelor Uncle Doo while their parents enjoy a vacation. While in Doo's garden, Marcus turns a sundial and suddenly Mr. Bros appears with his van that reads "Twentieth Century Bros Removers, Your Hearts Desire, Just Dial." The children are soon accompanying Mr. Bros on a series of time travels that take them from the childhood of their uncle to their own future as adults. Along the way Dawn and Marcus alter some events and provide their uncle with a happier life. While reviews of the book were mixed, there were several critics who perceived the book as worthwhile. *Voice of Youth Advocates* reviewer Nancy Choice favorably compared *The Shadow on the Dial* to the popular movie *Back to the Future,* stating that the book "should appeal to younger YAs" who are fans of the movie. A review in *Publishers Weekly* termed the novel an "entrancing" and "believable fantasy." Reviewing the book in *Horn Book,* Nancy Vasilakis called the book "a time-warp fantasy of appealing complexity" that is presented "in the classic tradition."

Sapieyevski also published *Next Time, Take Care* in 1987, a story about a young boy left with his knitting-obsessed aunt. The following year, she published *The Prisoner of Pineapple Place,* a sequel to *The People of Pineapple Place.* As in the first book, the invisible neighborhood on Pineapple Place has continued to move about. This time it has landed in Connecticut, where one of its residents, Jeremiah Jenkins, befriends a local girl named Ruby. Jeremiah is bored with his life as a perpetual nine-year-old, and he feels trapped in the street's repetitive environment—he had been through the fourth grade fifty times! He is excited when he discovers that Ruby can see and hear him, and he is eager to join the world and grow up. The only problem is that his defection may change the magic of Pineapple Place forever. Constance A. Mellon wrote in the *School Library Journal* that *The Prisoner of Pineapple Place* is "written with a style and balance that marks all good writing." And a reviewer for *Publishers Weekly* stated that "the logic of the story is flawless."

Sapieyevski followed *The Prisoner of Pineapple Place* with *Tidy Lady* in 1989. The environmentally conscious story is about a group of children who help a neighbor lady clean her yard—right down to the removal of the trees, the grass, and even the stars above. Fortunately, the children replace the natural items once the lady has moved. Sapieyevski followed this book with two publications in 1991, *Dearly Beloved* and *Gift from the Sea.*

## Time Travel

One of two books by Sapieyevski published in 1992, *Three Lives to Live* explores one of the author's favorite themes: time travel. In this story, twelve-year-old Garet relates, in the form of a school assigned autobiography, the sudden appearance of her twin sister Daisy at the age of twelve. It seems that the laundry chute in Garet's house is actually a portal to different time periods. It is soon discovered that Daisy is actually a twelve-year-old version of Garet's sole surviving relative, the grandmother with whom she lives. Then why is Daisy the spitting image of Garet? The answer is that Garet popped down the laundry chute ten years ago as a two-year-old version of her grandmother. The story goes on to explain that while they are technically three version of the same person, their separate experiences and choices make Garet, Daisy, and Grandma clear individuals. A writer for *Kirkus Reviews* called *Three Lives to Live* "lively and entertaining," while Deborah Stevenson wrote in the *Bulletin of the Center for Children's*

**Making a wish on a magical sundial isn't as simple as it at first seems to Dawn and Marcus, even when they unselfishly ask that their uncle find happiness.** (Cover illustration by Richard Jesse Watson.)

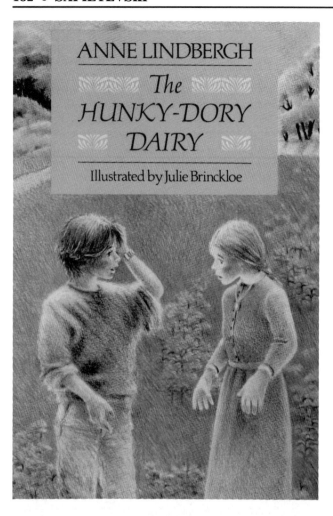

ANNE LINDBERGH
The
HUNKY-DORY
DAIRY

Illustrated by Julie Brinckloe

**Zannah and her mother Patty discover a peaceful, romantic world at an isolated dairy, where a family from the past has been trapped in the present.** (Cover illustration by Julie Brinkloe.)

*Books* that Sapieyevski's novel is "a funny and interestingly offbeat story."

Sapieyevski's second book of 1992 is *Travel Far, Pay No Fare,* which tells the story of displaced city boy Owen Noonan. Owen is in Vermont because his mother is marrying his deceased aunt's husband, making Owen's bothersome cousin Parsley his stepsister. What promises to be an unhappy, boring summer soon takes an unexpected twist when Parsley reveals to Owen that she has a magic bookmark. This bookmark will enable them to enter the world of whatever book it is placed in. Owen and Parsley take advantage of this magic to enter such classic books as *Alice's Adventures in Wonderland, The Yearling,* and others. While in the stories, the pair attempt to save doomed animals, bringing them back into their world. While they are successful in bringing the animals back, when they reread the book, the story does not change. This teaches the pair to accept things for what they are—especially the marriage of their respective parents. In another *Bulletin of the Center for Children's Books* review, Stevenson admired Sapieyevski's "surprisingly successful" combination of her characters with the characters and stories from classic

literature and termed the book "a satisfying substitute" for children searching for their own mystical excursions. Writing in *Voice of Youth Advocates,* Jane Chandra called *Travel Far, Pay No Fare* "an imaginative, well-written" story.

The book *Nick of Time,* which was published after Sapieyevski's death in 1993, returns again to the theme of time travel. Set in New Hampshire, the story tells about four children, Jericho, Alison, and Bunny, who are from the present, and Nick, who is from the year 2094. Nick is able to travel back to the twentieth century by walking through a portal in the kitchen wall of Jericho's house, where his father runs a school. The children soon discover that they can travel to Nick's time as easily as he can visit theirs. A conflict arises, however, when Alison begins to long for a life with Nick's family in the future, but Jericho has a crush on Alison and wants her to stay. *School Library Journal* contributor Mary Jo Drungil praised the "fast pace and fresh, funny delivery," calling the book a "must-read for fans of light fantasy."

For Anne Sapieyevski the creative process began well before she put pen to paper. "I write very quickly, but writing comes only at the end of a long process of 'walking out' the book," she once commented, "A basic idea comes first, along with one or two central characters. It then takes me several months to 'learn' my characters. During this time I wander around outside a lot, while the characters become clear and real to the point where I begin to imagine how they would react in whatever circumstances come up in my everyday life. The action of the completed book is, in a way, only an incident in the lives of my characters." Sapieyevski continued: "Once the characters are ready, I work out the plot. I try to avoid note-taking, as this tends to confuse me later; I do not allow myself to sit down and write until each chapter is totally thought through. Then I scribble. The reason for all the walking is that if I stay home, I am willingly distracted by the slightest temptation unless the story is really ready to go down on paper."

Sapieyevski refused to structure her writing around a set daily routine. "I enjoy writing," she commented, "and in the case of children's books, would rather be writing than not writing, but to write at all I need enormous amounts of space. For years I made the mistake of shutting myself up in a special room at a special time to write. This didn't work. It was boring and unproductive and made me feel guilty. Then I learned that the time and place I write don't really matter. When something is ready to be written I *always* get it down on paper somehow. The important thing is the time and place I *don't* write: hours alone in my house or outside, emptying out all formulated thoughts, leaving my mind free to fill up with what I didn't know I knew. Of course there are drawbacks to this state of mind. This is the period when I throw ice cubes in the waste paper basket rather than the sink because they are apparently solid and forget to feed the children dinner (which they don't mind) and dye all the laundry green (which they do). But without this space, I don't think I could write at all."

## ■ Works Cited

Review of *Bailey's Window, Publishers Weekly,* April 27, 1984, p. 87.

Berkowitz, Nancy, review of *Bailey's Window, School Library Journal,* May, 1984, p. 82.

Bruner Katharine, review of *Nobody's Orphan, School Library Journal,* November, 1983, p. 79.

Chandra, Jane, review of *Travel Far, Pay No Fare, Voice of Youth Advocates,* April, 1993.

Choice, Nancy, review of *The Shadow on the Dial, Voice of Youth Advocates,* June, 1987, pp. 90-91.

Drungil, Mary Jo, review of *Nick of Time, School Library Journal,* April, 1994, p. 128.

Leverich, Kathleen, review of *The People in Pineapple Place, New York Times Book Review,* March 20, 1983, p. 30.

Mellon, Constance A., review of *The Prisoner of Pineapple Place, School Library Journal,* August, 1988, p. 96.

Mercier, Jean F., "PW Interviews Anne Lindbergh," *Publishers Weekly,* July 27, 1984, pp. 147-148.

Review of *The People of Pineapple Place, Publishers Weekly,* August 6, 1992, p. 69.

Review of *The Prisoner of Pineapple Place, Publishers Weekly,* June 10, 1988, p. 81.

Review of *The Shadow of the Dial, Publishers Weekly,* June 12, 1987, p. 97.

Stevenson, Deborah, review of *Three Lives to Live, Bulletin of the Center for Children's Books,* June, 1992, p. 269.

Stevenson, Deborah, review of *Travel Far, Pay No Fare, Bulletin of the Center for Children's Books,* November, 1992.

Review of *Three Lives to Live, Kirkus Reviews,* May 15, 1992, p. 672.

Vasilakis, Nancy, review of *The Shadow on the Dial, Horn Book,* July/August, 1987, p. 463.

Review of *The Worry Week, Publishers Weekly,* March 22, 1985, p. 60.

## ■ For More Information See

*PERIODICALS*

*Bulletin of the Center for Children's Books,* October, 1982, p. 30; November, 1983, p. 53; July, 1984, p. 208; September, 1986, p. 12.

*Horn Book,* December, 1982, p. 650.

*Kirkus Reviews,* November 1, 1983; May 15, 1988; October 15, 1988; August 1, 1989; November 1, 1992, p. 1308.

*New York Times Book Review,* August 10, 1986, p. 25; January 17, 1988, p. 28.

*Publishers Weekly,* November 11, 1983, p. 47; March 22, 1985, p. 60; April 25, 1986, p. 79; May 13, 1988, p. 279; November 11, 1988, p. 60; August 25, 1989, p. 63; March 30, 1990, p. 65; May 4, 1992, p. 57; October 12, 1992, p.80.

*School Library Journal,* October, 1982, p. 153; August, 1985, p. 67; August, 1986, p. 95; July/August, 1987,

p. 97; December, 1988, p. 89; November, 1989, p. 88; June, 1992, p. 121; December, 1992, p. 113.

*Washington Post,* March 18, 1983.

*Washington Post Magazine,* February 6, 1983.

*OBITUARIES:*

*PERIODICALS*

*Chicago Tribune,* December 13, 1993, Section 4, p. 8.

*New York Times,* December 12, 1993, p. 60.

*Publishers Weekly,* January 24, 1994, p. 25.

*School Library Journal,* February, 1994, p. 18.

*Washington Post,* December 13, 1993, p. D6.*

\*          \*          \*

## SARGENT, Pamela 1948-

## ■ Personal

Born March 20, 1948, in Ithaca, NY. *Education:* State University of New York, Binghamton, B.A., 1968, M.A., 1970.

## ■ Addresses

*Home*—Box 486, Johnson City, NY 13790. *Agent*—Joseph Elder Agency, 150 West 87th St., Suite 6-D, New York, NY 10024.

## ■ Career

Honigsbaum's, Albany, NY, model and sales clerk, 1965-66; Endicott Coil Company, Albany, solderer on

**PAMELA SARGENT**

assembly line, 1966; Towne Distributors, Albany, sales clerk, 1966; Harpur College Library, State University of New York, Binghamton, typist in cataloging department, 1966-67; Webster Paper Company, Albany, office worker and receptionist, 1969; State University of New York, Binghamton, teaching assistant in philosophy, 1969-71; writer, 1969—. *Member:* Amnesty International, Authors Guild, Authors League of America, National Wildlife Federation, Science Fiction and Fantasy Writers of America.

## ■ Awards, Honors

Best Books for Young Adults citation, American Library Association, 1983, for *Earthseed;* Nebula Award (best novelette), Science Fiction and Fantasy Writers of America, 1992, LOCUS Award (best novelette), 1993, and Hugo Award nomination, all for "Danny Goes to Mars."

## ■ Writings

*FICTION*

*Cloned Lives,* Fawcett, 1976.
*Starshadows* (short stories), Ace, 1977.
*The Sudden Star,* Fawcett, 1979, published in England as *The White Death,* Fontana, 1980.
*The Golden Space,* Simon & Schuster, 1982.
*The Alien Upstairs,* Doubleday, 1983.
*The Mountain Cage,* illustrated by Judy King-Rieniets, Cheap Street, 1983.
*The Shore of Women,* Crown, 1986.
*Venus of Dreams,* Bantam, 1986.
*The Best of Pamela Sargent,* edited by Martin H. Greenberg, Academy, 1987.
*Venus of Shadows,* Doubleday, 1988.
*Ruler of the Sky: A Novel of Genghis Khan,* Crown, 1993.

*YOUNG ADULT FICTION*

*Earthseed,* Harper, 1983.
*Alien Child,* Harper, 1988.

*"EARTHMINDS" TRILOGY*

*Watchstar,* Pocket Books, 1980.
*Eye of the Comet,* Harper, 1984.
*Homesmind,* Harper, 1984.

*EDITOR AND CONTRIBUTOR*

*Women of Wonder: Science Fiction Stories by Women about Women,* Random House, 1975.
*Bio-Futures: Science Fiction Stories about Biological Metamorphosis,* Random House, 1976.
*More Women of Wonder: Science Fiction Novelettes by Women about Women,* Random House, 1976.
*The New Women of Wonder: Recent Science Fiction Stories by Women about Women,* Random House, 1978.

*OTHER*

(Editor with Ian Watson) *Afterlives: Stories about Life after Death,* Random House, 1986.

Contributor to numerous anthologies and science fiction and fantasy magazines. *Bulletin of the Science Fiction Writers of America,* managing editor, 1970-73, assistant editor, 1973-75, market report editor, 1973-76, co-editor, 1983-1992. Sargent's manuscripts are held by the David Paskow Science Fiction Collection, Temple University.

## ■ Sidelights

"Most of my writing has been science fiction and fantasy, a form that, by distancing the reader from our world as it is, can also bring certain aspects of it into sharper focus," says author, editor and anthologist Pamela Sargent of her chosen genre. Writing in the afterword to *The Work of Pamela Sargent: An Annotated Bibliography and Guide*—an annotated bibliography of the author's work compiled by Jeffrey M. Elliot—Sargent contends that "a genre sometimes unfairly labeled 'escape fiction' can give us a sense of our own possibilities."

Sargent spent most of her early childhood in Ithaca, New York, where her parents had attended Cornell University and settled after Sargent's father's service in the U.S. Marine Corps. The author's interest in reading and writing began at an early age. Sargent could read before she started school, and in grade school she wrote plays for her friends. During her adolescent years, Sargent wrote autobiographical short stories modeled after the work of J. D. Salinger (the author of *Catcher in the Rye*). She also loved to tell stories, often making up tales to entertain both her brothers and sister, as well as fellow campers at summer camp.

Sargent read her first science fiction book, *Man of Many Minds* by E. Everett Evans, by accident. When she was twelve years old, Sargent ordered several paperback books. When they arrived, she discovered that the science fiction book had been included by mistake. "It was a revelation," she told Elliot. "Here was a protagonist who could read other minds, who boarded a spaceship and traveled to another planet, who met aliens—it all struck me as terribly original.... I didn't know there was a tradition of writing where such notions were commonplace." Sargent later read *The Stars My Destination* by Alfred Bester and discovered H. G. Wells, whose work she chose as the topic for her senior high school English paper. During her teens, she was also a regular viewer of the television series *The Twilight Zone.*

Sargent's love for reading and writing continued to grow while she attended preparatory school. At the Albany Academy for Girls, she developed a reputation as a class comic and prankster, but still found the time to contribute stories and artwork to the school literary magazine. The school yearbook predicted Sargent would someday be a successful writer, but she was unsure about her writing abilities. When she enrolled at the State University of New York (SUNY) at Binghamton, she entered the philosophy program although the school offered creative writing courses. "I still didn't know what I wanted to do," Sargent admitted to Elliot, "but at least philosophy could train me in how to think."

While Sargent's interest in science fiction had just begun to emerge in her teen years, it leapt to life while she was in college. While studying for her bachelor's degree, and later her master's degree in philosophy, Sargent became an avid science fiction reader. During those days, she once commented, "I made up for lost time. I read SF compulsively, everything from E. E. Smith's *Lensmen Series* to J. G. Ballard. I read Robert Heinlein's SF novels for young people while recovering from bronchitis, and thus remember the illness as a pleasant interlude. I read Kurt Vonnegut while recovering from pneumonia. I gobbled up books by John Brunner, Arthur C. Clarke, Philip K. Dick, and Isaac Asimov. I discovered writers such as Thomas M. Disch, R. A. Lafferty, and Ursula Le Guin."

## Publishes First Work

Sargent credits her start in professional writing to George Zebrowski, whom she met as a fellow SUNY student. Also an aspiring writer at the time, Zebrowski inspired Sargent to attempt writing her first science fiction story. After Sargent tossed it into the wastebasket, he retrieved it and urged her to submit it. That story became Sargent's first published work, "Landed Minority," which was bought by the *Magazine of Fantasy & Science Fiction.*

Sargent entered graduate school at SUNY anticipating that she would eventually become a philosophy teacher, but her writing often took precedence over school. Sargent's first long work of fiction, *Cloned Lives,* was published in 1976. A well-received debut novel, *Cloned Lives* explores the moral and psychological consequences of cloning as a means to achieve immortality. A *Publishers Weekly* reviewer called the novel "the kind of [science fiction] that should appeal even to non-genre readers."

While writing *Cloned Lives,* Sargent also compiled a science fiction anthology entitled *Women of Wonder.* Published in 1975, the anthology is significant among Sargent's work because it highlights the contributions of women science fiction writers and provides a forum for attempting to correct the sexual stereotyping the author feels has dominated traditional science fiction literature. With the publication of *Women of Wonder* and her next anthology, *Bio-Futures,* Sargent began to establish herself as a prominent science fiction anthologist.

The *Women of Wonder* anthologies highlight Sargent's perspective that, as a genre, science fiction has been dominated by men. "Most science fiction has been written by men, and they still form a majority of the writers today," she wrote in her introduction to the first *Women of Wonder* anthology. With most traditional science fiction written by white males and containing white male characters, Sargent contended, minorities and women have been relegated to unimportant roles. "If more women begin to take an interest in SF and the

scientific and futurological ideas involved, publishers will have an interest in publishing and writers in writing novels exploring such ideas from different perspectives," she concluded.

In the *Women of Wonder* anthologies, Sargent presents collections of stories that center on strong female protagonists in dominant and responsible roles. Many critics have praised the author for her efforts to counteract sexual stereotypes in the genre, while others have criticized her methods. In a series of reviews in the *Magazine of Fantasy and Science Fiction,* Algis Budrys commented that *Women of Wonder* "contains few clinkers and many stories well worth reading," but also called some of the selections "highly questionable," describing some stories as "blows against the masculine [science fiction] establishment.... [Sargent] uses the sledgehammer approach as basic to her method of argument." Several critics perceived the second *Women of Wonder* anthology as being more successful; Budrys

**Nita and Sven, the last living humans on an Earth now inhabited by aliens, must decide whether repopulating the world will lead to another cataclysmic war.** (Cover illustration by Vincent Nasta.)

**In a world where almost everyone is a telepath, Anra is rejected because she lacks the ability to mindspeak. But when an evil force begins to dominate people's minds, only Anra and others like her can defend Earth.** (Cover illustration by David Palladini.)

called it "a good book, a valuable book, and in the bargain a very nice collection of reading."

While devoting much of her time to editing anthologies, Sargent was also busy with her own science fiction writing, publishing short stories for adults and young people, and writing several novels. Sargent's second novel, *The Sudden Star,* published three years after *Cloned Lives,* uses multiple and overlapping points of view to tell the story of two survivors of a violent future Earth disintegrating in the wake of a mysterious plague and nuclear war. *The Sudden Star* was followed by *Watchstar,* the first in a futuristic trilogy about the descendants of Earth inhabitants, and *The Golden Space,* whose characters search for meaning in the immortality gained through biological advances.

## Young Adults in Outer Space

Along with her anthology and adult fiction work, Sargent has published a number of books for younger readers that feature science fiction and fantasy themes. Her first novel for young adults is *Earthseed,* which tells

the story of young Zoheret and her shipmates, all of whom have been created from the genetic banks stored aboard Ship, a cybernetic machine hurtling through space. Raised inside the motherlike Ship, the crew of young people is destined to colonize an Earthlike, uninhabited planet. Before they can settle the planet, however, the group must learn how to survive on their own and to control their darker instincts. In *The Alien Upstairs,* two young protagonists take it upon themselves to investigate a self-proclaimed alien who lives on an upper floor of their apartment building. In 1984, Sargent concluded her *Watchstar* trilogy with the young adult novels *Eye of the Comet* and *Homesmind,* both of which reinforce Sargent's reputation as a creator of strong feminine characters.

In 1986, Sargent's *The Shore of Women*—a strongly feminist work—was published. The novel tells the story of a post-nuclear Earth in which women, determined that men will never again have the power to destroy, control all technology and advanced knowledge. The story is told through the eyes of three women: city-dweller Laissa, Avril, a huntress who lives in the wilderness, and Birana, an exile from the city. Reviewing *The Shore of Women* in the *Magazine of Fantasy & Science Fiction,* Orson Scott Card called the work "one of the few perfect novels of the 1980s. [Sargent's] story of a woman exiled from a safe high-tech city of women, the man ordered by the gods to kill her, and [the duo's] search for a place of safety is powerful, beautiful, and true."

Sargent's 1993 novel *Ruler of the Sky* marks a departure from her science fiction work. A novel about the Mongol leader Genghis Khan, *Ruler of the Sky* pieces together the life of one of the world's most historically controversial leaders, telling his story from the points-of-view of the women surrounding him. "To enter Mongol minds and to tell their stories, the women's in particular, was still an act of imagination," Sargent once commented, "and when the story required that I take some liberties with the facts, I took them. But the tale I told is rooted in what some of the Mongols remembered and believed about their great leader." Kerri Kilbane, writing in *Booklist,* called *Ruler of the Sky* "an impressive novel from a veteran writer."

In her body of science fiction novels, short fiction and other writings, Sargent's stories have covered a wide range of scientific issues—from genetic engineering to immortality, from the decline of societies to space colonization—but always with a focus on the human condition. Her primary tools are strong characterization and an exploration of the range of human emotions, experiences, and relationships. *Fantasy Review* critic Michael M. Levy commented, "Although her books deal intelligently with a variety of scientific issues, Sargent's main interests have always been character development and the complexity of human relationships."

Sargent's concern with creating strong, believable characters is tied directly to her perspective that science fiction has too long been dominated by men. Philip M.

Rubens summed up the author's self-assigned role to "restructure" science fiction in the *Dictionary of Literary Biography:* "What Sargent does is to depict a world in which human potential can be realized by anyone ... woman, in her empathetic state, cuts through to truth, to new realities, new possibilities. It is also woman, in a somewhat refashioned traditional role as mother, who tries to awaken everyone—male and female—to these new potentials, and who triumphs over old ways. This particularly cogent vision of woman's great potential has garnered a very special niche in science fiction (and indeed in belles lettres) for Pamela Sargent. Her own writings as well as her editorial work in women's themes has done much to alter old concepts of woman's role in science fiction."

### ■ Works Cited

Budrys, Algis, review of *Women of Wonder, Magazine of Fantasy & Science Fiction,* November, 1975, pp. 53-58.

Card, Orson Scott, review of *The Shore of Women, Magazine of Fantasy & Science Fiction,* June, 1987, pp. 53-54.

Review of *Cloned Lives, Publishers Weekly,* April 26, 1976, p. 57.

Elliot, Jeffrey M., editor, *The Work of Pamela Sargent: An Annotated Bibliography and Guide,* Borgo Press, 1990.

Kilbane, Kerri, review of *Ruler of the Sky, Booklist,* November 15, 1992.

Levy, Michael M., review of *Venus of Dreams, Fantasy Review,* January, 1986, pp. 24-25.

Rubens, Philip M., "Pamela Sargent," *Dictionary of Literary Biography,* Volume 8: *Twentieth-Century American Science-Fiction Writers,* Gale, 1981, pp. 96-99.

Sargent, Pamela, editor, *Women of Wonder: Science Fiction Stories by Women about Women,* Vintage, 1975.

### ■ For More Information See

*BOOKS*

*Science Fiction and Fantasy Literature,* Volume 2: *Contemporary Science Fiction Authors,* Gale, 1979, pp. 1064-1065.

*Twentieth Century Science-Fiction Writers,* St. James, 1991, pp. 689-691.

*PERIODICALS*

*Booklist,* August 1987, p. 1722.

*Houston Post,* February 28, 1993.

*       *       *

# SAUL, Carol P. 1947-

### ■ Personal

Born September 3, 1947, in New York City, NY; married Mark E. Saul (a teacher), 1968; children: Susanna, Michael, Peter. *Education:* Barnard College, B.A., 1969; Bank Street College of Education, M.S., 1977.

### ■ Addresses

*Office*—c/o Publicity Director, Simon and Schuster Children's Books, 15 Columbus Cir., New York, NY 10023.

### ■ Career

Day care teacher and elementary school teacher in New York City; also worked as an accompanist; author of books for children. Resources for Children with Special Needs advocate, New York City; volunteer in schools. *Member:* Society of Children's Book Writers and Illustrators.

### ■ Awards, Honors

*Peter's Song* was named one of the Best Books of 1992 by the Oppenheim List, 1992.

### ■ Writings

*Peter's Song,* illustrated by Diane de Groat, Simon & Schuster, 1992.

Contributor of articles to periodicals, including *Sesame Street.*

### ■ Work in Progress

*Some Place Else,* a picture book to be published in 1994; several young adult novels, a series of original folk tales, and a fantasy novel.

### ■ Sidelights

Carol P. Saul told *SATA:* "I have always made up stories, either on paper or in my head. At camp, I loved making up song parodies with my friends. My parents encouraged drawing, painting, and writing, and they provided my brother and me with music lessons. So there was always some messy creativity happening.

"I am thrilled when a person tells me that my story has touched them. I love to hear other people talk—and not only about my book. I love hearing other people's stories. I think if more people were allowed to speak the words in their heart and were able to listen to other people's stories, we'd have a lot more peace and understanding. And it wouldn't hurt for schools and governments to provide more opportunities for creativity: more arts education, more writing time, more showcases for young talent."

*Peter's Song* is the tale of a singing piglet who is proud of his song and is ignored by the animals in his barnyard. Determined to share his music with someone, Peter goes to the pond and meets Frank the frog. Frank is eager to hear Peter's song and share his own music. After appreciating each other's creations, the new friends compose music together. Peter sings the piggy highs and Frank takes the froggy lows, beginning a partnership in music and a wonderful friendship.

\* \* \*

## SCOFIELD, Penrod 1933-1993

*OBITUARY NOTICE*—See index for *SATA* sketch: Born June 18, 1933, in Stamford, CT; died of cancer, November 5, 1993, in Yonkers, NY. Artist, muralist, and illustrator. An illustrator of various books, including some children's works, Scofield trained for an artistic career at the Parsons School of Design and at the Art Students League in New York City. During his career, he created works in a number of media, including paintings and large-scale murals. In addition he illustrated filmstrips and animated Walt Disney films. His pictures appear in books such as Derek Tangye's *Monty: The Biography of a Marmalade Cat,* his companion Paul Kresh's *Isaac Bashevis Singer,* and the story collection *Your Own Word.*

*OBITUARIES AND OTHER SOURCES:*

*PERIODICALS*

*New York Times,* November 11, 1993, p. D23.

\* \* \*

## SHEPHERD, Donna Walsh
## See WALSH SHEPHERD, Donna

\* \* \*

## SHETTERLY, Will(iam Howard) 1955-

### ■ Personal

Born August 22, 1955, in Columbia, SC; son of Bob E. (an entrepreneur) and Joan Mary (an entrepreneur; maiden name, Fikkan) Shetterly; married Emma Lucinda Bull (a writer, editor, publisher, and musician), October 17, 1981. *Education:* Attended New College of the University of South Florida, 1973-74; Beloit College, B.A., 1976. *Politics:* "Whimsical." *Religion:* "Disorganized." *Hobbies and other interests:* "Life."

### ■ Addresses

*Home*—P.O. Box 7253, Powderhorn Station, Minneapolis, MN 55407. *Agent*—Valerie Smith, P.O. Box 278, Milford, PA 18337.

### ■ Career

Berkley Publishing Corp., New York City, editorial assistant, 1976; actor in New York City, 1977-78; Albany River Outfitters, New Osnaburgh, Ontario, entrepreneur, 1979-83; SteelDragon Press, Minneapolis, MN, founder and publisher, 1984—. *Member:* Interstate Writers Workshop.

### ■ Awards, Honors

Minnesota Book Award for Fantasy and Science Fiction, 1992, for *Elsewhere.*

### ■ Writings

*FANTASY*

*Cats Have No Lord,* Ace Books, 1985.
*Witch Blood,* Ace Books, 1986.
*The Tangled Lands,* Ace Books, 1989.
*Elsewhere,* Harcourt Brace, 1991.
*Nevernever,* Harcourt Brace, 1993.
*Dogland,* Tor Books, in press.

*OTHER*

Also contributor of short stories to anthologies, including *Bordertown,* edited by Terri Windling, Signet, 1986; *Life on the Border,* edited by Windling, Tor Books, 1991; *Xanadu,* edited by Jane Yolen and Martin Greenberg, Tor Books, 1992; *Xanadu 2,* edited by Yolen and Greenberg, Tor Books, 1993; *A Wizard's Dozen,* edited by Michael Stearns, Harcourt, 1993; *Bruce Coville's Book of Aliens,* edited by Bruce Coville, Scholastic, 1994, and *The Armless Maiden,* edited by Windling, Tor Books, 1994.

*CO-EDITOR OF ANTHOLOGIES; WITH WIFE, EMMA BULL*

(And contributor) *Liavek,* Ace Books, 1985.
(And contributor) *Liavek: The Players of Luck,* Ace Books, 1986.
*Liavek: Wizard's Row,* Ace Books, 1987.
*Liavek: Spells of Binding,* Ace Books, 1988.
(And contributor) *Liavek: The Grand Festival,* Ace Books, 1990.

*COMIC BOOKS AND GRAPHIC ALBUMS*

*Captain Confederacy,* Numbers 1-12, SteelDragon Press, 1986-88.
*Captain Confederacy,* Numbers 1-4, Epic/Marvel Comics, 1991.
*Gettysburg,* Epic/Marvel Comics, 1993.

Also author of "In Charge," *Grimjack,* Number 39, First Comics, 1987, and "Home is a Hard Place," *Open Space* Number 3, Marvel Comics, 1990.

*OTHER*

Contributor of articles to periodicals, including *The Utne Reader* and *Artpaper.*

### ■ Work in Progress

*Seven with One Blow.*

### ■ Sidelights

"I don't know why I write," Will Shetterly once reflected. "Perhaps it's because writing allows more procrastination than any other occupation." Procrastination not withstanding, Shetterly has written several fantasy novels, short stories, and comic books, edited a fantasy anthology series, and has even become a publisher in his own right. Shetterly and his wife, Emma Bull, who is also a writer, operate SteelDragon Press, which he describes as "a tiny publishing house specializing in fantasy and science fiction comic books, trade hardcovers, and collectors' edition hardcovers." Of his own writing, Shetterly commented: "If I have a primary theme, it's redemption; I hope this is always present and never explicit in my work."

Born in Columbia, South Carolina, and reared in northern Florida, Shetterly held various jobs prior to becoming a full-time writer, including a year spent as an actor in New York City, during which he appeared as Sloane in the film *Toxic Zombies* and played the role of Nureyev in *Little Blue Stars,* "an Off-Off-Broadway play." Shetterly's first novel, *Cats Have No Lord,* was published in 1985. The novel brings together four unlikely heroes—a circus girl, a priest, a barbarian, and a half-elf—in a fantasy setting in which they are led through a series of adventures that include a war of the gods. It soon becomes clear to the adventurers, who begin their journey in search of magical knowledge, that the fate of their world depends on the outcome of their quest. According to a *Booklist* reviewer, the book is not particularly original, but the inventive fantasy setting, the unusual characters, "and the author's clever whimsy make absorbing entertainment."

A later novel, *Elsewhere,* follows its fourteen-year-old protagonist, Ron, through his search for his brother, Tony, who has disappeared in the fantastic Bordertown on the edge of the Faerie lands. "Despite its fantastic setting," writes Kathryn Pierson Jennings in the *Bulletin of the Center for Children's Books,* "this is a biting street story, complete with gangs, bikers, prejudice, and fictional drugs." Ron finds some relief from the chaos of Bordertown in a mysterious bookstore called Elsewhere, which becomes the single constant aspect of his life during rapidly changing situations. After being befriended by a half-elf and inducted into a gang, Ron experiences a series of upheavals, including a near-tragic fire, alienation from the only friends he has in Bordertown, and a bout with drugs. Finally he confronts these problems, as he must also confront the discovery that his brother committed suicide well before Ron's arrival in Bordertown.

Ron is a well-drawn fourteen-year-old boy, notes Joyce Davidson in a *Voice of Youth Activists* review: "When things become too tough he tries to take the easy way out, but he discovers that you can't run from yourself." Although a *Kirkus* reviewer found the other characters underdeveloped, critics have generally praised the engaging setting and Ron's maturation in the course of the novel.

Shetterly and his wife Emma edit and often contribute to the well-known fantasy anthology series *Liavek.* The series brings together short works of fantasy fiction by several authors, all set in the port town of Liavek. The stories often overlap in detail and characters, and as a result are "amazingly well integrated," according to

THE BORDERLANDS SERIES CREATED BY TERRI WINDLING

ELSEWHERE

BY WILL SHETTERLY

A NOVEL OF THE BORDERLANDS —WHERE MAGIC MEETS ROCK & ROLL

US/52003-3 • $3.99 • ($4.99 CAN)

**While searching for his brother Tony, Ron travels to Bordertown, a bizarre city where gangs, drugs, elves, and magic coexist, and where a fantastic book store may hold the answers to Ron's quest.** (Cover illustration by Dennis Nolan.)

Brooke Selby Dillon in a *Voice of Youth Advocates* review of the first book in the series. Many of the *Liavek* stories revolve around "luck," which figures as a magical power possessed in varying degrees by the inhabitants of Liavek. Luck is particularly strong on one's birthday, when one may also "invest" one's luck in some object for safeguarding and further use. In a *Voice of Youth Advocates* review of *Wizard's Row,* the third volume in the series, Marian Rafal praises the variety of stories in the collection, all of which keep "the reader in taut suspense until each is resolved."

## ■ Works Cited

Review of *Cats Have No Lord, Booklist,* June 1, 1985, p. 1374.

Davidson, Joyce, review of *Elsewhere, Voice of Youth Advocates,* December, 1991, p. 326.

Dillon, Brook Selby, review of *Liavek, Voice of Youth Advocates,* December, 1985, p. 325.

Review of *Elsewhere, Kirkus Reviews,* November 1, 1991.

Jennings, Kathryn Pierson, review of *Elsewhere, Bulletin of the Center for Children's Books,* November, 1991, pp. 74-75.

Rafal, Marian, review of *Liavek: Wizard's Row, Voice of Youth Advocates,* February, 1988, p. 289.

### ■ For More Information See

*PERIODICALS*

*Booklist,* November 1, 1988, p. 452.
*Fantasy Review,* July/August, 1986, p. 33.
*Locus,* January, 1992, p. 33.
*School Library Journal,* November, 1991, p. 134.
*Science Fiction Chronicle,* spring, 1990, p. 36.
*Voice of Youth Advocates,* August, 1986, p. 165; December, 1990, p. 270.

\*    \*    \*

## SHIRER, William L(awrence) 1904-1993

*OBITUARY NOTICE*—See index for *SATA* sketch: Born February 23, 1904, in Chicago, IL; died December 28, 1993, in Boston, MA. Journalist, radio commentator, and author. Among a select group of journalists, Shirer is credited with transposing news events into the stuff of history. He started his career in journalism in 1925 as a European correspondent for the *Chicago Tribune.* In the early 1930s, he spent time with Indian leader Mohandas K. Gandhi and later published a book, *Gandhi: A Memoir,* about the famed pacifist. His experiences reporting on the rise of Nazi Germany and its leader Adolph Hitler resulted in the book *Berlin Diary: The Journal of a Foreign Correspondent, 1934-1941.* Shirer, who had been covering the early years of World War II from Berlin, fled Germany in 1940 when he was accused of spying and in danger of being arrested. During his time in Germany, he also broadcast reports on the war for CBS, sometimes resorting to American slang to confuse Nazi censors. Along with broadcasting contemporaries Edward R. Murrow and Eric Sevareid, he helped to define a new, hard-boiled style of radio news that, in addition to relaying events with unprecedented verisimilitude, created the news media's first celebrities. In the 1950s Shirer was blacklisted as a suspected communist sympathizer, and he resorted to lecturing at colleges to support his family. He credited this period, however, with providing the time to complete the highly-praised history *The Rise and Fall of the Third Reich,* which won the National Book Award in 1961. Of Nazi Germany, Shirer also wrote two books for children: *The Rise and Fall of Adolf Hitler* and *The Sinking of the Bismark.* Other books he has written include the novels *Stranger Come Home* and *The Consul's Wife,* and a three-volume set of memoirs, *Twentieth Century Journey.* His last work was a book on the Russian author Leo Tolstoy, which was published by Simon & Schuster in the spring of 1994.

*OBITUARIES AND OTHER SOURCES:*

*BOOKS*

*Who's Who in America,* 48th edition, Marquis, 1994.

*PERIODICALS*

*Chicago Tribune,* January 2, 1994, p. 6.
*Los Angeles Times,* December 29, 1993, p. A3.
*New York Times,* December 30, 1993, p. B7; January 17, 1994, p. A15.
*Times* (London), December 30, 1993, p. 17.
*Washington Post,* December 30, 1993, p. B6.

\*    \*    \*

## SILVERMAN, Erica 1955-

### ■ Personal

Born May 21, 1955, in Brooklyn, NY; daughter of Harold (in sales) and Gloria (Phillips) Silverman. *Education:* Attended State University of New York, Albany; University of California, Los Angeles, B.A. (magna cum laude), 1982. *Politics:* Democrat. *Religion:* Jewish. *Hobbies and other interests:* Psychology, politics, wildlife, ecology, social history.

### ■ Addresses

*Home*—c/o Publicity Director, Macmillan Publishing Co., 866 3rd Ave., New York, NY 10022.

**ERICA SILVERMAN**

# ■ Career

Freelance writer, 1982—. Teacher of English as second language, Los Angeles, CA, 1982—. Manuscript consultant and speaker. *Member:* Society of Children's Book Writers and Illustrators, National Association for the Preservation and Perpetuation of Storytelling, Sierra Club, Southern California Council on Literature for Children and Young People.

# ■ Awards, Honors

*On Grandma's Roof* was included in *Reading Rainbow*'s review section, 1992; *Big Pumpkin* was nominated for a North Carolina Children's Book Award and was selected as one of the Library of Congress' "Books for Children," 1992, and was selected as a "Children's Choice" by both the Children's Book Council and the International Reading Association, 1993.

# ■ Writings

*Warm in Winter,* illustrated by M. Deraney, Macmillan, 1989.
*On Grandma's Roof,* illustrated by Deborah Kogan Ray, Macmillan, 1990.
*Big Pumpkin,* illustrated by S. D. Schindler, Macmillan, 1992.
*Mrs. Peachtree and the Eighth Avenue Cat,* illustrated by Ellen Beier, Macmillan, 1993.
*Don't Fidget a Feather,* illustrated by Schindler, Macmillan, 1993.
*At the Crack of Dawn,* illustrated by Sandra Spiedel, Bridgewater Books, 1994.
*Mrs. Peachtree's Bicycle,* illustrated by Beier, Macmillan, 1995.

Contributor of stories to periodicals, including *Scholastic Scope* and *Schofar.*

# ■ Sidelights

"As an only child, I spent a lot of time in pretend worlds, talking to imaginary animals and people," Erica Silverman told *SATA.* "Now, many years later, when I am working on a story, I feel the same sense of total absorption as I create a world, fill it with characters and watch and listen to them interact.

"Mother Goose rhymes gave me my first awareness of the pleasure of language. My father had a big reel-to-reel tape recorder. Together we recited Mother Goose rhymes onto tape. As I grew older, our reciting material changed to include all kinds of poems and stories. Those hours of reciting onto tape nurtured in me a love for the sounds and rhythms of language."

In Silverman's first book, *Warm in Winter,* Rabbit tells her friend Badger that the best experience of warmth comes in winter. Badger finds this difficult to believe on a sunny, summer day. However, Badger learns the truth of Rabbit's claim when she visits Rabbit during the winter's first snow. After Badger travels through the

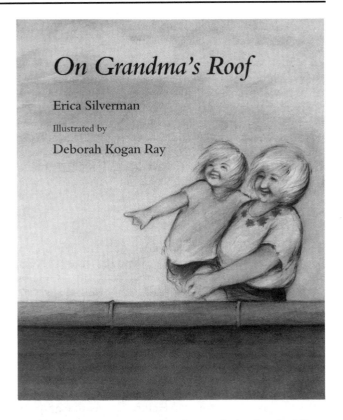

**Emily and her grandmother form a loving bond while doing everyday chores in this story reflecting Silverman's childhood memories.** (Cover illustration by Deborah Kogan Ray.)

blustery storm and is offered a seat next to the fire, she agrees warmth is best appreciated during winter. Commenting on the relationship between Badger and Rabbit in a *Booklist* review, Julie Corsaro called *Warm in Winter* an "affectionate tale of friendship." In a *School Library Journal* review, Marianne Pilla found the "narration descriptive," and also complemented the witty conversations between Rabbit and Badger.

Silverman described her work to *SATA:* "Without consciously deciding on it, my books seem to touch on the need to be connected; my characters seem to be concerned with the question of needing others and being needed.... In *Warm in Winter,* a lonely Badger must confront a blizzard in order to find the warmth of friendship."

Silverman's second book, *On Grandma's Roof,* follows a young girl and her grandmother through the day's single activity: hanging laundry out to dry. Emily and her grandmother take a picnic basket along with the laundry, and spend the day on the roof of the grandmother's apartment building, where the chore is transformed into an expression of the loving relationship between the two. Mary M. Burns, writing in *Horn Book Magazine,* described the combination of text and illustrations as "superb," and went on to praise the "childlike celebration of life and love" as particularly suited for its intended audience. The story "vibrates with the delight the characters feel in each other," noted Virginia Opocensky in a *School Library Journal* review.

"My grandmother started me on the road to reading before I was in school," Silverman told *SATA*. "She took me to the public library on 23rd street in Manhattan, up the endless staircase to the children's room and let me pick out books to take home. I particularly loved folk tales. One of my favorites was an East European folk tale called 'The Turnip.' Years later, I walked into a library and heard a librarian reading 'The Turnip' to a group of children. I started wondering how I could adapt it in order to tell my own story."

In Silverman's *Big Pumpkin,* based on "The Turnip," a witch grows a pumpkin too large to move. After encounters with a cast of Halloween characters, none of whom can move the pumpkin either, a little bat suggests that they all work together to move the pumpkin. "It is only by working together that the boastful characters can finally have their pumpkin pie," Silverman commented for *SATA*. A *Publishers Weekly* reviewer felt that the dialogue created "a pleasantly sinister mood that stops just short of being scary," while in the *School Library Journal* Elizabeth Hanson called the book "rousing good fun for the Halloween season and far beyond."

"I didn't set out to write stories about teamwork or interdependence," Silverman concluded for *SATA*. "That would have resulted in an essay rather than a picture book. I generally start with a setting, the voices of characters, and an unidentified mood or feeling that I am trying to bring into focus. Part of the fun of starting a new book is finding out something new about myself along the way."

## ■ Works Cited

Review of *Big Pumpkin, Publishers Weekly,* July 20, 1992, p. 248.
Burns, Mary M., review of *On Grandma's Roof, Horn Book Magazine,* July, 1990, p. 448.
Corsaro, Julie, review of *Warm in Winter, Booklist,* December 1, 1989.
Hanson, Elizabeth, review of *Big Pumpkin, School Library Journal,* September, 1992, p. 211.
Opocensky, Virginia, review of *On Grandma's Roof, School Library Journal,* March, 1990, p. 201.
Pilla, Marianne, review of *Warm in Winter, School Library Journal,* October, 1989, p. 1332.

## ■ For More Information See

*PERIODICALS*

*Booklist,* March 1, 1990, p. 1349.
*Kirkus Review,* September 1, 1989, p. 1332; July 15, 1992, p. 925.

## SMITH, Marya 1945-

### ■ Personal

Born November 12, 1945, in Youngstown, OH; daughter of Cameron Reynolds (an attorney) and Jean (a community volunteer; maiden name, Sause) Argetsinger; married Arthur B. Smith, Jr. (an attorney), December 30, 1968; children: Arthur Cameron, Sarah Reynolds. *Education:* Cornell University, B.A. (English literature), 1967. *Politics:* Democrat. *Religion:* Roman Catholic. *Hobbies and other interests:* Horseback riding, running, tennis, reading.

### ■ Addresses

*Home and office*—714 Gunderson Ave., Oak Park, IL 60304. *Agent*—Perry Browne, Pema Browne Ltd., Pine Rd., HCR 104-B, Neversink, NY 12765.

### ■ Career

*Seventeen* magazine, New York City, editorial assistant, 1967-68; University of Chicago Press, Chicago, IL, copywriter, 1968-70; Drucilla Handy Co., Chicago, publicity writer, 1970-72; freelance writer, Chicago, 1972-74; Cornell University, Ithaca, NY, Department of Communications, lecturer in magazine writing, 1976-77; freelance writer, Chicago, 1978—. Reading tutor, Oak Park Public Library. *Member:* Society of Children's Writers and Illustrators, Authors Guild, Authors League of America, National Writers Union, Children's Reading Round Table, Chicago Women in Publishing.

**MARYA SMITH**

## ■ Awards, Honors

Finalist, Prix de Paris writing contest for college seniors, *Vogue* magazine, 1967; second prize, George A. McCalmon playwrighting competition, Cornell University, 1967; Associated Church Press news writing award, 1986, for article "What to Expect When You Shelter an Unwed Mother," published in *Salt* magazine; poetry awards from Triton College's Salute to the Arts and Poets and Patrons' annual poetry contests, 1986, 1987, and 1989.

## ■ Writings

*Across the Creek,* Arcade, 1989.
*Winter-Broken,* Arcade, 1990.

Also author of three one-act comedies produced at Playwrights' Center Theatre, Chicago, IL. Contributor to various periodicals, including *Chicago, Ingenue, Sphere, Chicago Tribune Magazine,* and *Salt.*

## ■ Work in Progress

*Hire Power,* a two-act play.

## ■ Sidelights

Marya Smith's first novel, *Across the Creek,* follows twelve-year-old Ryerson, who is sent to his grandmother's farm after his mother's death. Rye is uncomfortable in this unfamiliar rural setting, removed from the possessions and friends that defined the happy life he led before his mother's death. Rye simultaneously discovers a creek on the property and a younger girl, with whom he develops a relationship through the construction of a stone altar on the creek-bank. In this nameless girl, Rye perceives a striking resemblance to childhood pictures of his mother, and he eventually convinces himself that she actually is his mother, returned in her youth to guard over him. When school begins, however, Rye finds that the girl attends classes for the developmentally disabled, and the subsequent dissipation of his fantasy provides Rye with both a crisis and the opportunity for personal growth.

In a *Horn Book* review, Martha V. Parravano noted that the book ran into some difficulty in its depiction of peer pressure and developmental disability, but maintained that "as a portrait of an unusual friendship and a young boy's response to loss, *Across the Creek* is sure-footed and strong." A reviewer for *Publishers Weekly* similarly commended the portrayal of "grief and longing that give rise to the protagonist's romantic fantasy."

Smith's second book, *Winter-Broken,* broached another highly emotional topic. Twelve-year-old Dawn prides herself on her ability to remain silent in the face of, and in avoidance of, her alcoholic father's physical abuse. Dawn escapes the traumas of her home life by making regular visits to a nearby farm, where she develops an attachment to a horse she names Wildfire. Eventually the man in charge of the farm notices Dawn's interest, and she is invited to tend to the horse. When Mr. Everly has a heart attack and Wildfire is sold, Dawn finds the resolve to seek help for the problems brought on by her family.

In a review for the *Bulletin of the Center for Children's Books,* Kathryn Pierson likened *Winter-Broken* to *Across the Creek,* finding both "powerful but slow-moving." Nancy Vasilakis noted in a *Horn Book* review that the novel "reveals many of the grim facts of child abuse," but considered the ending "optimistic," yet "not unrealistic."

## ■ Works Cited

Review of *Across the Creek, Publishers Weekly,* December 22, 1989.
Parravano, Martha V., review of *Across the Creek, Horn Book,* March/April, 1990, p. 204.
Pierson, Kathryn, review of *Winter-Broken, Bulletin of the Center for Children's Books,* November, 1990, p. 71.
Vasilakis, Nancy, review of *Winter-Broken, Horn Book,* November/December, 1990, p. 744.

## ■ For More Information See

*PERIODICALS*

*Booktalker,* March, 1991, p. 16.
*Bulletin of the Center for Children's Books,* January, 1990, p. 121.

\*    \*    \*

# SPARKS, Barbara 1942-

## ■ Personal

Born December 7, 1942, in Council Bluffs, IA; daughter of Harley (a soldier) and Thelma Sampson; married Richard Sparks (a freelance illustrator), June 1, 1968; children: Cinnamon, Allison, Lily Rose. *Education:* University of Texas at Arlington, B.F.A. *Politics:* "Undeclared." *Religion:* First Congregationalist. *Hobbies and other interests:* Reading, gardening, hiking.

## ■ Addresses

*Office*—c/o Publicity Director, Atheneum Publishers, 866 3rd Ave., New York, NY 10022.

## ■ Career

Freelance illustrator. Adjunct professor at University of Bridgeport, CT, 1991. Board member, Norwalk Youth Symphony; co-president, Tracey School Parent-Teacher Organization.

## ■ Awards, Honors

*Ganzy Remembers* was named to the "Children's Books of the Year" list of Bank Street College.

# ■ Illustrator

Mary Grace Ketner, *Ganzy Remembers,* Atheneum, 1991.

Also contributor of illustrations to *MotorHome* and *Humpty Dumpty Magazine.*

# ■ Work in Progress

Writing and illustrating for magazines.

# ■ Sidelights

Barbara Sparks told *SATA:* "*Ganzy Remembers,* by Mary Grace Ketner, was my first book to illustrate. It was a glorious experience. I wasn't expecting it to be so satisfying. The process was a multi-layered one: there was approaching publishers with a portfolio, for years; there was revising my portfolio, for years; there was finding the editor that was willing to take a chance with me. That was Gail Paris at Atheneum. Her confidence included the direction to work independently from the 'writer's vision,' which gave me the ability to rely on my own interpretation of Ganzy. So I began.

"The first step in the creation of the illustrations for *Ganzy Remembers* was a long one. We went all the way back from Connecticut to Texas, and back from the 1990s to the 1910s. Mary Grace Ketner's story was not just set in the Texas hill country, it was the Texas hill country as seen through the eyes of her grandmother. My editor had selected me as the illustrator without knowing I was raised in Texas, married to a Texan, and our families still live there. My husband and daughters and I had a magical time researching for *Ganzy.* We traveled through a Texas we had never seen before. The roadsides were covered with Lady Bird Johnson's wildflowers. There seemed to be bluebonnets and the slanting rays of the golden setting sun everywhere we went. I collected piles of snapshots I could use for reference for my watercolors.

"The second step was a totally different experience. This step was downward and into our cellar studio in Connecticut. By the time the sketches and design of the book had been approved, it was wintery and cold. Our attic studio had been dissembled while a roof was being repaired and our basement newly renovated. By renovations, let me be precise, the dirt floor had been newly layered with concrete and the fieldstone walls of our ninety-year-old cellar had been painted white. It was warm; it was cozy. I was glad of my husband's companionship as he worked on his assignments across the room. Once I began painting, I was back in Texas. It was startling. I came back to Connecticut for household and mother duties and meals, but I stepped into Texas when I picked up my brush. I was sorry when the last painting was done and the book ended.

"The third step to bookmaking is a lively one. It is the welcoming of the finished book into the world. The appearance of *Ganzy Remembers* was almost exactly a

year after the paintings were finished. We had a party of the many friends, neighbors, and family members who had participated in the pictures. They had taken on roles as characters in the story and let me take snapshots of them. I was particularly pleased to use my mother as the mother in the story. The role of Ganzy was 'played' by my dear neighbor, Mrs. Donofree. Mrs. Donofree was recovering from a heart attack and she had about her a beauty and glow that seemed to find its way into my pictures of her. My youngest daughter, Lily, was on practically every page of the book. She was the perfect age and size. Her sisters, Cinnamon and Allison, are almost the only family members not included. I consoled them with the promise that I am saving them for my next book. I can hardly wait to begin."

\* \* \*

# SPRINGER, Margaret 1941-

# ■ Personal

Born January 9, 1941, in England; emigrated to Canada, 1952, naturalized Canadian citizen; married Christopher Springer, May, 1966; children: Colin, Alison. *Education:* McGill University, B.A., 1961; B.L.S., 1964.

# ■ Addresses

*Home and office*—91 Blythwood Rd., Waterloo, Ontario N2L 4A1, Canada. *Agent*—David Bennett, Transatlantic Literary Agency, 72 Glengowan Rd., Toronto, Ontario M4N 1G4, Canada.

# ■ Career

McGill School of Library Science, librarian, 1964-66; St. Paul's United College, librarian, 1966-74, 1977-80; free-

**MARGARET SPRINGER**

lance writer, 1982—. Faculty member for the Institute of Children's Literature, 1988—, *Highlights for Children* Writer's Workshop, 1988 and 1993, and Conestoga College Continuing Education Department, 1993—; Boyds Mills Press, consulting editor, 1990—; judge for fiction contests. *Member:* Canadian Authors Association, Canadian Society of Children's Authors, Illustrators, and Performers, Society of Children's Book Writers and Illustrators, The Writer's Union of Canada.

## ■ Awards, Honors

Winner of two Pewter Plate Awards, *Highlights for Children* magazine, both 1990, for Author of the Month (September), and for Arts Feature of the Year.

## ■ Writings

*A Royal Ball,* illustrated by Tom O'Sullivan, Bell Books, 1992.

Contributor of children's fiction, nonfiction, and poetry to periodicals, including *Highlights for Children, Turtle, Pennywhistle Press,* and *Clubhouse.* Contributor of articles on writing for children to *Canadian Author, SCBWI Bulletin,* and *Children's Writer.*

## ■ Work in Progress

Stories and articles for children's magazines; articles on writing for adults; junior novel and picture book texts.

## ■ Sidelights

*A Royal Ball* may be Margaret Springer's first children's book, but it is not her first venture into children's literature. Since 1982, her poetry, fiction, and nonfiction have appeared in such magazines as *Highlights for Children, Turtle, Pennywhistle Press,* and *Clubhouse.* To date, she has published over seventy stories and articles.

*A Royal Ball* is the story of Queen Zygoma and King Mervin. Although their realms are right next to each other, the queen and king, for reasons no one can remember, have long been enemies. However, Queen Zygoma's seven daughters and King Mervin's seven sons conspire to bring peace between their parents.

The inspiration for Springer's stories come in various ways. She often keeps newspaper clippings that interest her and uses them as the basis for her stories. She also keeps a jar filled with words written on scraps of paper, and picks them out for story ideas. For instance, "Dishpan Ducks," published in *Highlights for Children* in 1990, was inspired by newspaper clippings about oil spills. Another story, "Elephant Yoga," came about when she reached into her jar and drew the words "jungle," "waterfall," and "mouse." Springer even keeps a file of names for her characters. She collects names from birth notices in the paper, concert programs, and lists of contest winners. She even collects names when she travels so that she has a diversity of names to choose from. She once came upon the name

The children of two warring royal families bring peace to their bordering countries in Springer's first published book. (Cover illustration by Tom O'Sullivan.)

Ryoji in a school program and decided to use it in a story. It took her a long time to find out whether it was a boy's name or a girl's, though she eventually learned that it was a boy's.

When it comes to the actual writing, Springer works in a number of different ways. She explained to *SATA,* "I write on a computer or laptop, but sometimes I still use scrap paper and pencil at the picnic table." Whatever tools she uses for her writing, Springer enjoys the imaginative thinking that goes into creating stories for children. "I love the sense of wonder and fun that is natural to all young children," she stated in an interview published in *Institute of Children's Literature Anthology,* "and I try to recapture that in myself."

## ■ Works Cited

"First Time Authors," *Institute of Children's Literature Anthology,* 1986.

## ■ For More Information See

*PERIODICALS*

*Inside Highlights for Children,* July-August, 1987.
*Kitchener-Waterloo Record,* March 30, 1990, p. C1.
*Quill & Quire,* January, 1993, p. 30.

**TRICIA SPRINGSTUBB**

# SPRINGSTUBB, Tricia 1950-

## ■ Personal

Born September 15, 1950, in New York, NY; daughter of Kenneth J. (an insurance manager) and Katherine (Hagerty) Carroll; married Paul Springstubb (a teacher), August 18, 1973; children: Zoe, Phoebe, Delia. *Education:* State University of New York, B.A., 1972.

## ■ Addresses

*Home*—1816 Wilton Rd., Cleveland Heights, OH 44118.

## ■ Career

Writer. *Member:* Authors Guild, Authors League of America.

## ■ Awards, Honors

*Give and Take* was selected one of New York Public Library's Books for the Teen Age, 1982; Ohioana Award for Juvenile Literature, 1991, for *With a Name Like Lulu, Who Needs More Trouble?*

## ■ Writings

*JUVENILE*

*My Minnie Is a Jewel,* illustrated by Jim LaMarche, Carolrhoda, 1980.
*The Blueberry Troll,* illustrated by Jeanette Swofford, Carolrhoda, 1981.
*The Magic Guinea Pig,* illustrated by Bari Weissman, Morrow, 1982.
*Which Way to the Nearest Wilderness?,* Little, Brown, 1984.

*Eunice Gottlieb and the Unwhitewashed Truth about Life,* Delacorte, 1987, published in England as *Why Can't Life Be a Piece of Cake?,* Collins, 1989.
*Eunice (the Egg Salad) Gottlieb,* Delacorte, 1988.
*With a Name Like Lulu, Who Needs More Trouble?,* illustrated by Jill Kastner, Delacorte, 1989.
*Lulu vs. Love,* illustrated by Kastner, Delacorte, 1990.
*Two Plus One Makes Trouble,* Scholastic, 1991.
*Pet Sitters Plus Five,* Scholastic, 1993.

*YOUNG ADULT*

*Give and Take,* Little, Brown, 1981.
*The Moon on a String: A Novel,* Little, Brown, 1982.

*NONFICTION*

*Cleveland for Kids: A Let's Have Fun Guide to Cultural Cleveland,* Cleveland Arts Consortium, 1993.

*OTHER*

Also contributor to *Short Takes* (college composition textbook), edited by Elizabeth Segel, Lothrup, 1986; contributor of articles and stories to *Redbook, McCall's, Woman's Day, Ohio Review,* and *The Writer.*

## ■ Sidelights

Ever since Tricia Springstubb was a child growing up in the New York suburb of Huntington, she loved stories. Whether she was eavesdropping on her many family members or reading the books her mother would bring home each week from the library, Springstubb had her ears and eyes open. However, she says she never thought of becoming a writer. At first, she wanted to be a dog, and later considered a career as a cowgirl, nun, archaeologist, or teacher. Ultimately, she became a social worker, teaching in the Head Start program and serving as a housemother to adolescent girls with emotional problems.

Reading case histories and listening to the many children she got to know through her work provided her with more stories. She wrote letters and a journal—but only for herself, until her husband encouraged her to try to get published. Springstubb once related to *SATA,* "It wasn't until, suffering from job burnout and encouraged by my husband, I submitted my first short story to *Redbook* and actually received a hand-written, friendly rejection, that I considered the possibility others might be interested in what I had to say. I continued to submit to *Redbook* and also to children's magazines and, lo and behold, eventually found myself being accepted. By then I knew I'd found the life I wanted, a life of wrestling and playing tag and, occasionally, sitting very quietly, with words."

Springstubb's first book, *My Minnie Is a Jewel,* is about an old woodcutter who is happy with his wife, even if she does get easily distracted and cook awful dinners. The loving couple reaps a prize for demonstrating their affection. A review in *School Library Journal* indicated the story is "told simply with gentle humor," and a *Publishers Weekly* critic deemed it "a tender, dizzy tale."

### Eunice Gottlieb and Lulu

Eunice Gottlieb is the main character in Springstubb's trilogy about relationships. The first book, *Which Way to the Nearest Wilderness?*, finds eleven-year-old Eunice planning to move to the woods to escape family tensions, until a turn of events alters her outlook. Called "a very funny novel, alive with ... wit and snappy dialogue" by a reviewer in the *Bulletin of the Center for Children's Books,* it was also heralded by Karen Stang Hanley in *Booklist* as "a smoothly developed, realistic family story bulwarked with engaging, multidimensional characters." In *Eunice Gottlieb and the Unwhitewashed Truth about Life,* the next work in the series, Eunice is twelve and is involved in helping her best friend, Joy, pay for ballet lessons. They start up a catering business, but Joy meets a boyfriend and Eunice feels left out. Although Eunice finds a new friend and partner, the company flounders and her friendship with Joy temporarily suffers. A *Kirkus Reviews* writer reported, "Springstubb's characters are believable, her writing economically witty." The third novel jumps back in time to take place prior to *Which Way to the Nearest Wilderness?*, the first in the trilogy. In *Eunice (the Egg Salad) Gottlieb,* nine-year-old middle child Eunice is ignored by her family, who directs all of the attention to Eunice's older sister and kindergarten-age brother, and she feels outshined by the athletically talented Joy, who receives gymnastics coaching from the new gym teacher. "Because the children are younger here," stated a writer in *Kirkus Reviews,* "the story will appeal to somewhat younger readers." Julie Corsaro, writing for *School Library Journal,* admired the "gentle humor, sprightly dialogue, strong characterizations (except for Mr. Gottlieb), and credible situations."

Springstubb introduces another character learning to deal with her family and understand herself in *With a Name Like Lulu, Who Needs More Trouble?* When ten-year-old Lulu catches a baby who jumped from a third-floor window, she becomes a heroine and gets involved in the lives of the toddler and her mother, eighteen-year-old Tilda. "There is plenty of action and humor here," commented Katharine Bruner in the *School Library Journal.* Lulu and Tilda are a year older and have become close pals in the sequel, *Lulu vs. Love.* Not unlike Eunice and Joy in *Eunice Gottlieb and the Unwhitewashed Truth about Life,* their friendship is tested when Tilda falls in love. Sally R. Dow, writing for *School Library Journal,* noted that "preadolescents will ... enjoy this lighthearted spoof," and Virginia Jescheling remarked in *Voice of Youth Advocates* that readers "who have lost a best friend or older favorite sibling to Cupid's arrows will identify with Lulu's painful acceptance of her changing relationship with Tilda."

Other books for young readers by Springstubb include *Two Plus One Makes Trouble* and *Pet Sitters Plus Five,* which also address the mishaps and adventures in growing up, including the difficulties of maintaining a three-way friendship, the joys and frustrations of the birth of a new brother, the meaning of responsibility, and discovering strengths and weaknesses. Springstubb

is also the author of *Cleveland for Kids: A Let's Have Fun Guide to Cultural Cleveland.* She told *SATA,* "The book grew out of the desire to send children and their grown-ups this message: Welcome to Cleveland's cultural scene. It features tips on preparing for visits to museums and performances, things to talk about and look for while you're there, and follow-up crafts and activities to extend the experience once you're back home. The book seems to be unique among city guidebooks, and has attracted a lot of attention."

Springstubb has also written novels for young adults. Her first, *Give and Take,* was praised by Holly Willett in *Horn Book* as "a subtly plotted story whose style is fresh, contemporary, and affectionate." Focusing on two teenage girls who are coping with their families and their first boyfriends, the tale explores the emotional ups and downs of friendship and love. *The Moon on a String,* another of Springstubb's works for older readers, introduces Deirdre Shea, who wishes to expand her horizons past her small hometown of Green River after her high school graduation. Her move to Boston and subsequent experiences there help her mature. In *Voice of Youth Advocates,* Jean S. Bolley lauded Deirdre as "a very real character" and commented that the "secon-

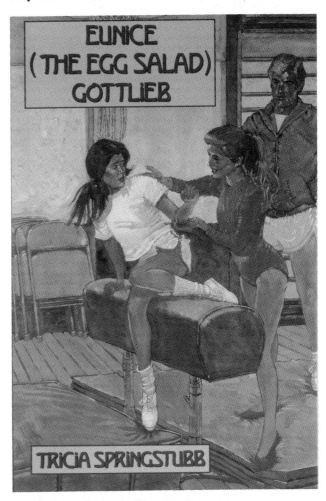

**Springstubb revisits pals Eunice and Joy as the arrival of a tough but talented gym teacher causes a rift in their friendship.** (Cover illustration by Don Dailey.)

dary characters are also well developed," while *Horn Book* contributor Ann A. Flowers called *The Moon on a String* "a well-written novel of self-discovery."

Springstubb once told *SATA,* "The 'moral' of all my work so far seems to be the necessity of extending ourselves. Taking risks, letting life surprise you: these seem to me key ingredients of happiness and, happily, of my craft."

## ■ Works Cited

Bolley, Jean S., review of *The Moon on a String, Voice of Youth Advocates,* April, 1983, p. 42.

Bruner, Katharine, review of *With a Name Like Lulu, Who Needs More Trouble?, School Library Journal,* November, 1989, p. 115.

Corsaro, Julie, review of *Eunice (The Egg Salad) Gottlieb, School Library Journal,* February, 1988, p. 75.

Dow, Sally R., review of *Lulu vs. Love, School Library Journal,* November, 1990, p. 119.

Review of *Eunice Gottlieb and the Unwhitewashed Truth about Life, Kirkus Reviews,* June 1, 1987, pp. 863-864.

Review of *Eunice (The Egg Salad) Gottlieb, Kirkus Reviews,* December 15, 1987, p. 1738.

Flowers, Ann A., review of *The Moon on a String, Horn Book,* February, 1983, p. 54.

Hanley, Karen Stang, review of *Which Way to the Nearest Wilderness?, Booklist,* July, 1984, p. 1552.

Jescheling, Virginia, review of *Lulu vs. Love, Voice of Youth Advocates,* February, 1991, p. 359.

Review of *My Minnie Is a Jewel, Publishers Weekly,* October 17, 1980, p. 66.

Review of *My Minnie Is a Jewel, School Library Journal,* December, 1980, p. 66.

Review of *Which Way to the Nearest Wilderness?, Bulletin of the Center for Children's Books,* June, 1984, p. 194.

Willett, Holly, review of *Give and Take, Horn Book,* October, 1981, p. 545.

## ■ For More Information See

*PERIODICALS*

*Booklist,* December 15, 1980; November 15, 1990, p. 658.

*Bulletin of the Center for Children's Books,* March, 1981, p. 140; June, 1984; June, 1987, pp. 197-198.

*Children's Book Review Service,* September, 1984, pp. 10-11.

*Junior Bookshelf,* June, 1989, pp. 136-137.

*Kirkus Reviews,* October 15, 1981, p. 1301; June 15, 1982, p. 676.

*Publishers Weekly,* July 30, 1982, p. 77; June 12, 1987, p. 85; November 24, 1989, p. 72.

*School Library Journal,* April, 1981, p. 143; October, 1982, pp. 146, 164; November, 1984, p. 129; August, 1987, p. 88.

*Tribune Books* (Chicago), May 29, 1988, Section 14, p. 4.

*Voice of Youth Advocates,* June, 1981, p. 31; August, 1981; February, 1990, p. 347.

# SPURLL, Barbara 1952-

## ■ Personal

Born December 22, 1952, in London, England; daughter of Geoffrey Blackman (a teacher) and Gladys Mary (an Anglican priest; maiden name, Peart) Spurll; married David C. K. Sin (an architect), August 28, 1981; children: Welland Theodore, Victoria Anne Spurll. *Education:* George Brown College, honors graduate, 1976. *Hobbies and other interests:* Reading (biographies, humor, human psychology, sociology), music (classical), martial arts.

## ■ Addresses

*Office*—366 Adelaide St. E., Suite 436, Toronto, Ontario M5A 3X9, Canada.

## ■ Career

Illustrator, 1975—. George Brown College, continuing education instructor of illustration, 1986-93. *Member:* Canadian Association of Photographers and Illustrators in Communications (CAPIC), Canadian Society of Children's Authors, Illustrators, and Performers (CANSCAIP).

## ■ Awards, Honors

First prize, Royal Ontario Museum ROMart Poster Competition, 1974; First prize, Metropolitan Citizen's Safety Council Logo Contest, 1974.

**BARBARA SPURLL**

# ■ Illustrator

Tololwa M. Mollel, *Rhinos for Lunch and Elephants for Supper!*, Oxford University Press, 1991, Clarion Books, 1992.
Betty Waterton, *Mustard,* Scholastic Canada, 1992.
Mollel, *The Flying Tortoise,* Clarion Books, 1993.

Contributor of illustrations to periodicals, including the *Toronto Star,* the *Financial Post,* and *Harrowsmith* magazine.

# ■ Sidelights

"I grew up in a house where the arts in general were very much respected, appreciated, and considered a worthy pursuit," Barbara Spurll told *SATA* of her childhood in Winnipeg, Canada. "I can remember watching my father painting watercolors of theatrical costumes and carefully constructing models of set designs. My mother, who has always loved literature, wrote poetry. My brother, Robert, and I spent hours filling large scrapbooks with all kinds of funny drawings."

Although, as a child, Spurll enjoyed the idea of becoming a comedian, her appreciation of art has shaped her life and career. She began by creating "character" maps of various cities and their most beloved and well-known landmarks. She then established herself as a free-lance illustrator and won regular assignments from the *Toronto Star,* the *Financial Post,* and *Harrowsmith* magazine. In addition to drawing caricatures and creating pieces for advertising, Spurll is developing a fine reputation as an illustrator for children's books. On top of all of this, she finds the time to teach an illustration course at George Brown College. As quoted by Bill Suddick in *Blotz,* Spurll tells her students to "Draw! You learn by doing—by drawing and painting as often as you can. You can't learn technique simply by looking over somebody's shoulder; you must do it yourself." Spurll elaborated to *SATA* that she believes aspiring artists must "draw every day without waiting for inspiration."

The first two children's books Spurll illustrated demonstrate her talent for drawing animals. In *Mustard,* Spurll colorfully displays the story of a mischievous puppy who needs a good home. Spurll explained the process of illustrating children's books like *Mustard* to *SATA:* "Illustrating children's books is what I enjoy doing the most and look forward to doing more of in the future. Illustrating a book is a large, involved project. The story takes on a life of its own which you can really become immersed in. Character development, the continuity of the characters and the flow of the pictures are additional challenges with children's books."

As she prepared illustrations for *Rhinos for Lunch and Elephants for Supper!,* a Massai tale told by Tololwa Mollel, Spurll was responsible for the development of many different animal characters. In this story, a hare, afraid of a monster that he thinks has inhabited his cave, finds bigger and bigger animal friends to force the monster out. It is a small female frog, in the end, which

**Spurll illustrated** *Mustard,* **the story of a troublesome pup written by Betty Waterton.**

has the cleverness and the courage to chase a tiny caterpillar out of the cave.

Critics almost unfailingly recognized the contribution of Spurll's illustrations to the book. Elizabeth MacCallum, writing for the Toronto *Globe and Mail,* praised Spurll's handling of the tale, noting that she "happily adopts the legend's fiercely satirical view of humanity." Most critics appreciated the captivating facial expressions and personalities Spurll gave each creature by including special touches like reading glasses. A critic in *Kirkus Reviews* added that the composition of the jungle background was carefully designed and also emphasized the "lively geometric design" of the border surrounding each illustration. More than any other scene, the illustration in which the animals roll on the ground laughing was lauded by critics.

Spurll told *SATA* that illustrating books for children is a rich and rewarding activity. "I'm delighted when people of all ages respond well to the books I've done. My guiding principle is that the intelligence and authenticity of my audience cannot be overestimated. Speaking from experience as the mother of two avid readers, children are very astute critics."

# ■ Works Cited

MacCallum, Elizabeth, review of *Rhinos for Lunch and Elephants for Supper!,* *Globe and Mail* (Toronto), October 3, 1992.
Review of *Rhinos for Lunch and Elephants for Supper!,* *Kirkus Reviews,* March 1, 1992.

Suddick, Bill, "Mom Knows Best," *Blotz,* April, 1990.

## ■ For More Information See

*PERIODICALS*

*Kitchener-Waterloo Record,* February 8, 1992.
*Los Angeles Times Book Review,* May 10, 1992, p. 11.

\*    \*    \*

## STARK, Evan 1942-

### ■ Personal

Born March, 10, 1942, in New York, NY; son of Irwin (a writer) and Alice (a teacher) Stark; married Anne Flitcraft (a physician); children: Aaron, Sam, Daniel, Rachel. *Education:* Attended Brandeis University, 1963; University of Wisconsin, M.S., 1967; State University of New York—Binghamton, Ph.D., 1984; Fordham University, M.S.W., 1990. *Hobbies and other interests:* Democratic town committee, coaching soccer.

### ■ Addresses

*Home*—201 West Park Ave., New Haven, CT 06511.

### ■ Career

Rutgers University, Newark, NJ, professor of public administration, 1986—; Shoreline Clinic, Madison, CT, psychotherapist; Domestic Violence Training Project, New Haven, CT, co-director. Consultant to Centers for Disease Control. *Member:* National Association of Social Workers.

### ■ Awards, Honors

Governor's Victim Service Award, 1990; Trend Setter Award, National Health Council, 1993; Sanctity of Life Award, Brandeis University, 1993.

### ■ Writings

*Everything You Need to Know about Family Violence,* Rosen Publishers, 1989, revised edition, 1991.
*Everything You Need to Know about Sexual Abuse,* Rosen Publishers, 1990, 2nd edition, 1992.
*Everything You Need to Know about Boys,* Rosen Publishers, 1992.
*Everything You Need to Know about Gangs,* Rosen Publishers, 1992.

Also editor of *Everything You Need to Know* series, Rosen Publishers, 1989-92. Author of more than fifty scholarly articles.

### ■ Work in Progress

Research on poverty, domestic violence, child abuse, youth violence.

### ■ Sidelights

"Most writing about social issues is moralistic, theoretically naive and one-dimensional, whether directed at children or adults," Evan Stark told *SATA.* "My purpose in writing for children is to make fairly sophisticated issues—like violence and sexual abuse—accessible through real-life stories and case histories. I am a feminist who has worked for many years as an activist and researcher in the battered women's movement."

\*    \*    \*

## STOOPS, Erik D. 1966-

### ■ Personal

Born November 18, 1966, in Cleveland, OH; son of Sherrie L. Stoops (an author). *Education:* Attended Scottsdale College and Phoenix College; Arizona State University, B.S., 1991, master's degree candidate. *Politics:* Republican. *Religion:* Jewish.

### ■ Addresses

*Home*—c/o 7123 North 11th Dr., Phoenix, AZ 85023.

### ■ Career

Metro Discovery Center, Phoenix, AZ, Living Treasures zoological center, vice-president of education center, 1989-93, museum director and curator of reptiles, 1990-92. Public speaker at schools for Outreach programs.

**ERIK D. STOOPS**

*Member:* American Zoological Parks and Aquariums, Society of Children's Book Writers and Illustrators.

## ■ Writings

*JUVENILE*

(With Annette T. Wright) *Snakes,* Sterling, 1992.
(With mother, Sherrie L. Stoops) *Sharks,* illustrated by Jeffrey L. Martin, Sterling, 1994.
(With Jeffrey L. Martin and Debbie Lynne Stone) *Dolphins,* Sterling, 1994.
(With Martin and Stone) *Whales,* Sterling, 1994.
*Penguins & Seals* (CD-ROM), Emerging Technology Consultants, 1994.

*OTHER*

(With Wright) *Snakes and Other Reptiles of the Southwest,* Golden West, 1991.
(With Wright) *Breeding Boas/Pythons,* TFH, 1992.
*Poisonous Animals of the Desert,* Golden West, 1993.
(With Martin) *Poisonous Insects of the Desert,* Golden West, 1994.

## ■ Work in Progress

Continuing a nature series for Sterling, to include forthcoming book *Alligators and Crocodiles.*

## ■ Sidelights

Erik D. Stoops is a specialist in herpetology, the study of reptiles and amphibians. In addition to writing articles and books on snakes, he is an expert in the care of boas and pythons in captivity, and he has bred and raised them and many other species of reptiles. His book *Snakes* is the first in a series of nature books dealing with many animal species.

Stoops works closely with registered nurse Annette Wright, coauthor of *Snakes,* in propagating certain reptiles that may be challenging to breed, especially endangered species. Together, they strive to protect wildlife, working with zoological agencies nationwide and even volunteering their own facilities as a holding or rehabilitation center.

Stoops's primary goal is to educate children about reptiles and their significance to the wildlife community. For two years, he worked at the Metro Discovery Center Children's Museum, where he curated the "Discover Living Treasures" exhibit about reptiles and wrote articles for the museum's educational programs. In addition, he is involved with the Phoenix chapter of the Boy Scouts, helping them earn merit badges by teaching them about wildlife conservation and proper care of neonates (newly born reptiles). With Wright, he conducts seminars that include hands-on contact with live animals.

## STOWE, Cynthia 1944-

## ■ Personal

Born September 7, 1944, in New Britain, CT; married Robert Stowe (a minister and director of a senior center), February 22, 1980. *Education:* University of Connecticut, B.A., 1966; University of Hartford, M.Ed., 1970. *Hobbies and other interests:* Swimming and quilt-making.

## ■ Addresses

*Agent*—Liza Voges, Kirchoff Wohlberg, Inc., 866 United Nations Plaza, New York, NY 10017.

## ■ Career

Board of Education, New Britain, CT, school psychologist, 1969-74; Rescue, Litchfield, CT, school psychologist, 1974-78; Northwest Regional Center, Torrington, CT, psychologist, 1979; Project Aware, Bath, ME, coordinator/teacher, 1980-81; Linden Hill, Northfield, MA, special education teacher, 1982-88; board of education psychologist, Greenfield, MA, 1988-89; board of education special education teacher, Shutesbury, MA, 1989-91; writer, 1991—. *Member:* Society of Children's Book Writers and Illustrators.

## ■ Writings

*Home Sweet Home, Good-bye,* Scholastic, 1990.
*Dear Mom, in Ohio for a Year,* Scholastic, 1992.

**CYNTHIA STOWE**

*Not So Normal, Norman,* A. Whitman, 1994.

## ■ Work in Progress

Continuing work on realistic, contemporary middle grade novels; fantasy and historical fiction; early chapter books, books for third and fourth graders, picture books, and adaptations of folk tales.

## ■ Sidelights

Cynthia Stowe told *SATA:* "I discovered my fascination with writing after I was forced to rest following surgery. Not able to work for a time, I took an oil painting class. My teacher told me to just keep painting, to let my creative self emerge. One day, when I was expressing dissatisfaction with my work, my teacher said, 'Take a week off from painting. Go home and write.' 'Write?' I asked. 'Why would I want to write?'

"I did, however, follow his advice. I remember the place where I first took up pencil and pad. On that day, I discovered that my creative self was a writer, and I have been seriously working every since.

"In my 'other' professional life, I have worked as a school psychologist and a special education teacher. Mostly, I've worked with people who have challenges in their lives. They've come in all ages and sizes, from preschoolers to adults. These people are represented in my books. I try to present them with the courage and honesty and, often, great senses of humor that so many of them possess.

"Many of my books deal with regular people in contemporary life. Humor is a big part of my work, because I feel that we can look at issues with humor that we might shy away from otherwise. I hope that kids who are dealing with major issues, such as the divorce of their parents, will read my books and feel a little less alone. I hope that all kids will gain understanding of others."

## ■ For More Information See

*PERIODICALS*

*Booklist,* April 1, 1990, p. 1560; November 15, 1992, p. 599.
*Bulletin of the Center for Children's Books,* January, 1993, p. 158.
*Childhood Education,* winter, 1990, p. 119.
*Children's Book Review Service,* April, 1990, p. 107; winter, 1993, p. 72.
*Children's Book Watch,* October, 1992, p. 5.
*Horn Book,* January, 1990, p. 246.
*Journal of Reading,* October, 1990, p. 154.
*Kirkus Reviews,* February 15, 1990, p. 271.
*Library Talk,* September, 1990, p. 34.
*Publishers Weekly,* September 21, 1992, p. 95.
*School Library Journal,* April, 1990, p. 126; March, 1993, p. 202.
*Voice of Youth Advocates,* June, 1990, p. 100; April, 1993, p. 30.
*Wilson Library Bulletin,* September, 1990, p. 12.

## STOWE, Leland 1899-1994

*OBITUARY NOTICE*—See index for *SATA* sketch: Born November 10, 1899, in Southbury, CT; died January 16, 1994, in Ann Arbor, MI. Journalist and author. Stowe's noteworthy career as a journalist was highlighted by his Pulitzer Prize-winning stories on the Paris Reparations Conference in 1929 for the *New York Herald Tribune* and his coverage of early World War II in Europe for the *Chicago Daily News.* His later articles on the war focused on events in Asia for both newspapers and radio. Among Stowe's major stories of this period was his discovery that the Chinese government was stockpiling U.S. lend-lease weapons for use against Communist insurgents rather than implementing them against their Japanese war enemy. In the late 1940s and early 1950s, he served as foreign editor of *Reporter* magazine and as the news director of Radio Free Europe. From 1956 to 1969 he taught journalism at the University of Michigan. During and after his academic career, Stowe served as a roving editor and writer for *Reader's Digest.* He published a number of books, including *Nazi Means War, Target: You, Crusoe of Lonesome Lake,* and the 1982 work, *The Last Great Frontiersman: The Remarkable Adventures of Tom Lamb.*

*OBITUARIES AND OTHER SOURCES:*

*BOOKS*

*Who's Who in America,* 48th edition, Marquis, 1994.

*PERIODICALS*

*Chicago Tribune,* January 17, 1994, Section 4, p. 9; January 23, 1994, Section 2, p. 6.
*New York Times,* January 18, 1993, p. B10.
*Washington Post,* January 18, 1993, p. D8.

\* \* \*

## STRAHINICH, H. C.
### See STRAHINICH, Helen C.

\* \* \*

## STRAHINICH, Helen C. 1949-
## (H. C. Strahinich)

## ■ Personal

Surname is pronounced "Stra-nich"; born March 11, 1949, in Columbus, OH; daughter of Herbert (a businessman and teacher) and Helene (in sales; maiden name, Goodman) Cummins; married John James Strahinich (a journalist), April 20, 1979; children: Nichola Montana. *Education:* Brandeis University, B.A. (cum laude), 1972; Harvard University, M.Ed., 1976.

## ■ Addresses

*Home and office*—32 Southbourne Rd., Jamaica Plain, MA 02130.

## ■ Career

Jamaica Plain High School, Boston, MA, special needs teacher, 1974-76; Belmont High School, Belmont, MA, learning disabilities specialist, 1976-77; Boston Center for Adult Education, Boston, teacher, 1977; University of Lowell, Lowell, MA, instructor, summer, 1977; The Reading Institute, Boston, supervisor and reading specialist, 1977-79; Holt, Rinehart and Winston, New York City, textbook editor, 1979-80; free-lance writer, 1980—.

## ■ Writings

*Guns in America,* Walker & Co., 1992.

Selector and adaptor of stories for *Sounds of Our Heritage* series, Holt, 1979-80; author of teacher's manual and skills component for *Scope English Anthology* series, Scholastic, 1982. Author, editor, and revisionist of materials for teachers and students, grades kindergarten through adult education courses, for numerous companies, including Economy Company; D.C. Heath; Houghton Mifflin; Silver Burdette and Ginn; First Teacher; Harcourt; Psych Corp.; Scott Foresman; Macmillan; and Charles Merrill. Contributor to periodicals, including *Boston Herald* and *Middlesex News.*

## ■ Work in Progress

A murder mystery (adult); an historical novel (young adult); a coming-of-age novel (young adult); and numerous short stories and picture books.

## ■ Sidelights

"I guess I'm a late bloomer," Helen C. Strahinich told *SATA.* "Nobody ever told me I was born to write, and it took me thirty years to find out.

"Through my twenties, I taught different subjects in different schools in Boston. I usually got bored with a job after a few years. One thing I never tired of, however, was writing materials to help my students become better readers and writers. When I moved to New York City, I stopped teaching and took a job as a textbook editor at Holt, Rinehart and Winston.

"At this time, I was also learning what it takes to become a writer by watching my husband. He was struggling to start a career in journalism. I discovered that it takes more than raw talent to make a writer. It also takes determination and sweat—lots of sweat.

"On my first project at Holt, I worked on a new folklore series for elementary schools—*Sounds of Our Heritage.* I collected and edited folk tales, poems, stories, articles, and photographs from different regions of the United States. I also got to write short articles for a few of these books, my first shot at professional writing.

"When I returned to Boston (where my husband landed his first job as a reporter), I became a free-lancer—a self-employed writer and editor, mostly for different textbook publishers—which is what I've been doing ever since. Two great things about free-lancing are freedom and variety. A third great thing is getting paid to write. I've written everything from video scripts to biology articles to science fiction stories. I've carved out time to write a book of nonfiction (*Guns in America*), to have a baby (my daughter Nicky), and to buy and remodel a house (in Jamaica Plain, Massachusetts). I've also done a stint as a journalist writing about family issues, children's entertainment, and children's books.

"Every morning I get up at 5:45 to work on special projects, such as *Guns in America.* I like early mornings when the house is quiet and my mind is fresh and uncluttered. During this time I also write fiction: novels, short stories, and children's books.

"I joined a writers group four years ago. We read and critique one another's stories and poetry. I find it helpful to give and get feedback about writing that may not be published right away. When I rewrite and revise this work I have my friends' ideas as well as my own to think about."

\*       \*       \*

# SUTCLIFF, Rosemary 1920-1992

## ■ Personal

Born December 14, 1920, in East Clanden, Surrey, England; died July 23 (one source says July 22), 1992; daughter of George Ernest (an officer in the Royal Navy) and Nessie Elizabeth (Lawton) Sutcliff. *Education:* Educated privately and at Bideford School of Art, 1935-39. *Politics:* "Vaguely Conservative." *Religion:* "Unorthodox" Church of England. *Hobbies and other interests:* Archaeology, anthropology, primitive religion, making collages and costume jewelry.

## ■ Career

Writer, 1945—. *Member:* PEN, National Book League, Society of Authors, Royal Society of Miniature Painters.

## ■ Awards, Honors

Carnegie Medal commendations, 1955, for *The Eagle of the Ninth,* 1957, for *The Shield Ring,* 1958, for *The Silver Branch,* and 1959, for *Warrior Scarlet;* Hans Christian Andersen Award honor book, 1959, International Board on Books for Young People honor list, 1960, and Highly Commended Author, 1974, all for *Warrior Scarlet;* Carnegie Medal, 1960, for *The Lantern Bearers; New York Herald Tribune*'s Children's Spring Book Festival Award, 1962, for *Dawn Wind;* Lewis Carroll Shelf Award, 1971, for *The Witch's Brat; Boston Globe-Horn Book* Award for outstanding text and Carnegie Medal runner-up, both 1972, for *Tristan and Iseult; Heather, Oak, and Olive: Three Stories* was selected one of Child Study Association's "Children's Books of the Year," 1972, and *The Capricorn Bracelet* was selected, 1973; Officer, Order of the British Empire,

**ROSEMARY SUTCLIFF**

1975; *Children's Book Bulletin* Other Award, 1978, for *Song for a Dark Queen;* Children's Rights Workshop Award, 1978; Royal Society of Literature fellow, 1982; Children's Literature Association Phoenix Award, 1985, for *The Mark of the Horse Lord;* Commander, Order of the British Empire, 1992.

*New York Herald Tribune*'s Children's Spring Book Festival honor book, 1957, for *The Shield Ring,* 1958, for *The Silver Branch;* American Library Association (ALA) notable book citations, 1960, for *Knight's Fee,* 1962, for *Beowulf,* 1963, for *The Hound of Ulster,* 1965, for *The Mark of the Horse Lord,* 1982, for *The Road to Camlann: The Death of King Arthur,* and *The Eagle of the Ninth, The Shield Ring, Warrior Scarlet, The Lantern Bearers, Dawn Wind, The Mark of the Horse Lord, The Witch's Brat,* and *Tristan and Iseult;* Horn Book honor list, 1962, for *Beowulf,* 1963, for *The Hound of Ulster,* 1965, for *The Mark of the Horse Lord,* 1967, for *The High Deeds of Finn MacCool,* 1978, for *Sun Horse, Sun Moon,* and *The Witch's Brat, Tristan and Iseult,* and *Blood Feud;* Boston Globe-Horn Book honor book for fiction, 1977, for *Blood Feud; Sword at Sunset* was a Literary Guild selection.

## ■ Writings

### *"ROMAN BRITAIN" TRILOGY*

*The Eagle of the Ninth,* illustrated by C. Walter Hodges, Oxford University Press, 1954, Walck, 1961.

*The Silver Branch,* illustrated by Charles Keeping, Oxford University Press, 1957, Walck, 1959.

*The Lantern Bearers,* illustrated by Keeping, Walck, 1959, revised edition, Oxford University Press, 1965.

*Three Legions: A Trilogy* (contains *The Eagle of the Ninth, The Silver Branch,* and *The Lantern Bearers*), Oxford University Press, 1980.

### *"ARTHURIAN KNIGHTS" TRILOGY*

*The Light beyond the Forest: The Quest for the Holy Grail,* illustrated by Shirley Felts, Bodley Head, 1979, Dutton, 1980.

*The Sword and the Circle: King Arthur and the Knights of the Round Table,* illustrated by Felts, Dutton, 1981.

*The Road to Camlann: The Death of King Arthur,* illustrated by Felts, Bodley Head, 1981, Dutton Children's Books, 1982.

### *FOR CHILDREN*

*The Chronicles of Robin Hood,* illustrated by C. Walter Hodges, Walck, 1950.

*The Queen Elizabeth Story,* illustrated by Hodges, Walck, 1950.

*The Armourer's House,* illustrated by Hodges, Walck, 1951.

*Brother Dusty-Feet,* illustrated by Hodges, Walck, 1952.

*Simon,* illustrated by Richard Kennedy, Walck, 1953.

*Outcast,* illustrated by Kennedy, Walck, 1955.

*The Shield Ring,* illustrated by Hodges, Walck, 1956.

*Warrior Scarlet,* illustrated by Charles Keeping, Walck, 1958, 2nd edition, 1966.

*The Bridge-Builders,* Blackwell, 1959.

*Knight's Fee,* illustrated by Keeping, Walck, 1960.

*Houses and History,* illustrated by William Stobbs, Batsford, 1960, Putnam, 1965.

*Dawn Wind,* illustrated by Keeping, Oxford University Press, 1961, Walck, 1962.

*Dragon Slayer,* illustrated by Keeping, Bodley Head, 1961, published as *Beowulf,* Dutton, 1962, published as *Dragon Slayer: The Story of Beowulf,* Macmillan, 1980.

*The Hound of Ulster,* illustrated by Victor Ambrus, Dutton, 1963.

*Heroes and History,* illustrated by Keeping, Putnam, 1965.

*A Saxon Settler,* illustrated by John Lawrence, Oxford University Press, 1965.

*The Mark of the Horse Lord,* illustrated by Keeping, Walck, 1965.

*The High Deeds of Finn MacCool,* illustrated by Michael Charlton, Dutton, 1967.

*The Chief's Daughter,* illustrated by Ambrus, Hamish Hamilton, 1967.

*A Circlet of Oak Leaves,* illustrated by Ambrus, Hamish Hamilton, 1968.

*The Witch's Brat,* illustrated by Richard Lebenson, Walck, 1970, illustrated by Robert Micklewright, Oxford University Press, 1970.

*Tristan and Iseult,* illustrated by Ambrus, Dutton, 1971.

*The Truce of the Games,* illustrated by Ambrus, Hamish Hamilton, 1971.

*Heather, Oak, and Olive: Three Stories* (contains *The Chief's Daughter, A Circlet of Oak Leaves,* and "A Crown of Wild Olive"), illustrated by Ambrus, Dutton, 1972.

*The Capricorn Bracelet* (based on BBC scripts for a series on Roman Scotland), illustrated by Richard Cuffari, Walck, 1973, illustrated by Keeping, Oxford University Press, 1973.

*The Changeling,* illustrated by Ambrus, Hamish Hamilton, 1974.

(With Margaret Lyford-Pike) *We Lived in Drumfyvie,* Blackie, 1975.

*Blood Feud,* illustrated by Keeping, Oxford University Press, 1976, Dutton, 1977.

*Shifting Sands,* illustrated by Laszlo Acs, Hamish Hamilton, 1977.

*Sun Horse, Moon Horse,* illustrated by Shirley Felts, Bodley Head, 1977, Dutton, 1978.

(Editor with Monica Dickens) *Is Anyone There?,* Penguin, 1978.

*Song for a Dark Queen,* Pelham Books, 1978, Crowell, 1979.

*Frontier Wolf,* Oxford University Press, 1980.

*Eagle's Egg,* illustrated by Ambrus, Hamish Hamilton, 1981.

*Bonnie Dundee,* Bodley Head, 1983, Dutton, 1984.

*Flame-Coloured Taffeta,* Oxford University Press, 1985, published in the United States as *Flame-Colored Taffeta,* Farrar, Straus, 1986.

*The Roundabout Horse,* illustrated by Alan Marks, Hamilton Children's, 1986.

*The Best of Rosemary Sutcliff,* Chancellor, 1987, Peter Bedrick, 1989.

*Little Hound Found,* Hamilton Children's, 1989.

*A Little Dog Like You,* illustrated by Jane Johnson, Simon & Schuster, 1990.

*The Shining Company,* Farrar, Straus, 1990.

*The Minstrel and the Dragon Pup,* illustrated by Emma Chichester Clark, Candlewick, 1993.

*Chess-Dream in a Garden,* illustrated by Ralph Thompson, Candlewick, 1993.

*Black Ships before Troy: The Story of the Iliad,* illustrated by Alan Lee, Delacorte, 1993.

OTHER

*Lady in Waiting* (novel), Hodder & Stoughton, 1956, Coward, 1957.

*The Rider of the White Horse* (novel), Hodder & Stoughton, 1959, abridged edition, Penguin, 1964, published in the United States as *Rider on a White Horse,* Coward, 1960.

*Rudyard Kipling,* Bodley Head, 1960, Walck, 1961, bound with *Arthur Ransome,* by Hugh Shelley, and *Walter de la Mare,* by Leonard Clark, Bodley Head, 1968.

*Sword at Sunset* (novel), illustrated by John Vernon Lord, Coward, 1963, abridged edition, Longmans, 1967.

*The Flowers of Adonis* (novel), Hodder & Stoughton, 1969, Coward, 1970.

*Blue Remembered Hills: A Recollection* (autobiography), Bodley Head, 1983, Morrow, 1984.

*Mary Bedell* (play), produced in Chichester, England, 1986.

*Blood and Sand,* Hodder & Stoughton, 1987.

Also coauthor with Stephen Weeks of a screenplay, *Ghost Story,* 1975, and author of radio scripts for BBC Scotland. A collection of Sutcliff's manuscripts is housed at the Kerlan Collection, University of Minnesota.

■ **Adaptations**

*Song for a Dark Queen* was adapted for stage by Nigel Bryant, Heinemann, 1984; *Dragon Slayer: The Story of Beowulf* has been recorded onto audio cassette (read by Sean Barrett), G. K. Hall Audio, 1986.

■ **Sidelights**

"For Rosemary Sutcliff the past is not something to be taken down from the shelf and dusted. It comes out of her pages alive and breathing and now," declared John Rowe Townsend in his *A Sense of Story: Essays on Contemporary Writers.* A Carnegie Medal-winning au-

*The future of a legion is in Marcus's hands*

**Part of Sutcliff's acclaimed "Roman Britain" trilogy, this story follows Marcus Flavius Aquila's search for the lost standard of his father's missing legion.** (Cover illustration by Charles Mikolaycak.)

thor, Sutcliff was essentially a storyteller, bringing history to life through her heroes and the settings she created. Many of her books present the history of England through the experiences of virtuous young men and women who overcome many difficulties despite their personal and physical limitations. Sutcliff also explored history through retellings of old legends or stories, such as those of King Arthur and the Knights of the Round Table and Beowulf, often adding a new dimension to their tales. "Most critics," contended May Hill Arbuthnot and Zena Sutherland in their *Children and Books,* "would say that at the present time the greatest writer of historical fiction for children and youth is unquestionably Rosemary Sutcliff."

Besides writing about historical and legendary characters, Sutcliff also recounted her personal history in *Blue Remembered Hills: A Recollection.* This autobiography describes her childhood feelings of isolation, which were caused by a severe case of rheumatoid arthritis, her father's career as a naval officer, and her mother's obsessive personality. Sutcliff's mother was a manic-depressive who became overprotective of her daughter during her illness. Never allowing anyone else to help her child, Sutcliff's mother doted on her—but at a price. She demanded nothing less than Sutcliff's unlimited love and loyalty in return and expected her daughter to want no other companions besides her.

The first eleven years of Sutcliff's life were spent hopping from one home to another because of the demands of her father's navy career. But when he retired the family settled down in an isolated moorland house in north Devon. Despite her arthritis, Sutcliff was able to attend a normal school for a few years. The onset of World War II forced her father to return to the navy, though, leaving mother and daughter alone again. Their house became a Home Guard signals post during the war, and it was at this time that Sutcliff's interest in battles and the military began to emerge.

Leaving school at the age of fourteen, Sutcliff began training as a miniature painter, a profession that was chosen for her because of her disability. Even though she had no inclination for the work, she made it through three years at Bideford Art School and became a professional. Eventually realizing that miniature painting was not the career for her, she began scribbling stories on pieces of paper she kept under her blotting paper. It was the pain of an early love that drove her to write her first published works, *The Chronicles of Robin Hood* and *The Queen Elizabeth Story.* These early books were only the beginning. It was not until such later stories as *Warrior Scarlet* and *The Lantern Bearers* that Sutcliff found her true voice.

## Sutcliff's Trilogies

Sutcliff began to win acclaim with the publication of her "Roman Britain" trilogy, which begins with *The Eagle of the Ninth.* The story concerns a young Roman centurion and his first few years spent in second-century Britain. Marcus Aquila is about to begin what he hopes

will be a lengthy and magnificent military career and is at the same time resolved to find his father, who mysteriously disappeared on his way to battle with the Ninth Legion ten years earlier. *The Eagle of the Ninth* "is one of the few good stories" covering the period of Roman rule in Britain, commented Ruth M. McEvoy in *Junior Libraries.* And a *Booklist* contributor concluded that the realistic background and characters make this a novel that "will reward appreciative readers."

*The Silver Branch,* the second book in the trilogy, takes place during the latter part of the third century and tells the story of Justin, a junior surgeon who has just arrived from Albion, and his centurion kinsman Flavius. The two young men are aware of the political turmoil around them, and when the emperor is killed, they are forced into hiding, eventually realizing that the hope of a unified Britain is at risk. "All the characters . . . are entirely credible," remarked Lavinia R. Davis in the *New York Times Book Review,* adding that the meticulous details "create a brilliant background for a vigorous and unusually moving narrative." And in a *Horn Book* review, Virginia Haviland recommended the novel for

Should Damaris risk helping the mysterious stranger?

**Venturing into the eighteenth century, Sutcliff weaves an exciting adventure of daring escapes and intrigue as two children rescue a Jacobite courier. (Cover illustration by Rachel Birkett.)**

those young people on their way "to becoming discriminating readers of adult historical fiction."

"*The Lantern Bearers* is the most closely-woven novel of the trilogy," Margaret Meek said of the trilogy's last book in her biography *Rosemary Sutcliff.* Meek added that "in it the hero bears within himself the conflict of dark and light, the burden of his time and of himself." The story presents the decline of Roman Britain through the character of Aquila, who deserts in order to remain in Britain when the last of the Romans pull out. "The characterizations are vivid, varied and convincing," maintained Margaret Sherwood Libby in the *New York Herald Tribune Book Review,* and "the plot, both interesting and plausible, has its significance heightened by the recurring symbolism of light in dark days." Meek recognized this theme of light and dark in all three of the books: "The conflict of the light and dark is the stuff of legend in all ages.... Sutcliff's artistry is a blend of this realization in her own terms and an instructive personal identification with problems which beset the young, problems of identity, of self-realization."

In Sutcliff's second trilogy, the "Arthurian Knights" stories, she focuses on the legends surrounding King Arthur, rather than simply using history as a background. The first book, *The Light beyond the Forest: The Quest for the Holy Grail,* relates the mystical search that Bors, Perceval, Galahad, and Lancelot conduct in an attempt to liberate the Wasteland from a religious curse. *The Sword and the Circle: King Arthur and the Knights of the Round Table* brings together thirteen Arthurian stories about such characters as Merlin, Morgan le Fay, and Sir Lancelot. The final book in the trilogy, *The Road to Camlann: The Death of King Arthur,* centers on Mordred's destruction of the round table, Lancelot's love of Guenevere, and the wars that lead to the final battle in which Lancelot dies. Sutcliff was able to relate the penetrating sadness of the story, as Marcus Crouch pointed out in a *Junior Bookshelf* review: "Here, young readers and their parents may be assured, is the best of a great and lasting story matched with the best of one of this age's great writers." Sutcliff's trilogy stands as "a valiant attempt to bring the often tragic, violent and sensual tales within the compass of children's understanding without cutting the heart from them," concluded *Times Educational Supplement* contributor Neil Philip.

## More Tales from Britain

With *Warrior Scarlet* and *Dawn Wind,* Sutcliff continued her tales of the making of Britain through two new young heroes. The story of the Bronze Age in England is told in *Warrior Scarlet* by focusing on a boy and his coming of age. In this heroic time, explained Meek, Drem must kill a wolf in single combat in order to hunt with the men, and if he fails, he is an outcast and must keep sheep with the Little Dark People. "Sutcliff has widened her range to cover the hinterland of history and realized," continued Meek, "with the clarity we have come to expect, every aspect of the people of the Bronze Age, from hunting spears and cooking pots to king-

**Based on a Welsh epic, this tale brings ancient England to life as young Prosper struggles to fight off the invading Saxons.** (Cover illustration by Charles Mikolaycak.)

making and burial customs, from childhood to old age. The book is coloured throughout with sunset bronze."

Chronologically, *Dawn Wind* follows *The Lantern Bearers,* because it deals with sixth-century Britain at the time of the invasion of the Saxons. The fourteen-year-old British hero, Owain, is the only survivor of a brutal battle with the Saxons that demolished his people. In the destroyed city, the only life Owain finds is Regina, a lost and half-starved girl. The two are bound by misery, then by mutual respect, and when Regina becomes ill Owain takes her to a Saxon settlement. The Saxons take care of Regina but sell Owain into slavery, and eleven years later he comes back for her. "So life is not snuffed out by the night," concluded Arbuthnot and Sutherland. "Sutcliff gives children and youth historical fiction that builds courage and faith that life will go on and is well worth the struggle."

*Flame-Coloured Taffeta* leaves the battle fields behind, returning to England and the Sussex Downs, between Chichester and the sea. Twelve-year-old Damaris Crocker of Carthagena Farm and Peter Ballard from the vicarage know the woods near their home very well, and it is here that they find Tom, a wounded "courier for the lost cause of the Jacobite court," as Joanna Motion explained in the *Times Literary Supplement.* The two children are not concerned with the rights and wrongs of the situation but feel they must protect and help the wounded man. Many adventures ensue, including a fox hunt, a midnight rescue of Tom, and an exciting escape through the woods. "A beautifully written and intricately woven tale, this novel should appeal to any lover of historical fiction," claimed *Voice of Youth Advocates* contributor Ellen Gulick. Motion concluded that *Flame-Coloured Taffeta* "succeeds as an enjoyable, soundly-crafted short novel where no whisker of plot or detail of character is wasted. And the sense of history under the lanes, the past seeped into the landscape, as Damaris looks out to sea from her farm house built of wrecked Armada timbers, will be familiar and satisfying to Sutcliff's many admirers."

## Sutcliff's Last Stories

The last book published before Sutcliff's death in 1992 was *The Shining Company,* set in the now-familiar age of post-Roman Britain. The plot is an adaptation of the Welsh epic *Y Gododdin,* the earliest surviving poem set in North Britain, and is told by Prosper, who joins Prince Gorthyn as a shield-bearer when the prince enlists in a company formed by the High Chief Mynyddog Mwynfawr to unite the Celtic tribes against the Saxon threat. Much of the story, related Christine Behrmann in the *School Library Journal,* is concerned with men from diverse parts of Britain coming together under a common cause. "Sutcliff has called all of her considerable talents into play here," said Behrmann, adding that readers who are willing to succumb to Sutcliff's "hypnotic language will be drawn into a truly splendid adventure."

Several works by Sutcliff have been published since her death, including *The Minstrel and the Dragon Pup, Chess-Dream in a Garden,* and *Black Ships before Troy: The Story of the Iliad.* Reviewers have been particularly impressed with *The Minstrel and the Dragon Pup,* a simple, completely original story about the friendship between a wandering minstrel and Lucky the dragon and how they save the life of a prince. Illustrated by Emma Chichester Clark, the story was written for children ages five and up. Although *School Library Journal* critic Lauralyn Persson wrote that the story is more suited to "sophisticated readers," she added that "all youngsters are sure to respond to the book's beauty and emotional power." And a *Publishers Weekly* reviewer called the story "captivating" and "timeless." Mary M. Burns concluded in a *Horn Book* article that it was "fitting that one of [Sutcliff's] last books" is about a minstrel, since the author was "a modern-day minstrel, celebrating noble deeds and re-creating times when heroes appeared larger than life."

Sutcliff's numerous historical adventures have been described by Sheila A. Egoff in her *Thursday's Child: Trends and Patterns in Contemporary Children's Literature* as "a virtually perfect mesh of history and fiction." Sutcliff "seems to work from no recipe for mixing fact and imagination and thus, like fantasy, which it also resembles in its magic qualities, her writing defies neat categorization." Similarly, Philip contended in another *Times Educational Supplement* article that "to call the books historical novels is to limit them disgracefully." Sutcliff "does not bring 'history' to the reader," continued Philip, "but involves the reader in the past—not just for the duration of a book, but for ever. She can animate the past, bring it to life inside the reader in a most personal and lasting way." Sutcliff immersed herself and the reader in the time periods that she described, and "her method of settling on the felt details that remain in the mind, driven along the nerves of the hero, is even more convincing than the historian's account," asserted Meek. "Sutcliff's name," Ann Evans declared in the *Times Literary Supplement,* "will be remembered and revered long after others have been forgotten."

## ■ Works Cited

Arbuthnot, May Hill, and Zena Sutherland, *Children and Books,* 4th edition, Scott, Foresman, 1972, pp. 508-509.

Behrmann, Christine, review of *The Shining Company, School Library Journal,* July, 1990, p. 90.

Burns, Mary M., review of *The Minstrel and the Dragon Pup, Horn Book,* July/August, 1993, p. 455.

Crouch, Marcus, review of *The Road to Camlann, Junior Bookshelf,* December, 1981, p. 251.

Davis, Lavinia R., "Turmoil in Britain," *New York Times Book Review,* June 29, 1958, p. 18.

Review of *The Eagle of the Ninth, Booklist,* February 1, 1955, p. 251.

Egoff, Sheila A., *Thursday's Child: Trends and Patterns in Contemporary Children's Literature,* American Library Association, 1981, pp. 159-192.

Evans, Ann, "The Real Thing," *Times Literary Supplement,* March 27, 1981, p. 341.

Gulick, Ellen, review of *Flame-Colored Taffeta, Voice of Youth Advocates,* February, 1987, p. 287.

Haviland, Virginia, review of *The Silver Branch, Horn Book,* June, 1958, pp. 209-210.

Libby, Margaret Sherwood, review of *The Lantern Bearers, New York Herald Tribune Book World,* February 14, 1960, p. 11.

McEvoy, Ruth M., review of *The Eagle of the Ninth, Junior Libraries,* January, 1955, p. 33.

Meek, Margaret, *Rosemary Sutcliff,* Walck, 1962.

Review of *The Minstrel and the Dragon Pup, Publishers Weekly,* April 12, 1993, p. 63.

Motion, Joanna, "Helping Out," *Times Literary Supplement,* September 19, 1986, p. 1042.

Persson, Lauralyn, review of *The Minstrel and the Dragon Pup, School Library Journal,* April, 1993, p. 103.

Philip, Neil, "Completing the Circle," *Times Educational Supplement,* October 23, 1981, p. 30.

Philip, Neil, "Romance, Sentiment, Adventure," *Times Educational Supplement,* February 19, 1982, p. 23.

Townsend, John Rowe, *A Sense of Story: Essays on Contemporary Writers for Children,* Lippincott, 1971, pp. 193-199.

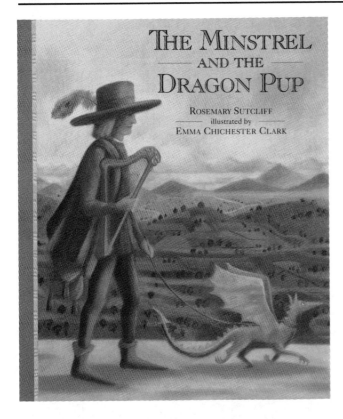

THE MINSTREL
— AND THE —
DRAGON PUP

ROSEMARY SUTCLIFF
illustrated by
EMMA CHICHESTER CLARK

**A wandering minstrel forms a close friendship with a dragon in this simple yet tender picture book for younger children.** (Cover illustration by Emma Chichester Clark.)

## ■ For More Information See

*BOOKS*

*Children's Literature Review,* Volume 1, Gale, 1976.

*Contemporary Literary Criticism,* Volume 26, Gale, 1983.

Crouch, Marcus, *Treasure Seekers and Borrowers: Children's Books in Britain 1900-1960,* Library Association, 1962.

Crouch, Marcus, *The Nesbit Tradition: The Children's Novel in England 1945-1970,* Benn, 1972.

Townsend, John Rowe, *Written for Children: An Outline of English Language Children's Literature,* Lippincott, 1974.

*PERIODICALS*

*Bulletin of the Center for Children's Books,* March, 1993, p. 226; November, 1993, pp. 102-103; January, 1994, p. 169.

*Horn Book,* June, 1958; February, 1968; April, 1970; December, 1971; August, 1980; February, 1982.

*Junior Bookshelf,* December, 1981.

*New Yorker,* October 22, 1984.

*New York Times Book Review,* October 26, 1952; January 9, 1955; March 17, 1957; January 4, 1959; April 22, 1962; November 11, 1962; May 26, 1963; May 3, 1964; November 7, 1965; January 30, 1966; February 15, 1970; September 30, 1973; April 5, 1987.

*Observer* (London), February 6, 1983.

*Publishers Weekly,* December 1, 1969; November 1, 1971; January 7, 1983; October 6, 1989; June 8, 1990; July 19, 1993, p. 254; October 11, 1993, p. 88.

*School Library Journal,* August, 1980; November, 1993, p. 110.

*Times* (London), January 26, 1983; June 9, 1990.

*Times Educational Supplement,* January 14, 1983, p. 24; January 13, 1984.

*Times Literary Supplement,* November 27, 1953; November 19, 1954; November 21, 1958; December 4, 1959; November 25, 1960; June 14, 1963; June 17, 1965; December 9, 1965; May 25, 1967; October 30, 1970; July 2, 1971; September 28, 1973; April 4, 1975; December 10, 1976; July 15, 1977; December 2, 1977; July 7, 1978; November 21, 1980; April 22, 1983; September 30, 1983.

*Tribune Books* (Chicago), March 8, 1987.

*Washington Post Book World,* November 5, 1967; September 9, 1990.

*OBITUARIES:*

*PERIODICALS*

*Junior Bookshelf,* October, 1992, pp. 181-184.

*School Library Journal,* September, 1992, p. 132.

*Times* (London), July 25, 1992, p. 17.*

# T

## TAYLOR, Dave 1948-
### (J. David Taylor, David Taylor)

### ■ Personal

Born July 6, 1948, in Ottawa, Canada; son of Wesley (a creator of greeting cards) and Edna (a housewife; maiden name, McMartin) Taylor; married Anne Mac-Pherson (a teacher), 1973; children: Liza, Ashley. *Education:* Received B.A., 1972; received teaching certification, 1972; received M.Ed., 1982.

### ■ Addresses

*Agent*—Crabtree Publishing Co. Ltd., 350 5th Ave., Suite 3308, New York, NY 10118.

### ■ Career

Peel Board of Education, Mississauga, Ontario, teacher, 1972—.

### ■ Writings

*SELF-ILLUSTRATED WITH PHOTOGRAPHS*

(As David Taylor) *Sharks (Nature's Children),* Grolier, 1987.
(As J. David Taylor) *Game Animals of North America,* Discovery Books, 1988.
*Ontario's Wildlife,* Boston Mills Press, 1988.
(With McClung, Caldwell, and Maplesden) *Cycles I & II,* Prentice Hall, 1990.
(With McClung, Caldwell, and Maplesden) *Cycles I & II Teacher's Guide,* Prentice Hall, 1990.
(With Kettle) *The Fishing Book,* Boston Mills Press, 1990.
*Safari: Journey to the End,* Boston Mills Press, 1990.
*The Alligator and the Everglades,* Crabtree, 1990.
*The Bison and the Great Plains,* Crabtree, 1990.
*The Elephant and the Scrub Forest,* Crabtree, 1990.
*The Lion and the Savannah,* Crabtree, 1990.
*Endangered Forest Animals,* Crabtree, 1992.
*Endangered Grassland Animals,* Crabtree, 1992.
*Endangered Wetland Animals,* Crabtree, 1992.

**DAVE TAYLOR**

*Endangered Mountain Animals,* Crabtree, 1992.
*Endangered Island Animals,* Crabtree, 1993.
*Endangered Ocean Animals,* Crabtree, 1993.
*Endangered Savannah Animals,* Crabtree, 1993.
*Endangered Desert Animals,* Crabtree, 1993.

## ■ Work in Progress

Books on bears and Algonquin Provincial Park, Ontario.

## ■ Sidelights

"I am a teacher first and foremost," Dave Taylor explained to *SATA*. "This desire on my part to help children and adults learn about their natural world is one of the main reasons why I write and illustrate books. I am also a classroom teacher and not surprisingly my subjects all include some aspect of science and outdoor education. My last teaching assignment was at the Britannia School Farm where I helped develop and implement a new program combining agriculture and environmental education. I have also worked as a science/social science consultant for my board of education. I began my teaching career in 1972 and have taught grades three through eight.

"I like to experience the things I write about and photography helps me to do this. Whether it is sitting in a blind watching ducks or following the wildebeest migration in Africa in a landcruiser, being there and seeing it helps me understand nature's complexity. While it is hard work it is also great fun.

"One of the questions I am often asked is 'Isn't it dangerous work?' Most of the time it is quite safe. After years of working with animals you get to a point where you can 'read' their behavior. However, I never take an animal for granted and always show them respect. Even so, I have been charged by moose, grizzlies, elephants, elk, and black bears. Fortunately, I did not panic and run and was literally able to talk my way out of it by speaking softly and backing slowly away to a point where the animal no longer considered me a danger.

"My family travels with me as often as we can afford it. Although I travel the world to do research, my favorite locations are the Southern and Western United States, Canada, and Alaska."

*     *     *

## TAYLOR, David
### See TAYLOR, Dave

*     *     *

## TAYLOR, J. David
### See TAYLOR, Dave

*     *     *

## TAYLOR, William 1938-

## ■ Personal

Born October 11, 1938, in Lower Hutt, Wellington, New Zealand; son of Alexander Ivan and Rosa Dorothea

**WILLIAM TAYLOR**

(Went) Taylor; married Delia Wellington, 1965 (divorced, 1976); children: Robin Alexander, Julian Alexander. *Education:* Attended Christchurch Teachers' College, New Zealand, 1957-58. *Hobbies and other interests:* Reading, music, gardening, skiing, hunting.

## ■ Addresses

*Home*—Kaitieke Rd., R.D. 2, Owhango, King Country, New Zealand.

## ■ Career

Primary school teacher in New Zealand, 1959-85; Ohakune School, Ohakune, New Zealand, principal, 1979-85; writer, 1985—. Mayor of Borough of Ohakune, New Zealand, 1981-88.

## ■ Awards, Honors

Choysa Bursary for Children's Writers, 1984; Esther Glen Medal, New Zealand Library Association, 1991, for *Agnes the Sheep;* Inaugural Children's Writing Fellowship, Palmerston North College of Education, New Zealand, 1992; *Agnes the Sheep* and *Knitwits* were cited by the American Library Association (ALA) and the New York Public Library.

# ■ Writings

*Pack Up, Pick Up and Off,* Price Milburn, 1981.
*My Summer of the Lions,* Reed Methuen, 1986.
*Possum Perkins,* Ashton Scholastic, 1986, published in the United States as *Paradise Lane,* Scholastic, 1987.
*Shooting Through,* Reed Methuen, 1986.
*Break a Leg!,* Reed Methuen, 1987.
*Making Big Bucks,* Reed Methuen, 1987.
*The Worst Soccer Team Ever,* Reed Methuen, 1987.
*I Hate My Brother Maxwell Potter,* Heinemann Reed, 1990.
*The Kidnap of Jessie Parker,* Heinemann Reed, 1990.
*Agnes the Sheep,* Ashton Scholastic, 1991.
*The Porter Brothers,* HarperCollins, 1991.
*Beth and Bruno,* Ashton Scholastic, 1992.
*Fast Times at Greenhill High,* Puffin, 1992.
*Knitwits,* Scholastic, 1992.
*Supermum and Spike the Dog,* HarperCollins, 1992.
*S.W.A.T.,* HarperCollins, 1993.
*The Blue Lawn,* HarperCollins, 1994.

Some of Taylor's works have been translated into Danish and French.

# ■ Work in Progress

*Dimwits* (tentative title), a sequel to *Knitwits,* for Scholastic; a humorous work for older readers.

# ■ Sidelights

"I grew up in rural New Zealand in the years immediately following World War II," William Taylor told *SATA.* "My family moved around a lot, and I was probably a fairly introverted child and adolescent. I have since made up for this! I am the eldest of four children, and we were blessed with loving, if somewhat feckless, parents. There was never much money. My father served for five years during the war in North Africa, the Middle East, and Europe. I didn't know him until I was seven years old. Our parents had wide interests in music, books, theater, and sports. As I get older I increasingly realize what a great debt I owe to them both. While it is true that I am what I have made of myself, the seeds of just whatever it is I have made, the beginnings, are right back there in my childhood and easily traceable to my mother and father."

After his rich and varied childhood, Taylor left home and school at age sixteen and began work in a bank. By the age of twenty-one he had become a teacher, a profession which then continued for more than twenty-five years. When he retired from teaching to pursue a full-time career as a writer, Taylor reflected on the time he had spent teaching and found that he had "loved every year." He also found plenty of inspiration. "In practical terms," he noted, "the immediate genesis of my writing is likely to be found in the hundreds of children I have taught and in my own two sons whom I brought up as a single parent from 1975."

Belinda and Joe inherit the responsibility of taking care of a surly sheep in this rollicking yarn. (Cover illustration by David Gaadt.)

## Wins American Readers with *Paradise Lane*

Taylor's first published work is titled *Pack Up, Pick Up and Off,* but he first became known to American audiences as the author of *Paradise Lane,* originally released in New Zealand under the title *Possum Perkins.* Because of her intelligence, her alcoholic mother, and her overbearing, potentially abusive father, Taylor's adolescent protagonist, Rosie Perkins, is isolated in the school community of her small town. Her only neighbor on Paradise Lane is Michael, a boisterous young man who seems her complete opposite. A grudging friendship develops between the two and is strengthened when Rosie finds an orphaned baby possum which she decides to keep and raise. Michael teases Rosie for her nurturing compassion, which he secretly admires, and he begins to feel a greater affection for her. The death of the possum and the support she eventually receives from Michael and his family are incentive for Rosie to confront her own family and seek help.

Ethel R. Twichell praised the convincing characters, "their psychological interaction, and the gentle flowering of Rosie and Michael's love" in a *Horn Book* review of *Paradise Lane.* A *Publishers Weekly* reviewer similarly praised the dramatic climax of the novel, and the tension that builds "as Rosie's independence begins to threaten her parents' status quo." A *Kirkus Reviews* contributor called the relationship between Rosie and Michael, and their subsequent emotional growth, "riveting—and unforgettable."

In 1991 Taylor won New Zealand's Esther Glen Medal for *Agnes the Sheep*. In this tale, Agnes is inherited by a pair of teenagers, Belinda and Joe, following the death of her previous owner, an ill-tempered old woman. A series of comic adventures ensues, during which the pair fight a constant battle to keep Agnes from friends and neighbors who think that she belongs on the dinner table. Agnes's tendency to misbehave reaches its peak in a wild chase through a supermarket. In the end, however, there is a note of sadness as Agnes dies and Belinda and Joe begin to lose interest in each other.

Critics generally praised the humor of *Agnes the Sheep*. In particular, Betsy Hearne claimed in a *Bulletin of the Center for Children's Books* review that the novel would serve as an introduction and means to "studying satirical literature." Taylor's satire spares no one, observed Connie Tyrell Burns in a *School Library Journal* review; he makes light of "teachers, education, priests, and the church in this zany and merry romp."

Among Taylor's more recent novels, *Knitwits* has also received approval for its quirky sense of humor. Chas bets his next-door-neighbor, Alice, that he can knit a sweater by the time his expectant mother has her baby. This results in a series of misadventures, including the discovery of his knitting by some male friends, who then become avid knitters themselves. "This blithe look at an expectant family has no dropped stitches," quipped a *Kirkus Reviews* contributor.

It was at the time of his grandson's birth that Taylor wrote *Knitwits*. "The whole notion behind that book rests very much on his small shoulders," the author recalled for *SATA*. "I watched the video of James's prenatal scan. I understand how very well that valiant knitter, Chas, in *Knitwits* must have felt when, halfway through the uphill garment-creating battle, he watched a strangely similar video of his yet-to-be-born sibling!"

### ■ Works Cited

Burns, Connie Tyrell, review of *Agnes the Sheep, School Library Journal*, March, 1991, p. 196.

Hearne, Betsy, review of *Agnes the Sheep, Bulletin of the Center for Children's Books*, March, 1991, p. 179.

Review of *Knitwits, Kirkus Reviews*, September 1, 1992, p. 1135.

Review of *Paradise Lane, Kirkus Reviews*, November 1, 1987, p. 1580.

Review of *Paradise Lane, Publishers Weekly*, September 11, 1987, p. 96.

Twichell, Ethel R., review of *Paradise Lane, Horn Book*, March, 1988, p. 212.

### ■ For More Information See

*PERIODICALS*

*Booklist*, May 15, 1991, p. 1794.

*Bulletin of the Center for Children's Books*, January, 1993, p. 158.

*School Library Journal*, December, 1987, p. 105.

*      *      *

## THOMAS, Joyce Carol 1938-

### ■ Personal

Born May 25, 1938, in Ponca City, OK; daughter of Floyd David (a bricklayer) and Leona (a housekeeper and hair stylist; maiden name, Thompson) Haynes; married Gettis L. Withers (a chemist), May 31, 1959 (divorced, 1968); married Roy T. Thomas, Jr. (a professor), September 7, 1968 (divorced, 1979); children: Monica Pecot, Gregory Withers, Michael Withers, Roy T. Thomas III. *Education:* Attended San Francisco City College, 1957-58, and University of San Francisco, 1957-58; College of San Mateo, A.A., 1964; San Jose State College (now University), B.A., 1966; Stanford University, M.A., 1967.

### ■ Addresses

*Home*—Caryville, TN. *Agent*—Mitch Douglas, International Creative Management, 40 West 57th St., New York, NY 10019.

**JOYCE CAROL THOMAS**

## ■ Career

Worked as a telephone operator in San Francisco, CA, 1957-58; Ravenwood School District, East Palo Alto, CA, teacher of French and Spanish, 1968-70; San Jose State College (now University), San Jose, CA, assistant professor of black studies, 1969-72; Contra Costa College, San Pablo, CA, teacher of drama and English, 1973-75; St. Mary's College, Moranga, CA, professor of English, 1975-77; San Jose State University, San Jose, reading program director, 1979-82, professor of English, 1982-83; full-time writer, 1982—. Visiting associate professor of English at Purdue University, spring, 1983; full professor of English, University of Tennessee, 1989—. *Member:* Dramatists Guild, Authors Guild, Authors League of America.

## ■ Awards, Honors

Danforth Graduate Fellow, University of California at Berkeley, 1973-75; Stanford University scholar, 1979-80, and Djerassi Fellow, 1982 and 1983; *New York Times* outstanding book of the year citation, American Library Association (ALA) best book citation, and Before Columbus American Book Award, Before Columbus Foundation (Berkeley, CA), all 1982, and the National Book Award for children's fiction, 1983, all for *Marked by Fire;* Coretta Scott King Award, ALA, 1984, for *Bright Shadow;* named Outstanding Woman of the Twentieth Century, Sigma Gamma Rho, 1986; *A Gathering of Flowers* was a National Conference of Christians and Jews recommended title for children and young adults, 1991; Coretta Scott King Honor Book Award, ALA, and Notable Children's Trade Book in the field of social studies, National Council for Social Studies and Children's Book Council, both 1994, for *Brown Honey in Broomwheat Tea.*

## ■ Writings

*YOUNG ADULT NOVELS*

*Marked by Fire,* Avon, 1982.
*Bright Shadow* (sequel to *Marked by Fire*), Avon, 1983.
*Water Girl,* Avon, 1986.
*The Golden Pasture,* Scholastic Books, 1986.
*Journey,* Scholastic Books, 1990.
*When the Nightingale Sings,* HarperCollins, 1992.

*POETRY*

*Bittersweet,* Firesign Press, 1973.
*Crystal Breezes,* Firesign Press, 1974.
*Blessing,* Jocato Press, 1975.
*Black Child,* illustrated by Tom Feelings, Zamani Productions, 1981.
*Inside the Rainbow,* Zikawana Press, 1982.
*Brown Honey in Broomwheat Tea,* illustrated by Floyd Cooper, HarperCollins, 1993.
*Gingerbread Days,* HarperCollins, 1994.

*PLAYS*

(And producer) *A Song in the Sky* (two-act), produced in San Francisco at Montgomery Theater, 1976.

The wise words of a kindly spider help Meggie Alexander years later when she and her friends try to solve a serial murder case in Thomas's unique mixture of fantasy and mystery. (Cover illustration by Paul Davis.)

*Look! What a Wonder!* (two-act), produced in Berkeley at Berkeley Community Theatre, 1976.
(And producer) *Magnolia* (two-act), produced in San Francisco at Old San Francisco Opera House, 1977.
(And producer) *Ambrosia* (two-act), produced in San Francisco at Little Fox Theatre, 1978.
*Gospel Roots* (two-act), produced in Carson, CA, at California State University, 1981.
*I Have Heard of a Land,* produced in Oklahoma City, OK, at Claussen Theatre, 1989.
*When the Nightingale Sings* (musical; based on Thomas's novel of the same title), produced in Knoxville, TN, at Clarence Brown Theatre, 1991.

*OTHER*

(Editor) *A Gathering of Flowers: Stories about Being Young in America,* HarperCollins, 1990.

Contributor to periodicals, including *American Poetry Review, Black Scholar, Calafia, Drum Voices, Giant Talk,* and *Yardbird Reader.* Editor of *Ambrosia* (women's newsletter), 1980.

## ■ Adaptations

*Marked by Fire* was adapted by James Racheff and Ted Kociolek for the stage musical *Abyssinia,* first produced in New York City at the C.S.C. Repertory Theatre in 1987.

## ■ Sidelights

Joyce Carol Thomas's background as a migrant farm worker in rural Oklahoma and California supplies her with the prolific stock of characters and situations that fill her novels. The author admittedly fell in love with words and with the songs she heard in church, and has spent much of her time as a writer trying to recreate the sounds of singing with her written language. She is well known for her book of poems, *Brown Honey in Broomwheat Tea;* her ground-breaking anthology, *A Gathering of Flowers: Stories about Being Young in America;* and her young adult novels *Marked by Fire* and *Bright Shadow,* which are set in Thomas's hometown and focus

After her face is scarred in a fire, Abyssinia Jackson is destined for a life of "unbearable pain and unspeakable joy."

on the indomitable spirit of Abyssinia Jackson and her people.

Thomas grew up in Ponca City, Oklahoma, a small, dusty town where she lived across from the school. This place has found a permanent home in Thomas's mind. "Although now I live half a continent away from my hometown," Thomas related in *Something about the Author Autobiography Series* (*SAAS*), "when it comes to my writing I find that I am still there." She has set three of her novels in her hometown: *Marked by Fire, Bright Shadow,* and *The Golden Pasture.*

Thomas loved school as a child and became anxious whenever it appeared she might be late because she didn't want to miss anything. However, she usually missed the first month of school in order to finish up her farm work. Times were lean for Thomas's family, but they always made do. This she attributes partly to her mother's genius at making healthy foods that weren't expensive; she has memories of huge spreads being laid out for Sunday dinners. These scenes of food have stuck with Thomas, for she finds food is one of the focuses in her novels. "Because in such a home food was another language for love, my books are redolent of sugar and spice, kale and collards," Thomas commented in *SAAS.*

When Thomas was ten years old, the family moved to rural Tracy, California. There Thomas learned to milk cows, fish for minnows, and harvest tomatoes and grapes. She also became intimately acquainted with black widow spiders—there was a nest of them under her bed. She was later to use this experience in her novel *Journey.* Likewise, she had a similar experience with wasps when her brother locked her in a closet containing a wasp nest; *Marked by Fire* contains some scary scenes with these insects.

In Tracy, California, Thomas continued her long summers harvesting crops. She worked beside many Mexicans and began a love affair with their language. "When the Spanish speakers talked they seemed to sing," Thomas remarked in *SAAS.* When she went to college—which she managed to do by working full-time as a telephone operator as well as raising her children—she majored in Spanish and French. "From this base of languages I taught myself all I know about writing," she related in *SAAS.* She went on to earn a master's degree from Stanford University, and then taught foreign languages in public school.

### *Marked by Fire* Reflects Heritage

From 1973 to 1978, Thomas wrote poetry and plays for adults and became a celebrated author. She traveled to conferences and festivals all over the world, including Lagos, Nigeria. In 1982, Thomas's career took a turn when she published *Marked by Fire,* a novel for a young adult audience. Steeped in the setting and traditions of her hometown, the novel focuses on Abyssinia Jackson, a girl who was born in a cotton field during harvest time. The title refers to the fact that she received a burn on her face from a brush fire during her birth. This leaves her "marked for unbearable pain and unspeakable joy," according to the local healer.

The pain begins when Abyssinia is raped by an elder in the church when she is ten. Abby becomes mute after the violent act and is nursed back to health through the strength of the local women and her family. Abby's mother is named Patience in honor of Thomas's mother, who was a very patient parent. Strong, the father, has left the family in their time of need, but returns to them later—ironically—because he is not strong enough to face a crisis in his life. When Abby eventually regains her voice, she is able to tell her friend Lily Norene that after the rape she "felt dirty. Dirtier than playing in mud. The kind of dirt you can't ever wash off.... But the worst part was I felt like I was being spit on by God." It is the seeming abandonment by God that strikes Abby to the core—she must work through the horror before she can recover completely. Mother Barker, the town's midwife and healer, has a special role in the rehabilitation of Abby. In a more macabre way, so does Trembling Sally, a frightening, crazy woman who assaults the young girl with strange trials of fire, water, and insects. Eventually, Abby recovers with Mother Barker's help.

*Marked by Fire* has been well received by critics. Wendell Wray wrote in *Best Sellers* that Thomas "captures the flavor of black folk life in Oklahoma.... [She] has set for herself a very challenging task.... [But] Thomas' book works." Critic Dorothy Randall-Tsuruta commented in the *Black Scholar* that Thomas's "poetic tone gives this work what scents give the roses already so pleasing in color. In fact often as not the lyrical here carries the reader beyond concerns for fast action. There too Thomas's short lived interest in writing plays figures in her fine regard and control of dialog." Hazel Rochman, writing in *School Library Journal,* admitted that "the lack of a fast-paced narrative line and the mythical overtones may present obstacles to some readers," but said that "many will be moved" by Abby's story.

The book was placed on required reading lists at many high schools and universities. Commenting on her stormy novel, Thomas once stated that "as a writer I work to create books filled with conflict.... I address this quest in part by matching the pitiful absurdities and heady contradictions of life itself, in part by leading the heroine to twin fountains of magic and the macabre, and evoking the holy and the horrible in the same breath. Nor is it ever enough to match these. Through the character of Abyssinia, I strive for what is beyond these, seeking, as do many writers, to find newer worlds."

### Abby Comes of Age in *Bright Shadow*

*Bright Shadow,* a sequel to *Marked by Fire,* was published in 1983. In this work, Abyssinia goes to college and ends up falling in love with Carl Lee Jefferson. Abby is a young woman now, searching for what she wants as she completes her pre-medical studies. For reasons she can't figure out, Abby's father disapproves

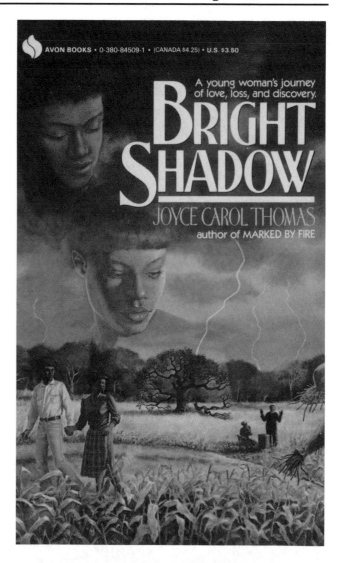

In this sequel to *Marked by Fire,* Abyssinia goes to college and falls in love, but tragedy soon looms over her good fortune.

of Carl Lee. She suspects, however, that it is because of Carl Lee's alcoholic father. At the same time, the psychically sensitive Abby begins to have forebodings about her Aunt's new husband. These feelings are validated when Aunt Serena is found brutally murdered.

Carl Lee begins to show his true colors when he is there to support Abby through her grief. Soon he has a revelation of his own when he finds out that the mysterious Cherokee woman that has been lurking around town is actually his mother. Despite these difficult hurdles, nothing is able to disrupt the young couple's love and support for one another. It is because of Carl Lee that Abby finds the light when all she can see are the dark shadows of her Aunt's death. *Bright Shadow* concludes when Abby has a dream in which her Aunt revisits her and gives her a lesson: "We are all taken from the same source: pain and beauty. One is the chrysalis that gives to the other some gift that even in death creates a new dimension in life."

Critical reaction to *Bright Shadow* was generally more mixed than for *Marked by Fire*. *School Library Journal* contributor Carolyn Caywood found the plot of *Bright Shadow* touched with melodrama and lacking in credibility, but admitted that Thomas's "story is readable and her sensuously descriptive passages celebrating the physical beauty of the black characters are a nice touch." In the *Bulletin of the Center for Children's Books,* Zena Sutherland said that *Bright Shadow* as "a love story ... is appealing, and the characterization is strong." However, she felt that "the often-ornate phraseology" sometimes weakens the story.

Several of Thomas's later books also feature the popular characters she created in *Marked by Fire* and *Bright Shadow,* including *The Golden Pasture,* which journeys back to Carl Lee's earlier life on his grandfather's ranch, and *Water Girl,* which tells the story of Abyssinia's teenage daughter Amber.

In 1990 Thomas edited the well-received anthology, *A Gathering of Flowers: Stories about Being Young in America.* The characters in these pieces represent various ethnic groups, including Native Americans, Asians, Hispanics, African Americans, and Anglos, and the authors include Gerald Vizenor, Jeanne Wakatsuki Houston, and Gary Soto. A critic noted in the *Bulletin of the Center for Children's Books,* "The collection is indeed rich and colorful, containing strong individual voices." *Voice of Youth Advocates* reviewer Judith A. Sheriff declared, "These stories will provide young adults with authentic glimpses of ethnic worlds they may seldom encounter personally."

In 1992 Thomas published *When the Nightingale Sings,* a young adult novel about the orphaned Marigold. The fourteen-year-old girl—a talented gospel singer—is living with a foster mother whose verbal abuse and bad temper make her less than an ideal parent. Although she is forced to spend her time cleaning and giving singing lessons to Ruby's unlikable children, Marigold resists believing in her foster mother's insults and instead concentrates on her singing. When the members of the Rose of Sharon Baptist Church hear her voice in the distance, their search for a new lead gospel singer just might be over. Although *Bulletin of the Center for Children's Books* contributor Betsy Hearne found the book's realistic plot to be at odds with its "fairy tale tone," Hazel S. Moore commented in *Voice of Youth Advocates,* "The element of suspension carries the story back to its roots—the African American family deeply involved with the African American Church."

Thomas's award-winning 1993 work, *Brown Honey in Broomwheat Tea,* is a collection of poetry illustrated by Floyd Cooper. *School Library Journal* reviewer Lyn Miller-Lachmann described it as "twelve short, interrelated poems about family, love, and African-American identity" which "are accessible, lyrical, and moving, with thought-provoking phrases and images." In the course of the book a family battles poverty and growing pains with love and pride. Cathy Collison, writing in the *Detroit Free Press,* commented on the recurring imagery that links the pieces: "The poems return often to tea, brewing the words into a blend as rich and seasoned as the warm Cooper portrait of a grandmother."

With her imagination and ability to bring authenticity to her novels, Thomas has been highly praised and often compared to other successful African-American women authors, like Maya Angelou, Toni Morrison, and Alice Walker. Thomas takes scenes and characters from her youth and crafts them into powerful fiction. "If I had to give advice to young people," Thomas commented in her *SAAS* essay, "it would be that whatever your career choice, prepare yourself to do it well. Quality takes talent and time. Believe in your dreams. Have faith in yourself. Keep working and enjoying today even as you reach for tomorrow. If you choose to write, value your experiences. And color them in the indelible ink of your own background."

### ■ Works Cited

Caywood, Carolyn, review of *Bright Shadow, School Library Journal,* January, 1984, pp. 89-90.

Collison, Cathy, "Picture Books beyond the Season," *Detroit Free Press,* December 22, 1993.

Review of *A Gathering of Flowers, Bulletin of the Center for Children's Books,* January, 1991.

Hearne, Betsy, review of *When the Nightingale Sings, Bulletin of the Center for Children's Books,* February, 1993, p. 194.

Miller-Lachmann, Lyn, review of *Brown Honey in Broomwheat Tea, School Library Journal,* November, 1993.

Moore, Hazel S., review of *When the Nightingale Sings, Voice of Youth Advocates,* June, 1993, p. 96.

Randall-Tsuruta, Dorothy, review of *Marked by Fire, Black Scholar,* summer, 1982, p. 48.

Rochman, Hazel, review of *Marked by Fire, School Library Journal,* March, 1982, p. 162.

Sheriff, Judith A., review of *A Gathering of Flowers, Voice of Youth Advocates,* December, 1990.

Sutherland, Zena, review of *Bright Shadow, Bulletin of the Center for Children's Books,* February, 1984, p. 119.

Thomas, Joyce Carol, *Marked by Fire,* Avon, 1982.

Thomas, Joyce Carol, *Bright Shadow,* Avon, 1983.

Thomas, Joyce Carol, essay in *Something about the Author Autobiography Series,* Volume 7, Gale, 1989, pp. 299-311.

Wray, Wendell, review of *Marked by Fire, Best Sellers,* June, 1982, pp. 123-124.

### ■ For More Information See

*BOOKS*

*Authors and Artists for Young Adults,* Volume 12, Gale, 1994.

*Children's Literature Review,* Volume 19, Gale, 1990.

*Contemporary Literary Criticism,* Volume 35, Gale, 1985.

*Dictionary of Literary Biography,* Volume 33: *Afro-American Fiction Writers after 1955,* Gale, 1984.

Pearlman, Mickey, and Katherine U. Henderson, editors, *Inter/view: Talks with America's Writing Women,* University Press of Kentucky, 1990.
Yalom, Margaret, editor, *Women Writers of the West,* Capra Press, 1982.

*PERIODICALS*

*Bakersfield Californian,* February 9, 1983.
*Berkeley Gazette,* July 21, 1983.
*New Directions,* January/February, 1984.
*Publishers Weekly,* October 11, 1993, p. 87.
*San Francisco Chronicle,* April 12, 1982.

\* \* \*

# TOLAN, Stephanie S. 1942-

## ■ Personal

Born October 25, 1942, in Canton, OH; daughter of Joseph Edward and Mary (Schroy) Stein; married Robert W. Tolan (a managing director of a theater), December 19, 1964; children: R. J.; stepchildren: Patrick, Andrew, Robert, Jr. *Education:* Purdue University, B.A., 1964, M.A., 1967.

## ■ Addresses

*Home*—50 Saratoga Ave., Waterford, NY 12188.
*Agent*—Marilyn Marlow, Curtis Brown Ltd., Ten Astor Pl., New York, NY 10010.

**STEPHANIE S. TOLAN**

## ■ Career

Purdue University, Fort Wayne, IN, instructor in continuing education, 1966-70; State University of New York College at Buffalo, faculty member in speech and theater, 1972; Franklin and Marshall College, Lancaster, PA, adjunct faculty member in English, 1973-75, coordinator of continuing education, 1974-75; writer, 1975—. Lecturer at Indiana University, 1966-70; participant, Artists-in-Education, Pennsylvania, 1974, Ohio, 1975, and North Carolina, 1984; faculty member, Institute of Children's Literature, 1988—. Member of literature panel, Ohio Arts Council, 1978-80. Actress, performing with Curtain Call Co., 1970-71. *Member:* Authors Guild, Authors League of America, Society of Children's Book Writers and Illustrators, Actors' Equity Association, Children's Book Guild of Washington, D.C.

## ■ Awards, Honors

Individual artist fellowships, Ohio Arts Council, 1978 and 1981; Post-Corbett awards finalist, 1981; Ohioana Book Award for juvenile fiction, 1981, for *The Liberation of Tansy Warner;* Bread Loaf Writers' Conference fellowship, 1981; American Psychological Association media award for best book of 1983, for *Guiding the Gifted Child; School Library Journal* Best Book of 1988 for *A Good Courage; Grandpa—and Me* was nominated for the Sequoyah Children's Book Award and the Georgia Children's Book Award.

## ■ Writings

*NOVELS FOR YOUNG READERS*

*Grandpa—and Me,* Scribner's, 1978.
*The Last of Eden,* Warne, 1980.
*The Liberation of Tansy Warner,* Scribner's, 1980.
*No Safe Harbors,* Scribner's, 1981.
*The Great Skinner Strike,* Macmillan, 1983.
*A Time to Fly Free,* Scribner's, 1983.
*Pride of the Peacock,* Scribner's, 1986.
*The Great Skinner Enterprise,* Four Winds, 1987.
*The Great Skinner Getaway,* Macmillan, 1987.
*A Good Courage,* Morrow, 1988.
*The Great Skinner Homestead,* Macmillan, 1988.
*Plague Year,* Morrow, 1990.
*Marcy Hooper and the Greatest Treasure in the World,* Morrow, 1991.
*Sophie and the Sidewalk Man,* Macmillan, 1992.
*The Witch of Maple Park,* Morrow, 1992.
*Save Halloween!,* Morrow, 1993.

*PLAYS*

*The Ledge* (one-act), Samuel French, 1968.
*Not I, Said the Little Red Hen* (one-act), first produced in New York City, 1971.
(With Katherine Paterson) *Bridge to Terabithia* (based on Paterson's novel), music by Steven Liebman, first produced in Louisville, KY, 1990.

*OTHER*

(With James T. Webb and Elizabeth Mechstroth) *Guiding the Gifted Child,* Ohio Psychology Publishing, 1982.

Contributor of poems to more than a dozen literary magazines, including *Roanoke Review, Descant,* and *Green River Review.*

## ■ Adaptations

*The Great Skinner Strike* was adapted as *Mom's on Strike,* a 1988 ABC-TV *After-School Special.*

## ■ Work in Progress

*Regions Unexplored: A Guidebook for Parents of Gifted Children,* nonfiction; a novel for young readers.

## ■ Sidelights

Stephanie S. Tolan is concerned about the rights of young people in a society that she feels cares less and less about children and their needs. Poverty, education,

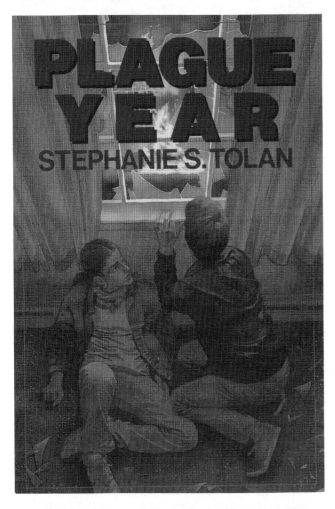

When David's friend Molly decides to help social outcast Bran Slocum, David slowly begins to sympathize with Bran ... and then a terrible secret is revealed. (Cover illustration by Ellen Thompson.)

housing, and abuse are some of the social issues that concern her, and she has dealt with some of these concerns in her books. Tolan feels that by writing about these problems she can do something to help change this trend. She also raises these issues when she speaks to parents, educators, librarians, and other audiences.

In *Sophie and the Sidewalk Man,* for instance, Tolan tells the story of an eight-year-old girl who is saving her allowance and collecting cans to buy Weldon, a stuffed hedgehog she sees in the window of a toy store. On one of her visits to see Weldon before she has enough money to buy him, Sophie sees a ragged, dirty man sitting on the sidewalk holding a sign that asks for help because he is hungry. Buying Weldon is important to Sophie because she cannot have a pet since her mother suffers from allergies. To help get the forty dollars she needs to buy Weldon, Sophie begins to skip lunch to add her lunch money to her savings. As Sophie experiences hunger, she becomes sympathetic to the "sidewalk man." Her sympathy for the man grows even stronger one day when she sees him giving half a sandwich to a stray cat. After having a discussion with her mother about giving handouts to the homeless, Sophie makes her difficult choice and helps the man.

Tolan has received praise from several reviewers for *Sophie and the Sidewalk Man.* One *Kirkus Reviews* critic calls the story "a thoughtful, intelligent, and appealing book, with respect for its young readers and for the problem it explores." In the *Horn Book Guide,* Elizabeth S. Watson comments that Sophie's progress toward growing up is admirable, and "no adult moralizing clouds the simple solution." Susannah Price, writing in *School Library Journal,* similarly finds the story "a meaningful novel that is infused with the spirit of Christmas.... This story will really hit home, right where kids' feelings are." As *Booklist* contributor Deborah Abbott states, "Tolan draws her characters carefully, making them believable and likable," and adds that the story's theme is "a welcome change of pace."

*Sophie and the Sidewalk Man* was published in 1992, but Tolan has been writing about significant social problems since she began writing. The author's first published work, *Grandpa—and Me,* discusses the important social issue of dealing with aging family members. The central character, Kerry, grows to understand how age is affecting her grandfather's behavior and also comes to a new understanding of her place within her family. In the *Plague Year,* Tolan writes about prejudice, ignorance, and hysteria, creating a compelling but frightening story about a maverick high school student whose appearance and personal background inspire hostility from the community.

In *Pride of the Peacock,* Tolan tells the story of Whitney and her fear of nuclear disaster. Whitney becomes preoccupied with the way the value and beauty of the earth are threatened by people. She meets a sculptor, Theodora Bourke, who is trying to escape the violent atmosphere of New York, where her husband lost his life. They meet at an abandoned estate where the neglected garden has become overgrown with weeds. Together they clean out the garden and their friendship helps both Whitney and Theodora to cope in a troubled world. According to an *English Journal* reviewer, teens should relate to Whitney and her strong emotions, "her fear in grappling with unsolvable real-life problems, and her inability to own the solutions acceptable to her parents and peers."

Tolan deals with a number of social problems even in her Skinner series of books, which are lighter in tone and have a lot more humor than her other works. One of her Skinner stories, *The Great Skinner Strike,* deals with Michael Skinner's involvement in a nationally publicized strike, while *The Great Skinner Enterprise* centers around running a home business. These books focus on issues about making a living that many middle-class people face in times of changing technology. Even *The Great Skinner Getaway* touches on the disillusionments of travelling, exploring, camping, and small-town American life. But despite their serious undertones, the Skinner series fulfills Tolan's interest in writing stories that will bring joy and adventure to reading for children.

*Marcy Hooper and the Greatest Treasure in the World,* a chapter book for young readers, is a fairy tale story with nymphs and dragons, but it also shows how a little girl can gain courage and become self-reliant. Marcy is having trouble at school and runs off toward the hills near her house to forget spelling tests, two-wheeled bikes, and tripping on jump ropes. She feels like a failure. By the end of her adventure, during which she finds a treasure and encounters a dragon who would swallow her up if given the chance, Marcy finds the treasure of her own courage. Jana R. Fine, reviewing the book in *School Library Journal,* says that Tolan's story "will attract those searching for mild adventure."

As with *Marcy Hooper and the Greatest Treasure in the World, The Witch of Maple Park* is "a semi-scary story with a happy ending," as Kathryn Jennings describes it in the *Bulletin of the Center for Children's Books.* The story is told by Casey, but the central character is her friend Mackenzie, who is a psychic. Mackenzie is afraid that Barnaby, the little boy she is baby-sitting, is in danger of being kidnapped by a "witch" who seems to be following them. All ends well when the "witch" turns out to be an herbalist who helps Mackenzie's mother in her failing catering business. *School Library Journal* contributor Lisa Dennis calls the book "a light, engaging read, jammed full of incidents and mild excitement, well blended into a pleasing whole." A *Kirkus Reviews* critic also writes that "quick pacing makes this a prime candidate for readers, including reluctant ones, who enjoy a frothy mystery." And Carolyn Phelan concludes in *Booklist* that "this entertaining book is a cut above most middle-grade fare."

As a child Tolan loved stories and spent many evenings under the covers finishing a good book with the help of a flashlight. "That joy in reading," she once told *SATA,* "made me want to be a writer, and from the time I was nine years old, I never doubted that I would be one." By

Even though Mackenzie has psychic powers, her friend Casey has doubts when Mackenzie tells her there's a witch in the neighborhood, until the evidence become too compelling to dismiss. (Cover illustration by Helen Cogancherry.)

the time she was eleven, Tolan had already received her first rejection slips, but continued to write throughout her junior and senior high school years. After college, Tolan became a teacher, but by 1976 she began to write full time. Participating in the National Endowment for the Arts Poets-in-the-Schools projects in 1974 and 1975 had helped her to realize that there was a new generation of children who read books under the covers with a flashlight. The experience helped her find what she called "my real audience. It is for them that I write now, as well as for myself, hoping all the time that I can make my stories worth staying up late to finish."

## ■ Works Cited

Abbott, Deborah, review of *Sophie and the Sidewalk Man, Booklist,* March 1, 1992, p. 1281.

Dennis, Lisa, review of *The Witch of Maple Park, School Library Journal,* October, 1992, p. 122.

Fine, Jana R., review of *Marcy Hooper and the Greatest Treasure in the World, School Library Journal,* January, 1992, p. 99.

Jennings, Kathryn, review of *The Witch of Maple Park,
Bulletin of the Center for Children's Books,* December, 1992, p. 125.

Phelan, Carolyn, review of *The Witch of Maple Park,
Booklist,* September 1, 1992, p. 62.

Price, Susannah, review of *Sophie and the Sidewalk
Man, School Library Journal,* May, 1992, p. 116.

Review of *Pride of the Peacock, English Journal,* October, 1987, p. 97.

Review of *Sophie and the Sidewalk Man, Kirkus Reviews,* March 15, 1992, p. 400.

Watson, Elizabeth S., review of *Sophie and the Sidewalk
Man, Horn Book Guide,* fall, 1992, p. 259.

Review of *The Witch of Maple Park, Kirkus Reviews,*
September 15, 1992, p. 1194.

## ■ For More Information See

*PERIODICALS*

*Bulletin of the Center for Children's Books,* October, 1993, pp. 59-60.
*New York Times Book Review,* April 30, 1978.
*Publishers Weekly,* September 20, 1993, p. 31.
*School Library Journal,* October, 1993, p. 133.
*Washington Post Book World,* June 10, 1990.\*

—*Sketch by Vita Richman*

\*      \*      \*

**NELLY S. TOLL**

## TOLL, Nelly S. 1935-

## ■ Personal

Born 1935, in Lwow, Poland; daughter of Zygmunt and Rose Mieses; married Erv Toll; children: Sharon, Jefferey. *Education:* Rowan College, B.A.; Rutgers University, M.A.; also attended Hahnaman University. *Religion:* Jewish.

## ■ Addresses

*Agent*—Cindy Kane, Dial Books, 2 Park Ave., New York, NY 10016.

## ■ Career

Worked as a tour guide for the Philadelphia Museum of Art. Creative writing instructor, Rowan College, Glassboro, NJ. Frequent lecturer at public schools, colleges and universities.

## ■ Awards, Honors

Children's Book Award, International Reading Association, 1994, for *Behind the Secret Window.*

## ■ Writings

(With W. Keedoner) *Behind the Closed Window* (play), produced at Princeton McCarther Theatre, Princeton, NJ, 1978.

(And contributor of illustrations) *Without Surrender:
Art of the Holocaust,* Running Press, 1982.
(And illustrator) *Behind the Secret Window: Memories
of a Hidden Childhood,* Dial Books, 1993.

Also contributor of articles and short stories to publications, including *Stone Soup.* Some of Toll's illustrations have been released as postcards, and are sold by the U.S. Holocaust Museum in Washington, DC.

## ■ Sidelights

In her 1993 book *Behind the Secret Window: Memories
of a Hidden Childhood,* Nelly S. Toll describes the Nazi's invasion of Lwow, Poland in 1941, and how it sent her Jewish family into hiding. Toll, who was six years old at the time of the invasion, recalls vividly her mother's attempts to hide them—first in the home of a Christian family and later in a cramped, bricked-up room in a gentile section of the city. During their thirteen months of hiding, Toll's father and younger brother were caught and murdered. Still, she and her mother persevered. Toll spent much of her time writing in her diary, which served as inspiration for *Behind the
Secret Window.* "Nelly Toll is a riveting companion to Anne Frank," Judy Silverman writes in *Voice of Youth
Advocates,* going on to describe Toll's book as "a very important story that needed to be told."

*Behind the Secret Window* stands out from other Holocaust tales in that it includes twenty-nine full-color watercolor illustrations that the six-year-old Toll had painted while in hiding. Though some indirectly portray the loneliness and fear she and her mother felt, most of these illustrations depict the young girl's normal daily activities, void of war and violence, while others display the child's hopeful longings for her family's happy reunion after the war. (Eight of Toll's paintings are displayed in Israel's Yad Vashem Holocaust Museum.) Ellen Fader, reviewing *Behind the Secret Window* for *School Library Journal*, claims that readers "will gain a new perspective on growing up during wartime." "Without emphasizing horror and loss," a *Publishers Weekly* critic concludes, "Toll conveys the effects of human evil and human folly, summoning up the forces of tragedy and courage."

Toll told *SATA:* "We must not forget how low human beings can stoop, so that this catastrophe will not happen again."

## ■ Works Cited

Review of *Behind the Secret Window, Publishers Weekly,* April 19, 1993, p. 63.
Fader, Ellen, review of *Behind the Secret Window, School Library Journal,* March, 1993, p. 232.
Silverman, Judy, review of *Behind the Secret Window, Voice of Youth Advocates,* February, 1993.

## ■ For More Information See

*PERIODICALS*

*Bulletin of the Center for Children's Books,* March, 1993, p. 227.
*Kirkus Reviews,* March 15, 1993.

\*      \*      \*

## TOPEK, Susan Remick 1955-

## ■ Personal

Born February 13, 1955, in Dayton, OH; daughter of Russell L. Remick and Betty K. Remick; married Joseph S. Topek (a rabbi), May 22, 1977; children: Leah Elsa, Sara Gila, Chana Malka. *Education:* Attended Young Judaea Year Course, 1973-74; University of Texas at Austin, B.A., 1977; attended Hebrew College, 1978. *Religion:* Jewish.

## ■ Addresses

*Home*—75 Sheep Pasture Rd., Setauket, NY 11733.

## ■ Career

Jewish Community Center, Boston, MA, group social worker, 1977-79; Temple Isaiah, Stony Brook, NY, Sunday and after school Hebrew teacher, 1985—; North Shore Jewish Center Pre-School, Pt. Jeff, NY, camp

director and teacher, 1986—. *Member:* Jewish Early Childhood Association, NAEC, Hadassah.

## ■ Writings

(And illustrator) *Israel Is,* Kar-Ben Copies, 1988.
*A Holiday for Noah,* Kar-Ben Copies, 1990.
*Ten Good Rules,* Kar-Ben Copies, 1991.
*A Turn for Noah,* Kar-Ben Copies, 1992.
*A Taste for Noah,* Kar-Ben Copies, 1993.

## ■ Sidelights

Susan Topek told *SATA:* "Finding interesting and appropriate Jewish books for two- and three-year-olds is always a problem. I wrote my first book after I went looking for a book on Israel. When I couldn't find one, I wrote it and illustrated it myself. From that one, stories from my toddler or pre-kindergarten classes came to me. Sometimes ideas would come from things the children said—as in *A Holiday for Noah*—and sometimes I'd design a book because I could not find one I liked. I write stories that I like to read and hear. I try to listen as a child would, so that my stories make children smile, think, and feel good. I feel that I am very lucky and that writing books for children is a gift. Writing Jewish books makes me feel proud and hopefully the children feel that also."

\*      \*      \*

## TRIPP, Valerie 1951-

## ■ Personal

Born September 12, 1951, in Mount Kisco, NY; daughter of Granger (an advertising executive) and Kathleen (a teacher; maiden name, Martin) Tripp; married Michael Petty (a teacher), June 25, 1983; children: Katherine. *Education:* Yale University, B.A. (with honors), 1973; Harvard University, M.Ed., 1981. *Hobbies and other interests:* Reading, hiking, conversation.

## ■ Addresses

*Home*—1007 McCeney Ave., Silver Spring, MD 20901. *Office*—c/o Pleasant Co., 8400 Fairway Pl., Middleton, WI 53562.

## ■ Career

Worked at Little, Brown, and Co., Boston, MA, 1973; Addison-Wesley, Menlo Park, CA, writer in language arts program, 1974-80; freelance writer, 1981—.

## ■ Awards, Honors

Children's Choice Award, International Reading Association, 1987, for *Meet Molly: An American Girl.*

# ■ Writings

*"AMERICAN GIRLS COLLECTION" SERIES*

*Meet Molly: An American Girl,* illustrated by C. F. Payne, vignettes by Keith Skeen and Renee Graef, Pleasant Co., 1986.

*Molly Learns a Lesson: A School Story,* illustrated by Payne, vignettes by Skeen and Graef, Pleasant Co., 1986.

*Molly's Surprise: A Christmas Story,* illustrated by Payne, vignettes by Skeen, Pleasant Co., 1986.

*Happy Birthday, Molly!: A Springtime Story,* illustrated by Nick Backes, vignettes by Skeen, Pleasant Co., 1987.

*Happy Birthday Samantha!: A Springtime Story,* illustrated by Robert Grace and Nancy Niles, vignettes by Jana Fothergill, Pleasant Co., 1987.

*Changes for Samantha: A Winter Story,* illustrated by Luann Roberts, Pleasant Co., 1988.

*Changes for Molly: A Winter Story,* illustrated by Nick Backes, vignettes by Skeen, Pleasant Co., 1988.

*Molly Saves the Day: A Summer Story,* illustrated by Backes, vignettes by Skeen, Pleasant Co., 1988.

*Samantha Saves the Day: A Summer Story,* illustrated by Grace and Niles, vignettes by Roberts, Pleasant Co., 1988.

*Felicity's Surprise: A Christmas Story,* illustrated by Dan Andreasen, vignettes by Roberts and Skeen, Pleasant Co., 1991.

*Felicity Learns a Lesson: A School Story,* illustrated by Andreasen, vignettes by Roberts and Skeen, Pleasant Co., 1991.

*Meet Felicity: An American Girl,* illustrated by Andreasen, vignettes by Roberts and Skeen, Pleasant Co., 1991.

*Changes for Felicity: A Winter Story,* illustrated by Andreasen, vignettes by Roberts and Skeen, Pleasant Co., 1992.

*Felicity Saves the Day: A Summer Story,* illustrations by Andreasen, vignettes by Roberts and Skeen, Pleasant Co., 1992.

*Happy Birthday Felicity!: A Springtime Story,* illustrated by Andreasen, vignettes by Roberts and Skeen, Pleasant Co., 1992.

*"JUST ONE MORE STORIES" SERIES*

*The Singing Dog,* illustrated by Sandra Kalthoff Martin, Children's Press, 1986.

*Baby Koala Finds a Home,* illustrated by Martin, Children's Press, 1987.

*The Penguins Paint,* illustrated by Martin, Children's Press, 1987.

*Squirrel's Thanksgiving Surprise,* illustrated by Martin, Children's Press, 1988.

*Sillyhen's Big Surprise,* illustrated by Martin, Children's Press, 1989.

*Happy, Happy Mother's Day!,* illustrated by Martin, Children's Press, 1989.

*OTHER*

*An Introduction to Williamsburg* (nonfiction), Pleasant Co., 1985.

*Home Is Where the Heart Is* (play), Pleasant Co., 1990.

**VALERIE TRIPP**

*Actions Speak Louder Than Words* (play), Pleasant Co., 1990.

*War on the Homefront* (play), Pleasant Co., 1990.

*Baby Koala Finds a Home* has been translated into Spanish.

# ■ Work in Progress

"Ten books about girls in the fourth grade today."

# ■ Sidelights

Valerie Tripp grew up in a large family, sandwiched between two older sisters and one younger sister and brother. The Tripp children were a close-knit group, spending their free time playing games, riding bikes, and, when winter came, sledding and ice skating. "We were a noisy, rambunctious, rag-taggle bunch," she explains in publicity brochure issued by the Pleasant Company. But their favorite activity was reading. Tripp learned to read while playing school with her older sisters, and she, in turn, taught her younger siblings. Tripp's parents encouraged the family's love of books.

Tripp has vivid and mostly fond memories of school. "I liked school, especially reading. I was like [my character] Molly in that I loved the teachers and always wanted to be the star of the school play . . . . Also, unfortunately, just like Molly, I was terrible at multiplication."

Tripp was one of the first women to be admitted to Yale University; she graduated with honors in 1973. After college, she worked in publishing, first at Little, Brown, and Co., and later at Addison-Wesley, where she wrote educational materials, such as songs, stories, and skills exercises for the language arts division.

In 1981, she received her Masters of Education degree from Harvard University. Since then, she has developed educational programs for such companies as Houghton Mifflin, Macmillan, and Harcourt Brace Jovanovich. Her children's books provide her with the greatest opportunity to combine her background in education and her love of writing. She has written six books of verse for the "Just One More Stories" series, which is aimed at beginning readers. However, she is best known for her "American Girls Collection."

The "American Girls" books focus on young women growing up during different periods in American History. Tripp has thus far written about three girls: Molly, a nine-year-old whose father serves in England during World War II; Samantha, an orphan who lives with her aunt and uncle in turn-of-the-century New York City; and Felicity, who lives in Williamsburg, Virginia, and whose life changes drastically during the outbreak of the American Revolution.

Tripp draws on events from her own childhood experiences when writing. Samantha's adventures in New York City are based on Tripp's own visits to the city. "Sometimes my whole family would go into the city to see a Broadway show, or go to a museum or a concert or the ballet," she remarks. "When I was writing *Happy Birthday Samantha!*, I remembered the feeling of exhilaration of being in the busy, fast-moving, enormous city. I knew just how Samantha felt."

Felicity's adventures reflect Tripp's fascination with colonial history. When the author was ten, she visited Williamsburg with her family. She uses her experience of attending a concert at the Governor's Palace as the basis for Felicity's night of dance at the same facility. For both writer and character, their respective evenings are among their most memorable ones.

### ■ Works Cited

*Pleasant Company Introduces an American Girls Author: Valerie Tripp* (publicity brochure), Pleasant Co., 1992.

### ■ For More Information See

PERIODICALS

*Booklist,* November 1, 1991, p. 523; May 1, 1992, p. 1603.

*Bulletin of the Center for Children's Books,* October, 1991, p. 51.
*School Library Journal,* January, 1992, p. 116; February, 1992, p. 90.

\*    \*    \*

# TUBB, Jonathan N. 1951-

### ■ Personal

Born in 1951; married; children: three.

### ■ Addresses

*Home*—3 Leighton Gardens, London NW10 3PX, England. *Office*—Western Asiatic Department, British Museum, London WC1B 3DG, England.

### ■ Career

British Museum, London, England, curator of Syria-Palestine section, and director of Museum's excavations at Tell es-Sa'idiyeh (ancient Zarethan) in Jordan. *Member:* Society of Antiquaries (fellow).

### ■ Writings

(Editor) *Palestine in the Bronze and Iron Ages: Papers in Honour of Olga Tufnell,* University of London, Institute of Archaeology, 1985.
*Archeology and the Bible,* British Museum Publications, 1990.
*Excavations at the Early Bronze Age Cemetery of Tiwal esh-Sharqi,* British Museum Publications, 1990.
*Bible Lands,* Knopf, 1991.

Contributor of scholarly articles to journals.

### ■ For More Information See

PERIODICALS

*Times Literary Supplement,* September 12, 1986, p. 1010.
*Voice of Youth Advocates,* April, 1992, p. 60.\*

\*    \*    \*

# TWOHILL, Maggie
## See ANGELL, Judie

# U

## URE, Jean 1943-
### (Jean Gregory; Ann Colin, Sarah McCulloch, pseudonyms)

### ■ Personal

Surname sounds like "Ewer"; born January 1, 1943, in Surrey, England; daughter of William (an insurance officer) and Vera (Belsen) Ure; married Leonard Gregory (an actor and writer), 1967. *Education:* Attended Webber-Douglas Academy of Dramatic Art, 1965-67. *Religion:* None. *Hobbies and other interests:* Reading, writing letters, walking dogs, playing with cats, music, working for animal rights.

### ■ Addresses

*Home*—88 Southbridge Rd., Croydon, Surrey CR0 1AF, England. *Agent*—Maggie Noach, 21 Redan St., London W14 0AB, England.

### ■ Career

Writer. Worked variously as a waitress, cook, washer-up, nursing assistant, newspaper seller, shop assistant, theater usherette, temporary shorthand-typist, translator, secretary with NATO and UNESCO, and television production assistant. *Member:* Society of Authors, Vegan Society, Animal Aid.

### ■ Awards, Honors

American Library Association best book for young adult citation, 1983, for *See You Thursday; See You Thursday* and *Supermouse* were Junior Literary Guild selections.

### ■ Writings

#### FOR CHILDREN

*Ballet Dance for Two,* F. Watts, 1960, published in England as *Dance for Two,* illustrated by Richard Kennedy, Harrap, 1960.
*Hi There, Supermouse!,* illustrated by Martin White, Hutchinson, 1983, published in the United States as *Supermouse,* illustrated by Ellen Eagle, Morrow, 1984.
*You Two,* illustrated by Eagle, Morrow, 1984, published in England as *The You-Two,* illustrated by White, Hutchinson, 1984.
*Nicola Mimosa,* illustrated by White, Hutchinson, 1985, published in the United States as *The Most Important Thing,* illustrated by Eagle, Morrow, 1986.
*Megastar,* Blackie, 1985.
*Swings and Roundabouts,* Blackie, 1986.
*A Bottled Cherry Angel,* Hutchinson, 1986.
*Brenda the Bold,* illustrated by Glenys Ambrus, Heinemann, 1986.
*Tea-Leaf on the Roof,* illustrated by Val Sassoon, Blackie, 1987.
*War with Old Mouldy!,* illustrated by Alice Englander, Methuen, 1987.
*Who's Talking?,* Orchard, 1987.
*Frankie's Dad,* Hutchinson, 1988.
(With Michael Lewis) *A Muddy Kind of Magic,* Blackie, 1988.
(With Lewis) *Two Men in a Boat,* Blackie, 1988.
*Cool Simon,* Orchard, 1990.
*Jo in the Middle,* Hutchinson, 1990.
*The Wizard in the Woods,* Walker, 1990.
*Fat Lollipop,* Hutchinson, 1991.
*William in Love,* Blackie, 1991.
*Wizard in Wonderland,* Walker, 1991.
*Spooky Cottage,* Heinemann, 1992.
*The Unknown Planet,* Walker, 1992.
*Wizard in the Woods,* Walker, 1992.
*The Ghost That Lives on the Hill,* Methuen, 1992.
*Bossyboots,* Hutchinson, 1993.
*Captain Cranko and the Crybaby,* Walker, 1993.
*Phantom Knicker Nicker,* Blackie, 1993.
*Star Turn,* Hutchinson, 1994.

#### FOR YOUNG ADULTS

*A Proper Little Nooryeff,* Bodley Head, 1982, published in the United States as *What If They Saw Me Now?,* Delacorte, 1984.
*If It Weren't for Sebastian,* Bodley Head, 1982, Delacorte, 1985.

**JEAN URE**

*You Win Some, You Lose Some,* Bodley Head, 1984, Delacorte, 1987.
*The Other Side of the Fence,* Bodley Head, 1986, Delacorte, 1988.
*One Green Leaf,* Bodley Head, 1987, Delacorte, 1989.
*Play Nimrod for Him,* Bodley Head, 1990.
*Plague 99,* Methuen, 1990, Harcourt, 1991.
*Dreaming of Larry,* Doubleday, 1991.
*Come Lucky April,* Methuen, 1992.
*Always Sebastian,* Bodley Head, 1993.
*A Place to Scream,* Doubleday, 1993.

*"WOODSIDE SCHOOL" SERIES*

*The Fright,* Orchard Books, 1987.
*Loud Mouth,* Orchard Books, 1988.
*Soppy Birthday,* Orchard Books, 1988.
*King of Spuds,* Orchard Books, 1989.
*Who's for the Zoo?,* Orchard Books, 1989.

*"THURSDAY" TRILOGY*

*See You Thursday,* Kestrel, 1981, Delacorte, 1983.
*After Thursday,* Kestrel, 1985, Delacorte, 1987.
*Tomorrow Is Also a Day,* Methuen, 1989.

*"VANESSA" TRILOGY*

*Trouble with Vanessa,* Transworld, 1988.
*There's Always Danny,* Transworld, 1989.
*Say Goodbye,* Transworld, 1989.

*FOR ADULTS*

*The Other Theater,* Transworld, 1966.
*The Test of Love,* Corgi, 1968.
*If You Speak Love,* Corgi, 1972.
*Had We but World Enough and Time,* Corgi, 1972.
*The Farther Off from England,* White Lion, 1973.
*Daybreak,* Corgi, 1974.
*All Thy Love,* Corgi, 1975.
*Marriage of True Minds,* Corgi, 1975.
*No Precious Time,* Corgi, 1976.
*Hear No Evil,* Corgi, 1976.
*Curtain Fall,* Corgi, 1978.
*Masquerade,* Corgi, 1979.
*A Girl Like That,* Corgi, 1979.
(Under pseudonym Ann Colin) *A Different Class of Doctor,* Corgi, 1980.
(Under pseudonym Ann Colin) *Doctor Jamie,* Corgi, 1980.
(Under name Jean Gregory) *Love beyond Telling,* Corgi, 1986.

*"RIVERSIDE THEATER ROMANCE" SERIES*

*Early Stages,* Corgi, 1977.
*Dress Rehearsal,* Corgi, 1977.
*All in a Summer Season,* Corgi, 1977.
*Bid Time Return,* Corgi, 1978.

*GEORGIAN ROMANCES; UNDER PSEUDONYM SARAH McCULLOCH*

*Not Quite a Lady,* Corgi, 1980, Fawcett, 1981.
*A Most Insistent Lady,* Corgi, 1981.
*A Lady for Ludovic,* Corgi, 1981.
*Merely a Gentleman,* Corgi, 1982.
*A Perfect Gentleman,* Corgi, 1982.

*TRANSLATOR*

Henri Vernes, *City of a Thousand Drums,* Corgi, 1966.
Vernes, *The Dinosaur Hunters,* Corgi, 1966.
Vernes, *The Yellow Shadow,* Corgi, 1966.
Jean Bruce, *Cold Spell,* Corgi, 1967.
Bruce, *Top Secret,* Corgi, 1967.
Vernes, *Treasure of the Golcondas,* Corgi, 1967.
Vernes, *The White Gorilla,* Corgi, 1967.
Vernes, *Operation Parrot,* Corgi, 1968.
Bruce, *Strip Tease,* Corgi, 1968.
Noel Calef, *The Snare,* Souvenir Press, 1969.
Sven Hassel, *March Battalion,* Corgi, 1970.
Hassel, *Assignment Gestapo,* Corgi, 1971.
Laszlo Havas, *Hitler's Plot to Kill the Big Three,* Corgi, 1971.
Hassel, *SS General,* Corgi, 1972.
Hassel, *Reign of Hell,* Corgi, 1973.

*OTHER*

Contributor of articles to periodicals, including *Vegan, Writers' Monthly, Books for Keeps,* and *School Librarian.*

## ■ Sidelights

Jean Ure's young adult books combine her lively sense of humor with unique stories that often contain off-beat situations and characters. Ure is a vegetarian who is

**This award-winning book about the love that emerges between a blind pianist named Abe and the much younger Marianne is an important benchmark in Ure's career.**

avid about animal rights, and while her books make references to these tendencies among her characters, they are never preachy. Class struggles, homosexuality, sexual awakenings, and feminism are also among her topics, all of which she delivers with freshness and currency.

Ure doesn't remember a time when she didn't want to be a writer. Born in Surrey, England, as a young girl she would steal notebooks from her school in order to fill them with imaginative stories. "I was brought up in a tradition of writing, inasmuch as my father's family were inveterate ode writers, sending one another long screeds of poetry on every possible occasion," Ure recalled in an essay for the *Something about the Author Autobiography Series* (*SAAS*). Amongst her family, she was also happy to read poetry or dance in front of a room of adoring relatives.

Going to school, however, was painful for Ure. She constantly felt like she didn't fit in. Ure humorously speculated in *SAAS* on the reasons why she never felt a part of the crowd: "The more I think about it, the more it seems to me that hair was the root cause of all my problems," she said, citing limp and unmanageable locks. "I am almost seriously persuaded that had it not been for hair I would have gone to the party along with everyone else."

Being outside of the popular crowd caused Ure to fantasize about many things, including being in love and dancing. Being a compulsive writer, Ure wrote down these fantasies. She sent the manuscript off to a publisher, and at the age of sixteen she became a published writer. "Writing *Dance for Two* was a very cathartic exercise and brought me great solace," she related in *SAAS*. "I almost managed to believe that ... I really *did* have a sweetheart called Noel, that I really *was* a ballet dancer."

Ambition and not wanting to continue on with the pain of school life were reasons why Ure chose to try writing as a profession rather than go to college. Unfortunately, she spent much time doing menial jobs while she tried to get her work published, and at first she didn't have much luck. Discouraged, Ure enrolled in a drama class and found within herself a hidden talent to entertain. She also met her husband, Leonard Gregory, at one of the few parties she attended. And suddenly her writing career took off. She started writing romantic novels as well as translating books. While these didn't stimulate her intellectually, they helped her learn her craft and earn a living at the same time. After a few years, however, she began to feel like she was compromising herself by writing these books.

### *See You Thursday* Marks Turning Point

The year 1980 was a turning point for Ure. She wrote in *SAAS:* "I really emerged as myself, with a book for young adults called *See You Thursday*." It focuses on a blind pianist named Abe and a sixteen-year-old rebel named Marianne. Although Abe is eight years older, wiser, and from a different background than Marianne, the pair become attracted to each other, and the relationship blossoms as Marianne sheds her shyness and finds a new maturity. In *After Thursday,* the sequel that followed this popular book, the romance of Abe and Marianne is further tested by their differing perspectives on independence. Ure was extremely happy to have found this fresh audience for her writing. "The reason I turned to writing for young adults was, basically, that it offered a freedom which 'genre' writing does not allow," she related in *SAAS*. Ure used her instinctive talent for writing to create these books. She commented, "When I created Abe, my blind pianist, I did the very minimum of research into blindness but was able to gain direct knowledge, albeit to a severely limited extent, of how it would be to be blind by tying a scarf about my eyes and blundering around the house." *See You Thursday* won the American Library Association's best book for young adults citation in 1983.

# Hi There, Supermouse!

## JEAN URE

**Published in the United States as *Supermouse*, this novel tells of the rivalry between sisters Nicola and Rose when they compete for a part in a ballet.**

Ure returned to the themes of autonomy and awakening sexuality in the "Vanessa" trilogy—which includes *Trouble with Vanessa, There's Always Danny,* and *Say Goodbye*—as well as in *The Other Side of the Fence.* Describing the first two books of the "Vanessa" trilogy as more than a romantic tale, Stephanie Nettell in the *Times Literary Supplement* labelled Ure's novels "intelligent, spiky and imaginative." Similarly enthusiastic about *The Other Side of the Fence,* reviewers such as *Bulletin of the Center for Children's Books* contributor Zena Sutherland praised the novel as "mature and sensitive.... [It is] told with both momentum and nuance." This romance is unusual, however, because it concerns a young homosexual, Richard, who meets and finds friendship with Bonny, a girl who is attracted to him but cannot understand—until the end—why her sexual advances are not returned. Although one critic, *School Library Journal* writer Karen K. Radtke, questioned Bonny's "naivete" regarding Richard (when she is otherwise street-smart), Radtke admitted that the story may be satisfying to teenagers who "harbor secret fantasies about ... flaunting parental authority."

Ure's sensitive treatment of relationships is often the focus of critical reviews. The special rivalry among sisters is explored in *Supermouse* when a shy but talented girl, Nicola, is offered a dancing role over her more favored younger sister, Rose. Mary M. Burns in *Horn Book* wrote that even though the story is told from the point of view of an eleven-year-old, "the author has managed to suggest subtle emotions which underlie the family's values and actions." The story is continued in *The Most Important Thing* when Nicola, now fourteen, must decide whether her future career will include ballet, or whether she should concentrate instead on science and maybe become a doctor. Cynthia K. Leibold concluded in the *School Library Journal* that "Ure is skillful at creating colorful characters ... and her characters execute their roles perfectly."

Using insight and sometimes humor, Ure's novels often question values and touch upon subjects such as social standards. In one such book, *What If They Saw Me Now?,* an athletic young man is caught in an amusing dilemma when he is asked to dance the male lead in a ballet. Described by Sutherland in the *Bulletin of the Center for Children's Books* as "a funny and liberating" novel, Ure's treatment of the subject may appeal to both boys and girls as they appreciate Jamie's predicament— to overcome his own and others' "macho" stereotypes.

Coping with illness is the theme of two of Ure's contemporary works, *If It Weren't for Sebastian* and *One Green Leaf*—the first focusing on mental illness and the latter on a fatal physical sickness. Sebastian is an intense but peace-loving young man whose "strangeness" is an object of scorn and misunderstanding to others in *If It Weren't for Sebastian.* Maggie becomes his friend and soon discovers that Sebastian is being treated as an out-patient at a mental health clinic. Ure "here explores the borderline psychotic and his relationships with great sensitivity and understanding," declared Sutherland in a *Bulletin of the Center for Children's Books* review. Fatal illness is similarly treated with sympathy and skill in *One Green Leaf.* After an unsuccessful surgery, it becomes obvious that David's cancer is terminal. Ure's emphasis, however, is on how David copes, and on the affection of his friends during his illness. According to Tess McKellen in the *School Library Journal,* the author "dramatizes successfully the effect of unexpected tragedy on young minds and emotions" in the novel.

Other topics for Ure's creative energy often center around her current passions: music, vegetarianism, animal rights, books, and theater. Her main motive is not to convert people, but to stimulate them. She confessed in *SAAS* that when writing she sets out "to make people think: to make them examine their motives and question their assumptions." She concluded by summing up her reasons for writing, explaining that "it will always be my characters who interest me the most; and my aim, if conscious aim I have ..., will still be to stimulate and entertain."

# ■ Works Cited

Burns, Mary M., review of *Supermouse, Horn Book,* June, 1984, p. 334.

Leibold, Cynthia K., review of *The Most Important Thing, School Library Journal,* May, 1986, p. 110.

McKellen, Tess, review of *One Green Leaf, School Library Journal,* May, 1989, p. 128.

Nettell, Stephanie, review of *Trouble with Vanessa* and *There's Always Danny, Times Literary Supplement,* June 9, 1989, p. 648.

Radtke, Karen K., review of *The Other Side of the Fence, School Library Journal,* April, 1988, p. 114.

Sutherland, Zena, review of *What If They Saw Me Now?, Bulletin of the Center for Children's Books,* June, 1984, p. 195.

Sutherland, Zena, review of *If It Weren't for Sebastian, Bulletin of the Center for Children's Books,* June, 1985, p. 197.

Sutherland, Zena, review of *The Other Side of the Fence, Bulletin of the Center for Children's Books,* February, 1988, p. 127.

Ure, Jean, essay in *Something about the Author Autobiography Series,* Volume 14, Gale, 1992.

# ■ For More Information See

### BOOKS

Chevalier, Tracy, editor, *Twentieth-Century Children's Writers,* 3rd edition, St. James Press, 1989.
*Children's Literature Review,* Volume 34, Gale, 1994.

### PERIODICALS

*British Book News,* March, 1985.
*Bulletin of the Center for Children's Books,* December, 1983, p. 79; May, 1984, p. 176; October, 1984, p. 36; April, 1986, p. 160; June, 1986, p. 198; May, 1987, p. 180; May, 1989, p. 238; October, 1991, p. 52.
*Horn Book,* December, 1983, p. 720; August, 1984, p. 479; March, 1988, p. 212.
*Publishers Weekly,* November 25, 1983, p. 64; April 13, 1984, p. 72; February 8, 1985, p. 77; May 30, 1986, p. 68; June 12, 1987, p. 86.
*School Library Journal,* August, 1984, p. 87; October, 1984, p. 163; August, 1985, p. 82; August, 1986, p. 108; October, 1991, p. 150; October, 1992, pp. 122-123; July, 1993, p. 87.
*Times Literary Supplement,* July 16, 1985, p. 910; November 28, 1986, p. 1347; September 1, 1989, p. 957.
*Voice of Youth Advocates,* August-October, 1986, p. 152; October, 1989, p. 218.

# V

**LAUREL van der LINDE**

## van der LINDE, Laurel 1952-

### ■ Personal

Born March 7, 1952, in Cleveland, OH; daughter of Donald (a Navy pilot) and Shirley (an opera singer; maiden name, Handel) van der Linde; children: Gower. *Education:* University of California at Los Angeles, B.A. (cum laude), 1974; studied ballet with Mia Slavenska, Michael Pancrieff, Rosemary Valeve, and Irina Kosmouska, 1966-70.

### ■ Addresses

*Home*—30841 Gilmour Rd., Castaic, CA 91384.

### ■ Career

Actress and dancer in Broadway plays, including *Annie, Seven Brides for Seven Brothers,* and *A Chorus Line,* 1976-82; cofounder of Landmark Entertainment Group (multimedia entertainment), North Hollywood, CA, 1982-86; author, 1991—; founder of Carousel Classics (audio books), 1992—. Trainer and breeder of Arabian and Lipizzan horses, 1984—. *Member:* American Book Association, Society of Children's Book Writers and Illustrators.

### ■ Writings

*The Devil in Salem Village,* Millbrook Press, 1992.
*The Pony Express,* Macmillan, 1993.
*The White Stallions: The Story of the Dancing Horses of Lipizza,* Macmillan, 1994.
*Legends in Their Own Time,* Millbrook Press, 1994.

Contributor to periodicals, including *California Arabian, Arabian Horse Times,* and *Equus.*

### ■ Sidelights

Horses are Laurel van der Linde's passion, and the animals have been the subject of two of her books for children. When she isn't writing, she trains and breeds Arabian and Lipizzan horses at her California ranch. Nevertheless, horses are but one aspect of van der Linde's background. Trained as a ballet dancer, she later had a successful career on the Broadway stage, appearing in such musicals as *Annie, A Chorus Line, Seven Brides for Seven Brothers, Annie Get Your Gun,* and a revival of *My Fair Lady.* Later, van der Linde decided to explore other aspects of the entertainment industry and cofounded the multimedia entertainment company Landmark Entertainment Group. Always fascinated with children's media, she also formed a children's audio book company, Carousel Classics. The company's first release was *The Juicy Truth about Johnny Appleseed,* with the titles *The Legend of Sleepy Hollow* and *The New Adventures of Paul Bunyan* following soon after.

Taking a cue from her interest in the genre, van der Linde began to write her own children's books. Her first work, 1992's *The Devil in Salem Village,* is a recounting of the witch trials that took place in Salem, Massachusetts, in 1692. These trials occurred when members of the Salem community began accusing a group of young women with consorting with the devil. As a result several young women were convicted as witches and subsequently burned at the stake. In *Voice of Youth Advocates,* Victoria Yablonsky called the book "an excellent introduction" to this episode of American colonial life.

Following *The Devil in Salem Village,* van der Linde focused her writing on her beloved horses. One of the resulting books is 1993's *The Pony Express,* a chronicle of the early western American service that employed horsemen to carry letters. Covering such topics as the diet of the horses and skirmishes with hostile Indians, van der Linde provides a chronology of the famous mail carriers and their mounts. She also provides photographs from the time, samples of the mail the Pony Express carried, and locations of the various stations that were scattered throughout the frontier. A reviewer for the *Bulletin of the Center for Children's Books* remarked that *The Pony Express* makes for "lively reading," and stands as a "thoroughly enjoyable account" of that part of American history. Van der Linde also published *The White Stallions: The Story of the Dancing Horses of Lipizza* and *Legends in Their Own Time,* a biography about famous horses, both in 1994.

### ■ Works Cited

Review of *The Pony Express, Bulletin of the Center for Children's Books,* July/August, 1993.

Yablonsky, Victoria, review of *The Devil in Salem Village, Voice of Youth Advocates,* August, 1992.

### ■ For More Information See

*BOOKS*

Willis, John, editor, *Theatre World,* Volume 39: *1982-1983,* Crown, 1984, pp. 11, 223, 225.

*PERIODICALS*

*Horse Illustrated,* July, 1990.

\*      \*      \*

# VERBA, Joan Marie 1953-

### ■ Personal

Born December 12, 1953, in Waltham, MA; daughter of Bennie Arthur (a computer marketer) and Mildred Maurine (a homemaker; maiden name, Whetstine)

**JOAN MARIE VERBA**

Verba. *Education:* University of Minnesota, B.S., 1975; graduate study at Indiana University, 1975-77. *Politics:* Democrat. *Religion:* United Methodist.

### ■ Addresses

*Office*—P.O. Box 1363, Minnetonka, MN 55345.

### ■ Career

Control Data Corporation and Unisys, computer programmer, 1978-87; Lerner Publications, word processor, 1989—. *Member:* Society of Children's Book Writers and Illustrators, Minnesota Science Fiction Society (past member of board of directors), SF Minnesota, Mythopoeic Society (member of board of directors).

### ■ Writings

*Voyager: Exploring the Outer Planets,* Lerner Publications, 1991.
*North Dakota,* Lerner Publications, 1992.

### ■ Work in Progress

A history of "Star Trek" fanzines, covering the years 1967-87, and a biography of C. S. Lewis, tentatively titled *Myth Made Real.*

# ■ Sidelights

Joan Marie Verba told *SATA:* "My interest in science and science fiction began when I was in second grade. The teacher placed a map of the solar system on a bulletin board, which led me to read everything I could find on space and space travel. In junior high and high school, J. R. R. Tolkien's *The Hobbit* and C. S. Lewis's *Out of the Silent Planet* were required reading, and that expanded my interest in fantasy studies as well, though I had been reading fantasy on my own much earlier.

"I had an interest in writing stories before I graduated from high school, and began having my stories published in amateur publications starting in 1973, but did not have any professional ambitions until 1978 when I attended the World Science Fiction Convention. I started my first novel in 1982, saw my first magazine article published in 1984, and published my first professional short story in 1985. When the opportunity came to write a book about Voyager, I was more than happy to put my knowledge and love of science to work. My current writing projects also relate to my interests in fantasy and science fiction, which I believe help society to understand its past and anticipate its future."

\*　　\*　　\*

# VERTREACE, Martha M. 1945-

# ■ Personal

Born November 24, 1945, in Washington, D.C.; daughter of Walter Charles (a supply officer) and Modena (a supervisor in a Washington, D.C., Recreation Warehouse; maiden name, Kendrick) Vertreace. *Education:* District of Columbia Teachers College, B.S., 1967; Roosevelt University, M.A., 1971, Mp.H., 1972; Mundelein College, M.S., 1981. *Politics:* Democratic Socialist. *Religion:* Roman Catholic. *Hobbies and other interests:* Knitting, photography, water colors.

# ■ Addresses

*Home*—1157 East 56th St., Chicago, IL 60637. *Office*—Kennedy-King College, 6800 South Wentworth, Chicago, IL 60621. *Agent*—James Plath, 1108 North Clinton, Bloomington, IL 61701.

# ■ Career

Kennedy-King College, Chicago, IL, associate professor and poet in residence, 1977—. Board of trustees, Illinois Writers Review Advisory Board. Judge, Illinois Arts Council and Wisconsin Arts Board grants; Ariel judge, Triton College. Minister of care, Saint Thomas the Apostle Church. *Member:* National Council of Teachers of English, Midwest Modern Language Association, Illinois Association for Teachers of English.

**MARTHA M. VERTREACE**

# ■ Awards, Honors

Excellence in Professional Writing award, Illinois Association for Teachers of English, 1987; Illinois Arts Council Literary award (poetry), 1987 and 1988; Hawthornden International Writers' Retreat fellowship, 1992; honorable mention, White Eagle Coffee Store Press Contest, 1992, for *Oracle Bones;* Eastern Washington University fellowship, 1993; Creative Writing fellowship, National Endowment for the Arts, and Illinois Arts Council fellowship, both 1993; Significant Illinois Poet award (established by Gwendolyn Brooks), 1993.

# ■ Writings

*JUVENILE*

*Kelly in the Mirror,* A. Whitman, 1993.

*ADULT POETRY*

*Second House from the Corner,* Kennedy-King College, 1986.
*Under a Cat's Eye Moon,* Clockwatch Review Press, 1991.
*Oracle Bones,* White Eagle Coffee Store Press, 1994.

Also contributor of poems to *Benchmark: An Anthology of Contemporary Illinois Poets,* Stormline Press.

*OTHER*

Contributor of essays to anthologies, including *American Women Writing Fiction,* University Press of Kentucky, 1989; and *The Anna Book,* Greenwood Press, 1993. Poetry editor, *Oyez Review;* book review editor,

**Kelly** *in the* **Mirror**

Martha M. Vertreace

*Illustrated by*
Sandra Speidel

**Although Vertreace usually writes adult poetry, her use of visual imagery lends itself well to this story of a young girl's search for identity.** (Cover illustration by Sandra Speidel.)

*Community* magazine; co-editor, *Rhino;* editor, *Class Act;* member of editorial board, *Seams* magazine.

## ■ Sidelights

"For me, writing is fun, although it is not necessarily easy," Martha Vertreace told *SATA*. "I began writing after the sudden death of my father when I was sixteen. It was a way to ease the tension, to focus on something else. I try not to judge my writing by asking whether or not the piece gets published; rather, my concern is that it express whatever I am after." She further explained her career by noting: "When I write, my primary goal is to enjoy the experience. Perhaps, therefore, my work can bring joy to someone else. I write whenever I get the chance. I enjoy working in various forms; consequently, although most of my writing is poetry, I have published short stories, reviews, and critical essays. If I spoke of influences on my work, I would think of various poets—Richard Wilbur, Rita Dove, Amy Clampitt, Derek Walcott, Mona Van Duyn, Seamus Heaney—many others."

Vertreace's success in writing for adults eventually led to her first book for children, *Kelly in the Mirror*. "My entry into writing children's books was quite by accident," the author related. "An editor read some of my poems and decided that I wrote with strong images. She invited me to try to write a picture book." In Vertreace's tale, Kelly is disturbed when her parents discuss the resemblance of her brother and sister to themselves. Because she does not look like anyone in her family, Kelly feels left out. After a trip up to the attic and a look through family albums, however, Kelly finds photos of her mother as a child and realizes that she *does* look like someone after all.

Reviewers of *Kelly in the Mirror* praised the concept of the story as well as its prose. A reviewer for *Publishers Weekly* wrote, "Every detail of [Vertreace's] deceptively simple narrative will grab and hold youngsters' attentions." And Mary Harris Veeder, writing in the *Chicago Tribune,* praised the author's "strength ... the feel [she] has for the small moment."

## ■ Works Cited

Review of *Kelly in the Mirror, Publishers Weekly,* March 29, 1993, p. 56.
Veeder, Mary Harris, review of *Kelly in the Mirror, Chicago Tribune,* May 9, 1993, p. 6.

# W

## WALLACE, Barbara Brooks 1922-

### ■ Personal

Born in Soochow, China; daughter of Otis Frank (a businessman) and Nicia E. Brooks; married James Wallace, Jr., February 27, 1954; children: James. *Education:* Attended schools in Hankow, Tientsin, and Shanghai, China; in Baguio, Philippines; and in Claremont, CA. Attended Pomona College, 1940-41; University of California, Los Angeles, B.A., 1945. *Religion:* Episcopalian.

### ■ Addresses

*Home*—2708 George Mason Pl., Alexandria, VA 22305.

### ■ Career

Author of books for children. *Member:* Children's Book Guild of Washington, D.C., Alpha Phi.

### ■ Awards, Honors

National League of American PEN Women Juvenile Book Award, 1970, for *Claudia,* and 1974, for *The Secret Summer of L. E. B.; Julia and the Third Bad Thing* was named an International Youth Library Choice Book, 1975; *Claudia* was included in the International Youth Library's "Best of the Best" list, 1975; William Allen White Children's Book Award, 1983, for *Peppermints in the Parlor; Booklist* Editor's Choice Book, 1993, and Edgar Allan Poe Award for best juvenile mystery from the Mystery Writers of America, 1994, both for *The Twin in the Tavern.*

### ■ Writings

*FOR YOUNG READERS*

*Claudia,* Follett, 1969.
*Andrew the Big Deal,* Follett, 1971.
*The Trouble with Miss Switch,* Abingdon, 1971.
*Victoria,* Follett, 1972.
*Can Do, Missy Charlie,* Follett, 1974.

**BARBARA BROOKS WALLACE**

*The Secret Summer of L. E. B.,* Follett, 1974.
*Julia and the Third Bad Thing,* Follett, 1975.
*Palmer Patch,* Follett, 1976.
*Hawkins,* Abingdon, 1977.
*Peppermints in the Parlor,* Atheneum, 1980.
*The Contest Kid Strikes Again,* Abingdon, 1980.
*Hawkins and the Soccer Solution,* Abingdon, 1981.
*Miss Switch to the Rescue,* Abingdon, 1981.
*Hello, Claudia!,* Modern Curriculum Press, 1982.
*Claudia and Duffy,* Modern Curriculum Press, 1982.
*The Barrel in the Basement,* Atheneum, 1985.
*Argyle,* Abingdon, 1987.
*The Interesting Thing That Happened at Perfect Acres, Inc.,* Atheneum, 1988.
*The Twin in the Tavern,* Atheneum, 1993.

**Julia is frightened by an ominous premonition in Wallace's story based on her mother's experiences in Russia.** (Cover illustration by Mike Eagle.)

## ■ Sidelights

"Nothing in my childhood that I can think of pointed toward an interest in writing," author Barbara Brooks Wallace once told *SATA*. "Though I treasured books (the newest *Oz* book from Grandmother in America or the latest *Tiger Tim Annual* from England—both books that were joyfully discovered under the Christmas tree each year), I didn't read avidly, at least not hundreds of books. Nor did I start writing at eight, or some other wonderfully early age. I envy all writers who have done both of these things, as so many have.

"It was my sister, Connie," Wallace continued, "who finally persuaded me to start writing, something I had been told I should do when in college. Connie apparently managed to do what a college professor had not succeeded in doing. Perhaps not a surprise. I had idolized my older sister as a child, managing to spend a great deal of time haunting her and her friends. Not the kind of thing, I might say, that adds to a younger sister's popularity, although I believe I've now been forgiven for that!"

Both sisters were born and spent their childhood years in China, where their father was a businessman. They attended schools in several cities in China and the Philippines before moving back to the United States. Wallace attended college in California, studying for one year at Pomona College and earning her bachelor of arts degree at the University of California at Los Angeles in 1945. But it was not until some fifteen years later, after

working in radio, television, and for the Red Cross in San Francisco, that Wallace—by then married and with a young son—began writing. She worked on adult short stories until she discovered her love of writing for children.

Wallace's first children's book, *Claudia,* was published in 1969 and included in the International Youth Library's "Best of the Best" list of 1975. *Claudia* tells of the often hilarious adventures of an eleven-year-old girl and her relationships with friends and family. Claudia reappears in *Hello, Claudia!* and *Claudia and Duffy. Hello, Claudia!,* in which the action occurs before the events of the first Claudia book, begins as Claudia's best friend moves away. Claudia, who is eight, is reluctant to become friends with the new boy next door, the precocious, six-year-old Duffy. The friendship, of course, blooms and carries on through all three books. "All of the [Claudia] books have a good balance of interests (home, friends, school) as well as warm familial relationships; all are discerning in their characterizations and have good dialogue," commented a reviewer in the *Bulletin of the Center for Children's Books.* A review of *Claudia and Duffy* in the same issue of the *Bulletin* called the three books "brisk, bouncy, warm in family relationships and often very funny."

Wallace's 1972 book, *Victoria,* tells the story of an eleven-year-old girl who dominates her three roommates at a boarding school by convincing them of the powers of a little book she owns. Trouble follows Victoria's adventures and she makes increasing demands on her three roommates. Only after the three reject Victoria do they learn of her unhappy background and her need for attention and importance. In reviewing *Victoria,* a *Bulletin of the Center for Children's Books* critic called it "a perceptive story, adroitly written; perhaps not since *Harriet (the Spy)* has there been a young heroine so self-centered, so complex, and so touching." And a *Publishers Weekly* contributor praised the work as "an unusual and entertaining novel."

### Fantasies, Fables, and Furkens

Wallace followed *Victoria* with *Can Do, Missy Charlie,* a book inspired by her childhood in China, *The Secret Summer of L.E.B., Julia and the Third Bad Thing,* an International Youth Library Choice Book of 1975, and *Palmer Patch,* an animal fantasy about which a critic wrote in the *Bulletin of the Center for Children's Books:* "For children who love animal stories, this has a sure appeal." These books were followed by the first in a series of lively, humorous books about a young American boy, Harvey, who inadvertently wins the services of a British gentleman's gentleman—*Hawkins, The Contest Kid Strikes Again,* and *Hawkins and the Soccer Solution.* Two other purely humorous books by Wallace, *The Trouble with Miss Switch* and *Miss Switch to the Rescue,* are fantasies, both featuring the popular teacher/witch, Miss Switch.

Courage is the primary theme in *The Barrel in the Basement,* a *Borrowers*-like story of Pudding and Mud-

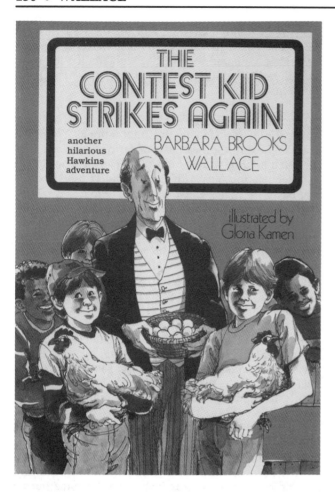

**Harvey Small suspects foul play when the town's new assistant to the mayor starts to interfere in rich Mrs. Mosely's business affairs.** (Cover illustration by Gloria Kamen.)

dle, two elves—called "Furkens"—looking for a new basement dwelling. They meet Old Toaster, a Furken who lives in a barrel provided by Noah, an elderly human scholar of all things elfin, and they become friends. When Noah embarks on a trip and mysteriously doesn't return, Pudding discovers that he has been placed in a nursing home, gathers up his courage, and sets out to rescue his friend. "These endearing creatures are fully developed," said reviewer Claudia W. Draper in *Horn Book*, expressing a hope for "further exploits of these newest denizens of Faerie."

*Argyle,* published in 1987, is a humorous, nonsensical, fable-like story about the comfort of sameness and the fickleness of fame. A sheep named Argyle is happiest when he blends in with the rest of the flock, but when he finds a patch of strange little colored flowers and eats them, his wool coat turns multi-colored—thus leading to the invention of argyle socks and a lucrative business for his owners. But fame is sometimes painful, and passes quickly. Without the enchanted flowers, Argyle loses his colors and happily returns to the security of the fold. Calling the book "delightful nonsense," a *Bulletin of the Center for Children's Books* reviewer described Wallace's writing as "honed to simplicity and . . . given

humor by the union of fantastic development and bland style."

Following *Argyle* was *The Interesting Thing That Happened at Perfect Acres, Inc.,* the story of ten-year-old Perfecta Deportmenta, the only child living in a sterile housing development owned by the evil Mr. Snoot, who hates animals and children. One lovely old house in the neighborhood is not controlled by Mr. Snoot, and it is there that Perfecta, with her new friend Puck, discovers that Mr. Snoot is imprisoning story book characters, zoo animals, and other creatures in an attempt to make children's literature boring. A lively adventure follows, complete with magically appearing helpers, cloaks of invisibility, and wallpaper animals coming to life. The adventure has an important meaning, leading Perfecta to a surprising—and welcome—discovery. "The book's intriguing beginning will capture readers' imaginations," asserted a reviewer in *Booklist*.

## Gothic Myseries

*Peppermints in the Parlor,* which won the William Allen White Children's Book Award in 1983, is a Gothic mystery set in San Francisco in the 1890s. Wallace's eleven-year-old heroine, Emily, has been orphaned and

**When Rupert's friend Amelia is kidnapped by the warlock Mordo it's up to him and the magical Miss Switch to rescue her.** (Cover illustration by Kathleen Garry McCord.)

sent to the mansion of her wealthy aunt and uncle. She is horrified to find her uncle missing and her aunt practically enslaved by two evil women who have turned the mansion into a home for the elderly. Emily, too, is forced into near slavery but she sets out to help the old people, who are locked in a dungeon-like cell called the Remembrance Room if they take a peppermint from a tantalizing dish kept in the parlor. Horror builds upon horror in the shadowy mansion as Emily tries to solve the mystery of her uncle's disappearance and thus obtain the key that will unlock all the other mysteries haunting Sugar Hill Hall. A reviewer in *Horn Book,* likening *Peppermints in the Parlor* to Frances Hodgson Burnett's *A Little Princess* and Joan Aiken's *The Wolves of Willoughby Chase,* described it as "an amusing Gothic romp with a shadowy, gaslit atmosphere, moving briskly and sweeping the reader along with it."

Wallace's Edgar Award-winning novel, *The Twin in the Tavern,* is another Victorian mystery in which a young boy, Taddy, is twice orphaned, first by the death of his parents, and then by the sudden death of his aunt and uncle. He ends up the captive of two villainous thieves, and is taken to live as an unpaid servant at the Dog's Tail, a grim tavern owned by one of the crooks on the Alexandria, Virginia, waterfront. Taddy has been warned by his dying uncle that he must find his twin to know who he is—and thereby hangs the tale and the mystery. Writing in *School Library Journal,* Sally Margolis called *The Twin in the Tavern* "a worthy successor to *Peppermints in the Parlor*" and praised Wallace's "fine hand for Gothic embroidery" and the book's "nifty surprise conclusion."

"I have a clear recollection of how I felt as a child about many things," Wallace told *SATA* in explanation of her ability to relate to her young audience. "Christmas, the terror of waking alone at night, having a friend, and an understanding, I believe, of why I felt as I did. And I love children, especially the ages of seven to twelve. They are eager, enthusiastic, and so tremendously responsive." Another inspiration has been her son Jimmy. "My husband and I have only one child, Jimmy, who has been my main source of material for almost all my book children, three-year-old girls, twelve-year-old boys, all of them. (Even my witches, dragons, and talking mushrooms tend to sound like Jimmy.)" Wallace also told *SATA* that children are her most valuable critics. "One little girl brought back a manuscript she was trial-reading for me and said, 'I never got past chapter one because I didn't know what you were talking about.' Just like that!

"The book I had most fun writing was *Peppermints in the Parlor,*" Wallace continued. "I didn't know what the ending was going to be until the ending arrived. I often didn't know what was going to happen from page to page, and would sit up late at night writing because I couldn't wait until the next morning to find out. I guess my readers must have felt the same way in reading it as I did in writing it, or so I'm told. *The Twin in the Tavern* wasn't fun to write, the first half anyway, but the end result has been wonderful. I hope I'll be lucky enough to

**Something wicked is slowly destroying the once happy home of Emily Luccock's Aunt and Uncle Twice in this chilling tale.** (Cover illustration by Richard Williams.)

create another Victorian mystery, another book that's pure humor, or another fantasy, all my favorites to write. But whatever I do write, I know it will always be for children and will always have a happy ending. And that's the wonderful thing about being a writer—*I* get to choose!"

## ■ Works Cited

Review of *Argyle, Bulletin of the Center for Children's Books,* September, 1987, pp. 19-20.

Review of *Claudia and Duffy, Bulletin of the Center for Children's Books,* February, 1983, p. 119.

Draper, Charlotte W., review of *The Barrel in the Basement, Horn Book,* September/October, 1985, p. 561.

Review of *Hello, Claudia!, Bulletin of the Center for Children's Books,* February, 1983, p. 119.

Review of *The Interesting Thing That Happened at Perfect Acres, Inc., Booklist,* March 15, 1988, p. 1269.

Margolis, Sally, review of *The Twin in the Tavern, School Library Journal,* October, 1993, p. 134.

Review of *Palmer Patch, Bulletin of the Center for Children's Books,* March, 1977, p. 116.

Review of *Peppermints in the Parlor, Horn Book,* October, 1980, pp. 522-523.
Review of *Victoria, Bulletin of the Center for Children's Books,* March, 1973, pp. 114-115.
Review of *Victoria, Publishers Weekly,* January 22, 1973, p. 71.

■ **For More Information See**

*PERIODICALS*

*Booklist,* May 1, 1985, p. 1260.
*Bulletin of the Center for Children's Books,* April, 1988, p. 172.
*Publishers Weekly,* July 24, 1987, pp. 185-186.

\* \* \*

# WALSH SHEPHERD, Donna 1948-

■ **Personal**

Born October 29, 1948, in Centralia, WA; daughter of Maurice R. (an educator) and Bernice Olivia (an artist; maiden name, Swearingen) Walsh; married Morris W. Shepherd (a certified public accountant), June 10, 1972; children: Chadney, Shane, Aaron. *Education:* Olympic College, A.A.; Central Washington University, B.A.; University of Alaska, Anchorage, M.F.A. *Hobbies and other interests:* Traveling, hiking, gardening.

■ **Addresses**

*Office*—Department of English, University of Alaska at Anchorage, 3211 Providence Dr., Anchorage, AK 99504.

■ **Career**

University of Alaska, Anchorage, instructor in literature and writing, 1988—; technical writing consultant; children's book author. *Member:* Society of Children's Book Writers and Illustrators, Alaska Press Women.

■ **Awards, Honors**

Best children's book, National Press Women, 1993, for *The Aztecs;* Excellence in Journalism Award—Pacific Northwest division, 1993; awards from Alaska Press Women; award for University of Alaska, Anchorage and *Anchorage Daily News* writing contest.

■ **Writings**

*Trixie Belden and the Mystery at Mead's Mountain,* Western, 1978.
*The Aztecs,* F. Watts, 1992.
*Uranus,* F. Watts, 1994.
*Auroras,* F. Watts, in press.

Also contributor to periodicals.

**DONNA WALSH SHEPHERD**

■ **Work in Progress**

*Tundra,* for F. Watts, 1996.

■ **Sidelights**

Donna Walsh Shepherd told *SATA:* "So often children consider nonfiction boring. Really, all the adventures and possibilities of the world live in nonfiction. I want my subject, whatever it is, to come alive and connect to the rest of the world. To do this, I try to experience as much of my subject as possible, whether it's walking where the ancient Aztecs walked and were killed, or looking through a telescope at Uranus and talking with *Voyager* scientists, or sleeping outside at thirty degrees below zero to watch the auroras catch fire to the sky. I believe in adventure, and the best of life's adventures begin in books.

"My writing career began with a book. One Christmas I took my children to visit my parents. Late one night I pulled an old Trixie Belden mystery off the shelf and read it with the same devouring delight I had as a child. As I put the book back on the shelf at three in the morning, I thought, 'That really was a good book. I could never write anything like that.' But my mind answered back, 'Well of course I could.' By morning I had plotted a whole new Trixie Belden mystery. Although very little of that ended up in print, I did get to write a Trixie Belden book. Later I began writing for magazines and newspapers and am now returning to children's books, which are so much fun and lead to so many wonderful adventures."

\*     \*     \*

# WATSON, Carol 1949-
   (Harriet Hains)

## ■ Personal

Born in 1949.

## ■ Addresses

*Home*—3 Geraldine Rd., Strand-on-the-Green, Chiswick, London W4 3PA, England.

## ■ Career

Free-lance writer and editor.

## ■ Writings

*The House*, illustrated by Colin King, Usborne, 1980.
*The Shop*, illustrated by King, Usborne, 1980.
*The Town*, illustrated by King, Usborne, 1980.
(With D. Bareijo) *Round the World in Spanish*, Usborne, 1980.
(With Katherine Folliot) *Round the World in French*, Usborne, 1980.
(With Mariolina Freeth) *Round the World in Italian*, Usborne, 1980.
(With Cornelie Tucking) *Round the World in German*, Usborne, 1980.
*Robbers*, illustrated by Stephen Cartwright, Usborne, 1981.
(Reteller) *Aesop's Fables*, illustrated by Nick Price, Usborne/Hayes, 1982.
(Reteller) *Animal Legends*, illustrated by Price, Usborne/Hayes, 1982.
(Reteller) *Magical Animals*, illustrated by Price, Usborne/Hayes, 1982.
(Editor) *The Usborne Book of Animal Stories*, Usborne, 1982.
*Opposites*, illustrated by David Higham, Usborne, 1983.
*Shapes*, illustrated by Higham, Usborne, 1983.
*Sizes*, illustrated by Higham, Usborne, 1983.
(With Robyn Gee) *Better English* (contains *English Grammar*, *English Spelling*, and *English Punctuation*), illustrated by Kim Blundell, Usborne, 1983.
*1 2 3*, illustrated by Higham, Usborne, 1984.
(With Heather Amery) *Colours*, illustrated by Higham, Usborne, 1984.
*Telling the Time*, illustrated by Higham, Usborne, 1984.
*Simple Sums*, illustrated by Higham, Usborne, 1984.
*Shire Horse*, illustrated by Sally Fear, A & C Black, c. 1988.
*If You Were a Guinea Pig*, Collins, 1988.
*If You Were a Rabbit*, Collins, 1988.
*If You Were a Hamster*, Collins, 1988.

(Editor) *Please God . . .: B.B.C. Radio Leicester's Book of Children's Prayers*, Fount Publications, 1989.
(Author and compiler) *365 Children's Prayers*, Lion Publishing, 1989.
*If You Were a Kitten*, illustrated by Sue Cony, Dinosaur, 1989.
*If You Were a Puppy*, illustrated by Valerie Petrone, Dinosaur, 1989.
*My Little Christmas Box*, Lion Publishing, 1990.
*Write-a-Story: At the Seaside*, CollinsEducational, 1990.
*Write-a-Story: Charlie's Chickenpox*, CollinsEducational, 1990.
*Write-a-Story: It's Snowing*, CollinsEducational, 1990.
*Write-a-Story: Moving Day*, CollinsEducational, 1990.
*Write-a-Story: The Invitation*, CollinsEducational, 1990.
*Read French: A Bilingual Picture Wordbook*, French translations by M. L. Sharp, Usborne, 1991.
(Author and compiler) *Prayers for a Fragile World*, illustrated by Rhian Nest James, Lion Publishing, 1991.
*If You Were a Photographer*, illustrated by Petrone, Belitha, 1992.
*If You Were a Pilot*, illustrated by Petrone, Belitha, 1992.
(With Brian Jones) *Space Activity Book*, Gollancz, 1992.
(Under pseudonym Harriet Hains) *My Baby Brother*, photography by Steve Shott, illustrations by Conny Jude, Dorling Kindersley, 1992.
(Under pseudonym Harriet Hains) *My New Puppy*, photography by Shott, illustrations by Jude, Dorling Kindersley, 1992.
(Under pseudonym Harriet Hains) *My New School*, Dorling Kindersley, 1992.
(Under pseudonym Harriet Hains) *Our New Kitten*, Dorling Kindersley, 1992.

Also author of *English Grammar*, *English Spelling*, and *English Punctuation*, all for Usborne; *Mouse House*, Octopus Books; and *Write Your Own Storybooks* (four books), *First Facts*, *First Skills*, *Glue*, *Water*, *Paint*, and *Scissors*, all for Collins. Reteller for *Giants*, Collins. Reteller of fairy tales for *Storyteller* magazine. Some of Watson's books have been translated into Gaelic or Welsh.

## ■ Sidelights

Carol Watson has collected and retold ancient legends and moral tales for young children which are presented in a comic-book style, including *Aesop's Fables*, *Animal Legends*, and *Magical Animals*. The use of nonlinear storytelling and the simplification required by the comic format have led some reviewers to express doubts about the treatments, but others have noted that the less formal style might make the books appealing to readers not yet old enough for standard versions. Watson's *Robbers* is presented in a similar format, which *School Librarian* reviewer Cliff Moon commented achieves "the perfect balance" between text and illustration.

Watson has also written the text for a number of books through which the youngest of children can learn simple concepts and vocabulary. Her concept books for preschoolers include *Opposites, Shapes, Sizes,* and *Simple Sums. Opposites* introduces children to its basic concept through a comparison of two friends, one fat and one thin. In *Sizes* Watson uses the animals on Farmer Jo's farm to compare big, bigger, small, and smaller. *Simple Sums* is a "first-rate" introduction to mathematics, asserted a reviewer for the *Junior Bookshelf,* and Watson's vocabulary books *The Shop, The House,* and *The Town* are "definitely the best of their type," according to Moon.

For *If You Were a Kitten* and *If You Were a Puppy,* factual books in which Watson teaches how to care for their pets, reviewers have recommended that adults supervise their children due to the difficulty of some of the vocabulary. *School Librarian* contributor Irene Babsky praised the books for their "imaginative insight into the world and needs of the animals" and the "wealth of information" they convey. Both books were praised for their charming illustrations and for the inclusion of a resource section in the back with advice, details of common health problems, and addresses for further information.

Watson's *Shire Horse* describes the life of a cart horse named Gilbert, and, like *If You Were a Kitten* and *If You Were a Puppy,* is intended for slightly older children. The stages of Gilbert's life are described in a manner which has been praised for both its simplicity and its clarity, including the training and grooming needed to prepare for showing the horse. A reviewer for *Books for Your Children* concluded that *Shire Horse* is "a very pleasing book both to look at and to think about."

### ■ Works Cited

Babsky, Irene, review of *If You Were a Kitten* and *If You Were a Puppy, School Librarian,* November, 1989, p. 146.

Moon, Cliff, review of *The Shop, The House,* and *The Town, School Librarian,* March, 1981, p. 24.

Moon, Cliff, review of *Robbers, School Librarian,* June, 1982, p. 127.

Review of *Shire Horse, Books for Your Children,* summer, 1988, p. 16.

Review of *Simple Sums, Junior Bookshelf,* February, 1985, p. 32.

### ■ For More Information See

*PERIODICALS*

*Booklist,* November 1, 1982, p. 364.
*Junior Bookshelf,* October, 1989, p. 233.
*School Librarian,* December, 1982, p. 328.
*School Library Journal,* February, 1983, pp. 63-64, p. 86; March, 1984, p. 167; April, 1984, pp. 109-110.

**April Halprin Wayland and her cat, Lucy**

## WAYLAND, April Halprin 1954-

### ■ Personal

Born April 20, 1954, in Los Angeles, CA; daughter of Leahn J. (a farmer) and Saralee (a concert pianist; maiden name, Konigsberg) Halprin; married Gary Carlton Wayland (a certified public accountant), October 17, 1981; children: Jeffrey. *Education:* University of California, Davis, B.S. (cum laude), 1976. *Religion:* Jewish.

### ■ Addresses

*Home*—143 South Kenter Ave., Los Angeles, CA 90049. *Agent*—Curtis Brown, Ltd., 10 Astor Place, New York, NY, 10003.

### ■ Career

Children's book writer and speaker. Has worked variously as a farmer, a government housing study worker for the Rand Corporation, a governess for comedian and talk show host Joan River's daughter, and a marketing manager for Pacific Bell. Cofounded Positive Education Inc., a nonprofit tutorial agency. *Member:* Authors Guild, Authors League of America, PEN, Society of Children's Book Writers and Illustrators,

Association of Booksellers for Children, Southern California Children's Booksellers Association, Southern California Council on Literature for Children and Young People, Santa Monica Traditional Folk Music Club (founder, 1978).

## ■ Awards, Honors

*To Rabbittown* was named a Junior Literary Guild selection, 1989, and was selected as a "Book of the Year" by Mommycare.

## ■ Writings

*To Rabbittown,* illustrated by Robin Spowart, Scholastic, 1989.
*The Night Horse,* illustrated by Vera Rosenberry, Scholastic, 1991.
*It's Not My Turn to Look for Grandma!,* illustrated by George Booth, Knopf, in press.

Contributor to anthologies, including *Poems for Mothers,* edited by Myra Cohn Livingston, McElderry Books, 1990; *If the Owl Calls Again,* edited by Livingston, McElderry Books, 1990; *Poems for Brothers, Poems for Sisters,* edited by Livingston, Holiday House, 1991; and *Roll Along: Poems on Wheels,* edited by Livingston, McElderry Books, 1993. Wayland's stories for children are also presented on the *Halfway Down the Stairs* radio program for KPFK-FM.

## ■ Work in Progress

"A billion books."

## ■ Sidelights

"To rebel in my family, you had to join management in a Fortune 500 company and wear a suit every day," April Halprin Wayland told *SATA.* The daughter of a farmer and a concert pianist, Wayland grew up in Santa Monica, California, and spent her holidays and vacations at the family farm in Yuba City, five hundred miles north.

Wayland began writing when she was thirteen years old. "I learned to type and I was bitten by the writing bug," she confessed. "My bedroom was downstairs, so after everyone was asleep, I would type poems and stories late into the night and then hide them away in my desk drawer." Music was another of Wayland's interests. She began playing the violin at age ten, became interested in folk music in college, and founded the Santa Monica Traditional Folk Music Club in her late twenties. "Between fifty and one hundred of us still meet once a month with banjos, dulcimers, harmonicas, guitars, fiddles, mandolins, spoons, and bones—to play and sing and learn new tunes," she said.

After she graduated from college, Wayland held an assortment of jobs. She helped run the family farm after her father's death, worked as a governess for the daughter of comedian Joan Rivers, and cofounded a nonprofit tutorial organization called Positive Education, Inc. Finally, however, she settled into the corporate workforce. She went to work for Pacific Bell, eventually being promoted to marketing manager. Wayland's mother was skeptical about this career choice. "As I moved up in the corporate world," Wayland recalls, "my mother would stand in the doorway and sigh, 'You should quit and become a children's book writer—you'd be much happier.' Why are mothers always right?"

One of Wayland's first ventures into children's reading was a picturebook for her nephew, Joshua. "It wasn't brilliant literature, but I illustrated, xeroxed, laminated, and bound it," she noted. "The night I finished it, I was so jazzed, I couldn't sleep."

Wayland decided to become a full-time writer. She has issued three picture books, *To Rabbittown, The Night Horse,* and *It's Not My Turn to Look for Grandma!* In each volume she explores children's relation to animals using humor and whimsy. "I see my books as mixtures of colors," she explained. "I want each to be as clear and as strong and as beautiful as it can be. I love the picture book format."

Wayland remarked, "I can't say enough about the community of children's book writers in Southern California. Teachers have become mentors and friends—everyone generously shares his/her knowledge. I thrive in groups, and this community (in addition to my husband) has had much to do with the joy I find in my career." She added, "I once decided that I wanted to publish 133 children's books by my ninetieth birthday. Then I re-read *Charlotte's Web* by E. B. White and I realized that *one* wonderful book was enough. So my new goal is to write each book as brilliantly as I can."

## ■ For More Information See

*PERIODICALS*

*Publishers Weekly,* January 13, 1989, p. 87.
*School Library Journal,* April, 1989, p. 92; April, 1991, p. 104.

*   *   *

# WEGMAN, William 1943-

## ■ Personal

Born December 2, 1943, in Holyoke, MA; married Gayle Schneider (an artist; divorced, 1978); married Laurie Jewell (a graphic designer; divorced, 1982). *Education:* Massachusetts College of Art, B.F.A., 1965; University of Illinois at Champaign-Urbana, M.F.A., 1967.

## ■ Addresses

c/o Pace/MacGill Gallery, 32 East 57th St., New York, NY 10022.

# ■ Career

Artist, photographer, and author. Associate professor at University of Wisconsin, Madison, 1968-70, and California State University, Long Beach, 1970. *Exhibitions:* Sonnabend Gallery, New York and Paris, 1971-73; University of Colorado Art Gallery, Boulder, 1980; Museum of Modern Art, New York City, 1980 and 1993; Hayward Gallery, London, 1980; Root Art Center, Clinton, NY, 1981; Whitney Museum of American Art, 1981 and 1992; Art Institute, Chicago, 1981; Delahunty Gallery, Dallas, 1981. Items held in collections at Whitney Museum of Art, New York; Museum of Modern Art, New York and Paris; Los Angeles Contemporary Museum of Art; and International Museum of Photography, Rochester, NY.

# ■ Awards, Honors

Guggenheim fellowships, 1975, 1986; National Endowment for the Arts grants, 1975-76, 1982.

# ■ Writings

*Man's Best Friend: Photographs and Drawings,* introduction by Laurence Wieder, Abrams, 1982.
*Everyday Problems* (drawings), Brightwaters Press, 1984.
*The History of Travel: The Catalogue of an Exhibition of Paintings by William Wegman,* Taft Museum/Butler Institute of American Art, 1990.
*William Wegman: Paintings, Drawings, Photographs, Videotapes,* edited by Martin Kunz, Abrams, 1990.
*William Wegman Photographic Works 1969-1976,* Fonds Regional d'Art Comtemporain (Limousin, France), 1991.
(With Carole Kismaric and Marvin Heiferman) *Cinderella,* Hyperion, 1993.
(With Kismaric and Heiferman) *Little Red Riding Hood,* Hyperion, 1993.
*ABC,* Hyperion, 1994.

Also creator of several videos featuring Man Ray, including *Spelling Lesson, Smoking,* and *New & Used Car Salesman.*

# ■ Sidelights

William Wegman, an artist who works in video, photography, painting, and drawing, is best known for his Polaroids of dogs posed in surprising outfits and settings. Wegman's works in each of these media exhibit his sense of humor, which pokes fun at all levels of society and art. *Contemporary Photographers* contributor Marina Vaizey finds that "his imagery, often hilarious, sardonic, and ironical, can be rather emotional too, and intricately baroque. The deliberate set-ups that he creates to photograph can be elaborate put-downs, a visual commentary on Madison Avenue culture laced with West Coast exuberance."

Wegman's first and most famous subject, a weimaraner named Man Ray after the dadaist and surrealist photog-

**William Wegman chats with a model**

rapher, is featured in much of his work from 1970 to 1982. Among the well-known images of Man Ray are "Fey Ray," in which the dog preens while his pink nail polish dries, "Brooke," a parody of actress Brooke Shields' designer jeans ads, and "The Kennebago," featuring Man Ray wearing a Native American headdress and drifting in a bright blue canoe. These and Wegman's other works made from 1979 to 1982 are included in the collection *Man's Best Friend: Photographs and Drawings,* which *New York Review of Books* contributor Sanford Schwartz noted "may be the most original book of photographs since Robert Frank's *The Americans* (1959). Like *The Americans,* it is a rarity in photography, a true book—an arrangement of individual shots that, taken together, enrich each other and leave a distinct, large impression."

Wegman's relationship with Man Ray has been a subject of interest to reviewers. Schwartz found significance in "Dusted," "the single most powerful image in *Man's Best Friend*" and the last image of the book, in which Man Ray sits while flour rains down onto him. "Working with his dog for so many years, Wegman may have felt he was under a spell," Schwartz remarked. "He may even have wanted all along to create an image that would express the spell—the attachment he and Ray had for each other, which continually prompted Wegman, in one cycle of work after another, to release more of his talent. Whether or not he wanted to create such an image, no other picture shows how much his dog meant to him as 'Dusted.'"

**Fay Ray and Battina are two of the stars in Wegman's canine version of *Little Red Riding Hood*.**

The accessibility and popularity of Wegman's photographs of Man Ray and later a female weimaraner named Fay Ray have brought the artist a success he sometimes finds frustrating: the popularity of the dog photos has led to an overidentification of Wegman's art with his dogs. Man Ray's fame was recognized after his death in 1982, when *Village Voice* named the dog its "Man of the Year."

Wegman continued producing oversized Polaroids featuring his weimaraners in the 1990s, culminating in the publication of two children's books. Based on popular fairy tales, *Cinderella* and *Little Red Riding Hood* are lushly illustrated with photographs of Fay Ray and her daughter Battina and son Chundo dressed as the title characters. "Campiness is the order of the day" in *Little Red Riding Hood,* which appeals to both children and adults, a *Publishers Weekly* reviewer commented.

## ■ Works Cited

Review of *Little Red Riding Hood, Publishers Weekly,* October 4, 1993, p. 77.
Schwartz, Sanford, review of *Man's Best Friend: Photographs and Drawings, New York Review of Books,* August 18, 1983, p. 44.
Vaizey, Marina, essay in *Contemporary Photographers,* St. James Press, 1988, pp. 1100-1101.

## ■ For More Information See

*PERIODICALS*

*Booklist,* November 15, 1982, p. 422.
*Voice Literary Supplement,* February, 1983, p. 4.

\*    \*    \*

## WELLS, Susan (Mary) 1951-

### ■ Personal

Born December 12, 1951, in Bath, England. *Education:* New Hall College, Cambridge University, B.A. with honors, 1973; M.S., 1977. *Hobbies and other interests:* Scuba diving.

### ■ Addresses

*Home*—56 Oxford Rd., Cambridge CB4 3PW, England.

### ■ Career

Natural History Museum, London, England, scientific officer, 1974; Station Biologique de la Tour du Valat, Camargue, France, researcher, 1974-77; International Union for Conservation of Nature and Natural Resources (IUCN) SSC Traffic Group, London, researcher, 1978-80; IUCN Conservation Monitoring Centre, Cambridge, England, research officer, 1980-83; senior research officer and senior editor of IUCN/United Nations Environment Programme (UNEP) Directory of Coral Reefs of International Importance, 1983-87. International Council for Bird Preservation (ICBP), Cam-

Susan Wells used her extensive experience as a research scientist to reveal the world of oceans to young readers.

bridge, assistant director of information and editor of *World Birdwatch,* 1988; independent environmental consultant, 1989-91; University of Newcastle-upon-Tyne, Newcastle-upon-Tyne, England, research associate, 1991-92; International Center for Living Aquatic Resources Management (ICLARM), Manila, Philippines, consultant, 1992. Scientific advisor for television programs on coral reefs, invertebrates, and birds; speaker on conservation issues on radio programs and at professional conferences. *Member:* International Society for Reef Studies, IUCN/SSC Mollusc Specialist Group (co-chair), IUCN Coral Reef Fish Group, IUCN/SSC Invertebrate Task Force, Unitas Malacologia, Marine Conservation Society Coral Reef Team, NGO Forum for U.K. Dependent Territories Forum.

### ■ Awards, Honors

Second place award, Sir Peter Kent Conservation Book Prize, 1992, for *The Greenpeace Book of Coral Reefs.*

### ■ Writings

(With R. M. Pyle and N. M. Collins) *The IUCN Invertebrate Red Data Book,* IUCN (England and Switzerland), 1983.
(With M. Haywood) *Manual of Marine Invertebrates,* Salamander Books, 1989.
(Editor and contributor) *Coral Reefs of the World,* Volume 1: *Atlantic and Eastern Pacific,* Volume 2: *Indian Ocean, Red Sea and Gulf,* Volume 3: *Central*

*and Western Pacific,* United Nations Environment Programme, 1989.

*The Illustrated World of Oceans,* Simon and Schuster, 1991.

*Explore the World of Mighty Oceans,* Western, 1992.

(With N. Hanna) *The Greenpeace Book of Coral Reefs,* Sterling, 1992.

*Coral Reef* (pop-up book), HarperCollins Children's Books, in press.

Contributor to *Encyclopaedia of the Animal Kingdom,* edited by R. Burton, Optimum Books, 1982, and *The Atlas of Endangered Species,* edited by J. Burton, Macmillan, 1991. Also editor of newsletters, including *Reef Encounter* and *Tentacle.* Contributor to scientific journals and periodicals, including *New Science, Scientific Approaches to Management of Shellfish Resources,* and *Biology and Conservation of Sea Turtles.*

## ■ Work in Progress

Researching coral reef conservation.

\*     \*     \*

## WHITE, Dana
## See LARSEN, Anita

\*     \*     \*

## WILLIAMS, Sherley Anne 1944-
## (Shirley Williams)

## ■ Personal

Born August 25, 1944, in Bakersfield, CA; daughter of Jessee Winson (a laborer) and Lelia Marie (Siler) Williams; children: John Malcolm. *Education:* Fresno State College (now California State University, Fresno), B.A., 1966; Howard University, graduate study, 1966-67; Brown University, M.A., 1972.

## ■ Addresses

*Office*—Department of Literature, University of California, San Diego, La Jolla, CA 92093.

## ■ Career

Fresno State College (now California State University, Fresno), co-director of tutorial program, 1965-66, lecturer in ethnic studies, 1969-70; Miles College, Atlanta, GA, administrative internal assistant to president, 1967-68; affiliated with Systems Development Corporation, Santa Monica, CA, 1968-69; Federal City College, Washington, D.C., consultant in curriculum development and community educator, 1970-72; California State University, Fresno, associate professor of English, 1972-73; University of California, San Diego, La Jolla, assistant professor, 1973-76, associate professor, 1976-82, professor of Afro-American literature, 1982—, department chair, 1976-82. Fulbright lecturer, University

of Ghana, 1984; *Member:* Poetry Society of America, Modern Language Association.

## ■ Awards, Honors

National Book Award nomination, 1976, for *The Peacock Poems; Dessa Rose* was named a notable book in 1986 by the *New York Times; Working Cotton,* illustrated by Carole M. Byard, was named a Ralph Caldecott Medal honor book by the American Library Association, 1993.

## ■ Writings

*Give Birth to Brightness: A Thematic Study in Neo-Black Literature,* Dial, 1972.

(Under name Shirley Williams) *The Peacock Poems* (also see below), Wesleyan University Press, 1975.

*Some One Sweet Angel Chile* (poems), Morrow, 1982.

*Dessa Rose* (novel), Morrow, 1986.

*Working Cotton* (picture book; based on "The Trimming of the Feathers" and "Conejo" originally published in *The Peacock Poems*), illustrated by Carole M. Byard, Harcourt, 1992.

Also author of *Ours to Make,* 1973, and *The Sherley Williams Special,* 1977, both for television; *Traveling Sunshine Good Time Show and Celebration,* 1973, a stage show; and *Letters from a New England Negro,* a full-length drama produced in 1982. Contributor to books, including *Midnight Birds,* edited by Mary Helen Washington, Anchor Press, 1980; *The Third Woman: Minority Women Writers of the United States,* edited by Dexter Fisher, Houghton, 1980; and *Black Sister: Poetry by Black American Women, 1746-1980,* edited by Erlene Stetson, Indiana University Press, 1981.

## ■ Sidelights

Sherley Anne Williams is a critic, poet, novelist, and educator, whose early experiences, while providing the inspiration for much of her work, made her an unlikely candidate for fame. As a girl, she lived in a Fresno, California, housing project and worked with her parents in fruit and cotton fields. Her father died of tuberculosis before her eighth birthday, and her mother, a practical woman from rural Texas who had tried to discourage Williams' early interest in reading, died when Williams was sixteen. "My friends were what you would call juvenile delinquents. Most of them didn't finish school," and her future, as she told Mona Gable in a *Los Angeles Times Magazine* interview, amounted to having children. But a series of events, including guidance from a science teacher and the discovery of books by black authors about their lives, including Richard Wright's *Black Boy,* and Ertha Kitt's *Thursday's Child,* stimulated her desire to write. "It was largely through these autobiographies I was able to take heart in my life," she told Gable.

The publication of *Give Birth to Brightness: A Thematic Study in Neo-Black Literature* encouraged Williams to pursue a writing career. The essays are, she wrote in the

Mamma keep the baby, Leanne, and the water jug on the row we be working. Mamma sing; Daddy hum.

**Sherley Anne Williams and illustrator Carole Byard portray a day in the fields with a family of migrant workers in this glimpse of a way of life unfamiliar to many of today's children.**

book's dedication, "a public statement of how I feel about and treasure one small aspect of Blackness in America." According to *Dictionary of Literary Biography* contributor Lillie P. Howard, Williams attempts in these essays "to recreate 'a new tradition built on a synthesis of black oral traditions [such as the blues] and Western literate forms.'" Williams discusses both the Harlem Renaissance (in which black writers spoke to white audiences) and the protest literature of the 1960s, noting that the writers of the 1970s and beyond "speak directly *to* Black people *about themselves* in order to move them toward self-knowledge and freedom." Reviewers found some fault with *Give Birth to Brightness,* but the volume was generally well received. Mel Watkins commented in the *New York Times,* "Miss Williams has written a readable and informative survey of black literature."

*The Peacock Poems,* Williams' second published book, also received a warm reception and was nominated for a National Book Award. In this volume of autobiographi-

cal poems, Williams expresses her feelings about her early family life and about being a single mother; in other poems collected in this work, the author depicts experiences of black women after the Civil War and in more recent times. In an interview with Claudia Tate published in *Black Women Writers at Work,* Williams remarked: "I wanted specifically to write about lower-income black women .... We were missing these stories of black women's struggles and their real triumphs .... I wanted to write about them because they had in a very real sense educated me and given me what it was going to take to get me through the world."

Williams' next publication, *Some One Sweet Angel Chile,* is a collection of poetry that again exhibits the author's ability to speak convincingly in a variety of voices. In the first section of the work, Williams writes of the experience of post-Civil War black women; in the second section, her poetry takes on the blues, focusing on Bessie Smith, the legendary singer. The final section features more autobiographical poems. Holly Prado, reviewing *Some One Sweet Angel Chile* for the *Los Angeles Times,* remarked that Williams' "descriptions and observations speak for themselves. Yet the writing carries a strong undercurrent of feeling ... a subtlety only good poetry can offer."

### Dessa Rose

Two economically disadvantaged women tell their stories in Williams' first novel and most highly acclaimed book, *Dessa Rose.* The book recounts the tragic, violent life of its title character, a whip-scarred, pregnant slave woman in jail for crimes committed against white men. Dessa recalls her life on the plantation with her lover, a life that ended when he was killed by their master. In turn, Dessa had killed the master, was arrested and chained to other slaves in a coffle, from which she escaped, again by violence to her white captors. Tracked down and sentenced to die after the birth of her child, who was considered valuable property by the whites, Dessa is interviewed by Adam Nehemiah, a white author who hopes to gain fame by publishing an analysis of Dessa's crimes. When asked why she kills white men, Dessa replies evenly, "Cause I can."

Dessa escapes again and is given refuge by Rufel Sutton, a white woman who offers refuge to other runaway slaves simply because she can. In a scam designed by the slaves, Rufel sells the runaways as slaves, waits for them to escape, and then sells them again—in order to gain them all enough money to start a new life elsewhere. All goes well until Rufel and Dessa are arrested by the enraged Nehemiah, but the two women elude his grasp with the aid of a female officer who is sent to verify Dessa's identity by examining her scars. When the group disbands, Rufel goes off to prosperity in the East; the blacks go west to the hardships of prejudice on the frontier. "Thus has Sherley Anne Williams breathed wonderful life into the bare bones of the past," commented *New York Times* reviewer Christopher Lehmann-Haupt. "And thus does she resolve more issues than are dreamed of in most history books."

*Dessa Rose* was widely acclaimed for its "unflinchingly realistic portrayal of American slavery," as Gable observed. For instance, the sexual exploitation of black men and women that was common to the condition of slavery is fully drawn in "a plot dealing with all the [sadism and lust] that Harriet Beecher Stowe [the author of *Uncle Tom's Cabin*] did not dare to mention," as London *Times* reviewer Andrew Sinclair attested. Furthermore, Jane Perliz noted in the *New York Times Books Review* that Williams intends Dessa's rebellion—based on an actual uprising led by a pregnant slave in 1829—to refute the myth that black women were the passive collaborators of their abusive masters. "Sherley Anne Williams's accomplishment," Michele Wallace added in the *Women's Review of Books,* "is that she takes the reader someplace we're not accustomed to going, someplace historical scholarship may never take us—into the world that black and white women shared in the antebellum South. But what excites me the most, finally, about this novel is its definition of friendship as

the collective struggle that ultimately transcends the stumbling-blocks of race and class." *New York Times Book Review* contributor David Bradley concluded, "Like Alice Walker [author of *The Color Purple*], Sherley Anne Williams has written a novel that is artistically brilliant, emotionally affecting and totally unforgettable."

In *Working Cotton,* Williams has devised a book for young children based on two works from *The Peacock Poems,* "The Trimming of the Feathers" and "Conejo." *Working Cotton* describes a day in the life of a young girl from a close-knit family of African-American migrant workers. Illustrated with double-page spreads that critics note enhance the heat and exhausting nature of the work, the book has been praised for its impressionistic portrayal of a rarely depicted life-circumstance. *Bulletin of the Center for Children's Books* contributor Betsy Hearne called *Working Cotton* "a slice of life presented without judgment or story" that brings home "an organic experience of work that few children have known or even imagined." *School Library Journal* contributor Lyn Miller-Lachmann noted that the rhythm of the workday is echoed in the story, beginning slowly, intensifying with the heat of the day, and "winding down with a portrait of hope for a better tomorrow." Miller-Lachmann concluded that while younger children "will enjoy listening to the story," older children will also have much "to ponder."

### ■ Works Cited

Bradley, David, "On the Lam from Race and Gender," *New York Times Book Review,* August 3, 1986, p. 7.

Gable, Mona, interview with Sherley Anne Williams, *Los Angeles Times Magazine,* December 7, 1986.

Hearne, Betsy, review of *Working Cotton, Bulletin of the Center for Children's Books,* October, 1992, p. 58.

Howard, Lillie P., "Sherley Anne Williams," *Dictionary of Literary Biography,* Volume 41: *Afro-American Poets since 1955,* Gale, 1985, pp. 343-350.

Lehmann-Haupt, Christopher, review of *Dessa Rose, New York Times,* July 12, 1986.

Miller-Lachmann, Lyn, review of *Working Cotton, School Library Journal,* November, 1992, p. 81.

Perliz, Jane, review of *Dessa Rose, New York Times Book Review,* August 3, 1986.

Prado, Holly, "The Tentative, Poetic Lives of Black Women," *Los Angeles Times,* July 4, 1982, p. 6.

Sinclair, Andrew, review of *Dessa Rose, Times* (London), March 19, 1987.

Tate, Claudia, editor, *Black Women Writers at Work,* Continuum, 1983.

Wallace, Michelle, review of *Dessa Rose, Women's Review of Books,* October, 1986.

Watkins, Mel, review of *Give Birth to Brightness, New York Times,* July 8, 1982.

Williams, Sherley Anne, *Dessa Rose,* Morrow, 1986.

### ■ For More Information See

*PERIODICALS*

*Kirkus Reviews,* May 15, 1986, p. 748.

*Library Journal,* May 1, 1972, p. 1720; April 1, 1982, pp. 733-734; June 15, 1986, p. 80.
*New Statesman,* April 24, 1987, p. 29.
*New Yorker,* September 8, 1986, p. 136.
*Publishers Weekly,* August 28, 1972, p. 265; February 19, 1982, p. 55; May 30, 1986, p. 53.
*Times Literary Supplement,* July 17, 1987, p. 765.*

\*     \*     \*

## WILLIAMS, Shirley
### See WILLIAMS, Sherley Anne

\*     \*     \*

## WINDSOR, Patricia 1938-
### (Colin Daniel)

### ■ Personal

Born September 21, 1938, in New York, NY; daughter of Bernhard Edward and Antoinette (Gaus) Seelinger; married Laurence Charles Windsor, Jr., 1959 (divorced, 1978); married Steve Altman, 1986 (divorced, 1987); children: Patience Wells, Laurence Edward. *Education:* Attended Bennington College and Westchester Community College; New York University, A.A.

PATRICIA WINDSOR

### ■ Addresses

*Agent*—Amy Berkower, Writers House, Inc., 21 West 26th St., New York, NY 10010; and Patricia White, 20 Powis Mews, London W11 1JN, England.

### ■ Career

Novelist. Windsor-Morehead Associates (advertising agency), New York City, vice president, 1960-63; American Telephone and Telegraph, Washington, D.C., editor-in-chief of *Easterner* (company publication), 1979-81. Teacher of creative writing, Westchester, NY, 1975-78; Institute of Children's Literature, Redding Ridge, CT, faculty member, 1976—; instructor, University of Maryland Writers Institute, 1981-83, and OPEN University, Washington, D.C. Family Planning Association, London, England, assistant director of central inquiries, 1972-73, counselor, 1974-75; correspondent, National Council of Social Service, London, 1974—; director, Wordspring Literary Consultants, 1987-90; counselor, First Call for Help, 1990-91; director, Summertree Studios, 1992—; active in YWCA and North Westchester Association for Retarded Children. Actress under the name Katonah Summertree for City Lights Productions. *Member:* PEN American Centre, Children's Book Guild, Poetry Society of Georgia, Georgia Historical Society, Savannah Storytellers, City Lights Theatre Guild.

### ■ Awards, Honors

*Chicago Tribune Book World* Honor Book award and Best Books for Young Adults award, American Library Association, both 1973, and Austrian State award for Books for Children and Youth, 1981, all for *The Summer Before; Diving for Roses* was named a notable book of 1976 by the *New York Times;* best newspaper story, United Way of National Capital Area, 1979; best photo presentation, United Way, 1980; Edgar Allan Poe Award, Mystery Writers of America, 1985, for *The Sandman's Eyes;* Edgar Allan Poe Award nomination, 1992, for *The Christmas Killer.*

### ■ Writings

*YOUNG ADULT NOVELS*

*The Summer Before,* Harper, 1973.
*Something's Waiting for You, Baker D,* Harper, 1974.
*Home Is Where Your Feet Are Standing,* Harper, 1975.
*Diving for Roses,* Harper, 1976.
*Mad Martin,* Harper, 1976.
*Killing Time,* Harper, 1980.
*The Sandman's Eyes,* Delacorte, 1985.
*How a Weirdo and a Ghost Can Change Your Entire Life,* illustrated by Jacqueline Rogers, Delacorte, 1986.
*The Hero,* Delacorte, 1988.
*Just Like the Movies,* Pan Macmillan, 1990.
*The Christmas Killer,* Scholastic, Inc., 1991.
*Two Weirdos and a Ghost,* Dell, 1991.
*Very Weird and Moogly Christmas,* Dell, 1991.

*OTHER*

*Old Coat's Cat* (short stories), Macmillan, 1974.
*Rain* (short stories), Macmillan, 1976.
*The Girl with the Click Click Eyes* (short stories), Heinemann, 1977.
(Under pseudonym, Colin Daniel) *Demon Tree,* Dell, 1983.

Columnist, *Blood Review,* 1988-89, and *Savannah Parent,* 1990—. Lyricist for popular songs composed by Yseult Freilicher. Contributor of short stories to periodicals (in Sweden, Denmark, South Africa, Australia, England, and the United States), including *Seventeen* and *Scholastic Scope.*

Windsor's manuscripts are included in the Kerlan Collection, University of Minnesota.

## ■ Sidelights

Patricia Windsor began her interest in writing at an early age: when her parents gave her an old typewriter to bang on at age ten, her writing career was launched. She made long lists of titles and planned hundreds of novels. "By the time I was sixteen, I'd collected thirty-five rejection slips," she once recalled. Along with a rejection from *Seventeen* magazine, she also amassed rejection slips for her works of science fiction. In high school Windsor turned to writing poetry. After graduation she worked in the college department of *Mademoiselle* and *Living for Young Homemakers,* where she worked as a table-setting editor and did table setups for the magazine's photographers.

After she became a mother, Windsor worked at a variety of jobs, including teaching modern dance, free-lance art work, and finding jobs for released inmates from Chicago's Cook County Jail. While living in England, she worked for several social service agencies doing counseling, writing, and public relations. As a counselor for a walk-in advice bureau in London, Windsor gained a lot of experience with young adults. "Some of their concerns and worries have been explored in my books *Diving for Roses* and *Mad Martin,*" she once told *SATA.* When she returned to the United States, Windsor became editor of a corporate newspaper and resumed teaching at the University of Maryland and the OPEN University in Washington, D.C.

Windsor wants young people to see that "they are not alone ... that their heartaches, problems, pains and joys are shared by us all, adults included!" She once commented that she doesn't mind if readers don't like what she has written, as "long as I made them think and react a little." Besides Isaac Asimov and Theodore Sturgeon, Windsor feels that James Joyce, Dylan Thomas, J. D. Salinger, and T. S. Eliot have influenced her writing.

While critical reaction to Windsor's books has been mixed, most reviewers give her high marks for holding the interest of her young adult readers. In a *School Library Journal* article, Cynthia K. Leibold commends

Windsor for reaching middle graders who will go on to read her books when they are older. Reviewing *How a Weirdo and a Ghost Can Change Your Entire Life,* Leibold says the book is "an enticing introduction for younger readers to an author whom they will enjoy as adolescents." As in her other books, Windsor combines psychic elements of ghostly contact with the unraveling of a mystery. The lead character, Martha Lewis, learns through her relationship with the class weirdo that true friendship is unconditional.

Windsor's *The Hero* is a tale about the psychic abilities of Dale, the headmaster's son, which are exploited by adults for dubious purposes. Several critics have faulted the book for its overabundance of negative adult personalities. "All adults are portrayed as either weak or self-serving," writes Susan H. Williamson in *School Library Journal.* "If Dale's models are greedy, self-absorbed, manipulative, weak, and criminal, where did he get his strong sense of right and wrong?" asks Cathi Dunn MacRae in *Wilson Library Bulletin.*

However, other critics have praise for *The Hero.* Roger Sutton remarks in *Bulletin of the Center for Children's Books* that "this is always a page-turner, and the lonely ending makes no compromises." A *Kirkus Reviews* critic

When class weirdo Teddy the Windbag teaches Martha how to use a Ouija board, she becomes involved in some ghostly goings-on. (Cover illustration by Jacqueline Rogers.)

also praises *The Hero:* "Windsor views this well-explored territory with a fresh eye and builds the tension expertly." MacRae reports that young adult readers score *The Hero* high in both quality and popularity.

Critical response to Windsor's 1991 book, the Edgar Allan Poe award nominee *The Christmas Killer,* was generally positive. Discussing the relationship between the volume's central character, Rose Potter, and her twin brother, Jerram, MacRae writes in *Wilson Library Bulletin* that the "twins' struggle to adjust their relationship to new adolescent needs for both privacy and identity mirrors the killer's own trauma. This integrated subplot will absorb young adult readers." Jeanette Larson praises *The Christmas Killer* in a *School Library Journal* review for Windsor's side themes, which include people's tendency to be unfair to mentally unbalanced people. While she finds the book more gruesome than most young adult mysteries, Larson feels "this one is well plotted and has sufficient clues for astute readers."

However, a *Publishers Weekly* reviewer was critical of *The Christmas Killer* because of the book's tendency to

Everyone suspects Michael Thorn of murder, and even he can't remember exactly what happened the night a woman fell to her death, but to clear his name he'll have to find out!

fall somewhere between a ghost story and a work of detective fiction. "Still," the reviewer concludes, "readers are likely to enjoy the appealing characters, spooky atmosphere and aptly evoked small-town setting." Stephanie Zvirin writes in *Booklist* that the reader cares about Windsor's protagonist "more than we do about the protagonists of most of the recent young adult whodunits." Zvirin continues by noting Windsor's restraint in "incorporating grisly details" and finds the novel's focus on ghostly goings-on give it broad appeal among young adult readers.

Reviewer Pam Spencer includes Windsor's *The Sandman's Eyes* among works of such writers as Agatha Christie and Arthur Conan Doyle in her list of whodunits for teens in *School Library Journal.* The story concerns Michael Thorne, a young teen who is convicted of pushing a young woman over a wall to her death. As a result, he must serve a two-year sentence in a correctional facility. When he is released and returns

It's almost Christmas, but Rose can't enjoy the season when there's a killer on the loose and every time she goes to sleep her murdered friend Nancy invades her dreams.

home, he must sort out his life and find the real killer as well. "It's bona fide suspense," comments Spencer.

### ■ Works Cited

Review of *The Christmas Killer, Publishers Weekly,* October 25, 1991.
Review of *The Hero, Kirkus Reviews,* May 1, 1988.
Larson, Jeanette, review of *The Christmas Killer, School Library Journal,* November, 1991.
Leibold, Cynthia K., review of *How a Weirdo and a Ghost Can Change Your Entire Life, School Library Journal,* November, 1986.
MacRae, Cathi Dunn, review of *The Hero, Wilson Library Bulletin,* February, 1989.
MacRae, Cathi Dunn, review of *The Christmas Killer, Wilson Library Bulletin,* April, 1992.
Spencer, Pam, review of *The Sandman's Eyes, School Library Journal,* March, 1992.
Sutton, Roger, review of *The Hero, Bulletin of the Center for Children's Books,* July, 1988.
Williamson, Susan H., review of *The Hero, School Library Journal,* May, 1988.
Zvirin, Stephanie, review of *The Christmas Killer, Booklist,* October 15, 1991.

### ■ For More Information See

*PERIODICALS*

*Booklist,* April 1, 1988.

—*Sketch by Vita Richman*

\* \* \*

## WOJCIECHOWSKI, Susan (Susan Albertson)

### ■ Personal

Born in Rochester, NY; daughter of Michael and Regina (Stenclik) Osinski; married Paul Wojciechowski, November 26, 1966; children: Joel, Christian, Mary. *Education:* Nazareth College, B.A.

### ■ Addresses

*Home*—56 Reitz Pkwy., Pittsford, NY 14534.

### ■ Career

Elementary school teacher; free-lance writer, 1981—; school librarian, 1986—. *Member:* Society of Children's Book Writers and Illustrators, Rochester Area Children's Authors and Illustrators.

### ■ Awards, Honors

*And the Other, Gold* was named one of the best books of the year, Child Study Association, and was chosen as a recommended Book for the Teen Age by the New York City library, both 1988; *Patty Dillman of Hot Dog Fame*

was nominated for the Florida Sunshine State Young Readers' Award, 1992.

### ■ Writings

*And the Other, Gold,* Orchard Books, 1987.
*Patty Dillman of Hot Dog Fame,* Orchard Books, 1989.
*Promises to Keep,* Crown, 1991.
*The Best Halloween of All* (picture book), illustrated by Susan Meddaugh, Crown, 1992.

Contributor to periodicals and professional journals, including *Baby Talk, Times Union, National Catholic Education Association,* and *Upstate Magazine.* Has published writings in England under the name Susan Albertson.

### ■ Work in Progress

*Don't Call Me Beanhead,* to be published in 1994, and *The Christmas Miracle of Jonathan Toomey,* both to be published by Candlewick Press.

### ■ Sidelights

With her humorous, true-to-life portrayals of young adults, Susan Wojciechowski has been compared to such authors as Judy Blume and Paula Danziger. The best-known of all Wojciechowski's characters is thirteen-year-old Patty Dillman, a student at St. Ignatius Junior High. Wojciechowski's first three books follow Patty's adventures as she discovers boys, learns to value her friends, and becomes involved with social problems. Peer pressure is an issue of importance to Wojciechowski, who explained in a publicity brochure issued by her publisher: "When I was in school, fitting in, belonging, wearing the right clothes—these problems did not exist to the extent that they do today. Kids feel they have to

**SUSAN WOJCIECHOWSKI**

Susan Wojciechowski

And the Other, Gold

**Patty and Tracy's lifelong friendship is in danger of ending when Patty becomes involved with a football player and Tracy spends more and more time with her pals in the school musical.** (Cover illustration by Toby Gowing.)

grow up so fast today. I try to tell them that it's okay not to have a boyfriend at 12 or 13, that it's OK to be a kid."

In *And the Other, Gold* Patty is best friends with Tracy until Patty meets Tim, a school football star. Suddenly, the thrill of having a boyfriend overwhelms her, and she finds herself too busy to continue her friendship with Tracy. In the end Tracy realizes the truth of an old girl scout song, "Make new friends, but keep the old; one is silver and the other, gold." A reviewer for *Publishers Weekly* praised the book's "sweet blend of goofiness and grownup concerns," and Marcia Hupp in the *School Library Journal* called the book "a likable and breezy novel."

The sequel *Patty Dillman of Hot Dog Fame* finds Patty taking ski lessons in order to be with Tim and continuing to engage in lighthearted mischief-making with Tracy. Patty's outlook on life changes drastically, however, when she goes to work in a soup kitchen for a school project. Patty isn't too thrilled about serving food to homeless people, but her apprehension is soon replaced by compassion as she begins to care about the people she serves. What's more, she meets a boy named Alex, who seems to share some of her social interests. A

*Publishers Weekly* reviewer concluded that Patty has "honest concerns and humorous, realistic solutions" to her problems.

Wojciechowski told *SATA:* "As a mother, librarian, and former teacher as well as a children's author, I have always felt the need to touch the minds of children. Through my writing, I try to reach children in a special way, by portraying them as real people—warts and all—and showing them that they are more or less alike, despite their differences."

## ■ Works Cited

Review of *And the Other, Gold, Publishers Weekly,* November 13, 1987.
Hupp, Marcia, review of *And the Other, Gold, School Library Journal,* November 1987, pp. 107-108.
Review of *Patty Dillman of Hot Dog Fame, Publishers Weekly,* May 19, 1989, p. 85.
*Susan Wojciechowski* (publicity release), Crown/ Random House, c. 1993.

## ■ For More Information See

*PERIODICALS*

*Horn Book,* March/April, 1988, p. 205.
*Kirkus Reviews,* October 1, 1987, p. 1469.
*Publishers Weekly,* November 13, 1987, pp. 71-72; September 7, 1992, p. 59.
*School Library Journal,* September, 1992, p. 214.

\*     \*     \*

# WOLF, Janet 1957-

## ■ Personal

Born April 30, 1957, in New York, NY; daughter of Fred (a photographer and photo engraver) and Lotte (a bookkeeper) Wolf. *Education:* Attended Tyler School of Art (Rome), 1976; Wesleyan University, B.A. (with high honors), 1979; attended Radcliffe Extension School, 1980. *Politics:* Liberal/Democrat. *Religion:* Jewish. *Hobbies and other interests:* Adventure travel, film, "*parliamo Italiano*" [speaking Italian], "anything Italian," cooking, swimming, ballet, museums, cats.

## ■ Addresses

*Home*—147 Maple Ave., Sea Cliff, NY 11579. *Office*—Green Vale School, Valentines Ln., Glen Head, NY. *Agent*—Peter Elek, 457 Broome St., New York, NY 10013.

## ■ Career

Green Vale School, Glen Head, NY, art teacher, 1981—; children's book author and illustrator. Affiliated with American Field Service, WNYC Public Radio, and AIDS (acquired immunodeficiency syndrome) Dance-A-Thon. *Member:* Society of Children's Book Writers and Illustrators.

JANET WOLF

## ■ Awards, Honors

*Rosie and the Yellow Ribbon* received a Christopher Award, 1993.

## ■ Writings

*Her Book,* Harper, 1982.
*The Best Present Is Me,* Harper, 1984.
*Adelaide to Zeke,* Harper, 1987.
*Baby's Book,* New York Life Insurance, 1990.
*The Rosy Fat Magenta Radish,* Joy St./Little, Brown, 1990.
(Illustrator) Paula de Paola, *Rosie and the Yellow Ribbon,* Joy St./Little, Brown, 1992.

## ■ Work in Progress

*Bananas, Lemons, and Raincoats,* a story about the disappearance of the color yellow; "I have also begun direct painting on silk and am negotiating for commercial sale of these scarves."

## ■ Sidelights

Janet Wolf told *SATA:* "When I was a child, my favorite book was *Little Women.* I remember weeping over Beth's death and then reading as much Louisa May Alcott as I could possibly get my hands on. I always tried to find different editions of the books, in hopes of finding one in which the pictures matched those in my head. At this time, of course, being an illustrator was not in the picture. I was going to be a dancer.

"Appendicitis and Aunt Ida abruptly put an end to my ballet career in the sixth grade. I was forced to stop lessons for a while after the appendectomy, allowing Aunt Ida enough time to convince my mother that classes were too expensive anyway (probably not a great

loss to the dance world!). I started to paint and draw. My father's cousin, a painter herself, gave me a set of colored pencils, and I won an honorable mention in a local art contest. My teachers were very encouraging.

"At age sixteen an AFS [American Field Service] scholarship sent me to Italy. A lifelong love affair with that country and its art had begun. I studied mosaics and soaked up the culture like a sponge. I return as often as I can and plan to live there someday.

"At Wesleyan University I studied printmaking. My work always lent itself to narrative. I had wonderful teachers who were very supportive. I decided I wanted to illustrate children's books. Breaking into this field is difficult. I pounded the pavement with my portfolio for a year, barely supporting myself with odd jobs. Laura Geringer, an editor at Harper & Row, liked my work and brought me, step by step, through the publication of my first book, *Her Book.* She eventually directed me toward my agent, Peter Elek, who has believed in me even when I doubt myself."

In Wolf's *Her Book* the author matches softly drawn pictures and a simple text to tell the story of a day in the life of a little girl, from "Her time to wake up," to the arrival of "Her friend," and finally to her bath and bedtime. Wolf hides the identity of the main character until the end, when the little girl is seen cuddling her stuffed toys in "Her bed." Some reviewers felt that the book sent mixed messages regarding the intended age of its readership, even though they found the concept of the unseen character interesting. They judged the language too simple for the age of the child depicted and some of the activities too advanced for the youngest of children. Jean F. Mercier, reviewing *Her Book* for *Publishers Weekly,* noted occasional lapses in its logic, but she also observed its simplicity and charm and called it "a debut of rare promise."

"I think it is important as a children's writer/illustrator to be in touch with one's own childhood," Wolf told *SATA.* "I have strong feelings and memories about being a kid. Writing and illustrating is a distillation of these memories contained within the framework of a story. *The Best Present Is Me,* for example, is the story of visiting my grandmother, whom I called Oma, in New York City. The book grew from a list of smells, tastes, sights, and sounds associated with Oma. An inventory, even of lovely things, is not a story. Eventually the plot line developed—the little girl in the book would lose the present she'd brought for Oma's birthday. It didn't matter to Oma, though. In the words of the little girl, 'The best present is me.'"

Reviewers generally praised Wolf's *The Best Present Is Me* for its uplifting story portraying the warm relationship between a little girl and her grandmother. Lynne McKechnie, reviewing the book for *School Library Journal,* applauded the text's appropriate length and interesting detail, summarizing it as "a warm story about grandchild/grandparent relationships for both reading aloud and independent use."

*Adelaide to Zeke,* Wolf's next effort, is an alphabet book in which each character acts upon the next in a humorous way, leading the reader successively through the alphabet. For example, "A is for Adelaide, who bothered Benny." While the sometimes random action and nonsensical relationships depicted did not please all reviewers, *Publishers Weekly* critic Diane Roback found it an "alluring" book nonetheless. She suggested that its playfulness would win a place in readers' minds. Writing in the *School Library Journal,* Cathy Woodward especially noted Wolf's "appealing" illustrations, which she described as "almost life-like" in some cases.

In *The Rosy Fat Magenta Radish* Wolf tells the story of Nora's first garden, which she plants with the help of her adult neighbor, Jim. As the title implies, Nora is most excited about planting radishes, which are her favorite color, magenta. After they are planted, she waits in suspense for the day she can serve a salad topped with radishes to Jim when he comes to dinner. The book is rounded out by endpapers depicting garden tools labeled with their common uses. While some reviewers felt the story lacked significant action to propel the plot, Phyllis K. Kennemer commented in *School Library Journal* that the artwork "adds much to the joyful story about the rewards of gardening's labors."

Wolf remarked to *SATA,* "I feel very lucky to be able to create books. It has enabled me to be a working artist, communicate with lots of people, and touch some lives. I have been fortunate enough to meet some of the people in this field whom I admire, including Laurent de Brunhoff (who continued the saga of Babar the elephant that his father, Jean, had begun) and Quentin Blake (illustrator of Roald Dahl's books). Best of all, I get to create the pictures which the words suggest in my head."

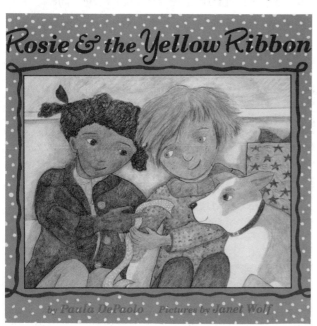

**Wolf illustrated this simple tale of a friendship put at risk by the loss of a yellow ribbon.**

## ■ Works Cited

Kennemer, Phyllis K., review of *The Rosy Fat Magenta Radish, School Library Journal,* May, 1990, pp. 93-94.

McKechnie, Lynne, review of *The Best Present Is Me, School Library Journal,* May, 1984, p. 74.

Mercier, Jean F., review of *Her Book, Publishers Weekly,* January 7, 1983, p. 73.

Roback, Diane, review of *Adelaide to Zeke, Publishers Weekly,* June 12, 1987, p. 83.

Wolf, Janet, *Her Book,* Harper, 1982.

Wolf, Janet, *Adelaide to Zeke,* Harper, 1987.

Woodward, Cathy, review of *Adelaide to Zeke, School Library Journal,* March, 1988, pp. 178-179.

## ■ For More Information See

*PERIODICALS*

*Children's Book Review Service,* July, 1984, p. 137; August, 1990, p. 163.

*Kirkus Reviews,* July 15, 1982, p. 797; June 15, 1987, p. 932.

*New York Times Book Review,* May 13, 1984, p. 20.

*Publishers Weekly,* June 8, 1990, p. 52.

*School Library Journal,* September, 1982, p. 113.

*        *        *

# WOLFF, Virginia Euwer 1937-

## ■ Personal

Born August 25, 1937, in Portland, OR, daughter of Eugene Courtney (a lawyer and rancher) and Florence (a teacher and rancher; maiden name, Craven) Euwer; married Art Wolff, July 19, 1959 (divorced, June, 1976); children: Anthony, Juliet. *Education:* Smith College, B.A., 1959. *Hobbies and other interests:* Playing the violin, swimming, hiking, gardening.

## ■ Career

The Miquon School, Philadelphia, PA, elementary school teacher, 1968-72; The Fiedel School, Glen Cove, NY, elementary school teacher, 1972-74; Hood River Valley High School, Hood River, OR, English teacher, 1976-86; Mount Hood Academy, Government Camp, OR, English teacher, 1986—. *Member:* Society of Children's Book Writers and Illustrators (national member and Northwest chapter member), Chamber Music Society of Oregon.

## ■ Awards, Honors

International Reading Association Award, young adult division, and PEN-West Book Award, both 1989, for *Probably Still Nick Swansen;* award from Child Study Children's Book Committee at Bank Street College, 1993, for *Make Lemonade;* Sixth Janusz Korczak Literary Competition honorable mention citation, Anti-Defamation League Braun Center for Holocaust Studies, for *The Mozart Season.*

**VIRGINIA EUWER WOLFF**

## ■ Writings

*Probably Still Nick Swansen,* Holt, 1988.
*The Mozart Season,* Holt, 1991.
*Make Lemonade,* Holt, 1993.

## ■ Work in Progress

A fourth young adult novel for Holt.

## ■ Sidelights

From Jolly, the single mother, to Nick Swansen, the learning-disabled teenager, to Allegra Shapiro, the violin prodigy, Virginia Euwer Wolff's characters are both unique and recognizable. Although they have special problems and interests, they also grapple with issues that many young readers understand.

Wolff's first novel, *Probably Still Nick Swansen,* is the poignant tale of a sixteen-year-old who attends special education classes in high school. Not only is he ridiculed by other students, but he is also haunted by memories of his older sister, who accidentally drowned seven years before. In addition to coping with these struggles, Nick also deals with situations typical to most teenagers, such as learning to drive and asking Shana, another special education student, to the prom. "Wolff has told a vivid, compassionate story," Barbara A. Lynn wrote in the *Voice of Youth Advocates.* Constance A. Mellon also

praised Wolff in *School Library Journal,* noting that the book "stresses the similarities between Nick and other teens rather than highlighting the differences."

Allegra Shapiro, the twelve-year-old heroine of *The Mozart Season,* is a violin student who is selected to be among six finalists in a prestigious competition for young musicians. Hence, she spends her summer trying to perfect Mozart's Fourth Violin Concerto in D. Wolff, like her character Allegra, is a violinist, and she has played with several community orchestras and both amateur and professional chamber ensembles.

In *Make Lemonade,* Wolff tells the story of the unique friendship between Jolly, a teenage mother, and La-Vaughn, the fourteen-year-old hired to care for young Jeremy and Jilly. LaVaughn takes the job to earn money for college, but in time she is drawn into Jolly and her children's lives. Jolly is poorly educated and has no family other than her children. She lives in a squalid apartment that reeks of garbage. To make matters worse, she is fired from her factory job after fighting off the sexual advances of a supervisor. LaVaughn provides her babysitting services for free while Jolly looks for another job. After a while, however, she encourages Jolly to take control of her life by returning to school. A reviewer for *Publishers Weekly* called *Make Lemonade* "a stellar addition to YA literature." And in the *School Library Journal,* Carolyn Noah called the book "a triumphant, outstanding story."

Wolff told *SATA:* "Here are some things I've learned as I've gone along: 1) nothing is as simple as it looks; 2) the events of childhood are the most emotionally convincing of any in our lifetimes; 3) it's easy to be compassionate with animals and strangers—with others it's more difficult; 4) the old idea of comforting the afflicted and afflicting the comfortable is still a valid one; 5) people with musical instruments in their hands are less likely to commit violence; and 6) I agree with author Eudora Welty that every story we write becomes our teacher."

## ■ Works Cited

Lynn, Barbara A., review of *Probably Still Nick Swansen, Voice of Youth Advocates,* June, 1989.
Review of *Make Lemonade, Publishers Weekly,* May 31, 1993.
Mellon, Constance A., review of *Probably Still Nick Swansen, School Library Journal,* December, 1988.
Noah, Carolyn, review of *Make Lemonade, School Library Journal,* July, 1993.

## ■ For More Information See

*PERIODICALS*

*Bulletin of the Center for Children's Books,* July, 1991, p. 279; July-August, 1993, p. 361.
*Horn Book,* September-October, 1991.
*School Library Journal,* November, 1989, pp. 42-43.
*Wilson Library Bulletin,* June, 1989.

**WOOD, Nuria**
  See NOBISSO, Josephine

# Y–Z

Herbert Wong Yee and his daughter, Ellen

## YEE, Wong Herbert 1953-

### ■ Personal

Born August 19, 1953, in Detroit, MI; son of Gee Hing (a restaurant owner) and Toy Wun (a restaurant owner/homemaker) Yee; married December 19, 1975; wife's name, Judy (a graphic artist); children: Ellen. *Education:* Wayne State University, B.F.A., 1975.

### ■ Addresses

*Agent*—c/o Houghton Mifflin Co., 222 Berkley St., Boston, MA 02116-3764.

### ■ Career

Graphic artist.

### ■ Writings

*SELF-ILLUSTRATED*

*Eek! There's a Mouse in the House,* Houghton, 1992.
*Big Black Bear,* Houghton, 1993.

### ■ Work in Progress

*Fireman Small.*

### ■ Sidelights

Wong Herbert Yee told *SATA:* "I remember what an art professor once said when I first started college: 'Everybody here is talented and thinks they can cut it. When you graduate, you will find things different; no more support group.' How true. I was cast out in 1975 with a degree in printmaking in hand. And like many other fine art graduates, drifted aimlessly for a long time. Fortunately a publisher purchased my first picture book. That's where my story begins.

"My advice to people starting out is that being an artist is not something you do. It's what you are. So stick with it! Find a way."

### ■ For More Information See

*PERIODICALS*

*School Library Journal,* October, 1992, p. 100.

\*    \*    \*

## ZAGWYN, Deborah Turney 1953-

### ■ Personal

Born August 14, 1953, in Cornwall, Ontario, Canada; daughter of Eugene (a professor) and Shirley Joan (a homemaker; maiden name, Johnston) Turney; married Leonardus Fredericus Zagwyn (a carpenter), March 18, 1978; children: Sonia Jessica, Graham Lee. *Education:* Attended Fraser Valley College. *Religion:* Agnostic.

**DEBORAH TURNEY ZAGWYN**

## ■ Addresses

*Office*—Box 472, Harrison Hot Springs, British Columbia, V0M 1K0, Canada.

## ■ Career

Writer, artist, and illustrator, 1985—. *Exhibitions:* Kent-Harrison Art Gallery, 1988, Chilliwack Museum, 1989, Prince George Art Gallery, 1989, Vancouver International Writer's and Reader's Festival, 1993. *Member:* Canadian Writer's Union, Canadian Society of Children's Authors, Illustrators, and Performers, Quill, Federation of British Columbian Writers, Canadian Children's Book Centre, Western Canada Wilderness Committee, Harrison Festival of the Arts (board member).

## ■ Awards, Honors

Amelia Frances Howard-Gibbon Illustrators Award finalist, 1986, for *A Winter's Yarn;* Sheila A. Egoff Children's Book Prize runner-up, 1989, for *Mood Pocket, Mud Bucket.*

## ■ Writings

*SELF-ILLUSTRATED*

*Mood Pocket, Mud Bucket,* Fitzhenry & Whiteside, 1988.
*The Pumpkin Blanket,* Fitzhenry & Whiteside, 1990.
*Long Nellie,* Orca Book Publishers, 1993.
*Hound without Howl,* Orca Book Publishers, 1994.

*ILLUSTRATOR*

Kathleen Waldron, *A Winter's Yarn,* RDC Press, 1986.

## ■ Sidelights

Deborah Turney Zagwyn told *SATA:* "When I was a kid, the public library was my entrance to another world. It was the drab ticket booth I passed through on my way to a circus tent full of marvels. Mrs. Slye (my librarian friend) was ticket-taker and usher to the various performances all between the covers of books. I was mesmerized by the Red, Yellow, Blue, and Green Fairy Tale books. I joined Lucy and Edmund in Narnia and later traveled with Bilbo Baggins through Mirkwood.

"In the picture book section, I became furious at the cutesy pictures of princesses who didn't fit their verbal descriptions and enamored with the homely-beautiful, cross-hatch characters of Maurice Sendak. I painstakingly copied his illustrations at home in my after-school time.

"Now I am mostly a grown-up and I know that fairy tales are flawed. I also know they are far more powerful than I ever realized. Mrs. Slye, my circus tent ticket-taker, lives only in my memory now. But when I visit a library and a librarian slips a card into a book for me, I still have the feeling it is a ticket. The magic lives on."

\*   \*   \*

# ZOLOTOW, Charlotte S(hapiro) 1915-
## (Sarah Abbott, Charlotte Bookman)

## ■ Personal

Born June 26, 1915, in Norfolk, VA; daughter of Louis J. and Ella (Bernstein) Shapiro; married Maurice Zolotow (a writer), April 14, 1938 (divorced, 1969); children: Stephen, Ellen (Crescent Dragonwagon). *Education:* Attended University of Wisconsin, 1933-36. *Religion:* Jewish.

## ■ Addresses

*Home*—29 Elm Pl., Hastings-on-Hudson, NY 10706. *Office*—HarperCollins Children's Books, 10 East 53rd St., New York, NY 10022.

## ■ Career

Harper & Row, New York, NY, senior editor of children's book department, 1938-44, 1962-76, vice-president and associate publisher of Junior Books division, 1976-81, consultant and editorial director of Charlotte Zolotow Books division, 1981-91, publisher emerita and editorial advisor, 1991—. University of Indiana Writers' Conference, lecturer, 1961 and 1962. Has also lectured at the University of Colorado. *Member:* PEN, Authors League of America.

■ **Awards, Honors**

*Indian, Indian* was named a Spring Book Festival honor book, *New York Herald Tribune,* 1952; *The Storm Book* and *Mr. Rabbit and the Lovely Present* were named Caldecott honor books, 1953 and 1963, respectively; *New York Times* outstanding book of the year and *School Library Journal* best book of the year awards, both 1972, both for *William's Doll;* Christopher Award, 1974, for *My Grandson Lew;* Harper Gold Medal Award for editorial excellence, 1974; Helen C. White tribute, 1982; Carolyn W. Field Award, Pennsylvania Library Association Youth Services Division, 1984, for *Some Things Go Together; Redbook* award, 1984, for *I Know a Lady,* and 1985, for *William's Doll;* Kerlan Award, University of Minnesota Children's Literature Research Collections, 1986; LMP Award, R. R. Bowker, 1990; University of Southern Mississippi Silver Medallion, 1990; American Library Association tribute, 1991; American Library Association notable book citations for *Do You Know What I'll Do?, Mr. Rabbit and the Lovely Present, William's Doll,* and *My Grandson Lew.*

■ **Writings**

*FICTION*

*The Park Book,* illustrated by H. A. Rey, Harper, 1944.
*But Not Billy,* illustrated by Lys Cassal, Harper, 1947, illustrated by Kay Chorao, 1983.
*The Storm Book,* illustrated by Margaret Bloy Graham, Harper, 1952.
*The Magic Word,* illustrated by Eleanor Dart, Wonder Books, 1952.
*Indian, Indian,* illustrated by Leonard Weisgard, Simon & Schuster, 1952.
(Under pseudonym Charlotte Bookman) *The City Boy and the Country Horse,* illustrated by William Moyers, Treasure Books, 1952.
*The Quiet Mother and the Noisy Little Boy,* illustrated by Kurt Werth, Lothrop, 1953, illustrated by Marc Simont, Harper, 1989.
*One Step, Two . . . ,* illustrated by Roger Duvoisin, Lothrop, 1955.
*Over and Over,* illustrated by Garth Williams, Harper, 1957.
*Not a Little Monkey,* illustrated by Duvoisin, Lothrop, 1957, illustrated by Michele Chessare, Harper, 1989.
*Do You Know What I'll Do?,* illustrated by Williams, Harper, 1958.
*Sleepy Book,* illustrated by Vladimir Bobri, Lothrop, 1958, illustrated by Ilse Plume, Harper, 1988.
*The Night When Mother Was Away,* illustrated by Reisie Lonette, Lothrop, 1958, published as *The Summer Night,* illustrated by Ben Shecter, Harper, 1974.

**CHARLOTTE ZOLOTOW**

*The Bunny Who Found Easter,* illustrated by Betty Peterson, Parnassus, 1959.
*Big Brother,* illustrated by Mary Chalmers, Harper, 1960.
*The Little Black Puppy,* illustrated by Lilian Obligado, Golden Press, 1960.
*The Three Funny Friends,* illustrated by Chalmers, Harper, 1961.
*The Man with the Purple Eyes,* illustrated by Joe Lasker, Abelard-Schuman, 1961.
*Mr. Rabbit and the Lovely Present,* illustrated by Maurice Sendak, Harper, 1962.
*Aren't You Glad?,* illustrated by Elaine Kurty, Lothrop, 1963.
*A Tiger Called Thomas,* illustrated by Werth, Lothrop, 1963, illustrated by Catherine Stock, 1988.
*The Sky Was Blue,* illustrated by Williams, Harper, 1963.
*The Quarreling Book,* illustrated by Arnold Lobel, Harper, 1963.
*The White Marble,* illustrated by Lilian Obligado, Abelard-Schuman, 1963, illustrated by Deborah K. Ray, Crowell, 1982.
*A Rose, a Bridge and a Wild Black Horse,* illustrated by Uri Shulevitz, Harper, 1964, illustrated by Robin Spowart, Harper, 1987.
*The Poodle Who Barked at the Wind,* illustrated by Duvoisin, Lothrop, 1964, illustrated by June Otani, Harper, 1987.
*I Have a Horse of My Own,* illustrated by Yoko Mitsuhashi, Abelard-Schuman, 1964.
*Someday,* illustrated by Lobel, Harper, 1965.
*When I Have a Little Girl,* illustrated by Hilary Knight, Harper, 1965.
*Flocks of Birds,* illustrated by Joan Berg, Abelard-Schuman, 1965, illustrated by Ruth Lercher Bornstein, Crowell, 1981.

*If It Weren't for You,* illustrated by Shecter, Harper, 1966.

*Big Sister and Little Sister,* illustrated by Martha Alexander, Harper, 1966.

*I Want to Be Little,* illustrated by Tony De Luna, Abelard-Schuman, 1966, published as *I Like to Be Little,* illustrated by Erik Blegvad, Crowell, 1987.

*When I Have a Son,* illustrated by Knight, Harper, 1967.

*Summer Is . . . ,* illustrated by Janet Archer, Abelard-Schuman, 1967, illustrated by Bornstein, Crowell, 1983.

*My Friend John,* illustrated by Shecter, Harper, 1968.

*The New Friend,* illustrated by Arvis L. Stewart, Abelard-Schuman, 1968, illustrated by Emily A. McCully, Crowell, 1981.

*The Hating Book,* illustrated by Shecter, Harper, 1969.

(Under pseudonym Sarah Abbott) *Where I Begin,* illustrated by Rocco Negri, Coward-McCann, 1970.

*You and Me,* illustrated by Robert Quackenbush, Macmillan, 1971, published as *Here We Are,* Macmillan, 1971.

*A Father Like That,* illustrated by Shecter, Harper, 1971.

*The Beautiful Christmas Tree,* illustrated by Ruth Robbins, Parnassus, 1972.

(Under pseudonym Sarah Abbott) *The Old Dog,* illustrated by George Mocniak, Coward-McCann, 1972.

*Hold My Hand,* illustrated by Thomas di Grazia, Harper, 1972.

*William's Doll,* illustrated by William Pene Du Bois, Harper, 1972.

*Janey,* illustrated by Ronald Himler, Harper, 1973.

(Editor) *An Overpraised Season: Ten Stories of Youth,* Harper, 1973.

*My Grandson Lew,* illustrated by Du Bois, Harper, 1974.

*The Unfriendly Book,* illustrated by Du Bois, Harper, 1975.

*May I Visit?,* illustrated by Erik Blegvad, Harper, 1976.

*It's Not Fair,* illustrated by Du Bois, Harper, 1976.

*Someone New,* illustrated by Blegvad, Harper, 1978.

*Say It!,* illustrated by James Stevenson, Greenwillow, 1980.

*If You Listen,* illustrated by Marc Simont, Harper, 1980.

*The Song,* illustrated by Nancy Tafuri, Greenwillow, 1982.

*I Know a Lady,* illustrated by Stevenson, Greenwillow, 1984.

*Timothy Too!,* illustrated by Ruth Robbins, Houghton, 1986.

(Editor) *Early Sorrow: Ten Stories of Youth,* Harper, 1986.

*Something Is Going to Happen,* illustrated by Catherine Stock, Harper, 1988.

*The Summer Night,* illustrated by Shecter, Harper, 1991.

*This Quiet Lady,* illustrated by Anita Lobel, Greenwillow, 1992.

*The Seashore Book,* illustrated by Wendell Minor, HarperCollins, 1992.

*The Moon Was the Best,* photographs by Tana Hoban, Greenwillow, 1993.

*Peter and the Pigeons,* illustrated by Martine Gourbault, Greenwillow, 1993.

*POETRY*

*All That Sunlight,* illustrated by Walter Stein, Harper, 1967.

*Some Things Go Together,* illustrated by Sylvie Selig, Abelard-Schuman, 1969, illustrated by Karen Bundersheimer, Crowell, 1983.

*River Winding,* illustrated by Regina Sherkerjian, Abelard, 1970, illustrated by Kazue Mizumura, Crowell, 1978.

*Wake Up and Goodnight,* illustrated by Weisgard, Harper, 1971.

*Everything Glistens and Everything Sings: New and Selected Poems,* illustrated by Margot Tomes, Harcourt, 1987.

*Snippets: A Gathering of Poems, Pictures, and Possibilities,* illustrated by Melissa Sweet, HarperCollins, 1993.

*OTHER*

*In My Garden,* illustrated by Duvoisin, Lothrop, 1960.

*When the Wind Stops,* illustrated by Lasker, Abelard-Schuman, 1962, illustrated by Howard Knotts, Harper, 1975.

*A Week in Yani's World: Greece,* photographs by Donald Getsug, Macmillan, 1969.

*A Week in Lateef's World: India,* photographs by Ray Shaw, Crowell-Collier, 1970.

Contributor to books, including *The Writer's Handbook,* 1968. Contributor to magazines, including *Writer's Yearbook, Prism,* and *McCall's.* Poems, stories, and articles are included in numerous magazines and anthologies for children.

Some of Zolotow's works are represented in the Kerlan Collection at the University of Minnesota and the de Grummond Collection at the University of Southern Mississippi.

## ■ Adaptations

*FILMS*

*My Grandson Lew,* Barr Films, 1976.

*William's Doll,* produced and directed by Robert Carlo Chiesa, Phoenix/BFA, 1981.

"Someone New," included in a CBS Library program, *The Wrong Way Kid,* produced by Busustow Entertainment, 1983.

*A Father Like That,* produced by Phil Marshall, Phoenix Films, 1983.

*The Hating Movie* (also available as videotape), Phoenix Films and Video, 1986.

*FILMSTRIPS*

*Mr. Rabbit and the Lovely Present,* Weston Woods, 1966.

*Someday,* Educational Enrichment Materials, 1976.

*When I Have a Little Girl,* Educational Enrichment Materials, 1976.

*When I Have a Son,* Educational Enrichment Materials, 1976.

*The Three Funny Friends,* Educational Enrichment Materials, 1976.

*A Father Like That,* Listening Library, 1978.

*The Hating Book* was made into a filmstrip by Harper Mediabook.

*OTHER*

A sound recording of some of Zolotow's stories was made by Vancouver Taped Books Project, 1972; an audiocassette of *Wake Up and Goodnight* was produced by Caedmon.

## ■ Sidelights

Charlotte Zolotow, author of more than sixty well-received picture books for younger readers, began her career as a writer after having served as a senior editor of Harper and Row's children's book department for several years. Through four decades she has combined her work as an author with her editorial duties, first at Harper and Row and more recently for her own imprint, Charlotte Zolotow Books. In 1974 she was honored with the Harper Gold Medal for editorial excellence, and her stories have received numerous awards, including the 1974 Christopher Award and "honor book" citations from the prestigious Caldecott and Newbery selection committees.

Asserting similarity in the feelings of young and old, Zolotow wrote in *Horn Book:* "We are all the same, except that adults have found ways to buffer themselves against the full-blown intensity of a child's emotions." Later in the article, the author stated that "a grown person's unrequited love evokes misery similar to a child's misery when a big sister or brother goes off without the child. The loss of a wanted job to someone else in the adult world can stir the same sense of rejection that a small child feels when the doll or dog he or she wanted is given to someone else. We are not different from the children we were—only more experienced, better able to disguise our feelings from others, if not from ourselves."

Several critics have indicated that Zolotow's empathy is what attracts the large number of youthful readers to her books. Marcus Crouch remarked in *School Librarian* that Zolotow "writes the kind of poetry that children write. She catches the fleeting moment as it passes and imprisons it in words. Her verses are frail and delicate. One readily acknowledges her sensitivity." May Hill Arbuthnot and Zena Sutherland expressed a similar view in their book *Children and Books:* "Few writers for small children so empathize with them as does Charlotte Zolotow, whose books—with some exceptions—are really explorations of relationships cast in story form and given vitality by perfected simplicity of style and by the humor and tenderness of the stories.... [Her] understanding of children's emotional needs and problems, and her ability to express them with candor have

Characteristic of Zolotow's tender and pure-of-heart characters, a girl promises her little brother she'll always think of him no matter where she is or what she's doing. (Cover illustration by Garth Williams.)

made her one of the major contemporary writers of realistic books for small children."

Zolotow, in an essay for *Books Are by People,* which she amended for *SATA,* discussed the way she begins work on many of her books: "My children and their friends have often reminded me of things from my childhood which become the theme of a book. Sometimes it is a kind of double-exposure—the adult awareness of a phenomenon and the memory of what it seemed to me as a child or seems to the children around me." She also stated that a "good picture book, I think, must be honest and unpretentious and direct. Whether it is funny or poetic (or both) there should be some universal truth or feeling in it, and what Margaret Wise Brown called the 'unexpected inevitable.'"

### From Editor to Author

While working as an editorial assistant to Ursula Nordstrom at Harper and Row, the author drafted an

**Zolotow shows how people like the woman in this story can make you feel special and loved.** (Cover illustration by James Stevenson.)

outline for a story that she thought could be well written by Brown. Nordstrom asked for clarification, and upon receiving a more detailed story, accepted the manuscript as Zolotow's first book. The author has credited her involvement with Nordstrom as the major influence in her writing and editing career. "[Nordstrom] taught me a fundamental lesson—the difference between being an editor and being a writer—early on in my career.... An editor *draws out* of an author—doesn't feed the editor's ideas *into* the creative person," Zolotow stated in an essay for *The Calendar,* which she amended for *SATA.* She further asserted in an interview with Justin Wintle for *Pied Pipers,* also amended for *SATA:* "I have to be careful if I see something isn't working: the temptation's very often there to say how it should be done, which is death to an author. You've got to let him solve his own problems."

In a *Publishers Weekly* interview with Jean Mercier, Zolotow described the changing focus in children's literature and her position as an editor: "We have to allow authors to put in their books all the information that's valid. We have to allow them to write about abortion, sex encounters, death, divorce and all kinds of problems if these are vital to the story. I don't believe any subject should be taboo if it's handled with taste. We have to tell young people the truth. I don't see how this position can be altered." Discussing what many people feel is the new trend in realism in youth books, Zolotow told Dolores Barclay in the *Los Angeles Times:* "What's called the 'new reality' is just common respect

for the child. Young people today are a great deal more sophisticated. Books we used to publish for 14-year olds are now being read by 10-year olds. In picture books for younger readers there was a time when death or divorce were never treated and everything worked out well." Writing for *Twentieth-Century Children's Writers,* Mercier noted that Zolotow herself was one of the first authors "to tackle the long-taboo subject of death in a picture book," referring to the author's 1974 book *My Grandson Lew,* in which a young boy struggles with his grandfather's death.

Another of Zolotow's books to address an unconventional topic was *William's Doll,* published in 1972. Exploring the topic of sex roles, the book relates William's enjoyment of dolls, an activity that his father and many of his friends consider appropriate only for girls. William's grandmother is supportive, however, believing that the boy can learn important lessons from this activity. Anita Silvey, reviewing *William's Doll* in *Horn Book,* praised the way in which Zolotow presented this controversial subject in the form of "an absolutely old-fashioned, charming book." Zena Sutherland was also enthusiastic, noting in the *Bulletin of the Center for Children's Books* that *William's Doll* is "as endearing for its tenderness as for the message it portrays."

Many observers feel one reason for Zolotow's success as an editor is her talent for linking the right artist with the right children's author. Zolotow told Mercier in *Publishers Weekly,* "We look for those who don't follow the text slavishly; they put in their own individual touches, their own viewpoints. Often the illustrators' work means that some of the text or dialogue can be eliminated. But it has to be there in the first place, so they can 'see' what's happening and get ideas." This stress on compatibility between picture and prose has benefitted Zolotow's authored works as well. For example, Neil Millar wrote in a *Christian Science Monitor* review of *River Winding:* "This is a near-perfect match of poet and illustrator. [The] poems, free verse or formal, are gems, glimpses of a gentle—most rustic—world seen through a gentle child's perception." Zolotow told Wintle, "I used to wish that I could paint myself, but as I've gotten older I've realized that I was very fortunate that I couldn't because I've had a much wider range of other people's talent and imagination than my own could have given me."

## Themes in Zolotow's Books

One of the many themes that reoccur in Zolotow's writings is her interest in expressing both the importance of family heritage and ways in which people change through time. This subject is explored in her 1963 book *The Sky Was Blue,* which focuses on a girl and her mother as they look at a picture album. As the two discuss the ancestors portrayed in the photographs, they come to understand that while things such as clothing styles may change over time, other elements— the repetition of the seasons and the feelings that tie a family together—remain the same. The issue of generations and heritage is also the subject of 1992's *This*

*Quiet Lady,* in which once again a picture book is central to the book's plot. Here a little girl views many photographs of her mother that were taken throughout the woman's life. In this way the girl comes to better understand the many events that led to her own birth. Sutherland found in the *Bulletin of the Center for Children's Books* that *This Quiet Lady* was "just right for the very young child being introduced to concepts of change and family continuity."

Another subject that reoccurs in Zolotow's books is her attention to the details of nature. Both her 1960 picture book *In My Garden* and the 1970 collection of poetry *River Winding* utilize the change of seasons to bring children in closer contact with the world around them. Other stories, such as *The Storm Book, Mr. Rabbit and the Lovely Present,* and *Flocks of Birds,* incorporate other elements of the natural world. More recently, *The Seashore Book* recreates an ocean beach for a child who has never seen one. Reviewing *The Seashore Book* in *New York Times Book Review,* Beth Dunlop noted that Zolotow's descriptions in the book "have a special caress, just like little waves lapping at the shore." Dunlop also praised the author's accomplishments in her many other books, proclaiming that Zolotow "is a wonderful writer; her words have a special lilt that lingers long after the book is closed."

## ■ Works Cited

Arbuthnot, May Hill, and Zena Sutherland, *Children and Books,* 4th edition, Scott, Foresman, 1972.

Barclay, Dolores, *Los Angeles Times,* February 29, 1980.

Crouch, Marcus, *School Librarian,* September, 1971.

Dunlop, Beth, review of *The Seashore Book, New York Times Book Review,* May 31, 1992, p. 38.

Mercier, Jean, *Twentieth-Century Children's Writers,* 3rd edition, St. James Press, 1989, p. 1080-1082.

Millar, Neil, *Christian Science Monitor,* November 13, 1978.

Silvey, Anita, review of *William's Doll, Horn Book,* December, 1972, p. 584.

Sutherland, Zena, review of *William's Doll, Bulletin of the Center for Children's Books,* July-August, 1972, p. 180.

Sutherland, Zena, review of *This Quiet Lady, Bulletin of the Center for Children's Books,* June, 1992, p. 286.

Zolotow, Charlotte, essay in *Books Are by People,* edited by Lee Bennett Hopkins, Citation Press, 1969; amended by Zolotow for *Something about the Author,* Volume 35, Gale, 1984.

Zolotow, Charlotte, interview with Jean Mercier for *Publishers Weekly,* June 10, 1974.

Zolotow, Charlotte, interview with Justin Wintle for *Pied Pipers,* edited by Wintle and Emma Fisher, Paddington Press, 1974; amended by Zolotow for *Something about the Author,* Volume 35, Gale, 1984.

Zolotow, Charlotte, "Ursula Nordstrom," *The Calendar,* November, 1981-June, 1982; amended by Zolotow for *Something about the Author,* Volume 35, Gale, 1984.

Zolotow, Charlotte, "Writing for the Very Young: An Emotional Deja Vu," *Horn Book,* September/October, 1985, p. 536-540.

## ■ For More Information See

*BOOKS*

Bader, Barbara, *American Picturebooks from Noah's Ark to the Beast Within,* Macmillan, 1976.

*Children's Literature Review,* Volume 2, Gale, 1976.

*Dictionary of Literary Biography,* Volume 52: *American Writers for Children since 1960: Fiction,* Gale, 1986.

Huck, Charlotte, *Children's Literature in the Elementary School,* Holt, 1976.

Huck, Charlotte, *Children's Literature,* 3rd edition, Holt, 1978.

Rudman, Masha, *Children's Literature,* 2nd edition, Longman, 1976.

Trelease, Jim, *The Read Aloud Handbook,* Penguin, 1982.

*PERIODICALS*

*Horn Book,* November, 1992, p. 753; May, 1993, p. 326.

*Ms.,* May, 1974.

*New Yorker,* December 17, 1966.

*New York Times Book Review,* November 11, 1984.

*Publishers Weekly,* May 25, 1992, p. 54; June 1, 1992, p. 61; December 14, 1992, p. 56.

*School Library Journal,* March, 1993, p. 195; June, 1993, pp. 92-93; November, 1993, p. 96.

**A little girl and her mother share special moments by looking through an old photograph book that helps the child understand her family better. (Cover illustration by Anita Lobel.)**